# Footprint Vietnam, Cambodia &

*Claire Boobbyer, Andrew Spooner an*
2nd edition

"... these incredible [monastery] buildings [are] unlike anything in the world, so that you are taken aback, and you cannot fit them into the scheme of things you know. It makes you laugh with delight to think that anything so fantastic could exist on this sombre earth".

Somerset Maugham, *The Gentlemen in the parlour*

# Vietnam, Cambodia & Laos Highlights

See colour maps at back of book

**❶ Sapa**
Perched on a mountainside high above the clouds and home to the Hmong people, page 111.

**❷ Halong Bay**
Limestone towers rise out of the waters of Halong Bay, a World Heritage Site, page 93.

**❸ My Son**
The core seat of the Champa Empire immortalized in stone, page 145.

**❹ Kontum**
A wooden church, bishop's seminary and ethnic minority villages, page 158.

**❺ Nha Trang**
Beachside hangout with restaurants, cafés and bars, page 158.

**❻ Cu Chi**
Viet Cong tunnel complex, page 181.

**❼ Phu Quoc**
Unspoilt island with few resorts and miles of white-sand beaches, page 198.

**❽ Kep**
Wonderful small coastal town with beautiful blooming gardens. Quiet alternative to Sihanoukville, page 298.

**❾ Bokor Mountain National Park**
Visit the colonial hill station, where French officers escaped from the heat of the plains, page 297.

**❿ Royal Palace and Silver Pagoda, Phnom Penh**
The capital's 19th-century concoction of temples, summerhouses and palaces, page 273.

**⓫ Tuol Sleng Museum, Phnom Penh**
To remember the dead and remind the living, page 277.

**⓬ Irrawaddy dolphins**
Use Kratie as a base to see these endangered mammals, page 306.

**⓭ Angkor Wat**
The largest religious monument in the world, page 325.

**⓮ Royal city of Angkor Thom and the Bayon**
Simply awesome, page 327.

**⓯ Mekong Islands**
Land-locked Laos' very own tropical archipelago, page 475.

**⓰ Wat Phou**
Stupendous 12th-century Khmer archaeological site, page 470.

**⓱ That Luang**
Symbol of Lao nationhood and the country's holiest site, page 390.

**⓲ Vang Vieng**
Adventure capital en route to Luang Prabang, with caves, rafting and elephant trekking, page 395.

**⓳ Plain of Jars**
Perplexing giant stone jars littered over US-bombed grasslands, page 446.

**⓴ Luang Prabang**
Perfectly formed little city with UNESCO World Heritage status, page 416.

MYANMAR (BURMA)

N

100 km
100 miles

# Contents

## Phnom Penh

## Southern Cambodia

## Northeast Cambodia

## Angkor

## Background

6

# Laos

## Vientiane & around

## Northern Laos

## Southern Laos

## Background

## Footnotes

## Inside front cover

Sleeping and eating
price codes

## Inside back cover

Author biographies
Acknowledgements

**Fantasia of the East**
*The Cao Dai Great Temple at Tay Ninh. "The most outrageously vulgar building ever to have been erected with serious intent..." Norman Lewis.*

**The smile of Angkor**
There are over 2000 large faces carved throughout the Bayon temple, which sits in the centre of the Angkor Thom complex.

# A foot in the door

Vietnam, Cambodia and Laos offer unrivalled attractions in the form of ruins, colonial remnants, stunning scenery, ethnic diversity and exotic food. Their shared history as part of Indo-china is still evident in the fading French architecture, the cuisine and the ubiquitous reminders of bloody wars, but it is their distinct differences that render the area such a fantastic travel experience.

In Vietnam, vivid rice paddies climb up mountainsides or sit alongside beautiful coastal scenery; feverish Ho Chi Minh City plays noisier, more moneyed brother to the enchanting, romantic capital, Hanoi. Cambodia is home to the magnificent Angkor Wat, the zenith of Southeast Asian architecture, and a multitude of other awe-inspiring monuments. Phnom Penh, the fascinating modern-day capital, offers the glistening Royal Palace, eclectic markets and poignant relics of a turbulent past. Laid-back Laos, rousing after years of isolation, provides a beautiful, postcard-like backdrop. From the picturesque gilded temples of the former royal capital, Luang Prabang, to the chilled-out Mekong islands of Siphandon, it's hard not to be inspired by this exquisite country and its charming people.

In modern-day Vietnam one thing in particular stands out. It is, quite simply, the remarkable speed at which the country is developing and the extraordinary ambitions its leaders are planning to achieve. Vietnam now hovers in an enigmatic and paradoxical time zone, somewhere between the late Industrial Revolution and the post-industrial age. High school children in Ho Chi Minh City vie for the trendiest motorbikes, mobile phones and trainers, while children in the Northern Highlands are happy with a pair of sandals. Youngsters in the Mekong Delta have email accounts, yet 10 years ago they didn't have a telephone. And while staff in call centres gossip about the latest fashions, their parents harvest rice by hand. Vietnam has experienced war and bloody revolution in the past 100 years. But the revolution it is now undergoing is peaceful and prosperous. Vast strides in economic development are apace with the government hoping to be crowned a middle income country by 2020. It is, in part, these changes that make Vietnam the absorbing and gripping place that it is.

War? Yes, Vietnam survived several, in fact, over the last century. The Vietnamese people have seen much water flow under the bridge since the last war ended but the government will not let it drop. Even now, 30 years on, new war memorials are being erected. It is as if the

**Motorbike heaven or hell**
*Thousands of motorbikes, hundreds of bicycles and dozens of cars swarm around Ho Chi Minh City in a never-ending stream of wheels and exhaust smoke.*

legitimacy of the government somehow depends on having won the war resulting in an odd mixture of war legacy in modern Vietnam. Heroic Communist monuments and war memorabilia abound in museums but the Vietnamese people have set their sights firmly on the future. There is no looking back, no nostalgia for the past. And this explains the lack of fuss every time an old building is flattened. Forget yesterday, look to tomorrow.

## Cambodia

Impenetrable jungles; abandoned temples smothered in centuries of foliage; arcing white-sand beaches fringed with swaying palms; exotic, smiling locals – in almost every respect Cambodia satisfies the hackneyed expectations of Southeast Asia. And, if you get off the beaten track, Cambodia also offers that increasingly elusive feeling of discovery; the feeling that you are entering into arcane and unknown worlds where few Westerners have been before. But this is a country that is still trying to make sense of itself after the horrors of the genocidal Khmer Rouge rule. While the UN-sponsored trial of the former leaders finally got underway in 2007, many of its minor officials still hold positions of influence and power in Cambodia and you don't have to spend long in the country to see the gulf between the indifferent rich and the absolute poor.

**Put out to pasture**
*Traditionally elephants were used as transport and to clear forests but today they are more commonly found working the tourist trail.*

Yet, without doubt, ancient Cambodia produced one of the world's greatest civilizations at Angkor. This temple complex near Siem Reap is truly breathtaking. But don't just stop there; Angkor Wat is merely one temple lying at the heart of a thousand others.

Today's capital, Phnom Penh, with its charming riverside setting is rapidly shedding its laid-back dusty charm and becoming a dynamic city complete with Hummer-driving Khmer yuppies, chic bars serving cocktails, clubs with designer interiors and hangouts filled with the great and the gorgeous.

On the beaches of the south you can find relaxed resort towns like Kep. In the northeastern provinces, tracts of red earth cut through hills carpeted in jungle. Elephant rides are the order of the day around Sen Monorom, and at Ban Lung you won't be disappointed by the waterfalls, boat rides and the stunning, bottle-green waters of Yaek Lom Lake.

## Laos

Laos is fast becoming the darling of Southeast Asia, satisfying all the romantic images of perfumed frangipani trees, saffron-robed monks, rusty old bicycles and golden temples, all set amongst a rich tapestry of tropical river islands, ethnic minority villages, cascading waterfalls and vivid, green rice paddies, and bound together by the mighty Mekong River, the country's lifeline. The vernacular architecture that other countries have swept away in a maelstrom of redevelopment survives in Laos. Simple wooden village homes, colonial-era brick-and-stucco shophouses and gently mouldering monasteries mark Laos out as different. Traditional customs are also firmly intact: incense wafts out of streetside wats, monks collect alms at daybreak and the clickety-clack of looms weaving richly coloured silk can be heard in most villages.

As compelling as these sights and sounds are, the lasting impression for most visitors is of the people and their overwhelming friendliness. Many believe the best thing about Laos is the constant chimes of '*sabaidee*' ringing out from schoolchildren, monks and other passers-by, extending an invitation to join their meal. This is a land that endures the terrible legacy of being the most bombed country per capita in the world, yet its people transform bomb casings into flower pots and bomb craters into fish ponds. Regardless of their history and their poverty, people here radiate a sunny, happy disposition.

Life is simple in Laos but the people share with their former French colonists an infectious *joie de vivre* that ensures that good food and great company are the pinnacle of enjoyment. If you're seeking a relaxed life-style and a warm welcome, you've come to the right place.

**The Akha Way**
The Akha live around Muang Sing, in northwest Laos. The women wear elaborate headdresses decorated with jewellery and silver coins.

1  An enormous beast is said to have careered into the sea here, cutting Halong Bay from the rocks. ▸▸ See page 93.

2  Rice, a staple food crop, accounts for a quarter of Laos' GDP. ▸▸ See page 528.

3  Monkeys roam the Angkor complex, an added attraction for tourists. ▸▸ See page 325.

4  Floating villages hug the shore of the Tonlé Sap and most services, including police, health, religion, retail and karaoke, are provided on the water. ▸▸ See page 316.

5  China Beach offers miles of soft white sand, clean water and a glorious setting. ▸▸ See page 143.

6  Patuxai, the Victory Monument in Vientiane. ▸▸ See page392.

7  A deep-fried spider vendor in Cambodia. ▸▸ See page 31.

8  Flower Hmong hats for sale at the Bac Ha Sunday market. ▸▸ See page 114.

9  Saffron-robed monks collect offerings from residents and pilgrims during the Boun That Luang festival. ▸▸ See page 405.

10 Hundreds of these ancient and mysterious jars still dot the landscape of Xieng Khouang Province, despite intensive bombing during the Secret War. ▸▸ See page 447.

11 The glass tower at Choeung Ek is a memorial to those people who died during Cambodia's genocide. It contains skulls from 129 mass graves uncovered on the site, south of Phnom Penh. ▸▸ See page 278.

12 Reproduction propaganda posters are sold in galleries and shops from Hanoi to Ho Chi Minh City. ▸▸ See page 99.

**A capital idea**
Monks wander past the gleaming Royal Palace and Silver Pagoda, the most impressive of Phnom Penh's cultural sites.

# Essentials

---

## ⚡ Footprint features

# Planning your trip

## Where to go

If time is limited, by far the best option is to get an open-jaw flight where you fly into one city and out of another or fly into Bangkok, the cheapest point of entry, and use the **Bangkok Airways** regional 'Discovery Airpass', which includes **Siem Reap Airways** routes and **Lao Airlines** primary routes. **Vietnam Airlines** has a good domestic network, too. Distances are huge in this region and in Cambodia and Laos, especially, roads are not always sealed, making overland journey times lengthy and sometimes tortuous, especially in the wet season. Note that there are strict regulations concerning visas that need to be noted before planning your trip, see Visas, page 49.

### One week

A one-week trip will require careful planning and prioritizing. Either take internal flights, if you want to cover a lot of ground, or limit yourself to just one area. In Vietnam, fly from energetic and historic **Ho Chi Minh City** to the imperial city of **Hué**, followed by a trip to enchanting **Hoi An** and its beach. Then fly on to cultured **Hanoi**. If the countryside is of more interest, the **Mekong Delta** can be visited in a day trip from Ho Chi Minh City; magical **Halong Bay** can be done in a day/night trip from Hanoi but in order to visit **Sapa**, known for its stunning scenery and hilltribes, you'll have to spend two nights on a train. In Cambodia, up to four days could be spent around the exceptional ruins of **Angkor**, with one day in **Phnom Penh** and one in either the laid-back beaches of **Sihanoukville** or in colonial-inspired **Kampot**. For Laos, fly from Bangkok to **Vientiane** before heading north to wonderfully preserved **Luang Prabang** via **Vang Vieng**. Or fly from Vientiane to **Luang Namtha** to access the interesting trekking region in the north before overlanding it back to Luang Prabang. Alternatively, after visiting Luang Prabang, fly back to Vientiane and on to Pakse for a trip to the tranquil, laid-back **Siphandon** (4000 islands) in the south.

### Two weeks

Building on the one-week options, you have the chance to cross a border or two. If you fly into **Ho Chi Minh City** you could see the war relic of the **Cu Chi tunnels** and the fantastical **Cao Dai Temple** before making your way through the **Mekong Delta** (visiting the floating markets at **Can Tho**) to **Phnom Penh**, **Choeung Ek** and onto **Siem Reap (Angkor)** by boat, where you will have more time to visit some of the outlying ruins such as **Koh Ker** and **Beng Melea** and, at a push, the brilliant, clifftop temple of **Preah Vihear**. You could then fly from Siem Reap to **Pakse** for **Wat Phou**, the sublime **Tad Lo** and **Tad Fan falls** and **Siphandon**, or to **Vientiane** to access northern Laos. Alternatively, you could fly to Cambodia first and then fly from either Phnom Penh to Vientiane or Ho Chi Minh City or from Siem Reap to Ho Chi Minh City. If you fly into **Hanoi** you could visit both **Sapa** (by train) and **Halong Bay** and then fly to **Vientiane** in Laos continuing to Siem Reap or Phnom Penh by plane.

### One month

With one month you can take things a little more slowly. Having explored **Sapa**, **Dien Bien Phu** and the area around **Mai Chau** in northwest Vietnam you could take an overnight train from **Hanoi** to **Hué**. You could either travel west into **central Laos** here or take the splendid **train journey from Hué to Danang**. Close by is **Hoi An**. From there,

travel to coastal **Nha Trang** for its islands or to the quieter, lovely resort of **Mui Ne**.
From Nha Trang you could go to **Dalat**, the hub of the Central Highlands and the towns
of **Buon Ma Thuot**, **Play Ku** and **Kontum**, then continue by air or overland to **Ho Chi
Minh City**, from where a side trip to the unspoilt beaches of **Phu Quoc** is possible.
To reach Cambodia, fly on to **Phnom Penh** or **Siem Reap** or go by bus and boat
through the **Mekong Delta**. Visit **Angkor** and then, from Phnom Penh, go south to
**Sihanoukville** and explore the beaches and outlying islands. A day or two can also be
spent visiting **Kampot** and the seaside town of **Kep**, as well as exploring the eerie
**Bokor Mountain National Park**. With one month it is better to start at the extreme
north or the south of Laos to cover as much territory as possible. From Phnom
Penh you could travel overland to **Siphandon** in southern Laos via Stung Treng.
Before heading north take a side trip to the interesting **Boloven Plateau** with its
stunning coffee plantations and ubiquitous falls. Overland it to **Thakhek** and do the
motorcycle loop around the limestone scenery of central Laos, visiting the **Kong Lor**
River Cave en route. Or fly direct to **Vientiane** in order to catch a flight to **Phonsavanh**
and explore the mysterious **Plain of Jars**, then overland it to **Xam Neua** to see the
ancient rock formations at **Suan Hin** and the Pathet Lao caves at **Vieng Xai**. A long but
interesting overland route will take you west from here via increasingly popular
**Nong Khiaw** to **Luang Prabang**, from where you can head north to the trekking areas
of **Luang Namtha**, **Muang Sing** and **Phongsali**, or catch a boat up the Mekong
towards the Thai border. A flight from Vientiane to Xam Neua will save two days' travel
and from Vientiane to Phongsali, four days' travel.

# When to go

Climatically the best time to visit the region is between November and April when it
should be dry and not too hot. In the southern part of the region it is warm but not too
hot with lovely cool evenings. However, in Cambodia wind-blown dust invades
everything at this time of year. In the north of Vietnam and Laos the highlands will be a
bit chilly but they should be dry with clear blue skies. However, temperatures in
upland areas like the Plain of Jars, the Boloven Plateau and some towns in the north
of Laos can be extraordinarily cold.

From late-March to April the region heats up and temperatures can exceed 40°C.
In northern Laos, the months from March through to the first rains in May or June can
be very hazy as smoke from burning off the secondary forest hangs in the air. On the
worst days this can cause itchiness of the eyes. It also means that views are restricted
and sometimes flights are cancelled. Travel on the region's mud and laterite roads is
difficult and sometimes impossible by June and July; transport will be slower and may
cease altogether in some parts. It is also impossible to do any outdoor activities in
June and July because of the rain. However, the area is at its most beautiful then.
Travel in the south and Mekong Delta can be difficult at the height of the monsoon
(particularly during September, October and November). The central regions and
north of Vietnam sometimes suffer tropical storms from May to November. Hué is at
its wettest wet from September to January.

**Tet**, Vietnamese new year, is not really a good time to visit. This movable feast
usually falls between late January and March and lasts for about a fortnight. It is the
only holiday most Vietnamese get in the year so popular destinations are packed,
roads are jammed and, for a couple of days, almost all hotels and restaurants are
shut. All hotel prices increase and car hire prices rise by 50% or more. Problems also
occur during **Khmer New Year** in Cambodia and **Pi Mai** in Laos, when public transport
is full and and hotels booked out in popular places.

## § Visiting ethnic minorities: house rules

Scores of different ethnic minority groups inhabit northern Vietnam, the Central Highlands of Vietnam and northern Laos, in particular, and their distinctive styles of dress and age-old rituals may be of special interest to Western travellers. If you choose to visit or stay in a minority village, please remember that it is not a human zoo. Etiquette and customs vary between the minorities, but the following are general rules of good behaviour that should be adhered to whenever possible.

→ Organize your visit through a local villager or a travel agency that supports the village.
→ Inform yourself of local trekking rules and guidance. See in particular page 113.

→ Dress modestly and avoid undressing/changing in public.
→ Ask permission before entering a house.
→ Ask permission before photographing anyone (old people and pregnant women often object to having their photograph taken). Be aware that villagers are unlikely to pose out of the kindness of their hearts so don't begrudge them the money; for many, tourism is their livelihood.
→ Buy handicrafts that support local industry.
→ Avoid sitting or stepping on door sills.
→ Avoid excessive displays of wealth and do not hand out gifts.
→ Avoid introducing Western medicines.
→ Do not touch or photograph village shrines.

# Activities and tours

Vietnam and Laos are well known for their wonderful trekking opportunities amid stunning mountainous landscape, which is home to a variety of ethnic minorities. Other activities, such as rafting, kayaking and cycling, are fairly recently established or slowly emerging and are not as developed as they are in a place like Thailand. Safety is always an issue when participating in adventurous sports: make sure you are fully covered by your travel insurance; check the credentials of operators offering adventure activities; and make sure that vehicles and safety equipment are in a good condition. Note that medical care in Camboda and Laos is very limited, see page 39.

## Caving

Laos has some of the most extensive and largest caves in the region. Some of the best can be found around Vang Vieng, where caving tourism has been developed. Another highlight is the amazing Kong Lor River Cave in the centre of the country. There are hundreds of caves around Vieng Xai but only a few open to tourists, for those interested in history these caves should be a first stop.

★ Head for ...
Vang Vieng ›› *page 395* Tham Kong Lor ›› *page 460*

ⓘ **Green Discovery**, Vang Vieng, T023-511230, www.greendiscoverylaos.com.

## Cycling and mountain biking

Large parts of Vietnam are flat so cycling is a popular activity, although the traffic on the roads can be hazardous. It's therefore recommended that any tour is planned off-road or on minor roads. In Cambodia and Laos, cycling is offered by several tour agencies; Luang Namtha is a popular place to start, and Green Discovery run excellent cycling tours. Many cyclists prefer to bring their own all-terrain or racing bikes but it's also possible to rent them from tour organizers.

**Head for ...**
Hué▶ *page 122* **Dalat**▶ *page 152*
**Mekong Delta** ▶ *page 193* **Luang**
**Namtha** ▶ *page 431*
ⓘ **Asian Trails**, www.asiantrails.com.
**Exotissimo**, Hanoi, T04-8282150; HCMC,
T08-8251723, www.exotissimo.com.
**Green Discovery**, Luang Namtha, T086-
211484, www.greendiscoverylaos.com.

## Diving and snorkelling

Underwater adventures are limited in
the seas around Vietnam, since much
of the coast is a muddy deltaic swamp
and, elsewhere, the water is turbid from
high levels of soil erosion. In those places
where snorkelling and diving is good (Nha
Trang, Phu Quoc and Danang) it is possible
for a few months of the year in the dry
season only (Nov-Apr). The dive industry
in Cambodia is in its infant years, but the
coast boasts lots of pristine coral reefs
and unexplored areas. There are several
dive operators in Sihanoukville.

**Head for ...**
Danang▶ *page 142* **Nha Trang**
▶ *page 158* **Phu Quoc** ▶ *page 198*
**Sihanoukville** ▶ *page 275*
ⓘ **Rainbow Divers**, Nha Trang,
T058-829946, T091-3408146 (mob),
www.divevietnam.com.
**Scuba Nation Diving Centre**,
Sihanoukville, T012-604680.

## Kayaking

Kayaking in Vietnam is centred around
Halong Bay. This World Heritage Site,
crammed with islands and grottoes, is a
fantastic place to explore by kayak. Head
to the Nam Song River at Vang Vieng for
kayaking, rafting and tubing in Laos.
There is also excellent kayaking around
the Boloven Plateau.

**Head for ...**
Halong Bay▶ *page 93* **Vang Vieng**
▶ *page 395*
ⓘ **Buffalo Tours**, Hanoi, T04-8280702;
Ho Chi Minh City, T08-8279169,
www.buffalotours.com.

**Exotissimo**, Hanoi, T04-8282150; HCMC,
T08-8251723, www.exotissimo.com.
**Green Discovery**, Vang Vieng, T023-
511230, www.greendiscoverylaos.com.
**Xplore-Asia**,www.xplore-asia.com.
**Riverside tours**, www.riversidetourlaos.com.

## Kitesurfing and windsurfing

Kitesurfing and windsurfing are found
largely in Mui Ne, Vietnam, which offers
just about perfect conditions throughout
the year. The wind is normally brisk over
many days and the combination of powerful
wind and waves enables good kite surfers
to get airborne for several seconds at a
time. Equipment can be rented at many
places. Windsurfing is popular in Nha
Trang where dive schools offer this and
other watersports.

**Head for ...**
Nha Trang▶ *page158* **Mui Ne**▶ *page161*
ⓘ **Jibe's Beach Club**, Mui Ne, T062-847405,
www.windsurf-vietnam.com.

## Rock climbing

Laos has stunning karst rock formations,
caves and cliffs. Vang Vieng is the hot spot
for this activity.

**Head for ...**
Vang Vieng▶ *page 395*
ⓘ **Green Discovery**, Vang Vieng, T023-
511230, www.greendiscoverlaos.com.

## Spas

The only devoted spa resorts in Vietnam are
the **Ana Mandara** in Nha Trang, the **Evason**
**Hideaway** in Ninh Van Bay and the **Evason**
**Villas** Dalat in the Central Highlands, www.six
senses.com. There are other good hotels such
as the **Life Wellness Resorts** and the **Victoria**
**Hotels** that offer spa facilities. Hotels offering
massage, treatments and therapies exist
across the region and are good value
for money.

There are also some wonderful spas in
Luang Prabang; for extreme indulgence try
the Spa at **La Residence Phou Vao** or for a
cheaper luxury alternative the **Spa Garden**.

★ **Head for ...**
**Dalat** ⏩ *page 152* **Nha Trang** ⏩ *page 158*
**Luang Prabang** ⏩ *page 416*
ⓘ **Spa Garden**, Luang Prabang, T071-212325, spagardenlpb@hotmail.com.

## Trekking

The main focus for trekking in Vietnam is Sapa but some trekking is also organized around Dalat. Some treks are straightforward and can be done without guides or support, whereas others need accommodation and there may be a legal requirement to take a licensed guide. If staying with ethnic minorities in homestays this must be organized through a tour operator. In Laos, Luang Namtha, Muang Sing and Phongsali all offer trekking in areas inhabited by a diverse range of ethnicities. There are also treks from Luang Prabang and Vang Vieng. For a different perspective on the landscape, **elephant trekking** is possible in Yok Don National Park, Vietnam, and around Vang Vieng and Tad Lo in Laos.

★ **Head for ...**
**Sapa** ⏩ *page 111* **Dalat** ⏩ *page 152* **Yok Don National Park** ⏩ *page 157* **Phou Khao Khouay** ⏩ *page 394* **Vang Vieng** ⏩ *page 395* **Luang Namtha** ⏩ *page 431* **Muang Sing** ⏩ *page 433* **Phongsali** ⏩ *page 436* **Tad Lo** ⏩ *page 474*
ⓘ T021-212251, www.trekkingcentrallaos.com.

# Taking a tour

Numerous operators offer organized trips to this region, ranging from a whistle-stop tour of the highlights to specialist trips that focus on a specific destination or activity. The advantage of travelling with a reputable operator is that your transport, accommodation and activities are all arranged for you in advance – particularly valuable if you only have limited time. By travelling independently, however, you can be more flexible and spontaneous about where you go and what you do. You will be able to explore less-visited areas and you will save money, if you budget carefully. On arrival in Vietnam, many travellers hire operators to take them on day and week-long trips. These tours cater for all budgets and you will benefit from an English-speaking guide and safe vehicles. Some of the most popular trips include week-long tours around the northwest or into the Mekong Delta. A list of specialist tour operators can be found in Essentials A-Z, page 47.

# Ecotourism

Since the early 1990s there has been a phenomenal growth in 'ecotourism', which promotes and supports the conservation of natural environments and is also fair and equitable to local communities. While the authenticity of some ecotourism operators needs to be interpreted with care, there is clearly both a huge demand for this type of activity and also significant opportunities to support worthwhile conservation and social development initiatives by this means. **Green Globe** (T020-77304428, www.greenglobe21.com) and **Responsible Travel** (www.responsibletravel.com) offer advice for travellers on selecting destinations and sites focused on conservation and sustainable development.

In addition, the **International Eco-Tourism Society** (www.ecotourism.org), **Tourism Concern** (T020-7753 3330, www.tourismconcern.org.uk), and **Planeta** (www.planeta.com) develop and promote ecotourism projects in destinations all over the world and their websites provide details for initiatives throughout Southeast Asia.

For opportunities to participate directly in scientific research and development projects, contact **Earthwatch** (www.earthwatch.org), **Discovery International** (www.discoveryinitiatives.com) and the **Nautilus Institute** (www.nautilus.org), which focuses on environmental and sustainability issues in the Asia-Pacific region. See also How big is your footprint?

# ⁝ How big is your footprint?

The benefits of international travel are self-evident for both hosts and travellers: employment, increased understanding of different cultures, business and leisure opportunities. At the same time there is clearly a downside to the industry. Where visitor pressure is high or poorly regulated, adverse impacts to society and the natural environment may occur. In order to ensure your contribution to the host nation is a positive one, follow these guidelines, taken from the Tourism Concern website, www.tourismconcern.org.uk.

→ Learn about the country you're visiting. Before you leave tap into as many sources of information as you can.

→ Think about where your money goes – be fair and realistic about how cheaply you travel. Try and put money into local people's hands; drink local beer or fruit juice rather than imported brands, and stay in locally owned accommodation.

→ Open your mind to new cultures and traditions. It can transform your holiday experience and you'll earn respect and be more readily welcomed by local people.

→ Think about what happens to your rubbish: take biodegradable products and a water filter bottle. Be sensitive to limited resources like water, fuel and electricity.

→ Help preserve local wildlife and habitats by respecting rules and regulations, such as sticking to footpaths, not standing on coral and not buying products made from endangered plants or animals.

→ Use your guidebook as a starting point, not the only source of information. Talk to local people, then discover your own adventure!

→ Don't treat people as part of the landscape; they may not want their picture taken. Put yourself in their shoes, ask first and respect their wishes. See also Visiting ethnic minorities: house rules, page 20.

# Getting there and flying around

## Arriving by air

The easiest – and cheapest – way to access the region is via **Bangkok** or **Hong Kong**. Most major airlines have direct flights from Europe, North America and Australasia to these hubs. International airports are at Tan Son Nhat Airport (SGN) in **Ho Chi Minh City** and Noi Bai Airport (HAN) in **Hanoi** (also **Danang** for some flights from the rest of Asia). **Cambodia and Laos** are only accessible from within Asia. The most important entry point for Cambodia remains **Phnom Penh** though there are now more flights to **Siem Reap** (REP). Both are connected to Bangkok, Singapore, Hong Kong, Ho Chi Minh City and Vientiane and Pakse in Laos. For Laos, there are direct flights to **Vientiane** from Phnom Penh, Siem Reap, Bangkok, Chiang Mai, Kunming Hanoi and Ho Chi Minh City. There are also flights from Bangkok and Chiang Mai to **Luang Prabang**. A cheaper option for getting to Laos from Bangkok is to fly to **Udon Thani**, Thailand, about 50km south of the border and travel overland via the Friendship Bridge. For full details, see page 393. An alternative route is to fly from Bangkok to **Chiang Rai**, Thailand, before overlanding it to **Chiang Khong** and crossing into northern Laos at **Houei Xai**. From Houei Xai there are flights to Vientiane and boats to Luang Prabang via Pak Beng. See regional flights page 24. ⇥ *For further details, see Ins and outs sections throughout the guide.*

**Flights from Europe**

There are direct flights to Vietnam only from Paris, with **Vietnam Airlines/Air France**. These code-shared flights last 12 hours. **Vietnam Airlines** has an office in the UK at Flighthouse, Fernhill Rd, Horley, Surrey RH6 9SY, T0871-2229233, www.vietnam airlines.uk.com, or flights can be booked online. There are also direct **Vietnam Airlines** flights from Moscow. Flights from London and other European hubs go via Bangkok, Singapore, Kuala Lumpur, or Hong Kong. From London to Vietnam takes around 16-18 hours, depending on the length of stopover. Airlines include **Cathay Pacific, Thai Airways, Singapore Airlines, Malaysia Airlines** and **Air France**. It is also possible to fly into Hanoi and depart from Ho Chi Minh City. Check details with flight agents and tour operators (page 47). The best deals usually involve flying to Bangkok and then on from there to your destination. There are countless airlines flying to Bangkok from Europe and lots of good deals, so shop around.

## Flights from the USA and Canada

There are flights to Vietnam from several major US hubs but these are very expensive. By far the best option is to fly via **Bangkok, Taipei** or **Hong Kong** and from there to Vietnam, Cambodia or Laos. The approximate flight time from Los Angeles to **Bangkok** is 21 hours. **United** flies from San Francisco and from LA via Tokyo and from Chicago via Hong Kong to Vietnam. **Thai, Delta, Northwest, United** and **Air Canada** fly to Bangkok from a number of US and Canadian cities.

## Flights from Australia and New Zealand

There are direct flights to **Bangkok** from all major Australian and New Zealand cities with **Cathay Pacific, Korean Airlines, Qantas, Malaysia Airlines, Singapore Airlines** and **Thai,** among others. There are direct flights to Vietnam from Adelaide, Melbourne, Sydney, Perth, Auckland and Wellington with **Cathay Pacific, Malaysia Airlines, Singapore Airlines** and **Thai.** There is also the option of flying into Hanoi and out of Ho Chi Minh City, or vice versa.

## ... and leaving again

**Airport tax** International departure taxes for Vietnam are now included in the airline ticket price. In Cambodia the international departure tax is US$25, domestic tax is US$6. In Laos it is US$15 for international; domestic airport tax is 5000 kip.

## Regional flights

If you have two weeks or less to spend in the region, it's important to factor in some flights if you want to cover a lot of ground. **Bangkok Airways,** www.bangkokair.com, offers a Discovery Airpass in cooperation with **Siem Reap Airways** (www.siemreap airways.com) and **Lao Airlines** (www.laoairlines.com), which permits several flights within the region at reduced rates. National carriers **Vietnam Airlines** (www.vietnam airlines.com) and **Lao Airlines** also offer regional flights.

Within Vietnam, **Vietnam Airlines** flies from Hanoi or Ho Chi Minh City to Dien Bien Phu, Hué, Danang, Nha Trang, Dalat, Buon Ma Thuot, Play Ku, Rach Gia and Phu Quoc. They also fly to Phnom Penh, Siem Reap and Bangkok. From Hanoi they fly to Luang Prabang. Flights can subsequently be altered at no cost at Vietnam Airlines booking offices, seat availability permitting. Within Vietnam there are two other domestic carriers, **Pacific Airlines** (www.pacificairlines.com.vn) and **Vasco Airlines**.

At the moment the only domestic route within Cambodia which operates safely and with any frequency is between Phnom Penh and Siem Reap, with **Siem Reap Airways** (www.siemreapairways.com). However, there are connections with Thailand (Bangkok), Malaysia (Kuala Lumpur), Singapore, Hong Kong, China (Guangzhou and Shanghai), Vietnam (Ho Chi Minh City), Taiwan (Taipei) and Laos (Vientiane and Pakse) from Phnom Penh. The following airlines currently operate international services to Phnom Penh's Pochentong Airport: **Bangkok Airways**; **Silk Air**; **Dragon Air**; **Thai**; **Malaysia Airlines**; **Vietnam Airlines**; **Siem Reap Airways**; **Lao Airlines**; **China Southern Airlines** and **Shanghai Airlines**. **Bangkok Airways, Vietnam Airlines, Silk Air** and **Lao Airlines** all operate flights to Siem Reap.

**Lao Airlines** flies internationally to Vientiane, Hanoi, Bangkok, Siem Reap, Kunming, Chiang Mai, Phnom Penh, They also run domestic flights to Phonsavanh (Xieng Khouang), Houei Xai, Oudom Xai and Pakse. All flights using **Lao Airlines**, whether domestic or international, have to be paid for in US dollars by foreigners. **Lao Airlines** flies three types of aeroplane: French-built *ATR-72s*, and Chinese-built *Y-7s* and *Y-12s*. The latter two are a risk. The most reliable, comfortable and newest machines – the *ATR-72s* – operate on the most popular routes (Vientiane-Bangkok, Vientiane-Luang Prabang, Vientiane-Pakse). Within Laos there is also a smaller, newer carrier, **Lao Air** (laoair@laopdr.com), which run flights to Xam Neua and Phongsali.

**Thai** (www.thaiair.com) flies to Ho Chi Minh City, Phnom Penh and Vientiane from Bangkok. Bangkok Airways flies daily between Bangkok and Luang Prabang. **Air Asia** (www.airasia.com) and **Nok Air** (www.nokair.com) fly to Udon Thani in northern Thailand for overland connections to Vientiane, see page 393. **Air Asia** also flies from Bangkok to Chiang Rai, Hanoi and Phnom Penh. Thai also flies to Chiang Rai.

# Getting around by land and river

## Vietnam

Open Tour Buses, see below, are very useful and cheap for bridging important towns. Train travel is exciting and overnight journeys are a good way of covering long distances. The Vietnamese rail network extends from Hanoi to Ho Chi Minh City. Many travellers opt to take a tour to reach remote areas because of the lack of self-drive car hire and the dangers and slow speed of public transport.

**Boat** The Victoria hotel chain (www.victoriahotels-asia.com) runs a Mekong Delta service for its guests. There are also services from Chau Doc to Phnom Penh, see border box, page 197.

**Bus** Since Highway 1 is so dangerous and public transport buses are poor and slow, most travellers opt for the cheap and regular Open Tour Bus (private mini-bus or coach) that covers the length of the country. Almost every Vietnamese tour operator/travellers' café listed in this guide will run a minibus service or act as an agent. The ticket is a flexible, one-way ticket from Ho Chi Minh City to Hanoi and vice versa. The buses run daily from their own offices and include the following stops: Ho Chi Minh City, Mui Ne, Nha Trang, Dalat, Hoi An, Hué, Ninh Binh and Hanoi. They will also stop off at tourist destinations along the way such as Lang Co, Hai Van Pass, Marble Mountains and Po Klong Garai. You may join at any leg of the journey, paying for one trip or several as you go. The Hanoi to Hué and vice versa is an overnight trip but although you might save on a night's accommodation you are unlikely to get much sleep. Note that bus listings in this guide refer to Open Tours Buses unless otherwise stated.

**Car hire** Self-drive car hire is not available in Vietnam. It is, however, possible to hire cars with drivers and this is a good way of getting to more remote areas with a group of people. Cars with drivers can be hired for around US$50-70 per day. All cars are modern and air-conditioned. Car hire prices increase by 50% or more during Tet. A standard, air-conditioned modern car including the driver, fuel, road fees and food and accommodation for the driver in and around Hanoi and the north would cost around US$250 for one week. For travelling the length of the country the cost could escalate to around US$1200 for a week including fuel, driver and food and accommodation for the driver or a discount may be offered for a one-way service where a company has multiple branches throughout the country.

**Motorbike and bicycle hire** Most towns are small enough for bicycles to be an attractive option but if taking in a sweep of the surrounding countryside (touring around the Central Highlands, for example) then a motorbike will mean you can see more. Motorbikes can be rented easily and are an excellent way of getting off the beaten track. You do not need a driver's licence or proof of motorbike training to hire a motorbike in Vietnam. It is only compulsory for motorcyclists riding on highways to wear helmets. Take time to familiarize yourself with road conditions and ride slowly.

Bicycles can be rented by the day in the cities and are useful for getting out into the countryside. Hotels often have bicycles for hire and there is usually someone willing to lend their machine for a small charge (US$1-2 per day). Many travellers' cafés rent out bicycles and motorbikes too, the latter for around US$6 a day. Motorbikes are hired out with helmets and bicycles with locks. Always park your bicycle or motorbike in a guarded parking place (*gui xe*). Ask for a ticket. The 2000d this costs is worth every dong, even if you are just popping in to the post office to post a letter.

**Motorbike taxi and cyclo** Motorcycle taxis, known as *honda ôm* or *xe ôm* are ubiquitous and cheap. You will find them on most street corners, outside hotels or in the street. With their uniform baseball caps and dangling cigarette, *xe ôm* drivers are readily recognizable. If they see you before you see them, they will shout 'moto' to get your attention. In the north and upland areas the Honda is replaced with the Minsk. The shortest hop would be at least 5000d. Always bargain though.

Cyclos are bicycle trishaws. Cyclo drivers charge double that of a *xe ôm*. A number of streets in the centres of Ho Chi Minh City and Hanoi are one-way or out of bounds to cyclos, necessitating lengthy detours which add to the time and cost. Do not take a cyclo after dark unless the driver is well known to you or you know the route. It is a wonderful way to get around the Old Quarter of Hanoi, though, and for those with plenty of time on their hands it is not so hazardous in smaller towns.

**Taxi** Taxis ply the streets of Hanoi and Ho Chi Minh City and other large towns and cities. They are cheap, around 12,000d per kilometre, and the drivers are better English speakers than cyclo drivers. See page 83 for an explanation of Vietnamese addresses. Always keep a small selection of small denomination notes with you so that when the taxi stops you can round up the fare to the nearest small denomination. At night use the better known taxi companies rather than the unlicensed cars that often gather around popular nightspots.

**Train Vietnam Railways** (www.vr.com.vn) runs the 2600-km rail network. With overnight stays at hotels along the way to see the sights, a rail sight-seeing tour from Hanoi to Ho Chi Minh City should take a minimum of 10 days but you would need to buy tickets for each separate journey. The difference in price between first and second class is small and it is worth paying the extra. There are three seating classes and four sleeping classes. The kitchen on the Hanoi-Ho Chi Minh City service serves soups and simple, but adequate, rice dishes (it is a good idea to take additional food and drink on long journeys though). First-class long-distance tickets include the price of meals. Six trains leave Hanoi for Ho Chi Minh City daily and vice versa. The express trains (**Reunification Express**) take between an advertised 29-39 hours. Most ticket offices have some staff who speak English. Queues can be long and sometimes confusing and some offices keep unusual hours. If you are short of time and short on patience it may well pay to get a tour operator to book your ticket for a small fee. All sleepers should be booked three days in advance.

## ⁞ Main border crossings

**Vietnam/Cambodia**
Moc Bai – Bavet, page 197
Kaam Samnor – Chau Doc
(Vinh Xuong crossing), page 197
Ha Tien – Kep, reference
page 290

**Vietnam/Laos**
Tay Trang – Muang Khua,
page 111
Nam Xoi – Nameo, page 452
Lao Bao – Savannakhet
(Dansavanh crossing), page 131

**Laos/Cambodia**
Voen Kham – Stung Treng
(Don Kralor crossing), page 307

**Laos/Thailand**
Houei Xai – Chiang Kong, page 434
Tha Na Leng – Nong Khai
(Friendship Bridge), page 393
Savannakhet – Mukdahan, page 467

**Cambodia /Thailand**
Koh Kong (Cham Yem crossing) –
Hat Lek, page 296

## Cambodia

Over the last few years the road system in Cambodia has dramatically improved. By the end of 2008 a trunk route of international standards, apart from a few gnarly stretches, from Stung Treng to Koh Kong will be fully open. Much of the rest of the network is pretty basic and journeys can sometimes be long and labourious. Also, to some parts, such as Ratanakiri, the road is a graded, laterite track, untarmacked and potholed. In the rainy season expect to be slowed down on many roads to slithering muddy crawl. The Khmer-American Friendship Highway (Route 4), which runs from Phnom Penh to Sihanoukville, is entirely tarmacked, as is the NH6 between Siem Reap and Phnom Penh. The infamous National Highway 6 between Poipet and Phnom Penh via Siem Reap has also had extensive work, as has National Highway 1. The Japanese in particular have put considerable resources into road and bridge building.

**Boat** All the Mekong towns and settlements around the Tonlé Sap are accessible by boat. It is a very quick and relatively comfortable way of travel and much cheaper than flying. The route between Siem Reap and Phnom Penh is very popular while the route between Siem Reap and Battambang is one of the most scenic. For those on a budget it is the best way to go. With the new road opening, boats are no longer used as a main form of transport along the Mekong and in the northeast.

**Bus and shared taxi** There are buses and shared taxis to most parts of the country. Shared taxis (generally Toyota Camrys) or pickups are usually the quickest and most reliable public transport option. The taxi operators charge a premium for better seats and you can buy yourself more space. It is not uncommon for a taxi to fit 10 people in it, including two sitting on the driver's seat. Fares for riding in the back of the truck are half that for riding in the cab. The Sihanoukville run has an excellent and cheap air-conditioned bus service.

**Car hire and taxi** A few travel agents and hotels may be able to organize self-drive car hire and most hotels have cars for hire with a driver (US$30-50 per day). There is a limited taxi service in Phnom Penh.

**Motorbike and bicycle hire** Motorbikes can be rented from between US$5 and US$8 per day and around US$1 per day for a bicycle. If riding either a motorbike or bicycle be aware that the accident rate is very high. This is partly because of the poor condition of many of the cars, trucks and other vehicles on the road; partly because of poor roads; and partly because of horrendously poor driving. If you do rent a motorbike ensure it has a working horn (imperative) and buy some rear-view mirrors so you can keep an eye on the traffic. Wear a helmet (even if using a motodop); it may not be cool but neither is a fractured skull.

**Moto** The most popular and sensible option is the motorbike taxi, known as 'moto'. This costs around the same as renting your own machine and with luck you will get a driver who speaks a bit of English and who knows where he's going. Once you have found a good driver stick with him: handing out the odd drink, a packet of cigarettes or an extra dollar or two is a good investment. Outside Phnom Penh and Siem Reap, do not expect much English from your moto driver.

## Laos

The roads are not good, but they are slowly improving. Many have been repaired or upgraded in recent years, making journeys infinitely more comfortable, as well as faster. Quite a few bus, truck, tuk-tuk, songthaew (see below) and taxi drivers understand the rudimentaries of English, French or Thai, although some of them (especially tuk-tuk drivers) aren't above forgetting the lowest price you thought you'd successfully negotiated before hopping aboard! It is best to take this sort of thing in good humour. Even so, in order to travel to a particular destination, it is a great advantage to have the name written out in Lao. Many people will not know road names, even if it's the road right outside their front door. However, they will know where all the sights of interest are – for example wats, markets, monuments, waterfalls, etc. In city centres make sure you have the correct money for your tuk-tuk as they are often conveniently short of change. Also opt to flag down a moving tuk-tuk rather than selecting one of the more expensive ones that sit out the front of tourist destinations.

**Boat** It is possible to take river boats up and down the Mekong and its main tributaries. Boats stop at Luang Prabang, Pak Beng, Houei Xai, around Don Deth, Don Khong, and other smaller towns and villages. Apart from the main route, Houei Xai to Luang Prabang, there are often no scheduled services and departures may be limited during the dry season. Take food and drink and expect somewhat crowded conditions aboard. The most common riverboats are the *hua houa leim*, with no decks, the hold being enclosed by side panels and a flat roof (note that metal boats get very hot). Speedboats also chart some routes, but are very dangerous and never enjoyable. Prices vary according to size of boat and length of journey.

**Bus/truck** It is now possible to travel to most areas of the country by bus, truck or songthaew (converted pickup truck) in the dry season, although road travel in the rainy season can be tricky if not impossible. VIP buses are very comfortable night buses, usually allowing a good sleep during the trip – but watch out for karaoke on board. In the south of Laos there is a night bus that plies the route from Pakse to Vientiane; make sure you book a double bed, otherwise you could end up sleeping next to a stranger. Robberies have been reported on the night buses so keep your valuables secure.

On certain long routes, such as Vientiane/Luang Prabang to Xam Neua, big Langjian (Chinese) trucks are sometimes used. These trucks have been colourfully converted into buses with a wooden structure on the back, divided wooden seats and glassless windows. In more remote places (Xam Neua to Vieng Xai, for instance), ancient jeeps are common.

In the south of the country, Japanese-donated buses are used although you may see the occasional shiny Volvo bus. Few of the roads are now unsealed, and breakdowns, though not frequent, aren't uncommon either. For some connections you may need to wait a day. During the rainy season (June to December) expect journey times to be longer than those quoted; indeed some roads may be closed altogether.

**Car hire** This costs anything from US$40-100 per day, depending on the vehicle, with first 150 km free, then US$10 every 100 km thereafter. The price includes a driver. For insurance purposes you will probably need an international driver's permit. Insurance is generally included with car hire but it's best to check the fine print. A general rule of thumb: if you are involved in a car crash, you, the foreigner, will be liable for costs as you have more money.

**Motorbike and bicycle hire** There are an increasing number of motorcycles available from guesthouses and other shops in major towns. 110cc bikes go for around US$4-10 a day, while 250cc Hondas are around US$20 per day. Bicycles are available in many towns and are a cheap way to see the sights. Many guesthouses have bikes for rent for US$1-2 per day.

**Tuk-tuk** The majority of motorized three-wheelers known as 'jumbos' or tuk-tuks are large motorbike taxis with two bench seats in the back. You'll find them in most cities and metropolitan areas; expect to pay around 10,000-15,000 kip for a short ride. They can also be hired by the hour or the day to reach destinations out of town.

# Sleeping

## Vietnam

Accommodation ranges from luxury suites in international five-star hotels and spa resorts to small, family hotels (mini hotels) and homestays with local people in the Mekong Delta and with the ethnic minorities in the Central Highlands and northwest Vietnam. During peak seasons – especially December to March and particularly during busy holidays such as Tet, Christmas, New Year's Eve and around Easter – booking is essential. Expect staff to speak English in all top hotels. Do not expect it in cheaper hotels or in more remote places, although most places employ someone with a smattering of a foreign language.

Private, mini hotels are worth seeking out as, being family-run, guests can expect quite good service. Mid-range and tourist hotels may provide a decent breakfast which is often included in the price. Many luxury and first-class hotels charge extra for breakfast and, on top of this, also charge VAT and service charge. There are some world-class beach resorts in Nha Trang, Mui Ne, Hoi An and Danang. In the northern uplands, in places like Sapa and Mai Chau, it is possible to stay in an ethnic minority house. Bathrooms are basic and will consist of a cold shower and a natural toilet. To stay in a homestay, you must book through a tour operator or through the local tourist office; you cannot just turn up. Homestays are also possible on farms and in orchards in the Mekong Delta. Here, guests sleep on camp beds and share a Western bathroom with hot and cold water. National parks offer everything from air-conditioned bungalows to shared dormitory rooms to campsites where, sometimes, it is possible to hire tents. Visitors may spend a romantic night on a boat in Halong Bay or on the Mekong Delta. Boats range from the fairly luxurious to the basic. Most people book through tour operators.

You will have to leave your passport at hotel reception desks for the duration of your stay. It will be released to you temporarily for bank purposes or buying an air ticket. Credit cards are widely accepted but there is often a 2-4% fee for paying in this manner. Tipping is not expected in hotels in Vietnam. See the box below for details of what to expect within each price category.

## Cambodia

Accommodation standards in Cambodia have greatly improved over the last couple of years. Phnom Penh now has a good network of genuine boutique hotels – arguably they are overpriced and sometimes management can be a bit Fawlty Towers but

## ⁝ Sleeping price codes

LL **Over US$200  Luxury**: mostly found in Bangkok with some in Ho Chi Minh City, Hanoi, Phnom Penh and Siem Reap. Some beach and mountain resorts also fall into this category.

L **US$100-199  First class plus**: there are a number of hotels in this category found in all the major cities and some smaller ones plus resorts across the region. Laos' top hotels fall into this category. A full range of facilities will be included.

A **US$50-99  First class**: these hotels are increasingly found in towns across Vietnam but less so in Cambodia and Laos. Hotels in this category should offer reasonable business services, a range of recreational facilities, restaurants and bars, although these services will be more limited in Cambodia and Laos. From this category upwards a 5-10% service and 10% VAT will be added to the bill in Vietnam.

B **US$25-49  Tourist class**: all rooms will have air-conditioning and an attached bathroom with hot water. Other services should include one or more restaurants, a bar and room service. In Bangkok and Vietnamese beach resorts a swimming pool may be available. Service charges may be added to the bill in Vietnam.

C **US$15-24  Economy**: rooms should be air-conditioned in Vietnam and Laos but not necessarily in Cambodia and will have attached bathrooms with hot water and Western toilets. A restaurant and room service will probably be available.

D **US$8-14  Medium budget**: air-conditioned rooms quite likely in Vietnam although not necessarily in Cambodia and Laos, also rooms may have an attached bathroom. Toilets should be Western-style. Bed linen will be provided, towels perhaps. There may be a restaurant.

E **US$4-7  Budget**: usually fan-cooled rooms and often shared bathrooms with cold water only and basic facilities. Bathrooms are more likely to have squat toilets. Bed linen should be provided, towels may not be. Rooms are small and facilities few.

F **Less than US$4  Dormitory/ guesthouse**-type accommodation, with shared bathroom facilities, squat toilets, fan-cooled and probably cold-water showers. Cleanliness will vary.

the bar has certainly been raised. Siem Reap, without doubt, has now become a destination for the upmarket international traveller. The range, depth and quality of accommodation here is of an excellent standard and is on a par with anywhere else in Asia. Even if you travel to some of the smaller, less visited towns, family-run Chinese style hotels should now provide hot water, a/c and cable TV even if they can't provide first class service. These places are often the best bargains in the country as many of the cheap backpacker places, while very, very cheap, are mostly hovels.

## Laos

Rooms in Laos are rarely luxurious and standards vary enormously. You can end up paying double what you would pay in Bangkok for similar facilities and service. However, the hotel industry is expanding rapidly. There is a reasonable choice of hotels of different standards and prices in Vientiane, Luang Prabang and Pakse and an expanding number of budget options in many towns on the fast-developing tourist trail. First-class hotels exist in Vientiane and Luang Prabang. The majority of guesthouses and hotels have fans and attached bathrooms, although more and more are providing air conditioning where there is a stable electricity supply, while others are installing their own generators to cater

## ⁞ Restaurant codes

| ♙♙♙ | Expensive | Over US$12 |
|---|---|---|
| ♙♙ | Moderate | US$6-12 |
| ♙ | Cheap | under US$6 |

Prices refer to the cost of a meal for one, without a drink.

for the needs of the growing tourist trade. Smaller provincial towns, having previously had only a handful of hotels and guesthouses – some of them quaint French colonial villas – are now home to a growing number of rival concerns as tourism takes off. In rural villages, people's homes are enthusiastically transformed into bed and breakfasts on demand. While Vientiane may still have little budget accommodation, many towns in the north, such as Vang Vieng, Muang Ngoi, Muang Sing and Luang Namtha, have a large choice of very cheap, and in some cases very good accommodation, including dorm beds. In the southern provinces, upmarket and boutique accommodation has popped up in Pakse and Don Khong. There are several excellent eco-lodges in the country, most notably the Boat Landing at Luang Namtha and the Kingfisher Ecolodge at Ban Kiet Ngong in the south. Many tour companies offer homestay in ethnic minority villages and camping as part of a package tour.

# Eating and drinking

## Vietnam

Vietnam offers outstanding Vietnamese, French and international cuisine in restaurants that range from first class to humble foodstalls. At either the quality will be, in the main, exceptional. The accent is on local, seasonal and fresh produce and the rich pickings from the sea, along Vietnam's 2000-km coastline will always make it far inland too. You will find more hearty stews in the more remote north and more salad dishes along the coast. All restaurants offer a variety of cuisine from the regions and some specialize in certain types of food – Hué cuisine, Cha Ca Hanoi etc. *Pho* (pronounced *fer*), noodle soup, is utterly delicious.

All Vietnamese food is dipped, whether in fish sauce, soya sauce, chilli sauce, peanut sauce or pungent prawn sauce (*mam tom* – avoid if possible) before eating. As each course is served so a new set of dips will accompany. Follow the guidance of your waiter or Vietnamese friends to get the right dip with the right dish.

Locally produced fresh beer is called *bia hoi*. Bar customers have a choice of • Tiger, Heineken, Carlsberg, San Miguel, 333, Saigon Beer or Huda. Rice and fruit wines are produced and consumed in large quantities in upland areas, particularly in the north of Vietnam. The Chinese believe that snake wines increase their virility and as such are normally found in areas of high Chinese concentration. Soft drinks and bottled still and sparkling mineral water are widely available. Tea and coffee is widely available. Coffee is drunk with condensed milk.

## Cambodia

For a country that has suffered and starved in the way Cambodia has, eating for fun as opposed to eating for survival, has yet to catch on as a pastime. There are some good restaurants and things are improving but don't expect Cambodia to be a smaller version of Thailand, or its cuisine even to live up to the standards of Laos. Cambodian food shows clear links with the cuisines of neighbouring countries: Thailand, Vietnam, and to a lesser extent, Laos. The influence of the French colonial period is also in evidence, most clearly in the availability of good French bread. Chinese food is also available owing to strong business ties between Cambodia and China. True Khmer food is difficult to find and much that the Khmers would like to claim as indigenous food is actually of Thai, French or Vietnamese origin. Curries, soups, rice and noodle-based dishes, salads, fried vegetables and sliced meats all feature in Khmer cooking.

Phnom Penh and Siem Reap have the best restaurants with French, Japanese, Italian and Indian food being available. But those who want to sample a range of dishes and get a feel for Khmer cuisine should head for the nearest market where dishes will be cooked on order in a wok – known locally as a *chhnang khteak*.

International soft drink brands are widely available in Cambodia. Tea is drunk without sugar or milk. Coffee is also served black, or 'crème' with sweetened condensed milk. Bottled water is easy to find, as is local mineral water. Fruit smoothies – known locally as *tikalok* – are ubiquitous. Local and imported beers are also available everywhere.

## Laos

Lao food is similar to that of Thailand, although the Chinese influence is slightly less noticeable. Lao dishes are distinguished by the use of aromatic herbs and spices such as lemon grass, chillies, ginger and tamarind. The best place to try Lao food is often from roadside stalls or in the markets. The staple Lao foods are *kao niao* (glutinous rice), which is eaten with your hands and fermented fish or *pa dek* (distinguishable by its distinctive smell), often laced with liberal spoons of *nam pa*, fish sauce. Being a landlocked country, most of the fish is fresh from the Mekong. One of the delicacies that shouldn't be missed is *Mok Pa* steamed fish in banana leaf. Most of the dishes are variations on two themes: fish and bird. *Laap*, also meaning 'luck' in Lao, is a traditional ceremonial dish made from (traditionally) raw fish or meat crushed into a paste, marinated in lemon juice and mixed with chopped mint. It is called *laap sin* if it has a meat base and *laap paa* if it's fish based. Beware of *laap* in cheap street restaurants. It is sometimes concocted from raw offal and served cold and should be consumed with great caution. Overall though laap is cooked well for the falang palate.

Restaurant food is, on the whole, hygienically prepared, and as long as street stall snacks have been well cooked, they are usually fine and a good place to sample local specialities. Really classy restaurants are only to be found in Vientiane and Luang Prabang . Good French cuisine is available in both cities. Salads, steaks, pizzas and more are all on offer. A better bet in terms of value for money are the Lao restaurants.

Far more prevalent are lower-end Lao restaurants which can be found in every town. Right at the bottom end – in terms of price if not necessarily in terms of quality – are stalls that charge a US$1-2 for filled baguettes or simple single-dish meals.

Soft drinks are expensive as they are imported from Thailand. Bottled water is widely available and produced locally, so it is cheap (about 3000 kip for a litre). *Nam saa*, weak Chinese tea, is free. Imported beer can be found in hotels, restaurants and bars but is not particularly cheap. *Beer Lao* is a light lager (although the alcohol content is 5%). The local brew is rice wine (*lao-lao*) which is drunk from a clay jug with long straws.

# Festivals and events

Colourful and serious ceremonies take place throughout the lunar calender in Vietnam. To help you work out on which day these events fall, check out the following website, which covert the Gregorian calendar to the lunar calendar: http://umunhum.stanford.edu/~lee/chicomp/lunar.html; consult also www.vietnamtourism.com. There are some 30 public holidays celebrated each year in Cambodia. Most are celebrated with public parades and special events to commemorate the particular holiday. The largest holidays also see many Khmers – although less than used to be the case – firing their guns, to the extent that red tracer fills the sky. Being of festive inclination, the Lao celebrate New Year four times a year: the international New Year in January, Chinese New Year in January/February, Lao New Year (Pi Mai) in April and Hmong New Year in December. The Lao Buddhist year follows the lunar calendar, so many of the festivals are movable.

## Bangkok

**Apr** (movable, public holiday). Songkran marks the beginning of the Buddhist New Year. It is a 3- to 5-day celebration, with parades, dancing and folk entertainment.

## Vietnam

**Late Jan-Mar** (movable, 1st-7th day of the new lunar year): **Tet** is the traditional new year. The big celebration of the year, the word Tet is the shortened version of tet nguyen dan ('first morning of the new period'). Tet is the time to forgive and forget and to pay off debts. It is also everyone's birthday – everyone adds one year to their age at Tet. Enormous quantities of food are consumed and new clothes are bought. It is believed that before Tet the spirit of the hearth, Ong Tao, leaves on a journey to visit the palace of the Jade Emperor where he must report on family affairs. To ensure that Ong Tao sets off in good cheer, a ceremony is held before Tet, Le Tao Quan, and during his absence a shrine is constructed (Cay Neu) to keep evil spirits at bay until his return. On the afternoon before Tet, Tat Nien, a sacrifice is offered at the family altar to dead relatives who are invited back to join in the festivities. Great attention is paid to preparations for Tet, because it is believed that the first week of the new year dictates the fortunes for the rest of the year. The first visitor to the house on New Year's morning should be an influential, lucky and happy person, so families take care to arrange a suitable caller.
**Apr** (5th or 6th of the 3rd lunar month): **Thanh Minh** (**New Year of the Dead** or **Feast of the Pure Light**). The Vietnamese walk outdoors to evoke the spirit of the dead and family shrines and tombs are cleaned and decorated.
**Aug** (movable, 15th day of the 7th lunar month): **Trung Nguyen** (**Wandering Souls Day**). During this time, prayers can absolve the sins of the dead who leave hell and return, hungry and naked, to their relatives. The Wandering Souls are those with no homes to go to. There are celebrations in Buddhist temples and homes, food is placed out on tables and money is burnt.

**Sep** (movable, 15th day of the 8th month): **Tet Trung Thi** (**Mid-Autumn Festival**). This festival is particularly celebrated by children. It is based on legend. In the evening families prepare food including sticky rice, fruit and chicken to be placed on the ancestral altars. Moon cakes (egg, green bean and lotus seed) are baked, lanterns are made and painted, and children parade through town with music.

## Cambodia

**Apr** (13-15): **Bonn Chaul Chhnam** (**Cambodian New Year**). A 3-day celebration to mark the turn of the year when predictions are made for the forthcoming year. The celebration is to show gratitude to the departing demi-god, filled with offerings of food and drink. Homes are spring cleaned. Householders visit temples and traditional games like both angkunh and chhoal chhoung are plaed and festivities are performed.
**Apr/May** Visak Bauchea (dates vary with the full moon), the most important Buddhist festival; a triple anniversary commemorating Buddha's birth, enlightenment and his Paranirvana (state of final bliss).
**Oct/Nov** (movable) **Bon Om Tuk** (**Water Festival** or **Festival of the Reversing Current**). Celebrates the movement of the waters out of the Tonlé Sap with boat races in Phnom Penh. Boat races extend over 3 days with more than 200 competitors but the highlight is the evening gala in Phnom Penh when a fleet of boats, studded with lights, row out under the full moon. Under the Cambodian monarchy, the king would command the waters to retreat.

## Laos

**Jan/Feb** (movable): **Chinese New Year**. Celebrated by Chinese and Vietnamese communities. Many businesses shut down for 3 days.
**Apr** (13-15): **Pi Mai** (**Lao New Year**). The first month of the Lao new Year is actually Dec but it is celebrated in Apr when days are longer than nights. One of the most important annual festivals, particularly in Luang Prabang. Statues of Buddha (in the

'calling for rain' posture) are ceremonially doused in water, which is poured along an intricately decorated trench (*hang song nam pha*). The small stupas of sand, decorated with streamers, in wat compounds are symbolic requests for health and happiness over the next year. It is celebrated with traditional Lao folksinging (*mor lam*) and the circle dance (*ramwong*). There is usually a 3-day holiday. 'Sok Dee Pi Mai' (good luck for the New Year) is usually said to one another during this period.

**May** (movable): **Boun Bang Fai**. The rocket festival, is a Buddhist rain-making festival. Large bamboo rockets are built and decorated by monks and carried in procession before being blasted skywards. The higher a rocket goes, the bigger its builder's ego gets. Designers of failed rockets are thrown in the mud. The festival lasts 2 days.

**Sep** (movable): **Boun Ok Phansa**. The end of the Buddhist Lent when the faithful take offerings to the temple. It is the '9th month' in Luang Prabang and the '11th month' in Vientiane, and marks the end of the rainy season. Boat races take place on the Mekong River with crews of 50 or more men and women. On the night before the race small decorated rafts are set afloat on the river.

**Nov** (movable): **Boun That Luang**. Celebrated in all Laos' *thats*, most enthusiastically and colourfully in Vientiane (see page 388).

# Shopping

## Vietnam

Vietnam is increasingly a good destination for shopping. A wide range of designer clothing, silk goods, high quality handicrafts, ceramics and lacquerware are available at excellent value. The main shopping centres are Hanoi, Ho Chi Minh City and Hoi An. Hoi An is the best place to get clothes made. Do not buy any marine turtle products. The majority of shops and markets in Vietnam are open from early in the morning to late at night every day of the week and do not close for lunch. Shops and markets will accept US dollars and Vietnamese dong and most shops also accept credit cards. Export of wood or antiques is banned and anything antique or antique-looking will be seized at customs. In order to avoid this happening you will need to get an export licence from the **Customs Department** ① *162 Nguyen Van Cu St, Hanoi, T04-8265260.*

## Cambodia

Phnom Penh's markets are highly diverting. Cambodian craftsmanship is excellent and whether you are in search of silverware, *kramas* – checked cotton scarves – hand-loomed sarongs or bronze buddhas you will find them all in abundance. A great favourite for its range and quality of antiques, jewellery and fabrics is the **Russian Market** (Psar Tuol Tom Pong). Silverware, gold and gems are available in the **Central Market** (Psar Thmei). *Matmii* – ikat – is also commonly found in Cambodia. It may have been an ancient import from Java and is made by tie-dyeing the threads before weaving. It can be bought throughout the country. Other local textile products to look out for are silk scarves bags and traditional wall-hangings. Colourful *kramas* can be found in local markets across the country and fine woven sarongs in cotton and silk are available in Phnom Penh and Siem Reap. Silk and other textiles products can be bought throughout the country. There has been a strong revival of pottery and ceramics in Cambodia in the last 30 years. Other crafts include bamboo work, wooden panels with carvings of the *Ramayana* and temple rubbings.

## Laos

Popular souvenirs from Laos include handicrafts and textiles, which are sold pretty much everywhere. The market is usually a good starting point as are some of the minority villagers. The smaller, less touristy towns will sell silk at the cheapest price (at about 40,000 kip a length). The best place to buy naturally dyed silk in Laos is in Xam Neua. This high quality silk often makes its way to Luang Prabang and Vientiane but usually at much greater cost. Most markets offer a wide selection of patterns and embroidery though amongst the best places to go are **Talaat Sao** (Vientiane Morning Market) or, behind it, the cheaper **Talaat Kudin**, which has a textile section in the covered area. If you wish to have something made, most tailors can whip up a simple *sinh* (Lao sarong) in a day but you might want to allow longer for adjustments or other items. **Ock Pop Tok** in Luang Prabang also has a fantastic reputation for producing top-shelf, naturally dyed silk. Vientiane and Luang Prabang offer the most sophisticated line in boutiques, where you can get all sorts of clothes from the utterly exquisite to the frankly bizarre. Those on a more frugal budget will find some tailors who can churn out a decent pair of trousers on Sisavangvong in Luang Prabang and around Nam Phou in Vientiane. If you get the right tailor, they can be much better than those found in Thailand both in terms of price and quality but you do need to be patient and allow time for multiple fittings. It is also a good idea to bring a pattern/picture of what you want.

**Silverware**, most of it is in the form of jewellery and small pots (though they may not be made of silver), is traditional in Laos. The finest silversmiths work out of Vientiane and Luang Prabang. Chunky antique ethnic-minority jewellery, bangles, pendants, belts and earrings are often sold in markets in the main towns, or antique shops in Vientiane, particularly congregating around Nam Phou. Xam Neua market also offers a good range of ethnic minority-style silver jewellery. Look for traditional necklaces that consist of wide silver bands, held together by a spirit lock (a padlock to lock in your scores of souls). Gold jewellery is the preference of the Lao Loum (lowland Laos) and its bright yellow colour is associated with Buddhist luck (often it is further dyed to enhance its orange goldness), this is best bought in Vientiane. Craftsmen in Laos are still producing **wood carvings** for temples and coffins. Designs are usually traditional, with a religious theme.

# Essentials A-Z

## Accident and emergency

Contact the relevant emergency service and your embassy. Make sure you obtain police/medical records in order to file insurance claims. If you need to report a crime visit your local police station and take a local with you who speaks English.
**Vietnam** Ambulance T115, Fire T114, Police T113.
**Cambodia** Ambulance T119 /724891, Fire T118, Police T117/112/012-999999.
**Laos** Ambulance T195, Fire T190, Police T191.

## Children

The region is not particularly geared up for visiting children but there are activities that will appeal to both adults and children alike.

Some attractions in **Vietnam** offer a child's concession. In terms of discounts, **Vietnam Airlines** offers under 12s a reduced fare. The railways allow children under 5 to travel free and charge 50% of the adult fare for those aged 5-10. The Open Tour

Bus tickets and tours are like-wise free for children under 2 but those aged 2-6 pay 75% of the adult price. Baby products are found in major supermarkets in the main cities. In the remoter regions, such as the north and the Central Highlands and smaller towns, take everything with you.

In **Cambodia** be aware that expensive hotels as well as market stalls may have squalid cooking conditions and try to ensure that children do not drink any water (especially important when bathing). For babies, powdered milk is available in provincial centres, although most brands have added sugar. Breast feeding is strongly recommended if possible. Baby food can also be bought in some towns – the quality may not be the same as equivalent foods bought in the West, but it is perfectly adequate for short periods. Disposable nappies can be bought in Phnom Penh, but are often expensive.

In **Laos**, disposable nappies can be bought in Vientiane and other larger provincial capitals, but again are often expensive.

Public transport may be a problem; long bus journeys are restrictive and uncomfortable. Chartering a car is the most convenient way to travel overland but rear seatbelts are scarce and child seats even rarer. Lao people love children and it is not uncommon for waiters and waitresses to spend the whole evening looking after your child.

## Customs and duty free

### Vietnam

Duty-free allowance is 400 cigarettes, 50 cigars or 100 g of tobacco, 1.5 litres of spirits, plus items for personal use. You cannot import pornography, anti-government literature, photographs or movies nor culturally unsuitable children's toys.

### Cambodia

A reasonable amount of tobacco products and spirits can be taken in without incurring customs duty – roughly 200 cigarettes or the equivalent quantity of tobacco, 1 bottle of liquor and perfume for personal use. Taking any Angkorian era images out of the country is strictly forbidden.

### Laos

Duty-free allowance is 500 cigarettes, 2 bottles of wine and a bottle of liquor. Laos has a strictly enforced ban on the export of antiquities and all Buddha images.

## Disabled travellers

Considering the proportion of the region's population that are seriously disabled, foreigners might expect better facilities for the immobile. However, some of the more upmarket hotels do have a few designated rooms for the disabled. For those with walking difficulties many of the better hotels have lifts. Wheelchair access is improving with more shopping centres, hotels and restaurants providing ramps for easy access. People sensitive to noise will find **Vietnam**, for example, at times, almost intolerable. The general situation in **Cambodia** is no better. The Angkor Complex can be a real struggle for disabled or frail persons. The stairs are 90 degrees steep and semi-restoration of areas means that visitors will sometimes need to climb over piles of bricks. Hiring an aide to help you climb stairs and generally get around is a very good ideaand can be hired for around US$5-10 a day. In **Laos** pavements are often uneven, there are potholes and missing drain covers galore, pedestrian crossings are ignored, ramps are unheard of, lifts are few and far between and escalators are seen only in magazines and high end hotels and a sprinkling of shopping complexes.

**RADAR**, 12 City Forum, 250 City Rd, London, EC1V 8AF, T0207-2503222, www.radar.org.uk. **SATH**, 347 Fifth Avenue, Suite 605, New York City, NY 10016, T0212-4477284, www.sath.org.

## Drugs

### Vietnam

Drugs are common and cheap and the use of hard drugs by Vietnamese is a rapidly growing problem. Attitudes towards users are incredibly lax and the worst that will happen is that certain bars and nightclubs may be closed for a few weeks. In such an atmosphere of easy availability and tolerance, many visitors may be tempted to indulge, and to excess, but beware that the end result can be disastrous. Attitudes to traffickers on the other hand are harsh, although the death penalty is usually reserved for Vietnamese and other Asians whose governments are less likely to kick up a fuss.

### Cambodia

Drug use is illegal in Cambodia but drugs are a big problem. Many places use marijuana in their cooking and the police seem to be quite ambivalent to dope smokers (unless they needto supplement their income with bribe money, in which case – watch out). The backpacker areas near the lake in Phnom Penh and Sihanoukville are particularly notorious for heavy drug usage by Westerners, some of whom have actually died as a result of mistakenly overdosing on heroin. It is important to note that cocaine and ecstasy do not really exist in Cambodia, despite what you may be told. Avoid *yaa baa*, a particularly insidious amphetamine. It has serious side effects and can be lethal.

### Laos

Drug use is illegal and there are harsh penalites ranging from fines through to imprisonment or worse. Police have been known to levy heavy fines on people in Vang Vieng for eating so-called 'happy' foods, see page 395, or for being caught in possession of drugs. Note that 'happy' food can make some people extremely sick. Though opium has in theory been eradicated it is still for sale in northern areas and people have died from over-dosing.*Yaa baa* is also available here and should be avoided at all costs.

## Electricity

**Vietnam** Voltage 110. Sockets are round 2-pin. Sometimes they are 2 flat pin. A number of top hotels now use UK 3 square-pin sockets.
**Cambodia** Voltage 220. Sockets are usually round 2-pin.
**Laos** Voltage 220, 50 cycles in the main towns. 110 volts in the country; 2-pin sockets. Blackouts are common outside Vientiane and many smaller towns are not connected to the national grid and only have power during the evening.

## Embassies and consulates

**Vietnamese**
**Australia**, 6 Timbarra Cres, O'Malley Canberra, ACT 2606, T+61-2-6286 6059/2.
**Cambodia**, 436 Monivong, Phnom Penh, T+855-23-364741.
**Canada**, 470 Wilbrod St, Ottawa, Ontario, K1N 6M8, T+1-613-236 0772.
**France**, 62-66 R Boileau-75016, Paris, T+33-1-4414 6447.
**Laos**, That Luang Rd, Vientiane, T+856-21-413409; 118 Si-Sa-Vang-Vong Moung Khanthabouli, Savannakhet, T+856-41-212418.
**South Africa**, 87 Brooks St, Brooklyn, Pretoria, T+27-12-362 8119.
**Thailand**, 83/1 Wireless Rd, Lumpini, Pathum-wan, Bangkok 10330, T+66-2-2515838.
**United Kingdom**, 12-14 Victoria Rd, London W8 5RD, T+44-(0)207 937 1912.
**USA**, 1233, 20th St, NW Suite 400 Washington DC, 20036, T+1-202-861 0737.

**Cambodian**
**Australia**, 5 Canterbury Cres, Deakin, ACT 2600, Australia, T+61-2-6273 1259.
**Laos**, Thadeua Rd, KM2 Vientiane, BP34 T+856-21-314950.

**New Zealand**, see Australia.
**Thailand**, 185 Rajdamri Rd, Lumpini Patumwan, Bangkok 10330, T+66-2-254 6630, recbkk@cscoms.com.
**United Kingdom**, 64 Brondesbury Park, Willesden Green, London NW6 7AT, T+44-(0)207 451 7850.
**USA**, 4530, 16th St NW, Washington DC 20011, T1-202 726 8042.
**Vietnam**, 41 Phung Khac Khoan, HCMC, T0848-829 2751, cambocg@hcm.vmn.vn; 71 Tran Hung Dao St, Hanoi, T+844-942 4789, arch@fpt.vn.

**Laos**
**Australia**, 1 Dalman Cres, O' Malley Canberra, ACT 2606, T+61-2-864595.
**Cambodia**, 15-17 Mao Tse Toung Bvd, Phnom Penh, T+855-23-982632.
**France**, 74 Ave Raymond-Poincaré 75116 Paris, T+33-1-4553 0298.
**Thailand**, 502/1 Soi Ramkamhaeng 39, Thanon Pracha Uthit, Wangthonglang, Bangkok 10310, T+66-2-539 6667.
**Vietnam**, 22 Tran Binh Trong, Hanoi, T04-2854576; 181 Hai Ba Trung, Ho Chi Minh City, T+844-829 7667.

## Gay and lesbian

**Vietnam**
The Vietnamese are tolerant of homo-sexuality. There are no legal restraints for 2 people of the same sex co-habitating in the same room be they Vietnamese or non-Vietnamese. There are several bars in central HCMC popular with gays. Cruising in dark streets is not advised. An Asian online resource for gays and lesbians which includes a list of scams and warnings in Vietnam as well as gay-friendly bars in Hanoi and HCMC is www.utopia-asia.com.

**Cambodia**
Gay and lesbian travellers will have no problems in Cambodia. Men often hold other men's hands as do women, so this kind of affection is nothing short of commonplace. Any kind of passionate kissing or sexually orientated affection in public is taboo – both for straight and gay people. The gay scene is just starting to develop in Cambodia but there is definitely a scene in the making. **Linga**

*Essentials A-Z*

Barin Siem Reap and the **Salt Lounge** in Phnom Penh are both gay bars and are excellent choices for a night out.

## Laos

Gay and lesbian travellers should have no problems in Laos. It does not have a hot gay scene per se and the Lao government is intent on avoiding the mushrooming of the gay and straight sex industry. Officially it is illegal for any foreigner to have a sexual relationship with a Lao person they aren't married to. Openly gay behaviour is contrary to local culture and custom and visitors, whether straight or gay, should not flaunt their sexuality. Any overt display of passion or even affection in public is taboo. In Vientiane there aren't any gay bars, although there are some bars and clubs where gays congregate. Luang Prabang has a few more options and is fast becoming one of Southeast Asia's most gay friendly destinations.

## Health

See your doctor or travel clinic at least 6 weeks before your departure for general advice on travel risks, malaria and vaccinations. Make sure you have travel insurance, get a dental check (especially if you are going to be away for more than a month), know your own blood group and if you suffer a long-term condition such as diabetes or epilepsy make sure someone knows or that you have a Medic Alert bracelet/necklace with this information on it (www.medicalert.co.uk).

### Vaccinations

The following are advised:
**BCG** It is not known how much protection this vaccination gives the traveller against lung tuberculosis but it is currently advised that people have it in the absence of any better alternative.
**Hepatitis A** Yes, as the disease can be caught easily from food/water.
**Japanese Encephalitis** May be advised for some areas, depending on the duration of the trip and proximity to rice growing and pig-farming areas.
**Polio** Yes, if no booster in last 10 years.
**Rabies** Advised if travelling to jungle and/or remote areas

**Tetanus** Yes, if not vaccinated in last 10 years (but after 5 doses you've had enough for life).
**Typhoid** Yes, if none in last 3 years.
**Yellow Fever** The disease does not exist in Vietnam, Cambodia or Laos. However, the authorities may wish to see a certificate if you have recently arrived from an endemic area in Africa or South America.

### Health risks

**Malaria** exists in rural areas in **Vietnam**. However, there is no risk in the Red River Delta and the coastal plains north of Nha Trang. Neither is there a risk in Hanoi, Ho Chi Minh City, Danang and Nha Trang. Malaria exists in most of **Cambodia**, except the capital Phnom Penh. Malaria is prevalent in **Laos** and remains a serious disease; about a third of the population contracts malaria at some stage in their lives. The choice of malaria prophylaxis will need to be something other than chloroquine for most people, since there is such a high level of resistance to it. Always check with your doctor or travel clinic for the most up-to-date advice.

Malaria can cause death within 24 hrs. It can start as something just resembling an attack of flu. You may feel tired, lethargic, headachy, feverish; or more seriously, develop fits, followed by coma and then death. Have a low index of suspicion because it is very easy to write off vague symptoms, which may actually be malaria. If you have a temperature, go to a doctor as soon as you can and ask for a malaria test. On your return home if you suffer any of these symptoms, get tested as soon as possible, even if any previous test proved negative, the test could save your life.

The most serious viral disease is **dengue fever**, which is hard to protect against as the mosquitos bite throughout the day as well as at night. Bacterial diseases include **tuberculosis** (TB) and some causes of the more common traveller's **diarrhoea**. Each year there is the possibilty that **avian flu** or **SARS** might rear their ugly heads. Check the news reports. If there is a problem in an area you are due to visit you may be advised to have an ordinary flu shot or to seek expert advice. There are high rates of

HIV in the region, especially among sex workers. Rabies and **schistosomiasis** (bilharzia, a water-borne parasite) may be a problem in Laos.

## Medical services
### Vietnam
Western hospitals exist in Hanoi and Ho Chi Minh City in Vietnam.
**International SOS**, Central Building, 31 Hai Ba Trung St, Hanoi, T04-934066, www.internationalsos.com/countries/Vietnam/. Open 24 hrs for emergencies, routine and medical evacuation. Dental service too.
**Columbia Asia** (Saigon International Clinic), 8 Alexander de Rhodes St, HCMC, T08-8238455 (T08-8238888, 24-hr emergency), www.columbiaasia.com. International doctors offering a full range of services.

### Cambodia
Hospitals are not recommended anywhere in Cambodia (even at some of the clinics that profess to be 'international'). If you fall ill or are injured the best bet is to get yourself quickly to either Bumrungrad Hospital or Bangkok Nursing Home, both in **Bangkok**. Both hospitals are of an exceptional standard, even in international terms.

### Laos
Hospitals are few and far between and medical facilities are poor in Laos. Emergency treatment is available at the Mahosot Hospital and Clinique Setthathirath in Vientiane. The Australian embassy also has a clinic for Commonwealth citizens with minor ailments (see page 411); US$60 per consultation. Better facilities are available in Thailand; emergency evacuation to **Nong Khai** or **Udon Thani** (Thailand) can be arranged at short notice.

### Thailand
**Aek Udon Hospital**, Udon Thani, Thailand T+66-42-342555. A 2½-hr trip from Vientiane.
**Bumrungrad Hospital**, Soi 3 Sukhumvit, Bangkok, T+66-2-667 1000, www.bumrungrad.com. The best option: a world-class hospital with brilliant medical facilities.
**Nong Khai Wattana General Hospital**, T+66-42-465201, is a better alternative to the hospitals in Vientiane and only a 40-min trip from the capital.

## Useful websites
**www.btha.org** British Travel Health Association (UK). This is the official website of an organization of travel health professionals.
**www.cdc.gov** US Government site which gives excellent advice on travel health and details of disease outbreaks.
**www.fitfortravel.scot.nhs.uk** A-Z of vaccine/health advice for each country.
**www.who.int** The WHO Blue Book lists the diseases of the world.

# Insurance

Always take out travel insurance before you set off and read the small print carefully. Check that the policy covers the activities you intend or may end up doing. Also check exactly what your medical cover includes, eg ambulance, helicopter rescue or emergency flights back home. Also check the payment protocol. You may have to cough up first before the insurance company reimburses you. It is always best to dig out all the receipts for expensive personal effects like jewellery or cameras. Take photos of these items and note down all serial numbers. You are advised to shop around. **STA Travel** and other reputable student travel organisations offer good value policies. Young travellers from North America can try the **International Student Insurance Service** (ISIS), which is available through **STA Travel**, T01-800-7770112, www.sta-travel.com. Other recommended travel insurance companies in North America include: **Travel Guard**, www.noelgroup.com; **Access America**, www.accessamerica.com; **Travel Insurance Services**, www.travelinsure.com; and **Travel Assistance International**, www.travelassistance.com. Older travellers should note that some companies will not cover people over 65 years old, or may charge higher premiums. The best policies for older travellers (UK) are offered by **Age Concern**, www.ageconcern.org.uk.

# Internet

### Vietnam
Although emailing is now usually easy enough in Vietnam, access to the internet from within Vietnam is restricted as the

authorities battle vainly to firewall Vietnam-related topics. Access has greatly improved with broadband available in many places in Hanoi and HCMC and there are internet cafés in nearly every town. Rates are 3000-30,000d per hr.

### Cambodia

Cambodia is surprisingly well-connected and most medium-sized to large towns have internet access. Not surprisingly, internet is a lot more expensive in smaller towns, up to a whopping US$5 per hr. In Phnom Penh internet rates are US$1-2 per hr and in Siem Reap should be US$1 per hr or under.

### Laos

Internet cafés have been popping up all over Laos over the last few years. The connections are surprisingly good in major centres. Fast, cheap internet is available in Vientiane, Luang Prabang, Vang Vieng and Savannakhet for around 100-200 kip per minute. Less reliable and more expensive internet (due to long-distance calls) can be found in Phonsavanh, Don Khone, Don Deth, Luang Namtha, Thakhek, Savannakhet and Udomxai. Many internet cafés also offer international phone services.

## Language

### Vietnam

You are likely to find a smattering of English wherever there are tourist services but outside tourist centres communication can be a problem for those who have no knowledge of Vietnamese. Furthermore, the Vietnamese language is not easy to learn. For example, pronunciation presents enormous difficulties as it is tonal. On the plus side, Vietnamese is written in a Roman alphabet making life much easier: place and street names are instantly recognizable. French is still spoken and often very well by the more elderly and educated.

### Cambodia

In Cambodia the national language is Khmer (pronounced Khmei). It is not tonal and the script is derived from the southern Indian alphabet. French is spoken by the older generation who survived the Khmer Rouge

era. English is the language of the younger generations. Away from Phnom Penh, Siem Reap and Sihanoukville it can be difficult to communicate with the local population.

### Laos

Lao is the national language but there are many local dialects, not to mention the ubiquitous languages of the minority groups. Lao is closely related to Thai and, in a sense, is becoming more so as the years pass. Though there are important differences between the languages, they are mutually intelligible – just about. French is spoken, though only by government officials, hotel staff and many educated people over 40. However, most government officials and many shopkeepers have some command of English.

## Media

### Vietnam

Unlike western newspapers, Vietnamese papers are less interested in what has happened (that is to say, news), preferring instead to report on what will happen or what should happen, featuring stories such as 'Party vows to advance ethical lifestyles' and 'Output of fertilizer to grow 200%'. The English language daily *Vietnam News* is widely available. Inside the back page is an excellent 'What's on' section. *The Guide*, a monthly magazine on leisure and tourism produced by the *Vietnam Economic Times*, can be found in tourist centres. Good hotels will have cable TV with a full range of options.

### Cambodia

Cambodia has a vigorous English-language press which fights bravely for editorial independence and freedom to criticize politicians. The principal English-language newspapers are the fortnightly *Phnom Penh Post*, which many regard as the best and the *Cambodia Daily*, published 5 times a week. There are also several tourist magazine guides. The BBC World Service provides probably the best news and views on Asia (available on 100 FM).

### Laos

The *Vientiane Times*, is published 5 times a week and provides some interesting cultural and tourist-based features, as well as quirky stories translated from the local press and wire service. Television is becoming increasingly popular as more towns and villages get electricity. The national TV station broadcasts in Lao. In Vientiane, CNN, BBC, ABC and a range of other channels are broadcast. Thailand's Channel 5 subtitles the news in English. The Lao National Radio broadcasts news in English. The BBC World Service can be picked up on shortwave.

## Money

### Vietnam

The unit of currency is the dong. The exchange rate at the time of going to press was US$1 = 16,027d; £1 = 31,840d, €1 = 23,036d. Under law, shops should only accept dong but in practice this is not enforced and dollars are accepted almost everywhere. If possible, however, try to pay for everything in dong as prices are usually lower and in more remote areas people may be unaware of the latest exchange rate. Also, to ordinary Vietnamese, 15,000d is a lot of money, while US$1 means nothing. ATMs are plentiful in HCMC and Hanoi and can also be found in other major tourist centres, but it is a good idea to travel with US$ cash as a back up. Banks in the main centres will change other major currencies including UK pound sterling, Hong Kong dollar, Thai baht, Swiss franc, Euros, Australian dollars, Singapore dollars and Canadian dollars. **Credit cards** are increasingly accepted, particularly Visa, MasterCard, Amex and JCB. Large hotels, expensive restaurants and medical centres invariably take them but beware a surcharge of between 2.5 and 4.5%. Most hotels will not add a surcharge onto your bill if paying by credit card. Traveller's cheques are best denominated in US$ and can only be cashed in banks in the major towns. Commission of 2-4% is payable if cashing into dollars but not if you are converting them direct into dong.

### Cambodia

The riel is the official currency though US dollars are widely accepted and easily exchanged. At the time of going to press the exchange rates were US$1 = 3946, £1= 7800, €1 = 5810.

In Phnom Penh and other towns most goods and services are priced in dollars and there is little need to buy riel. In remote rural areas prices are quoted in riel (except accommodation). Money can be exchanged in banks and hotels. US$ traveller's cheques are easiest to exchange – commission ranges from 1 to 3%. Cash advances on credit cards are available. Credit card facilities are limited but some banks, hotels and restaurants do accept them, mostly in the tourist centres.

ANZ Royal Bank has recently opened a number of ATMs throughout Phnom Penh. Machines are also now appearing in other towns and a full ATM network should be established in the next couple of years.

### Laos

The kip is the official currency. At the time of going to press the exchange rate was US$1 = 9559 kip, £1 = 19,044 kip, €1 = 13,728 kip. The lowest commonly used note is the 500 kip and the highest, the recently introduced 50,000 kip tends to shadow the Thai baht but with a rather quaint one week delay. It is getting much easier to change currency and traveller's cheques. Banks are generally reluctant to give anything but kip in exchange for hard currency. US dollars and Thai baht can be used as cash in most shops, restaurants and hotels and the Chinese Yuan is starting to be more widely accepted in northern parts of Laos (closer to the Chinese border). A certain amount of cash (in US dollars or Thai baht) can also be useful in an emergency. Banks include the Lao Development Bank and Le Banque pour Commerce Exterieur Lao (BCEL), which change most major international currencies (cash) and traveller's cheques denominated in US dollars and pounds sterling. Many of the BCEL branches offer cash advances on Visa/MasterCard. Note that some banks charge a hefty commission of US$2 per TC. While banks will change traveller's cheques and cash denominated in most major currencies into kip, some will only change US dollars into Thai baht, or into US dollars cash.

Thai baht are readily accepted in most towns but it is advisable to carry kip in rural areas (buses, for example, will usually only accept kip).

The BCEL has distributed several ATMs across the country but at the time of publication the majority of these were MasterCard only. Multi-card ATMS (only Visa and MasterCard) are only available in Vientiane but several more are planned in the future. At the time of writing, there were only a sprinkling of international multi-card ATMs in Vientiane (at the **BCEL** bank in Vientiane on Fa Gnum, near the Novotel and 500 m from Wat Simuang temple and across from the Lao Plaza Hotel), but will only dispense a maximum of 700,000 kip at a time. On weekends, the only other options for exchange or obtaining cash are the **BCEL** booth along the river.

Payment by credit card is becoming easier – although beyond the larger hotels and restaurants in Vientiane and Luang Prabang do not expect to be able to get by on plastic. American Express, Visa, MasterCard/Access cards are accepted in a limited number of more upmarket establishments. Note that commission is charged by some places on credit card transactions. If they can route the payment through Thailand then a commission is not levied; but if this is not possible, then 3% is usually added.

Many BCEL banks will now advance cash on credit cards in Luang Prabang, Vientiane, Pakse, Phonsavanh, Savannakhet and Vang Vieng (not all cards are accepted at these banks, so it's better to check in advance).

#### Cost of travelling
**Vietnam** is better overall value than Cambodia and Laos as it has a better established tourism infrastructure and more competitive services. On a budget expect to pay around US$6-12 per night for accommodation and about the same each day for food. A good mid-range hotel will cost US$12-30. There are comfort and cost levels anywhere from here up to US$200 per night. For travelling many use the Open Tour Buses as they are inexpensive and, by Vietnamese standards, 'safe'. Slightly more expensive are trains followed by planes. The budget traveller will find that a little goes a long way in **Cambodia**. Numerous guesthouses offer accommodation at around US$3-7 a night.

Food-wise, the seriously strapped can easily manage to survive healthily on US$4-5 per day, so an overall daily budget (not allowing for excursions) of US$7-9 should be enough or the really cost-conscious. For the less frugally minded, a daily allowance of US$30 should see you relatively well-housed and fed, while at the upper end of the scale, there are, in Phnom Penh and Siem Reap, plenty of restaurants and hotels for those looking for Cambodian levels of luxury. A mid-range hotel (attached bathroom, hot water and a/c) will normally cost around US$25 per night and a good meal at a restaurant around US$5-10.

The variety of available domestic flights means that the bruised bottoms, dust-soaked clothes and stiff limbs that go hand-in-hand with some of the longer bus/boat rides can be avoided by those with thicker wallets in **Laos**. Note that foreigners pay more than locals for flights in Laos. As the roads improve and journey times diminish, buses have emerged as the preferred (not to mention most reasonably priced) transportation option. Budget accommodation costs US$3-10 with a mid-range hotel costing from US$20-30. Local food is very cheap and it is possible to eat well for under US$2. Most Western restaurants will charge between US$2-5.

## Opening hours

### Vietnam
**Shops** Daily 0800-2000. Some stay open for another hour or two, especially in tourist centres.
**Banks** Mon-Fri 0800-1600. Many close 1100-1300 or 1130-1330.
**Offices** Mon-Fri 0730-1130, 1330-1630.
**Restaurants, cafés, bars** Daily from 0700 or 0800 although some open earlier. Bars are meant to close at 2400 by law.

### Cambodia
**Shops** Daily from 0800-2000. Some, however, stay open for a further hour or two, especially in tourist centres. Most markets open daily between 0530/0600-1700.
**Banks** Mon-Fri 0800-1600. Some close 1100-1300. Some major branches are open until 1100 on Sat.

**Offices** Mon-Fri 0730-1130, 1330-1630.
**Restaurants**, **cafés** and **bars** Daily from
0700-0800 although some open earlier.
Bars are meant to close at 2400 by law.

### Laos

**Banks** Mon-Fri 0830-1600 (some close
at 1500).
**Offices** Mon-Fri 0900-1700; those that
deal with tourists stay open a bit later and
are also usually open over the weekends.
Government offices close at 1600.
**Bars** and **nightclubs** Usually close around
2200-2300 depending on how strictly the
curfew is being inforced. In smaller towns,
most restaurants and bars will be closed
by 2200.

## Police and the law

### Vietnam

If you are robbed in Vietnam, report the
incident to the police (for your insurance
claim). Otherwise, the police are of no use
whatsoever. They will do little or nothing
(apart from log the crime on an incident
sheet which you will need for your insurance
claim). Vietnam is not the best place to
come into conflict with the law. Avoid
getting arrested. If you are arrested,
however, ask for consular assistance
immediately and English-speaking staff.

Involvement in politics, possession of
political material, business activities that
have not been licensed by appropriate
authorities, or non-sanctioned religious
activities (including proselytizing) can
result in detention. Sponsors of small,
informal religious gatherings such as
bible-study groups in hotel rooms, as
well as distributors of religious materials,
have been detained, fined and expelled.
(Source: US State Department.) The army
are extremely sensitive about all their
military buildings and become exceptionally
irate if you take a photo. There are signs to
this effect outside all military installations,
of which there are hundreds.

### Cambodia

A vast array of offences are punishable in
Cambodia, from minor traffic violations
through to possession of drugs. If you are
arrested or are having difficulty with the
police contact your embassy immediately.
As the police only earn approximately
US$20 a month, corruption is a problem
and contact should be avoided, unless
absolutely necessary. Most services,
including the provision of police reports,
will require paying bribes. Law enforcement
is very haphazard, at times completely
subjective and justice can be hard to
find. Some smaller crimes receiving large
penalties while perpetrators of greater
crimes often get off scot-free.

### Laos

If you are robbed insurers will require that
you obtain a police report. The police may
try to solicit a bribe for this service. Although
not ideal, you will probably have to pay this
fee to obtain your report. Laws aren't strictly
enforced but when the authorities do
prosecute people the penalties can be harsh,
ranging from deportation through to prison
sentences. If you are arrested seek embassy
and consular support. People are routinely
fined for drugs possession, having sexual
relations with locals (when unmarried) and
proselytizing. If you are arrested or
encounter police, try to remain calm and
friendly. Although drugs are available
throughout the country, the police levy
hefty fines and punishments if caught.

## Post

### Vietnam

Postal services are pretty good. Post offices
open daily 0700-2100; smaller ones close
for lunch.

### Cambodia

International service is unpredictable but it
is reasonably priced and fairly reliable (at
least from Phnom Penh). Only send mail
from the GPO in any given town rather
than sub POs or mail boxes. **Fedex** and **DHL**
also offer services.

### Laos

The postal service is inexpensive and reliable
but delays are common. As the National
Tourism Authority assures: in Laos the
stamps will stay on the envelope. Contents
of outgoing parcels must be examined by
an official before being sealed. Incoming

mail should use the official title, Lao PDR. There is no mail to home addresses or guesthouses, so mail must be addresses to a PO Box. The post office in Vientiane has a poste restante service. EMS (Express Mail Service) is available from main post offices in larger towns. In general, post offices open 0800-1200, 1300-1600. In provincial areas, **Lao Telecom** is usually attached to the post office. **DHL**, **Fedex** and **TNT** have offices in Vientiane.

## Public holidays

### Vietnam

**1 Jan**  New Year's Day.
**3 Feb**  Founding anniversary of the Communist Party of Vietnam.
**30 Apr**  Liberation Day of South Vietnam and HCMC.
**1 May**  International Labour Day.
**19 May**  Anniversary of the Birth of Ho Chi Minh (this is a government holiday). The majority of state institutions will be shut but businesses in the private sector carry on regardless.
**2 Sep**  National Day.
**3 Sep**  President Ho Chi Minh's Anniversary.

### Cambodia

**1 Jan**  National Day and Victory over Pol Pot.
**7 Jan**  Celebration of the fall of the Khmer Rouge in 1979.
**8 Mar**  Women's Day. Processions, floats and banners in main towns.
**17 Apr**  Independence Day.
**1 May**  Labour Day.
**9 May**  Genocide Day.
**1 Jun**  International Children's Day.
**18 Jun**  Her Majesty Preah Akkaek Mohesey Norodom Monineath Sihanouk's Birthday.
**Sep** (movable)  End of Buddhist 'lent'.
**24 Sep**  Constitution Day.
**23 Oct**  Paris Peace Accord.
**30 Oct-1 Nov**  King's Birthday.
**9 Nov**  Independence Day (1953).
**10 Dec**  Human Rights Day.

### Laos

**1 Jan**  New Year's Day.
**6 Jan**  Pathet Lao Day. Parades and holidays in some towns.
**20 Jan**  Army Day.
**8 Mar**  Women's Day.

**22 Mar**  People's Party Day.
**1 May**  Labour Day.
**1 Jun**  Children's Day.
**2 Dec**  Independence Day.

## Safety

### Travel advisories

The US State Department's travel advisories: **Travel Warnings & Consular Information Sheets**, www.travel.state.gov/travel_warnings.html.
The **UK Foreign and Commonwealth Office**'s travel warning section, www.fco.gov.uk/travel/.

### Vietnam

Do not take any valuables on to the streets of HCMC as bag and jewellery snatching is a common and serious problem. Thieves work in teams, often with beggar women carrying babies as a decoy. Beware of people who obstruct your path (pushing a bicycle across the pavement is a common ruse); your pockets are being emptied from behind. Young men on fast motorbikes also cruise the central streets of HCMC waiting to pounce on unwary victims. The situation in other cities is not as bad but take care in Nha Trang and Hanoi. Never go by cyclo in a strange part of town after dark.

Lone women travellers have fewer problems than in many other Asian countries. The most common form of harassment usually consists of comic and harmless displays of macho behaviour.

Unexploded ordnance is still a threat in some areas. It is best not to stray too far from the beaten track and don't unearth bits of suspicious metal.

Single western men will be targeted by prostitutes on street corners, in tourist bars and those cruising on motorbikes.

### Cambodia

Cambodia is not as dangerous as some would have us believe. The country has really moved forward in protecting tourists and violent crime towards visitors is comparatively low. Since large penalties have been introduced for those who kill or maim tourists, random acts of violence aren't as common these days. Safety on the night-time streets of Phnom Penh is a problem. Robberies and hold-ups are common. Many robbers are armed, so do not resist. As Phnom Penh has a limited taxi service, travel after dark poses a problem. Stick to moto drivers you know. Women are, obviously, particularly targeted by bag snatchers. Khmer New Year is known locally as the 'robbery season'. Theft is endemic at this time of year so be on red alert. A common trick around New Year is for robbers to mess around with tourists (usually throwing water and talcum powder in the eyes) and rob them blind. Leave your valuables in the hotel safe or hidden in your room. Sexual harassment is not uncommon. Many motos/tour guides will try their luck with women but generally it is more macho posturing than anything serious.

Outside Phnom Penh safety is not as much of a problem. Visitors should be very cautious when walking in the countryside, however, as landmines and other unexploded ordnance is a ubiquitous hazard. Stick to well worn paths, especially around Siem Reap and when visiting remote temples. Motorbike accidents have serious fatality rates as they do in Vietnam.

**Laos**

Crime rates are very low but it is advisable to take the usual precautions. Most areas of the country are now safe – a very different state of affairs from only a few years ago when foreign embassies advised tourists not to travel along certain roads and in certain areas (in particular Route 13 between Vientiane and Luang Prabang, and Route 7 between Phonsavanh and Route 13). Today these risks have effectively disappeared. However, the government will sometimes make areas provisionally off-limits if they think there is a security risk – take heed!

There has been a reported increase in motorcycle drive-by thefts in Vientiane, but these and other similar crimes are still at a low level compared with most countries. If riding on a motorbike or bicycle, don't carry your bag strap over your shoulder – as you could get pulled off the bike if someone goes to snatch your bag. In the Siphandon and Vang Vieng areas, theft seems more common. Use a hotel security box if available.

Road accidents are on the increase. The hiring of motorbikes is becoming more

popular and consequently there are more tourist injuries. Wear a helmet.

Be careful around waterways, as drowning is one of the primary causes of tourist deaths. Be particularly careful during the rainy season (May-Sep) as rivers have a tendency to flood and can have extremely strong currents. Make sure if you are kayaking, tubing, canoeing, travelling by fast-boat, etc, that proper safety gear, such as life jackets, is provided. 'Fast-boat' river travel can be dangerous due to excessive speed and the risk of hitting something in the river and capsizing.

Xieng Khouang Province, the Boloven Plateau, Xam Neua and areas along the Ho Chi Minh Trail are littered with bombies (small anti-personnel mines and bomblets from cluster bomb units). There are also numerous, large, unexploded bombs; in many villages they have been left lying around. They are very unstable so DO NOT TOUCH. Only walk on clearly marked or newly trodden paths.

## Student travellers

There are discounts available on some **Vietnam Airlines** routes and the train in **Vietnam**. Discount travel is provided to those under 22 and over 60. There are no specific student discounts in **Cambodia** or **Laos**. Anyone in full-time education is entitled to an International Student Identity Card (www.isic.org). These are issued by student travel offices and travel agencies and offer special rates on all forms of transport and other concessions and services. They sometimes permit free admission to museums and sights, at other times a discount on the admission.

## Telephone

**Vietnam**

To make a domestic call dial 0 + area code + phone number. Note that all numbers in this guide include the 0 and the area code. Most shops or cafés will let you call a local number for 2000d: look for the blue sign 'dien thoai cong cong' (meaning public telephone). All post offices provide international telephone services. The cost of calls has greatly reduced but some post offices and hotels still insist on charging for a minimum of 3 mins. You start paying for an overseas call from the moment you ring even if the call is not answered. By dialling 171 or 178 followed by 0 or 00 to make an international call, it is approximately 30% cheaper. Vietnam's country code is +84; IDD is 0084; directory enquires 1080; operator-assisted domestic long-distance calls 103; international directory enquiries 143; Yellow pages 1081. Numbers beginning with 091 or 090 are mobile numbers. Pay-as-you-go sim cards are available.

### Cambodia
Landline linkages are so poor in Cambodia that many people and businesses prefer to use mobile phones instead. The 3-digit prefix included in a 9-digit landline telephone number is the area (province) code. If dialling within a province, dial only the 6-digit number. International calls can be made from most guesthouses, hotels and phone booths. Don't anticipate being able to make international calls outside Phnom Penh, Siem Reap and Sihanoukville. Use public MPTC or Camintel card phone boxes dotted around Phnom Penh to make international calls (cards are usually sold at shops near the booth). International calls are expensive, starting at US$4 per minute in Phnom Penh, and more in the provinces. To make an overseas call from Cambodia, dial 007 or 001 + IDD country code + area code minus first 0 + subscriber number. Internet calls are without a doubt the cheap-est way to call overseas. Pay-as-you-go sim cards are available. The country code for Cambodia is +855.

### Laos
Public phones are available in Vientiane and other major cities. You can also go to **Lao Telecom** offices to call overseas. Call 178 in Vientiane for town codes. Most towns in Laos have at least one telephone box with IDD facility. The one drawback is that you must buy a phonecard. Because these are denominated in such small units, even the highest-value card will only get you a handful of minutes talk time with Europe. Most call are charged between US$0.80 and US$2 per min. All post offices, telecoms offices and many shops sell phone cards.

Note: If ringing Laos from Thailand, dial 007 before the country code for Laos.

Mobile telephone coverage is now quite good. Pay-as-you-go sim cards are available for 30,000 kip to 50,000 kip. Coverage is available in most provincial capitals.

Many internet cafés have set up call facilities that charge US$0.20 per min and under to make a call. In Vientiane, Pakse, Luang Prabang and Vang Vieng most internet cafés are equipped with Skype, including headphones and web-cam, which costs a fraction of the price for international calls (as long as you have an account already established).

International operator: 170. Operator: 16. The IDD for Laos is 00856.

## Time

Vietnam, Cambodia and Laos are 7 hrs ahead of Greenwich Mean Time.

## Tipping

Vietnamese do not normally tip if eating in small family restaurants but may tip extravagantly in expensive bars. Foreigners normally leave the small change. Big hotels and some restaurants add 5-10% service charge and the government tax of 10% to the bill. Taxis are rounded up to the nearest 5000d, hotel porters 20,000d. Tipping is rare but appreciated in Cambodia. Neither is it common practice in Laos, even in hotels. However, it is a kind gesture to tip guides and some more expensive restaurants. If someone offers you a lift, it is a courtesy to give them some money for fuel.

## Tourist information

Contact details for tourist offices and other information resources are given n the relevant Ins and Outs sections throughout the text.

### Vietnam
The national tourist office is **Vietnam National Administration of Tourism** (www.vietnamtourism.com), whose role is to promote Vietnam as a tourist destination rather than to provide tourist information. Visitors to their offices can get some information and maps but are more likely

to be offered tours. There are exceptions eg **Saigontourist** (www.saigon-tourist.com). Good tourist information is available from tour operators in the main tourist centres.

## Cambodia
Government tourism services are minimal at best. The **Ministry of Tourism**, 3 Monivong Blvd, T023-426876, is not able to provide any useful information or services. The tourism office in Siem Reap is marginally better but will only provide services, such as guides, maps etc, for a nominal fee. In all cases in Cambodia you are better off going through a private operator for information and price.

## Laos
The **Laos National Tourism Authority**, Lane Xang, Vientiane, T021-212248, www.tourism laos.gov.la, provides maps and brochures. The provincial offices are usually excellent and as long as you are patient they will usually come through with the information you need. There are particularly good tourism offices in Thakhek, Vieng Xai, Savannakhet, Xam Neua and Luang Namtha.

The authority has teamed up with local tour operators to provide a number of ecotourism opportunities, such as trekking and village homestays, www.ecotourismlaos.com.

## Tour operators

For regional tour operators, such as **Asian Trails** (www.asiantrails.com), refer to the Activities and tours listings in the guide.

### In the UK
**Adventure Company**, Cross & Pillory House, Cross & Pillory Lane, Alton, Hampshire GU34 1HL, T0845-450 5316, www.adventurecompany.co.uk.
**Audley Travel**, New Mill, New Mill Lane, Whitney, Oxfordshire OX29 9SX, T01993-838100, www.audleytravel.com.
**Explore**, Nelson House, 55 Victoria Rd, Farnborough, Hants GU14 7PA, T0870-333 4002, www.explore.co.uk.
**Guerba Adventure & Discovery Holidays**, Wessex House, 40 Station Rd, Westbury, Wiltshire BA13 3JN, T01373-826611, www.guerba.co.uk.

Essentials A-Z

**48** **Regent Holidays**, Fromsgate House, Rupert St, Bristol BS1 2QJ, T0845-277 3317, www.regent-holidays.co.uk.

**Silk Steps**, Odyssey Lodge, Holy Well Rd, Edington, Bridgwater, Somerset TA7 9JH, T01278-722460, www.silksteps.co.uk.

**Steppes Travel**, 51 Castle St, Cirencester, Glos GL7 1QD, T01285-880980, www.steppestravel.co.uk.

**Symbiosis Expedition Planning**, Holly House, Whilton, Daventry, Northants, NN11 2NN, T0845-123 2844, www.symbiosis-travel.com.

**Trans Indus**, Northumberland House, 11 The Pavement, Popes Lane, London W5 4NG, T020-8566 2729, www.transindus.co.uk. Tailor-made holidays and group tours.

**Travel Indochina**, 2nd floor, Chester House, George St, Oxford 0X1 2AY, T01865-268940, www.travelindochina.co.uk. Small group journeys and tailor-made holidays.

**Travelmood**, 214 Edgware Rd, London W2 1DH; 1 Brunswick Court, Leeds LS2 7QU; 16 Reform St, Dundee, DD1 1RG, T0800-2989815, www.travelmoodadventures.com.

**Trips Worldwide**, 14 Frederick Pl, Clifton, Bristol BS8 1AS, T0117-311 4400, www.tripsworldwide.co.uk.

**Visit Asia (Tennyson Travel)**, 30-32 Fulham High St, London SW6 3LQ, T020-7736 4347, www.visitasia.co.uk. Specializes in tours throughout Asia.

**In North America**

**Adventure Center**, 1311 63rd St, Suite 200, Emeryville, CA, T+1-800 227 8747, www.adventurecenter.com.

**Global Spectrum**, 3907 Laro Court, Fairfax, VA 22031, T+1-800 -419 4446, www.globalspectrumtravel.com.

**Hidden Treasure Tours**, 509 Lincoln Blvd, Long Beach, NY 11561, T01-87-7761 7276 (USA toll free), www.hiddentreasure tours.com.

**Journeys**, 107 April Drive, Suite 3, Ann Arbor MI 46103, T+1-800-255 8735 (USA toll free), www.journeys-intl.com.

**Myths & Mountains**, 976 Tree Court, Incline Village, Nevada 89451, T1-800 670 6984, www.mythsandmountains.com. Organizes travel to all 3 countries.

**Nine Dragons Travel & Tours**, 1476 Orange Grove Rd, Charleston, SC 29407, T+1-317-281 3895, www.nine-dragons.com.

### In Australia and New Zealand
**Intrepid Travel**, 360 Bourke St, Melbourne, Victoria 3000, T+61-03-8602 0500, www.intrepidtravel.com.au
**Travel Indochina**, Level 10, HCF House, 403 George St, Sydney, NSW 2000, T+61-1-300-138755 (toll free), www.travel indochina.com.au. Small group journeys and tailor-made holidays.

## Visas and immigration

30-day tourist visas are granted on arrival in Bangkok.

### Vietnam
Valid passports with visas issued by a Vietnamese embassy are required by all visitors. Visas are normally valid only for arrival by air at Hanoi and HCMC.

Those wishing to enter or leave Vietnam by land must specify the border crossing when applying. It is possible to alter the point of departure at immigration offices in Hanoi and HCMC.

The standard tourist visa is valid for one month for 1 entry only. Tourist visas cost £38 (US$75) and generally take 5 days to process. Express visas cost £55 (2 days). If you are planning on staying for a while or making a side trip to Laos or Cambodia with the intention of coming back to Vietnam then a 1-month multiple entry visa, £70 (US$139) will make life much simpler. Visa regulations are ever changing: usually it is possible to extend visas within Vietnam. Travel agencies and hotels will probably add their own mark-up but for many people it is worth paying to avoid the difficulty of making 1 or 2 journeys to an embassy. Visas can be extended for 1 month for US$15-30. Depending on where you are it will take between 1 day and a week. A visa valid for 1 month can only be extended for 1 month.

Visas for a 30-day stay are available on arrival at Phnom Penh's airport and Siem Reap's airport. Fill in a form and hand over 1 photograph (4 cm x 6 cm). Tourist visas cost US$20 and your passport must be valid for at least 6 months from the date of entry.

Officially, visas are not available on the Lao border. Many people have reported successfully obtaining visas here but don't rely on it. Travellers using the Lao border should try to arrange visa paperwork in advance in either Phnom Penh, Bangkok or Vientiane. The **Cambodian Embassy** in Bangkok, 185 Rajdamri Rd, T+66-2546630, issues visas in 1 day if you apply in the morning, as does the **Consulate General** in HCMC, Vietnam, 41 Phung Khac Khoan, T+84-88292751, and in Hanoi at 71 Tran Hung Dao St, T+84-49424788. In both Vietnam and in Thailand travel agencies are normally willing to obtain visas for a small fee. Cambodia has a few missions overseas from which visas can be obtained.

Travellers leaving by land must ensure that their Vietnam visa specifies Moc Bai or Chau Doc as points of entry otherwise they could be be turned back. You can apply for a Cambodian visa in HCMC and collect in Hanoi and vice versa.

Extensions can be obtained at the Department for Foreigners on the road to the Airport, T023-581558 (passport photo required). Most travel agents arrange visa extensions for around US$40 for 30 days. Those overstaying their visas are fined US$5 per day, although officials at land crossings often try to squeeze out more.

## Laos

A 30-day tourist visa can be obtained at Vientiane's Wattay Airport; Luang Prabang International Airport; Pakse International Airport; along the Thai border at the Friendship Bridge crossing near Nong Khai/Vientiane, Chiang Khong/Houei Xai crossing; Chongmek/Vang Tao (near Pakse) crossing; Nakhon Phanom/Thakhek crossing; and Mukdahan/Savannakhet crossing. In China, Lao visas are available at the Mohan/Boten crossing. In Vietnam, they are available at the following crossings: Lao Bao/Dansavanh in Savannakhet; Cau Treo/Nam Phao (Khammouane Province); and Nam Khan/Nam Can in Xieng Khouang Province.

At the time of publication, Lao visas were not available at the following borders: the Vietnam crossing Nam Xoi/Nameo; Na Phao /Cha Lo, Attapeu/Quy Nhon and the Cambodian crossing at Dom Kralor. For these crossings, visas will need to be organized in advance. You will also need a passport photo, maybe 2.

Visa prices are based on reciprocity with countries and cost US$30-42. 'Overtime fees' are often charged if you enter after 1600 or at a weekend. To get a visa you need to provide a passport photograph and the name of the first hotel you plan on staying

The Lao government also issues business visas (US$35) that are available for 30-days with the possibility of extending for months beyond. This is a more complicated process and usually requires a note from an employer or hefty fees from a visa broker. These visas are best organized from your home country and can take a long time to process.

Tourist visa extensions can be obtained from the Lao Immigration Office in the Ministry of the Interior opposite the Morning Market in Vientiane, T021-212529. They can be extended for up to a month at the cost of US$2 per day (although if you want to extend for a month it works out cheaper to cross the border); you will need one passport photo. It takes a day to process the extension and if you drop the paperwork off early in the morning it will often be ready by the afternoon. Travel agencies in Vientiane and other major centres can also handle this service for you for a fee (eg an additional US$1-2 per day). Visitors who overstay their visas are charged US$10 for each day beyond the date of expiration, they will be asked to pay this on departure from Laos.

# Bangkok

## ♟ Footprint features

# Introduction

Thailand's capital is dirty, dynamic, wild and sweaty, a heaving scrum of humanity blended with ancient beauty, booming youth culture and the rituals of a bygone age. The Thais call it the City of Angels but there's nothing angelic about Bangkok. Don't arrive expecting an exotic, languid, dreamy place trapped in a traditional past. What will hit you is the size, pace, endless olfactory/oral cacophony, friendliness of the locals and gridlocked traffic.

Some of the old *King and I* romanticism does persist. There are the khlongs, palaces and temples but ultimately, what marks Bangkok out from the imaginings of its visitors, is its thrusting modernity in open struggle with the ancient, rural traditions of Thai culture. Neon, steel and glass and futuristic transport rubs shoulders with alms-collecting monks and crumbling teak villas. It's all here: poverty and wealth, smog-filled thoroughfares and backstreets smothered in alluring exotic aromas, cybercafés and fried-bug-laden barrows.

With your senses fully overloaded don't forget the sheer luxury that's on offer. Bangkok is home to some of the best, and most affordable, hotels in the world. Add the numerous spas, super-hip nightlife and the diverse range of markets, selling everything from amulets and sarongs to Prada and hi-tech, and your head will be spinning.

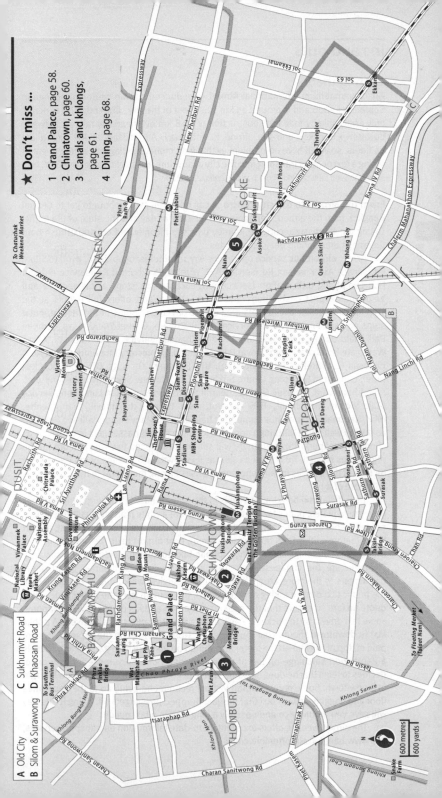

★ Don't miss ...

1 Grand Palace, page 58.
2 Chinatown, page 60.
3 Canals and khlongs, page 61.
4 Dining, page 68.

A Old City
B Silom & Surawong
C Sukhumvit Road
D Khaosan Road

To Chatuchak
Weekend Market

DIN DAENG

ASOKE

PUSIT

BANGLAMPHU

OLD CITY

Grand Palace

CHINATOWN

THONBURI

PATPONG

Chao Phraya River

Expressway
Second Stage Expressway
Chalem Mahanakhon Expressway

New Phetburi Rd
Rama IV Rd
Sukhumvit Rd
Witthayu (Wireless) Rd
Phetchaburi
Phra Ram 9
Phetchaburi
Sukhumvit
Phrom Phong
Thonglor
Ekkamai
Sol 63
Sol Ekkamai
Asoke
Sol Asoke
Rachdaphisek Rd
Queen Sikrit
Khlong Toey
Rama IV Rd
Sol 26
Nana
Soi Nana Nua
Ploenchit Rd
Chitlom
Rachdamri
Ploenchit
Lumpini
Sol Sribamphen
Nang Linch Rd
Lumpini Park
Rachdarnri Rd
Henri Dunant Rd
Phayathai Rd
Rachprarop Rd
Phetburi Rd
Phayathai Rd
Victory Monument
Victory Monument
Phayathai
Ratchathewi
Siam
Siam Square
Siam Tower & Discovery Centre
Jim Thompson's House
National Stadium
MBK Shopping Centre
Rama VI Rd
Rachwith Rd
Chitralada Palace
National Assembly
Vimanmek Palace
National Library
Tewes Market
Chitsanulok Rd
Sri Ayutthaya Rd
Lan Luang Rd
Krung Kasem Rd
Government House
Rachdamnern Nok Av
Samsen Rd
Krung Kasem Rd
Wisutkasat Rd
Rachdamnern Klang Av
Phra Athit Rd
Phra Pinklao Bridge
Phra Pinklao Nor
Khlong Bangkok Noi
Khlong Banglamphu
Sanaam Luang
Wat Mahathat
Wat Phra Kaeo
Wat Arun
Wat Phra Chetuphon (Wat Pho)
Charoen Krung
Tri Phet Rd
Memorial Bridge
Maharat Rd
Mahachai Rd
Chakrawat Rd
Nakhon Kasem
Yaowarat Rd
Songwat Rd
Wat Traimitr (Temple of the Golden Buddha)
Hualamphong Station
Hualamphong
Krung Kasem Rd
Worachak Rd
Luang Rd
Golden Mount
Rama I Rd
Rama IV Rd
Si Phraya Rd
Samyan
Surawong Rd
Silom Rd
Chongnonsi
Sala Daeng
Patpong
Chaoren Krung
Sathon Nua Rd
Sathorn Rd
Surasak
Surasak Rd
Taksin Bridge
Charoen Nakorn Rd
Chaoren Krung (New Rd)
Lat Ya Rd
Taksin Rd
To Floating Market (Talaat Nam)
To Southern Bus Terminal
Charan Sanitwong Rd
Itsaraphap Rd
Inthraphitak Rd
Khlong Mon
Khlong Samre
Khlong Bangkok Yai
Khlong Bangnam Chai
Snake Farm
Charan Sanitwong Rd
Phet Kasem Rd

N

600 metres
600 yards

# Ins and outs

## Getting there

**Air** **Suvarnabhumi International Airport** (pronounced su-wan-na-poom) opened in September 2006 and is around 25 km southeast of the city. Currently, the airport is only accessible by road but construction of a 28-km overhead city rail link between downtown Bangkok and the airport is underway. All facilities at the airport are 24 hours, so you'll have no problem exchanging money, getting something to eat or taking a taxi or other transport into the city at any time. ▸▸ *For details of onward flights from Suvarnabhumi International Airport, see Essentials, page 24.*

**From the airport to the city centre** It can take well over an hour to get to Central Bangkok from the airport, depending on the time of day and the state of the traffic. Taking the expressway cuts the journey time significantly and outside of rush-hour the transit time should be 35-45 minutes.

An a/c **airport bus service** operates every 15 minutes, 0500-2400, ฿100 to Silom Rd (service A1), Khaosan Rd (service A2), Wireless/Sukhumvit Rd (service A3) and Hua Lumphong train station (service A4). Each service stops at between 12 and 20 popular tourist destinations and hotels. The airport offers full details at the stop located outside the Arrivals area on the pavement. Some of the more popular stops on each line are: **Silom service (A1):** Pratunam, Central World Plaza, Lumpini Park, Sala Daeng, Patpong, Sofitel Silom. **Khaosan service (A2):** Pratunam, Amari Watergate Hotel, Asia Hotel, Royal Princess Hotel, Democracy Monument, Phra Artit, Khaosan Rd. **Wireless Rd service (A3):** BTS (Skytrain) On Nuts, BTS Thonglor, Rex Hotel, Emporium Shopping Centre Sukhumvit 24, Novotel Sukhumvit, Westin Hotel, Amari Boulevard, Majestic Grande, Central Silom and Nana. **Hua Lumphong service (A4):** Victory Monument, BTS On Nut, Asia Hotel Ratchathewi, Siam Centre, MBK/National Stadium, Hua Lumphong train station. Many visitors will see the ฿100 as money well spent (although note that for three or four passengers in a taxi it is as cheap or cheaper). However, there will still be a hardened few who will opt for the **regular bus service**. This is just as slow as it ever was, 1½ to three hours (depending on time of day), prices for air-conditioned buses linking the airport to the city are now a flat rate of ฿35.

The official **taxi** booking service is in the arrivals hall. Official airport limousines have green plates, public taxis have yellow plates; a white plate means the vehicle is not registered as a taxi. There are three sets of taxi/limousine services. First, **airport limos** (before exiting from the restricted area), next **airport taxis** (before exiting from the terminal building), and finally, a **public taxi counter** (outside, on the slipway). The latter are the cheapest. Note that airport flunkies sometimes try to direct passengers to the more expensive 'limousine' service: walk through the barriers to the public taxi desk. If taking a metered taxi, the coupon from the booking desk will quote no fare so ensure that the meter is turned on and keep hold of your coupon – some taxi drivers try to pocket it – as it details the obligations of taxi drivers. A public taxi to downtown should cost roughly ฿300. Note that tolls on the expressways are paid on top of the fare on the meter and should be no more than ฿40 per toll. There is a ฿50 airport surcharge on top of the meter cost. Don't be surprised if your driver decides to feign that he does not know where to go: it's all part of being a new boy/girl in a new town. Some regular airport visitors recommend going up to the departures floor and flagging down a taxi that has just dropped passengers off. Doing it this way will save you around ฿50 and possibly a long wait in a taxi queue.

The airport website offers excellent up-to-date information on transport services, see www.bangkokairportonline.com.

# Getting around

Bangkok has the unenviable reputation of having some of the worst traffic in the world. The **Skytrain** – an elevated railway – along with the newer **Metro** have made things a lot easier for those areas of the city they cover. Plentiful **buses** travel to all city sights and offer the cheapest way to get around. A **taxi** or **tuk-tuk** ride within the centre should cost ฿50-100. All taxis now have meters. Tuk-tuk numbers are dwindling and the negotiated fares often work out more expensive than a taxi. Walking can be tough in the heat and fumes, although there are some parts of the city where this can be the best way to get around. For an alternative to the smog of Bangkok's streets, hop onboard one of the express **river taxis**, which ply the Chao Phraya River and the network of khlongs (canals) that criss-cross the city; it's often quicker than going by road.

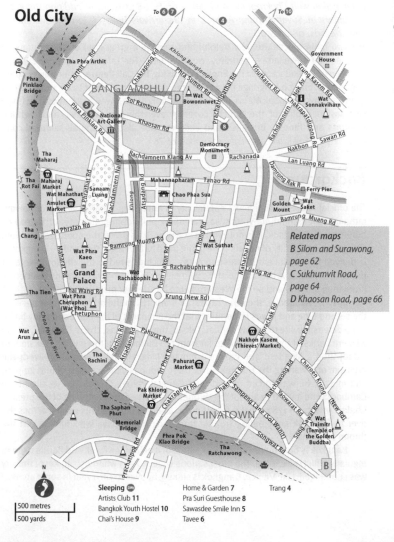

**Old City**

*Related maps*
*B Silom and Surawong,*
*page 62*
*C Sukhumvit Road,*
*page 64*
*D Khaosan Road, page 66*

**Sleeping**
Artists Club **11**
Bangkok Youth Hostel **10**
Chai's House **9**

Home & Garden **7**
Pra Suri Guesthouse **8**
Sawasdee Smile Inn **5**
Tavee **6**

Trang **4**

500 metres
500 yards

Begin in the bejewelled beauty of the **Old City**. The charming **Golden Mount** is a short hop to the east, while to the south are the bewildering alleyways and gaudy temples of Bangkok's frenetic **Chinatown**. Head west over the Chao Phraya River to the magnificent spire of **Wat Arun** and the **khlongs of Thonburi**. To the north are the broad, leafy avenues of **Dusit**, the home of the Thai parliament and the King's residence. Carry on east and south and you'll reach modern Bangkok. A multitude of mini-boutiques forms **Siam Square** and the Thai centre of youth fashion; **Silom** and **Sukhumvit roads** are vibrant runs of shopping centres, restaurants and hotels, while the **Chatuchak Weekend Market** (known to locals as JJ), in the northern suburbs, is one of Asia's greatest markets.

## Tourist information

Tourist Authority of Thailand (TAT) ① *main office at 1600 New Phetburi Rd, Makkasan, Ratchathewi, T02-2505500, www.tourismthailand.org; also at 4 Rachdamnern Nok Av (intersection with Chakrapatdipong Rd), Mon-Fri 0830-1630; in addition there are 2 counters at Suvarnabhumi Airport, in the arrivals halls of Terminals 1 and 2, T02-5042701, 0800-2400.*

The two main offices are very helpful and provide a great deal of information for independent travellers – certainly worth a visit. For information, phone T1672 between 0800 and 2200 for the English-speaking **TAT Call Centre**. A number of good, informative, English-language magazines provide listings of what to do and where to go in Bangkok: *Bangkok Metro*, published monthly (฿100, www.bkkmetro.com) is the well-designed pick of the bunch, covering everything from music and nightlife to sports and fitness, business and children. See also www.khao-san-road.com.
▶▶ *For Sleeping, Eating and other listings, see pages 65-76.*

# Background

The official name for Thailand's capital city is Krungthep-phramaha-nakhonbawon-rathanakosin-mahinthara-yutthayaa-mahadilok-phiphobnobpharaat-raatchathaani-buriiromudomsantisuk. It is not hard to see why Thais prefer the shortened version, Krungthep, or the 'City of Angels'. The name used by the rest of the world – Bangkok – is derived from 17th-century Western maps, which referred to the city (or town as it then was) as *Bancok*, the 'village of the wild plum'. This name was only superseded by Krungthep in 1782, and so the Western name has deeper historical roots.

In 1767, Ayutthaya, then the capital of Siam, fell to the marauding Burmese for the second time and it was imperative that the remnants of the court and army find a more defensible site for a new capital. Taksin, the Lord of Tak, chose Thonburi, on the western banks of the Chao Phraya, far from the Burmese. In three years, Taksin had established a kingdom and crowned himself king. His reign was short-lived; the pressure of thwarting the Burmese over three arduous years caused him to go mad and in 1782 he was forced to abdicate. General Phraya Chakri was recalled from Cambodia and invited to accept the throne. This marked the beginning of the present Chakri Dynasty. In 1782, Chakri (now known as Rama I) moved his capital across the river to Bangkok anticipating trouble from King Bodawpaya who had seized the throne of Burma.

Bangkok is built on unstable land, much of it below sea level, and floods used to regularly afflict the capital. The most serious were in 1983 when 450 sq km of the city was submerged. Like Venice, Bangkok is sinking by over 10 cm a year in some areas.

## ❖ The Thai Ramayana: the Ramakien

The *Ramakien* – literally the 'Story of Rama' – is an adaptation of the Indian Hindu classic, the *Ramayana*, which was written by the poet Valmiki about 2000 years ago. This 48,000-line epic odyssey, often likened to the works of Homer, was introduced into mainland Southeast Asia in the early centuries of the first millennium. The heroes were simply transposed into a mythical, ancient, Southeast Asian landscape. In Thailand, the *Ramakien* quickly became highly influential, and the name of the former capital of Siam, Ayutthaya, is taken from the legendary hero's city of Ayodhia in the epic. Unfortunately, these early Thai translations of the *Ramayana* were destroyed following the sacking of Ayutthaya by the Burmese in 1767. The earliest extant version was written by King Taksin in about 1775, although Rama I's rather later rendering is usually regarded as the classic interpretation.

In many respects, King Chakri's version closely follows that of the original Indian story. It tells of the life of Ram (Rama), the King of Ayodhia. In the first part of the story, Ram renounces his throne following a long and convoluted court intrigue, and flees into exile. With his wife Seeda (Sita) and trusted companion Hanuman (the monkey god), they undertake a long and arduous journey. In the second part, his wife Seeda is abducted by the evil king Ravana, forcing Ram to wage battle against the demons of Langka Island (Sri Lanka). He defeats the demons with the help of Hanuman and his monkey army, and recovers his wife. In the third and final part of the story – and here it diverges sharply from the Indian original – Seeda and Ram are reunited and reconciled with the help of the gods (in the Indian version there is no such reconciliation). Another difference with the Indian version is the significant role played by the Thai Hanuman – here an amorous adventurer who dominates much of the third part of the epic.

There are also numerous sub-plots which are original to the *Ramakien*, many building upon events in Thai history and local myth and folklore. In tone and issues of morality, the Thai version is less puritanical than the Indian original. There are also, of course, differences in dress, ecology, location and custom.

# Old City and around

Filled with palaces and temples the Old City is the ancient heart of Bangkok. These days it is the premium destination for the Thai capital's visitors and controversial plans are afoot to change it into a 'tourist zone'. This would strip the area of the usual chaotic charm that typifies Bangkok, moving out the remaining poor people who live in the area and creating an ersatz, gentrified feel.

## Wat Phra Chetuphon (Wat Pho)

ⓘ *Entrance on the south side of the monastery, www.watpho.com; 0900-1700, ฿20.*

Wat Phra Chetuphon, or Wat Pho, is the largest and most famous temple in Bangkok. The 'Temple of the Reclining Buddha' was built in 1781 and houses one of the largest reclining Buddhas in the country. The soles of the Buddha's feet are decorated with mother-of-pearl, displaying the 108 auspicious signs of the Buddha. The bustling grounds of the wat contains more than 1000 bronze images, mostly rescued from the ruins of Ayutthaya and Sukhothai, while the bot houses the ashes of Rama I. The bot is enclosed by two galleries which house 394 seated bronze Buddha images. Around the exterior base of the bot are marble reliefs telling the story of the abduction and recovery of Ram's wife Seeda from the second section of the *Ramakien* (see page 57), as adapted in the Thai poem, 'The Maxims of King Ruang'.

One of Wat Pho's biggest attractions is its role as a respected centre of **traditional Thai massage**. Thousands of tourists, powerful Thai politicians, businessmen and military officers come here to escape the tensions of modern life. The Burmese destroyed most medical texts when they sacked Ayutthaya in 1776 but, in 1832, to help preserve the ancient medical art, Rama III had what was known about Thai massage inscribed onto a series of stones, which were then set into the walls of Wat Pho.
➤➤ *For further information, see Activities and tours, page 73.*

## Wat Phra Kaeo and Grand Palace

ⓘ *Main entrance is the Viseschaisri Gate, Na Phralan Rd, T02-2220094, www.palaces.thai.net. Admission to the Grand Palace complex ฿250 (ticket office open daily 0830-1130, 1300-1530 except Buddhist holidays when Wat Phra Kaeo is free but the rest of the palace is closed), includes a free guidebook to the palace (with plan), admission to the Coin Pavilion and to the Vimanmek Palace in the Dusit area (see page 61). No photography allowed inside the bot. All labels in Thai. Free guided tours in English throughout the day; personal audio guides in several languages ฿100 (2 hrs). No shorts, short skirts, sleeveless shirts, flip flops or sandals; plastic shoes and trousers are available for hire near the entrance.*

The Grand Palace is situated on the banks of the Chao Phraya River and is the most spectacular – some say 'gaudy' – collection of buildings in Bangkok. The complex, which began life in 1782, covers an area of over 1.5 sq km and the architectural plan is almost identical to that of the Royal Palace in the former capital of Ayutthaya.

The buildings of greatest interest are clustered around **Wat Phra Kaeo**, or the **Temple of the Emerald Buddha** (see opposite). The glittering brilliance of sunlight bouncing off the coloured glass mosaic exterior of Wat Phra Kaeo creates a gobsmacking initial impression for visitors to the Grand Palace. Built by Rama I in imitation of the royal chapel in Ayutthaya, Wat Phra Kaeo was the first of the buildings within the Grand Palace complex to be constructed. While it was being erected, the king lived in a small wooden building in one corner of the palace compound.

The **ubosoth** is raised on a marble platform with a frieze of gilded garudas holding nagas running round the base. Mighty, bronze *singhas* (lions) act as door guardians. The inlaid mother-of-pearl door panels date from Rama I's reign (late 18th century) while the doors are watched over by Chinese door guardians riding on lions. Inside the temple, the Emerald Buddha peers down on the gathered throng from a lofty, illuminated position above a large golden altar. Facing the Buddha on three sides are dozens of other gilded Buddha images, depicting the enlightenment of the Buddha when he subdues the evil demon Mara, the final temptation of the Buddha and the subjugation of evil spirits.

Around the walls of the shaded **cloister** that encompasses Wat Phra Kaeo, is a continuous mural depicting the *Ramakien* (see page 57). There are 178 sections in all, which were first painted during the reign of King Rama I but have since been restored.

To the north of the ubosoth on a raised platform is the **Royal Pantheon**, with gilded kinarees at the entrance. The Royal Pantheon is only open to the public once a year on Chakri Day, 6 April (the anniversary of the founding of the present Royal Dynasty). On the same terrace there are two gilt stupas built by King Rama I in commemoration of his parents. The **Phra Mondop** (library) was also built by Rama I to house the first revised Buddhist scriptural canon. To the west of the mondop is the large **Golden Stupa** or chedi, with its circular base, in Ceylonese style. To the north of the mondop is a model of Angkor Wat constructed during the reign of King Mongkut (1851-68) when Cambodia was under Thai suzerainty. To the north again from the Royal Pantheon is the **Supplementary Library** and two viharns – **Viharn Yod** and **Phra Nak**. The former is encrusted with pieces of Chinese porcelain.

## ⁝ The Emerald Buddha

Wat Phra Kaeo was specifically built to house the Emerald Buddha, the most venerated Buddha image in Thailand. It is carved from green jade (the emerald in the name referring only to its colour) and is a mere 75 cm high, seated in an attitude of meditation.

The image is believed to have been found in 1434 in Chiang Rai, and stylistically belongs to the Late Chiang Saen or Chiang Mai schools. Since then, it has been moved on a number of occasions: to Lampang, Chiang Mai and Laos (both Luang Prabang and Vientiane). It stayed in Vientiane for 214 years before being recaptured by the Thai army in 1778 and placed in Wat Phra Kaeo on 22 March 1784.

The image wears seasonal costumes of gold and jewellery; one each for the hot, cool and the rainy seasons. The changing ceremony takes place three times a year in the presence of the King of Thailand.

Buddha images are often thought to have personalities and the Phra Kaeo is no exception to this. It is said that such is the antipathy between the Pra Bang image in Luang Prabang (Laos, see page 420) and the Phra Kaeo that the images can never reside in the same town.

To the south of Wat Phra Kaeo are the buildings of the **Grand Palace**. These are interesting for the contrast that they make with those of Wat Phra Kaeo. Walking out through the cloisters, on your left is the French-style **Boromabiman Hall**, which was completed during the reign of Rama VI. The **Amarinda Hall** has an impressive, airy interior, with chunky pillars and gilded thrones. The **Chakri Mahaprasart** (Palace Reception Hall) stands in front of a carefully manicured garden with topiary. It was built and lived in by King Chulalongkorn (Rama V) shortly after he had returned from a trip to Java and Singapore in 1876, and it shows: the building is a rather unhappy amalgam of colonial and traditional Thai styles of architecture. Rama V found the overcrowded Grand Palace oppressive and after a visit to Europe in 1897 built himself a new home at Vimanmek (see page 61) in Dusit where the present King, Bhumibol, lives in the Chitralada Palace. The Grand Palace is now only used for state occasions.

Next to the Chakri Mahaprasart is the raised **Dusit Hall**, a cool, airy building containing mother-of-pearl thrones. Near the Dusit Hall is a **museum** ① *daily 0900-1600, ฿50*, which has information on the restoration of the Grand Palace, models of the Palace and many more Buddha images. There is also a collection of old cannon, mainly supplied by London foundries.

### Sanaam Luang and around

To the north of the Grand Palace, across Na Phralan Road, lies the large open space of the Pramane Ground (the Royal Cremation Ground), better known as **Sanaam Luang**. This area was originally used for the cremation of kings, queens and important princes. It is the place in Bangkok to eat charcoal-grilled dried squid and have your fortune told by the *mor duu* (seeing doctors), who sit in the shade of the tamarind trees along the inner ring of the southern footpath. Each *mor duu* has a 'James Bond case' – a black briefcase – and having your fortune told costs around ฿30-60, or ฿100 for a full consultation.

North along Na Phrathat Road, on the river side of Sanaam Luang is **Wat Mahathat** (the Temple of the Great Relic) ① *daily 0900-1700*, a temple famous as a meditation centre; walk under the archway marked 'Naradhip Centre for Research in Social Sciences' to reach the wat. At No 24 Maharaj Road a narrow *soi* (lane) leads down towards the river and a large daily **market** selling exotic herbal cures, amulets, clothes and food. At weekends, the market spills out onto the surrounding streets (particularly Phra Chan Road) and amulet sellers line the pavement, their magical and holy talismen carefully displayed.

## Banglamphu

Northeast of the National Art Gallery is the district of Banglamphu and the legendary **Khaosan Road** (see map, page 66), backpacker haunt and epicentre of Bangkok's travellers' culture.

## Golden Mount and around

This area, to the east of the Old City, is where ancient Bangkok begins to give way to the modern thrust of the bewildering 21st-century city. Apart from the Golden Mount there's little reason to hang around here but with the area's history of demonstrations and cries for democracy, it beats a defining pulse in the hearts of most Thais. The Golden Mount itself (also known as the Royal Mount) is an impressive artificial hill nearly 80 m high. The climb to the top is exhausting but worth it for the fabulous views of Bangkok.

# Chinatown

South of the Old City, Chinatown covers the area from Charoen Krung (or New Road) down to the river. Few other places in Bangkok match Chinatown for atmosphere. The warren of alleys, lanes and tiny streets are cut through with an industrious hive of shops, temples and restaurants. Weird food, neatly arranged mountains of mechanical parts, gaudy temple architecture, gold, flowers and a constant frenetic bustle will lead to many hours of happy wandering. This is an area to explore on foot, getting lost in the many nooks and crannies.

## Nakhon Kasem (Thieves' Market)

Nakhon Kasem, strictly speaking Woeng Nakhon Kasem (Thieves' Market), lies between Charoen Krung and Yaowarat Road, to the east of the khlong that runs parallel to Mahachai Road. Its boundaries are marked by archways. As its name suggests, this market used to be the centre for the fencing of stolen goods. It is not quite so colourful today but there remain a number of second-hand and antique shops, such as the **Good Luck Antique Shop**, which are worth a browse. Among other things, musical instruments, brass ornaments, antique (and not so antique) coffee grinders are all on sale here.

## Wat Traimitr (Temple of the Golden Buddha)

ⓘ *Traimitr Rd, Chinatown; daily 0900-1700, ฿20.*

The most celebrated example of the goldsmith's art in Thailand sits within Wat Traimitr (Temple of the Golden Buddha). The Golden Buddha is housed in a small, rather gaudy and unimpressive room. Although the leaflet offered to visitors says the 3-m-high, 700-year-old image is 'unrivalled in beauty', be prepared for disappointment; it's featureless. What makes it special, drawing large numbers of visitors each day, is that it is made of 5½ tonnes of solid gold. Apparently, when the East Asiatic Company was extending the port of Bangkok, they came across a huge stucco Buddha image, which they obtained permission to move. However, during the move in 1957, it fell from the crane and the stucco cracked to reveal a solid gold image. During the Ayutthayan period it was the custom to cover valuable Buddha images in plaster to protect them from the Burmese and this example had stayed that way for several centuries.

# Thonburi and the khlongs

Thonburi is Bangkok's little-known alter ego. Few people cross the Chao Phraya to see this side of the city and, if they do it is usually only to catch a glimpse from the seat of a speeding *hang yaaw* (long-tailed boat) and then climb the steps of **Wat Arun**. But Thonburi, during the reign of King Taksin, was once the capital of ancient Siam. King Rama I believed the other side of the river – present-day Bangkok – could be more easily defended from the Burmese and so, in 1782, he switched riverbanks.

## Exploring the khlongs

One of the most enjoyable ways to see Bangkok is by boat – and particularly by the fast and noisy *hang yaaws*, powerful, lean machines that roar around the river and the khlongs at breakneck speed. There are innumerable tours around the khlongs of Thonburi taking in a number of sights which include the floating market, snake farm and Wat Arun. Boats go from the various piers located along the east bank of the Chao Phraya River. The route skirts past laden rice-barges, squatter communities on public land and houses overhanging the canals. On private tours the first stop is usually the **Floating Market** (Talaat Nam). This is now an artificial, ersatz gathering which exists purely for the tourist industry. The nearest functioning floating market is at Damnoen Saduak (see page 64). ▸▸ *For further information, see Activities and tours and Transport, page 73.*

## Wat Arun

ⓘ *Daily 0830-1730, ฿20. Water-taxi from Tha Tien pier (at the end of Thai Wang Rd near Wat Pho) or from Tha Chang (at the end of Na Phralan near Wat Phra Kaeo).*
Facing Wat Pho across the Chao Phraya River is the famous Wat Arun (Temple of the Dawn). The wat stands 81 m high, making it the highest *prang* (tower) in Thailand. It was built in the early 19th century on the site of Wat Chaeng, the Royal Palace complex when Thonburi was briefly the capital of Thailand. Wat Chaeng housed the Emerald Buddha before the image was transferred to Bangkok and it is said that King Taksin vowed to restore the wat after passing it one dawn. The prang is completely covered with fragments of Chinese porcelain and includes some delicate gold and black lacquered doors. The temple is really meant to be viewed from across the river; its scale and beauty can only be appreciated from a distance. The best view of Wat Arun is in the evening from the Bangkok side of the river when the sun sets behind the prang.

# Dusit area

The present home of the Thai royal family and the administration is located north of Banglamphu in an area of wide, tree-lined boulevards, more in keeping with a European city. It is grand but lacks the usual bustling atmosphere found in the rest of Bangkok.

## Vimanmek Palace

ⓘ *Just off Rachvithi Rd, to the north of the National Assembly, T02-2811569, www.palaces.thai.net. Daily 0900-1600 (last tickets sold at 1500), ฿50, ฿20 for children, admission by guided tour only (1 hr). Tickets to the Grand Palace include entrance to Vimanmek Palace. Dance shows 1030 and 1400. No shorts or short skirts; sarongs available for hire (฿100, refundable).*
The Vimanmek Palace is the largest golden teakwood mansion in the world, but don't expect to see huge expanses of polished wood – the building is almost entirely painted. It was built by Rama V in 1901 who was clearly taken with Western style. It looks like a large Victorian hunting lodge and is filled with china, silver and paintings from all over the world (as well as some gruesome hunting trophies).

# East of the Old City

## Siam Square

A 10-minute walk east along Rama I Road is the biggest and busiest modern shopping area in the city, centred on a maze of tiny boutiques and a covered market known as Siam Square. Head to this area if you want to be at the apex of Thai youth culture and the biggest spread of shopping opportunities in the city. Whether you visit the hi-tech market at Panthip Plaza, the host of upmarket stores at one of Southeast Asia's largest malls, Siam Paragon and neighbour Siam Discovery, pure silk at Jim Thompson's House or the warren of tiny boutiques, you should leave with a big hole in your bank account. Thronged with young people, Siam Square plays host to Bangkok's burgeoning youth culture; cutting-edge contemporary and experimental fashions, Thai-style fast food and dozens of urban stylists keep the kids entertained. On the corner of Rama 1 and Phayathri Rd is **MBK**, Bangkok's largest indoor shopping area. Crammed with bargains and outlets of every description this is one of the Thai capital's most popular shopping spots.

## Jim Thompson's House

ⓘ *Soi Kasemsan Song (2), opposite the National Stadium, Rama I Rd, www.jimthompson.com. Mon-Sat 0900-1630, ฿100, children ฿25 (profits to charity). Shoes must be removed before entering; walking barefoot around the house adds to*

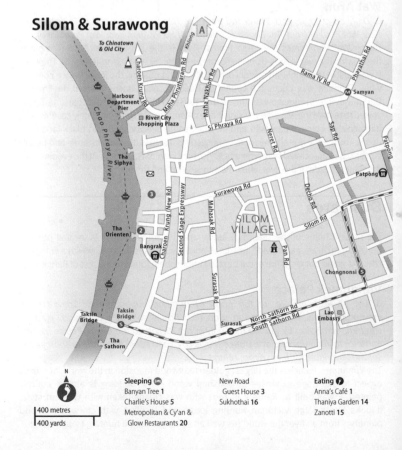

**Silom & Surawong**

| Sleeping | New Road | Eating |
| --- | --- | --- |
| Banyan Tree **1** | Guest House **3** | Anna's Café **1** |
| Charlie's House **5** | Sukhothai **16** | Thaniya Garden **14** |
| Metropolitan & Cy'an & | | Zanotti **15** |
| Glow Restaurants **20** | | |

400 metres
400 yards

Jim Thompson's House is an assemblage of traditional teak northern Thai houses, some more than 200 years old, transported here and reassembled. Jim Thompson arrived in Bangkok as an intelligence officer attached to the United States' OSS (Office of Strategic Services) and then made his name by reinvigorating the Thai silk industry after the Second World War. He disappeared mysteriously in the Malaysian jungle on 27 March 1967 but his silk industry continues to thrive. Jim Thompson chose this site for his house partly because a collection of silk weavers lived nearby on Khlong Saensaep. The house contains an eclectic collection of antiques from Thailand and China, with work displayed as though it was still his home. There is a sophisticated little café attached to the museum as well as a shop selling Jim Thompson products.

## Silom and Patpong

Hi-tech, high-rise and clad in concrete and glass, Silom, south of Siam Square, is at the centre of booming Bangkok. Banks, international business and many media companies are based in this area, as is the heart of Bangkok's gay community. Stylish, tacky and sweaty, head down the length of Silom for a full slice of contemporary Bangkok life.

The seedier side of Bangkok life has sadly always been a crowd-puller to the Western tourist. Most people flock to the red-light district of **Patpong**, which runs along two lanes (Patpong 1 and 2) linking Silom to Surawong. These streets were transformed

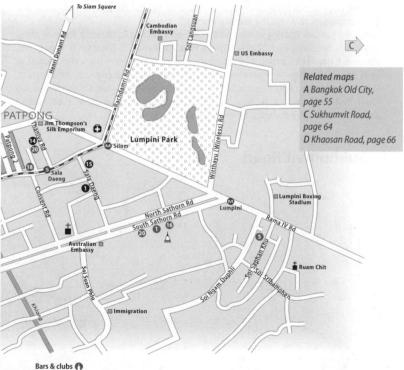

Related maps
A Bangkok Old City, page 55
C Sukhumvit Road, page 64
D Khaosan Road, page 66

Bars & clubs 🍸
Bamboo at Oriental Hotel **2**
Noriega's **20**
Tapas **18**

from a row of 'tea houses' (brothels serving local clients) into a high-tech lane of go-go bars in 1969 when an American entrepreneur made a major investment. Patpong 1 is the larger and more active of the streets, with a famous market running down the middle at night, and is largely recognized as the eponymous home of Bangkok's notorious girly shows, complete with acrobatic vaginas. Patpong two supports cocktail bars, pharmacies and clinics for STDs, as well as a few go-go bars. There are also restaurants and bars here. Patpong is home to a night market infamous for its line in copied designer handbags, some of which are better made than the originals.

## Sukhumvit Road

With the Skytrain running its length, Sukhumvit Road, east of Siam Square and Silom, has developed into Bangkok's most vibrant strip. Shopping centres, girly bars, some of the city's best hotels and awesome places to eat have been joined by futuristic nightclubs. The grid of sois that run off the main drag are home to a variety of different communities including Arab, African and Korean, as well as throngs of Westerners.

# Around Bangkok

## Damnoen Saduak floating market

ⓘ *109 km west of Bangkok, 1½ hrs by bus No 78 from the Southern bus terminal in Thonburi (T02-4355031 for booking) every 40 mins from 0600 (₿30-49); ask the conductor to drop you at Thanarat Bridge in Damnoen Saduak, then either walk down the lane (1.5 km) that leads to the market or take a river taxi for ₿10, or a minibus, ₿2. Tour companies also visit the floating market.*

Damnoen Saduak floating market in Ratchaburi Province is (almost) the real thing. Sadly, it is becoming increasingly like the Floating Market in Thonburi (see page 61), although it does still function as a legitimate market. Aim to get to Damnoen Saduak as early as possible, as the market winds down after 0900, leaving only trinket stalls. There are a number of floating markets in the maze of khlongs – Ton Khem, Hia Kui and Khun Phithak – and it is best to hire a *hang yaaw* to explore them (about ₿300 per hour; agree the price before setting out).

## Sukhumvit Road

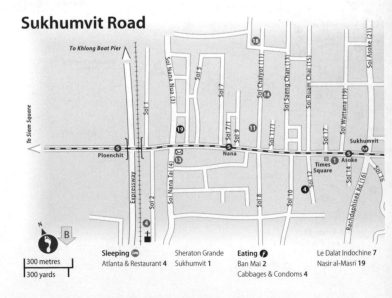

**Sleeping** 🛏
Atlanta & Restaurant 4
Sheraton Grande Sukhumvit 1

**Eating** 🍴
Ban Mai 2
Cabbages & Condoms 4
Le Dalat Indochine 7
Nasir al-Masri 19

# Chatuchak Weekend Market

ⓘ *Just off Phahonyothin Rd. Take a Skytrain to Mo Chit station or Chatuchak Park and Kampaeng Phet Metro stations. At the weekend the market is officially open from 0800-1800 (although some shops open earlier about 0700, some later about 0900), it's best to go early in the day or after 1500.*

Chatuchak is a huge conglomeration of 15,000 stallholders spread over an area of 14 ha selling virtually everything under the sun. There are antique stalls, basket stalls, textile sellers, carvers and painters along with the usual array of fishmongers, vegetable hawkers, butchers and candlestick makers. Beware of pickpockets. The head office and information centre can be found opposite Gate 1 off Kampaengphet Road. The clock tower serves as a good reference point should visitors become disoriented.

---

## 🛏 Sleeping

From humble backstreet digs to opulent extravagence, Bangkok has an incredibly diverse range of hotels, guesthouses and serviced apartments. The best bargains are often to be had in the luxury sector; you'll find some of the best hotels in the world here, many offer their rooms at knock-down prices.

### Old City and Banglamphu *p57, maps p55 and p66*

The guesthouses of Khaosan are cheapish but far more expensive than what you'll find in other parts of the country. Note that rooms facing on to Khaosan Rd tend to be very noisy; the sois off the main road, such as Soi Chana Songkhran or Soi Rambutri, are often quieter.

Sri Ayutthaya, north of Banglamphu, is emerging as an 'alternative' area for budget travellers. It is a central location, with restaurants and foodstalls nearby, but does not suffer the overcrowding and sheer pandemonium of Khaosan Rd.

**A Buddy Lodge**, 265 Khaosan Rd, T02-6294477, www.buddylodge.com. One of the more upmarket options around the Khaosan Rd area and one of the first to use the now ubiquitous term 'boutique', Buddy Lodge actually deserves the title with rooms featuring relatively plush modern interiors and chic fittings as well as home comforts like a fridge and TV. There is also a Japanese restaurant, a coffee shop and a pool.

**A Trang Hotel**, 99/1 Visutkaset Rd, T02-28221414, www.tranghotelbangkok.com. A/c, restaurant, pool. Friendly, well priced hotel popular with regular visitors to Bangkok. Set around a relaxing courtyard a little way from the action and major sights.

*Bangkok Listings*

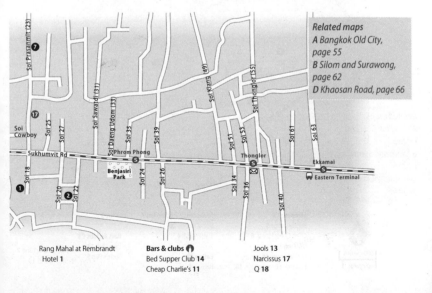

**Related maps**
A Bangkok Old City, page 55
B Silom and Surawong, page 62
D Khaosan Road, page 66

Rang Mahal at Rembrandt Hotel 1

**Bars & clubs** 🎵
Bed Supper Club 14
Cheap Charlie's 11

Jools 13
Narcissus 17
Q 18

**B Chart Guest House**, 62 Khaosan Rd, T02-2820171. Very clean airy rooms, cosmopolitan feel, with winding staircase and retro-style bar with movies. Friendly, English-speaking staff.

**B-D D&D Inn**, 68-70 Khaosan Rd, T02-6290526, www.khaaosanby.com. Large, purpose-built hotel with lift, neat if slightly soulless a/c rooms, and hot showers. The small swimming pool and bar on the roof offers a fine view. Very centrally located.

**B-D Orchid House**, Rambutri St, T02-2802619. Fan and a/c rooms with attached showers. Cosy, clean and safe with pretty interior touches in the rooms and communal areas. The ground floor terrace restaurant is a nice quiet spot for reading or people watching. Internet café and travel agent. Recommended.

**B-D Sawasdee Bangkok Inn**, 126/2 Khaosan Rd, T02-2801251. Good value, clean, fair-sized rooms with wooden floors and some with a/c. A vibrant, popular bar, and friendly staff. Free safety deposit and left luggage.

**B-D Sawasdee Smile Inn**, 35 Soi Rongmai, T02-629321. Restaurant and 24-hr bar, so ask for a room at the back if you want an early night. Rooms are clean and simple, all with cable TV. Free safety boxes available.

**B-D Siam Oriental**, 190 Khaosan Rd, T02-6290312, siam_oriental@hotmail.com. Fine, clean rooms (some a/c), smart tiled corridors, and very friendly staff. Internet facilities downstairs, along with a very popular restaurant. Free safety box.

**B-E Sawasdee Krungthep Inn**, 30 Praathi Rd, T02-6290072. Clean and simple rooms, all with cable TV. A lively communal atmosphere. Family rooms available.

**B-E Tuptim Bed and Breakfast**, 82 Rambutri, T02-629153536, info@tuptim b-b.com. Recommended budget option some rooms with a/c and en suite shower, but even the shared facilities are exceptionally clean, breakfast included. Very friendly staff.

**B-F Tavee**, 83 Sri Ayutthaya Rd, Soi 14, T02-2825983. Restaurant, a quiet, relaxed, and respectable place with a small garden and a number of fish tanks. Friendly management – a world away from the chaos of Khaosan Rd. The Tavee family keep the rooms and shared bathrooms immaculately clean and are a good source of information for travellers. Dorms are also available for ฿80 per night. This place has been operating since 1985 and has managed to maintain a very high standard.

# Khaosan Road

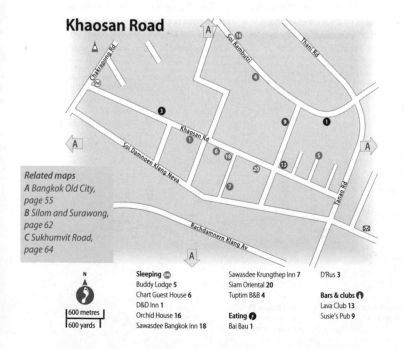

**Related maps**
*A Bangkok Old City,*
*page 55*
*B Silom and Surawong,*
*page 62*
*C Sukhumvit Road,*
*page 64*

N

| 600 metres |
| 600 yards |

**Sleeping**
Buddy Lodge **5**
Chart Guest House **6**
D&D Inn **1**
Orchid House **16**
Sawasdee Bangkok Inn **18**

Sawasdee Krungthep Inn **7**
Siam Oriental **20**
Tuptim B&B **4**

**Eating**
Bai Bau **1**

D'Rus **3**

**Bars & clubs**
Lava Club **13**
Susie's Pub **9**

C-E **Home and Garden**, 16 Samphraya Rd (Samsen 3), T02-2801475. Away from the main concentration of guesthouses, down a quiet soi (although the roosters tend to ensure an early start for light sleepers). This small house in a delightful leafy compound has a homely atmosphere. The rooms are a fair size with large windows, some face onto a balcony. Friendly owner, excellent value.

C-E **Pra Suri Guesthouse**, 85/1 Soi Pra Suri (off Dinso Rd), 5 mins east of Khaosan Rd not far from the Democracy Monument, T/F02-2801428. Fan, restaurant, own bathrooms (no hot water), clean, spacious and quiet, very friendly and helpful family-run travellers' guesthouse with all the services to match.

D-E **Chai's House**, 49/4-8 Chao Fa Soi Rongmai, T02-2814901. The last house down Soi Rambutri, so away from the competition. Some a/c, friendly atmosphere. Rooms are in traditional Thai-style, with wood panelling. They vary in size but are clean and the a/c rooms are good value. Balconies and orchid-filled restaurant make it a quiet and relaxing place. Recommended.

D-F **Bangkok Youth Hostel**, 25/2 Phitsanulok Rd (off Samsen Rd), T02-2820950. North of the Khaosan Rd, away from the bustle, the dorm beds are great value (฿120) being newly furnished and with a/c. Other rooms are clean and basic but still a bargain for those who don't mind a few hardships. If you don't have a valid YHA membership card, it will cost an extra ฿50 per night.

**Thonburi and the khlongs** *p61*
B-D **The Artists Club**, 61 Soi Tiem Boon Yang, T02-8620056. Run by an artist, this is a guesthouse-cum-studio-cum-gallery buried deep in the khlongs with clean rooms, some with a/c. It makes a genuine alternative with concerts, drawing lessons and other cultural endeavours.

**East of the Old City** *p62, maps p55, p62 and p64*
In all Bangkok, the Silom area most resembles a Western city, with its international banks, skyscrapers, first-class hotels, shopping malls, pizza parlours and

**67**

Bangkok Listings

pubs. It is also home to one of the world's best-known red-light districts – Patpong.

Sukhumvit is now one of Bangkok's premier centres of accommodation and is a great place for restaurants and night-life with several good bars and clubs. This is also a good area for shopping for furniture: antique and reproduction.

Soi Ngam Duphli to the east is much the smaller of Bangkok's two main centres of guesthouse accommodation. This area has seen better days but still makes a viable alternative for budget travellers.

**LL Metropolitan**, 27 South Sathorn Rd T02-6253333, www.metropolitan.como.bz. From its funky members/guest-only bar through to the beautiful, contemporary designer rooms and the awesome restaurants (**Glow** and **Cy'an**) this is one of Bangkok's hippest hotels.

**LL-L Sheraton Grande Sukhumvit**, 250 Sukhumvit, T02-6498888, www.luxury collection.com/bangkok. Superbly managed business and leisure hotel. Service, food and facilities are impeccable. The rooftop garden is an exotic delight and the spa offers some of the best massage in town. The **Rossini** and **Basil** restaurants are also top class. Great location and, if you can afford it, the best place to stay on Sukhumvit.

**LL-L Sukhothai**, 13/3 South Sathorn Rd, T02-2870222, www.sukhothai.com. A competitor for the **Metropolitan**'s crown as the sleekest, chicest place to sleep in the city. Stunning, modern oriental interiors set in landscaped gardens complete with decadent pool area. Recommended.

**L Banyan Tree**, 21/100 South Sathorn Rd, T02-6791200, www.banyantree.com. Glittering sumptuous surrounds immediately relax the soul here. Famous for its divine luxury spa and literally breathtaking roof-top **Moon Bar**, all rooms are suites with a good location and set back from busy Sathorn Rd.

**A-E New Road Guest House**, 1216/1 Charoen Krung Rd, T02-2371094. This Danish-owned place provides a range of accommodation from decent budget rooms to hammocks on the roof. A restaurant serves inexpensive Thai dishes and there's a free fruit buffet breakfast. A bar provides a pool table and darts and there's a small outdoor sitting area.

**B-D Atlanta**, 78 Sukhumvit Soi 2, T02-2521650, www.theatlanta hotel.bizland. com. Basic a/c or fan-cooled rooms. A good large pool and children's pool. Good restaurant. Prides itself on its literary, peaceful atmosphere. Appears to be the cheapest and is certainly the most appealing hotel in the area at this price, particularly suited for families, writers and dreamers, 24-hr email available.

**B-D Charlie's House**, Soi Saphan Khu, T02-6798330, www.charlieshouse thailand.com. Helpful owners create a friendly atmosphere and the rooms are carpeted and very clean. This is probably the best of the budget bunch. There is a restaurant and coffee corner with good food at reasonable prices. Recommended.

## ● Eating

Bangkok is one of the greatest food cities on earth. You could spend an entire lifetime finding the best places to eat in this city that seems totally obsessed with its tastebuds. Many restaurants, especially Thai ones, close early (between 2200 and 2230). Street food can be found across the city and a rice or noodle dish will cost ฿25-40 instead of a minimum of ฿50 in the restaurants. Some of the best can be found on the roads between **Silom** and **Surawong Rd**, **Soi Suanphlu** off South Sathorn Rd, down **Soi Somkid**, next to Ploenchit Rd, or opposite on **Soi Tonson**.

### Old City and Banglamphu *p57, maps p55 and p66*

Travellers' food such as banana pancakes and muesli is available in the guesthouse/travellers' hotel areas (see Sleeping, above). However, the Thai food sold along Khaosan Rd is some of the worst and least authentic in town, watered down to suit the tastebuds of unadventurous backpackers.

**D'Rus**, Khaosan Rd, T02-2810155, 0700-2400. A typical big-screen sports and sofas Khaosan place, but the Thai/Western food is decent and cheap and the coffee is freshly brewed.

**Bai Bau**, 146 Rambutri St. Tasty Thai food in a quiet corner; best bet for a relaxed authentic meal in a friendly environment. Good value.

### East of the Old City p62, maps p55, p62 and p64

**Anna's Café**, 118 Silom Soi Sala Daeng, T02-6320619, daily 1100-2200. Great Thai-cum-fusion restaurant in a villa off Silom Rd named after Anna of *King & I* fame. Some classic Thai dishes like *larb, nua yaang* and *som tam* along with fusion dishes and Western desserts such as apple crumble and banoffee pie.

**Cy'an**, Metropolitan Hotel, 27 South Sathorn Rd, T02-6253333, www.metropolitan.como.bz. With a menu concocted by one of Asia's leading chefs, Amanda Gale, **Cy'an** is a scintillating dining experience the like of which is not matched in the entire Thai capital. This is international cuisine of the highest order: the almond-fed Serrano ham and Japanese *wagyu* beef are highlights in a stunning menu. Strangely ignored by wealthy Thais, this is a restaurant at the cutting edge of Bangkok eating, miles ahead of the competition.

**Glow**, Metropolitan Hotel, 27 South Sathorn Rd, T02-6253333, www.metropolitan.como.bz. An organic lunch bar. Feast on spirulina noodles and tuna sashimi, all washed down with fresh beetroot and ginger juice.

**Rang Mahal**, Rembrandt Hotel, Sukhumvit Soi 18, T02-2617107. Some of the finest Indian food in town, award-winning and very popular with the Indian community. Spectacular views from the rooftop position, sophisticated, elegant and expensive.

**Thaniya Garden Restaurant**, Thaniya Plaza, 3rd floor, Room 333-335, 52 Silom Rd, T02-2312201, Mon-Sat 1100-2200. Excellent Thai food and enormous portions.

**Zanotti**, Sala Daeng, Soi 2 (off Silom Rd), T02-6360002, open daily for lunch and dinner. Extremely popular, sophisticated Italian restaurant serving authentic Italian cuisine, including wonderful Italian breads, salads, pizzas, risotto and exceptional pasta.

**Nasir al-Masri**, 4-6 Sukhumvit Soi Nana Nua, T02-2535582. Reputedly the best Arabic food in Bangkok, falafel, tabouleh, hummus, frequented by lots of Arabs who come for a taste of home.

**Le Dalat Indochine**, 47/1 Sukhumvit Soi 23, T02-6617967, daily for lunch and dinner. Reputed to serve the best Vietnamese food in Bangkok. Not only is the food good, but the ambience is satisfying too.

**Ban Mai**, 121 Sukhumvit Soi 22, Sub-Soi 2. Thai food served amongst Thai-style decorations in an attractive house with a friendly atmosphere. Good value.

**Cabbages and Condoms**, Sukhumvit Soi 12 (around 400 m down the soi). Population and Community Development Association (PDA) Thai restaurant, so all proceeds go to this charity. Eat rice in the Condom Room, drink in the Vasectomy Room. Good *tom yam khung* and honey-roast chicken, curries all rather similar, good value. Very attractive courtyard area .

## ● Bars and clubs

The city has some fantastic nightlife – everything from boozy pubs through to über-trendy clubs. You can listen to decent jazz and blues or get into the latest overseas DJs spinning the hippest beats. Groovy Map's *Bangkok by Night*(฿120) includes information on bars and dance clubs, the city's gay scene, as well as music venues and drinking spots. Check the Bangkok listing magazines for the latest information on who's spinning and what's opening.

### Old City and Banglamphu p57, maps p55 and p66

**Brick Bar at Buddy Lodge**, 365 Khaosan Rd, T02-6294477. A relatively recently refurbished up-market and pleasant venue overlooking Khaosan Rd, competitive prices and a mixed crowd of travellers and hip young locals looking to test out their English skills. Worth a trip, great live bands at night, open all day.

**Lava Club**, 249 Khaosan Rd, T02-2816565, daily 2000-0100. Playing the ubiquitous Bangkok mixture of hip-hop and house, this large and deeply cavernous venue looks not unlike a heavy metal club, decked out as it is in nothing but black with red lava running down the walls and floors.

**Saxophone**, 3/8 Victory Monument, Phayathai Rd, Golden Mount, daily 1800-0300. Series of alternating house bands, including jazz, blues, ska and soul. Another place with a long-standing – and deserved – reputation for delivering the music goods.

**Susie's Pub**, turn right between **Lava Club** and **Lek GH**, 2000-0200. This is the place for a more alternative Thai experience of what it is to go clubbing down Khaosan, as its always absolutely heaving, more with locals than travellers. Top decibel thumping local tunes and all sorts of flashing neon outside announce its presence, but while it might be easy to find, it's not always such a simple thing to get in, as there's a seething mass of bodies to negotiate from relatively early on right up until closing.

### East of the Old City *p62, maps p55, p62 and p64*

The greatest concentration of bars in this area are to be found in the 'red-light' districts of Patpong.

**Bamboo Bar**, Oriental Hotel, 48 Oriental Av, T02-2360400. Sun-Thu 1100-0100, Fri-Sat 1100-0200. One of the best jazz venues in Bangkok, classy and cosy with good food and pricey drinks – but worth it if you like your jazz and can take the hit.

**Bed Supper Club**, 26 Sukhumvit Soi 11, T02-6513537, www.bedsupperclub.com, daily 2000-0200. A futuristic white pod, filled with funky beats, awesome cocktails, superb food, gorgeous designer furniture and hordes of Bangkok's beautiful people.

**Cheap Charlie's**, 1 Sukhumvit Soi 11, 1500 until very late. Very popular with expats, backpackers and locals. Lively, cheap and unpretentious open-air bar in kitsch faux-tropical surrounds.

**Jools Bar**, 21/3 Nana Tai, Sukhumvit Soi 4, daily 0900-0100. A favourite watering hole for Brits. Serves classic English food.

**Narcissus**, 112 Sukhumvit Soi 23, T02-258 2549, daily 2100-0200. The classy, art deco **Narcissus** was awarded Metro's Best Night-club award in 2001. The music here is trance, house and techno and the clientele are office types trying to hold on to their youth.

**Noriega's Bar**, 106/108 Soi 4, Silom Rd, T02-2332814, daily 1800-0200. Words like minimalist and Zen spring to mind in this relatively quiet watering hole on an otherwise bustling strip. Live acts on Sat, Sun and Mon nights help cater for the guys, gays and gals this place targets with its promise of booze, broads, bites and blues.

**Q Bar**, 34 Sukhumvit Soi 11, T02-2523274, www.qbarbangkok.com. Housed in a modern building, it is the reincarnation of photographer David Jacobson's bar of the same name in HCMC. Good beats, great drinks menu and sophisticated layout.

**Tapas**, 114/17 Silom Soi 4, T02-2344737. A very popular, sophisticated bar with contagious beats and atmosphere. Attracts a friendly mix of expats and locals. The bar upstairs caters for the dancing crowds at the weekends with live drumming sessions and guest Djs.

### Gay and lesbian bars and clubs

The hub of Bangkok's gay scene can be found among the clubs, bars and restaurants on Silom, Sois 2 and 4. If it's your first time in Thailand, **Utopia Tours**, www.utopia-tours.com, are specialists in organizing gay travel, including tours of Bangkok. Its website also contains a huge number of listings, contacts and insights for gay and lesbian travellers.

**Balcony**, 86-8 Silom Soi 4, daily 1700-0200. Cute bar where you can hang out on the venues terraces watching the action below.

**DJ Station**, Silom Soi 2, www.dj-station.com, daily 2200-0200, ฿100 admission. This is the busiest and largest club on a busy soi. 3 floors of pumping beats and flamboyant disco. Essential and recommended.

**The Expresso**, 8/6-8 Silom Soi 2, daily 2200-0200. Good place to relax, with subdued lights and a lounge atmosphere.

**Freeman**, Silom Soi 2. Worth seeking out to find one of Bangkok's funniest **ka-toey** cabarets; it's mostly in Thai but the visual references leave little to the imagination. There's a dancefloor on the top floor but it's a little dark and seedy.

## ● Entertainment

### Thai Boxing (Muay Thai)

Thai boxing is both a sport and a means of self-defence and was first developed during the Ayutthaya period, 1351-1767. It differs from Western boxing in that contestants are allowed to use almost any part of their body. There are 2 main boxing stadiums in Bangkok: **Lumpini**, Rama 1V Rd, near Lumpini Park, T02-2514303, and **Rachdamnern Stadium**, Rachdamnern Rd (near TAT office), T02-2814205. At Lumpini, boxing nights are Tue and Fri (1700-2000) and Sat (2030-2400); tickets cost up to and over ฿1500 for a ringside seat; cheaper seats cost about ฿500-800. At Rachdamnern Stadium, boxing nights are Mon, Wed and Sun (1800-2230) and Sat (1700 and 2230), seats from ฿500-1500.

## ☸ Festivals and events

**Mar-Apr** International Kite Festival is held at Sanaam Luang when kite fighting and demonstrations by kite-flyers take place.
**Apr** Songkran. The beginning of the Buddhist New Year. Marked by excessive and exuberant water-throwing. The Khaosan Rd and Patpong/Silom are the places to head/ avoid depending on your chaos tolerance levels.

## O Shopping

From flowers and fruit sold at energetic all-night markets through to original and fake Louis Vuitton, Bangkok has the lot. Most street stalls will try and fleece you, so be prepared to shop around and bargain hard. Some arcades target the wealthier shopper and are dominated by brand-name goods and designer wear. Department stores tend to be fixed price. Most shops do not open until 1000-1100.

Sukhumvit Rd and the sois to the north are lined with shops and stalls, especially around the **Ambassador** and **Landmark** hotels. Many tailors and made-to-measure shoe shops are to be found in this area. Higher up on Sukhumvit Rd particularly around Soi 49 are various antique and furnishing shops.

### Antiques
**Jim Thompson's**, Surawong Rd, www.jimthomspon.com, for a range of antiques, wooden artefacts, furnishings and carpets.
**L'Arcadia**, 12/2 Sukhumvit Soi 23, Burmese antiques, beds, ceramics, doors, good quality and prices are fair.

**River City**, a shopping complex next to the **Royal Orchid Sheraton Hotel**, houses a large number of the more expensive antique shops and is an excellent place to start. Reputable shops here include **Verandah** on the top floor, the **Tomlinson Collection Room**, nos 427-428, and **Acala Room**, 312, for Tibetan and Nepalese art.

### Clothes and tailoring
Bangkok's tailors are skilled at copying anything, either from fashion magazines or from a piece of your own clothing. Always request at least 2 fittings, ask to see a finished garment and inspect it for stitching quality, ask for a price in writing and pay as small a deposit as possible. Tailors are concentrated along Silom, Sukhumvit and Ploenchit Roads and on Gaysorn Sq.

Cheap designer wear with meaningless slogans and a surfeit of labels is available just about everywhere, and especially in tourist areas like Patpong and Sukhumvit. Note that the less you pay, generally, the more likely that the dyes will run, shirts will downsize after washing, and buttons will eject themselves at will.
**Fly Now**, 2nd floor, Gaysorn Plaza, Ploenchit Rd. Directional but wearable designs blending Thai-style femininity and flair with current Western influences. As seen at London Fashion Week.
**Kai Boutique**, 187/1 Bangkok Cable Building, Thanon Rachdamri, www.kai boutique.com. This building is worth visiting for those interested in what the best designers in Thailand are doing. One of Bangkok's longest-standing high-fashion outlets.

### Handicrafts
**Cocoon**, 3rd floor, Gaysorn Plaza. Here, traditional Thai objects have been transformed by altering the design slightly and using bright colours. Great for unusual and fun gifts.

### Jewellery
Thailand has become the world's largest gem-cutting centre and it is an excellent place to buy both gems and jewellery. The best buy of the native precious stones is the sapphire. Modern jewellery is well designed and of a high quality. Always insist on a certificate of authenticity and a receipt.

Ban Mo, on Pahurat Rd, north of Memorial Bridge, is the centre of the gem business although there are shops in all the tourist areas particularly on Silom Rd near the intersection with Surasak Rd, eg **Rama Gems** 987 Silom Rd. **Uthai Gems**, 28/7 Soi Ruam Rudi, off Ploenchit Rd, just east of Witthayu Rd, is recommended, as is **P Jewellery** (Chantaburi), 9/292 Ramindra Rd, Anusawaree Bangkhan, T02-5221857.

For Western designs, **Living Extra** and **Yves Joaillier** are to be found on the 3rd floor of the Charn Issara Tower, 942 Rama IV Rd. **Jewellery Trade Centre** (aka Galleria Plaza), next door to the **Holiday Inn Crowne Plaza** on the corner of Silom Rd and Surasak Rd, contains a number of gem dealers and jewellery shops on the ground floor. **Tabtim Dreams** at Unit 109, is a good place to buy loose gems.

## Markets

The markets in Bangkok are an excellent place to browse, take photographs and pick up bargains.

**Khaosan Rd Market**, close to Banglamphu Market, is geared to the needs and desires of the foreign tourist: counterfeit CDs, DVDs, designer clothing, rucksacks, leather goods, jewellery, souvenirs and so on.

**Nakhon Kasem**, known as the **Thieves' Market**, in the heart of Chinatown (see page 60) houses a number of 'antique' shops selling brassware, old electric fans and woodcarvings (tough bargaining is needed and don't expect everything to be genuine).

**Pahurat Indian Market**, a small slice of India in Thailand, with mounds of sarongs, batiks, buttons and bows.

**Pak Khlong Market** is a wholesale market selling fresh produce, orchids and cut flowers and is situated near the Memorial Bridge on Tri Phet Rd. An exciting place to visit at night when the place is a hive of activity.

**Patpong Market**, arranged down the middle of Patpong Rd, linking Silom and Surawong roads, opens up about 1700 and is geared to tourists. Bargain hard.

**Tewes Market**, near the National Library, is a photographer's dream; a daily market, selling flowers and plants.

**Weekend Market** is the largest and is at Chatuchak Park (see page 65).

## Shopping malls

**The Emporium**, on Sukhumvit Soi 24, daily 1000-2200 (directly accessible from BTS Phrom Phong Station) is an enormous place with many clothes outlets as well as record and book shops, designer shops and more.

**Mah Boonkhrong Centre (MBK)** on the corner of Phayathai and Rama 1, is long established and downmarket and packed full of bargains with countless small shops/stalls.

**Peninsula Plaza**, between the **Hyatt Erawan** and **Regent** hotels, is considered one of the smarter shopping plazas in Bangkok.

**Siam Discovery Centre** (Siam Tower), 6 storeys of high-end fashion across the road from Siam Sq. All the top designers, both Thai and international names, have a presence here.

**Siam Square**, at the intersection of Phayathai and Rama I roads. For teenage trendy Western clothing, bags, belts, jewellery and some antique shops.

## Silk

Silk varies greatly in quality. Generally, the heavier the weight the more expensive the fabric. 1-ply is the lightest and cheapest (about ฿200 per m), 4-ply the heaviest and most expensive (about ฿300-400 per m). Silk also comes in 3 grades: Grade 1 is the finest and smoothest and comes from the inner part of the cocoon. There is also 'hard' and 'soft' silk, soft being rather more expensive. There are a number of specialist silk shops at the top of Surawong Rd (near Rama IV) and a number of shops along the bottom half of Silom Rd (towards Charoen Krung) and in the Siam Centre on Rama I Rd.

**Anita Thai Silk**, 294/4-5 Silom Rd, slightly more expensive than some, but the extensive range makes it worth a visit.

**Cabbages and Condoms**, Sukhumvit Soi 12 and Raja Siam, Sukhumvit Soi 23. Village-made silks.

**Jagtar**, 37 Sukhumvit Soi 11, has some lovely silk curtain fabrics as well as cushion covers in unusual shades and other accessories made from silk. Originality means prices are high.

**Jim Thompson's**, top of Surawong Rd, www.jimthompson.com, daily 0900-2100. Famous silk shop which is expensive, but has the best selection.

## ▲ Activities and tours

### Boat tours

Either book a tour at your hotel or go to one of the piers and organize your own trip. The most frequented piers are located between the **Oriental Hotel** and the Grand Palace, or under Taksin Bridge (which marks the end of the Skytrain line). The pier just to the south of the **Royal Orchid Sheraton Hotel** is recommended. Organizing your own trip gives greater freedom to stop and start when the mood takes you. It is best to go in the morning (0700).

### City tours

Bangkok has innumerable tour companies that can take visitors virtually anywhere. If there is not a tour to fit your bill – most run the same range of tours – many companies will produce a customized one for you, for a price. Most top hotels have their own tour desk and it is probably easiest to book there (arrange to be picked up from your hotel as part of the deal). Prices per person are about ฿400-800 for a half day, ฿1000-2000 for a full day (including lunch).

### Massage

**Wat Pho**, T02-2212974, www.watpho.com (see page 57). The centre is located at the back of the wat, on the opposite side from the entrance. The school offers body massage with or without herbs, and foot massage. The service is available 0800-1700 and costs from ฿250 for a 30-min body massage to ฿350 for an 1-hr body massage with herbal compress. A foot massage is ฿250 for 45 mins. For Westerners wishing to learn the art of traditional Thai massage, special 30-hr courses can be taken for ฿7000, stretching over either 15 days(2 hrs per day) or 10 days (3 hrsper day). There is also a foot massage course at ฿3600, 15 hrs over 3 days.

### Tour operators

Asian Trails, 9th floor, SG Tower, 161/1 Soi Mahadlek, Luang 3, Rajdamri Rd, T02-6262000, www.asiantrails.com. Southeast Asia specialist.
Bangkok Tourist Bureau, 17/1 Phra Arthit Rd, under Phra Pinklao Bridge, T02-2257612, www.bangkoktourist.com, 0900-1900.

Offers every imaginable tour of Bangkok by river, bike and even bus. Knowledgeable and reliable. Their white booths are found in popular tourist areas and are easy to spot. **Real Asia**, T02-7129301, www.realasia.net. Cycling and walking tours around the city's 'greenbelt' including the less-explored rural riverside areas of Bang Kra Jao and Phra Padaeng.

## ⊖ Transport

### Air

For airport information, see page 54; for flight information, see Essentials page 23.

**Airline offices**  Air France, Vorawat Building, 20th floor, 849 Silom Rd, T02-635 1199. **Alitalia**, SSP Tower 3, 15th floor, Unit 15A, 88 Silom Rd, T02-6341800. **American Airlines**, 518/5 Ploenchit Rd, T02-2511393. **Bangkok Airways**, Queen Sirikit National Convention Center, New Rajdapisek Rd, Klongtoey, T02-2293456, www.bangkok air.com. **British Airways**, 14th floor, Abdulrahim Place, 990 Rama 1V Rd, T02-6361747. **Canadian Airlines**, 6th floor, Maneeya Building, 518/5 Ploenchit Rd, T02-2514521. **Cathay Pacific**, 11th floor, Ploenchit Tower, 898 Ploenchit Rd, T02-2630606. **Continental Airlines**, CP Tower, 313 Silom Rd, T02-2310113. **Delta Airlines**, 7th floor, Patpong Building, Surawong Rd, T02-2376838. **Eva Airways**, Green Tower, 2nd floor, 425 Rama IV Rd, opposite Esso Head Office. **Finnair** 6th floor, Vorawat Building, 849 Silom Rd, T02-635 1234. **Gulf Air**, 12th floor, Maneeya Building, 518 Ploenchit Rd, T02-2547931. **KLM**, 19th floor, Thai Wah Tower 11, 21/133-134 South Sathorn Rd, T02-6791100. **Lufthansa**, 18th floor, Q-House (Asoke), Sukhumvit Rd Soi 21, T02-2642400. **Qantas**, 14th floor, Abdulrahim Place, 990 Rama IV Rd, T02-6361747. **SAS**, 8th floor, Glas Haus I, Sukhumvit Rd Soi 25, T02-2600444. **Singapore Airlines**, 12th floor, Silom Centre, 2 Silom Rd, T02-2365295/6. **Swiss**, 21st floor Abdulrahim Place, 990 Rama 1V Rd, T02-6362160. **THAI**, 485 Silom Rd, T02-2343100 and 89 Vibhavadi-Rangsit Rd, T02-5130121. **Vietnam Airlines**, 7th floor, Ploenchit Centre, 1202 Sukhumvit 2 Rd, T02-6569056.

## Metro (MRT) and Skytrain (BTS)

The new **Metro**, www.bangkokmetro.co.th, loops through 18 stations and also intersects with the Skytrain. The entire network is a/c, the comfortable trains run regularly and stations are well-lit and airy. There is a lack of integration with the Skytrain – separate tickets are needed and interchanges are awkward and badly planned. At present, fares for the Metro are cheap, ฿14-36.

The **Skytrain**, T02-6177300, www.bts.co.th, runs on an elevated track through the most developed parts of the city – it is quite a ride, veering between the skyscrapers. Trains run 0600-2400, every 3-5 mins during peak periods and every 10-15 mins out of the rush hour. Fares are ฿10 for one stop, ฿40 for the whole route. Multi-trip tickets can also be purchased, which makes things slightly cheaper.

### Motorcycle taxi

These are used to run up and down the long sois that extend out of the main thoroughfares. Riders wear numbered vests and tend to congregate at the end of the busiest sois. The short-hop fare is about ฿10 and there is usually a price list (in Thai) at the gathering point. Some riders will take you on longer journeys across town and fares will then need to be negotiated – expect to pay ฿25-100, dependent on your negotiating skills.

## Bangkok Skytrain & Metro

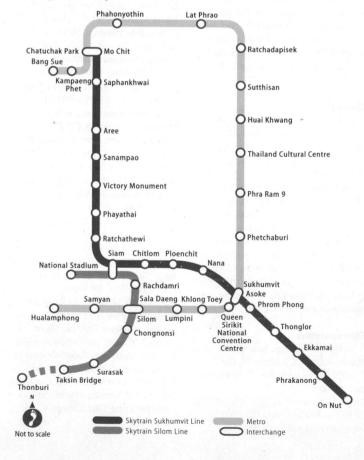

# Chao Phraya River Express

*Rua duan* (boats) link almost 40 *tha* (piers) along the Chao Phraya River from Tha Rajburana (Big C) in the south to Tha Nonthaburi in the north. Selected piers and places of interest, travelling upstream are as follow:

**Tha Sathorn** Pier with the closest access to the Skytrain (Taksin Bridge, S6).

**Tha Orienten** By the Oriental Hotel; access to Silom Road.

**Tha Harbour Department** In the shadow of the Royal Orchid Hotel, on the south side and close to River City shopping centre.

**Tha Ratchawong** Access to Chinatown and Sampeng Lane.

**Tha Saphan Phut** Under the Memorial Bridge and close to Pahurat Indian Market.

**Tha Rachini** Pak Khlong Market; just upstream, the Catholic seminary surrounded by high walls.

**Tha Tien** Close to Wat Pho; Wat Arun on the opposite bank; and,

just downstream from Wat Arun, the Vichaiprasit Fort (headquarters of the Thai navy), lurking behind crenellated ramparts.

**Tha Chang** Just downstream is the Grand Palace; Wat Rakhang with its white corn-cob prang lies opposite.

**Tha Maharaj** Access to Wat Mahathat and Sanaam Luang.

**Tha Phra Arthit** Access to Khaosan Road.

**Tha Visutkasat** Just upstream from the elegant central Bank of Thailand.

**Tha Thewes** Just upstream are boatsheds with royal barges.

**Tha Wat Chan** Just upstream is the Singha Beer Samoson brewery.

**Tha Wat Khema** Wat Khema in large, tree-filled compound.

**Tha Wat Khian** Wat Kien, semi-submerged.

**Tha Nonthaburi** Last stop on the express boat route.

Bangkok Listings

### River transport

The cheapest way to travel on the river is by regular water taxi. There are 3 types. The Chao Phraya Express River Taxi (*rua duan*) runs between Nonthaburi in the north and Rajburana (Big C) in the south. Fares are calculated by zone and range from ฿4-10 for the daily **Standard Express Boat** and ฿10 for the **Special Express Boat**. At peak hours boats leave every 10 mins, off-peak about 15-25 mins. **Standard Express Boats** operate daily 0600-1840, and **Special Express Boats** Mon-Fri 0600-0900, 1200-1900 (see above). The journey from one end of the route to the other takes 75 mins. **Special Express Boats**, flying either a red/orange or a yellow pennant, do not stop at all piers; boats without a flag are the **Standard Express Boats** and stop at all piers. Also, boats will only stop if passengers wish to board or alight, so make your destination known. Be warned that Thais trying to sell boat tours will tell you Express Boats are not running and will try

to extort grossly inflated prices. Walk away and find the correct pier!

**Ferries** also ply back and forth across the river, between Bangkok and Thonburi.

**Khlong or long-tailed boats** (*hang yaaw*) can be rented for ฿200 per hr, or more if you feel like splashing out in more ways than one. See the khlong trips outlined on page 61 for information on what to see on the river. A good map, 'Rivers and Khlongs', is available from the TAT office.

### Taxi

Taxis are usually metered (they must have a/c to register) – look for the 'Taxi Meter' illuminated sign on the roof. Check that the meter is 'zeroed' before setting off.

Fares are ฿35 for the first 2 km, ฿4.50 per km up to 12 km, and ฿5 per km thereafter. Most trips in the city should cost ฿40-100. If the travel speed is less than 6 kph – always a distinct possibility in the traffic choked capital – a surcharge of ฿1.25 per min is automatically added. Passengers also pay the tolls for using the expressway. Taxi drivers sometimes refuse to use the meter despite the fact that they are required to do so by law. Tipping, though not expected, is much appreciated. It is usual to round fares up to the nearest ฿5. To call a taxi **Siam Taxis** T1661 or **Radio Taxi** T1681, they charge ฿20 plus the fare on the meter.

### Tuk-tuk

Best for short journeys, they are uncomfortable and, being open to the elements, you are likely to be asphyxiated by car fumes. Bargaining is essential and the fare should be negotiated before boarding, though most tuk-tuk drivers try to rip tourists off and taking a metered taxi will be less hassle and cheaper. Expect to pay anything from ฿30-100 for a short hop across town.

## ● Directory

### Banks

There are countless exchange booths in all the tourist areas open 7 days a week, mostly 0800-1530, some 0800-2100. Rates vary only marginally between banks, although if changing a large sum, it is worth shopping around. ATMs abound in Bangkok and most can be used with credit cards and bank cards. Open 24 hrs a day.

### Embassies and consulates

**Australia**, 37 South Sathorn Rd, T02-2872680. **Cambodia**, 185 Rachdamri Rd, T02-2546630. **Canada**, 15th floor Abdulrahim Place, 990 Rama IV Rd, T02-6360541. **Laos**, 502/1-3 Soi Ramkhamhaeng 39,T02-5396667. **New Zealand**, 93 Wireless Rd, T02-2542530. **South Africa**, 6th floor,Park Place, 231 Soi Sarasin, Rachdamri Rd, T02-2538473. **UK**, 1031 Wireless Rd, T02-2530191/9. **USA**, 95 Wireless Rd, T02-2054000. **Vietnam**, 83/1 Wireless Rd, T02-2517202, 2 photos required, same-day visas available for ฿2700.

### Internet

There are thousands of internet cafés. Most offer hi-speed access and away from the tourist areas will cost from ฿10 per hr while along Khaosan and Sukhumvit prices are ฿30-60 per hr.

### Immigration

Sathorn Tai Soi Suanphlu, Silom district, T02-2873101.

### Medical services

**Bangkok Adventist Hospital**, 430 Phitsanulok Rd, Dusit, T02-2811422/ 2821100. Efficient vaccination service and 24-hr emergency unit. **Bangkok General Hospital**, New Phetburi Soi 47, T02-3180066.

### Post

**Central GPO** (Praysani Klang for taxi drivers): 1160 Charoen Krung, opposite the Ramada Hotel. Mon-Fri 0800-2000, Sat, Sun and holidays 0800-1300.

### Tourist police

24-hr hotline T1155, 4 Rachadamnoen Nol Av, Dusit.

# Vietnam

# Vietnam

# Hanoi & around

## ☻ Footprint features

# Introduction

Hanoi is a small city of broad, tree-lined boulevards, lakes, parks, weathered colonial buildings, elegant squares and some of the newest office blocks and hotels in Southeast Asia. It lies nearly 100 km from the sea on a bend in the Red River and from this geographical feature the city derives its name – Hanoi – meaning 'within a river bend'.

Hanoi is the capital of the world's 14th most populous country, but, in an age of urban sprawl, the city remains small and compact, historic and charming. Much of its charm lies not so much in the official 'sights' but in the unofficial and informal: the traffic zooming around the broad streets or the cyclos taking a mellow pedal through the Old Quarter, small shops packed with traders' goods or stacks of silk for visitors, skewered poultry on pavement stalls, mobile flower stalls piled on the backs of bikes, the bustle of pedestrians, the ubiquitous tinkle of the ice cream man's bicycle, and the political posters, now raised to an art form, dotted around the city.

At the heart of the city is Hoan Kiem Lake and the famous Sunbeam Bridge. The Old Quarter (36 Streets and Guilds) area, north of the lake, is densely packed and bustling with commerce, its ancient buildings crumbling from the weight of history and activity. The French Quarter, which still largely consists of French buildings, is south of the lake. Here you'll find the Opera House and the grandest hotels, shops and offices.

Accessible on a tour from the city, the primates at Cuc Phuong National Park and the waters of Halong Bay make this area one of the most visited in Vietnam.

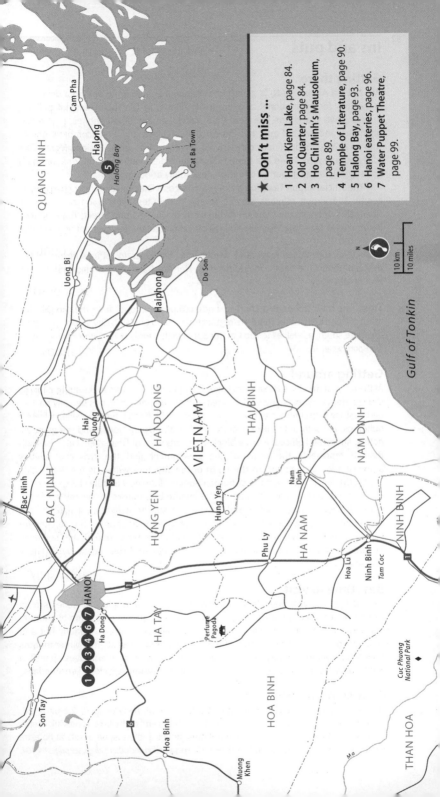

**★ Don't miss ...**

1 Hoan Kiem Lake, page 84.
2 Old Quarter, page 84.
3 Ho Chi Minh's Mausoleum, page 89.
4 Temple of Literature, page 90.
5 Halong Bay, page 93.
6 Hanoi eateries, page 96.
7 Water Puppet Theatre, page 99.

Gulf of Tonkin

QUANG NINH
Cam Pha
Halong
Halong Bay
Cat Ba Town
Uong Bi
Haiphong
Do Son
Bac Ninh
BAC NINH
Hai Duong
HAI DUONG
HUNG YEN
Hung Yen
VIETNAM
THAI BINH
NAM DINH
Nam Dinh
Phu Ly
HA NAM
Hoa Lu
Ninh Binh
Tam Coc
NINH BINH
HANOI
Ha Dong
HA TAY
Perfume Pagoda
Son Tay
Muong Khen
Hoa Binh
HOA BINH
Cuc Phuong National Park
THAN HOA
Ma

N

10 km
10 miles

# Ins and outs

## Getting there

**Air** **Noi Bai Airport** (HAN) is 35 km from Hanoi, a 45-minute to one-hour drive, and is the hub for international and domestic flights. In the main terminal building there are two snack bars, the Aero Café, toilets, a bank of telephones, post office, pharmacy and first-aid unit, two bureaux de changes and a Vietcombank branch with an ATM (Monday-Friday 0730-1600). Incombank accepts Visa and MasterCard (daily 0600-2400). There is a tourist information desk with scant information (daily 0700-1700) and an airport information desk (daily 0600-2300).

The official **Airport Taxi**, T04-8733333, charges a fixed price of US$7.50 to the city centre. The airport minibus service (every 30 minutes, daily 0900-2000, US$2), terminates opposite the **Vietnam Airlines** office, Quang Trung Street, T04-8250872. Return buses leave the Vietnam Airlines office at regular intervals from 0500-1800.

**Bus** Open Tour Buses leave and depart from tour operator offices in the city for destinations in the south, including Hué, Hoi An, Dalat, Nha Trang, Mui Ne and Ho Chi Minh City.

**Train** The train station is a short taxi ride (40,000-65,000d) from the Old Quarter, north of Hoan Kiem Lake. There are regular trains to Ho Chi Minh City, and all points on the route south, as well as to Lao Cai (for Sapa) in the north. ▶ *For further information, see Transport, pages 103-104.*

## Getting around

At the heart of the city is Hoan Kiem Lake. The majority of visitors make straight for the Old Quarter (36 Streets and Guilds) area north of the lake, which is densely packed and bustling with commerce. The French Quarter, which still largely consists of French buildings, is south of the lake. Here you'll find the Opera House and the grandest hotels, shops and offices. A large block of the city west of Hoan Kiem Lake (Ba Dinh District) represents the heart of the government and the civil and military administration of Vietnam. To the north of the city, meanwhile, is the West Lake, Tay Ho District, fringed with the suburban homes of the new middle class.

Hanoi is getting more frenetic by the minute but, thanks to the city's elegant, tree-lined boulevards, walking and cycling can still be delightful. If you like the idea of being pedalled around town, then a cyclo is the answer but be prepared for some concentrated haggling. There are also motorbike taxis (*xe ôm*), and self-drive motorbikes for hire as well as a fleet of metered taxis. Local buses have also improved.

## Best time to visit

For much of the year Hanoi's weather is decidedly non-tropical. It benefits from glorious Europe-like springs and autumns, when temperatures are warm but not too hot and not too cold. From May until early November Hanoi is fearfully hot and steamy. You cannot take a step without breaking into a sweat. The winter months from November to February can be chilly and Hanoians wrap themselves up well in warm coats, woolly hats, gloves and scarves. Most museums are closed on Mondays.

## Tourist information

The new privately run **Tourist Information Center** ⓘ *7 Dinh Tien Hoang St, T04-9263366, www.vntourists.com, daily 0800-2200,* at the northern end of the lake, is proving useful. It provides information and maps and will book hotels and transport tickets at no extra cost; also currency exchange and ATM. ▶ *For Sleeping, Eating and other listings, see pages 94-104.*

## Street smart in Vietnam

Odd numbers usually run consecutively on one side of the street, evens on the other; *bis* after a number, as in 16 bis Hai Ba Trung Street, means there are two houses with the same number and *ter* after the number means there are three houses with the same number. Large buildings with a single street number are usually subdivided 21A, 21B, etc; some buildings may be further subdivided 21C1, 21C2, and so on. An oblique (/ – *sec* or *tren* in Vietnamese) in a number, as in 23/16 Dinh Tien Hoang Street, means the address is to be found in a small side street (*hem*) – in this case running off Dinh Tien Hoang by the side of no 23: the house in question will probably be signed 23/16 rather than just 16. Usually, but by no means always, a hem will be quieter than the main street. Q stands for *quân* (district); this points you in the right general direction and will be important in locating your destination as a long street may run through several quan.

**Hanoi Administration of Tourism** ① *3 Le Lai St, T04-8247652*. Good tourist information is available from the multitude of tour operators in the city. ‣ *For a list of tour operators, see page 100.*

# Background

The origins of Hanoi as a great city lie with a temple orphan, Ly Cong Uan. Ly rose through the ranks of the palace guards to become their commander and in 1010, four years after the death of the previous King Le Hoan, was enthroned, marking the beginning of the 200-year Ly Dynasty. On becoming king, Ly Cong Uan moved his capital from Hoa Lu to Dai La, which he renamed **Thang Long** (Soaring Dragon). Thang Long is present-day Hanoi.

During the period of French expansion into Indochina, the Red River was proposed as an alternative trade route to that of the Mekong. The French attacked and captured the citadel of Hanoi under the dubious pretext that the Vietnamese were about to attack. Recognizing that if a small expeditionary force could be so successful, then there would be little chance against a full-strength army, Emperor Tu Duc acceded to French demands. At the time that the French took control of Annam, Hanoi could still be characterized more as a collection of villages than a city. From 1882 onwards, Hanoi, along with the port city of Haiphong, became the focus of French activity in the north. Hanoi was made the capital of the new colony of Annam and the French laid out a 2 sq km residential and business district, constructing mansions, villas and public buildings incorporating both French and Asian architectural styles. At the end of the Second World War, with the French battling to keep Ho Chi Minh and his forces at bay, Hanoi became little more than a service centre. After the French withdrew in 1954, Ho Chi Minh concentrated on building up Vietnam and in particular Hanoi's industrial base.

Although Ho Chi Minh City has attracted the lion's share of Vietnam's foreign inward investment, Hanoi, as the capital, also receives a large amount. But whereas Ho Chi Minh City's investment tends to be in industry, Hanoi has received a great deal of attention from property developers, notably in the hotel and office sectors.

# Central Hanoi

## Hoan Kiem Lake

Hoan Kiem Lake, or Ho Guom (Lake of the Restored Sword) as it is more commonly referred to in Hanoi, is named after an incident that occurred during the 15th century. Emperor Le Thai To (1428-1433), following a momentous victory against an army of invading Ming Chinese, was sailing on the Lake when a golden turtle appeared from the depths to take back the charmed sword which had secured the victory and restore it to the Lake from whence it came. Like the sword in the stone of British Arthurian legend, Le Thai To's sword assures the Vietnamese of divine intervention in time of national crisis and the story is graphically portrayed in water puppet theatres across the country. There is a modest and rather dilapidated tower (the **Tortoise Tower**) commemorating the event on an islet in the southern part of the lake. In fact, the lake does contain large turtles, believed to be a variety of Asian softshell tortoise; one captured in 1968 was reputed to have weighed 250 kg.

Located on a small island on the lake, the **Ngoc Son Temple** ① *daily 0730-1800, 3000d*, was constructed in the early 19th century on the foundations of the old Khanh Thuy Palace, which had been built in 1739. The temple is dedicated to Van Xuong, the God of Literature, although the 13th-century hero Tran Hung Dao, the martial arts genius Quan Vu and the physician La To are also worshipped here. The island is linked to the shore by a red, arched wooden bridge, **The Huc (Sunbeam) Bridge**, constructed in 1875.

The park that surrounds the shore is used by the residents of the city every morning for jogging and t'ai chi (Chinese shadow boxing) and is regarded by locals as one of the city's beauty spots.

## Old Quarter and 36 Streets

Stretching north from the Lake is the Old Quarter (36 Streets and Guilds or 36 Pho Phuong), the most beautiful area of the city. The narrow streets are each named after the products that are (or were) sold there (**Basket Street, Paper Street, Silk Street**, etc) and create an intricate web of activity and colour. By the 15th century there were 36 short lanes here, each specializing in a particular trade and representing one of the 36 guilds. Among them were the **Phuong Hang Dao (Dyers' Guild Street)**, and the **Phuong Hang Bac (Silversmiths' Street)**. Some of the area's past is still in evidence: at the south end of **Hang Dau Street**, for example, is a mass of stalls selling nothing but shoes, while Tin Street is still home to a community of pot and pan menders (and sellers). Generally, however, the crafts and trades have given way to new activities – karaoke bars and tourist shops – but it is remarkable the extent to which the streets still specialize in the production and sale of just one type of merchandise.

The dwellings in this area are known as *nha ong* (**tube houses**); they have narrow shop fronts, sometimes only 3 m wide, but can stretch back from the road for up to 50 m. In the countryside the dimensions of houses were calculated on the basis of the owner's own physical dimensions; in urban areas the tube houses evolved so that each house could have an, albeit very small, area of shop frontage facing onto the main street, its width determined by the social class of the owner. The houses tend to be interspersed by courtyards or 'wells' to permit light into the house and allow some space for outside activities like washing and gardening. The structures were built of bricks 'cemented' together with sugar-cane juice. The older houses tend to be lower; commoners were not permitted to build higher than the Emperor's own residence. Other regulations prohibited attic windows looking down on the street; this was to prevent assassination and to stop people from looking down on a passing king. As far as colour and decoration were concerned, purple and gold were strictly for royal use only, as was the decorative use of the dragon.

By the early 20th century, inhabitants were replacing their traditional tube houses with buildings inspired by French architecture. Many fine buildings from this era remain and are best appreciated by standing back and looking upwards. Shutters, cornices, columns and wrought-iron balconies and balustrades are common decorative features. An ornate façade sometimes conceals a pitched roof behind. There are some good examples on **Nguyen Sieu Street**. The house at **87 Ma May Street** ① *daily 0800-1200, 1300-1700, 5000d, guide included*, is a wonderfully preserved example of an original shop house.

Further north is the large and varied **Dong Xuan Market**, on Dong Xuan Street. This covered market was destroyed in a disastrous fire in 1994 but has since been rebuilt. It specializes mainly in clothes and household goods.

## St Joseph's Cathedral

To the west of Hoan Kiem Lake, in a little square stands the rather sombre, twin-towered neo-Gothic **Saint Joseph's Cathedral**. Built in 1886, the cathedral is important as one of the very first colonial-era buildings in Hanoi finished, as it was, soon after the Treaty of Tientsin which gave France control over the whole of Vietnam. Some fine stained-glass windows remain.

## Opera House

① *Not open to the public except during public performances. See the billboards outside or visit the box office for details.*

To the south and east of Hoan Kiem Lake is the proud-looking French-era Opera House. It was built between 1901 and 1911 by François Lagisquet and is one of the finest French colonial buildings in Hanoi. Some 35,000 bamboo piles were sunk into the mud of the Red River to provide foundations for the lofty edifice. The exterior is a delightful mass of shutters, wrought-iron work, little balconies and a tiled frieze. The top balustrade is capped with griffins. Inside, there are dozens of little boxes and fine decoration evocative of the French era. Having suffered years of neglect, the Opera House was eventually lavishly restored, opening in time for the Francophone Summit held in 1997. The restoration cost US$14 million, a colossal sum to spend on the reappointment of a colonial edifice.

## Museum of Vietnamese History

① *1 Trang Tien St, Tue-Sun 0800-1130, 1330-1630; 15,000d.*

The history museum (**Bao Tang Lich Su**) is housed in a splendid building, completed in 1931. It was built as the home of the École Française d'Extrême-Orient, a distinguished archaeological, historical and ethnological research institute, by Ernest Hébrard. The collection spans Vietnamese history from the Neolithic period to the 20th century of Ho Chi Minh and is arranged in chronological order.

Galleries on the first floor lead from the Neolithic (Bac Son) represented by stone tools and jewellery to the Bronze Age (Dong Son) with some finely engraved ceremonial bronze drums, symbolizing wealth and power. Wooden stakes that were used to impale invading Chinese forces in 1288 were found in 1976 at the cross of the Chanh River and Bach Dang River – a photo of some remaining in the river bed is interesting and a giant oil painting depicting the famous battle is hypnotically fascinating. The giant turtle, a symbol of longevity, supports a vast stela which praises the achievements of Le Loi (reigned 1428-1433), founder of the Le Dynasty who harnessed nationalist sentiment and succeeded in repelling the war-hungry Chinese. A replica of the oldest Buddha Amitabha statue dominates the far end of the first floor. Amitabha is the Buddha of Infinite Light and the original dates from 1057 and was from Phat Tich Pagoda in Bac Ninh Province. Opposite the statue the oldest minted coins in Vietnam are displayed. They date from AD 968 and were minted by the Dinh Dynasty. A collection of outsized paper currency from the French colonial

# Hanoi

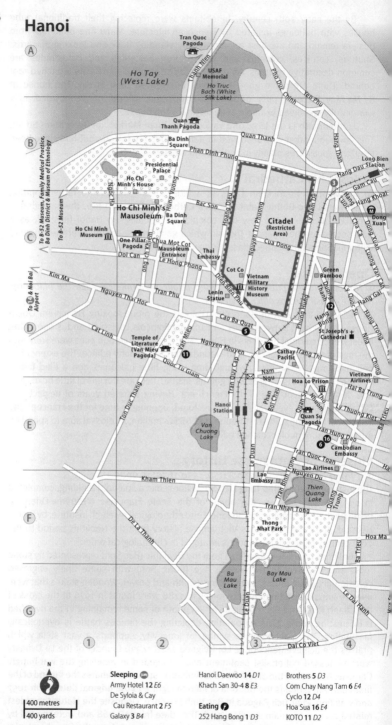

N

400 metres
400 yards

**Sleeping**
Army Hotel **12** *E6*
De Syloia & Cay
 Cau Restaurant **2** *F5*
Galaxy **3** *B4*

Hanoi Daewoo **14** *D1*
Khach San 30-4 **8** *E3*

**Eating**
252 Hang Bong **1** *D3*

Brothers **5** *D3*
Com Chay Nang Tam **6** *E4*
Cyclo **12** *D4*
Hoa Sua **16** *E4*
KOTO **11** *D2*

days is also interesting. These date from 1875 when the French established the Bank of Indochina. The second floor begins with the 15th century to the present day; Champa is represented by some remarkably well-preserved stone carvings of apsaras, mythical dancing girls and a head of Garuda, found at Quang Nam. There are relics such as 18th-century, unusually shaped, bronze pagoda gongs and urns of successive royal dynasties from Le to Nguyen. Unfortunately, some of the pieces are reproductions, including a number of the stelae.

## Hoa Lo Prison

ⓘ *1 Hoa Lo, Tue-Sun 0800-1130, 1330-1630, 5000d which includes a useful pamphlet; 10,000d for a larger one.*

Hoa Lo Prison (Maison Centrale), better known as the **Hanoi Hilton**, is the prison where US POWs were incarcerated, some for six years, during the Vietnamese War. Up until 1969, prisoners were also tortured here. Two US Airforce officers, Charles Tanner and Ross Terry, rather than face torture, concocted a story about two other members of their squadron who had been court-martialled for refusing to fly missions against the north. Thrilled with this piece of propaganda, visiting Japanese Communists were told the story and it filtered back to the US. Unfortunately for Tanner and Terry, they had called their imaginary pilots Clark Kent and Ben Casey (both TV heroes). When the Vietnamese realized they had been made fools of, the two prisoners were again tortured. The final prisoners of war were not released until 1973, some having been held in the north since 1964. At the end of 1992, a US mission was shown around the prison where 2000 inmates had been housed in cramped and squalid conditions.

Despite pleas from war veterans and party members, the site was sold to a Singapore-Vietnamese joint venture and is now a hotel and shopping complex, **Hanoi Towers**. As part of the deal the developers had to leave a portion of the prison for use as a museum. There are recreations of conditions under colonial rule when the French incarcerated patriotic Vietnamese from 1896: by 1953 they were holding 2000 prisoners in a space designed for 500. Less prominence is given to the role of the prison for holding American pilots, but

*Related maps*
*A Hanoi centre, page 88*

Douglas 'Pete' Peterson, the first post-war American Ambassador to Vietnam (1997-2001), who was one such occupant (imprisoned 1966-1973), has his mug-shot on the wall, as does John McCain (imprisoned 1967-1973), now a US senator.

# Hanoi centre

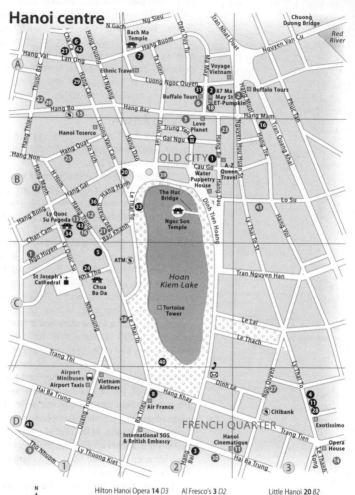

200 metres
200 yards

**Sleeping**
Artist **11** D3
Eden Hanoi & A Little
  Italian Restaurant **9** D1
Freedom **12** B1
Gold Spring **2** A3
Hang Trong **13** B1
Hanoi Backpacker's
  Hostel **1** C1

Hilton Hanoi Opera **14** D3
Hoa Linh **15** A1
Ho Guom **16** B1
Hong Ngoc **17** B1
Hong Ngoc 2 **6** A2
Hong Ngoc 3 **3** B2
My Lan **20** A1
Nam Phuong **21** B1
Ngoc Diep **22** A1
Real Darling Café **25** B1
Sofitel Metropole Hanoi
  & Le Beaulieu
  Restaurant **27** D3

**Eating**
69 **2** A2

Al Fresco's **3** D2
Au Lac **4** D3
Baan Thai **5** C1
Baguette & Chocolat **42** A1
Bit Tet **7** A2
Bobby Chinn **8** D2
Café Moca **24** C1
Café Puku **43** B1
Cha Ca La Vong **21** A1
Club Opera **11** D3
Dakshin **5** C1
Green Tangerine **1** B2
Hanoi Press Club **28** D3
Highlands Coffee **40** C2
Highway 4 **16** B3
Lá **34** B1

Little Hanoi **20** B2
Pepperonis **36** B1
Restaurant 22 **29** A1
San Ho **41** D1
Tamarind & Handspan
  Adventure Travel **31** A2
Thuy Ta **33** B2

**Bars & clubs**
Ho Guom Xanh **38** C2
Legends **39** B2
Le Pub **23** B2
R&R Tavern **45** B3
Red Beer **18** A2
Spotted Cow **30** D2

# West from the Citadel

## Vietnam Military History Museum

ⓘ *28 Dien Bien Phu St, Tue-Thu, Sat and Sun 0800-1130, 1300-1630; 5000d, camera use, 20,000d. ATM and Highlands Coffee Café on site.*

Tanks, planes and artillery fill the courtyard of the Army Museum (Bao Tang Quan Doi). Symbolically, an untouched Mig-21 stands at the museum entrance while wreckage of B-52s, F1-11s and Q2Cs is piled up at the back. The museum illustrates battles and episodes in Vietnam's fight for independence, from the struggles with China through to the resistance to the French and the Battle of Dien Bien Phu (illustrated by a good model). Inevitably, of course, there are lots of photographs and exhibits of the American war and although much is self-evident, unfortunately a lot of the explanations are in Vietnamese only.

In the precincts of the museum is the **Cot Co**, a flag tower, raised up on three platforms. Built in 1812, it is the only substantial part of the original **citadel** still standing. There are good views over Hanoi from the top. The walls of the citadel were destroyed by the French between 1894 and 1897, presumably as they symbolized the power of the Vietnamese emperors. The French were highly conscious of the projection of might, power and authority through large structures, which helps explain their own remarkable architectural legacy. Other remaining parts of the citadel are in the hands of the Vietnamese army and out of bounds to visitors. Across the road from the museum's front entrance is a **statue of Lenin**.

## Ho Chi Minh's Mausoleum and Ba Dinh Square

ⓘ *1 Apr-1 Oct Tue-Thu 0730-1100, 1400-1600, Fri 0730-1100, Sat and Sun 0730-1100, 1400-1630; 30 Nov-31 Mar Tue-Thu 0800-1100, 1330-1600, Fri 0800-1100, Sat and Sun 0800-1100, 1330-1630; closed Oct and Nov for conservation. Before entering the mausoleum, visitors must leave possessions at the office (Ban To Chuc) on Huong Vuong, just south of and a few mins' walk from the Mausoleum. Visitors must be respectful: dress neatly, walk solemnly, do not talk and do not take anything in that could be construed as a weapon, for example a penknife.*

The Vietnamese have made the mausoleum housing Ho Chi Minh's body a holy place of pilgrimage and visitors march in file to see Ho's embalmed corpse inside the mausoleum (Lang Chu Tich Ho Chi Minh). The embalming and eternal display of Ho Chi Minh's body was contrary to Ho's own wishes: he wanted to be cremated and his ashes placed in three urns to be positioned atop three unmarked hills in the north, centre and south of the country. He once wrote that "cremation is not only good from the point of view of hygiene, but it also saves farmland". The embalming of Ho's body was undertaken by the chief Soviet embalmer, Dr Sergei Debrov, who also pickled such Communist luminaries as Klenient Gottwald (President of Czechoslovakia), Georgi Dimitrov (Prime Minister of Bulgaria) and Forbes Burnham (President of Guyana). Debrov was flown to Hanoi from Moscow as Ho lay dying, bringing with him two transport planes packed with air conditioners (to keep the corpse cool) and other equipment. To escape US bombing, the team moved Ho to a cave, taking a full year to complete the embalming process. Russian scientists still check-up on their handiwork, servicing Ho's body regularly. Their embalming methods and the fluids they use are still a closely guarded secret. In an interview, Debrov noted with pleasure the poor state of China's Chairman Mao's body, which was embalmed without Soviet help.

The mausoleum, built between 1973 and 1975, is a massive, square and forbidding structure and must be among the best constructed, maintained and air-conditioned buildings in Vietnam. Opened in 1975, it is a modelled closely on Lenin's Mausoleum in Moscow. Ho lies with a guard at each corner of his bier and visitors march past in file to see his body.

In front of Ho Chi Minh's Mausoleum is **Ba Dinh Square** where Ho read out the Vietnamese Declaration of Independence on 2 September 1945. Following Ho's declaration, 2 September became Vietnam's National Day. Coincidentally, 2 September was also the date on which Ho died in 1969, although his death was not officially announced until 3 September in order not to mar people's enjoyment of National Day in the beleaguered north of the country.

## Ho Chi Minh's house and the Presidential Palace

ⓘ *1 Bach Thao St, T04-08044529, summer Tue-Thu, Sat and Sun 0730-1100, 1400-1600, Fri 0730-1100; winter Tue-Thu, Sat and Sun 0800-1100, 1330-1600, Fri 0800-1100; 5000d. The Presidential Palace is not open to the public.*

From the mausoleum, visitors are directed to Ho Chi Minh's house built in the compound of the former Presidential Palace. The palace, now a party guesthouse, was the residence of the Governors-General of French Indochina and was built between 1900 and 1908. In 1954, when North Vietnam's struggle for independence was finally achieved, Ho Chi Minh declined to live in the palace, saying that it belonged to the people. Instead, he stayed in what is said to have been an electrician's house in the same compound. He lived here from 1954 to 1958, before moving to a new stilt house built on the other side of the small lake (Ho Chi Minh's 'Fish Farm', swarming with massive and well-fed carp). The house was designed by Ho and an architect, Nguyen Van Ninh. This modest house made of rare hardwoods is airy and personal and immaculately kept. Ho conducted meetings under the house, which is raised up on wooden pillars, and slept and worked above from May 1958 to August 1969. Behind the house is Ho's bomb shelter and, behind that, the hut where he died in 1969.

## One Pillar Pagoda and Ho Chi Minh Museum

Close by is the **One Pillar Pagoda** (Chua Mot Cot), one of the few structures remaining from the original foundation of the city. It was built in 1049 by Emperor Ly Thai Tong, although the shrine has since been rebuilt on several occasions, most recently in 1955 after the French destroyed it, before withdrawing from the country. The emperor built the pagoda in a fit of religious passion after he dreamt that he saw the goddess Quan Am (Vietnam's equivalent of the Chinese goddess Kuan-yin, see box, page 91), sitting on a lotus and holding a young boy, whom she handed to the Emperor. On the advice of counsellors who interpreted the dream, the Emperor built a little lotus-shaped temple in the centre of a water-lily pond and shortly afterwards his queen gave birth to a son. As the name suggests, it is supported on a single (concrete) pillar with a brick and stone staircase running up one side. The pagoda symbolizes the 'pure' lotus sprouting from the sea of sorrow. Original in design, with dragons running along the apex of the elegantly-curved tiled roof, the temple is one of the most revered monuments in Vietnam.

Overshadowing the One Pillar Pagoda is the **Ho Chi Minh Museum** ⓘ *19 Ngoc Ha St, T04-8463752, Tue-Thu and Sat 0800-1130, 1400-1600, Fri 0800-1130, 10,000d, 40,000d for guide,* opened in 1990 in celebration of the centenary of Ho's birth. Contained in a large and impressive modern building, it is the best arranged and most innovative museum in Vietnam. The displays trace Ho's life and work from his early wanderings around the world to his death and final victory over the south.

## Temple of Literature

ⓘ *Entrance on Quoc Tu Giam St, T04-8452917, open daily summer 0730-1730, winter 0730-1700; 5000d, 45-min tour in French or English 50,000d, 3000d for brochure. ATM inside.*

The Temple of Literature (Van Mieu Pagoda) is the largest and, probably, the most important, temple complex in Hanoi. It was founded in 1070 by Emperor Ly Thanh Tong, dedicated to Confucius who had a substantial following in Vietnam, and modelled, so it is said, on a temple in Shantung, China, the birthplace of the sage.

## The story of Quan Am

Quan Am was turned onto the streets by her husband for some unspecified wrong-doing and, dressed as monk, took refuge in a monastery. There, a woman accused her of fathering, and then abandoning, her child. Accepting the blame (why, no one knows), she was again turned out onto the streets, only to return to the monastery much later when she was on the point of death – to confess her true identity. When the Emperor of China heard the tale, he made Quan Am the Guardian Spirit of Mother and Child, and couples without a son now pray to her.

Quan Am's husband is sometimes depicted as a parakeet, with the Goddess usually holding her adopted son in one arm and standing on a lotus leaf (the symbol of purity).

Some researchers, while acknowledging the date of foundation, challenge the view that it was built as a Confucian institution pointing to the ascendancy of Buddhism during the Ly Dynasty. Confucian principles and teaching rapidly replaced Buddhism, however, and Van Mieu subsequently became the intellectual and spiritual centre of the kingdom as a cult of literature and education spread amongst the court, the mandarins and then among the common people. At one time there were said to be 20,000 schools teaching the Confucian classics in northern Vietnam alone.

The temple and its compound are arranged north-south; visitors enter at the southern end from Quoc Tu Giam Street. On the pavement two pavilions house stelae bearing the inscription *ha ma* (climb down from your horse), a nice reminder that even the most elevated dignitaries had to proceed on foot. The main **Van Mieu Gate** (Cong Van Mieu Mon) is adorned with 15th-century dragons. Traditionally, the large central gate was opened only on ceremonial occasions. The path leads through the Cong Dai Trung to a second courtyard and the **Van Khue Gac Pavilion**, which was built in 1805 and dedicated to the Constellation of Literature. The roof is tiled according to the yin-yang principle.

Beyond lies the **Courtyard of the Stelae** at the centre of which is the rectangular pond or Cieng Thien Quang (**Well of Heavenly Clarity**). More important are the stelae themselves, on which are recorded the names of 1306 successful examination scholars (*tien si*). Of the 82 stelae that survive (30 are missing), the oldest dates back to 1442 and the most recent to 1779. Each stela is carried on the back of a tortoise, symbol of strength and longevity. The stelae are arranged in no order but three chronological categories can be identified. Fourteen date from the 15th and 16th centuries; they are the smallest and embellished with floral motifs and yin-yang symbols but not dragons (a royal emblem). Twenty-five stelae are from the 17th century and ornamented with dragons (by now permitted), pairs of phoenix and other creatures mythical or real. The remaining 43 stelae are of 18th-century origin; they are the largest and decorated with two stylized dragons, some merging with flame clouds.

Passing the examination was not easy: in 1733, out of some 3000 entrants only eight passed the doctoral examination (*Thai Hoc Sinh*) and became Mandarins, a task that took 35 days. This tradition was begun in 1484, on the instruction of Emperor Le Thanh Tong, and continued through to 1878, during which time 116 examinations were held. The Temple of Literature was not used only for examinations, however: food was also distributed from here to the poor and infirm, 500 g of rice at a time. In 1880, the French Consul Monsieur de Kergaradec recorded that 22,000 impoverished people came to receive this meagre handout.

Continuing north, the **Dai Thanh Mon** (Great Success Gate) leads on to a courtyard flanked by two buildings which date from 1954, the originals having been destroyed in 1947. These buildings were reserved for 72 disciples of Confucius. Facing is the **Dai Bai**

**Duong** (Great House of Ceremonies) which was built in the 19th century but in the earlier style of the Le Dynasty. The carved wooden friezes with their dragons, phoenix, lotus flowers, fruits, clouds and yin-yang discs are all symbolically charged, depicting the order of the universe and by implication reflecting the god-given hierarchical nature of human society, each in his place. It is not surprising that the Communist government has hitherto had reservations about preserving a temple extolling such heretical doctrine. Inside is an altar on which sit statues of Confucius and his closest disciples. Adjoining is the **Dai Thanh Sanctuary** (Great Success Sanctuary), which also contains a statue of Confucius.

## B-52 Museum
① *157 Doi Can St, free.*
The remains of downed B-52s have been hawked around Hanoi over many years but seem to have found a final resting place at the **Bao Tang Chien Tang B-52** (B-52 Museum). This curious place is not really a museum but this doesn't matter because what everyone wants to do is to walk over the wings and tail of a shattered B-52, and the B-52 in question lies scattered around the yard. As visitors to Vietnamese museums will come to expect, any enemy objects are heaped up as junk while the Vietnamese pieces are painted, cared for and carefully signed with the names of whichever heroic unit fought in them. There are anti-aircraft guns, the devastating SAMs that wreaked so much havoc on the US Airforce and a Mig-21. Curiously the signs omit to mention the fact that all this hardware was made in Russia.

## Vietnam Museum of Ethnology
① *Nguyen Van Huyen Rd, some distance west of the city centre in Cau Giay District, T04-7562193; Tue-Sun 0830-1730, 20,000d; photography 50,000d; tour guide 50,000d. Take a taxi or catch the No 14 minibus from Dinh Tien Hoang St, north of Hoan Kiem Lake, to the Nghia Tan stop; turn right and walk down Hoang Quoc Viet St for 1 block, before turning right at the Petrolimex station down Nguyen Van Huyen; the museum is on the left.*
The collection here of some 25,000 artefacts, 15,000 photographs and documentaries of practices and rituals is excellent and, more to the point, is attractively and informatively presented with labels in Vietnamese, English and French. It displays the material culture (textiles, musical instruments, jewellery, tools, baskets and the like) of the majority Kinh people as well as Vietnam's 53 other designated minority peoples. While much is historical, the museum is also attempting to build up its contemporary collection. There is a shop attached to the museum and ethnic minorities' homes have been recreated in the grounds.

# Around Hanoi ⊛▲ ▸ *pp94-104. Colour map 2, B4 and B5.*

There are a number of worthwhile day and overnight trips from Hanoi: the Perfume Pagoda lies to the southwest; Tam Coc and Cuc Phuong National Park are some three hours south, while Halong Bay, best visited on an overnight trip, is three hours to the east.

## Perfume Pagoda → *Colour map 2, B4.*
① *A tour from Hanoi costs about US$30 and includes the return boat trip along the Yen River.*
The Perfume Pagoda (Chua Huong or Chua Huong Tich) is 60 km southwest of Hanoi. A sampan takes visitors along the Yen River, a diverting 4-km ride through a flooded landscape to the Mountain of the Perfume Traces. From here it is a 3-km hike up the mountain to the cool, dark cave where the Perfume Pagoda is located. The stone statue of Quan Am in the principal pagoda was carved in 1793 after Tay Son rebels

had stolen and melted down its bronze predecessor to make cannon balls. Dedicated
to Quan Am (see page 91), it is one of a number of shrines and towers built amongst limestone caves and is regarded as one of the most beautiful spots in Vietnam. Emperor Le Thanh Tong (1460-1497) described it as *"Nam Thien de nhat dong"* or "foremost cave under the Vietnamese sky". It is a popular pilgrimage spot, particularly during the festival months of March and April.

## Tam Coc → *Colour map 2, B4.*

ⓘ *The turning to Tam Coc is 4 km south of Ninh Binh on Highway 1. US$2 plus US$1.50 per person for the boat ride. Tam Coc can easily be reached from Hanoi on a day trip, either as part of an organized tour or by hiring a car and driver. Take plenty of sun cream and a hat.*

An area of enchanting natural beauty, Tam Coc means literally 'three caves'. Those who have seen the film *Indochine*, some of which was shot here, will be familiar with the nature of the beehive-type scenery created by limestone towers, similar to those of Halong Bay. The highlight of this excursion is an enchanting boat ride up the little Ngo Dong River through the eponymous three caves. The exact form varies from wet to dry season; when flooded, the channel disappears and one or two of the caves may be drowned; in the dry season, the shallow river meanders between fields of golden rice. Women punt pitch-and-resin tubs that look like elongated coracles through the tunnels. It is a leisurely experience and a chance to observe at close quarters the extraordinary method of rowing with the feet. The villagers have a rota to decide whose turn it is to row and, to supplement their fee, will try and sell visitors embroidered tablecloths. Enterprising photographers snap you setting off from the bank and will surprise you 1 km upstream with copies of your cheesy grin already printed. On a busy day the scene from above is like a two-way, nose-to-tail procession of waterboatmen, so to enjoy Tam Coc at its best, make it your first port of call in the morning.

## Cuc Phuong National Park → *Colour map 2, B4.*

ⓘ *Nho Quan district, 120 km south of Hanoi and 45 km west of Ninh Binh, T030-848006, www.cucphuongtourism.com; 40,000d. Cuc Phuong can be visited as a day trip from Hanoi (early start), either on an organized tour (a sensible option for lone travellers or pairs) or by hiring a car with driver or a motorbike.*

Located in an area of deeply-cut limestone and reaching elevations of up to 800 m, this park is covered by 22,000 ha of humid tropical montagne forest. It is home to an estimated 2000 species of flora, including the giant parashorea, cinamomum and sandoricum trees. Wildlife, however, has been much depleted by hunting, so that only 117 mammal, 307 bird species and 110 reptiles and amphibians are thought to remain. April and May sees fat grubs and pupae metamorphosing into swarms of beautiful butterflies that mantle the forest in fantastic shades of greens and yellows. The government has resettled a number of the park's 30,000 Muong minority people but Muong villages do still exist and can be visited. The **Endangered Primate Rescue Centre** ⓘ *www.primatecenter.org, 0900-1100, 1330-1600, limited entrance every 30 mins, 10,000d,* is a big draw in the park, with more than 30 cages, four houses and two semi-wild enclosures for the 130 animals in breeding programmes.

## Halong Bay → *Colour map 2, B5.*

ⓘ *Most boats depart from Halong City, 110 km east of Hanoi. Http://halongbay. halong.net.vn/ has comprehensive information on the area, including transport details. US$1 admission for each cave and attraction. You need 4-5 hrs to see the bay properly but an overnight stay aboard a boat is enjoyable. The majority of people visit on an all-inclusive tour with tourist cafés or tour operators from Hanoi (see page 100). It can be stormy in Jun, Jul and Aug; Jul and Aug are also the wettest months; winter is cool and dry; rain is possible at all times of year.*

Halong means 'descending dragon'. An enormous beast is said to have careered into the sea at this point, cutting the fantastic bay from the rocks as it thrashed its way into the depths. Vietnamese poets, including the 'Poet King' Le Thanh Tong, have traditionally extolled the beauty of this romantic area, with its rugged islands that protrude from a sea dotted with sailing junks. Artists, too, have drawn inspiration from the crooked islands, seeing the forms of monks and gods in the rock faces, and dragon's lairs and fairy lakes in the depths of the caves. Another myth says that the islands are dragons sent by the gods to impede the progress of an invasion flotilla. The area was the location of two famous sea battles in the 10th and 13th centuries and is now a UNESCO World Heritage Site.

Geologically, the tower-karst scenery of Halong Bay is the product of millions of years of chemical action and river erosion working on the limestone to produce a pitted landscape. At the end of the last ice age, when the glaciers melted, the sea level rose and inundated the area turning hills into islands. The islands of the bay are divided by a broad channel: to the east are the smaller outcrops of Bai Tu Long, while to the west are the larger islands with caves and secluded beaches. Rocks can be treacherously slippery, so sensible footwear is advised. Many of the caves are a disappointment, with harrying vendors, mounds of litter and disfiguring graffiti. Among the more spectacular, however, are **Hang Hanh**, which extends for 2 km. Tour guides will point out fantastic stalagmites and stalactites which, with imagination, become heroes, demons and animals. **Hang Luon** is another flooded cave, which leads to the hollow core of a doughnut-shaped island. It can be swum or navigated by coracle. **Hang Dau Go** is the cave in which Tran Hung Dao stored his wooden stakes prior to studding them in the bed of the Bach Dang River in 1288 to destroy the boats of invading Mongol hordes. **Hang Thien Cung** is a hanging cave, a short 50-m haul above sea level, with dripping stalactites, stumpy stalagmites and solid rock pillars.

## ● Sleeping

Old Quarter buildings are tightly packed and have small rooms, sometimes without windows. Hotels in this area offer the best value for money.

**Central Hanoi** *p84, maps p86 and p88*
**LL Hilton Hanoi Opera**, 1 Le Thanh Tong St, T04-9330500, www1.hilton.com. Built adjacent to and architecturally in keeping with the Opera House, this is a splendid building and provides the highest levels of service and hospitality. The stylishly furnished rooms enjoy separate bathtubs and showers and broadband internet access. There is a French restaurant, Chinese restaurant, bakery and sports bar.
**LL-L Hanoi Daewoo**, 360 Kim Ma St, T04-8315000, www.hanoi-daewoo.com. A giant hotel with an adjoining apartment complex and office tower. The hotel is one of Vietnam's most luxurious with plushly decorated rooms, a large pool, shops and four restaurants. The **Edo** is considered as serving some of the finest Japanese food in town.

**LL-L Sofitel Metropole Hanoi**, 15 Ngo Quyen St, T04-8266919, www.accor hotels-asia.com. The only hotel in its class in central Hanoi and often full. It boasts a diversity of bars and restaurants: the **Met Pub** is a popular live music bar; **Le Beaulieu** is one of the finest restaurants in Hanoi; a pianist plays at 1800 nightly at **Le Club bar**. There is also a business centre, a cluster of shops and a small pool with attractive poolside Bamboo Bar. 2007 saw the introduction of a spa. The hotel has retained most of its business despite competition from newer business hotels away from the city centre and remains a hub of activity. Graham Greene, Charlie Chaplin and Somerset Maugham have all stayed here.
**L-A De Syloia**, 17A Tran Hung Dao St, T04-8245346, www.desyloia.com. An attractive and friendly small boutique, business hotel south of the lake. 33 rooms and suites, a business centre and gym in good central location. The popular **Cay Cau** restaurant specializes in Vietnamese dishes and the daily set-lunch is excellent value.

**L-A Ho Guom**, 76 Hang Trong St, T04-824 3565, hoguomtjc@hn.vnn.vn. Very near the lake and set back from the road in a quiet courtyard with a nice position. All rooms are furnished in Hué imperial style and are fully equipped. Staff are friendly and helpful. This hotel is upgrading to 4 stars and prices were not available at the time of going to press.

**A Army Hotel**, 33C Pham Ngu Lao St, T04-8252896, armyhotel@fpt.vn. Owned and run by the Army, this is a suprisingly pleasant and attractive hotel. Set around a decent-sized swimming pool, it is quiet and comfortable. The hotel has a total of 69 a/c rooms and a restaurant.

**A Galaxy**, 1 Phan Dinh Phung St, T04-8282888, www.tctgroup.com.vn. Well-run 3-star business hotel (built in 1918) with 50 carpeted rooms and full accessories including the all-important bedside reading lights which too many expensive hotels forget.

**A Hong Ngoc**, 30-34 Hang Manh St, T04-8285053, hongngochotel@hn.vnn.vn. This is a real find. A small, family-run hotel, with comfortable rooms and huge bathrooms with bathtubs. It is spotlessly clean throughout and run by cheerful and helpful staff. Breakfast included.

There are 2 other Hong Ngoc's in the Old Quarter: Hong Ngoc 2, 99 Ma May St, T04-8283631, hongngochotel@hn.vnn.vn, and **Hong Ngoc 3** (see below).

**A-B Eden Hanoi**, 78 Tho Nhuom St, T04-9423273, www.edenhanoihotel.com. Good location but small rooms; worth paying more for the suites. Popular and handy for **A Little Italian** restaurant.

**B Gold Spring Hotel**, 22 Nguyen Huu Huan St, T04-9263057, www.goldenspringhotel.com.vn. On the edge of the Old Quarter. 22 fine rooms that are attractively decorated. Breakfast and free internet included.

**B Hang Trong**, 56 Hang Trong St, T04-8251346, thiencotravelvn@yahoo.com. A/c and hot water (showers only), a few unusual and quite decent rooms set back from the road, either on a corridor or in a courtyard. The ones that don't overlook the courtyard are dark and airless. Very convenient position for every part of town.

Internet and booking office for Sinh Café tours.

**B Hong Ngoc 3**, 39 Hang Bac St, T04-9260322, hongngochotel@hn.vnn.vn. Some staff here are exceptionally helpful, others are not. A real mixed bag. Rooms are clean and comfortable with TVs, a/c and bathtubs. It's in a great central location and surprisingly quiet. You may want to pass on the breakfast.

**B-D Freedom**, 57 Hang Trong St, T04-8267119, freedomhotel@hn.vnn.vn. Not far from Hoan Kiem lake and the cathedral. 11 spacious rooms with desks. Some have bathtubs; those without have small bathrooms. Friendly family.

**B-D Hoa Linh**, 35 Hang Bo St, T04-8243887, hoalinhhotel@hn.vnn.vn. Right in the centre of the Old Quarter, this hotel has lovely bedrooms decked out in the dark wood of Hué imperial style: bedsteads are ornately carved with dragons; screens and bedside tables are inlaid with mother-of-pearl. The larger, more expensive rooms have a double and a single bed and a balcony. It is worth paying extra for a view of the decoration on the crumbling buildings opposite. Bathrooms are basic with plastic showers and no curtains. Breakfast included.

**B-E Hanoi Backpacker's Hostel**, 48 Ngo Huyen St, T04-8285372 (last minute reservations 1800 1552 toll free), www.hanoibackpackershostel.com. Dorm rooms (with bedside lights, lockers and a/c) and double suites in a house that belonged to the Brazilian ambassador. This is a friendly and busy place to stay with plenty of opportunities to meet other travellers and gather advice. Breakfast, internet, tea and coffee and luggage store is included. Don't miss the BBQs on the roof terrace and the Sunday sessions.

**C-D Artist Hotel**, 22A Hai Ba Trung St, T04-8244433, artist_hotel@yahoo.com. This small hotel is set above the pleasant and quiet courtyard of the Hanoi Cinematique. Some of the rooms, all with a/c, are a little dark but the price is great for such a central and unusual location.

**Vietnam** Hanoi & around Listings

For an explanation of sleeping and eating price codes used in this guide, see inside the front cover. Other relevant information is found in Essentials, see pages 29-32.

**C-D Nam Phuong**, 16 Bao Khanh St, T04-8258030, www.ktscom@vnn.vn. Pleasant position near Hoan Kiem Lake, 9 a/c rooms with good soundproofing. Rooms at the back are cheaper. Breakfast and free internet included.

**C-E Khach San 30-4**, 115 Tran Hung Dao St, T04-9420807. Opposite railway station with cheap and good-value rooms; cheaper fan rooms have shared bathroom facilities.

**C-F Real Darling Café**, 33 Hang Quat St, T04-8269386, darling_cafe@hotmail.com. Travellers' café which has 16 rooms, a/c and a 6 bed dorm with fan for US$3 per person. Friendly.

**D-E My Lan**, 70 Hang Bo St, T04-8245510, hotelmylan@yahoo.com. Go through the dentist's surgery where an elderly French-speaking doctor has 10 rooms to rent, a/c or fans. Rather tightly packed but light and breezy; also 1 nice rooftop apartment with kitchen and terrace, US$400 a month. Recommended.

**D-F Ngoc Diep**, 83 Thuoc Bac St, through the Chinese pharmacy, T04-8250020, thugiangguesthouse@yahoo.com. Cheaper rooms all have fan; more expensive rooms a/c. All rooms have hot water and TV, and free internet; breakfast can be included. Bus station and railway station pick up. Popular and friendly, long-stay discounts available.

## Eating

Hanoi has Western-style coffee bars, restaurants and watering holes that stand up well to comparison with their equivalents in Europe. It also has a good number of excellent Vietnamese restaurants.

**Note**: dog (*thit chó* or *thit cay*) is an esteemed delicacy in the north but is mostly served in shacks on the edge of town – so you are unlikely to order it inadvertently.

**Central Hanoi** *p84, maps p86 and p88*

**Hanoi Press Club**, 59A Ly Thai To St, Hoan Kiern District, T04-340888, www.hanoi-pressclub.com. There are 3 good food outlets in this stylish complex directly behind the **Sofitel Metropole Hotel: The Restaurant** has remained consistently one of the most popular dining experiences in Hanoi. The dining room is luxuriously furnished with polished, dark wood floors and print-lined walls. The food is imaginative and superb and there's a fine wine list. The service is faultless. This is a memorable dining experience. In the same building is **The Deli**, T04-8255337; keep its delivery menu by the telephone for pizza, pasta, salads, sandwiches; or fill up in the canteen area with fat stuffed sandwiches and cakes. **The Library Bar** stocks a good range for cigars and whiskies.

**Le Beaulieu**, 15 Ngo Quyen St (in the **Metropole Hotel**), T04-8266919. A good French and international restaurant open for breakfast, lunch and dinner; last orders 2200. Its Sun brunch buffet is regarded as one of the best in Asia. A great selection of French seafood, oysters, prawns, cold and roast meats and cheese. All for US$35.

**Bobby Chinn**, 1 Ba Trieu St, T04-9348577, www.bobbychinn.com. Bobby Chin is one of Hanoi's better known and more expensive fusion restaurants blending Western and Asian ingredients and flavours; it has an award-winning wine list. It is stylish, with hanging rosebuds dropped from the ceiling but the sparkle and warmth has gone. The popular bar has been moved from the centre of the restaurant to the side leaving a lacklustre air.

**Club Opera**, 59 Ly Thai To St, T04-8246950, clubopera@fpt.vn, daily 1100-1400 and 1730-2230. A small, cosy restaurant with an extensive Vietnamese menu in the attractive setting of a restored French villa. The menu is varied, the tables are beautifully laid and the food is appealingly presented.

**San Ho**, 58 Ly Thuong Kiet St, T04-9349184, ando@hn.vnn.vn. 1100-1400, 1700-2200. Live piano music 1900-2100. Vietnamese food. This is Hanoi's most popular seafood restaurant which offers a series of set menus for US$15, 20 and 37.

**Al Fresco's**, 23L Hai Ba Trung St, T04-8267782. A popular Australian grill bar serving ribs, steak, pasta, pizza and fantastic salads. Giant portions, lively atmosphere, a memorable experience. Recommended.

**Hoa Sua**, 28A Ha Hoi St (off Tran Hung Dao St), T04-9424448, www.hoasua school.com, daily 1100-2200. French training restaurant for disadvantaged youngsters, where visitors eat excellently prepared French and Vietnamese cuisine in an attractive and secluded courtyard setting. Reasonably cheap and popular. Cooking classes now available.

**¶ Pepperonis**, 31 Bao Khanh St, T04-9287030, Mon-Sat 1130-1330. A popular pizza and pasta place right in the heart of a busy bar/restaurant area. Cheap and cheerful. A great all-you-can-eat lunch.

**¶-¶ 69 Restaurant Bar**, 69 Ma May St, T04-9261720, daily 0700-2300. The restaurant is up a steep flight of wooden stairs in a restored 19th-century house in the Old Quarter, with 2 tables on the tiny shuttered balcony. Plenty of Vietnamese and seafood dishes, including Hong Kong duck (chargrilled and stuffed with five spices, ginger, onion and garlic) and sunburnt beef: beef strips deep fried in five spice butter. Special mulled wine is offered on cold nights.

**¶-¶ Baan Thai**, 3B Cha Ca St, T04-8288588, daily 1030-1400, 1630-2200. Authentic Thai fare that has received good reviews.

**¶-¶ Brothers**, 26 Nguyen Thai Hoc St, T04-7333866, 1100-1400, 1830-2200. Set in a restored villa, part of the pleasure of dining here is the sumptuous surroundings. An extensive menu of delicious Vietnamese food forms the buffet lunches and dinner. Lunch is remarkable value at US$6 and one of the best deals in the country. Visitors may be inclined to try the **Brothers** restaurant in Hoi An which, like this one, is part of the Khai Silk empire.

**¶-¶ Cay Cau**, De Syloia Hotel, 17A Tran Hung Dao St, T04-9331010. Good Vietnamese fare at reasonable prices in this popular place. Daily set lunch at 130,000d is good value.

**¶-¶ Cyclo**, 38 Duong Thanh St, T04-8286844. Nicely furnished restaurant (diners sit in converted cyclos) with garden bar. Vietnamese and French dishes on offer.

**¶-¶ Dakshin**, 94 Hang Trong St, T04-9286872, daily 1000-1430, 1800-2230. This upstairs Indian vegetarian restaurant is popular and well worth a visit. Elegant with rattan furniture and nicely attired waitresses, it specializes in southern Indian dosas, pancakes served with different sauces. The menu provides a useful glossary of the many unusual dishes served. All come on stainless-steel platters lined with a banana leaf. Prices are reasonable, just a couple of US dollars for a light dosa and less for starters.

T04-8251286, greentangerine@vnn.vn. This is a gorgeous French restaurant with a lovely spiral staircase, wafting fans, tasselled curtain cords, abundant glassware and a gleaming black sidecar on display. The US$7.50 set lunch menu with 2 courses is excellent value. Try boneless froglegs, candid duck leg or anything from the sumptuous dessert list.

**¶-¶ Highway 4**, 5 Hang Tre St, T04-9260639, daily 0900-0200. A second branch is open at 54 Mai Hac De St. This restaurant specializes in ethnic minority dishes from North Vietnam. The fruit and rice wines – available in many flavours – are the highlight of this place. On the upper 2 floors guests sit cross-legged on cushions; downstairs there's conventional dining. There's plenty to eat – ostrich, fried scorpions, bull's penis steamed with Chinese herbs. Quite a remarkable experience.

**¶ Au Lac**, 57 Ly Thai To St, T04-8257807, daily 0700-2300. Nice café in the garden of a French villa. Breakfasts, sandwiches, pizzas, soups and pastas are available. The green papaya salad with grilled beef and sesame seeds is recommended as are the sautéed oysters with turmeric and lemon grass.

**¶ Bit Tet** (Beefsteak), 51 Hang Buom St, T04-8251211, 1700-2100. If asked to name the most authentic Vietnamese diner in town it would be hard not to include this on the list. The soups and steak frites are simply superb; it's rough and ready and you'll share your table as, at around US$2-3 per head, it is understandably crowded. (Walk to the end of the alley and turn right for the dining room.)

**¶ Café Moca**, 14-16 Nha Tho, T04-8256334, daily 0700-2400. This open space has big windows, wafting fans, marble-topped tables and modern urban touches, including exposed red-brick walls and a chrome flue. Cinnamon-flavoured cappuccino, smoked salmon and Bengali specials are all served on pretty, brown floral crockery. It's a favourite for coffee on rainy afternoons.

**¶ Cha Ca La Vong**, 14 Cha Ca St, T04-8253929, daily 1100-2100. Serves one dish only, the eponymous *cha ca Hanoi*, fried fish fillets in mild spice and herbs served with noodles. It's delicious and popular with both visitors and locals, although expensive at 70,000d for the meal.

¶ **Com Chay Nang Tam**, 79A Tran Hung Dao St, T04-9424140, daily 1100-1400, 1700-2200. This popular little a/c vegetarian restaurant is down an alley off Tran Hung Dao St and serves excellent and inexpensive 'Buddhist' dishes in a small, family-style dining room.

¶ **Lá**, 25 Ly Quoc Su St, T04-9288933. This restaurant serves up marvellous Vietnamese and international food. Try the fillet of salmon with passion fruit and sauvignon blanc glaze or the lamb shank braised in orange, sweet capiscum and espresso. Do not leave Hanoi without sampling the sherry fool. For those in the know these are the people who used to run **Café Thyme** on Lo Su St.

¶ **Little Hanoi**, 21 Hang Gai St, T04-8288333, daily 0730-2300. An all-day restaurant/café serving outstanding sandwiches. The cappuccinos, home-made yoghurt with honey and the apple pie are also top class.

¶ **Restaurant 22**, 22 Hang Can St, T04-8267160, daily 1200-2100. Good menu, popular and tasty Vietnamese food, succulent duck. At just a couple of dollars per main course it represents excellent value for money.

¶ **Tamarind**, 80 Ma May St, T04-9260580, tamarind_café@yahoo.com. This sets a whole new standard in travel café food. There is a comfortable café at the front and a smart restaurant behind in the **Handspan Adveture Travel** office. There's a lengthy vegetarian selection, delicious juices and the recommended Thai glass noodle salad.

**West of the Citadel** *p89, map p86*

¶¶¶ **KOTO**, 59 Van Mieu St, T04-7470337, www.koto.com.au, Mon 0730-1800, Tue-Sun 0730-2230. A training restaurant for under-privileged young people. Next to the Temple of Literature, pop in for lunch after a morning's sightseeing. The food is inter-national, filling and delicious. Upstairs is the new **Temple Bar** with Wi-Fi. Recommended.

**Cafés**

**252 Hang Bong**, actually in what is now Cua Nam St. Pastries, yoghurt and crème caramel, very popular for breakfast.

**Baguette and Chocolat**, 11 Cha Ca St, T04-9231500, 0700-2200. Part of the Hoa Sua restaurant training school for under-privileged youngsters. This is really nothing more than a café-cum-bakery but meals are available. Good for breakfast.

**Café Puku**, upstairs 60 Hang Trong St, T04-9285244. Funky arty hang-out with tiny stalls on a balcony or inside on the blue and orange sofas or at big tables. An unobtrusive hideaway. Daily specials and a variety of snacks.

**Highlands Coffee**, southwest corner of Hoan Kiem Lake. Lovely spot under the trees overlooking the lake. Great place for a coffee or a cold drink.

**Thuy Ta**, 1 Le Thai To St, T04-8288148. Nice setting on the northwest corner of Hoan Kiem Lake and a popular meeting place for Vietnamese and travellers. Snacks, ice creams and drinks served.

## ⊙ Bars and clubs

**Hanoi** *p84, maps p86 and p88*

The Bao Khanh and Hang Hanh area is packed with bars. It's very lively all day and evening but, like most places in Hanoi, shuts down around midnight.

**Apocalypse Now**, 2 Pho Dong Tac, daily 2000-0200. Like its HCMC counterpart this is popular with a wide cross-section of society. Music, pool and dancing. However, it has moved from its central location to way out of town making it a less obvious nightstop.

**Ho Guom Xanh**, 32 Le Thai To St, T04-8288806, daily 1600-2400. From outside it's impossible to imagine the colourful and operatic stage shows this nightclub puts on nightly. It's loud, packed and popular with a mainly local crowd but a real visual treat. Drinks are fairly expensive for what is a predominantly Vietnamese menu.

**Legends**, 1-5 Dinh Tien Hoang St, T04-9360345, www.legendsbeer.com.vn, daily 0800-2300. One of Hanoi's popular micro-breweries. The German helles bier (light) and particularly the dunkels bier (dark) are strong and tasty. This café bar has views over Hoan Kiem Lake. An exten-sive food menu too and good for snacks and ice cream.

**Le Pub**, 25 Hang Be St, T04-9262104, www.lepub.org. Photos and artwork on the deep-red walls here make an interesting change. Drink well or plump for the all-day breakfast or gorge yourself on comfort food – burgers, pizzas, nachos and chicken nuggets. This place has outdoor seating on one of the Old Quarter's busiest streets and is an increasingly popular place to hang out.

**Mao's Red Lounge**, 7 Ha Tien St, T04-9263104. The beers are 15,000d in this all-red cubby hole on a tiny street. Duck in after a meal and chat to the friendly staff. Don't miss the hilarious photomontage of Prince Charles with a mop of ginger hair.

**R & R Tavern**, 47 Lo Su St, T04-9344109, daily 0730-2400; live music Thu, Fri and Sat evenings. A popular and lively bar with a great selection of bar food. Noticeboards and leaflets; good for picking up information.

**Red Beer**, 97 Ma May St, T04-8260247, daily 1000-2300. This microbrewery serves outstanding Belgian brews, 28,000d for 650ml glass. The smell of hops hits you as you walk through the door. Copper vats and stainless steel vessels line the back wall.

**Spotted Cow**, 23C Hai Ba Trung St, T04-8241028, 1130-0300. Cheerful and lively pub decorated in Friesian cows. Happy hour until 1800, food until 2400. The Hash House Harriers bus leaves from here on Sun.

## Entertainment

**Hanoi** *p84, maps p86 and p88*
**Dance and theatre**
**Opera House**, T04-9330113, nthavinh@ hn.vn.vn, box office daily 0800-1700. Housed in an impressive French-era building at the east end of Trang Tien St (see page 85). A variety of Vietnamese and Western concerts, operas and plays are staged. Schedule in *Vietnam News* or from the box office.

**Water puppet theatre**
**Water Puppetry House**, 57 Dinh Tien Hoang St, www.thanglong waterpuppet.org, box office daily 0830-1200, 1530-2000. Fabulous shows with exciting live music and beautiful comedy: the technical virtuosity of the puppeteers is astonishing. Performances Mon-Sat 1715, 1830 and 2000, plus an additional matinee on Sun 0930. Admission 40,000d (1st class), 20,000d (2nd class); children 10,000d and 5000d. This is not to be missed.

## Festivals and events

**Around Hanoi** *p92*
**Perfume Pagoda Festival** – from 6th day of the 1st lunar month to end of 3rd lunar month (15th-20th day of 2nd lunar month is the main period). This festival focuses on the worship of the Goddess of Mercy (Quan Am), see page 91. Thousands flock to this famous pilgrimage site during the festival period. Worshippers take part in dragon dances and a royal barge sails on the river.

## Shopping

**Hanoi** *p84, maps p86 and p88*
The city is a shopper's paradise with cheap silk and expert tailors, handicrafts and antiques and some good designer shops. Hang Gai St is well geared to the souvenir hunter and stocks an excellent range of clothes, fabrics and lacquerware.

**Art and Antiques**
Shops along Hang Khay and Trang Tien streets, on the south edge of Hoan Kiem Lake, sell silver ornaments, porcelain, jewellery and carvings. Not everything is either antique or silver; bargain hard.

Art shops abound near Hoan Kiem Lake, especially on Trang Tien St and on Dinh Tien Hoang St at the northeast corner.
**Apricot Gallery**, 40B Hang Bong St, T04-8288965, www.apricot-artvietnam.com. High prices but spectacular exhibits.
**Dien Dam Gallery**, 4B Dinh Liet St and 60 Hang Hom St, T04-8259881, www.diendamgallery.com. Beautiful photographic images in black and white and colour.
**Hanoi Gallery**, 17 Nha Chung St, T04-9287943, propaganda_175@yahoo.com. This is a great find: hundreds of propaganda posters for sale. Original posters cost US$200 upwards; US$8 for a rice paper copy. Some of the reproductions aren't faithful to the colours of the originals, choose carefully.

**Clothes, fashions, silk and accessories**
The greatest concentration is in the Hoan Kiem Lake area particularly on Nha Tho, Nha Chung, Hang Trong and Hang Gai.
**Co**, 18 Nha Tho, T04-289925, conhatho@ yahoo.com, daily 0830-1900. This tiny clothes shop has a very narrow entrance.

It has some unusual prints and the craftsmanship is recommended.

**Ipa Nima**, 34 Han Thuyen St, T04-9334000, www.ipa-nima.com. Enter the glittering and sparkling world of Ipa Nima. Shiny shoes, bags, clothes and jewellery boxes. Hong Kong designer Christina Yu is the creative force behind the label. Some shoe sizes are not available.

**Song**, 27 Nha Tho, T04-9288733, www.asia songdesign.com, daily 0900-2000. The Song shop is run by friendly staff and has beautiful designer clothes, accessories and homeware but its floor space is much smaller than the HCMC store (see page 190).

**Tina Sparkle**, 17 Nha Tho St, T04-9287616, tinasparkle@ipa-nima.com, daily 0900-2000. Funky boutique that sells mostly bags in a glittering array of designs, from tropical prints to big sequinned flowers. Also, divine sequinned shoes by Christina Yu. Occasional sales will save you 50%.

**Handicrafts**

**Chi Vang**, 17 Trang Tien, T04-9360027, chivang@fpt.vn. A beautifully restored building selling exquisitely embroidered cloths, babies' bed linen and clothing, cushion covers, tablecloths and unusual-shaped cushions artfully arranged in the spacious interior. All the goods displayed are embroidered by hand.

**Mosaique**, 22 Nha Tho St, T04-9286181, mosaique@fpt.vn, daily 0830-2000. An Aladdin's cave of embroidered table runners, lamps and stands, beautiful silk flowers for accessorizing, silk curtains, furry silk cushions, metal ball lamps, pillow cushions and lotus flower-shaped lamps.

---

## ▲▲ Activities and tours

**Hanoi** *p84, maps p86 and p88*
**Tour operators**
The most popular option for travellers are the budget cafés, which offer reasonably priced tours and an opportunity to meet fellow travellers. Operators match their rivals' prices and itineraries closely and indeed many operate a clearing system to consolidate passenger numbers to more profitable levels. Many Hanoi tour operators run tours to **Halong Bay** (see page 94). Some also offer kayaking trips.

**A-Z Queen Travel**, 49 Hang Be St, T04-9262734, www.azqueencafe.com. A well-connected organization capable of handling tailor-made as well as standard tours for individuals or small groups, visas.

**Buffalo Tours Vietnam**, 94 Ma May St, T04-8280702, www.buffalotours.com. Well-established and well-regarded organization. It has its own boat for Halong Bay trips and offers tours around the north as well as day trips around Hanoi. Staff are friendly and the guides are informative and knowledgeable.

**Diethelm Travel**, HCO Building, Suite 1701, 44B Ly Thuong Kiet St, T04-9344844. A well-known and long-established tour operator.

**Discovery Indochina**, 63A Cua Bac St, T04-7164132, www.discoveryindochina.com. Private and customized tours throughout Vietnam, Cambodia and Laos.

**Ethnic Travel**, 35 Hang Giay St, T04-9261951, www.ethnictravel.com. Little more than a one-man show but, to judge by the comments of satisfied customers, it is well worth investigating. The owner, Mr Khanh, runs individual tours to Bai Tu Long Bay (next to Halong Bay) and to Ninh Binh. Also offers homestays and always tries, in a non-gimmicky way, to show travellers the 'real' Vietnam. Book exchange inside.

**ET-Pumpkin**, 89 Ma May St, T04-9260739, www.et-pumpkin.com. Very professional in attitude, offering a good selection of travel services, particularly for visitors to the northwest. Now offering motorbiketours of the north. Good place for jeep hire.

**Exotissimo**, 26 Tran Nhat Duat St, T04-8282150, www.exotissimo.com. Specializes in more upmarket tours, good nationwide service.

**Green Bamboo**, 2A Duong Thanh St, T04-8286504, www.greenbamboo travel.com. Another well-established leader in the budget market, organizes tours of Halong Bay and Sapa.

**Haivenu Tours**, 12 Nguyen Trung Truc St, Ba Dinh, T04-9272917, www.haivenu-vietnam.com. Tailor-made tours.

**Handspan Adventure Travel**, 78-80 Ma May St, T04-9262828, www.handspan.com. Reputable business specializing in adventure tours, trekking in the north, mountain biking and kayaking in Halong Bay. Also has its own junk in Halong Bay.

**Hanoi Toserco**, 18 Luong Van Can St, T04-8287552, www.tosercohanoi.com. It runs an efficient Open Tour service.

**Love Planet**, 25 Hang Bac St, T04-8284864, www.loveplanettravel.com. Individual and small group tours; also organizes visas. Very helpful and patient service; good book exchange too.

**Luxury Travel Co, Ltd**, 35 Hong Phic St, T04-9274120, www.LuxuryTravel Vietnam.com. Offers luxury tours to Vietnam, Cambodia and Laos.

**Real Darling Café**, 33 Hang Quat St, T04-8269386, darling_café@hotmail.com. Long-established and efficient. Concentrates on tours of the north and has a visa service.

**Sinh Café**, 52 Luong Ngoc Quyen St, T04-9261568. This is the one and only official branch of **Sinh** in Hanoi. It is only listed here so you know it is the official office. However, it is not recommended. There are dozens of far superior, switched on and efficient tour operators in the city far more deserving of your patronage.

**Topas**, 52 To Ngoc Van St, Tay Ho, T04-7151005, www.topasvietnam.com. Good, well-run tour operator.

**Trekking Travel**, 108 Hang Bac St, T04-9260572, www.trekkingtravel.com.vn. Small group tours to Halong Bay and Sapa, and one-day tours around Hanoi.

**Vietnam Indochine**, 5-118/239/71 Nguyen Van Cu St, T04-8722319, www.vietnamholidays.biz. Organizes a range of trips throughout Vietnam.

**Voyage Vietnam Co**, MOTOTOURS ASIA, 1-2 Luong Ngoc Quyen St, T04-9262616, www.voyagevietnam.net. Well-organized, reliable, good fun and knowledgeable motorbiking, trekking and kayaking tours, especially of the north. The super-friendly and knowledgeable Tuan will take professional bikers to China, Laos and the Golden Triangle. 4WD car hire also available. This is the only company permitted to import your bike into Vietnam and to organize trips from Vietnam through to China and Tibet.

## ⊖ Transport

**Hanoi** *p84, maps p86 and p88*

### Air

For airport information, see page 54; for details of international and domestic flights, see page 23.

**Airline offices** Air France, 1 Ba Trieu St, T04-8253484. **Cathay Pacific**, 49 Hai Ba Trung St, T04-8267298. **Lao Airlines**, 40 Quang Trung St, T04-9425362. **Malaysian Airlines**, 49 Hai Ba Trung St, T04-8268820. **Pacific Airlines**, 36 Dien Bien Phu St, Ba Dinh District, T04-7339999. **Singapore Airlines**, 17 Ngo Quyen St, T04-8268888. **Thai**, 44B Ly Thuong Kiet St, T04-8267921. **Vietnam Airlines**, 1 Quang Trung St, T04-8320320.

### Bicycle

This is the most popular form of local mass transport and is an excellent way to get around the city. Bikes can be hired from the little shops at 29-33 Ta Hien St and from most tourist cafés and hotels; expect to pay about US$2 per day.

### Bus

Tour operators run Open Tour Buses from offices in the Old Quarter to major tourist destinations in the south. See Getting around, page 25.

### Cyclo

Cyclos are ubiquitous especially in the Old Quarter. A trip from the railway station to Hoan Kiem Lake should not cost more than 15,000d. The same trip on a *xe ôm* would be 10,000d.

### Motorbike

Hiring a motorbike is a good way of getting to some of the more remote places. Tourist cafés and hotels rent a variety of machines for US$5-40 per day. Note that hire shops insist on keeping the renter's passport, so it can be hard to rent other than at your hotel.

### Taxi and private car

There are plenty of metered taxis in Hanoi, the following companies are recommended: **Airport Taxi**, T04-8733333; **City Taxi**,

**Vietnam** Hanoi & around Listings

---

### SUGGESTED TOUR ORGANIZER

One of the prestige tour operators in Hanoi is Trekking Travel. They organize small group tours and use their own vehicles and guides. Here, you can book most of the tours in Vietnam especially tours in the North Vietnam like Halong bay, Sapa or one day tours around Hanoi. The company has daily Open Bus (seat and sleeper) go from Hanoi to Sai Gon and return. By this way, you can stop at many tourist attractions along the country and continue your trip whenever you like.

Trekking Travel
Add:108 Hang Bac str, Hoan Kiem dist, Hanoi, Vietnam.
Tell: +84.4.9260572    Fax: +84.4.9260617
Website: www.trekkingtravel.com.vn

---

T04-8222222; **Hanoi Taxi**, T04-8535353; **Mai Linh Taxi**, T04-8222666. Private cars with drivers can be chartered from most hotels and from many tour operators, see page 100.

**Train**

The **central station** (*Ga Hanoi*) is at 120 Le Duan St (a 10-min taxi ride from the centre of town), T04-7470666. For trains to **H CMC** and the south, enter the station from Le Duan St. For trains to **Lao Cai** (for Sapa) enter the station from Tran Quy Cap St. It is possible to walk to get to these platforms from the main entrance if you go to the wrong part. There are regular daily connections with **HCMC**; advance booking required.

Overnight trains from Hanoi to **Lao Cai**, 8½-10 hrs, from where a fleet of minibuses ferries passengers on to **Sapa**. The train carriages are run by different companies, as follows. The very popular **Victoria Express**, with dining carriage, is for Victoria Hotel guests only, and departs Hanoi Sun-Fri at 2155), arriving 0630 the following morning. The dining carriage is only available Mon, Wed and Fri. The return trip departs from Lao Cai on Tue 1845 (LC2) arriving 0400, on Thu and Sat at 0915 (LC4) arriving 1955, and on Sun at 1930 (LC6) arriving 0415. Prices vary. **Royal Train**, T04-8245222, leaves Hanoi daily at 2115 (SP1) arriving at 1535. **Tulico** carriages, T04-8287806, leave on the 2040 (LC5), arriving at Lao Cai at 0455. This service returns on the LC6 at 1930 Sun arriving 0415. **Ratraco** (part of Vietnam Railways), 2F Vietnam Railtour Building, 95-97 Le Duan St, T04-9422889, ratraco@hn.vnn.vn, has berths on several trains.

## ● Directory

**Hanoi** *p84, maps p86 and p88*
**Banks**
Commission is charged on cashing TCs into US$ but not into dong. It is better to withdraw dong from the bank and pay for everything in dong. Most hotels will change dollars, often at quite fair rates. ATMs are now to be found in most large hotels and in some post offices. **ANZ Bank**, 14 Le Thai To St, T04-8258190, Mon-Fri 0830-1600.

Provides full banking services including cash advances on credit cards, 2% commission on TCs, 24-hr ATMs. **Citibank**, 17 Ngo Quyen St, T04-8251950. Cashes TCs into dong. **Incombank**, 37 Hang Bo St, T04-8254276. Dollar TCs can be changed here. Deals with Amex, Visa, MasterCard and Citicorp. **Vietcombank**, 198 Tran Quang Khai St, T04-8243108. 2% commission if converted to dollars cash.

**Embassies and consulates**
**Australia**, 8 Dao Tan St, T04-8317755. **Cambodia**, 71 Tran Hung Dao St, T04-9427646. **Canada**, 31 Hung Vuong St, T04-8235500. **Laos**, 22 Tran Binh Trong St, T04-9424576. **Thailand**, 63-65 Hoang Dieu St, T04-8235092. **UK**, Central Building, 31 Hai Ba Trung St, T04-9360500. **USA**, 7 Lang Ha St, T04-7721500.

**Medical services**
**Family Medical Practice Hanoi**, Van Phuc Compound, 298 I Kim Ma Rd, Ba Dinh, T04-8430748, 24 hour emergency (T090401919), www.vietnammedicalpractice.com. 24-hr medical service, dental care. **Hospital Bach Mai**, Giai Phong St, T04-8693731. English-speaking doctors. Dental service. **International SOS**, Central Building, 31 Hai Ba Trung St, T04-9340555, www.internationalsos.com/countries/Vietnam/. 24-hr, emergencies and medical evacuation. Dental service too.

**Immigration**
**Immigration Dept**, 40A Hang Bai St, T04-8266200.

**Internet**
Internet access is cheap and easy. The cheapest rates are about 3000d per hr, the most expensive are 200-300d/min.

**Post office**
GPO, 75 Dinh Tien Hoang St. International telephone service also available at the PO at 66-68 Trang Tien St and at 66 Luong Van Can St and at the PO on Le Duan next to the train station. DHL, at the GPO.

## ⚬ Footprint features

# Introduction

The north is a mountainous region punctuated by limestone peaks and luscious valleys of terraced paddy fields, tea plantations, stilt houses and water hyacinth-quilted rivers. Sapa, in the far northwest, is a former French hill station, home of the Hmong and set in a stunning valley, carpeted with Alpinese flowers. It is a popular centre for trekking. Scattered around are market towns and villages populated by Vietnam's ethnic minorities such as the Black Hmong, Red Dao, Flower Hmong, Phu La, Dao Tuyen, La Chi and Tay – the latter being Vietnam's largest ethnic minority.

Nor is the region without wider significance; the course of world history was altered at Dien Bien Phu in May 1954 when the Vietnamese defeated the French. In 2004 a vast bronze statue commemorating the victory was erected; it towers over the town. Closer to Hanoi is Hoa Binh where villages of the Muong and Dao can be seen and the beautiful Mai Chau Valley, home to the Black and White Thai whose attractive houses nestle amid the verdant paddies of the hills.

The geology of much of northwest Vietnam is limestone; the humid tropical climate and the resulting streams and rivers have a remarkable effect on this soft rock. Large cones and towers, some with vertical walls and overhangs, rise dramatically from the flat alluvial plains. This landscape, dotted with bamboo thickets, is one of the most evocative in Vietnam; its hazy images seem to linger deep in the collective Vietnamese psyche and perhaps symbolize a sort of primaeval Garden of Eden, an irretrievable age when life was simpler and more innocent.

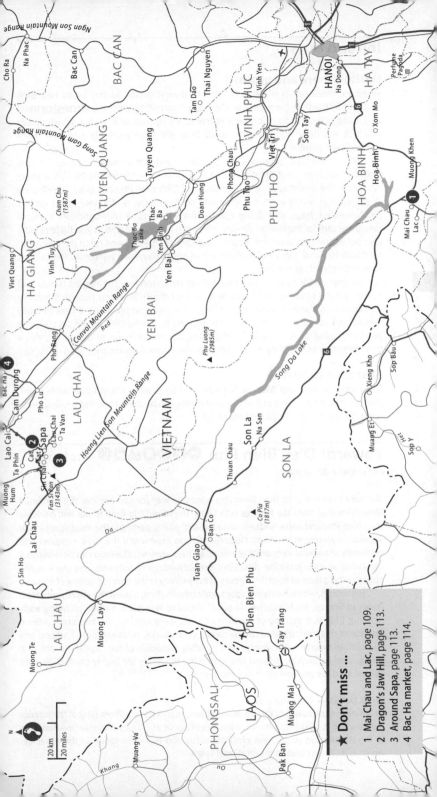

★ **Don't miss ...**

1  Mai Chau and Lac, page 109.
2  Dragon's Jaw Hill, page 113.
3  Around Sapa, page 113.
4  Bac Ha market, page 114.

# Ins and outs

## Getting there and around

There are three points of entry for the northwest circuit: to the south **Hoa Binh** (reached by road); to the north **Lao Cai/Sapa** (reached by road or preferably by train) and, bang in the middle, **Dien Bien Phu** reached by road or by plane. Which option you pick will depend upon how much time you have available and how much flexibility you require.

Expect overland journeys to be slow and sometimes arduous in this mountainous region but the discomfort is more than compensated for by the sheer majesty of the landscapes. The road south of Dien Bien Phu has been significantly upgraded over recent years but the route north to Sapa is still poor and a 4WD is recommended. Jeeps with driver can be hired from some tour operators in Hanoi (see page 100) for the five- or six-day round trip for US$330-370. A good and slightly cheaper option is to leave the jeep in Sapa (about US$275) and catch the overnight train back to Hanoi from Lao Cai. For those willing to pay more, Japanese land cruisers offer higher levels of comfort.

Another option is to do the whole thing by motorbike. The rugged terrain and relatively quiet roads make this quite a popular choice for many people. It has the particular advantage of allowing countless side trips and providing access to really remote and untouched areas. It is not advised to attempt the whole circuit using public transport as this would involve fairly intolerable levels of discomfort and a frustrating lack of flexibility. ▸▸ *For further information, see Transport, page 117.*

## Best time to visit

The region is wet from May to September. This makes travel quite unpleasant. Owing to the altitude of much of the area winter can be quite cool, especially around Sapa, so make sure you go well prepared.

---

# Towards Dien Bien Phu 🖰🚲🍴🛏▲🚌🅘 ▸▸ *pp114-118.*
*Colour map 2, B2, B3 and B4.*

The road from Hanoi to Dien Bien Phu winds its way for 420 km into the Annamite Mountains that mark the frontier with Laos. The round trip from Hanoi and back via Dien Bien Phu and Sapa is about 1200 km and offers, perhaps, the most spectacular scenery anywhere in Vietnam. Opportunities to experience the lives, customs and costumes of some of Vietnam's ethnic minorities abound. The loop can be taken in a clockwise or anti-clockwise direction; the advantage of following the clock is the opportunity to recover from the rigours of the journey in the tranquil setting of Sapa.

Highway 6, which has been thoroughly rebuilt along almost the entire route from Hanoi to Son La, leads southwest out of Hanoi to Hoa Binh. Setting off in the early morning (this is a journey of dawn starts and early nights), the important arterial function of this road to Hanoi can be clearly seen: ducks, chickens, pigs, bamboo and charcoal all pour in – the energy and building materials of the capital – much of it transported by bicycle. Beyond the city limits, the fields are highly productive, with market gardens and intensive rice production.

## Hoa Binh → *Colour map 2, B4.*
Hoa Binh, on the banks of the Da (Black) River, marks the southern limit of the interior highlands. It is 75 km from Hanoi, a journey of about 2½ hours. Major excavation sites of the Hoabinhian prehistoric civilization (10,000 BC) were found in the province, which is its main claim to international fame.

# People of the north

Ethnic groups belonging to the Sino-Tibetan language family such as the Hmong and Dao, or the Ha Nhi and Phula of the Tibeto-Burman language group are relatively recent arrivals. Migrating south from China only within the past 250-300 years, these people have lived almost exclusively on the upper mountain slopes, practising slash-and-burn agriculture and posing little threat to their more numerous lowland-dwelling neighbours, notably the Thai.

Thus was established the pattern of human and political settlement that would persist in North Vietnam for more than 1000 years right down to the colonial period – a centralized Viet state based in the Red River Delta area, with powerful Thai vassal lordships dominating the Northwest. Occupying lands located in some cases almost equidistant from Hanoi, Luang Prabang and Kunming, the Thai, Lao, Lu and Tay lords were obliged during the pre-colonial period to pay tribute to the royal courts of Nam Viet, Lang Xang (Laos) and China, though in times of upheaval they could – and frequently did – play one power off against the other for their own political gain. Considerable effort was thus required by successive Viet

kings in Thang Long (Hanoi) and later in Hué to ensure that their writ and their writ alone ruled in the far north. To this end there was ultimately no substitute for the occasional display of military force, but the enormous cost of mounting a campaign into the northern mountains obliged most Viet kings simply to endorse the prevailing balance of power there by investing the most powerful local lords as their local government mandarins, resorting to arms only when separatist tendencies became too strong. Such was the political situation inherited by the French colonial government following its conquest of Indochina in the latter half of the 19th century. Its subsequent policy towards the ethnic minority chieftains of North Vietnam was to mirror that of the Vietnamese monarchy whose authority it assumed; throughout the colonial period responsibility for colonial administration at both local and provincial level was placed in the hands of seigneurial families of the dominant local ethnicity, a policy which culminated during the 1940s in the establishment of a series of ethnic minority 'autonomous zones' ruled over by the most powerful seigneurial families.

**Hoa Binh Province Museum** (Bao Tang Tinh Hoa Binh) ⓘ *daily 0800-1030, 1400-1700, 10,000d*, contains items of archaeological, historical and ethnographical importance. Relics of the First Indochina War, including a French amphibious landing craft, remain from the bitterly fought campaign of 1951-1952 which saw Viet Minh forces successfully dislodge the French.

**Muong** and **Dao minority villages** are accessible from Hoa Binh. **Xom Mo** is 8 km from Hoa Binh and is a village of the Muong minority. There are around 10 stilt houses, where overnight stays are possible (contact **Hoa Binh Tourism**, T018-854374, www.hoahbintourism.com), and there are nearby caves to visit. **Duong** and **Phu** are villages of the Dao Tien (Money Dao), located 25 km up river. Boat hire (US$25) is available from **Hoa Binh Tourism**. A permit is required for an overnight stay.

## Mai Chau and Lac → *Colour map 2, B3 and B4.*

After leaving Hoa Binh, Highway 6 heads in a south-southwest direction as far as the Chu River. Thereafter it climbs through some spectacular mountain scenery before descending into the beautiful Mai Chau Valley. During the first half of this journey, the turtle-shaped roofs of the Muong houses predominate but, after passing Man Duc, the road enters the territory of the Thai, northwest Vietnam's most prolific ethnic minority, heralding a subtle change in the style of stilted-house architecture. This region is dominated by Black Thai communities (a sub-ethnic group of the Thai) but White Thai also live in the area.

The growing number of foreign and domestic tourists visiting the area in recent years has had a significant impact on the economy of Mai Chau and the lifestyles of its inhabitants. Some foreign visitors complain that the valley offers a manicured hill-tribe village experience to the less adventurous tourist who wants to sample the quaint lifestyle of the ethnic people without too much discomfort. There may be some truth in this allegation, yet there is another side to the coin. Since the region first opened its doors to foreign tourists in 1993, the **Mai Chau People's Committee** has attempted to control the effect of tourism on the valley. **Lac** (White Thai village) is the official tourist village to which tour groups are led and, although it is possible to visit and even stay in the others, the committee hopes that by 'sacrificing' one village to tourism, the impact on other communities will be limited. Income generated from tourism by the villagers of Lac has brought about a significant enhancement to the lifestyles of people throughout the entire valley, enabling many villagers to tile their roofs and purchase consumer products such as television sets, refrigerators and motorbikes.

Lac is easily accessible from the main road from the direction of Hoa Binh. Take the track to the right, immediately before the ostentatious, red-roofed **People's Committee Guesthouse**. This leads directly into the village. You can borrow or rent a bicycle from your hosts and wobble across narrow bunds to the neighbouring hamlets, enjoying the ducks, buffalos, children and lush rice fields as you go – a delightful experience.

About 5 km south of Mai Chau on Route 15A is the Naon River on which, in the dry season, a boat can be taken to visit a number of large and impressive grottoes. Others can be reached on foot. If you wish to visit them, ask your hosts or at the **People's Committee Guesthouse** for details, see page 114.

## Dien Bien Phu → *Colour map 2, B2.*

ⓘ *The airport is 2 km north of town. The battlefield sites, most of which lie to the west of the Nam Yum River, are a bit spread out and best visited by car or by motorbike. Since the majority of visitors arrive in Dien Bien Phu using their own transport, this is not normally a problem.*

Dien Bien Phu lies in the Muong Thanh valley, a region where, even today, ethnic Vietnamese still represent less than one-third of the total population. For such a remote and apparently insignificant little town to have earned itself such an important place in the history books is a considerable achievement. And yet, the Battle of Dien Bien Phu in 1954 was a turning point in colonial history. It was the last calamitous battle between the French and the forces of Ho Chi Minh's Viet Minh and was waged from March to May 1954. The French, who under Vichy rule had accepted the authority of the Japanese during the Second World War, attempted to regain control after the Japanese had surrendered. Ho, following his Declaration of Independence on 2 September 1945, thought otherwise, heralding nearly a decade of war before the French finally gave up the fight after their catastrophic defeat here. It marked the end of French involvement in Indochina and heralded the collapse of its colonial empire. Had the Americans, who shunned French appeals for help, taken more careful note of what happened at Dien Bien Phu they might have avoided their own calamitous involvement in Vietnamese affairs just a decade later.

**To Laos via Tay Trang**

The **Lao border** is only 34 km from Dien Bien Phu, at Tay Trang.
This border crossing has only recently been opened to foreign tourists.

**Transport** There's a bus to the border crossing at Tay Trang to Muang Khua (Laos) every other day leaving at 0500.

**Note** A Laos visa is not available at the border and must be bought in Hanoi or at the Lao embassy.

**General de Castries' bunker** ① *daily 0700-1100, 1330-1700, 5000d*, has been rebuilt on the sight of the battlefield and eight of the 10 French tanks are scattered over the valley, along with US-made artillery pieces. East of the river, **Hill A1** ① *daily 0700-1800*, known as Eliane 2 to the French, was the scene of the fiercest fighting. Remains of the conflict include a bunker, the bison (tank) known as Gazelle, a war memorial dedicated to the Vietnamese who died on the hill and, around at the back, the entrance to a tunnel dug by coal miners from Hon Gai. Their tunnel ran for several hundred metres to beneath French positions and was filled with 1000 kg of high explosives. It was detonated at 2300 on 6 May 1954 as a signal for the final assault. The huge crater is still there. Opposite the hill, the renovated **Historic Victory Exhibition Museum** (Nha Trung Bay Thang Lich Su Dien Bien Phu) ① *daily 0700-1100, 1330-1800, 5000d*, has a good collection of assorted Chinese, American and French weapons and artillery in its grounds. Inside are photographs and other memorabilia, together with a large illuminated model of the valley illustrating the course of the campaign and an accompanying video. While every last piece of Vietnamese junk is carefully catalogued, displayed and described, French relics are heaped into tangled piles. The **Revolutionary Heroes' Cemetery** ① *opposite the Exhibition Museum next to Hill A1, daily 0700-1100, 1330-1800*, contains the graves of 15,000 Vietnamese soldiers killed during the course of the Dien Bien Phu campaign. At the north end of town, the **Victory monument** (Tuong Dai Chien Dien Bien Phu) ① *entrance next to the TV station on 6 Pho Muong Thanh; look for the tower and large pond*, erected on D1 at a cost of US$2.27 million, is the largest monument in Vietnam. The enormous, 120-tonne bronze sculpture was created by former soldier Nguyen Hai and depicts three Vietnamese soldiers standing on top of de Castries' bunker. It was commissioned to mark the 50th anniversary of the Vietnamese victory over the French.

# Sapa and around 🟢🟡🔵🟠⚪🔺🚌🟤 ➡ *pp114-118. Colour map 2, A2 and A3.*

Despite the countless thousands of tourists who have poured in every year for the past decade, Sapa retains great charm. Its beauty derives from two things: the impressive natural setting high on a valley side, with Fan Si Pan, Vietnam's tallest mountain either clearly visible or brooding in the mist; and the clamour and colour of the ethnic minorities selling jewellery and clothes. Distinctly oriental but un-Vietnamese in manner and appearance are the Hmong, Dao and other groups who come to Sapa to trade. Interestingly, the Hmong (normally so reticent) have been the first to seize the commercial opportunities presented by tourism. Saturday night is always a big occasion for Black Hmong and Red Dao teenagers in the Sapa area, as youngsters from miles around come to the so-called 'Love Market' to find a partner. The market proved so popular with tourists that the teenagers now arrange their trysts and liaisons in private. Sapa's regular market is at its busiest and best on Sunday mornings, when most tourists scoot off to Bac Ha (see page 114).

**Getting there and around** Travel to Sapa is either by road on the northwest circuit or by overnight train from Hanoi, via Lao Cai. A fleet of minibuses ferries passengers from Lao Cai railway station to Sapa. Sapa is a charming town, small enough to walk around easily. From Sapa there are a great many walks and treks to outlying villages.

▶▶ *For further information, see Transport, pages 104 and 118.*

**Best time to visit** At 1650 m Sapa enjoys warm days and cool evenings in the summer but gets very cold in winter. Snow falls, on average, every couple of years and settles on the surrounding peaks of the Hoang Lien Son Mountains. Rain and cloud can occur at any time of year but the wettest months are May to September with nearly 1000 mm of rain in July and August alone, the busiest months for Vietnamese tourists. December and January can be pretty miserable with mist, low cloud and low temperatures. Spring blossom is lovely but even in March and April a fire or heater may be necessary in the evening.

## Background

Originally a Black Hmong settlement, Sapa was first discovered by Europeans when a Jesuit missionary visited the area in 1918. By 1932 news of the quasi-European climate and beautiful scenery of the Tonkinese Alps had spread throughout French Indochina. By the 1940s an estimated 300 French buildings, including a sizeable prison and the summer residence of the Governor of French Indochina, had sprung up. Until 1947 there were more French than Vietnamese in the town, which became renowned for its many parks and flower gardens. However, as the security situation

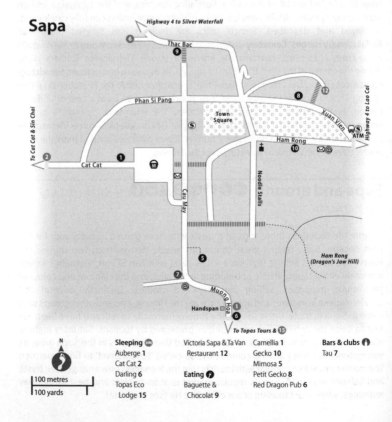

**Sapa**

*Highway 4 to Silver Waterfall*

Thac Bac

Phan Si Pang

*To Cat Cat & Sin Chai*

Cat Cat

Town Square

Ham Rong

Xuan Vien

*Highway 4 to Lao Cai*

ATM

Cau May

Noodle Stalls

Ham Rong
(Dragon's Jaw Hill)

Muong Hoa

Handspan

*To Topas Tours & 15*

N
100 metres
100 yards

**Sleeping**
Auberge **1**
Cat Cat **2**
Darling **6**
Topas Eco
Lodge **15**

Victoria Sapa & Ta Van
Restaurant **12**

**Eating**
Baguette &
Chocolat **9**

Camellia **1**
Gecko **10**
Mimosa **5**
Petit Gecko **8**
Red Dragon Pub **6**

**Bars & clubs**
Tau **7**

## ⦂ Trekking rules

Tourists wanting to trek around Sapa are no longer allowed to go it alone. Visitors must now have a touring card, sightseeing ticket and a licensed tour guide to trek six permitted routes in the area, although it is possible to trek to Cat Cat, Sin Chai and the silver waterfall without a guide and permit. Additional routes may be added in the future. Ticket checkpoints have been set up at starting points. Tour guides who violate these new rules will have their licences withdrawn and tourists who do so will be disciplined, according to the People's Committee of Sapa District. The following are permitted routes from Sapa:

⦿ Round trip to Cat Cat and Sin Chai
⦿ Round trip to Cat Cat, Y Linh Ho, Lao Chai and Ta Van
⦿ Round trip to Lao Chai, Ta Van, Ban Ho, Thanh Phu and Nam Cang
⦿ Round trip to Lao Chai, Ta Van, Su Pan and Thanh Kim
⦿ Round trip to Ta Phin, Mong Sen and Takco
⦿ Ascent of Mount Fan Si Pan

began to worsen during the latter days of French rule, the expatriate community steadily dwindled, and by 1953 virtually all had gone. Immediately following the French defeat at Dien Bien Phu in 1954, victorious Vietnamese forces razed a large number of Sapa's French buildings to the ground.

## Sights

Sapa is a pleasant place to relax in and unwind. Being comparatively new it has no important sights but several French buildings in and around are worth visiting. The huge scale of the Fan Si Pan range gives Sapa an Alpine feel and this impression is reinforced by *haut savoie* vernacular architecture, with steep pitched roofs, window shutters and chimneys. Each house has its own neat little garden of temperate flora – foxgloves, roses, apricot and plum trees – carefully nurtured by generations of gardeners. But in an alluring blend of European and Vietnamese vegetation, the gardens are cultivated alongside thickets of bamboo and delicate orchids, just yards above the paddy fields.

The small **church** in the centre of Sapa was built in 1930. In the churchyard are the tombs of two former priests, including that of Father Thinh, who was brutally murdered. In the autumn of 1952, Father Thinh confronted a monk named Giao Linh who had been discovered having an affair with a nun at the Ta Phin seminary. Giao Linh obviously took great exception to the priest's interference, for shortly after this, when Father Thinh's congregation arrived at Sapa church for mass one foggy November morning, they discovered his decapitated body lying next to the altar.

**Ham Rong (Dragon's Jaw Hill)** ① *daily 0600-1800, 30,000d, free for children under 5*, offers excellent views of the town. The path winds its way through a number of interesting limestone outcrops and miniature grottoes as it nears the summit. Traditional dance performances take place on the mountain. ⊳ *For further information, see Entertainment, page 117.*

## Around Sapa → *Colour map 2, A2 and A3.*

Trekking to the villages around Sapa is a highlight of this region. It is a chance to observe rural life led in reasonable prosperity. Wet rice forms the staple income, weaving for the tourist market puts a bit of meat on the table. Here, nature is kind: there is rich soil and no shortage of water. It's clear how the landscape has been engineered to suit man's needs: the terracing is on an awesome scale (in places more than 100 steps), the result of centuries of labour to convert steep slopes into level fields which can be flooded to grow rice. Technologically, and in no sense pejoratively, the villages might be described as belonging to a bamboo age: bamboo trunks carry water huge distances from spring to village; water flows across barriers and tracks in bamboo aqueducts; mechanical rice huskers made of bamboo are driven by water requiring no human effort; houses are held up with bamboo; bottoms are parked on bamboo chairs; and tobacco and other substances are inhaled through bamboo pipes. In late 2004, regulations were brought in, which mean that trekking without a licensed guide is no longer possible, see Trekking regulations, above.

The track heading west from Sapa through the market area offers either a short 5-km round-trip walk to the Black Hmong village of **Cat Cat** (accessible without a guide) or a longer 10-km round-trip walk to **Sin Chai** (Black Hmong). Both options take in some beautiful scenery; foreigners must pay 15,000d to use the track. The path to Cat Cat leads off to the left of the Sin Chai track after about 1 km, following the line of pylons down through the rice paddies to Cat Cat village; beyond the village over the river bridge you can visit the **cascade waterfall** (from which the village takes its name) and an old French hydro-electric power station that still produces electricity. Sin Chai village is 4 km northwest of here. Walking to **Lau Chai village** (Black Hmong) and **Ta Van village** (Zay or Giay) with a licensed guide is a longer round trip of 20 km taking in minority villages and beautiful scenery. **Mount Fan Si Pan**, at a height of 3143 m, is Vietnam's highest mountain and is a three-day trek from Sapa. It lies on a bearing of 240° from Sapa; 9 km as the crow flies but 14 km by track. The route involves dropping to 1200 m and crossing a rickety bamboo bridge before ascending.

North of Sapa is an abandoned **French seminary**, where the names of the bishop who consecrated it and the presiding Governor of Indochina can be seen engraved on stones at the west end. Built in 1942 and under the ecclesiastical jurisdiction of the Parish of Sapa, the building was destroyed 10 years later by militant Vietnamese hostile to the intentions of the order. Beyond the seminary, the path descends into a valley of beautifully sculpted rice terraces and past Black Hmong settlements, with their shy and retiring inhabitants, to **Ta Phin**, a Red Dao village.

**Bac Ha**, located to the northeast of Sapa, is really only notable for one thing and that is its Sunday morning market. That 'one thing', however, is very special. Hundreds of local minority people flock in from the surrounding districts to shop and socialize, while tourists from all corners of the earth pour in to watch them do it. The market draws in the Flower Hmong, Phu La, Dao Tuyen, La Chi and Tay, and is a riot of colour and fun. While the women trade and gossip, the men consume vast quantities of rice wine; by late morning they can no longer walk so are heaved onto donkeys by their wives and led home. If you have your own transport arrive early; if you haven't, nearly all the hotels and all the tour operators in Sapa organize trips. ▸▸ *For further information, see Activities and tours, page 117.*

## ● Sleeping

### Hoa Binh *p108*
**B Hoa Binh 1**, 54 Phuong Lam, T018-852051. On Highway 6 out of Hoa Binh towards Mai Chau. Clean rooms with a/c and TV; some rooms built in minority style. There's also an ethnic minority dining experience complete with rice drunk through bamboo straws. Gift shop stocks local produce.
**B Hoa Binh 2**, 160 An Duong Vuong, T018-852001. Has the same facilities as its sister hotel but no restaurant.

### Mai Chau and Lac *p109*
**L Mai Chau Lodge**, a short walking distance southwest of Lac village, T018-868959, www.maichaulodge.com. Owned and operated by Buffalo Tours and staffed by locals, there are 16 rooms with modern facilities. The attractive lodge has 2 restaurants, a bar, swimming pool, sauna and jacuzzi. Bicycling and trekking tours are offered. The price includes a 2-day 1-night trip with accommodation, tours and other services.

**C-D Ethnic Houses**, Lac Village. Trips to homestays must be booked by tour operators, usually in Hanoi. In Mai Chau, visitors can spend the night in a White Thai ethnic house on stilts. Mat, pillow, duvet, mosquito net, communal washing facilities (some hot showers) and sometimes fan provided. This is particularly recommended as the hospitality and easy manner of the people is a highlight of many visitors' stay in Vietnam. Food and local rice wine provided. Avoid the large houses in the centre if possible. **Guesthouse No 6**, T018-867168, is popular, with plentiful food and rice wine. The owner fought the French at Dien Bien Phu. Minimal English is spoken.

**Dien Bien Phu** *p110*
**B May Hong**, Tran Dang Ninh, T023-826300. Opposite Vietnam Airlines booking office. Standard rooms with a/c and hot water.
**B-D Muong Thanh Hotel**, 25 Him Lam-TP, T023-810043. Breakfast included with the more expensive rooms. 62 standard rooms with TV, a/c, minibar and fan. Internet service, swimming pool (10,000d for non-guests), karaoke, Thai massage and free airport transfer. Souvenir shop and bikes for rent.
**D-E Brewery**, 62 Muong Thanh 10 St (Hoang Van Thai St), T023-824635. Out beyond Hill A1 at the east end of town. 10 rooms, basic and clean, with fan or a/c, no restaurant but, as the name suggests, beer and plenty of it. A little *bia hoi* next to the gate offers fresh cool beer at 1500d a glass.

**Sapa** *p111, map p112*
A host of guesthouses has sprung up to cater for Sapa's rejuvenation and the appeal of the town has, perhaps, been a little compromised by the new structures. (Certainly none of them can compare with the style of the lovely old French buildings.) Prices tend to rise Jun-Oct to coincide with northern hemisphere university holidays and at weekends. Hoteliers are accustomed to bargaining; healthy competition ensures fare rates in Sapa.
**L Topas Eco Lodge**, Than Kimh, Lao Cai, 18 km from Sapa, T020-872404, www.topas-eco-lodge.com. Vietnam's

first eco-lodge is perched on a plateau overlooking the Hoang Vien Valley. Palm-thatched bungalows, each with its own bathroom and porch, run on solar power, enjoy fantastic views over the valley. Trekking, horse riding, mountain biking and handicraft workshops are organized daily for guests and are included in the full-board price. Free transport from Sapa; discounts available.
**L-A Victoria Sapa**, T020-871522, www.victoriahotels-asia.com. Opened in 1998 with 77 rooms, a nice position above the town and a pleasant aspect: this hotel is easily the best in town. Comfortable, with well-appointed rooms, it is a lovely place in which to relax and enjoy the peace. In winter there are warming open fires in the bar and dining rooms. The food is very good and the set buffets are excellent value. The Health Centre offers everything from the traditional massage to reflexology. The centre, pool, tennis courts and sauna are open to non-guests. Packages are available.
**B-D Darling**, Thac Bac St, T020-871349, www.tulico-sapa.com.vn. It's a short walk from town to this secluded building but for those seeking peace it's worth every step. Simple and clean with a warm welcome, stunning views and a colourful garden. There are 45 rooms, most with fabulous views. The top terrace bedroom has the best view in all of Sapa. Swimming pool, gym and pool table.
**C-D Auberge**, Muong Hoa St, T020-871243, www.sapanowadays.com. Mr Dang Trung, the French-speaking owner, shows guests his wonderful informal garden with pride: sweet peas, honeysuckle, snap dragons, foxgloves, roses and irises – all familiar to visitors from temperate climes – grow alongside sub-Alpine flora and a fantastic collection of orchids. The rooms are simply furnished but clean and boast bathtubs and log fires in winter. There's a restaurant on the lovely terrace.
**C-E Cat Cat**, Cat Cat St, through the market, T020-871387, www.catcathotel.com. The guesthouse has expanded up the hillside, with new terraces and small bungalows with balconies all with views down the valley. A friendly and popular place, its 40 rooms span the price range but all

represent good value for money. Some of its rooms enjoy the best views in Sapa. The hotel has a good restaurant and, like most others, arranges tours and provides useful information.

### Around Sapa *p113*

It is possible to spend the night in one of the ethnic houses in the Sapa district. However, in line with the trekking rules (see page 113), homestays must be organized through reputable tour operators and are only permitted in the following villages: **Ta Van Giay**, **Ban Den**, **Muong Bo**, **Ta Phin Commune Central Area**, **Sa Xeng Cultural Village** and **Sin Chai**, as well as at **Topas Eco Lodge**. The Black Hmong villages are probably the best bet, though facilities are considerably more basic than in the Muong and Thai stilted houses of Hoa Binh and Mai Chau and travellers will need to bring their own bedding materials and mosquito net. A contribution of around 30,000d should be made (or more if dinner is included).

## ● Eating

### Hoa Binh *p108*

¶ **Thanh Toi**, 22a Cu Chinh Lan, T018-853951. Local specialities, wild boar and stir-fried aubergine.

### Mai Chau and Lac *p109*

Most people will eat with their hosts. Mai Chau town itself has a couple of simple *com pho* places near the market. The rice wine in Mai Chau is excellent, particularly when mixed with local honey.

### Dien Bien Phu *p110*

¶ **Lien Tuoi**, 27 Muong Thanh 8 St, next to the Vietnamese cemetery and Hill A1, T023-824919, daily 0700-2200. Delicious local fare in a family-run restaurant.
¶ **Muong Thanh Hotel Restaurant**, 25 Him Lam-TP, T023-810043, daily 0600-2200. Breakfasts, plenty of Vietnamese dishes and a few pasta dishes. Also duck, boar, pork, frog, curry and some tofu dishes and quite a bit of seafood.

### Sapa *p111, map p112*

There are rice and noodle stalls in the market and along the path by the church.
¶¶¶ **Ta Van**, in **Victoria Sapa**, see Sleeping, T020-871522. The food is very good, served in the large dining room with an open fire, and the set buffets are excellent value.
¶¶-¶ **The Gecko**, T020-871504, daily 0730-2230. Attractive with dining room and tables on its front terrace. Good French as well as Vietnamese food is served. Pizzas go from US$5; main courses around US$6. Delicious with the restaurant's home-made bread. The daily set lunch at US$11 is good value. Opposite is the **Petit Gecko** offering snacks and takeaway sandwiches. It's cosier than its big brother and serves the best hot chocolate in town.
¶ **Baguette & Chocolat**, Thac Bac St, T020-871766, www.hoasuaschool.com, daily 0700-2100. The ground floor of the guesthouse comprises a stylish restaurant and café, with small boulangerie attached; lovely home-made cakes for exhausted trekkers go down a treat. Picnic kits from 32,000d are a useful and welcome service.
¶ **Camellia**, Cat Cat St, just through market on the right, T020-871455. Long menu, delicious food, rice and fruit wine. They'll actually warm the rice bowls for you in winter. The beef steak is rather like dried buffalo but the grilled deer is good, the **Camellia** salad is spicy and excellent, and the apple wine warm and strong (much better value by the bottle than by the glass).
¶ **Mimosa**, up a small path off Cay Mau St, T020-871377, daily 0700-2300. A small, slightly chaotic, family-run restaurant. Sit cosy indoors or in the fresh air on a small terrace. A long menu of good Western and Asian dishes. Very popular and service is incredibly slow when busy. Pizzas, pastas and burgers as well as boar, deer, pork and vegetarian dishes.
¶ **Red Dragon Pub**, 21 Muong Hoa St, T020-872085, reddragonpub@hn.vnn.vn, daily 0750-2300 (food until 2230). Done out like an English tearoom with mock Tudor beams and red and white checked table-cloths. Tea, cornflakes, and a mean shepherd's pie. Pub upstairs. Fantastic views of the valley.

● *For an explanation of sleeping and eating price codes used in this guide, see inside the*
● *front cover. Other relevant information is found in Essentials, see pages 29-32.*

## ❶ Bars and clubs

**Sapa** *p111, map p112*
**Red Dragon Pub**, see Eating. The balcony
is perfect for a sunset drink.
**Tau Bar**, 42 Cau May St, beneath the Tau
Hotel, T0912-927756, funkybarsapa@
yahoo.com, daily 1500-late. It must have
the longest bar made of a single tree trunk
in the world and worth a beer just to see it.
Minimalist, with white walls, stools, darts
board and pool table. Range of beers
and spirits.

## ❻ Entertainment

**Hoa Binh** *p108*
**Hoa Binh Ethnic Minority Culture Troupe**,
Hoa Binh 1 Hotel. 1-hr shows featuring
dance and music of the Muong, Thai,
Hmong and Dao.

**Mai Chau and Lac** *p109*
**Mai Chau Ethnic Minority Dance Troupe**.
Thai dancing culminating in the communal
drinking of sweet, sticky rice wine through
straws from a large pot. This troupe performs
most nights in Lac in one of the large stilt
houses. Admission is included for people on
tours; otherwise give a small contribution.

**Sapa** *p111, map p112*
**Ethnic minority dancing**, Dragon's Jaw Hill,
daily at 0930 and 1500, 10,000d. Also at the
**Bamboo Hotel**, 2030-2200; free as long as
you support the bar and at the **Victoria Sapa**
every Sat at 2030.

## ❻ Shopping

**Mai Chau and Lac** *p109*
Villagers offer a range of woven goods
and fabrics on which they are becoming
dependent for a living. There are also local
paintings and well-made wicker baskets,
pots, traps and pouches. Mai Chau is
probably the best place for buying
handicrafts in the northwest.

**Sapa** *p111, map p112*
Sapa is the place for buying ethnic clothes
but it is not possible to buy walking shoes,
rucksacks, coats, jackets or any
mountaineering equipment here.

**Wild Orchid**, 3 shops on Cau May St,
T020-871665. Really beautiful wall
hangings starting from around US\$15
and clothes.

## ▲ Activities and tours

**Hoa Binh** *p108*
**Hoa Binh Tourism**, next to the Hoa
Binh 1 hotel, T018-854374, daily 0730-
1100, 1330-1700, www.hoabinh
tourism.com. Can arrange boat hire
as well as visits to minority villages,
trekking and transport.

**Mai Chau and Lac** *p109*
Hanoi tour operators run overnight tours
to the area.

**Sapa** *p111, map p112*
**Therapies**
**Victoria Sapa**. Massage and other treatments are available in the hotel treatment
centre, US\$19. The hotel also has an indoor
swimming pool. The pool area is being
renovated to accommodate a better spa.

**Tour operators**
**Handspan**, 8 Cau May St, T020-872110,
www.handspan.com, daily 0730-1130,
1330-1830. Offers a diverse range of tours
in the vicinity of Sapa, including a range of
treks, mountain bike excursions, homestays
and jeep expeditions.
**Topas**, 24 Muong Hoa St, T020-871331,
www.topas-adventure-vietnam.com.
A combined Danish and Vietnamese
operator offering treks from fairly leisurely
1-day walks to an arduous 4-day assault on
Mount Fan Si Pan. Also organizes bicycling
tours, horse riding and familytours. Well-
run operation, with an office in Hanoi.

## ❻ Transport

For overland transport, see page 108.

**Dien Bien Phu** *p110*
**Air**
The airport (T023-824416) is 2 km north
of town, off Highway 12. Flights to and
from **Hanoi** with **Vietnam Airlines**, office
inside Airport Hotel, daily 0700-1100,
1330-1630.

**Sapa** *p111, map p112*
**Train**

For all train details, see Hanoi Transport, page 104. Passengers alighting at Lao Cai will either be met by their hotel (eg Victoria Sapa) or there is a desk selling minibus tickets to Sapa. Tour operators in Hanoi can also book your ticket for you for a small fee from the top of the class – the Victoria Sapa carriage – downwards. It is often less hassle than organizing it yourself and, if you are in a hurry, it's a great time saver.

## ● Directory

**Dien Bien Phu** *p110*
**Banks** Vietcombank and Nong Nghiep Bank. **Internet**  Muong Thanh Hotel, 25 Him Lam-T.

**Sapa** *p111, map p112*
**Banks** Agribank, 1 Pho Cau May St, T020-871206, Mon-Fri and Sat morning. The bank will change US dollars, euros, Australian dollars, Chinese yuan and Canadian dollars cash, as will most hotels but at poor rates. It will also change US dollar and euro TCs. **BIDV**, Ngu Chi Son St, T020-872569, opposite the lake, has a visa ATM and will change cash and TCs. Convert before you travel; as elsewhere in the Northwest beads and gold go further than plastic. **Internet**  Many of the better hotels have email and allow their customers to use it. There is an internet café opposite the Delta Restaurant. **Post office**  There are 2 in Sapa from where international phone calls can be made. The main post office offers internet.

## Footprint features

# Introduction

The central region extends over 1000 km north to south. It includes the mountains of the Annamite chain, which form a natural frontier with Laos to the west and, in places, extends almost all the way to the sea in the east. This hinterland is the domain of numerous ethnic minorities and is peppered with former French hill stations. The narrow, coastal strip, sometimes only a few kilometres wide, supported the former artistically accomplished Kingdom of Champa.

The middle part of the central region is home to World Heritage Sites: the gracious imperial city of Hué stands on the Perfume River, with the artistic tomb complexes of the emperors – built in accordance with the rules of geomancy – resting along the banks. Inland are the brick-carved towers of My Son, spiritual capital of the Cham Kingdom; and, close to the coast, Hoi An is an old mercantile port town that retains traditional architecture and overflows with great shops and restaurants. Its silk shops are famed and its food is fêted. Just 5 km away are the bright sands of Cua Dai Beach.

The southern part of this diverse region is garlanded with stunning coast and beaches: Nha Trang and Mui Ne are ideal spots for a few days by the sea.

★ **Don't miss ...**

# Hué and around

*Hué, an imperial city that housed generations of the country's most powerful emperors, was built on the banks of the Huong Giang (Perfume River), 100 km south of the 17th parallel. The river is named after a scented shrub which is supposed to grow at its source.*

*In many respects, Hué epitomizes the best of Vietnam and, in a country that is rapidly disappearing under concrete, it represents a link to a past where people live in old buildings and don't lock their doors. Whether it is because of the royal heritage or the city's Buddhist tradition, the people of Hué are the gentlest in the country. They speak good English and drive their motorbikes more carefully than anyone else.*

*Just south of the city are the last resting places of many Vietnamese emperors (page 126). A number of war relics in the Demilitarized Zone (DMZ) can be easily visited from Hué (page 130).* ▸▸ *For Sleeping, Eating and other listings, see pages 133-136.*

## Ins and outs → *Colour map 3, B5.*

**Getting there** Hué's Phu Bai airport is a 25-minute drive from the city. There are daily connections with Hanoi and Ho Chi Minh City. **Vietnam Airlines** runs a bus service in to town which costs 30,000d; a taxi costs 125,000d. The railway station is more central. The trains tend to fill up, so advance booking is recommended, especially for sleepers. ▸▸ *For further information, see Transport, page 136.*

**Getting around** For the city itself, walking is an option, interspersed, perhaps, with the odd cyclo journey. However, most guesthouses hire out bicycles and this is a very pleasant and slightly more flexible way of exploring Hué and some of the surrounding countryside. A motorbike provides even more independence and makes it possible to visit many more sights in a day. There is also the usual array of *xe ôm* motorbike taxis. The many tour operators in the city will also provide plenty of information and advice.

Getting to and around the **Imperial Tombs** is easiest by motorbike or car as they are spread over a large area. Most hotels and cafés organize tours either by minibus, bike or by boat. Sailing up the Perfume River is the most peaceful way to travel but only a few of the tombs can be reached by boat so *xe ôm* wait at the riverbank to take passengers on to the tombs. All the tombs are accessible by bicycle but you'll need to set out early. It is also possible to go on the back of a motorbike taxi. Further details are given for each individual tomb. ▸▸ *For further information, see Activities and tours, page 135.*

**Best time to visit** Hué has a reputation for bad weather. Rainfall of 2770 mm has been recorded in a single month. The rainy season runs from September to January and rainfall is particularly heavy between September and November; the best time to visit is therefore between February and August. However, even in the 'dry' season an umbrella is handy. Temperatures in Hué can also be pretty cool in winter, compared with Danang, Nha Trang and other places to the south, as cold air tends to get bottled here, trapped by mountains to the south. For several months each year neither fans nor air-conditioning are required.

## Background

Hué was the capital of Vietnam during the Nguyen Dynasty, which ruled Vietnam between 1802 and 1945. For the first time in Vietnamese history a single court controlled the land from Yunnan (southern China) southwards to the Gulf of Siam. To link the north and south (more than 1500 km), the Nguyen emperors built and maintained the Mandarin Road (Quan Lo), interspersed with relay stations. Even in 1802, when it was not yet complete, it took couriers just 13 days to travel between Hué and Ho Chi Minh City, and five days between Hué and Hanoi. If they arrived more than two days late, couriers were punished with a flogging. There cannot have been a better road in Southeast Asia nor a more effective incentive system.

Although the Confucian bureaucracy and some of the dynasty's technical achievements may have been remarkable, there was continual discontent and uprisings against the Nguyen emperors. The court was packed with scheming mandarins, princesses, eunuchs and scholars writing wicked poetry.

In 1883 a French fleet assembled at the mouth of the Perfume River and opened fire. After taking heavy casualties, Emperor Hiep Hoa sued for peace and signed a treaty making Vietnam a protectorate of France. As French influence over Vietnam increased, the power and influence of the Nguyen waned. The undermining effect of the French presence was compounded by significant schisms in Vietnamese society. In particular, the spread of Christianity was undermining traditional hierarchies. Despite the

## Hué

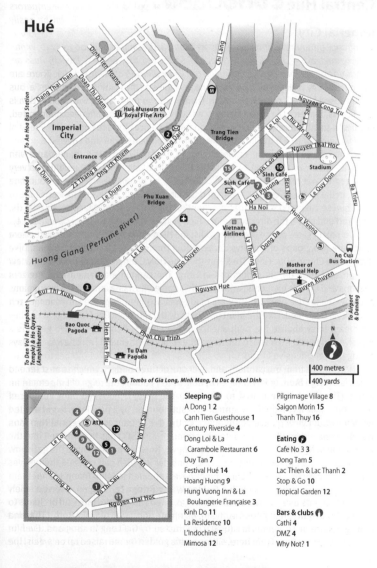

**Sleeping**
A Dong 1 **2**
Canh Tien Guesthouse **1**
Century Riverside **4**
Dong Loi & La
  Carambole Restaurant **6**
Duy Tan **7**
Festival Hué **14**
Hoang Huong **9**
Hung Vuong Inn & La
  Boulangerie Française **3**
Kinh Do **11**
La Residence **10**
L'Indochine **5**
Mimosa **12**

Pilgrimage Village **8**
Saigon Morin **15**
Thanh Thuy **16**

**Eating**
Cafe No 3 **3**
Dong Tam **5**
Lac Thien & Lac Thanh **2**
Stop & Go **10**
Tropical Garden **12**

**Bars & clubs**
Cathi **4**
DMZ **4**
Why Not? **1**

impressive tombs and palace around Hué, many scholars maintain that the Nguyen Dynasty was simply too short-lived to have ever had a 'golden age'. Although the French and then the Japanese found it to their advantage to maintain the framework of Vietnamese imperial rule, the system became hollow and, eventually, irrelevant. The last Nguyen Emperor, Bao Dai, abdicated on 30 August 1945.

During the 1968 Tet offensive, Viet Cong soldiers holed up in Hué's Citadel for 25 days. The bombardment which ensued, as US troops attempted to root them out, caused extensive damage to the Thai Hoa Palace and other monuments. During their occupation of Hué, the NVA forces settled old scores, shooting, beheading and even burning alive 3000 people, including civil servants, police officers and anyone connected with, or suspected of being sympathetic to, the government in Ho Chi Minh City.

# Central Hué ⬛⚡️🏠️🔄️⭕️🔺️🚌️☕️ ➡ *pp133-136*.

## Imperial City
① *Entrance through the Ngo Mon Gate, 23 Thang 8 St, summer daily 0630-1730, winter daily 0700-1700; 55,000d. Guided tour US$3 for 1½ hrs; English, French, Russian, Mandarin and Japanese spoken. Guiding can last until 1900 after the ticket desk closes.*
The Imperial City at Hué is built on the same principles as the Forbidden Palace in Beijing. It is enclosed by thick outer walls (**Kinh Thanh**), 7-10 m thick, along with moats, canals and towers. Emperor Gia Long commenced construction in 1804 after geomancers had decreed a suitable location and orientation for the palace. The site enclosed the land of eight villages (for which the inhabitants received compensation) and covered 6 sq km, sufficient area to house the emperor and all his family, courtiers, bodyguards and servants. It took 20,000 men to construct the walls alone. Not only has the city been damaged by war and incessant conflict, but also by natural disasters such as floods which, in the mid-19th century, inundated the city to a depth of several metres.

Chinese custom decreed that the 'front' of the palace should face south (like the Emperor) and this is the direction from which visitors approach the site. Over the outer moat, a pair of gates pierce the outer walls: the **Hien Nhon** and **Chuong Duc** gates. Just inside are two groups of massive cannon; four through the Hien Nhon Gate and five through the Chuong Duc Gate. These are the Nine Holy Cannon (**Cuu Vi Than Cong**), cast in bronze in 1803 on the orders of Gia Long. The cannon are named after the four seasons and the five elements, and on each is carved its name, rank, firing instructions and how the bronze of which they are made was acquired. They are 5 m in length but have never been fired. Like the giant urns outside the Hien Lam Cac (see page 126), they are meant to symbolize the permanence of the empire. Between the two gates is a massive **flag tower**, from which the flag of the National Liberation Front flew for 24 days during the Tet Offensive in 1968.

Northwards from the cannon, and over one of three bridges which span a second moat, is the **Ngo Mon**, or Royal Gate (**1**), built in 1833 during the reign of Emperor Minh Mang. (The ticket office is just to the right.) The gate, remodelled on a number of occasions since its original construction, is surmounted by a pavilion from where the emperor would view palace ceremonies. Of the five entrances, the central Ngo Mon was only opened for the emperor to pass through. UNESCO has thrown itself into the restoration of Ngo Mon with vigour and the newly finished pavilion atop the gate now gleams and glints in the sun; those who consider it garish can console themselves with the thought that this is how it might have appeared in Minh Mang's time.

North from the Ngo Mon is the **Golden Water Bridge** (**2**) – again reserved solely for the emperor's use – between two tanks (**3**), lined with laterite blocks. This leads to the **Dai Trieu Nghi** (Great Rites Courtyard, **4**), on the north side of which is the **Thai Hoa Palace** (Palace of Supreme Harmony), constructed by Gia Long in 1805 and used for his coronation in 1806. From here, sitting on his golden throne raised up on a dais, the emperor would receive ministers, foreign emissaries, mandarins and military officers during formal ceremonial occasions. In front of the palace are 18 stone stelae, which stipulate the arrangement of the nine mandarinate ranks on the Great Rites Courtyard: the upper level was for ministers, mandarins and officers of the upper grade; the lower for those of lower grades. Civil servants would stand on the left and the military on the right. Only royal princes were allowed to stand in the palace itself, which is perhaps the best-preserved building in the Imperial City complex. Its red and gold columns, tiled floor and fine ceiling have all been restored.

North of the Palace of Supreme Harmony is the **Tu Cam Thanh** (Purple Forbidden City **5**), reserved for the use of the emperor and his family, and surrounded by walls, 1 m thick, to form a city within a city. Tragically, the Forbidden City was virtually destroyed during the 1968 Tet offensive. The two **Mandarin Palaces** and the **Royal Reading Pavilion (10)** are all that survive. The Royal Reading Pavilion has been rebuilt but, needless to say, has no books.

At the far side of Thai Hoa Palace are two enormous **bronze urns** (Vac Dong) decorated with birds, plants and wild animals, and weighing about 1500 kg each. On either side are the **Ta (6)** and **Huu Vu (7)** pavilions, one converted into a souvenir art shop, the other a mock throne room in which tourists can pay US$5 to dress up and play the part of king. On the far side of the palace are the outer northern walls of the citadel and the north gate.

# Hué Imperial City

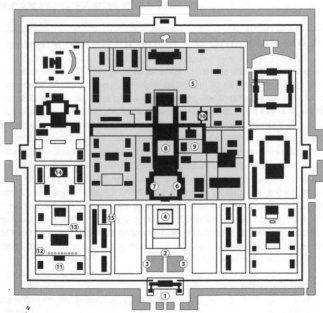

**N**

| 100 metres |
| 100 yards |

1 Ngo Mon (Royal Gate)
2 Golden Water Bridge

3 Tanks
4 Dai Trieu Nghi (Great
  Rites Courtyard) & Thai
  Hoa Palace (Palace of
  Supreme Harmony)
5 ☐ Tu Cam Thanh
  (Purple Forbidden City)
6 Ta Pavilion

7 Huu Vu Pavilion
8 Central Pavilion,
  private apartments
  of the Emperor
9 Quang Minh Palace
10 Royal Reading
  Pavilion
11 Hien Lam Cac

12 9 Bronze urns
13 Thé Temple (Temple
  of Generations)
14 Hung Temple
15 Waiting Pavilion (Huu
  Ta Dai Lam Vien)

Most of the surviving buildings of interest are to be found on the west side of the palace, running between the outer walls and the walls of the Forbidden City. At the southwest corner is the well-preserved and beautiful **Hien Lam Cac (12)**, a pavilion built in 1821, in front of which stand nine massive **bronze urns (13)** cast between 1835 and 1837 on the orders of Emperor Minh Mang. It is estimated that they weigh between 1500 kg and 2600 kg, and each has 17 decorative figures, animals, rivers, flowers and landscapes representing between them the wealth, beauty and unity of the country. The central, largest and most ornate urn is dedicated to the founder of the empire, Emperor Gia Long. Next to the urns walking northwards is **Thé Temple** (Temple of Generations, **14**). Built in 1821, it contains altars honouring 10 of the kings of the Nguyen Dynasty (Duc Duc and Hiep Hoa are missing) behind which are meant to be kept a selection of their personal belongings. It was only in 1954 that the stelae depicting the three Revolutionary emperors, Ham Nghi, Thanh Thai and Duy Tan, were brought into the temple. The French, perhaps fearing they would become a focus of discontent, prevented the Vietnamese from erecting altars in their memory. North of the Thé Temple is **Hung Temple (15)**, built in 1804 for the worship of Gia Long's father, Nguyen Phuc Luan, the father of the founder of the Nguyen Dynasty.

## Hué Museum of Royal Fine Arts
ⓘ *3 Le Truc St, Tue-Sun 0700-1700, until 1730 in summer (14 Apr-14 Oct); 35,000d. No cameras or video cameras; over shoes are provided; information in English.*
Housed in the Long An Palace, the museum contains a reasonable collection of ceramics, furniture, screens and bronzeware and some stunning, embroidered imperial clothes. The building itself is worthy of note for its elegant construction. Built by Emperor Thieu Tri in 1845, it was dismantled and erected on the present site in 1909.

---

# Perfume River and the imperial tombs » *Colour map 3, B5.*

As the geographical and spiritual centre of the Nguyen Dynasty, Hué and the surrounding area is the site of numerous pagodas, seven imperial tombs and the tombs of numerous other royal personages, countless courtiers and successful mandarins. Many of these are located close to the Perfume River.

Each of the tombs follows the same stylistic formula, although they also reflect the individual tastes and predilections of the emperor in question. The tombs were built during the lifetime of each emperor, who took a great interest in their design and construction; they were, after all, meant to ensure his comfort in the next life. Each mausoleum, variously arranged, has five design elements: a courtyard with statues of elephants, horses and military and civil mandarins (usually approached through a park of rare trees); a stela pavilion (with an engraved eulogy composed by the king's son and heir); a Temple of the Soul's Tablets; a pleasure pavilion, and a grave. Geomancers decreed that they should also have a stream and a mountainous screen in front. The tombs faithfully copy Chinese prototypes, although most art historians claim that they fall short in terms of execution.

## Thien Mu Pagoda → *Colour map 3, B5.*
ⓘ *An easy 4-km bicycle (or cyclo) ride from the city, following the north bank of the river upstream (west).*
Thien Mu Pagoda (the Elderly Goddess Pagoda), also known as the Thien Mau Tu Pagoda, and locally as the **Linh Mu Pagoda** (the name used on most local maps), is the finest in Hué and beautifully sited on the north bank of the Perfume River. It was built in 1601 by Nguyen Hoang, the governor of Hué, after an old woman appeared to him and said that the site had supernatural significance and should be marked by the construction of a pagoda. The monastery is the oldest in Hué, and the seven-storey

**Phuoc Duyen** (Happiness and Grace Tower), built later by Emperor Thieu Tri in 1844, is 21 m high, with each storey containing an altar to a different Buddha. The summit of the tower is crowned with a water pitcher to catch the rain, water representing the source of happiness. Arranged around the tower are four smaller buildings one of which contains the **Great Bell**, cast in 1710 under the orders of the Nguyen Lord, Nguyen Phuc Chu, and weighing 2200 kg. Beneath another of the surrounding pavilions is a monstrous **marble turtle** on which is a stela, carved in 1715 and 2.6 m high, recounting the development of Buddhism in Hué. Beyond the tower, the entrance to the pagoda is through a triple gateway patrolled by six carved and vividly painted guardians, two on each gate. The roof of the sanctuary itself is decorated with jataka stories (birth stories of the Buddha). At the front of the sanctuary is a laughing Buddha in brass. Behind that are an assortment of gilded Buddhas and a crescent-shaped gong, cast in 1677 by Jean de la Croix. Thich Quang Duc, the first monk to commit suicide through self immolation, came from this pagoda (see page 178); the grey Austin in which he made the journey to his death in Ho Chi Minh City is still kept here in a garage in the temple garden.

## Tomb of Emperor Gia Long → Colour map 3, B5.

ⓘ *South of town on a tributary of the Perfume River, daily 0630-1730; 55,000d for the upkeep of the tomb. Get there by bicycle or motorbike.*

The Tomb of Emperor Gia Long is the most distant from Hué and is rarely visited. Overgrown with venerable mango trees and devoid of tourists, touts and ticket sellers, it is the most atmospheric of all the tombs. And, given the historical changes that were to be wrought by the dynasty Gia Long founded, this is arguably the most significant tomb in Hué.

Nguyen Anh, or Gia Long as he was crowned in 1802, came to power with French support. His reign was despotic: when his European advisers suggested that encouragement of industry would lead to the betterment of his poorer subjects, Gia Long replied that he preferred them poor. In fact, the poor were virtual slaves during his reign: the price for one healthy young buffalo was one healthy young girl. It's not surprising, then, that a study by a Vietnamese scholar estimated that there were 105 peasant uprisings between 1802 and 1820 alone. The Vietnamese have never forgiven Gia Long for his despotism nor for the fact that he gave the French a foothold in Vietnam; they still say of him that "*cong ran can ga nha*" (he carried home the snake that killed the chicken).

To reach Gia Long's tomb, take Dien Bien Phu Street out of town. After a couple of kilometres turn right at the T-junction facing pine-shrouded Dan Nam Giao Temple and take the first left onto Minh Mang. Continue past the sign marking your departure from Hué and take the right-hand branch of the fork in the road. After a short distance the road joins the riverbank and heads for some 2 km towards the new Hué bypass (Highway 1) across the river. Follow the riverbank directly underneath this bridge and continue straight on as the road begins to deteriorate. A few metres beyond the Ben Do 1 km milestone is a red sign for 'Gia Long Tomb'. Down a steep path a sampan waits to ferry passengers across this tributary of the Perfume River (bargain but expect to pay US$2-3 return); on the far side, follow the track upstream for about 1 km. Turn right by a café with two billiard tables and then, almost immediately, turn left. Keep on this path. Ask for directions along the way!

Gia Long's geomancers did a great job finding this site: with the mountainous screen in front of it is a textbook example of a final resting place. Interestingly, although they had first choice of all the possible sites, this is the furthest tomb from the palace: clearly they took their task seriously. Gia Long's mausoleum was built between 1814 and 1820 (see page 128, for an account of the emperor's burial) and, as the first of the dynasty, set the formula for the later tombs. There is a surrounding lotus pond and steps lead up to a courtyard, where the Minh Thanh ancestral temple stands resplendent in red and gold.

## The burial of Emperor Gia Long

When the Emperor Gia Long died on 3 February 1820, the thread on the ancestors' altar (representing his soul) was tied. The following day the corpse was bathed and clothed in rich garments, and precious stones and pearls were placed in his mouth. Then a ritual offering of food, drink and incense was made, before the body was placed in a coffin made of catalpa wood (*bignonia catalpa*) – a wood impervious to insect attack. At this point, the crown prince announced the period of mourning that was to be observed, a minimum of three years. Relatives of the dead emperor, mandarins and their wives each had different forms and periods of mourning to observe, depending upon their position.

Three days after Gia Long's death, a messenger was sent to the Hoang Nhon Pagoda to inform the dead empress of the demise of her husband. Meanwhile, the new Emperor Minh Mang had the former ruler's deeds recorded and engraved on golden sheets which were bound together as a book. Then astrologers selected an auspicious date for the funeral. After some argument they chose 27 May, although 11 May also had its supporters. On 17 May, court officials told the heaven, the earth and the dynastic ancestors of the details for the funeral and at the same time opened the imperial tomb. On 20 May, the corpse was informed of the ceremony. Four days later the coffin left the palace for the three-day journey to its final resting place. Then, at the appointed time, the coffin was lowered into the sepulchre – its orientation correct – shrouded in silk cloth, protected by a second outer coffin, covered in resin and, finally, bricked in. Next to Gia Long, a second grave was dug into which were placed an assortment of objects useful in his next life. The following morning, Emperor Minh Mang, in full mourning robes, stood outside the tomb facing east, while a mandarin facing in the opposite direction inscribed ritual titles on the tomb. The silk thread on the ancestors' altar, the symbol of the soul, was untied, animals slaughtered and the thread was then buried in the vicinity of the tomb.

(This account is adapted from James Dumarçay's *The palaces of South-East Asia*, 1991.)

To the right is a double burial chamber, walled and locked, where Gia Long and his wife are interred (the emperor's tomb is fractionally the taller). The chamber is perfectly lined up with the two huge obelisks on the far side of the lake. Beyond this is a courtyard with five, now headless, mandarins, horses and elephants on each side; steps lead up to the stela eulogizing the emperor's reign, composed, presumably, by his eldest son, Minh Mang, as was the custom. This grey monolith, engraved in Chinese characters, remained miraculously undisturbed during two turbulent centuries.

### Tomb of Emperor Minh Mang → Colour map 3, B5.
ⓘ *12 km south of Hué. Daily 0630-1730; 55,000d. To get there by bicycle or motorbike follow the directions for Gia Long's tomb (page 127) but cross the Perfume River using the new road bridge; on the far side of the bridge turn left.*

The Tomb of Emperor Minh Mang is possibly the finest of all the imperial tombs. Built between 1841 and 1843, it is sited among peaceful ponds south of the city. In terms of architectural poise and balance, and richness of decoration, it has no peer in the area. The tomb's layout, along a single central and sacred axis (*Shendao*), is unusual in its symmetry; no other tomb, with the possible exception of Khai Dinh (page 129), achieves the same unity of constituent parts, nor draws the eye onwards so easily and pleasantly from one visual element to the next. The tomb was traditionally approached through the **Dai Hong Mon**; today, visitors pass through a side gate into the ceremonial courtyard, which contains an array of statuary. Next is the stela pavilion in which there is a carved eulogy to the dead emperor composed by his son, Thieu Tri. Continuing downwards through a series of courtyards visitors see, in turn, the **Sung An Temple** dedicated to Minh Mang and his empress; a small garden with flower beds that once formed the Chinese character for 'longevity', and two sets of stone bridges. The first consists of three spans, the central one of which (**Trung Dao Bridge**) was for the sole use of the emperor. The second, single bridge, leads to a short flight of stairs with naga balustrades at the end of which is a locked bronze door (no access). The door leads to the tomb itself which is surrounded by a circular wall.

## Tomb of Tu Duc → Colour map 3, B5.

① *7 km south Hué, daily 0630-1730; 55,000d. If you're travelling by boat, a return xe ôm trip from the riverbank is 20,000d.*

The Tomb of Tu Duc was built between 1864 and 1867 in a pine wood. The complex is enclosed by a wall and encompasses a lake, with lotus and water hyacinth. An island on the Lake has a number of replicas of famous temples, built by the king, which are now rather difficult to discern. Tu Doc often came here to relax and, from the pavilions that reach out over the lake, composed poetry and listened to music. The **Xung Khiem Pavilion**, built in 1865, has recently been restored with UNESCO's help and is the most attractive building here.

West of the lake, the tomb complex follows the formula described above: ceremonial square, mourning yard with pavilion and then the tomb itself. To the left of Tu Duc's tomb are the tombs of his Empress, Le Thien Anh, and adopted son, Kien Phuc. Many of the pavilions are crumbling and ramshackle, lending the complex a rather tragic air. This is appropriate since, though he had 104 wives, Tu Duc fathered no sons and was therefore forced to write his own eulogy, a fact which he took as a bad omen. The eulogy itself recounts the sadness in Tu Duc's life. It was shortly after Tu Duc's reign that France gained full control of Vietnam.

## Tomb of Khai Dinh

① *10 km south of Hué, daily 0630-1730; 55,000d. To get there by motorbike or bicycle follow the directions for Gia Long's tomb (page 127) but turn immediately left past small shops after the new river crossing (Highway 1) and head straight on, over a small crossroads, parallel to the main road. If you're travelling by boat, a return xe ôm trip from the riverbank is 25,000-30,000d.*

The Tomb of Khai Dinh was built between 1920 and 1932 and is the last mausoleum of the Nguyen Dynasty. By the time Khai Dinh was contemplating the afterlife, brick had given way in popularity to concrete, so the structure is now beginning to deteriorate. Nevertheless, it occupies a fine position on the Chau Mountain facing southwest towards a large white statue of Quan Am (see p91), also built by Khai Dinh. The valley, used for the cultivation of cassava and sugar cane, and the pine-covered mountains, make this one of the most beautifully sited and peaceful of the tombs. Indeed, before construction could begin, Khai Dinh had to remove the tombs of Chinese nobles who had already selected the site for its beauty and auspicious orientation. A total of 127 steep steps lead up to the Honour Courtyard with statuary of mandarins, elephants and horses. An octagonal stela pavilion in the centre of the mourning yard contains a stone stela engraved with a eulogy to the emperor. At the top of some more stairs, are the tomb and shrine of Khai Dinh, containing a bronze statue of the emperor sitting on his throne and holding a jade sceptre. The body is interred 9 m below ground level. The interior is richly decorated with ornate and colourful murals (the artist incurred the wrath of the emperor and only just escaped execution), floor tiles, and decorations built up with fragments of porcelain. It is the most elaborate of all the tombs and took 11 years to build. Such was the cost of construction that Khai Dinh had to levy additional taxes to fund the project. The tomb shows distinct European stylistic influences.

## Amphitheatre and Elephant Temple
① *South bank of the river, about 3 km west of Hué railway station. Free. To get there by bicycle or motorbike turn left up a paved track opposite 203 Bui Thi Xuan St; the track for the Elephant Temple runs in front of the amphitheatre (off to the right).*

The Ho Quyen (Amphitheatre) was built in 1830 by Emperor Minh Mang as a venue for the popular duels between elephants and tigers. This royal sport was in earlier centuries staged on an island in the Perfume River or on the riverbanks themselves but, by 1830, it was considered desirable for the royal party to be able to observe the duels without placing themselves at risk from escaping tigers. The amphitheatre is said to have been last used in 1904 when, as was usual, the elephant emerged victorious. The walls of the amphitheatre are 5 m high and the arena is 44 m in diameter. On the south side, beneath the royal box, is one large gateway (for the elephant) and, to the north, five smaller entrances for the tigers.

**Den Voi Re**, the Temple of the Elephant Trumpet, dedicated to the call of the fighting elephant, is a few hundred metres away. It is a modest little place and fairly run down, with a large pond in front and two small elephant statues. Presumably this is where elephants were blessed before battle or perhaps where the unsuccessful ones were mourned.

## Thanh Toan Covered Bridge
① *8 km west of Hué.*

The bridge was built in the reign of King Le Hien Tong (1740-1786) by Tran Thi Dao, a childless woman, as an act of charity, hoping that God would bless her with a baby. The structure, with its shelter for the tired and homeless, attracted the interest of several kings who granted the village immunity from a number of taxes. Unfortunately, the original yin-yang tiles have been replaced with ugly green enamelled tube tiles but the bridge is still in good condition. The route to the bridge passes through beautiful countryside where ducks waddle along roads and paddy fields line the route. Travel there by bicycle or motorbike in the glow of the late afternoon sun.

# Around Hué ›› *Colour map 3, B4 and B5.*

## The Demilitarized Zone (DMZ) → *Colour map 3, B4.*
① *Most visitors see the sights of the DMZ, including Khe Sanh and the Ho Chi Minh Trail, on a tour. A 1-day tour of all the DMZ sights can be booked from any of Hué's tour operators for around US$10; depart 0600, return 1800-2000.* ›› *For further information, see Activities and tours, page 135.*

The incongruously named Demilitarized Zone (DMZ), scene of some of the fiercest fighting of the Vietnam War, lies along the **Ben Hai River** and the better-known **17th Parallel**. The **Hien Luong Bridge** on the 17th parallel is included in most tours. The DMZ was the creation of the 1954 Geneva Peace Accord, which divided the country into two spheres of influence prior to elections that were never held. Like its counterpart in Germany, the boundary evolved into a national border, separating Communist from Capitalist but, unlike its European equivalent, it was the triumph of Communism that saw its demise.

At **Dong Ha**, to the north of Hué, Highway 9 branches off the main coastal Highway 1 and heads 80 km west to the border with Laos (see below). Along this route is **Khe Sanh** (now called Huong Hoa), the site of one of the most famous battles of the war (see

### To Laos via Lao Bao

The **Vietnamese border** post is 3 km beyond Lao Bao village at the western end of Highway 9; Lao immigration is 500 m west at Dansavanh. Once in Laos, Route 9 heads west over the Annamite Mountains to Xepon (45 km) and on to Savannakhet (236 km from the border). We have received reports of long delays at this border crossing, particularly entering Vietnam, as paperwork is scrutinized and bags are checked and double-checked. Don't be surprised if formalities take 1 hr – and keep smiling! Expect to pay 'overtime fees' on the Lao side if you come through on a Saturday or Sunday or after 1600 on a weekday. Lao immigration can issue 30-day tourist visas for US$30-42. You can also get a Lao visa in advance from the Lao consulate in Danang (12 Tran Qui Cap St, T0511-821208, 0800-1100, 1400-1600); it takes 24 hrs to process. The closest Vietnamese consulate is in Savannakhet; see page 467 for visa application details and opening hours.

**Transport** There are buses from Hué direct to Savannakhet or buses to Khe Sanh where there are connections to Lao Bao. There are also buses direct to the border from Le Duan St in Dong Ha, 1-1.5 hrs. *Xe ôm* from Khe Sanh to the border costs US$3, or from Lao Bao village to the border, US$1. There are daily departures for the Lao town of Savannakhet from Dansavanh. Buses also depart from Xepon (45 km west of the border) to Savannakhet daily 0800, 30,000 kip. Those crossing into Vietnam from Laos may be able to get a ride with the DMZ tour bus from Khe Sanh back to Hué (see page 130) in the late afternoon. Otherwise, there are Vietnam-bound buses from Savannakhet (see page 466) and numerous songthaews to the border from the market in Xepon, 45 km, 1 hr, 20,000 kip but you'll need to get there by 0700 to ensure a space.

**Accommodation Mountain**, Lao Bao village. A simple, clean and friendly guesthouse.

page 132). The battleground is 3 km from the village. There's also a small **museum** ⓘ *25,000d* at the former Tacon military base, surrounded by military hardware.

A section of the **Ho Chi Minh Trail** runs close to Khe Sanh. This is another popular but inevitably disappointing sight, given that its whole purpose was to be as inconspicuous as possible and anything you see was designed to be invisible, from the air at least. However, it's worthy of a pilgrimage considering the sacrifice of millions of Vietnamese porters and the role it played in the American defeat (see page 182).

Tours to the DMZ usually also include the **tunnels of Vinh Moc** ⓘ *13 km off Highway 1 and 6 km north of Ben Hai River, 25,000d*, which served a similar function to the better known Cu Chi tunnels in the south. They evolved as families in the heavily bombed village dug themselves shelters beneath their houses and then joined up with their neighbours. Later the tunnels developed a more offensive role when Viet Cong soldiers fought from them. Some visitors regard these tunnels as more 'authentic' than the 'touristy' tunnels of Cu Chi.

The **Rock Pile** is a 230-m-high limestone outcrop just south of the DMZ. It served as a US observation post, with troops, ammunition, Budweiser and prostitutes all being helicoptered in. Jon Swain, the war correspondent, describes in his memoirs, *River of Time*, how his helicopter got lost around the Rock Pile and nearly came to disaster in this severely contested zone. Although it was chosen as an apparently unassailable position, the sheer walls of the Rock Pile were eventually scaled by the Viet Cong.

# ⁞ The battle at Khe Sanh

In early 1968, the North Vietnamese Army (NVA) tried to inflict a humiliating defeat on American forces at Khe Sanh (already the site of a bloody confrontation in April and May 1967). Their apparent aim was to replicate their victory over the French at Dien Bien Phu (see p110); one of the NVA divisions, the 304th, even had Dien Bien Phu emblazoned on its battle streamers.

The US Commander, General Westmoreland, in turn, hoped to bury Ho Chi Minh's troops under tonnes of high explosive and achieve a Dien Bien Phu in reverse. Unlike the French in the previous decade, however, the American high command had some warning of the attack: a North Vietnamese regimental commander was killed while surveying the base on 2 January and that was interpreted as a sign that the NVA were planning a major assault. Special US forces long-range patrols were dropped into the area around the base and photo reconnaissance increased. It became clear that 20,000-40,000 NVA troops were converging on Khe Sanh.

By January 1968 the US Marines were effectively surrounded in a place which the assistant commander of the 3rd Marine Division referred to as "not really anywhere". There was a heavy exchange of fire, with the Marine artillery firing 159,000 shells and B-52s carpet-bombing the surrounding area, obliterating each 'box' with 162 tonnes of bombs. However, the commanders of the NVA knew there was no chance of repeating their success at Dien Bien Phu against the US military; instead the attack on Khe Sanh was designed to distract US attention away from urban centres in preparation for the Tet offensive (see page 228).

The 77-day seige of Khe Sanh cost many thousands of NVA lives (one estimate is 10,000-15,000 as against only 248 Americans) but the Tet offensive proved to be a remarkable psychological victory for the NVA. Again, a problem for the US military was one of presentation. Even Walter Cronkite, the doyen of TV reporters, informed his audience that the parallels between Khe Sanh and Dien Bien Phu were "there for all to see".

## Hai Van Pass and Lang Co → Colour map 3, B5.

Between Hué and Danang a finger of the Truong Son Mountains juts eastwards, extending all the way to the sea: almost as though God were somewhat roguishly trying to divide the country into two equal halves. The mountains act as an important climatic barrier, trapping the cooler, damper air masses to the north and bottling them up over Hué, which accounts for Hué's shocking weather. They also mark an abrupt linguistic divide: the Hué dialect (the language of the royal court) to the north is still the source of bemusement to many southerners. The physical barrier to north-south communication has resulted in some spectacular engineering solutions: the single track and narrow gauge **railway line** closely follows the coastline, sometimes almost hanging over the sea while Highway 1 winds its way equally precariously over the Lang Co lagoon and Hai Van Pass.

The road passes through many pretty, red-tiled villages, compact and surrounded by clumps of bamboo and fruit trees, which provide shade, shelter and sustenance. And, for colour, there's the bougainvillea, which produces pink and white leaves on the same branch. Windowless jalopies from the French era trundle along picking up passengers and their bundles, while station wagons from the American era provide an inter-village shared taxi service. The idyllic fishing village of **Lang Co** is just off Highway 1, about 65 km south of Hué, and has a number of cheap and good seafood restaurants.

Shortly after crossing the Lang Co lagoon, dotted with coracles and fish traps, the road begins the long haul up to **Hai Van Pass** (Deo Hai Van or 'Pass of the Ocean Clouds'), known to the French as 'Col des Nuages'. The pass is 497 m above the dancing white waves that can be seen at its foot and once marked the border between the kingdoms of Vietnam and Champa. The pass is peppered with abandoned pillboxes and crowned with an old fort, originally built by the Nguyen Dynasty from Hué and used as a relay station for the pony express on the old Mandarin Road. Subsequently used by the French, it is a pretty shabby affair today, collecting wind-blown litter and sometimes used by the People's Army for a quiet brew-up and a smoke. Looking back to the north, stretching into the haze is the littoral and lagoon of Lang Co; to the south is Danang Bay and Monkey Mountain, and at your feet lies a patch of green paddies which belong to the leper colony, accessible only by boat.

# ● Sleeping

**Hué** *p122, map p123*

Most hotels lie to the south of the Perfume River, although there are a couple to the north in the old Vietnamese part of town. Hué still suffers from a dearth of quality accommodation but this has improved in recent years and more properties are planned.

**LL-L La Residence Hotel & Spa**, 5 Le Loi St, T054-837475, www.la-residence-hue.com. Anyone who knew this hotel before will be stunned at its fabulous makeover. For lovers of art deco, it is an essential place to stay and to visit. Home of the French governor of Annam in the 1920s, it has been beautifully and decadently restored with 122 rooms, restaurant, lobby bar, spa and swimming pool close to the Perfume River. The citadel can be seen from the hotel. The rooms in the original governor's residence are the most stylish, with 4-poster beds and lovely dark wood furnishings; other rooms are extremely comfortable too, with all mod cons. The breakfasts are very filling; guests also enjoy free internet. The hotel has a fascinating collection of old colonial-era photographs that are hung along the corridors. Highly recommended.

**LL-A The Pilgrimage Village**, 130 Minh Mang Rd, T054-885461, www.pilgrimage village.com. Beautifully designed rooms in a village setting ranging from honeymoon and pool suites to superior rooms. There are 2 restaurants, a number of bars, a gorgeous spa and 2 pools. Cooking and t'ai chi classes are available. There's a complimentary shuttle service to and from town.

**L Saigon Morin**, 30 Le Loi St, T054-823526, www.morinhotel.com.vn. The best hotel in Hué, this is still recognizable as the fine hotel built by the Morin brothers in the 1880s.

Arranged around a courtyard with a small pool, the rooms are large and comfortable. All have a/c, satellite TV and hot water. The courtyard, lit with candles, is a delightful place to sit in the evening and enjoy a quiet drink.

**A Century Riverside**, 49 Le Loi St, T054-823390, www.centuryriverside hue.com. Fabulous river views and comfortable, nicely furnished rooms in this very imposing building. Note that not all rooms have been renovated, so enquire before booking. Vietnamese and Western food is served at the restaurants. There's a pool, tennis courts and a massage service. The hotel is used by dozens of tour operators.

**A-B Duy Tan**, 12 Hung Vuong St, T054-825001, www.duytanhotel.com.vn. Large building in a bustling part of town, with comfortable superior rooms. The standard rooms are spartan but fully equipped.

**A-B Festival Hué Hotel**, 15 Ly Thuong Kiet St, T054-823071, www.festivalhuehotel.com.vn. The Festival hotel has now renovated all its rooms and is situated just outside the main bustle of downtown activity. Its wicker bedroom furniture makes a refreshing change from the heavy imperial dark wood furniture so favoured by many hotels in Hué. There's a very sheltered pool and breakfast is included.

**B-D L'Indochine** (formerly **Dong Duong**), 2 Hung Vuong St, T054-823866, indochine-hotel@dng.vnn.vn. Priciest rooms in the old villa in front with bathtubs in bathrooms; the building behind is sterile and modern and the cheapest rooms (with showers only) are here. The first-class rooms are looking a little worn around the edges. There are 3 restaurants and not much English is spoken.

**B-E Dong Loi**, 19 Pham Ngu Lao St, T054-822296, www.hoteldongloi.com. Well situated and surrounded by internet cafés, shops and restaurants, this is a bright, breezy, airy and comfortable hotel. All rooms have a/c and hot water and all except the cheapest have a bathtub. Family-run, friendly and helpful service. The excellent **La Carambole Restaurant** adjoins the hotel.

**C-D Kinh Do**, 1 Nguyen Thai Hoc St, T054-823566. Architecturally unattractive with 35 smallish rooms but comfortable, in a central location and quiet with friendly staff and 2 restaurants. The price includes breakfast.

**C-E A Dong 1**, 1 bis Chu Van An St, T054-824148, adongcoltd@dng.vnn.vn. 7 rooms in this friendly hotel, with a/c, fridge and bathtub; also has an attractive upstairs terrace. There's also an **A Dong 2** on Doi Cung St.

The little *hem* (alley) opposite the **Century Riverside** (see above) has some really nice rooms in comfortable and cheerful guesthouses – easily the best-value accommodation in Hué. Recommended are:

**C-E Canh Tien Guesthouse**, 9/66 Le Loi St, T054-822772, http://canhtienhotel. chez.tiscali.fr. 12 rooms with fan or a/c. Cheaper rooms have fans; the most expensive have a balcony. Welcoming family.

**C-F Mimosa**, 66/10 (10 Kiet 66) Le Loi St, T054-828068. French is spoken when the owner is here. 8 rooms, with a/c, hot water and bathtub that are quiet, simple and clean. Rooms with fan are cheaper.

**D-E Hung Vuong Inn**, 20 Hung Vuong St, T054-821068, truongdung2000@yahoo.com. Above **La Boulangerie**. There are 9 double and twin rooms above the shop that are all spotlessly clean. Rooms have a TV and minibar and bathtubs; some have a balcony. It is quieter on the back side of the building.

**D-E Thanh Thuy**, 66/4 (4 Kiet 66) Le Loi St, T054-824585, thanhthuy66@dng.vnn.vn. Small, peaceful, clean and friendly family-run guesthouse. 4 rooms, with a/c and hot water. Car hire at good rates (around US$25/day).

**D-F Hoang Huong**, 66/2 (2 Kiet 66) Le Loi St, T054-828509. Some a/c or cheaper rooms with fan; friendly and helpful family guesthouse. Cheap dormitories too and bicycles and motos rented.

## ● Eating

Hué cuisine is excellent. The influence of the royal court is evident in the large number of dishes served, each dish being relatively light. Hué food is also delicately flavoured and requires painstaking preparation in the kitchen: in short, it is a veritable culinary harem in which even the most pampered and surfeited emperor could find something to tickle his palate. Apart from this 'nibble' food, other Hué dishes are more robust, notably the famed *bun bo Hué* – round white noodles in soup, with slices of beef, laced with chilli oil of exquisite piquancy. Restaurants for local people usually close early; it's best to get there before 2000. Traveller cafés and restaurants tend to keep serving food until about 2200.

### Hué *p122, map p123*

♥♥ **La Carambole**,19 Pham Ngu Lao St, T054-810 491, la_carambole @hotmail.com, daily 0700-2300. One of the most popular restaurants in town and deservedly so. The ceiling is decorated with beautiful kites, shot through with sticks capped by feathers. It is incredibly busy especially for dinner when the imperial-style dinner is recommended.

♥♥ **Saigon Morin**, see Sleeping. Excellent buffets for US$12 in a lovely garden setting with a range of specialty Hué cuisine. While you dine, be entertained by Royal Music performers.

♥♥-♥ **The Tropical Garden Restaurant**, 27 Chu Van An St, T054-8471431, tropicalgarden@vnn.vn. Dine alfresco in a small leafy garden, just a short walk from the Perfume River. Beef soup with starfruit and mackerel baked in pineapple are among the flavoursome choices.

♥ **Café No 3**, 3 Le Loi St, T054-824514. Near the railway station, a cheap and popular café serving standard Vietnamese, Western and vegetarian food. A useful source of information and with bikes for rent.

♥ **Dong Tam**, 7/66 (7 Kiet 66) Le Loi St, T054-828403. Tucked away in the *hem* opposite **Century Riverside**, this is Hué's vegetarian restaurant. Sit in a pleasant and quiet yard surrounded by plants and topiary while choosing from the very reasonably

● *For an explanation of sleeping and eating price codes used in this guide, see inside the* ● *front cover. Other relevant information is found in Essentials, see pages 29-32.*

priced menu. Its credentials are reflected in its popularity with the city's monkish population.

**¶ La Boulangerie Française**, 20 Hung Vuong St, T054-821068, 0700-2030. There's a large range of Western and Vietnamese food served up by very friendly staff. Proceeds from the bakery go to help Vietnamese orphans via a French charity (AEVN-France).

**¶ Lac Thien**, 6 Dinh Tien Hoang St, T054-527348, and **¶ Lac Thanh**, 6A Dinh Tien Hoang St, T054-524674. Arguably Hué's most famous restaurants, run by schismatic branches of the same deaf-mute family in adjacent buildings. You go to one or the other: under no circumstances should clients patronize both establishments. **Lac Thien** (frequented by Footprint) serves excellent dishes from a diverse and inexpensive menu, its Huda beers are long and cold and the family is riotous and entertaining, but service has been known to be slack.

**¶ Stop and Go**, 18 Ben Nghe St, T054-827051, stopandgocafe@yahoo.com. Next door to **Ben Nghe Guesthouse**. Travel café run by the silver-haired Mr Do. Specialities include rice pancakes and the Hué version of spring rolls, excellent and cheap.

**¶ Y Thao Garden**, 3 Thach Han St, T054-523018, ythaogarden@gmail.com. Eating here is an extraordinary experience. The set menu of 8 courses is a culinary adventure with some amazing animals-from-food sculpture. The old house in a pretty garden is delightful. Recommended.

## 🍷 Bars and clubs

**Hué** p122, map p123
**Cathi**, 64 Le Lo Sti, T054-831210. Such a friendly place offering lots of titbits with drinks. Pretty coloured lantern shades inside and in the front yard and tree trunks to sit on inside for drinks and a garden at the back. Large drinks list including cocktail and teas – one, the polygonum, will cure "involuntary ejaculation" and improve "potency and longevity." Also yoghurts and a small menu of meat, noodles and rice.
**DMZ Bar**, 60 Le Loi St, T054-823414, www.dmz-bar.com, 0900-0200. Hué's first bar, with pool table, cold beer and spirits at

affordable prices. Good place to meet people **135** and pick up tourist information.
**Why Not?**, 21 Vo Thi Sau St. Slightly arty café bar, with a decent selection of food and drink.

## 🎭 Entertainment

**Hué** p122, map p123
Rent a **dragon boat** and sail up the Perfume River with your own private singers and musicians; tour offices and major hotels will arrange groups.

See a **Royal Court performance** in the Imperial City's theatre or listen to performers during the **Saigon Morin**'s occasional evening buffet.

## 🛍 Shopping

**Hué** p122, map p123
There is a much wider range of goods on sale in Hué now than was the case in the past. Shops around the **Century Riverside Hotel**, for example Le Loi and Pham Ngu Lao streets, sell ceramics, silk and clothes. The *non bai tho* or poem hats are also available. These are a unique Hué form of the standard conical hat (*non lá*), made from bamboo and palm leaves, with love poetry, songs, proverbs or simply a design stencilled on to them. The decoration is only visible if the hat is held up to the light and viewed from the inside.

No Vietnamese visitor would shake the dust of Hué off his feet without having previously stocked up on *me xung*, a sugary, peanut and toffee confection coated in sesame seeds; it's quite a pleasant energy booster to carry while cycling around the tombs.

## ⛰ Activities and tours

**Hué** p122, map p123
**Tour operators**
Almost every travellers' café acts as an agent for a tour operator and will take bookings. Bus and boat tours to the **Imperial Tombs** are organized by tour operators and hotels. Local tour operators charge around US$6 per person to visit Thien Mu Pagoda, Hon Chien Temple, Tu Duc, Minh Mang and Khai Dinh's Tombs, departing at 0800, returning 1530.

There are also day tours to some of the sights of the Vietnam War, US$10 for about 9 sights, including **Vinh Moc** tunnels and museum, the **Ho Chi Minh Trail** and **Khe Sanh**, depart 0600, return 1800-2000. Those wishing to travel overland to Laos can arrange to be dropped off in Khe Sanh and pay less.

**Lienhoang**, 12 Nguyen Thien Ke St, T054-823507/091-4147378 (mob), tienbicycles@gmail.com. Mr Tien runs recommended bicycling tours around the country, including one to the DMZ, costing US$12 a day including bike, support car, guide, accommodation and entrance fees.
**Stop and Go Café**, 18 Ben Nghe St, T054-827051/090-5126767 (mob), stopandgocafe@yahoo.com. Known for its tours of the DMZ (all-day tour, US$16 on a motorbike, US$60 in a car) which are led by ARVN veterans which brings the landscape to life and an insight you won't get on a cheaper tour. Highly recommended.
**Sinh Café**, 7 Nguyen Tri Phuong St, T054-848626, and at 12 Hung Vuong St, T054-8450222, www.sinhcafevn.com. A number of competitively priced tours and money changing facilities.

## ⊙ Transport

**Hué** *p122, map p123*
**Air**
There are flights to and from Hanoi and HCMC. **Phu Bai Airport** is a 25-min drive south of Hué. There is an airport bus, 1 hr, 30,000d run by Vietnam Airlines. **Airline offices** Vietnam Airlines, 23 Nguyen Van Cu St, 0715-1115, 1330-1630.

**Bicycle and motorbike**
Bikes and motorbikes (US$6 per day) can be hired from most hotels, guesthouses and cafés.

**Boat**
Boats can be hired through tour agents and from any berth on the south bank of the river, east of Trang Tien Bridge or through travel cafés. Good for either a gentle cruise, with singers in the evening, or an attractive way of getting to some of the temples and mausoleums, around US$5-10 depends on

time and if singers are employed. Note that if you travel by boat to the tombs you may have to pay a moto driver to take you to the tomb as they are often 1 km or so from the riverbank.

**Bus**
The An Cuu station at 43 Hung Vuong St serves destinations south of Hué. The An Hoa station up at the northwest corner of the citadel serves destinations to the north of Hué. Open Tour Buses can be booked from hotels or tour agencies. Tourist buses to **Savannakhet**, Laos, via Lao Bao, leave at 0600 arriving 1530, US$15. Buses to **Vientiane** leave at 1730 and arrive at 1430, US$18. Book with tour operators.

**Cyclo and xe ôm**
Cyclos and *xe ôm* are available everywhere. Cyclos are pleasant for visiting the more central attractions. *Xe ôm* are a speedier way to see the temples, as the terrain south of town is quite hilly.

**Taxi**
**Hué Taxi**, T054-833333; **Mai Linh Taxi**, T054-898989.

**Train**
Hué Railway Station, 2 Bui Thi Xuan, west end of Le Loi St, T054-830666, booking office open 0700-2200. It serves all stations south to **HCMC** and north to **Hanoi**. Advance booking, especially for sleepers, is essential. The 4-hr journey to **Danang** is recommended for its scenic views.

## ⊙ Directory

**Hué** *p122, maps p123*
**Banks** Incombank, 2A Le Quy Don St, 0700-1130, 1330-1700, closed Thu afternoon. Has a Visa and MasterCard ATM. Vietcom Bank, 78 Hung Vuong St, 0700-2200. There's a Visa ATM to the left of La Résidence hotel. **Internet** Most hotels and guesthouses listed here offer internet services. **Medical Services** Hué General Hospital, 16 Le Loi St, T054-822325. **Post office and telephone** 8 Hoang Hoa Tham St and 91 Tran Hung Dao, daily 0630-2130.

# Hoi An, Danang and around

*The city of Danang has no real charm and no sense of permanence but few cities in the world have such spectacular beaches on their doorstep, let alone three UNESCO World Heritage Sites – Hué, Hoi An and My Son – within a short drive. The ancient town of Hoi An (formerly Faifo) lies on the banks of the Thu Bon River. During its heyday 200 years ago, when trade with China and Japan flourished, it was a prosperous little port. Much of the merchants' wealth was spent on family chapels and Chinese clan houses which remain little altered today. The city of Hoi An is currently experiencing a revival: the river may be too shallow for shipping but it is perfect for tourist boats; the silk merchants may not export any produce but that's because everything they make leaves town on the backs of satisfied customers.* ➤➤ *For Sleeping, Eating and other listings, see pages 146-151.*

## Hoi An 🖃🏃🏦🎯🔊🔳🚌🛈 ➤➤ *p146-151. Colour map 3, B6.*

Hoi An's tranquil riverside setting, its diminutive scale, friendly people and its shops and galleries have made it one of the most popular destinations in Vietnam for foreign travellers. There is much of historical interest in the town, plus a nearby beach and plenty of superb, inexpensive restaurants. That said, Hoi An's historic character is being slowly submerged by the rising tide of tourism. Although physically intact, virtually every one of its fine historic buildings either markets some aspect of its own heritage or touts in some other way for the tourist dollar; increasingly it is coming to resemble the 'Vietnam' pavilion in a Disney theme park. Nevertheless, visitors to Hoi An are charmed by the gentleness of the people and the sedate pace of life.

Most of Hoi An's more attractive buildings and assembly halls (*hoi quan*) are found either on, or just off, Tran Phu Street, which stretches west to east from the Japanese Covered Bridge to the market, running parallel to the river.

### Ins and outs
**Getting there and around** There are direct minibus connections with Ho Chi Minh City, Hanoi, Hué and Nha Trang. The quickest way of getting from Hanoi or Ho Chi Minh City is by flying to Danang airport (see page 142) and then getting a taxi direct to Hoi An (40 mins, US$12-15). The town itself is compact, quite busy and best explored on foot, although guesthouses also hire out bicycles. ➤➤ *For further information, see Transport, page 150.*

**Best time to visit** On the 14th day of the lunar month the town converts itself into a Chinese lantern fest and locals dress in traditional costume. The old town is pedestrianized for the night and poetry and music are performed in the streets.

**Tourist information** Entrance to most historic buildings is by sightseeing ticket, 75,000d, on sale at **Hoi An Tourist Office** ①*12 Phan Chu Trinh St, T0510-861276, and at 1 Nguyen Truong To St, T0510-861327, www.hoianoldtown.vn, open 0630-1800,* has English-speaking staff and can arrange car and minibus hire as well as sightseeing guides. Sights in Hoi An are open September to March 0700-1730 and April to August 0630-1800. The sightseeing ticket is segregated into five categories of different sights, allowing visitors admission to one of each. It is valid for three days. If you want to see additional sights and have used up your tokens for that particular category you must buy additional tickets; 10,000d tokens for additional sights are no longer available. At least a full day is needed to see the town properly.

*Vietnam* Central Vietnam Hoi An, Danang & around

**Background**

Hoi An is divided into five quarters, or 'bangs', each of which would traditionally have had its own pagoda and supported one Chinese clan group. The Chinese, along with some Japanese, settled here in the 16th century and controlled trade between the islands of Southeast Asia, East Asia (China and Japan) and India. Portuguese and Dutch vessels also docked at the port. Chinese vessels tended to visit Hoi An during the spring, returning to China in the summer. By the end of the 19th century the Thu Bon River had started to silt up and Hoi An was gradually eclipsed by Danang as the most important port of the area.

## Japanese Covered Bridge (Cau Nhat Ban)

ⓘ *Tran Phu St, 1 'other' token; keep your ticket to get back across the bridge.*

The Japanese Covered Bridge – also known as the Pagoda Bridge and the Faraway People's Bridge – is Hoi An's most famous landmark and was built in the 16th century. Its popular name reflects a long-standing belief that it was built by the Japanese, although no documentary evidence exists to support this. One of its other names, the Faraway People's Bridge, is said to have been coined because vessels from far away would moor close to the bridge. On its north side there is a pagoda, Japanese in style, for the protection of sailors, while at each end of the bridge are statues of two dogs (at the west end) and two monkeys (at the east end). It is said that the bridge was begun in the year of the monkey and finished in the year of the dog, although some scholars have pointed out that this would mean a two-year period of construction, an inordinately long time for such

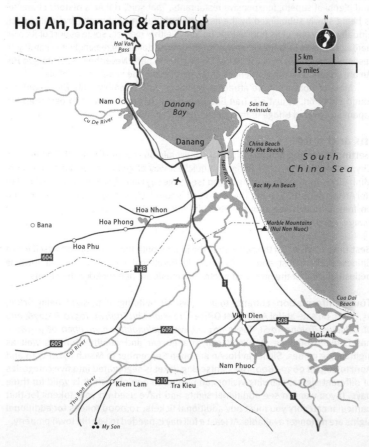

# Hoi An, Danang & around

a small bridge. They maintain, instead, that the two animals represent points of the compass, WSW (monkey) and NW (dog). Father Benigne Vachet, a missionary who lived in Hoi An between 1673 and 1683, notes in his memoirs that the bridge was the haunt of beggars and fortune tellers hoping to benefit from the stream of people crossing over it.

## Bach Dang Street and the French quarter

Just south of the Covered Bridge is Bach Dang Street, which runs along the bank of the Thu Bon River, where there are boats, activity and often a cooling breeze, before looping round to the Hoi An Market. Further on, the small but interesting French quarter around Phan Boi Chau Street is worth taking time over; it's not on the regular 'tourist circuit' and requires no entry fee but the colonnaded fronts here are particularly attractive. As in all historical quarters of Vietnamese towns, visitors should raise their gaze above street level to appreciate the architectural detail of upper floors, which is more likely to have survived, and less likely to be covered up.

## Assembly Halls (Hoi Quan)

Chinese traders in Hoi An (like elsewhere in Southeast Asia) established self-governing dialect associations or clan houses which owned their own schools, cemeteries, hospitals and temples. The clan houses (*hoi quan*) may be dedicated to a god or an illustrious individual and may contain a temple, although they are not themselves temples. There are five *hoi quan* in Hoi An, four for use by people of specific ethnicities – Fukien, Cantonese, Hainan, Chaozhou – and the fifth for use by any visiting Chinese sailors or merchants.

Strolling east from the Covered Bridge down Tran Phu Street all the assembly halls can be seen. Merchants from Guangdong would meet at the **Cantonese Assembly Hall** (Quang Dong Hoi Quan) ① *176 Tran Phu St, 1 'assembly hall' token*. This assembly hall is dedicated to Quan Cong, a Han Chinese general and dates from 1786. The hall, with its fine embroidered hangings, is in a cool, tree-filled compound and is a good place to rest.

Next is the **All Chinese Assembly Hall** (Ngu Bang Hoi Quan) ① *64 Tran Phu St, free*, sometimes referred to as **Chua Ba** (Goddess Temple). Unusually for an assembly hall, it was a mutual aid society open to any Chinese trader or seaman, regardless of dialect or region of origin. The assembly hall would help shipwrecked or ill sailors and also performed the burial rites of merchants with no relatives in Hoi An. Built in 1773 as a meeting place for all five groups (the four listed above plus Hakka) and also for those with no clan house of their own, today it accommodates a Chinese School, Truong Le Nghia, where children of the diaspora learn the language of their forebears.

The **Fukien Assembly Hall** (Phuc Kien Hoi Quan) ① *46 Tran Phu St, 1 'assembly hall' token*, was founded around 1690 and served Hoi An's largest Chinese ethnic group, those from Fukien. It is an intimate building within a large compound and is dedicated to Thien Hau, goddess of the sea and protector of sailors. She is the central figure on the main altar, clothed in gilded robes, who, together with her assistants, can hear the cries of distress of drowning sailors. Immediately on the right on entering the temple is a mural depicting Thien Hau rescuing a sinking vessel. Behind the main altar is a second sanctuary which houses the image of Van Thien whose blessings pregnant women invoke on the lives of their unborn children.

Further east, the **Hainan Assembly Hall** (Hai Nam Hoi Quan) ① *10 Tran Phu St, free*, has a more colourful history. It was founded in 1883 in memory of more than 100 sailors and passengers who were killed when three ships were plundered by an admiral in Emperor Tu Duc's navy. In his defence the admiral claimed that the victims were pirates; some sources maintain he even had the ships painted black to strengthen his case.

Exquisite wood carving is the highlight of the **Chaozhou (Trieu Chau) Assembly Hall** ① *362 Nguyen Duy Hieu St, 1 'assembly hall' token*. The altar and its panels depict images from the sea and women from the Beijing court, which were presumably intended to console homesick traders.

**Tan Ky House** ⓘ *101 Nguyen Thai Hoc St, 1 'old house' token*, dates from the late 18th century. The Tan Ky family had originally arrived in Hoi An from China 200 years earlier and the house reflects not only the prosperity the family had acquired in the intervening years but also the architecture of their Japanese and Vietnamese neighbours, whose styles had presumably influenced the aesthetic taste and appreciation of the younger family members.

At the junction of Le Loi and Phan Chu Trinh streets, the **Tran Family Temple** ⓘ *1 'old house' token*, has survived for 15 generations (although the current generation has no son, which means the lineage has been broken). The building exemplifies Hoi An's construction methods and the harmonious fusion of Chinese and Japanese styles. It is roofed with heavy yin and yang tiling, which requires strong roof beams; these are held up by a triple-beamed support in the Japanese style (also seen on the roof of the covered bridge). Some beams have Chinese-inspired ornately carved dragons. The outer doors are Japanese, the inner are Chinese. On a central altar rest small wooden boxes which contain the photograph or likeness of the deceased together with biographical details. Beyond, at the back of the house, is a small, raised Chinese herb, spice and flower garden with a row of bonsai trees. As at all Hoi An's

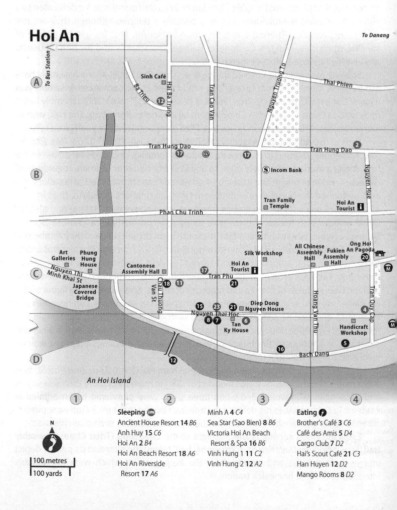

# Hoi An

To Danang

To Bus Station

(A) Sinh Café
Thai Phien
Ba Trieu
Hai Ba Trung
Tran Cao Van
Nguyen Truong To

Tran Hung Dao @ Tran Hung Dao **2**

(B) Ⓢ Incom Bank
Nguyen Hue

Tran Family Temple
Hoi An Tourist ℹ

Phan Chu Trinh

Le Loi

Art Galleries
Phung Hung House
Silk Workshop
All Chinese Assembly Hall
Fukien Assembly Hall
Ong Hoi An Pagoda **20**

Nguyen Thi Minh Khai St
Cantonese Assembly Hall
Hoi An Tourist ℹ

(C) Japanese Covered Bridge
Chau Thuong Van St
**18** **11**
Tran Phu
**17** **21**

**15** **23** **21**
Diep Dong Nguyen House
Nguyen Thai Hoc
**8** **7**
Tan Ky House
**6**
Hoang Van Thu
Tran Quy Cap
Handicraft Workshop
**5**
Ⓜ

(D) **16**
Bach Dang
**12**

*An Hoi Island*

(1)   (2)   (3)   (4)

N
▲
100 metres
100 yards

family houses, guests are received warmly and courteously and served lotus tea and
dried coconut.

**Diep Dong Nguyen House** ⓘ *80 Nguyen Thai Hoc St*, with two Chinese lanterns hanging outside, was once a Chinese dispensary. The owner is friendly, hospitable and not commercially minded. He takes visitors into his house and shows them everything with pride and smiles.

Just west of the Japanese Bridge is **Phung Hung House** ⓘ *4 Nguyen Thi Minh Khai St, 1 'old house' token*. Built over 200 years ago it has been in the same family for eight generations. The house, which can be visited, is constructed of 80 columns of ironwood on marble pedestals. During the floods of 1964, Phung Hung House became home to 160 locals who camped upstairs for three days as the water rose to a height of 2.5 m.

## Ong Hoi An Pagoda and around

At the east end of Tran Phu Street, at No 24, close to the intersection with Nguyen Hue Street, is the **Ong Hoi An Pagoda** ⓘ *1 'other' token*. This temple is in fact two interlinked pagodas built back-to-back: Chua Quan Cong, and behind that Chua Quan Am. Their date of construction is not known, although both certainly existed in 1653. In 1824 Emperor Minh Mang made a donation of 300 luong (1 luong being equivalent to 1½ oz of silver) for the support of the pagodas. They are dedicated to Quan Cong and Quan Am (see page 91) respectively.

Virtually opposite the Ong Hoi An Pagoda is **Hoi An Market** (Cho Hoi An). The market extends down to the river and then along the river road (Bach Dang Street, see page 139). At the Tran Phu Street end it is a covered market selling mostly dry goods. Numerous cloth merchants and seamstresses will produce made-to-measure shirts in a few hours but not all to the same standard. On the riverside is the local **fish market**, which comes alive at 0500-0600 as boats arrive with the night's catch.

## Cua Dai Beach

ⓘ *4 km east of Hoi An. You must leave your bicycle (5000d) or moto (1000d) just before Cua Dai beach in a car park.*

A very white sand beach with a few areas of shelter, Cua Dai Beach is a pleasant 20-minute bicycle ride or one-hour walk from Hoi An. Head east down Tran Hung Dao Street or, for a quieter route, set off down Nguyen Duy Hieu Street, which peters out into a walking and cycling path. This is a lovely route past paddy fields and ponds; nothing is signed but those with a good sense of direction will make their way back to the main road a kilometre or so before Cua Dai and those with a poor sense of direction can come to no harm. Behind the beach are a handful of hotels where food and refreshments can be bought.

Ly Thuong Kiet

Ngo Gia Tu

Cua Dai

Hoi An

Cyclos
Taxis
Shuttle Bus

Pham Hong Thai

Hoi An Tourist

Chaozhou Assembly Hall

Nguyen Duy Hieu

Hainan Assembly Hall ⓮

Hoang Dieu

Cloth Market

Phan Boi Chau ⓯

⓭ French Houses

Fish Market Ⓜ

To Cua Dai Beach & ⓭⓱⓰⓱⓲

To Cua Dai Beach (cycle route)

⑧

Cam Nam Bridge

Thu Bon River

Cam Nam Island

⑤ ⑥

Nhu Y **14** C5
Tam Tam Café **15** C2
Thanh **16** D3
Vinh Hung **18** C2
Yellow River **20** C4

**Bars & clubs** 🎵
Champa **6** D3
Sa Long **23** C2
Treat's **17** B2, B3, C2

# Danang 🚫🕖⚠🚉🛈 ›› pp146-151. Colour map 3, B5.

Danang, Vietnam's third-largest port and a trading centre of growing importance, is situated on a peninsula of land at the point where the Han River flows into the South China Sea. It was first known as Cua Han (Mouth of the Han River) and renamed Tourane (a rough transliteration of Cua Han) by the French. It later acquired the title, Thai Phien, and finally Danang. An important port from French times, Danang gained world renown when two US Marine battalions landed here in March 1965 to secure the airfield. They were the first of a great many more US military personnel who would land on the beaches and airfields of South Vietnam.

## Ins and outs
**Getting there** Flights from Bangkok, Hanoi, Ho Chi Minh City, Buon Ma Thuot, Dalat, Pleiku and Nha Trang arrive at Danang airport on the edge of the city; a taxi into town costs US$3 and takes five to 10 minutes. Danang is on the north-south railway line linking Hanoi and Ho Chi Minh City. Regular bus and minibus connections link Danang with all major cities in the south as far as Ho Chi Minh City, and in the north as far as Hanoi. There are also daily buses from Danang to the Lao town of Savannakhet on the Mekong via the border at Lao Bao (see page 131). Visas are available from the Lao consulate in Danang. ›› *For further information, see Transport, page 151.*

**Getting around** Danang is a sizeable town, rather too large to explore on foot, but there is abundant public transport, including cyclos, taxis and *Honda ôm*. Bicycles and motorbikes are available for hire from most hotels and guesthouses.

**Tourist information** An Phu Tourist ⓘ *20 Dong Da St, T0511-3818366,* can help with information as can tour operators.

## Museum of Champa Sculpture
ⓘ *Intersection of Trung Nu Vuong and Bach Dang streets, daily 0700-1700; 30,000d. The museum booklet (US$9) has been written as an art history, not as a guide to the collection, and is of little help. However, there are now books on Champa art which extensively catalogue the exhibits, US$8. Labels are in English.*

The museum (Bao Tang Dieu Khac Champa Da Nang) contains the largest display of Cham art anywhere in the world and testifies to a lively, creative and long-lasting civilization. Each room is dedicated to work from a different part of the Champa kingdom and, since different parts of Champa flowered artistically at different times from the fourth to the 14th centuries, the rooms reveal the evolution of Cham art and the prevailing outside influences, from Cambodia to Java.

Many pieces from **My Son** (page 145) illustrate the Hindu trinity: Brahma the Creator, Vishnu the Preserver and Siva the Destroyer. An altar is inscribed with scenes from the wedding story of Sita and Rama, taken from the *Ramayana*, the Hindu epic. Ganesh, the elephant-headed son of Siva, was a much-loved god and is also well represented here.

At the end of the ninth century **Dong Duong** replaced My Son as the centre of Cham art. At this time Buddhism became the dominant religion of court, although it never fully replaced Hinduism. The Dong Duong room is illustrated with scenes from the life of Buddha. Faces from this period become less stylistic and more human and the bodies of the figures are more graceful and flowing.

The subsequent period of Cham art is known as the late **Tra Kieu** style. In this section there are *apsaras* (celestial dancing maidens), whose fluid and animated forms are exquisitely captured in stone. Thereafter Cham sculpture went into artistic decline.

The **Thap Mam** style (late 11th to early 14th century) sees a range of mythical beasts whose range and style is unknown elsewhere in Southeast Asia. Also in this

room is a pedestal surrounded by 28 breast motifs. It is believed they represent
Uroha, the mythical mother of the Indrapura nation (incorporating My Son, Tra Kieu,
Dong Duong), but the meaning of the pedestal and others like it is unknown.

## China Beach (My Khe Beach)

ⓘ *With the opening of the new River Han Bridge, My Khe Beach is just a short ride from the centre of Danang by bicycle or motorbike (15-20 mins). Turn right just after the bridge, then take the first big turning on the left into Nguyen Cong Tru St; the beach is right at the end.*

Despite being only 20 minutes from Danang centre, **China Beach** is an 'undiscovered' and undeveloped asset, with the potential to transform Danang into the Río de Janeiro of Asia. It has miles and miles of fine white sand, clean water and a glorious setting: the hills of Monkey Mountain to the north and the Marble Mountains clearly visible to the south. There is a merciful absence of vendors, no litter and a number of excellent seafood restaurants. At times, though, there is a dangerous cross-current and undertow.

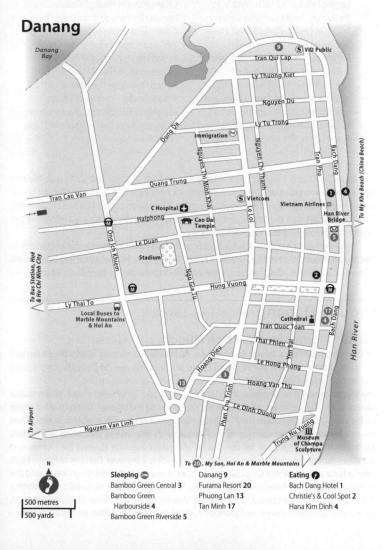

# Danang

**Sleeping** 😴
Bamboo Green Central **3**
Bamboo Green
  Harbourside **4**
Bamboo Green Riverside **5**
Danang **9**
Furama Resort **20**
Phuong Lan **13**
Tan Minh **17**

**Eating** 🍴
Bach Dang Hotel **1**
Christie's & Cool Spot **2**
Hana Kim Dinh **4**

500 metres
500 yards

*Vietnam* Central Vietnam Hoi An, Danang & around

## ⋮ Kingdom of Champa

The powerful kingdom of Champa was one of the most glorious in ancient Southeast Asia. Chinese texts suggest that in AD 192 a group of tribes, probably of Indonesian descent, formed a union known as Lin-Yi, later to become Champa. The first Champa capital, Tra Kieu (fourth to 10th centuries), was about 30 km from Danang, but the kingdom's territories extended far afield and other major sites included Dong Duong (eighth to 10th centuries), Po Nagar, Thap Mam and Cha Ban. Tra Kieu, My Son (p145) and Dong Duong were the three most important centres of the kingdom.

The polytheistic religion of Champa was a fusion of Buddhism, Sivaism, local elements and, later, Islam, and was expressed in an abundance of religious (and secular) sculptures and monuments. The kingdom reached its apogee in the 10th and 11th centuries but, unlike the Khmers, Champa never had the opportunity to create a capital city matching the magnificence of Angkor. For long periods the Cham were compelled to pay tribute to the Chinese and, after that, they were dominated in turn by the Javanese, Annamese (the Vietnamese) and then the Khmers. The Cham kingdom was finally eradicated in 1471, although there are still an estimated 90,000 Cham living in central Vietnam (mostly Brahmanists and Muslims). Given this turbulent history, it is perhaps surprising that the Cham found any opportunity for artistic endeavours. It should perhaps be added that since the demise of the kingdom, the number of Cham sculptures has increased enormously as forgers have carved more of these beautiful images.

As an R&R retreat during the Vietnam War, the white sand and surf made My Khe popular with American soldiers, who named it China Beach. It became a fabled resort celebrated in rock songs. Since 1975, however, it has been called T20 Beach, after the military code used by the North Vietnamese Army. Today the whole area including the hotels still belongs to the Vietnamese Army.

Two kilometres south of China Beach and eight km from the centre of Danang is **Bac My An Beach**, next to the **Furama Resort**. This is a clean and attractive beach with some seafood stalls. Most visitors here go direct to the resort from the airport.

# Around Danang  → *Colour map 3, B5 and B6.*

## Marble Mountains (Nui Non Nuoc) → *Colour map 3, B6.*
ⓘ *12 km from Danang, 20 km from Hoi An. Many visitors stop off at Marble Mountain en route to Hoi An; catch the red-and-white bus towards Hoi An from Danang's local bus station (opposite 350 Hung Vuong St), 25 mins, or take a xe ôm.*

The Marble Mountains overlook the city of Danang and its airfield, about 12 km to the west of town. The name was given to these five peaks by the Nguyen Emperor Minh Mang on his visit in 1825, although they are in fact limestone crags with marble outcrops. They are also known as the mountains of the five elements (fire, water, soil, wood and metal). An important religious spot for the Cham, the peaks became havens for Communist guerrillas during the war, owing to their commanding view over Danang airbase. From here, a force with sufficient firepower could control much of what went on below, and the guerrillas harried the Americans incessantly. The views from the mountain, overlooking Danang Bay, are impressive. On the Marble Mountains are a number of important sites, often associated with caves and grottoes formed by chemical action on the limestone.

Of the mountains, the most visited is **Thuy Son**. There are several grottos and cave pagodas in the mountain, which are marked by steps cut into the rock. The **Tam Thai Pagoda**, reached by a staircase cut into the mountain, is on the site of a much older Cham place of worship. Constructed in 1825 by Minh Mang, and subsequently rebuilt, the central statue is of the Buddha Sakyamuni (the historic Buddha) flanked by the Bodhisattva Quan Am (a future Buddha and the Goddess of Mercy, see page 91) and a statue of Van Thu (symbolizing wisdom). At the rear of the grotto is another cave, the **Huyen Khong Cave**. Originally a place of animist worship, it later became a site for Buddhist pilgrimage. The entrance is protected by four door guardians. The high ceiling of the cave is pierced by five holes through which the sun filters and, in the hour before midday, illuminates the central statue of the Buddha Sakyamuni. In the cave are various natural rock formations which, according to the young cave guides look like storks, elephants, an arm, a fish and a face.

A few hundred metres to the south on the right is a track leading to **Chua Quan The Am**, which has its own grotto, complete with stalactites, stalagmites and pillars.

## My Son → *Colour map 3, B5.*

ⓘ *60 km south of Danang via Tra Kieu or 45 km west of Hoi An via Nam Phuoc. From the ticket office (6 km beyond the village of Kiem Lam) it's a 2 km jeep ride (included in the ticket price) and a short walk to My Son. Daily 0630-1630. 60,000d. Tour operators in Hoi An and Danang offer tours. It is not clear how thoroughly the area has been de-mined so do not stray too far from the road and path. Take a hat, sun cream and water.*

My Son, with its detailed carved masonry, was the spiritual centre of the Cham empire (see page 144). Declared a World Heritage Site by UNESCO in 1999, it is one of Vietnam's most ancient monuments. Weather, jungle and years of strife have wrought their worst on My Son. But, arguably, the jungle under which My Son remained hidden to the outside world provided it with its best protection, for more has been destroyed in the past 40 years than the previous 400. Today, far from anywhere, My Son is a tranquil archaeological treasure. Not many visitors have time to make an excursion to see it which makes it all the more appealing to those that do. The thin red bricks of the towers and temples have been beautifully carved and the craftsmanship of many centuries still remains abundantly visible today. The trees and creepers have been pushed back but My Son remains cloaked in green; shoots and saplings sprout up everywhere and one senses that were its custodians to turn their backs for even a short time My Son would be quickly reclaimed by nature.

My Son consists of more than 70 monuments spread over a large area. It was rediscovered and investigated by French archaeologists of the École Française d'Extrême-Orient in 1898. Their excavations revealed a site that had been settled from the early eighth to the 15th centuries, the longest uninterrupted period of development of any monument in Southeast Asia. Its maximum population is unknown but it seems to have had a holy or spiritual function rather than being the seat of power and was, very probably, a burial place of its god kings. Unfortunately, My Son was a Viet Cong field headquarters, located within one of the US 'free fire' zones during the Vietnam War. The finest sanctuary in the complex was demolished by US sappers and temple groups A, E and H were badly damaged. Groups B and C have largely retained their temples but many statues, altars and linga have been removed to the Museum of Champa Sculpture in Danang (page 142). Currently Group C is being restored by UNESCO; the F building is covered in cobwebs and propped up by scaffolding.

It is important to see My Son in the broader context of Indian influence on Southeast Asia, not just in terms of architecture but also in terms of spiritual and political development around the region. Falling as it did so strongly under Chinese influence, it is all the more remarkable to find such compelling evidence of Indian culture and iconography in Vietnam. Indeed this was one of the criteria cited by UNESCO as justification for My Son's World Heritage listing.

Angkor in Cambodia, with which My Son is broadly contemporaneous, is the most famous example of a temple complex founded by a Hindu or Sivaist god king (*deva-raja*). The Hindu cult of *deva-raja* was developed by the kings of Angkor and later employed by Cham kings to bolster their authority but, because Cham kings were far less wealthy and powerful than the god kings of Angkor, the monuments are correspondingly smaller and more personal. One of the great joys of Cham sculpture and building is its unique feel, its graceful lines and unmistakable form.

The characteristic Cham architectural structure is the tower, built to reflect the divinity of the king: tall and rectangular, with four porticoes, each of which is 'blind' except for that on the west face. Orginally built of wood (not surprisingly, none remains), they were later made of brick, of which the earliest (seventh century) are located at My Son. The bricks are exactly laid and held together with a form of vegetable cement, probably the resin of the day tree. Sandstone is sometimes used for plinths and lintels but, overwhelmingly, brick is the medium of construction. It is thought that on completion, each tower was surrounded by wood and fired over several days in what amounted to a vast outdoor kiln. The red bricks at My Son have worn amazingly well and are intricately carved with Hindu, Sivaist and Buddhist images and ornaments. Sivaist influence at My Son is unmissable, with Siva often represented, as in other Cham relics thoughout Vietnam, by the linga or phallus.

## ● Sleeping

**Hoi An** *p137, map p140*
**LL-L Victoria Hoi An Beach Resort &
Spa**, Cua Dai Beach, T0510-927040,
www.victoriahotels-asia.com. A charming
and attractive resort right on the beach. It
has 105 beautifully furnished rooms facing
the sea or the river either in Vietnamese,
French or Japanese style. There is a large
pool, the **L'Annam Restaurant** (which serves
very tasty but expensive dishes), a couple of
bars, a kids' club, BBQ beach parties, live
music and dancing, a host of watersports
and all with charming service. Free shuttle
bus runs between the hotel and the town.
**L Hoi An Beach Resort**, 1 Cua Dai Beach Rd,
Cua Dai Beach, T0510-927011, www.hoian
tourist.com. A quiet, attractively designed
resort with its own stretch of private beach
just across the road. Its rooms are simply
designed and spacious with large
bathrooms; some enjoy little terraces or
balconies overlooking the river. The large
restaurant also overlooks the river, and the
pool, which is close to the restaurant, is
particularly inviting. A good choice for some
peace and quiet but with a free shuttle service
to town. **Rainbow Divers**, T09-4224102
(mob), www.divevietnam.com, is on site.
**L Hoi An Riverside Resort**, 175 Cua Dai Rd,
Cua Dai Beach, T0510-864800,
www.hoianriverresort.com  A short, 5 min
cycle ride from the beach and a 15-min

pedal from town, this Khai Silk hotel faces
the Thu Bon River with lovely views. There is
a dark, slate-lined pool surrounded by white
umbrellas and white seats, set in landscaped
gardens with hammocks. Standard rooms
have balconies with beautifully made beds,
decorated in tiny red and pink flowers and
plenty of cushions in wine, white and beige.
All rooms, with gorgeous ethnic drapes on
the walls, have showers. The **Song Do**
restaurant is the best place to be at sunset as
it has uninterrupted views of the river.
**A Ancient House Resort**, 377 Cua Dai St,
T0510-923377, www.ancienthouse
resort.com. This is a beautiful, small hotel
set around a small garden with a series of
landscaped ponds and potted frangipani. All
the 42 rooms are decorated in virginal white.
There is a pool, shop, billiards, free shuttle to
town and beach, free bicycle service and a
restaurant. Behind the hotel is a traditional
Ancient House. Below ground art work and
an unusual linga sculpture are displayed.
Breakfast is included.
**A Hoi An**, 10 Tran Hung Dao St,
T0510-861445, www.hoiantourist.com. An
attractive colonial building set well back
from the road in spacious grounds with
attractively furnished, comfortable rooms
with all mod cons and en suite bathrooms
with bathtubs. The pool is especially inviting
and the hotel has a new Zen spa and beauty

salon. Discounts are offered in Hoi An's summer low season. Staff are welcoming and there are a host of activities from Chinese lantern making to trips to local villages, see page 150.

**A Vinh Hung 1**, 143 Tran Phu St, T0510-861621, www.vinhhungresort.com. An attractive old building with a splendid and ornate reception room, decorated with dark wood in Chinese style. It is halving its room capacity and upgrading the 6 remaining.

**B Vinh Hung 2**, Ba Trieu St, T0510-863717, www.vinhhungresort.com. A sister hotel with 40 rooms, a short walk away, built in traditional style, with a pool and all mod cons but lacking the atmosphere of the original.

**B-D Sea Star (Sao Bien)**, 489 Cua Dai St, on the road to the beach, T0510-861589. A privately run hotel. Rooms with a/c and hot water. Travel services, bicycle, motor bike and car hire on offer. Efficient and popular but possibly a little complacent.

**C Anh Huy Hotel**, 30 Phan Boi Chau St, T0510-862116, www.anhuyhotel.com. A sweet little hotel, opposite **Brother's Café**, with courtyards that create a breeze and shutters that keep the noise out. Spacious rooms are beautifully decorated in Japanese style and the staff are very friendly. Breakfast and free internet is included.

**D-E Minh A**, 2 Nguyen Thai Hoc St, T0510-861368. This is a very special little place. An old family house with just 5 guestrooms that are all different. Guests are made to feel part of the family. Communal bathrooms have hot water and fan. Right next to the market in a busy part of town. Very welcoming, recommended.

**Danang** *p142, map p143*

**LL-L Furama Resort**, 68 Ho Xuan Huong St, Bac My An Beach, 8 km from Danang, T0511-3847888, www.furamavietnam.com. 198 rooms and suites beautifully designed and furnished. One of the most attractive aspects of Furama is its fabulously opulent foyer with smart seating and warm lighting. It has 2 pools, 1 of which is an infinity pool

overlooking the private beach. All its facilities are first class. Watersports facilities, diving, mountain biking, tennis and a health centre offering a number of massages and treatments. Operates a free and very useful shuttle to and from the town, Marble Mountains and Hoi An. Surprisingly the price does not include breakfast.

**A-B Bamboo Green**, there are 3 hotels in this chain: **Bamboo Green Central**, 158 Phan Chu Trinh St, T0511-3822996, **Bamboo Green Harbourside** (a somewhat tenuous claim), 177 Tran Phu St, T0511-3822722; and **Bamboo Green Riverside**, 68 Bach Dang St, T0511-3832591. All share the bamboogreen@dng.vnn.vn email address. All are well-run, well-equipped, comfortable, business-type hotels with efficient staff and in central locations offering excellent value for money. **Riverside** has a particularly attractive outlook.

**B Danang**, 50 Bach Dong St, T0511-3823649, bdhotel@dng.vnn.vn. Large and centrally located hotel. Rooms rather cramped for the price; some with river views; cheaper rooms in an older building at the back. All rooms have satellite TV and bathtubs. There's quite a good restaurant on site.

**C-D Phuong Lan**, 178 Hoang Dieu St, T0511-3820373. Rooms with a/c, satellite TV, and hot water. It's good value (after some bargaining), free airport pick-up and motorbikes for rent.

**C-D Tan Minh**, 142 Bach Dang St, T0511-3827456. On the riverfront, a small, well-kept hotel, friendly staff speak good English.

**China Beach (My Khe)** *p143*

**A-B Tourane**, My Khe Beach, T0511-3932666, touranehotel@dng.vnn.vn. A 'esort-type' hotel with accommodation in decent villa-type blocks. 30 rooms all with a/c and hot water.

**B-D My Khe Beach**, 241 Nguyen Van Thoai St, My Khe Beach, T0511-3836125. Accommodation here is in rather austere-looking blocks set among the sea pines. All with a/c and hot water, price includes breakfast. **Conroy's Bar** is on the ground floor of the block nearest the sea.

*For an explanation of sleeping and eating price codes used in this guide, see inside the front cover. Other relevant information is found in Essentials, see pages 29-32.*

## ❼ Eating

**Hoi An** *p137, map p140*

A Hoi An speciality is *cao lau*, a noodle soup with slices of pork and croutons, traditionally made with water from one particular well. The quality of food in Hoi An, especially the fish, is outstanding and the value for money is not matched by any other town in Vietnam. Bach Dang St is particularly pleasant in the evening, when tables and chairs are set up almost the whole way along the river.

**♥♥♥-♥♥ Brother's Café**, 27 Phan Boi Chau St, T0510-914150, www.brothercafehoian. com.vn. It is excellent news that these little cloistered French houses should have been put to such good use and renovated in such exquisite taste. The house and garden leading down to the river are beautifully restored. The menu is strong on Vietnamese specialities, especially seafood, and at US$12 the daily set menu still offers good value in such charming surroundings.

**♥♥-♥ Café des Amis**, 52 Bach Dang St, near the river, T0510-861616. The set menu of fish/seafood or vegetarian dishes changes daily and is widely acclaimed and excellent value. The owner, Mr Nguyen Manh Kim, spends several months a year cooking in Europe. Highly recommended.

**♥♥-♥ Mango Rooms**, 111 Nguyen Thai Hoc St, T0510-910839, www.mangorooms.com. With its bright, bold colours, superlative food and comfy seating out back overlooking the river, the Mango Rooms is a very welcome addition to Hoi An. The superior cooking makes a repeat visit a must. Enjoy slices of baguette layered with shrimp mousse served with a 'delectable' mango coconut curry or the delicious ginger and garlic-marinated shrimps wrapped in tender slices of beef and pan-fried with wild spicy butter and soy-garlic sauce; the seared tuna steak with mango salsa is outstanding. Complimentary tapas-style offerings such as tapioca crisps are a welcome touch. Highly recommended.

**♥♥ Nhu Y** (aka Mermaid), 2 Tran Phu St, T0510-861527, www.hoianhospitality.com. Miss Vy turns out all the local specialities as well as some of her own. The 5-course set dinner is particularly recommended.

**♥♥ Tam Tam Café**, 110 Nguyen Thai Hoc St, T0510-862212, tamtamha@dng.vnn.vn. This is a great little café in a renovated tea house. Cocktails, draft beer, music, book exchange, plus attached restaurant serving French and Italian cuisine. A relaxing place for a drink, espresso or meal.

**♥♥ Thanh**, 76 Bach Dang St, T0510-861366. A charming old house overlooking the river, recognizable by its Chinese style and flowering *hoa cat dang* creepers; the shrimp is excellent. Friendly service.

**♥♥ Vinh Hung**, 147B Tran Phu St, T0510-862203 (See Sleeping). Another attractive building with Chinese lanterns and traditional furniture. An excellent range of seafood dishes and Vietnamese specials at fair prices.

**♥ Cargo Club**, 107-109 Nguyen Thai Hoc St, T0510-910489. This extremely popular venue serves up filling Vietnamese and Western fodder including club sandwiches, Vietnamese salads and overpriced fajitas. The service is quicker downstairs than up on the balcony overlooking the river. The patisserie, groaning with cakes and chocolate is the best thing about this place.

**♥ Hai's Scout Café**, 111 Tan Phu St/98 Nguyen Thai Hoc St, T0510-863210, www.visit hoian.com. The central area of this back-to-back café has a photographic exhibition of the WWF's invaluable work in the threatened environment around Hoi An. It offers good food in a relaxing courtyard or attractive café setting. Cookery courses can be arranged.

**♥ Han Huyen**. This former floating restaurant has been moved to 35 Nguyen Phuc Chu St, across the river to make way for a bridge construction, T510-861462. Serves excellent seafood.

**♥ Yellow River**, 38 Tran Phu St, T0510-861053. Good Hoi An family eatery, the fried wanton is recommended. French is spoken.

**Danang** *p142, map p143*

Seafood is good here and Danang has its own beers, Da Nang 'Export' and Song Han. There are a number of cafés and restaurants along Bach Dang St, overlooking the river.

**♥♥ Hana Kim Dinh**, 7 Bach Dang St. This is a restaurant on a small pier shaped like a boat, opposite the **Bach Dang Hotel**. Western and Vietnamese menus; mainly seafood served.

**♥♥-♥ Christie's** and **Cool Spot**, 112 Tran Phu St, T0511-824040, ccdng@dng.vnn.vn. The old premises were demolished in the construction of the River Han Bridge, the new location is 1 block in from the river and has merged forces

with the **Cool Spot** bar. Frequented by expats from Danang and outlying provinces, it has a small bar downstairs and a restaurant upstairs. Cold beer, Western and Japanese food and tasty home-made pizzas.
❢ **Bach Dang Hotel**, 50 Bach Dang St. Informal restaurant, with glimpses of river and decent food.

### China Beach (My Khe) *p143*
The many restaurants here are virtually indistinguishable and it is impossible to single any one out for special mention. They all have excellent fish, prawn, crab, clams and cuttlefish, grilled, fried or steamed. 2 people can eat well for US$7-10 including local beers.

## ❶ Bars and clubs

**Hoi An** *p137, map p140*
**Champa**, 75 Nguyen Thai Hoc St, T0510-861159. This is a rambling place with pool tables and an upstairs cultural show in the evenings. Downstairs hits from the 1960s and 1970s predominate.
**Sa Long**, 102 Nguyen Thai Hoc St, T0913-684401, daily 1100-late. Formerly the **Lounge Bar**, this is one of the more popular places in town to hang at the bar or blend into the sofas. The wicked mojitos just go down too easily.
**Tam Tam Café**, 110 Nguyen Thai Hoc St. Mainly a café/restaurant but also has a good bar and a pool table. An attractive place to sit.
**Treat's**, 158 Tran Phu St, T0510-861125, open till late. One of Hoi An's few bars and a very well-run one. 2 pool tables, airy, attractive style: popular happy hour and attractive balcony. Also at 69 and 93 Tran Hung Dao St which are very popular at night.

## ❷ Entertainment

**Hoi An** *p137, map p140*
**Hoi An Handicraft Workshop**, 9 Ngyuen Thai Hoc St, T0510-910216, www.hoian handicraft.com. Traditional music performances at 1015 and 1515 Tue-Sun, with the Vietnamese monochord and dancers. At the back there is a potter's wheel, straw mat making, embroiderers, conical hat makers, wood carvers and iron ornament makers.

## ❸ Shopping

**Hoi An** *p137, map p140*
Hoi An is a shopper's paradise. Tran Phu and Le Loi are the main shopping streets. 2 items stand out, paintings and clothes.

### Accessories and handicrafts
Hoi An is the place to buy handbags and purses and attractive Chinese silk lanterns, indeed anything that can be made from silk, including scarves and shoes. The shop at **41 Le Loi Street** is a silk workshop where the whole process from silkworm to woven fabric can be seen and fabrics purchased, daily 0745-2200. There is also a lot of chinaware available, mostly modern, some reproduction and a few antiques.
**53a Le Loi**, 53a Le Loi, T091-4097344 (mob). A handbag and shoe shop unit with lots of choice. Have your bag made here but definitely not your shoes.
**Reaching Out, Hoa-nhap Handicrafts**, 103 Nguyen Thai Hoc, T0510-910168, Tue-Sun 0730-1930. Fair trade shop selling arts and crafts, cards and notebooks, textiles and silk sleeping bags all made by disabled artisans living in Hoi An. Profits support the disabled community. There is usually someone at work in the shop so you can see what they are getting up to.

### Art
Vietnamese artists have been inspired by Hoi An's old buildings and a Hoi An school of art has developed. Countless galleries sell original works of art but the more serious galleries are to be found in a cluster on Nguyen Thi Minh Khai St, west of the Japanese Bridge.

### Tailors
Hoi An is famed for its tailors – there are now reckoned to be more than 140 in town – who will knock up silk or cotton clothing in 24 hrs. The quality of the stitching varies from shop to shop, so see some samples first, and the range of fabrics is limited, so many people bring their own. A man's suit can cost anywhere from US$30-295 and a woman's from US$50-395, depending on fabric and quality of workmanship. Note that Thai silk costs more than Vietnamese silk and Hoi An silk is quite coarse.

Visitors talk of the rapid speed at which shops can produce the goods but bear in mind that, if every visitor to Hoi An wants something made in 12-24 hrs, this puts enormous strain on staff. Quite apart from the workers having to stay up all night, the quality of the finished garment could suffer. So, if you are in Hoi An for a few days, do your clothes shopping on the first day to give you time to accommodate second or third fittings which may be necessary.

**Lan Ha**, 1A Hai Ba Trung St, T0510-910706, leco50@hotmail.com, daily 0900-2200. This shop unit is recommended because of the speed of service, the quality of the goods, the excellent prices and the fact that, unlike many other tailors in town, second, third or even fourth fittings are usually not required.

**Yaly**, 47 Nguyen Thai Hoc St, T0510-910474, yalyshop@dng.vnn.vn, daily 0700-2030. Professional staff, very good, quality results across a range of clothing, including shoes, in a lovely old building. Women's blouses are around US$20 and dresses US$30-80. There are now 4 branches of **Yaly** in town but this is the original.

## ▲▲ Activities and tours

### Hoi An p137, map p140
### Boat rides
Boat rides are available on the Thu Bon River. Local boatwomen charge US$1 or so per hour – a tranquil and relaxed way of spending the early evening.

### Cookery classes
**Red Bridge Cooking School**, run out of the Hai Scout Café, 98 Nguyen Thai Hoc St, T0510-863210. Visit the market to be shown local produce, then take a 20-min boat ride to the cooking school where you're shown the herb garden. Next you watch a demonstration by chefs on how to make a number of dishes such as warm squid salad served in half a pineapple and grilled aubergine stuffed with vegetables. Move inside and you get to make your own fresh spring rolls and learn Vietnamese food carving, which is a lot harder than it looks. US$15. (Red Bridge Cooking School, Thon 4, Cam Thanh, T0510-933222, www.visithoian.com. Operates all year, 0815-1330. The restaurant is open to the public Fri, Sat, Sun).

### Tour operators
**An Phu Tourist**, 141 Tran Phu St, T0510-861447, www.anphutouristhoian.com. Several offices in town, offering a wide range of tour services and reliable Open Tour Buses.
**Hoi An Travel**, Hotel Hoi An, 6 Tran Hung Dao St, and at Hoi An Beach Resort, T0510-910400, www.hoiantravel.com, 0630-2200. Offers a variety of tours including some unusual ones: a visit to a vegetable village, fishing at Thanh Ha pottery village, and visiting the Cham Islands. You can also arrange trips to Savannakhet and Pakse, Laos and from Bangkok to Hoi An, Danang and Hué and returning to Laos and Thailand.
**Trekking Company-Mr Tung**, 1 Hai Ba Trung, T0510-14218, trekkingtravel_hoian@yahoo.com.vn. This small operation but does a good job booking bus tickets and arranging tours to My Son, etc. Tours to My Son US$2 by bus, US$3 by boat; taxi and minivan to Da Nang US$8-12; bus to Hanoi US$14; to Nha Trang US$16. Recommended.
**Sinh Café**, 18B Hai Ba Trung St, T0510-863948, www.sinhcafevn.com, daily 0630-2200. Branch of the ubiquitous chain offering tours, transport, reservations and internet use. Its Open Tour bus departs and arrives at the Phuong Nam Hotel, to the north of the office, off Hai Ba Trung St. My Son tour, US$3; with return boat trip via Kim Bong carpentry village, US$5.
**Son My Son Tours**, 17/2 Tran Hung Dao St, T0510-861121, mysontour@dng.vnn.vn. Cheap minibus tickets to Hué, Nha Trang and HCMC plus car and motorbike hire and useful advice.

### Danang p142, map p143
### Therapies
**Tamarind Spa, Victoria Hoi An Beach Resort & Spa**, Cua Dai Beach, T0510-927040, www.victoriahotels-asia.com, 0900-2100. A lovely, friendly spa centre with a wide range of treatments from body wraps to facials. The foot reflexology treatment is especially good.

## ⊖ Transport

### Hoi An p137, map p140
### Bicycle and motorbike
Hotels have 2WD and 4WD vehicles for hire. Bicycle hire, 10,000d per day, motorbike US$4-8 per day.

## Bus
The bus station is about 1 km west of the centre of town on Ly Thuong Kiet St. There are regular connections from **Danang**'s local bus station, from 0530 until 1800, 1 hr, 20,000d. Open Tour Buses go north to **Hanoi** and South to **HCMC**. Book through local tour operators (see above).

### Danang p142, map p143
### Air
The airport is 2.5 km southwest of the city. There are daily connections with **Bangkok, Phnom Penh, Siem Reap, Singapore, Hong Kong, Paris, Tokyo, Vientiane, Nha Trang, Hanoi, HCMC** and **Pleiku**. There are plans to expand the airport from 2008 to cater for 4 million passengers a year. A taxi from Danang airport to Hoi An will cost about US$15 or less (bargain hard), 40 mins.

**Airline offices** Vietnam Airlines Booking Office, 35 Tran Phu St, T0511-3821130. **Pacific Airlines**, 35 Nguyen Van Linh St, Hai Chau District, T0511-3583583.

### Bicycle
Bicycles are available from many hotels. Some cafés and hotels also rent motor-bikes for US$5-7 per day.

### Taxi
Airport Taxi, T0511-3825555. **Dana Taxi**, T0511-3815815.

## Train
Danang Railway Station, 122 Haiphong St, 2 km west of town, T0511-3750666. There are express trains to and from **Hanoi**, **HCMC** and **Hué**.

## ● Directory

**Hoi An** *p137, map p140*
**Banks** Hoi An Bank, 4 Hoang Dieu St. Accepts most major currencies, US dollar withdrawal from credit/debit card, no commission for cashing Amex TCs, daily 0730-1900. Hoi An Incombank, 9 Le Loi St, offers identical services and an ATM.
**Medical Services** 4 Tran Hung Dao St, T0510-864566, daily 0700-2200. Tram y Te Pharmacy, 72 Nguyen Thai Hoc St.
**Internet** Widely available in cafés and hotels. One internet café is **Nguyen Tan Hieu**, 89 Tran Hung Dao St. **Post office** 5 Tran Hung Dao St, T0510-861480. Has Poste Restante, international telephone, fax service and ATM.

**Danang** *p142, map p143*
**Banks** VID Public Bank, 2 Tran Phu St. Vietcombank, 104 Le Loi St. Will change most major currencies, cash and TCs.
**Medical services** C Hospital, 74 Haiphong St, T0511-3821480. **Internet** There are numerous internet cafés all over town.
**Post office** 60 Bach Dang St, corner of Bach Dang and Le Duan streets. Telex, fax and telephone facilities.

# Central Highlands and the coast

*The Central Highlands consist of the Truong Son Mountain Range and its immediate environs. The mountain range is commonly referred to as the backbone of Vietnam and borders Laos and Cambodia to the west. The highlands provide flowers and vegetables to the southern lowlands and have several tea and coffee plantations that supply the whole of Vietnam. Tourism is an additional source of revenue. Most highlanders belong to one of 26 indigenous groups and, beyond the main towns of Dalat, Buon Ma Thuot, Play Ku (Pleiku) and Kontum, their way of life remains unchanged.*

*East of the highlands, on the coast, Nha Trang is a seaside resort with diving, boat tours and spas to entice foreign visitors. Further south, Mui Ne has golden sands and the best kitesurfing in Vietnam.* ▸▸ *For Sleeping, Eating and other listings, see pages 162-168.*

**Best time to visit** In terms of climate, the best time to visit this region is from December to April. However, as there are many different indigenous groups within its borders, there are festivals in the region all year round.

## Background

The Central Highlands have long been associated with Vietnam's hilltribes. Under the French, the colonial administration deterred ethnic Vietnamese from settling here but missionaries were active among the minorities of the region, although with uneven success. Bishop Cuenot (page 158) dispatched two missionaries to Buon Ma Thuot, where they received a hostile reception from the M'nong, however in Kontum, among the Ba-na, they found more receptive souls for their evangelizing. Today many of the ethnic minorities in the Central Highlands are Roman Catholic, although some (such as the Ede) are Protestant.

At the same time French businesses were hard at work establishing plantations to supply the home market. Rubber and coffee were the staple crops. The greatest difficulty they faced was recruiting sufficient labour. Men and women of the ethnic minorities were happy in their villages drinking rice wine and cultivating their own small plots. They were poor but content and saw no reason to accept the hard labour and slave wages of the plantation owners. Norman Lewis travelled in the Central Highlands and describes the situation well in his book, *A Dragon Apparent*.

Since 1984 there has been a bit of a free-for-all and a scramble for land in the highlands. Ethnic Vietnamese have encroached on minority land and planted it with coffee, pepper and fruit trees. As an indicator of progress, Vietnam is now the second-largest producer of coffee in the world, although it produces cheaper robusta rather than arabica coffee. The way of life of the minorities is disappearing with the forests: there are no trees from which to build traditional stilt houses nor shady forests in which to live and hunt.

---

# Dalat ⊖⊘⊙⛰⊙⊙ ⟩⟩ *pp162-168. Colour map 4, B2.*

Dalat is situated on a plateau in the Central Highlands, at an altitude of almost 1500 m. The town itself, a former French hill station, is centred on a Lake – Xuan Huong – amidst rolling countryside. To the north are the five volcanic peaks of **Langbian Mountain**, rising to 2400 m. The ascent is recommended for stunning views and abundant birdlife. In the vicinity of Dalat are lakes, forests, waterfalls, and an abundance of orchids, roses and other temperate flora. Newly-weds should note that Dalat is the honeymoon capital of southern Vietnam and there is a quaint belief that unless you go on honeymoon to Dalat you are not really married at all.

## Ins and outs

**Getting there and around** There are daily direct flights to Dalat from Ho Chi Minh City and Hanoi. Open Tour Buses pass through Dalat heading to Nha Trang, Mui Ne and Ho Chi Minh City and innumerable local buses plough the inter-provincial routes between Dalat, Play Ku, Kontum, Ho Chi Minh City, Nha Trang, Buon Ma Thuot, Phan Thiet and Phan Rang. Alternatively it is possible to hire a car and driver. Taxis and *xe ôm* are available around town and the cool climate means that it is very pleasant to reach outlying attractions by bicycle. In fact a day spent travelling can be more enjoyable than the sights themselves. ⟩⟩ *For further information, see Transport, page 167.*

**Tourist information** Dalat Travel Bureau ① *www.dalattourist.com*, is the state-run travel company for Lam Dong Province. There are also a number of tour operators in town ⟩⟩ *For further information, see Activities and tours, page 166.*

# Background

Dr Alexandre Yersin, a protégé of Luis Pasteur, founded Dalat in 1893. He stumbled across Dalat as he was trying to find somewhere cool to escape from the sweltering summer heat of the coast and lowlands. The lush alpine scenery of Dalat impressed the French and it soon became the second city in the south after Saigon. In the summer months the government and bureaucrats moved lock, stock and barrel to Dalat where it was cooler. There are still plenty of original French-style villas in the town, many of which have been converted into hotels. The last Emperor of Vietnam Bao Dai also lived here.

Dalat soon took on the appearance of Paris in the mountains. A golf course was made and a luxurious hotel was built. In both the Second World War and the American War, high-ranking officials of the opposing armies would while away a pleasant couple of days playing golf against each other before having to return to the battlefields. Of all the highland cities, Dalat was the least affected by the American War. The main reason being that, at the time, the only way to Dalat was via the Prenn pass. There was a small heliport at Cam Ly and also a radio-listening station on Langbian Mountain but nothing else of note.

## Xuan Huong Lake and the centre

**Xuan Huong Lake** was created as the Grand Lake in 1919, after a small dam was constructed on the Cam Ly River, and renamed in 1954. It is a popular exercise area for the local inhabitants, many of whom walk around the lake first thing in the morning, stopping every so often to perform t'ai chi exercises. At the northeast end of the Lake is the **Dalat Flower Garden** ① *0700-1800, 8000d*. Established in 1966, it supports a modest range of temperate and tropical plants including orchids (of which Dalat is justly renowned throughout Vietnam), roses, camellias, lilies and hydrangeas.

**Dalat Cathedral** ① *Mass is held twice a day Mon-Sat 0515 and 1715 and on Sun at 0515, 0700, 0830, 1430 and 1600*, is a single-tiered cathedral, visible from the lake. It is referred to locally as the 'Chicken Cathedral' because of the chicken-shaped wind dial at the top of the turret. Construction began in 1931, although the building was not completed until the Japanese 'occupation' in the 1940s. The stained-glass windows, with their vivid colours and use of pure, clean lines, were crafted in France by Louis Balmet, the same man who made the windows in Nha Trang and Danang Cathedrals, between 1934 and 1940. Sadly, most have not survived the ravages of time. The cathedral has a good choir and attracts a large and enthusiastic congregation for mass.

At the end of Nguyen Thi Minh Khai Street, **Dalat Market (Cho Dalat)** sells an array of exotic fruits and vegetables: plums, strawberries, carrots, potatoes, loganberries, cherries, apples, onions and avocados. The forbidding appearance of the market is masked by the riot of colourful flowers also on sale, including gladioli, irises, roses, chrysanthemums and marigolds.

## Tran Hung Dao Street

Many of the large **colonial villas**, almost universally washed in pastel yellow, are 1930s and 1940s vintage. Some have curved walls, railings and are almost nautical in inspiration; others are reminiscent of houses in Provençe. Many of the larger villas can be found along **Tran Hung Dao Street**, although many have fallen into a very sorry state of repair. Perhaps the largest and most impressive house on Tran Hung Dao is the former residence of the Governor General at No.12. It occupies a magnificent position set among mountain pines, overlooking the town. The villa, now the **Hotel Dinh 2**, is 1930s in style, with large airy rooms and uncomfortable furniture.

## Summer Palace (Dinh 3)

① *Le Hong Phong St, about 2 km from the town centre, daily 0700-1700, 5000d; visitors have to wear covers on their shoes to protect the wooden floors.*

Vietnam's last emperor, Bao Dai, chose Dalat for his Summer Palace, built between 1933 and 1938 on a hill with views on every side, it is art deco in style, both inside and out, and rather modest for a palace. The stark interior contains little to indicate that this was the home of an emperor, especially since almost all of Bao Dai's personal belongings have been removed. The impressive dining room contains an etched-glass map of Vietnam, while the study has Bao Dai's desk, books, a few personal ornaments and, notably, photographs of the royal family, who were exiled permanently to France in 1954. One of the photos shows Bao Dai's son, the prince Bao Long, in full military dress uniform. He was a distinguished and gallant soldier who died during the war. Of all the members of the royal family, he is the only one regarded with respect by the government, as a good, patriotic Vietnamese who fought for his country. The emperor's bedroom, balcony and bathroom are also open to the public, as is the family drawing room. The gardens are colourful and well maintained.

## Lam Ty Ni Pagoda and around

Lam Ty Ni Pagoda, off Le Hong Phong St, is unremarkable save for the charming monk, Vien Thuc, who has lived here since 1968. He has created a garden, almost Japanese in inspiration, around the pagoda, known as the Divine Calmness Bamboo Garden. Vien Thuc is a scholar, poet, artist, philosopher, mystic, divine and entrepreneur but is best known for his paintings of which, by his own reckoning, there are more than

# Dalat

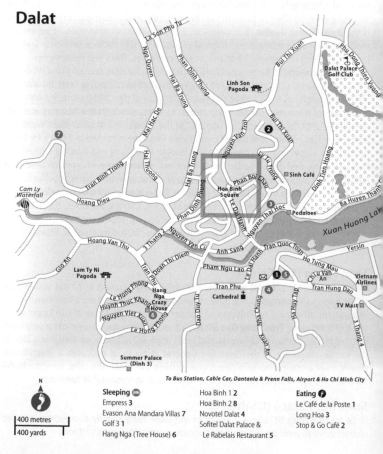

To Bus Station, Cable Car, Dantanla & Prenn Falls, Airport & Ho Chi Minh City

400 metres
400 yards

**Sleeping** 
Empress **3**
Evason Ana Mandara Villas **7**
Golf 3 **1**
Hang Nga (Tree House) **6**

Hoa Binh 1 **2**
Hoa Binh 2 **8**
Novotel Dalat **4**
Sofitel Dalat Palace &
  Le Rabelais Restaurant **5**

**Eating** 
Le Café de la Poste **1**
Long Hoa **3**
Stop & Go Café **2**

100,000. Wandering through the maze of rustic huts and shacks tacked on to the back of the temple you will see countless hanging sheets bearing his simple but distinctive calligraphy and philosophy: "Living in the present how beautiful this very moment is", "Zen painting destroys millennium sorrows", and so on. Vien Thuc's work is widely known and has been exhibited in Paris, New York and the Netherlands, as well as on the internet.

The slightly wacky theme is maintained at the nearby **Hang Nga Guest House and Art Gallery (Crazy House)** ① *3 Huynh Thuc Khang, T063-22070; art gallery 0700-1700, 8000d*, where Doctor Hang Viet Nga has, over a period of many years, built up a hotel in organic fashion. Rooms and gardens resemble scenes from the pages of a fairy storybook; guests sleep inside mushrooms, trees and giraffes, and sip tea under giant cobwebs. It is not a particularly comfortable place to stay and the number of visitors limits privacy but it is well worth visiting. ▸▸ *For further information, see Sleeping, page 162.*

## Bao Dai's hunting lodge (Dinh 1)

Emperor Bao Dai also had a hunting lodge that used to be a museum. East of the town centre, Dinh 1 sported 1930s furniture, antique telephone switchboards, and although it was not sumptuous, nevertheless had a feel of authenticity. It has now closed and there is talk of it reopening as a casino.

## Railway to Trai Mat Village

**Dalat Railway Station**, off Quang Trung Street to the east of the centre, was opened in 1938 and is the last station in Vietnam to retain its original French art deco architecture and coloured-glass windows. In 1991, a 7-km stretch of railway to the village of **Trai Mat** was reopened and every day a small Russian-built diesel car makes the journey ① *daily at 0630, 0805, 0940, 1115, 1405, 1545, US$5 return, 30 minutes, minimum 6 people*. The journey to Trai Mat takes you near the **Lake of Sighs**, 5 km northeast of Dalat. The Lake is said by some to be named after the sighs of the girls being courted by handsome young men from the military academy in Dalat. Another theory is that the name was coined after a young Vietnamese maiden, Mai Nuong, drowned herself in the Lake in the 18th century, believing that her lover, Hoang Tung, had rejected her. Not long ago the Lake was surrounded by thick forest but today it is a thin wood. The track also passes immaculately tended vegetable gardens; no space on the valley floors or sides is wasted and the high intensity agriculture is a marvellous sight. Trai Mat itself is a prosperous K'Ho village with a market selling piles of produce from the surrounding area. Walk 300 m up the road and take a narrow lane to the left to reach Chua Linh Phuoc, an attractive Buddhist temple, notable for its huge Buddha and mosaic-adorned pillars, made from broken rice bowls and fragments of beer bottle.

Vietnam Central Vietnam Central Highlands & the coast

**Waterfalls around Dalat**

**Cam Ly Waterfall** ⓘ *2 km from the centre of town, T063-824145, daily 0700-1700, 6000d*, is the closest waterfall to Dalat town centre. It is pleasant enough but should be avoided during the dry season, as it is the overflow for the sewerage system in Dalat. The falls are not particularly noteworthy but the gardens are peaceful and serene.

More cascades can be found south of town off Highway 20 towards Ho Chi Minh City. The first of these is **Datanla Falls** ⓘ *5 km out of town, T063-831804, 0700-1700; 5000d*. A path leads steeply downwards into a forested ravine; it is an easy hike to get there, but tiring on the return journey. However, the new Alpine Coaster, a toboggan on rails ⓘ *T063-831804, 35,000d return* makes the journey faster and easier. The falls are hardly spectacular but few people come here, except at weekends, so they are usually peaceful. Not far from the falls is the terminus of the **Dalat cable car** (**Càp Treo**) ⓘ *daily 0730-1700 but may be closed May-Nov if the wind is too strong, 35,000d one way, 50,000d return*, which starts from the top of Prenn Pass, about 100 m from the bus station. The journey from top to bottom takes about 15 minutes and gives a different perspective of the Dalat area.

**Prenn Falls**, next to Highway 20, 12 km south of Dalat, were dedicated to Queen Sirikit of Thailand when she visited in 1959. The area has recently undergone a large renovation and is cleaner and better equiped than it used to be. The falls are not that good but there is a rope bridge that can be crossed and pleasant views of the surrounding area. About 20 km north of Bao Loc on the Bao Loc Plateau are the **Dambri Falls** ⓘ *Highway 20, 120 km from Dalat, Jul-Nov only; get a xe ôm from Bao Loc or take a tour*. These are considered the most impressive falls in southern Vietnam and are worth an excursion for those who have time.

---

# Central provinces 🚌🚌  ▶ *pp162-168. Colour map 4, A2, B1 and B2.*

## Ins and outs

**Getting there and around** There are direct flights from Ho Chi Minh City and Danang to Buon Ma Thuot and Play Ku. Innumerable local buses plough the inter-provincial routes between Dalat, Play Ku, Kontum, Ho Chi Minh City, Nha Trang, Buon Ma Thuot, Phan Thiet and Phan Rang. Alternatively it is possible to hire a car and driver. ▶ *For further information, see Transport, page 167.*

## Buon Ma Thuot → *Colour map 4, B2.*

Buon Ma Thuot, the provincial capital of Daklak Province, is located at the junction of Highway 14 and Highway 26. Until the 1950s big game hunting was Buon Ma Thuot's main claim to fame but now the town has surpassed its illustrious and renowned neighbour of Dalat to be the main centre for tea and coffee production. With the rise of the Trung Nguyen coffee empire, Buon Ma Thuot has changed from a sleepy backwater to a thriving modern city. The government also instigated a resettlement programme here, taking land from the ethnic minority groups to give to Vietnamese settlers. The Ede did not take kindly to having their land encroached upon by outsiders; tensions reached their peak in late 2001 and early 2002, when there was widespread rioting in Buon Ma Thuot. Today, the best Ede village to visit is **Buon Tur**, southwest of Buon Ma Thuot, off Highway 14. Apart from the odd TV aerial, life has changed little in this community of 20 stilt houses and, despite the efforts of the government to stop it, Ede is still taught in school. **Daklak Tourist Office** ⓘ *3 Phan Chu Trinh St (within the grounds of Thang Loi Hotel), T050-852108, www.daklaktourist.com*, provides useful information about the province and has knowledgeable, English-speaking staff.

## Dray Sap waterfalls → *Colour map 4, B2.*

ⓘ *2 km off Highway 14 towards Ho Chi Minh City, 20 km from Buon Ma Thuot, daily 0700-1700; 6000-8000d.*

The waterfalls consist of several different cascades all next to each other. The 100-m-wide torrent is particularly stunning in the wet season when the spray justifies the name 'waterfall of smoke'. There are two paths to choose from: one down by the river and the other on the high ground. Note, though, that access may occasionally be limited in the wet season, if the paths are too treacherous to use.

## Lak Lake → *Colour map 4, B2.*

The serene Lak Lake is about 50 km southeast of Buon Ma Thuot and can be explored by dugout. It is an attraction in its own right but is all the more compelling on account of the surrounding **Mnong villages**. Early morning mists hang above the calm waters and mingle with the columns of woodsmoke rising from the longhouses. The Mnong number about 50,000 and are matriarchal. They have been famed as elephant catchers for hundreds of years, although the elephants are now used for tourist rides rather than in their traditional role for dragging logs from the forest. In order to watch the elephants taking their evening wallow in the cool waters and to appreciate the tranquility of sunrise over the lake, stay overnight at a Mnong village, **Buon Juin**. An evening supping with your hosts, sharing rice wine and sleeping in the simplicity of a Mnong longhouse is an ideal introduction to these genial people. ⏩ *For further information, see Sleeping, page 163.*

## Yok Don National Park → *Colour map 4, B1.*

ⓘ *40 km northwest of Buon Ma Thuot, T050-783049, yokdonecotourism@vnn.vn. Tour guide section Mr Hung 090-5197501 (mob), daily 0700-2200. Tours range from elephant riding (US$20 for 2 per hr; US$45 for 3hrs) to elephant trekking (US$190 for 2 for 3 days) to animal spotting by night (US$70). While there is a bridge under construction travellers must pay to cross the river on a pull boat, US$4 per group. Accommodation is available.*

This 115,000 ha wildlife reserve is home to 250 species of birds and at least 63 species of mammals, 17 of which are on the worldwide endangered list. It is believed that several rare white elephants survive here. The best chance of spotting wildlife is on an overnight guided hike or elephant safari. Within the park boundaries are also 17 different ethnic tribes.

## Play Ku (Pleiku) and around → *Colour map 4, A2.*

Nearly 200 km north of Buon Ma Thuot, Play Ku is located in a valley at the bottom of a local mountain and is visible from 12 kilometres away. It is a modern, thriving, bustling town, surrounded by rubber, pepper, coffee and tea plantations. There was fierce fighting here during the American War and, as a result, the town itself has little to offer the tourist but nearby are several Jarai villages that are worth a visit. Contact **Gia Lia Tourist** ⓘ *215 Hung Vuong St (in Hung Vuong Hotel), T059-874571, www.gialiatourist.com, daily 0730-1100, 1330-1630*, for information and, for the sake of preserving the traditional way of life, only visit those villages where foreigners no longer need a licence.

**Plei Fun** is about 16 km north of Play Ku and is the village **Gia Lai Tourist** will take you to if you book a tour through them. The local villagers have wised up to tourism and may try and charge you 30,000d to see their graveyard, in which tiled or wooden roofs shelter the worldly possessions of the deceased: bottles, bowls and even the odd bicycle. Traditional Jarai carved hardwood statues guard the graves. Push on to **Plei Mun**, another 5 km down the road and left 2 km down a dirt road, for some even finer examples. There is also a traditional wooden *rong* house here but it has a corrugated iron roof.

Kontum is a small, sleepy market town, 44 km north of Play Ku on Highway 14. There are a couple of notable sights that make a sidetrip to Kontum worthwhile, plus scores of Ba-na villages in the vicinity that can be reached by motorbike and on foot. Contact **Kontum Tourist Office** ① *2 Phan Dinh Phung St (on the ground floor of the Dakbla Hotel 1), T060-861626, www.kontumtourism.com, daily 0700-1100, 1300-1700,* for further information.

The French Bishop and missionary Stephano Theodore Cuenot founded Kontum in the mid 1800s and succeeded in converting many of the local tribespeople to Christianity. He was arrested on Emperor Tu Duc's orders but died in Binh Dinh prison on 14 November 1861, a day before the beheading instructions arrived. He was beatified in 1909. Cuenot and other French priests and missionaries slain by Emperor Tu Duc are commemorated by a plaque set into the altar of **Tan Huong Church** ① *92 Nguyen Hue St (if the church is shut ask in the office adjacent and they will gladly open it).* The whitewashed façade has an interesting depiction of St George and the dragon. It is not immediately evident that the church is built on stilts, but crouch down and look under one of the little arches that run along the side and the stilts, joists and floorboards are clear. Many of the windows are original but, unfortunately, the roof is a modern replacement, although the original style of fishscale tiling can still be seen in the tower. The interior of the church is exquisite, with dark wooden columns and a fine vaulted ceiling made of wattle and daub.

Further east (1 km) on the same street is the superb **Wooden Church**. Built by the French with Ba-na labour in 1913, it remains largely unaltered, with the original wooden frame and wooden doors. Inside, the blue walls combine with the dark-brown polished wood to produce a very serene effect. Unfortunately the windows are modern tinted glass and rather crude. In the grounds to the right stands a *rong* house and a statue of Cuenot, the first Catholic bishop of East Cochin China diocese.

---

# Nha Trang 🔲🚲🏃🏔️🚌🚐 ⇒ *pp163-168. Colour map 4, B3.*

Nha Trang is Vietnam's only real seaside town, with a long, golden beach. The centuries-old fishing settlement nestles in the protective embrace of the surrounding hills and islands at the mouth of the Cai Estuary. The light here has a beautifully radiant quality and the air is clear: colours are vivid, particularly the blues of the sea, sky and fishing boats moored on the river. The name Nha Trang is thought to be derived from the Cham word *yakram*, meaning bamboo river. Certainly, the surrounding area was a focal point of the Cham Kingdom (see page 144), with some of the country's best-preserved Cham towers located nearby.

Nha Trang's clear waters and offshore islands won wide acclaim in the 1960s and its current prosperity is based firmly on tourism. Word has spread and Nha Trang's days as an undiscovered treasure are over. The town is now a firmly established favourite of Vietnamese as well as foreign visitors. There is a permanent relaxed holiday atmosphere, the streets are not crowded and the motorbikes cruise at a leisurely pace. There are, in reality, two Nha Trangs: popular Nha Trang, which is a sleepy, sedate seaside town consisting of a long, palm and casuarina-fringed beach and one or two streets running parallel to it, and commercial Nha Trang to the north of Yersin Street, which is a bustling city with an attractive array of Chinese shophouses.

## Ins and outs
**Getting there** The airport is 34 km from Nha Trang at Cam Ranh. There are daily flights to Hanoi and Ho Chi Minh City and regular flights to Danang. The town is on the main north-south railway line, with trains to Ho Chi Minh City, Hanoi and stops

between. The main bus terminal is west of the town centre. Note that inter-provincial buses do not go into Nha Trang but drop off on Highway 1 which bypasses the town. *Xe ôms* take passengers into town. ▸▸ *For further information, see Transport, page 167* .

**Getting around** Nha Trang is just about negotiable on foot but there are also bicycles and motorbikes for hire everywhere and the usual cyclos.

**Tourist office** **Khanh Hoa Tourism** ① *1 Tran Hung Dao St, T058-526753, www.nha trangtourist.com.vn, daily 0700-1130, 1330-1700*, is the official tour office and can arrange visa extensions, car and boat hire and tours of the area. It's also **Vietnam Airlines** booking office.

# Nha Trang

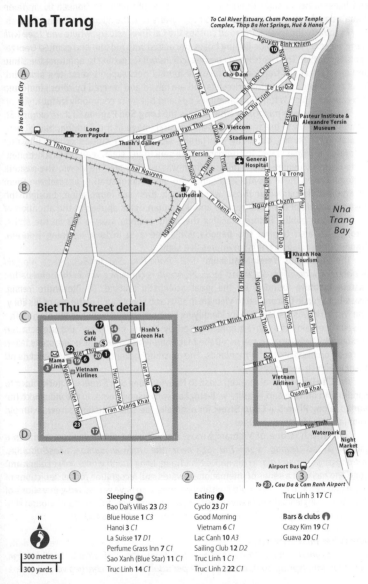

**Sleeping**
Bao Dai's Villas **23** *D3*
Blue House **1** *C3*
Hanoi **3** *C1*
La Suisse **1** *D1*
Perfume Grass Inn **7** *C1*
Sao Xanh (Blue Star) **11** *C1*
Truc Linh **14** *C1*

**Eating**
Cyclo **23** *D1*
Good Morning Vietnam **6** *C1*
Lac Canh **10** *A3*
Sailing Club **12** *D2*
Truc Linh **1** *C1*
Truc Linh 2 **22** *C1*
Truc Linh 3 **17** *C1*

**Bars & clubs**
Crazy Kim **19** *C1*
Guava **20** *C1*

Known as Thap Ba, the temple complex of **Cham Ponagar** ① *follow 2 Thang 4 St north out of town; Cham Ponagar is just over Xom Bong bridge, daily 0600-1800, 5000d,* is on a hill just outside the city. Originally the complex consisted of eight towers, four of which remain. Their stylistic differences indicate they were built at different times between the seventh and 12th centuries. The largest (23 m high) was built in AD 817 and contains a statue of Lady Thien Y-ana, also known as Ponagar (the beautiful wife of Prince Bac Hai), as well as a fine and very large linga. She taught the people of the area weaving and new agricultural techniques, and they built the tower in her honour. The other towers are dedicated to gods: the central tower to Cri Cambhu (which has become a fertility temple for childless couples); the northwest tower to Sandhaka (wood cutter and foster-father to Lady Thien Y-ana); and the south tower to Ganeca (Lady Thien Y-ana's daughter). The best time to visit the towers is in the afternoon, after 1600.

En route to the towers, the road crosses the **Cai River estuary**, where you'll see Nha Trang's elegant fleet of blue fishing boats, decorated with red trim and painted eyes for spotting the fish. The boats have coracles (*cái thúng*) for getting to and from the shore and mechanical fish traps, which take the form of nets supported by long arms; the arms are hinged to a platform on stilts and are raised and lowered by wires connected to a capstan which is turned, sometimes by hand but more commonly by foot.

The best known pagoda in Nha Trang is the **Long Son Pagoda** ① *23 Thang 10 St*, built in 1963. Inside the sanctuary is an unusual image of the Buddha, backlit with natural light. Murals depicting the jataka stories (birth stories of the Buddha) decorate the upper walls. To the right of the sanctuary, stairs lead up to a 9-m-high white Buddha, perched on a hill top, from where there are fine views. The pagoda commemorates those monks and nuns who died demonstrating against the Diem government, in particular those who, through their self-immolation, brought the despotic nature of the Diem regime and its human rights abuses to the attention of the American public. Before reaching the white pagoda, take a left on the stairs. Through an arch behind the pagoda you'll see a 14-m long reclining Buddha. Commissioned in 2003, it is an impressive sight.

The **Alexandre Yersin Museum** ① *8 Tran Phu St, T058-829540, Mon-Fri 0800-1100, 1400-1630, Sat 0800-1100, 26,000d,* is contained within the colonnaded **Pasteur Institute** founded by the great scientist's protégé, Dr Alexandre Yersin. Swiss-born Yersin first arrived in Vietnam in 1891 and spent much of the rest of his life in Nha Trang. He was responsible for identifying the bacillus which causes the plague. The museum contains the lab equipment used by Yersin, his library and stereoscope through which visitors can see in 3-D the black-and-white slides, including shots taken by Yersin on his visits to the highlands. The museum's curator is helpful, friendly, and fluent in French and English.

The **Cho Dam** (central market) close to Nguyen Hong Son Street is a good place to wander and browse and is quite well-stocked with useful items. In the vicinity of the market, along **Phan Boi Chau Street** for example, are some bustling streets with old colonial-style shuttered houses.

Long Thanh is one of Vietnam's most distinguished photographers and has a **gallery** ① *126 Hoang Van Thu St, near the railway station, T058-824875, lvntrang50@hotmail.com,* in his native Nha Trang. Long Thanh works only in black and white and has won a series of international awards and recognition for his depictions of Cham children and of wistful old men and women, who have witnessed generations of change in a single lifetime. Many of his famous pictures were taken in and around Nha Trang. Long Thanh speaks English and welcomes visitors to his gallery.

## Thap Ba Hot Springs
① *2 km beyond Cham Ponagar, not far from the Cai River, T058-835335, www.thapbahotspring.com, around US$3 per adult although charges vary.*

A soak in mineral water or a mud bath is a relaxing and refreshing experience. Baths and pools of differing sizes are available for individuals, couples and groups. The water is 40°C and is rich in sodium silicate chloride. Steam baths and massages are available.

## Islands around Nha Trang

ⓘ *The islands are reached on boat trips from Cau Da pier. Departures 0900. Around US$5 including a seafood lunch and snorkelling equipment; cold beers cost extra. Boat charters also available. Visitors must now pay a Nha Trang sightseeing fee.*

The **islands** off Nha Trang are sometimes known as the **Salangane** islands after the sea swallows that nest here in such profusion. The sea swallow (*yen* in Vietnamese) produces the highly prized bird's nest from which the famous soup is made.

There's an uninspiring aquarium on **Mieu Island** but no other sights, as such. The islands (including **Hon Mun, Hon Tam** and **Hon Mot**) are usually a bit of an anticlimax for, as so often in Vietnam, to travel is better than to arrive; it's often a case of lovely boat trip, disappointing beach. The best part is anchoring offshore and jumping into the exquisitely cool water while your skipper prepares a sumptuous seafood feast and the beers chill in the ice bucket. The best known boat trips to the islands are run by **Hanh's Green Hat** and **Mama Linh** ⤤ *For further information, see Activities and tours, page 167.*

## Mui Ne 🛏🚲🍴⛰🚌🍸

⤤ *pp164-168. Colour map 4, C2.*

Further down the coast and east of the small fishing town of **Phan Thiet** is Mui Ne, a 20-km sweep of golden sand where Vietnam's finest coastal resorts can be found. Watersports are available here as well as one of the country's most attractive golf courses. ⤤ *For further information, see Activities and tours, page 167.*

### Ins and outs

**Getting there** Open Tour Buses nearly all divert to Mui Ne and drop off/pick up from just about every hotel along the beach. It is also possible and quicker to hire a car; from Ho Chi Minh City to Mui Ne will cost approximately US$75. ⤤ *For further information, see Transport, page 168.*

**Best time to visit** The weather is best in the dry season, November to May. Mui Ne is most popular with overseas visitors in the Christmas to Easter period when

*Map labels:* Mui Ne, To Hon Rom, Sinh Café, Phan Thiet Bay, ATM, TM Brother's, To Phan Thiet

N
1 km
1 miles

Sea Breeze **12**
Small Garden (Vuon Nho) **14**
Thuy Thuy **17**
Victoria Phan Thiet Beach Resort & Spa **18**

**Sleeping** 🛏
Bamboo Village **1**
Coco Beach (Hai Duong) **3**
Full Moon Beach **4**
Hiep Hoa **5**
Mui Ne Resort **13**
Sailing Club **11**

**Eating** 🍴
Luna D'Autonno **3**
Sunset **5**

**Bars & clubs** 🍸
Guava **8**
Pogo **7**

*Side margin:* **Vietnam** Central Vietnam · Central Highlands & the coast prices at the some of the better hotels rise by 20% or more. From December to March, Mui Ne loses much of its beach to the sea.

## Sights

Mui Ne (Cape Ne) is the name of the famous sandy cape and the small fishing village that lies at its end. Mui Ne's two claims to fame are its *nuoc mam* (fish sauce) and its **beaches**, where it's possible to play a host of watersports, including kitesurfing for which it is justly famous. The cape is dominated by some impressive **sand dunes**, which are quite red in parts due to the underlying geology.

Around the village, visitors may notice a strong smell of rotting fish. This is the unfortunate but inevitable by-product of fish sauce fermenting in wooden barrels. The process takes a year but to Vietnamese palates it is worth every day. The *nuoc mam* of Phan Thiet is made from anchovies and is highly regarded but not as reverentially as that from the southern island of Phu Quoc.

## ● Sleeping

**Dalat** *p152, map p154*

**LL-L Evason Ana Mandara Villas & Six Senses Spa at Dalat**, Le Lai St, T063-555888, www.sixsenses.com. Restored French villas are perched on a hillside, surrounded by fruit farms. Each villa has a couple of bedrooms, a sitting room and dining room; guests have dedicated butlers. A number of pools are scattered about the hotel complex. There is also a central villa that houses a French bistro and wine bar. The Six Senses Spa experience has been created in one of the villas with river and mountain views, outdoor pools and hot tubs.

**LL-L Sofitel Dalat Palace**, 12 Tran Phu St, Dalat, T063-825444, www.sofitel.com. This rambling old building was built in 1922 and restored to its former glory in 1995. Those that knew it before the renovation will be amazed: curtains, furniture, statues, gilt mirrors and chandeliers adorn the rooms which are tastefully arranged as the French do best. The view over Xuan Huong Lake to the hills beyond is lovely and the extensive grounds of the hotel are beautifully laid out. Hotel restaurant Le Rabelais (ŸŸŸ) has a superb dining room with views down to the Lake and offers French specialities and an excellent wine list. Hotel guests get special green fees on the nearby golf course.

**A Empress Hotel**, 5 Nguyen Thai Hoc St, T063-833888, empressdl@hcm.vnn.vn. This is a particularly attractive hotel in a lovely position overlooking the lake. All rooms are arranged around a small courtyard which traps the sun and is a great place for breakfast or to pen a postcard. The rooms are large with very comfortable beds and the more expensive ones have luxurious bathrooms so try to get a room upgrade. Attentive and courteous staff. A great value hotel with the best view of Xuan Huong Lake.

**A Golf 3 Hotel**, 4 Nguyen Thi Minh Khai St, T063-826042, golf3.dalat@vinagolf.vn. Smart, centrally located hotel with comfortable rooms; cheaper rooms have showers only. It has a good range of facilities, including bar, restaurant, massage, nightclub and karaoke. The location by Dalat market is excellent. One drawback though is that because it is so near to the market the rooms facing the street are noisy. Breakfast is included.

**A Novotel Dalat**, 7 Tran Phu St, T063-825777, www.accorhotels-asia.com. The original hotel opened as the Hotel Du Parc in 1932 and was completely restored in 1995. It is opposite the post office and near the Sofitel, with which it shares its management and many facilities. Rooms nicely restored and comfortably furnished, although the standard rooms are small. There is no restaurant but breakfast is served here and Café de la Poste is just over the road.

**B-E Hang Nga (Tree House)**, 3 Huynh Thuc Khang St, T063-822070. If you fancy a fantasy night in a mushroom, a tree or a giraffe then this is the place for you. It is an architectural meander through curves, twists and bizarre rooms and ornamentation. The guesthouse was designed by Hang Nga, whose father, Truong Chinh, formed the triumvirate of power following the death of Ho Chi Minh. Prices are reasonable but the rooms tend to be visited by curious tourists and the furniture is sturdily made and not too comfortable.

**D-E Hoa Binh 1 (Peace Hotel 1)**, 64 Truong Cong Dinh St, T063-822787, peace12@hcm.vnn.vn. One of the better low-cost places with 16 rooms in a good location, including 5 at the back around a small yard, quiet but not much view. Rooms at the front have a view but can be a bit noisy. The rooms have TV, fan and mosquito nets. A friendly place with an all-day café.

**D-E Hoa Binh 2 (Peace Hotel 2)**, 67 Truong Cong Dinh St, T063-822982, peace12@hcm.vnn.vn. Almost opposite its sister hotel, this is rather an attractive 1930s building. It's clean and some rooms have small balconies.

**Buon Ma Thuot** *p156*
**B Thang Loi Hotel**, 1 Phan Chu Trinh St, T050-857615, www.daklaktourist.com.vn. A modern hotel in a central location, opposite the victory monument. The rooms are all large and come with en suite facilities. The staff speak good English. Food in the restaurant is fresh, well presented, good value and plentiful. ATM on site.

**D-F Duy Hoang Hotel**, 30 Ly Thuong Kiet St, T050-858020. Spacious, well-furnished rooms with en suite facilities and a/c. Cheaper rooms have fan and shared bathrooms. Staff are efficient and friendly and have a reasonable grasp of English. Excellent value for money.

**Lak Lake** *p157*
It costs US$5 to stay in a Mnong longhouse at **Buon Jun**; contact **Daklak Tourist** for arrangements.

**Play Ku** *p157*
**C-D Ialy Hotel**, 89 Hung Vuong St, T059-824843, ialyhotel@dng.vnn.vn. Excellent location opposite the main post office. Reasonable sized, good value rooms with en suite facilities, a/c and satellite TV. Staff are friendly enough but no English is spoken. The restaurant on the first floor is only open for breakfast. ATM in the lobby.

**Kontum** *p158*
**C-D Dakbla 1 Hotel**, 2 Phan Dinh Phung St, T060-863333. Set amid attractive grounds, this hotel has a small restaurant and jetty on the riverbank. Staff are friendly and helpful

and have a basic understanding of English and French. Rooms have minibars, satellite TV, a/c, hot water and en suite bathrooms. The restaurant provides good food at a reasonable price.

**Nha Trang** *p158, map p159*
**LL Evason Hideaway & Six Senses Spa at Ana Mandara**, Ninh Vinh Bay; 30 km north of Nha Trang, T058-728222, www.evasonhide aways.com. Beach Villas, Rock Villas and Hilltop Villas are laid out in the full dramatic curve of Ninh Van Bay. You can't get more exceptionally luxurious than this; the Rock Villas are perched on rocks at the tip of the bay with bathrooms overlooking the sea and fronted by small infinity pools. The resort is large; from the Rock Villas to the main restaurant is an enormous hike. Beach Villas are more centrally located. While your days away in the herb garden, **Six Senses Spa**, library or bar and be attended by your personal butler. It's highly romantic, very secluded and very expensive; the food is exceptional. The resort is 1 hr ahead of real time which is far too confusing.

**L Whale Island Resort**, off Nha Trang, T058-840501, www.whaleislandresort.com. This is a great place in which to relax amid the aquamarine waters of the South China Sea. Bungalows right on this island beach, 2½ hrs north of Nha Trang. The price includes full board and return transfers to Nha Trang and gets cheaper the longer you stay. Activities include diving, windsurfing, canoeing and catamaran sailing and there's plenty of wildlife to observe too. .

**A-C Bao Dai's Villas**, Tran Phu St (just before Cau Da village), T058-590147, http://vn realty.com/nt/baodai/index.html. Several villas of former Emperor Bao Dai, with magnificent views over the harbour and outlying islands, sited on a small promontory, with large elegant a/c rooms. There are an additional 40 rooms in assorted buildings that lack the scale and elegance, not surprisingly, of the emperor's own quarters. Overrun with sightseers during holiday periods.

**B-E Perfume Grass Inn (Que Thao)**, 4A Biet Thu St, T058-524286, www.perfume-grass.com. Well-run and friendly family hotel with 21 rooms. Restaurant and internet service. Good value for money. Book in advance.

C-D **La Suisse Hotel**, 34 Tran Quang Khai St, T058-524353, www.lasuissehotel.com. Excellent new hotel with 24 rooms on 5 floors, nicely built, and offering excellent value for money. The best rooms (VIP) are large and have attractive balconies with sea view. All rooms have bathtubs. Breakfast included.

C-E **Sao Xanh (Blue Star)**, 1B Biet Thu St, T058-525447, quangc@dng.vnn.vn. Another popular, clean and friendly family-run hotel. 23 rooms, free coffee and bananas, more expensive rooms have breakfast included. Near the beach and in a popular area.

D-E **Blue House**, 12/8 Hung Vuong St, T058-522505, ngothaovy1983@ yahoo.com.vn. Down a little alley in a quiet setting. 14 a/c and fan rooms in a small, neat blue building. Friendly and excellent value for money.

D-E **Hanoi**, 31C Biet Thu St, T058-525127, hanoihotel-nt@yahoo.com. Set in a quiet cul-de-sac at the end of the road, this small 12-room hotel has a/c and fan rooms. Breakfast costs US$2 extra, helpful.

D-E **Truc Linh**, 27B Hung Vuong St, T058-522201. Best known for its restaurant, this guesthouse is popular with budget travellers. It's moved from across the street. The 15 rooms have a/c, hot water, TV and minibar and some have a sea view. Try to opt for a room with external windows.

**Mui Ne** *p161, map p161*

L **Coco Beach (Hai Duong)**, T062-8471113, www.cocobeach.net. Coco Beach was the first resort on Mui Ne and remains among the best. Not luxurious but friendly and impeccably kept. Wooden bungalows and 2-bedroom 'villas' facing the beach in a beautiful setting with a lovely pool. Price includes a decent buffet breakfast. There are 2 restaurants: the French **Champa** (Tue-Sun 1500-2300 only) and **Paradise Beach Club** (open all day).

L **Victoria Phan Thiet Beach Resort & Spa**, T062-813000, www.victoriahotels-asia.com. Part of the French-run Victoria Group, the resort has 59 upgraded thatch-roof bungalows with outdoor rain showers and 3 villas, built in country-house style in an attractive landscaped setting. It is well equipped with restaurants, several bars, an attractive pool and a spa.

L-A **Bamboo Village**, T062-847007, www.bamboovillageresortvn.com. Attractive, simple, hexagonal bamboo huts peppered around a lovely shady spot at the top of the beach. More expensive rooms have a/c and hot-water showers. An excellent restaurant and attractive swimming pool.

L-A **Sailing Club**, T062-847440, www.sailingclubvietnam.com. This is a stunning resort, designed in the most charming style with bungalows and rooms that are simple and cool and surrounded by dense vegetation. Its pool has been extended and the bathrooms for the superior rooms enlarged. It has an excellent restaurant and bar. A good buffet breakfast is included. Western owned and managed.

A **Full Moon Beach**, T062-847008, www.windsurf-vietnam.com. Visitors are assured of a friendly reception by the French and Vietnamese couple who own and run the place. Accommodation is of a variety of types: some rooms are spacious, others a little cramped, some brick, some bamboo. The most attractive rooms have a sea view. There is a good restaurant.

A-D **Small Garden (Vuon Nho)**, T062-874012, nguyengrimm@yahoo.com. Run by a Vietnamese family, it consists of simple and cheap bamboo hut accommodation in well-cared for gardens near the road and new small a/c concrete bungalows nearer the beach. Although lacking in amenities it is in a good part of the beach with plenty of cafés and restaurants nearby.

B **Miu Ne Resort (Sinh Café)**, T062-847542, www.sinhcafevn.com. Large and new hotel that has cleverly packed the narrow site with 48 rooms and brick-built bungalows. It has a nice pool, bar and restaurant.

B **Sea Breeze**, T062-847373, www.muineseabreeze.com. This far north the beach is getting a bit narrow and the road is a little close to some of the rooms for comfort. Although they are slightly pricier, insist on a sea-view room of which there are 2 categories. The place is well kept, clean and comfortable. Breakfast included. Motorbike and bicycle rental.

B **Thuy Thuy**, T062-847357, T091-8160637 (mob), thuythuyresort2000@yahoo.com. Just 7 pleasant a/c bungalows with TV run by the friendly Elaine. Newer bungalows are a bit more expensive but the originals are perfectly comfortable. Set on the 'wrong' side of the road (eg away from the beach) this is nevertheless a rather charming and nicely run little place, highly praised by guests. Attractive pool.

**B-D Hiep Hoa**, T062-847262, T091-8124149 (mob), hiephoatourism@yahoo.com. Attractive and simple little place with 25 a/c rooms. It's quiet, clean and with its own stretch of beach. Popular and should be booked in advance. Its rate are excellent value for Mui Ne; they go down in the low season.

## ❼ Eating

### Dalat *p152, map p154*
In the evening, street stalls line Nguyen Thi Minh Khai St, leading to Dalat market, which is itself the ideal place to buy picnic provisions. Lakeside cafés and restaurants may look attractive but they serve indifferent food.

**♥♥-♥ Empress Restaurant**, Empress hotel. Open all day and specializing in Chinese fare but with a good selection of Vietnamese and Western dishes. Ideal breakfast setting, al fresco around the fountain in the courtyard of the hotel.

**♥♥-♥ Le Café de la Poste**, 12 Tran Phu St. Adjacent to the **Sofitel** and under the same management. International comfort food at near-Western prices in an airy and cool building. The 3-course lunch menu is great value. A pool table dominates the café. Upstairs is a Vietnamese restaurant.

**♥ Hoa Binh 1**, 67 Truong Cong Dinh St. An all-day eatery serving standard backpacker fare: fried noodles, vegetarian dishes and pancakes at low prices.

**♥ Long Hoa**, 6 3 Thang 2, T063-822934. In the best traditions of French family restaurants, this place has delicious food with fish, meat, venison and super breakfasts. Popular with Dalat's expats and visitors. The chicken soup and beefsteak are particularly recommended and sample Madame's homemade strawberry wine. Service is erratic.

**♥ Stop and Go Café**, 2A Ly Tu Trong St, T063-828458. A café and art gallery run by the local poet, Mr Duy Viet. Sit inside or on the terrace as he bustles around rustling up breakfast, pulling out volumes of visitors' books and his own collected works. The garden is an overrun wilderness where tall fir trees sigh in the breeze.

A local speciality is *nem nuong*, grilled pork wrapped in rice paper with salad leaves and *bun*, fresh rice noodles. The French bread in Nha Trang is also excellent. On the beach near **Nha Trang Waterpark** is a night market, where stalls serve freshly cooked fish and barbecued meat.

**♥♥-♥ Good Morning Vietnam**, 19B Biet Thu St, T058-815071, daily 1000-2300. Popular Italian restaurant, part of a small chain to be found in major tourist centres.

**♥♥-♥ Sailing Club**, 72-74 Tran Phu St, T058-524628, sailingnt@dng.vnn.vn, daily 0700-2300. Although best known as a bar, this busy and attractive beachfront area also includes several restaurants: Japanese, Italian and global cuisine. None is cheap but all serve good food and represent decent value.

**♥ Cyclo**, 130 Nguyen Thien Thuat St, T058-524208, khuongthuy@hotmail.com, daily 0700-2400. A really outstanding little family-run restaurant that has moved to new premises a few doors away. Italian and Vietnamese dishes. Real attention to detail in the bamboo decor and cooking.

**♥ Lac Canh**, 44 Nguyen Binh Khiem St, T058-821391. Specializes in beef, squid and prawns,which you barbecue at your table. Also excellent fish and a special dish of eel mixed with vermicilli. Smoky atmosphere and can be hard to get a table. Highly recommended.

**♥ Truc Linh**, 11 Biet Thu St, T058-526742. Deservedly popular with sensible prices. Good fruit shake and *op la* (fried eggs). There's also **Truc Linh 2**, at 21 Biet Thu St, T058-521089, and **Truc Linh 3**, at 80 Hung Vuong St, T058-525259. Nos 2 and 3 are recommended as the best.

### Mui Ne *p161, map p161*
Of the hotel restaurants the Sailing Club, Bamboo Village and Coco Beach stand out, see Sleeping, page 164.

**♥♥ Luna D'Autonno**, T062-847591. One of the best Italian restaurants in the country. Inspired menu that goes way beyond the standard pizzas and pasta with daily fish specials and BBQs. Huge portions and a good wine list.

**♥ Sunset**, T062-847605. Good Vietnamese food, especially fish. Efficient service and excellent value.

# ◐ Bars and clubs

**Nha Trang** *p158, map p159*
**Crazy Kim**, 19 Biet Thu St, T058-816072, open until late. A busy, lively bar in the heart of a popular part of town. Pool, table tennis, food.
**Guava**, 17 Biet Thu St, T058-524140, daily 1100-2400. Striking orange front. Stylish relaxing café, cocktail bar and lounge bar with garden. Good music and bar games.
**Sailing Club**, 74-76 Tran Phu St, T058-524628, open until late. Lively bar, especially on Sat nights when locals and visitors congregate to enjoy pool, cold beer, dancing and music.

**Mui Ne** *p161, map p161*
**Pogo beach bar**, www.thepogobar.com. Just down from **Sinh Café** with cocktails, movies, beer and local and international food.
**Guava**. Like its namesake in Nha Trang this is a large funky place in which to lounge or drink at the bar. Atmospherically candlelit at night. International food is served.

# ◑ Shopping

**Dalat** *p152, map p154*
Dalat has a well-deserved reputation for producing not only beautiful flowers but also some of the best handmade silk paintings in Vietnam.

# ▲ Activities and tours

**Dalat** *p152, map p154*
**Golf**
**Dalat Palace Golf Course**, 1 Phu Dong Thien Vuong St, T063-823507, www.vietnam golfresorts.com. Originally built for Emperor Bao Dai in 1922, it was rebuilt in 1994 and is now an 18-hole championship golf course. Rated by some as the finest in Vietnam and one of the best in the region. Beautiful setting with fairways, bent grass tees and greens overlooking Xuan Huong Lake. Green fees US$90, include caddie fee.

**Tour operators**
**Dalat Toserco**, No7, 3 Thang 2 St, T063-822125. Budget transport and a good selection of tours. Slightly more expensive than **Sinh Café** and **TM Brothers**.

**Dalat Travel Bureau**, 1 Nguyen Thi Minh Khai, T063-510104, www.dalattourist.com.vn. The state-run travel company for Lam Dong Province. Tours include: city, trekking, canyoning, rock climbing, exploring and biking; the majority of these tours cost US$10 per person.
**Phattire Adventures**, 73 Truong Cong Dinh St, T063-829422, www.phattire adventures.com. Canyoning, from US$24; rock climbing, US$30; mountain biking, from US$32; trekking from US$17; kayaking, US$27.
**Sinh Café**, 4a Bui Thi Xuan, T063-822663, www.sinhcafevn.com. Part of the nationwide Sinh Café chain. Primarily provides cheap travel to HCMC and Nha Trang. Also arranges local tours.
**TM Brothers**, 58 Truong Cong Dinh St, T063-828383, tmbrother_dalat@yahoo.com. Similar to **Sinh Café** in that they provide budget tours and transportation. Has a wide range of tours including to Yok Don National Park. Central Highlands tours range from US$45-100 per person. Motorbike rental US$4-6/day.

**Buon Ma Thuot** *p156*
**Tour operators**
Vietnam Highland Travel, 24 Ly Thuong Kiet, T050-855009, www.vietnamhighland travel.com.vn. Offer adventure packages, including elephant trekking and homestays.

**Nha Trang** *p158, map p159*
**Diving**
Dry season only (Jan-May). **Rainbow Divers**, 90A Hung Vuong St, T058-524351, T090-8781756 (mob), www.divevietnam.com. A full range of training and courses, including the National Geographic dive courses. Good reports regarding equipment and focus on safety. Qualified instructors speak a variety of European languages.
    **The Evason Hideaway** also offers diving packages.

**Fishing**
Boats and equipment can be hired from Cau Da Pier; contact **Khanh Hoa Tourism**, 1 Tran Hung Dao St, T058-526753, www.nhatrangtourist.com.vn, for details.

## Therapies
**Six Senses Spa**, Ana Mandara Resort, www.sixsenses.com. Exotic treatments: Japanese and Vichy showers, hot tubs and massages in beautiful surroundings. 2007 saw the resort introduce Life-style programmes for vitality, stress-management and meditation that include tailored spa treatments. 5-day lifestyle packages are US$990 not including accommodation.

## Watersports
The **Ana Mandara Resort** offers windsurfing, parasailing, hobiecats and fishing.

## Tour operators
The following tour operators also arrange trips to **Buon Ma Thuot** and the **Central Highlands**.
**Hanh's Green Hat**, 2C Biet Thu St, T058-526494, biendaotour@yahoo.com. Boat trips (US$5 including lunch and pick-up from hotel, excluding entrance fees and snorkelling fees). Also other local tours, car, motorbike and bicycle hire.
**Mama Linh**, 23C Biet Thu St, T058-522844, www.mamalinhvn@yahoo.com. Standard boat trips for US$6 and minibus tickets to Hoi An, Phan Thiet, HCMC and Dalat.
**Sinh Café**, 10 Biet Thu St, T058-524329, www.sinhcafevn.com. Offers tours and Open Bus Tour tickets. **Sinh Café** buses arrive and depart from here.

## Mui Ne *p161, map p161*
### Golf
**Ocean Dunes Golf Club**, 1 Ton Duc Thang St, T062-823366, www.vietnamgolfresorts.com. Phan Thiet's 18-hole golf course, designed by Nick Faldo, is highly regarded. Fully equipped club house with bar and restaurant. Green fee US$90 Mon-Fri, weekends and holidays US$100 including caddie fees.

### Therapies
**Lotus Day Spa**, Sailing Club, T062-847440, www.sailingclubvietnam.com. Massage treatments are available in special cabins in the grounds.

### Tour operators
**Sinh Café**, 144 Nguyen Dinh Chieu, T062-847542, muine@sinhcafevn.com. Good for Open Tour tickets and local tours.

**TM Brother's**, with several outlets, T062-847359, T098-4074507 (mob). Local tours and Open Tour Bus service.

## Watersports
Windsurfing, kitesurfing and other water-sports are popular in Mui Ne. The wind is normally brisk and the sight of the kitesurfers zooming around on the waves is great for those of us too cowardly to try. Equipment and training is offered by a couple of resorts.
**Airwaves**, T090-3308313 (mob), www.airwaveskitesurfing.com, has stations at the Sailing Club, Sea Horse Resort and Bon Bien Resort. There are also 2 Airwaves shops in town. Prices vary according to lessons and equipment needed. Kitesurfing lesson, US$100; windsurf lesson including equipment, US$20/hr; surf lesson, US$16/hr.
**Jibe's Beach Club**, T062-847405, T091-3162005 (mob), www.windsurf-vietnam.com, part of and close to **Full Moon Beach Resort**. Equipment is available for purchase or for hire by the hour, day or week. A 5-hr kitesurfing lesson is US$200; 5-hr windsurfing lesson, US$170; surfboard hire, US$5; kayaking, US$5/hr per person. Instruction available in 9 languages.

## ⦿ Transport

### Dalat *p152, map p154*
#### Air
See page 152. **Vietnam Airlines**, No 2 and No 40 Ho Tuong Mau St, T/F063-833499, open daily 0730-1130, 1330-1630, closes 30 mins earlier at weekends.

### Bus
Open Tour Bus companies operate daily trips to **HCMC**, 7hrs, **Nha Trang**, 6 hrs, and **Mui Ne**, 6 hrs.

### Car
It is possible to hire cars and taxis. Many tour operators have cars for hire and there are numerous taxis to choose from.

### Central provinces *p156*
#### Air
**Vietnam Airlines** has offices at Buon Ma Thuot (T050-954442) and Play Ku (T059-823058) airports and at 129 Ba Trieu St in Kontum, T060-862282.

Regular local buses link provincial centres throughout the region.

### Car

Cars with drivers are available for hire; contact the provincial tourist offices or your hotel. Play Ku to **Buon Ma Thuot**, 3½ hrs, US$50.

### Nha Trang *p158, map p159*
### Air

See page 158. Some hotels offer complimentary bus rides to town. The airport bus costs 70,000d from the airport and 25,000d from Nha Trang, 34 km. Taxis wait at the bus station to transport passengers to hotels. A taxi from the airport to town costs 200,000d.

   **Vietnam Airlines**, 91 Nguyen Thien Thuat St, T058-826768.

### Bicycles and motorbikes

Bicycles can be hired from almost every hotel and every café for around 20,000d per day for a bicycle. Motorbikes can be hired from hotels and cafés for around 64,000d per day.

### Bus

The long-distance bus station is out of town at 23 Thang 10 St and has connections with **HCMC, Phan Rang, Danang, Quy Nhon, Buon Ma Thuot, Dalat, Hué** and **Vinh**. Open Tour Buses arrive at and depart from their relevant operator's café (see Tour operators, above).

### Taxi
**Mai Linh**, T058-910910.

### Train

There are regular train connections with stops to and from **Hanoi** and **HCMC**. The station is at 17 Thai Nguyen St, T058-820666.

   **5 Star Express**, 15B Thai Nguyen St, T058-5621868, www.5starexpress.com.vn. This new and comfortable train departs Nha Trang at 1455, arriving in HCMC at 2318. There's also a day train leaving at 0500, arriving 1810, US$56. There are a variety of carriages, and tickets are priced according to the class; tickets range from US$10 one way for the entire route up to US$150. Highly recommended.

### Mui Ne *p161, map p161*
### Bus

A local bus plies the route from Phan Thiet bus station to **Mui Ne**, as do taxis. **Sinh Café** and **TM Brother's** Open Tour Buses drop off and pick up from all resorts on **Mui Ne**.

---

## ❶ Directory

### Dalat *p152, map p154*
**Banks** BIDV, 42 Hoa Binh Sq. **Incombank**, 46-48 Hoa Binh Sq, Mon-Fri 0700-1000, 1300-1600, Sat until 1100. It has a bureau de change, an ATM and also cashes TCs. **Medical services** 4 Pham Ngoc Thach St, T063-822154. Well-equipped hospital. The doctors speak English and French. **Internet** There are internet cafés galore along Nguyen Chi Thanh St, heading from Hoa Binh Sq to Xuan Huong Lake. **Post office and telephone** 14 Tran Phu St, opposite Novotel Hotel. Offers internet and IDD.

### Nha Trang *p158, map p159*
**Banks** Vietcombank, 17 Quang Trung St. Will change most major currencies, cash, TCs (2% commission), and arrange cash advances on some credit cards. There's a Vietcombank exchange bureau at 8A Biet Thu St. **Medical services** General Hospital, 19 Yersin St, T058-822168. **Internet** There are internet cafés all over town, particularly in Biet Thu St and Hong Vuong St. **Post office** GPO, 2 Le Loi St. Also in Biet Thu St, near Nguyen Thien Thuat St.

### Mui Ne *p161, map p161*
**Banks** There are no banks in Mui Ne but a couple of ATMs; the **Saigon Mui Ne Resort** has one and there is one in front of the **Ocean Star Resort** that is next to the Sailing Club. **Medical services** Polyclinic, next to **Swiss Resort**, T062-84749, 091-8210504 (mob), open daily 1130-1330, 1730-2100 **Internet** There are a few internet cafés, particularly the tour cafés, some of which offer free service to customers and almost all hotels offer internet access to their guests. Prices are quite high.

# Ho Chi Minh City & the south

## ⁝ Footprint features

# Introduction

Ho Chi Minh City is a manic, capitalistic hothouse, clogged with traffic, bustling with energy and enlivened by top restaurants, shops and bars. Its streets are evidence of a vibrant historical past with pagodas and temples and a bustling Chinatown. In more recent times it was the seat of the South Vietnam government until events in 1975 led to the country's reunification. Today, it is a burgeoning city, dedicated to commerce and hedonistic pleasures.

Ho Chi Minh City is surrounded by fascinating historical sights to the north and by the liquid fingers of the river delta to its south. The Mekong region is a veritable Garden of Eden, stuffed full of bountiful fruit trees, decorated in pink bougainvillea and carpeted with brilliant green rice paddies. Waterways are as busy as highways, with fishing boats chug chug chugging their way along the brown river. Elsewhere in the south, historical, cultural, religious and pleasurable treasures abound: the Viet Cong tunnels at Cu Chi, the fantastical Cao Dai temple at Tay Ninh and dazzling white, remote beaches at Phu Quoc.

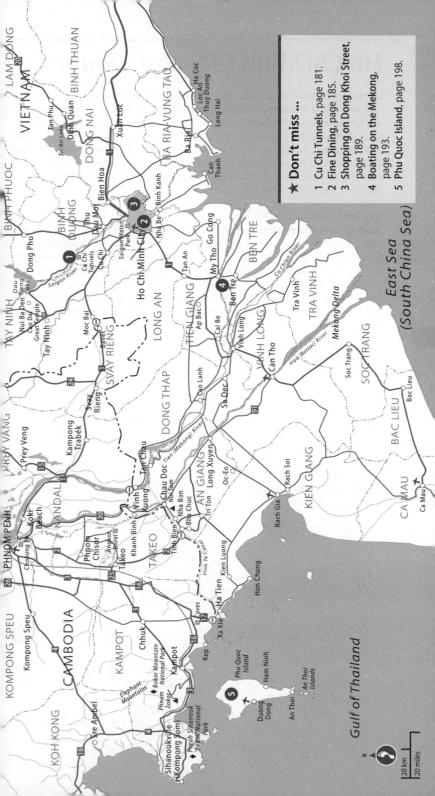

★ **Don't miss ...**

1 Cu Chi Tunnels, page 181.
2 Fine Dining, page 185.
3 Shopping on Dong Khoi Street, page 189.
4 Boating on the Mekong, page 193.
5 Phu Quoc Island, page 198.

# Ho Chi Minh City and around

*Officially renamed in 1975, Ho Chi Minh City remains to most the bi-syllabic, familiar 'Saigon'. During the 1960s and early 1970s, Saigon, the Pearl of the Orient, boomed and flourished under the American occupation. Today, it is the largest city in Vietnam and still growing at a prodigious rate. It is a place of remorseless, relentless activity and expanding urban sprawl. It is also the nation's foremost commercial and industrial centre. For the visitor, Ho Chi Minh City is a fantastic place to shop, eat and drink, while admiring its historical past and enjoying its energetic present.* ▸▸ *For Sleeping, Eating and other listings, see pages 183-192.*

## Ins and outs → *Colour map 6, C5.*

**Getting there** **Tan Son Nhat airport** (SGN), T08-848 5383/0832 0320, is 30 minutes from the centre. By taxi the cost is about US$5-7. Taxi drivers may try and demand a flat fee in US dollars but you should insist on using the meter, which is the law, and pay in dong. Facilities in arrivals include tourist information, two banks and a post office; in departures, there is a **Vietindebank**, post office, first-aid office and telephone service. There are also small duty-free shops and poor but expensive cafés and bars. On the right of the international terminal is the **domestic terminal**. It has toilets, a shop, telephones and a reasonable restaurant.

## Ho Chi Minh City

**Related maps**
**A** Ho Chi Minh City centre, page 175
**B** Ho Chi Minh City centre detail, page 176
**C** Pham Ngu Lao, page 179

**Open Tour Buses** generally depart and leave from offices in the Pham Ngu Lao district. There is also a daily bus service from Ho Chi Minh City to Phnom Penh (Cambodia). The **railway station** is northwest of the city centre. There are regular daily connections to/from Hanoi and all stops on the line north. ▸▸ *For further information, see Transport, page 191.*

**Getting around** Ho Chi Minh City has abundant transport. Metered taxis, motorcycle taxis and cyclos vie for business. Those who prefer some level of independence opt to hire (or even buy) a bicycle or motorbike. There are now so many motorbikes on the streets of Ho Chi Minh City that intersections seem lethally confused. Miraculously, the riders miss each other (most of the time), while pedestrians safely make their way through waves of machines (see Crossing the road, page 177). Take an organized tour to reach sights outside the city.

**Orientation** Virtually all of Ho Chi Minh City lies to the west of the Saigon River. Most visitors to Ho Chi Minh City head straight for hotels in Districts 1 or 3. Many will arrive on buses in De Tham or Pham Ngu Lao streets, the backpacker area, in District 1, not far from the city centre. Many of the sights are also in District 1 (also still known as Saigon). Cholon or Chinatown (District 5) is a mile west of the centre. All the sights of Central Ho Chi Minh City can be reached on foot or cyclo in no more than 30 minutes from the major hotels on Nguyen Hue, Dong Khoi and Ton Duc Thang streets.

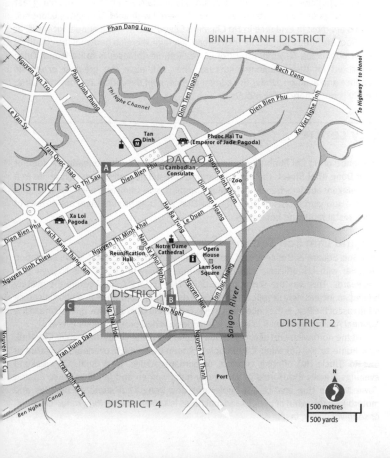

*Vietnam Ho Chi Minh City & around*

Before the 15th century, Ho Chi Minh City was a small village surrounded by a wilderness of forest and swamp. Through the years it was ostensibly incorporated into the Funan and then the Khmer empires but it's unlikely that these kingdoms had any lasting influence on the community. In fact, the Khmers, who called the region *Prei Nokor*, used it for hunting. By 1623 the town had become an important commercial centre and, in the mid-17th century, it became the residence of the so-called Vice-King of Cambodia. In 1698, the Viets managed to extend their control to the far south and Saigon was finally brought under Vietnamese control. By 1790, the city had a population of 50,000 and Emperor Gia Long made it his place of residence until Hué was selected as the capital of the Nguyen Dynasty.

In the middle of the 19th century, the French began to challenge Vietnamese authority in the south. Between 1859 and 1862, in response to Nguyen persecution of the Catholics in Vietnam, the French attacked and captured Saigon. The Treaty of Saigon in 1862 ratified the conquest and created the new French colony of Cochin China. Saigon was developed in French style, with wide, tree-lined boulevards, street-side cafés, elegant French architecture, boutiques and the smell of baking baguettes.

During the course of the Vietnam War, as refugees spilled in from a devastated countryside, the population of Saigon almost doubled from 2.4 million in 1965 to around 4.5 million by 1975. With reunification in 1976, the new Communist authorities pursued a policy of depopulation, believing that the city had become too large and parasitic, preying on the surrounding countryside.

The population of Ho Chi Minh City today is officially seven million and rising fast as the rural poor are lured by tales of streets paved with gold. Vietnam's economic reforms are most in evidence in Ho Chi Minh City, where average annual incomes, at US$1800, are more than double the national average. It is also here that the country's largest population (around 380,000) of Hoa (ethnic Chinese) is to be found. Once persecuted for their economic success, they still have the greatest economic influence and acumen. Under the current regime, best described as crony capitalist, the city is once more being rebuilt.

# City centre

The centre of Ho Chi Minh City is, in many respects, the most interesting. A saunter down **Dong Khoi Street**, the old rue Catinat, can still give an impression of life in a more elegant and less frenzied era. Much remains on a small and personal scale and within a 100 yard radius of Dong Khoi or Thai Van Lung streets there are dozens of cafés, restaurants and boutiques.

## Around Lam Son Square

Lam Son Square is the centre of Ho Chi Minh City. The **Rex Hotel**, a pre-Liberation favourite with US officers, stands at the intersection of Le Loi and Nguyen Hue boulevards. This was the scene of the daily 'Five O'clock Follies' where the military briefed an increasingly sceptical press corps during the Vietnam War. A short distance northeast of the **Rex**, is the once impressive, French-era **Opera House**, once home to the National Assembly. When it is open, it provides a varied programme of events.

At the northwest end of Nguyen Hue Boulevard is the yellow and white **City Hall**, now home to Ho Chi Minh City People's Committee, which overlooks a **statue of Bac Ho** (Uncle Ho) offering comfort, or perhaps advice, to a child. On weekend evenings literally thousands of young city men, women and families cruise up and down Nguyen Hue and Le Loi boulevards and Dong Khoi street on bicycles and motorbikes; this whirl of people and machines is known as *chay long rong*, 'cruising', or *song voi*, 'living fast'.

To the left of the Opera House is the **Continental Hotel**, built in 1880 and an integral part of the city's history. Graham Greene stayed here and the hotel features in the novel *The Quiet American*. The old journalists' haunt, the 'Continental Shelf', was described as "a famous veranda where correspondents, spies, speculators, traffickers, intellectuals and soldiers used to meet during the war to glean information and pick up secret reports, half false, half true or half disclosed. All of this is more than enough for it to be known as Radio Catinat".

## Cong Xa Pari (Paris Square)

In the middle of Cong Xa Pari is the imposing and austere **Notre Dame Cathedral** ① *open to visitors 0800-1100 and 1500-1600 on weekdays*, built between 1877 and 1880, allegedly on the site of an ancient pagoda. The red-brick, twin-spired cathedral overlooks a grassy square with a statue of the Virgin Mary holding an orb.

# Ho Chi Minh City centre

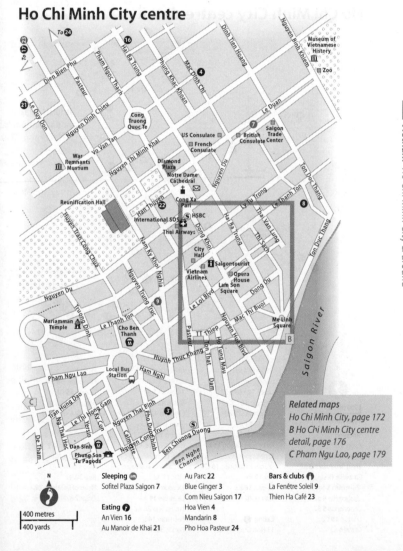

Related maps
Ho Chi Minh City, page 172
B Ho Chi Minh City centre detail, page 176
C Pham Ngu Lao, page 179

N

400 metres
400 yards

| Sleeping | Au Parc 22 | Bars & clubs |
|---|---|---|
| Sofitel Plaza Saigon 7 | Blue Ginger 3 | La Fenêtre Soleil 9 |
| | Com Nieu Saigon 17 | Thien Ha Café 23 |
| Eating | Hoa Vien 4 | |
| An Vien 16 | Mandarin 8 | |
| Au Manoir de Khai 21 | Pho Hoa Pasteur 24 | |

Facing onto Paris Square is the **General Post Office**, built in the 1880s, a particularly distinguished building despite the veneer of junk that has been slapped onto it. The front façade has attractive cornices with French and Khmer motifs and the names of distinguished French men of letters and science. Inside, the high, vaulted ceiling and fans create a deliciously cool atmosphere in which to scribble a postcard. Note the old wall-map of Cochin-China, which has miraculously survived.

## Reunification Hall

ⓘ *Nam Ky Khoi Nghia St, To8-8223652, daily 0730-1100, 1300-1600; 15,000d, children 2000d, brochure 5000d. Tours every 10 mins; the guides are friendly but their English is not always very good. The hall is sometimes closed for state occasions.*
The residence of the French governor was built on this site in 1868 and later became Ngo Dinh Diem's **Presidential Palace**. In February 1962, a pair of planes took off to

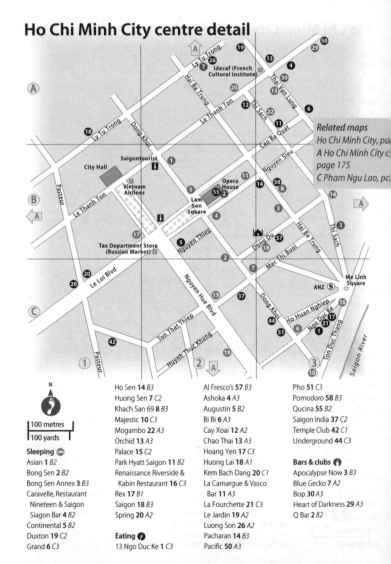

# Ho Chi Minh City centre detail

**Related maps**
Ho Chi Minh City, pa
A Ho Chi Minh City c
page 175
C Pham Ngu Lao, po

100 metres
100 yards

N

**Sleeping** 🛏
Asian **1** B2
Bong Sen **2** B2
Bong Sen Annex **3** B3
Caravelle, Restaurant
  Nineteen & Saigon
  Siagon Bar **4** B2
Continental **5** B2
Duxton **19** C2
Grand **6** C3

Ho Sen **14** B3
Huong Sen **7** C2
Khach San 69 **8** B3
Majestic **10** C3
Mogambo **22** A3
Orchid **13** A3
Palace **15** C2
Park Hyatt Saigon **11** B2
Renaissance Riverside &
  Kabin Restaurant **16** C3
Rex **17** B1
Saigon **18** B3
Spring **20** A2

**Eating** 🍴
13 Ngo Duc Ke **1** C3

Al Fresco's **57** B3
Ashoka **4** A3
Augustin **5** B2
Bi Bi **6** A3
Cay Xoai **12** A2
Chao Thai **13** A3
Hoang Yen **17** C3
Huong Lai **18** A1
Kem Bach Dang **20** C1
La Camargue & Vasco
  Bar **11** A3
La Fourchette **21** C3
Le Jardin **19** A2
Luong Son **26** A2
Pacharan **14** B3
Pacific **50** A3

Pho **51** C3
Pomodoro **58** B3
Qucina **55** B2
Saigon India **37** C2
Temple Club **42** C1
Underground **44** C3

**Bars & clubs** 🍸
Apocalypse Now **3** B3
Blue Gecko **7** A2
Bop **30** A3
Heart of Darkness **29** A3
Q Bar **2** B2

*Vietnam* Ho Chi Minh City & around

## ⁞ Crossing the road

Ho Chi Minh City's streets may look anarchic but they are not. A strict code of conduct applies: the main difference between Vietnam's roads and those of the west is that, in Vietnam, the individual abdicates responsibility for his personal safety and assumes an obligation on the part of everyone else; it is the closest Vietnam has ever come to true Communism!

Watch Vietnamese cross a busy street: unlike Westerners they do not wait for a lull in the traffic but launch themselves straight into the flow, chatting and laughing with their friends, eyes ahead so as to avoid walking into a passing bicycle (their sole duty), no looking left and right, no ducking and weaving – responsibility for their safety rests entirely with the oncoming cyclists. In order to make it easier for cyclists not to hit them they walk at a steady, even pace with no deviation from a clearly signalled route, as any slight change in trajectory or velocity would spell certain disaster.

attack Viet Cong emplacements but turned back to bomb the Presidential Palace in a futile attempt to assassinate President Diem who had been living there since 1954. The president escaped with his family to the cellar but the palace had to be demolished and replaced with a new building, now renamed Reunification Hall, or the **Thong Nhat Conference Hall**. One of the two pilots, Nguyen Thanh Trung, is now a Vice President of Vietnam Airlines and still flies government officials around to keep his pilot's licence current.

One of the most memorable photographs taken during the war was of a North Vietnamese Army (NVA) tank crashing through the gates of the Palace on 30 April 1975, symbolizing the end of South Vietnam and its government. A similar tank is now displayed in the forecourt. The President of South Vietnam, General Duong Van Minh, along with his entire cabinet, was arrested in the palace shortly afterwards but the hall has been preserved as it was found in 1975. In the Vice President's Guest Room is a lacquered painting of the Temple of Literature in Hanoi, while the Presenting of Credentials Room contains a fine 40-piece lacquer work showing diplomats presenting their credentials during the Le Dynasty (15th century). In the basement, there are operations rooms, military maps, radios and other official paraphernalia.

## War Remnants Museum

ⓘ *28 Vo Van Tan St, District 3, T08-9306325. Mon-Fri and public holidays 0730-1100, 1330-1715; 10,000d.*

All the horrors of the Vietnam War from the Vietnamese perspective are piled from floor to ceiling in this museum. The courtyard is stacked with tanks, bombs, planes and helicopters, while the museum, arranged in rooms around the courtyard, record man's inhumanity to man, with displays of deformed feotuses alongside photographs of atrocities and of military action. The exhibits cover the Son My (My Lai) massacre on 16 March 1968, the effects of napalm and phosphorous, and the after-effects of Agent Orange defoliation. Many of the pictures are horrific.

One of the most interesting rooms is dedicated to war photographers and their pictures. It is a requiem to those who died pursuing their craft and, unusually, depicts the military struggle from both sides. The war, as captured through the lens, is an Heironymous Bosch-like hell of mangled metal, suffocating mud and injured limbs. The wall-to-wall images include shots from Robert Capa's last roll of film (before the famous photographer stood on a land mine on 25 May 1954 and died); *Life* magazine's first colour coverage of the conflict, and quotes from those that perished, including a memorable one from Georgette Louise Meyer, aka Dickey Chapelle, who described the thrill of being on the "bayonet border" of the world. Understandably, there is no record of North Vietnamese atrocities carried out on US and South Vietnamese troops.

## Xa Loi Pagoda

ⓘ *89 Ba Huyen Thanh Quan St, daily 0630-1100, 1430-1700.*
The Xa Loi Pagoda is not far from the War Remnants Museum and is surrounded by foodstalls. Built in 1956, the pagoda contains a multi-storeyed tower, which is particularly revered, as it houses a relic of the Buddha. The main sanctuary contains a large, bronze-gilded Buddha in an attitude of meditation. Around the walls are a series of silk paintings depicting the previous lives of the Buddha (with an explanation of each life to the right of the entrance into the sanctuary). The pagoda is historically, rather than artistically, important as it became a focus of dissent against the Diem regime in 1963 when several monks committed suicide through self-immolation.

## Le Duan Street

Le Duan Street was the former corridor of power with Ngo Dinh Diem's Palace at one end, the zoo at the other and the former embassies of the three major powers, France, the US and the UK, in between. Nearest the Reunification Hall is the compound of the **French Consulate**. A block away is the **former US Embassy**. After diplomatic ties were resumed in 1995, the Americans lost little time in demolishing the 1960s embassy, which held so many bad memories. The US Consulate General now stands on this site. A **memorial** outside, on the corner of Mac Dinh Chi Street, records the attack by Viet Cong special forces during the Tet Offensive of 1968 and the final victory in 1975. On the other side of the road, a little further northeast at 25 Le Duan, is the **former British Embassy**, erected in the late 1950s, which now serves as the British Consulate General and British Council.

## Museum of Vietnamese History

ⓘ *2 Nguyen Binh Khiem St, To8-8298146, daily 0800-1100, 1330-1630; 5000d. No photograpy allowed. Labels in English and French. Water puppet shows are held here daily at 0900, 1000, 1400, 1500 and 1600, 15 mins; US$2.*
The history museum (Bao Tang Lich Su Viet Nam) occupies an elegant 1928 building with a pagoda-based design. The collection spans a wide range of artefacts from the prehistoric (300,000 years ago) and the Dong Son periods (3,500BC-AD100), right through to the birth of the Vietnamese Communist Party in 1930. Particularly impressive are the Cham sculptures, of which the standing bronze Buddha, showing Indian stylistic influence, is probably the finest. There is also a delicately carved Devi (goddess) dating from the 10th century, as well as the head of Siva (Hindu destroyer and creator) and Ganesh (elephant-headed son of Siva and Parvati) both dating from the eighth to the ninth century.

Representative pieces from the Chen-la, Funan, Khmer, Oc-eo and Han Chinese periods are also on display, along with items from the various Vietnamese dynasties and some ethnic minority artefacts. Other highlights include the wooden stakes planted in the Bach Dang riverbed to repel the war ships of the Mongol Yuan in the 13th century; a beautiful Phoenix head from the Tran Dynasty (13th to 14th century) and a Hgor (big drum) of the Jorai people, made from the skin of two elephants.

## Ben Thanh Market (Cho Ben Thanh)

A large, covered central market, Ben Thanh Market faces a statue of Tran Nguyen Han at a large and chaotic roundabout, known as the Ben Thanh gyratory system. Ben Thanh is well stocked with clothes, household goods, a good choice of souvenirs, lacquerware, embroidery and so on, as well as some terrific lines in food, including cold meats, fresh and dried fruits. It is not cheap (most local people window-shop here and purchase elsewhere) but the quality is high and the selection probably without equal. Outside the north gate (*cua Bac*) on Le Thanh Ton Street are some particularly tempting displays of fresh fruit (the oranges and apples are imported) and beautiful cut flowers. The **Ben Thanh Night Market** has flourished since 2003; starting at dusk and continuing until after midnight, it offers clothes and cheap jewellery and an abundance of food stalls.

## Phung Son Tu Pagoda and Dan Sinh market

On Nguyen Cong Tru Street is **Phung Son Tu Pagoda**, a small temple built just after the Second World War by Fukien Chinese; its most notable features are the wonderful painted entrance doors with their fearsome armed warriors. Incense spirals hang in the open well of the pagoda, which is dedicated to Ong Bon, the Guardian of Happiness and Virtue.

Close to the pagoda, on the same street, is the **War Surplus Market** (**Dan Sinh**). Merchandise on sale includes dog tags and military clothing and equipment (not all of it authentic). The market is popular with Western visitors looking for mementoes of their visit, so bargain particularly hard.

## Pham Ngu Lao

Most backpackers arriving overland in Ho Chi Minh City are dropped off in this bustling district, a 10 to 15-minute walk from downtown. There are countless hotels, guesthouses and rooms to rent and the area is peppered with restaurants, cafés, bars, email services, tour agencies and money changers, all fiercely competitive.

---

# Cholon (Chinatown)

Cholon (*Cho lon* or 'big market' or Chinatown), which encompasses District 5 to the southwest of the city centre, is inhabited predominantly by Vietnamese of Chinese origin. Since 1975, the authorities have alienated many Chinese, causing hundreds of thousands to leave the country. (Between 1977 and 1982, 709,570 refugees were recorded by the UNHCR as having fled Vietnam.) In making their escape many have died, either through drowning – as their perilously small and overladen craft foundered – or at the hands of pirates in the South China Sea. By the late 1980s, the flow of boat people was being driven by economic rather than by political forces: there was little chance of making good in a country as poor, and in an economy as

# Pham Ngu Lao

| Sleeping | Minh Chau 11 | Cay Bo De 3 |
| --- | --- | --- |
| 211 1 | Ngoc Dang 12 | Good Morning Vietnam 13 |
| Hong Hoa 3 | Que Huong (Liberty 3) 13 | Kim Café 4 |
| Huong 4 | Que Huong (Liberty 4) 14 | Lac Thien 10 |
| Linh 7 | Thanh Huyen 17 | |
| Linh Thu Guesthouse 8 | | Bars & clubs |
| Madame Cuc 20 | Eating | 163 Cyclo 14 |
| Mimi Guesthouse 10 | Cappuccino 2 | |

N
50 metres
50 yards

moribund, as that of Vietnam. Even with this exodus of Chinese out of the country, there is still a large population of Chinese Vietnamese living in Cholon, an area which, to the casual visitor, appears to be the most populated, noisiest and, in general, the most vigorous part of Ho Chi Minh City, if not of Vietnam. It is here that entrepreneurial talent and private funds are concentrated; both resources that the government are keen to mobilize in their attempts to reinvigorate the economy.

Cholon is worth visiting not only for the bustle and activity, but also because the temples and assembly halls found here are the finest in Ho Chi Minh City. As with any town in Southeast Asia boasting a sizeable Chinese population, the early settlers established meeting rooms which offered social, cultural and spiritual support to members of a dialect group. These assembly halls (*hoi quan*) are most common in Hoi An and Cholon. Temples within the buildings attract Vietnamese as well as Chinese worshippers and, today, the halls serve little of their former purpose.

## Assembly halls and temples

**Nghia An Assembly Hall** ① *678 Nguyen Trai St,* has a magnificent, carved, gold-painted wooden boat hanging over the entrance. To the left, on entering the temple, is a larger than life representation of Quan Cong's horse and groom. At the main altar are three figures in glass cases: the central red-faced figure with a green cloak is Quan Cong himself; to the left and right are his trusty companions, General Chau Xuong (very fierce) and the mandarin Quan Binh respectively. On leaving the temple, note the fine gold figures of guardians on the inside of the door panels.

**Thien Hau Temple** ① *710 and 802 Nguyen Trai St,* is one of the largest in the city. Constructed in the early 19th century, it is Chinese in inspiration and is dedicated to the worship of both the Buddha and the Goddess Thien Hau (goddess of the sea and the protector of sailors). Thien Hau was born in China and, as a girl, saved her father from drowning but not her brother. Thien Hau's festival is marked here on the 23rd day of the third lunar month. Inside, the principal altar supports the gilded form of Thien Hau, with a boat to one side. Silk paintings depicting religious scenes decorate the walls. By far the most interesting part of the pagoda is the roof, which can be best seen from the small open courtyard. It is one of the finest and most richly ornamented in Vietnam, with a high-relief frieze depicting episodes from the Legends of the Three Kingdoms. In the post-1975 era, many would-be refugees prayed here for safe deliverance before casting themselves adrift on the South China Sea. A number of those who survived the perilous voyage sent offerings to the merciful goddess and the temple has been well maintained since. Look up on leaving to see, over the front door, a picture of a boiling sea peppered with sinking boats. A benign Thien An looks down mercifully from a cloud.

**Ming Dynasty Assembly Hall** (Dinh Minh Huong Gia Thanh) ① *380 Tran Hung Dao St,* was built by the Cantonese community, which arrived in Ho Chi Minh City via Hoi An in the 18th century. The assembly hall was built in 1789 to the dedication and worship of the Ming Dynasty, although the building today dates largely from an extensive renovation carried out in 1960s. In the main hall there are three altars, which following imperial tradition: the central altar is dedicated to the royal family (Ming Dynasty in this case); the right-hand altar to two mandarin officers (military), and the left-hand altar to two mandarin officers (civil).

**Quan Am Pagoda** ① *12 Lao Tu St, just off Luong Nhu Hoc St,* is thought to be one of the oldest in the city. Its roof supports four sets of impressive mosaic-encrusted figures, while inside, the main building is fronted with gold and lacquer panels of guardian spirits. The altar supports a seated statue of A-Pho, the Holy Mother. In front of the main altar is a white ceramic statue of Quan Am, the Goddess of Purity and Motherhood (Goddess of Mercy), see page 91.

# Outer districts

The outlying areas of Ho Chi Minh City include a clutch of scattered pagodas in districts 3, 10, 11 and Binh Thanh. All are accessible by cyclo, moto or taxi.

## Pagodas

**Giac Vien Pagoda** (Buddha's Complete Enlightenment) ① *at the end of a narrow, rather seedy 400-m-long alley running off Lac Long Quan Street, District 11,* was built in 1771 and dedicated to the worship of the Emperor Gia Long. Although restored, Giac Vien remains one of the best preserved temples in Vietnam. It is lavishly decorated, with more than 100 carvings of various divinities and spirits, dominated by a large gilded image of the Buddha of the Past (Amitabha or *A Di Da Phat* in Vietnamese).

In District 10, the **Giac Lam Pagoda** (Forest of Enlightenment) ① *118 Lac Long Quan St, To8-8653933, daily 0500-1200, 1400-2100, through an arch and down a short track about 300 m from the intersection with Le Dai Hanh St,* was built in 1744 and is the oldest pagoda in Ho Chi Minh City. There is a sacred Bodhi tree in the temple courtyard and the pagoda is set among fruit trees and vegetable plots. The interior of Giac Lam feels, initially, like a rather cluttered private house. In one section, there are rows of funerary tablets with pictures of the deceased. The main altar is particularly impressive, with layers of Buddhas, dominated by the gilded form of the Buddha of the Past. Note the 49-Buddha oil lamp with little scraps of paper tucked in to it. On these scraps are the names of the mourned. Behind the main temple in the section with the funerary tablets is a bust of Ho Chi Minh. At the very back of the pagoda is a hall with murals showing scenes of torture from hell. Each sin is punished in a very specific and appropriate way. An unusual feature is the use of blue and white porcelain plates to decorate the roof and some of the small towers in the garden facing the pagoda. These towers are the burial places of former head monks.

**Phuoc Hai Tu** (Emperor of Jade Pagoda) ① *73 Mai Thi Luu St, off Dien Bien Phu St, 0700-1800* can be found, nestling behind low pink walls, just before the Thi Nghe Channel. The Emperor of Jade is the supreme god of the Taoists, although this temple, built in 1900, contains a wide range of other deities. These include the archangel Michael of the Buddhists, a Sakyamuni (historic) Buddha, statues of the two generals who tamed the Green Dragon (representing the east) and the White Dragon (representing the west) to the left and right of the first altar respectively and Quan Am (see page 91). The Hall of Ten Hells in the left-hand sanctuary has reliefs depicting the 1000 tortures of hell.

# Around Ho Chi Minh City ›› *Colour map 6, C5.*

The Cu Chi Tunnels are the most popular day trip, followed closely by an excursion to the Mekong Delta, especially My Tho (see page 194). ›› *For further information, see Activities and tours, page 190.*

## Cu Chi Tunnels → *Colour map 6, C5.*

① *About 40 km northwest of Ho Chi Minh City, daily 0700-1700. 70,000d. Most visitors reach Cu Chi on a tour or charter a car and include a visit to Tay Ninh.*
Begun by the Viet Minh in 1948, these tunnels were later expanded by the Viet Cong and used for storage and refuge. Between 1960-1970, 200 km of tunnels were built, containing sleeping quarters, hospitals and schools. The original tunnels were only 80 cm high and the width of the tunnel entry at ground level was 22 cm by 30 cm. The tunnels are too narrow for most Westerners, but a short section of the 250 km of tunnels has been especially widened to allow tourists to share the experience.

## Ho Chi Minh Trail

The Ho Chi Minh Trail was used by the North Vietnamese Army to ferry equipment from the North to the South via Laos. The road, or more accurately roads (there were between eight and 10 routes to reduce "choke points") were camouflaged in places, allowing the NVA to get supplies to their comrades in the South through the heaviest bombing by US planes. Even the USA's use of defoliants such as Agent Orange only marginally stemmed the flow. Neil Sheehan, in his book *A Bright Shining Lie*, estimates that at no time were more than one third of the supply trucks destroyed and, by marching through the most dangerous sections, the forces themselves suffered a loss rate of only 10-20%.

The Ho Chi Minh Trail was built and kept operational by 300,000 full-time workers and by another 200,000 part-time North Vietnamese peasants. Initially, supplies were carried along the trail on bicycles; later, as supplies of trucks from China and the Soviet Union became more plentiful, they were carried by motorized transport. By the end of the conflict the Trail comprised 15,360 km of all-weather and secondary roads. It One Hero of the People's Army is said, during the course of the war, to have carried and pushed 55 tonnes of supplies a distance of 41,025 km – roughly the circumference of the world.

The Ho Chi Minh Trail represents perhaps the best example of how, through revolutionary fervour, ingenuity and weight of people (not of arms), the Viet Cong were able to vanquish the might of the US. But American pilots did exact a terrible toll through the years. Again, Sheehan writes: "Driving a truck year in, year out with 20-25% to perhaps 30% odds of mortality was not a military occupation conducive to retirement on pension."

The cemetery for those who died on the trail covers 16 ha and contains 10,306 named head-stones; many more died unnamed and unrecovered.

Cu Chi was one of the most fervently Communist districts around Ho Chi Minh City and the tunnels were used as the base from which the VC mounted the operations of the Tet Offensive in 1968. When the Americans first discovered this underground network on their doorstep (Dong Du GI base was nearby) they would simply pump CS gas down the tunnel openings and then set explosives. They also pumped river water in and used German Shepherd dogs to smell out air holes, although the VC smothered the holes in garlic to deter the dogs. Around 40,000 VC were killed in the tunnels in 10 years but, later, realizing the tunnels might also yield valuable intelligence, the Americans sent volunteer 'tunnel rats' into the earth to capture prisoners.

Cu Chi district initially was a free-fire zone and was assaulted using the full battery of ecological warfare. Defoliants were sprayed and 20-tonne Rome Ploughs carved up the area in the search for tunnels. It was said that even a crow flying over Cu Chi district had to carry its own lunch. Later it was carpet bombed: 50,000 tonnes were dropped on the area in 10 years evidenced by the B-52 bomb craters.

At **Cu Chi 1** (Ben Dinh) ① *70,000d*, visitors are shown a somewhat antique but interesting film of the tunnels during the war before being taken into the tunnels themselves and seeing some of the rooms and the booby traps the GIs encountered. You will also be invited to a firing range to try your hand with ancient AK47s at a buck a bang. **Cu Chi 2** (Ben Duoc), has a temple, built in 1993, devoted to the memory of the

dead and visited by those whose relatives are still 'missing'. The sculpture behind the
temple is of a massive tear cradled in the hands of a mother.

## Cao Dai Great Temple → *Colour map 6, C5.*

ⓘ *Tay Ninh, 64 km beyond Cu Chi town (96 km northwest of Ho Chi Minh City). It can be visited on a day trip from the city and can easily be combined with a visit to the Cu Chi tunnels. Ceremonies 1 hr daily 0600, 1200, 1800 and 2400; visitors should not wander in and out during services but can watch from the cathedral's balcony. At other times keep to the side aisles and do not enter the central portion of the nave. Photography is allowed. Shoes must be removed.*

The Cao Dai religion was founded on Phu Quoc Island (page 198) in 1920, when civil servant Ngo Van Chieu communed with the spirit world and made contact with the Supreme Being. The idiosyncratic, twin-towered Cao Dai Great Temple, the 'cathedral' of the religion, was built from 1933 to 1955 and is European in inspiration but with distinct Oriental features. On the façade are figures of Cao Dai saints in high relief and, at the entrance to the cathedral, there is a painting depicting writer Victor Hugo flanked by the Vietnamese poet Nguyen Binh Khiem and the Chinese nationalist Sun Yat Sen.

The temple provokes strong reactions: Novelist Graham Greene in *The Quiet American* called it "The Walt Disney Fantasia of the East". Monsieur Ferry, an acquaintance of travel writer Norman Lewis, described the cathedral in even more outlandish terms, saying it "looked like a fantasy from the brain of Disney, and all the faiths of the Orient had been ransacked to create the pompous ritual...". Lewis himself was clearly unimpressed with the structure and the religion, writing in *A Dragon Apparent* that this "cathedral must be the most outrageously vulgar building ever to have been erected with serious intent".

After removing shoes and hats, women enter the cathedral through a door to the left, men to the right, and they then proceed down their respective aisles towards the altar, usually accompanied by a Cao Dai priest dressed in white with a black turban. During services they don red, blue and yellow robes signifying Confucianism, Taoism and Buddhism respectively. Two rows of pink pillars entwined with green, horned dragons line the nave, leading up to the main altar which supports a large globe on which is painted a single staring eye: the divine, all-seeing eye. Above the altar is the Cao Dai pantheon: at the top in the centre is Sakyamuni Buddha; next to him, on the left, is Lao Tzu, master of Taosim; left of Lao Tzu is Quan Am, Goddess of Mercy, sitting on a lotus blossom; on the other side of the Buddha statue is Confucius; right of the sage is the red-faced Chinese God of War, Quan Cong; below Sakyamuni Buddha is the poet and leader of the Chinese saints, Li Ti Pei; below him is Jesus, and, below Christ, is Jiang Zhia, master of Geniism.

## ● Sleeping

**City centre** *p174, maps p175 and p176*
**LL Caravelle**, 19-23 Lam Son Square, T08-823 4999, www.caravellehotel.com. Central and one of HCMC's top hotels. Comfortable with well-trained and friendly staff. **Restaurant Nineteen** serves a fantastic buffet lunch and dinner with free flow of fine French wine included (see Eating), and **Saigon Saigon**, the rooftop bar, draws the crowds until the early hours of the morning (see Bars and clubs). Also has a suite of boutique shops and ATM.

**LL Park Hyatt Saigon**, 2 Lam Son Sq, T08-8241234, www.saigon.park.hyatt.com. This new hotel is in a class of its own. It exudes elegance and style and its location north of the Opera House is unrivalled. Works of art are hung in the lobby, rooms are classically furnished in French colonial style but with modern touches; the pool area is lovely; the wonderful lounge area features a baby grand piano and there are a number of very good restaurants that incorporate jaw-dropping displays of floor-to-ceiling wines in a glass display. **Square One** is an excellent restaurant with open kitchens and displays. There's also a fitness centre and spa.

**LL-L Majestic**, 1 Dong Khoi St, T08-8295517, www.majesticsaigon.com. Built in 1925, this riverside hotel has character and charm and has been tastefully restored and recently expanded. More expensive and large rooms have superb views over the river; from the new bar on the top floor there are magnificent views of the riverfront, especially at night.

**LL-L Sofitel Plaza Saigon**, 17 Le Duan St, T08-8241555, www.sofitel.com. A smart, fashionable and comfortable hotel with a delicious rooftop pool.

**L Continental**, 132-134, Dong Khoi St, T08-8299201, www.continental-saigon.com. Built in 1880 and renovated in 1989, this is an integral part of the city's history (see page 175). It has an air of faded colonial splendour and its large but dated rooms need upgrading. The hotel boasts a couple of restaurants, a business centre, fitness room and a pool. Probably in an attempt to stamp out the theft of souvenirs, you can purchase every item in the room.

**L Duxton**, 63 Nguyen Hue Blvd, T08-8222999, www.duxton.com. The Duxton Hotel is a very attractively appointed and well finished hotel and popular with Japanese visitors. It has 198 finely decorated rooms, a health club, pool and a restaurant.

**L Grand**, 8 Dong Khoi St, T08-823 0163, www.grandhotel.vn. A 1930s building, extensively renovated but, happily, the stained glass and marble staircase have largely survived the process. A huge, modern featureless wing has been added. The pool is surrounded by a tiled and potted plant-filled patio. Good value hotel with a very reasonably priced restaurant. **Saigontourist** is to upgrade this hotel to 5 stars in 2009.

**L Renaissance Riverside**, 8-15 Ton Duc Thang St, T08-8220033, www.marriott.com. Despite its 21 floors and 349 rooms and suites this is, in style and feel, almost a boutique hotel. Very well run, comfortable and popular with its customers. It also boasts Vietnam's highest atrium. It has several excellent restaurants, including Kabin Chinese restaurant, and an attractive pool.

**L Rex**, 141 Nguyen Hue Blvd, T08-8292185, www.rexhotelvietnam.com. A historically important hotel with unusual interior decor and an expansion underway. The large lobby is decorated entirely in wood. Superior rooms have small bathtub and are interior facing. Deluxe rooms are double the size but those on the main road are noisy. The **Mimosa Club** has a pool, rooftop tennis court, fitness centre and beauty salon. It has the famous rooftop terrace bar, popular with journalists and upmarket tour groups.

**A Bong Sen**, 117-123 Dong Khoi St, T08-8291516, www.hotelbongsen.com. Operated by **Saigontourist**. Well-run and upgraded in a perfect location in the heart of the shopping district. Good value for the location but standard rooms are very small. Larger superior rooms are only slightly more expensive and have bathtubs. Few rooms have views. There is a restaurant and the **Green Leaf** café.

**A Bong Sen Hotel Annex**, 61-63 Hai Ba Trung St, T08-8235818, www.hotelbong sen.com. Sister hotel of the **Bong Sen**, this is a well-managed hotel with standard a/c rooms and a restaurant.

**A Huong Sen**, 66-70 Dong Khoi St, T08-8291415, huongsen@hcm.vnn.vn. This central hotel is popular with tour groups and good value on this street. A rooftop bar on the 7th floor is a nice place for a beer.

**A Palace**, 56-66 Nguyen Hue Blvd, T08-8292860, www.palacesaigon.com/. **Saigontourist**-run hotel with some decent-sized rooms. It's very central with a restaurant and small rooftop pool.

**A Saigon**, 45-47 Dong Du St, T08-8299734, saigonhotel@hcm.vnn.vn. Opposite the mosque in a good central location. Some rooms a bit dark and small, but it's popular and clean. Prices have risen which makes it not quite such good value.

**A-B Asian**, 146-150 Dong Khoi St, T08-8296979, asianhotel@hcm.fpt.vn. Rooms with a/c and satellite TV are a little small. There's a restaurant and breakfast is included. The location is central.

**A-B Ho Sen**, 4B-4C Thi Sach St, T08-8232281, www.hosenhotel.com.vn. This bland looking hotel in a very central location is a good find. Rooms are surprisingly very quiet, fairly spacious and comfortable with TVs. Staff are friendly and helpful and will store luggage.

**A-B Spring**, 44-46 Le Thanh Ton St, T08-8297362, springhotel@hcm.vnn.vn. Central, comfortable with charming and helpful staff. Book well in advance if you want to stay in this well-run family hotel that is excellent value; breakfast included. Recommended.

**B Mogambo**, 20Bis Thi Sach St, T08-8251311, mogambo@saigonnet.vn. A/c, satellite TV, a few good and fairly priced rooms above this popular American-run diner.

**B Orchid**, 29A Thai Van Lung St, T08-8231809. In a good, central spot, surrounded by restaurants and bars, worth taking a look at. Rooms have a/c and satellite TV.

**C-D Khach San 69**, 69 Hai Ba Trung St, T08-8291513, 69hotel@saigonnet.vn. Central location with clean a/c rooms that back onto HCMC's Indian mosque.

**Pham Ngu Lao** *p179, map p179*
Shared rooms can be had for as little as US$4-5 per night and dormitory rooms for less but facilities and comfort levels at the bottom end are very basic.

**A Que Huong** (Liberty 4), 265 Pham Ngu Lao St, T08-8365822, www.libertyhotel saigon.com. Formerly **Hoang Vu**, a perfectly comfortable hotel. It has had to moderate its prices which means it is now possibly fair value but priced way too high for this area. Breakfast is included.

**A Que Huong** (Liberty 3), 187 Pham Ngu Lao St, T08-8369522, www.liberty hotelsaigon.com. Less popular with travellers than previously as there is now more choice; cheapest rooms are on the upper floors, rather noisy.

**B Huong**, 40/19 Bui Vien St, T08-8369158. Rooms with a/c, hot water, private bathrooms.

**B-D 211**, 211-213 Pham Ngu Lao St, T08-8367353, hotelduy@hotmail.com. Some a/c, clean, rooftop terrace and rooms in 3 price categories.

**B-E Ngoc Dang**, 254 De Tham St, T08-8371896, www.ngocdanghotel.com. Clean, friendly and pleasant; some a/c and fan rooms.

**C-D Hong Hoa**, 185/28 Pham Ngu Lao St, T08-836 1915, www.honghoavn.com. A well-run family hotel with 9 rooms,

all a/c, hot water and private bathroom. Conveniently, the downstairs has banks of free email terminals and a supermarket.

**C-D Linh Thu Guesthouse**, 72 Bui Vien St, T08-8368421, linhthu72@saigonnet.vn. Fan rooms with bathroom and some more expensive a/c rooms too.

**C-D Thanh Huyen**, 175/1 Pham Ngu Lao St, T08-8370760. Above a small eatery and off the main drag, 3 clean and quiet rooms (1 a/c, 2 fan).

**C-E Hotel Madam Cuc**, 64 Bui Vien St, T08-8365073, 127 Cong Quynh St, T08-8368761, and 184 Cong Quynh St, T08-8361679, www.madamcuchotels.com. The reception staff at No 64 could be a lot friendlier. Rooms are quite small but the US$20 room is the bargain of the place.

**C-E Linh**, 40/10 Bui Vien St, T/F8-8369641, linh.hb@hcm.vnn.vn. Well-priced, clean, friendly, family-run hotel with a/c and hot water. Attracts some long-stay guests.

**C-E Mimi Guesthouse**, 40/5 Bui Vien St, T08-8369645, mimihotel405@yahoo.fr. 6 rooms with private bathroom, a/c, fan rooms and hot water. Motorbikes, bicycles and the internet.

**C-E Minh Chau**, 75 Bui Vien St, T08-8367588. Price includes breakfast, some a/c, hot water and private bathrooms. Spotlessly clean and run by 2 sisters. It has been recommended by lone women travellers.

## ● Eating

HCMC has a rich culinary tradition and, as home to people from most of the world's imagined corners, its cooking is diverse. Do not overlook street-side stalls whose staples consist of *pho* (noodle soup), *bánh xeo* (savoury pancakes), *cha giò* (spring rolls) and *banh mi pate* (baguettes stuffed with pâté and salad) all usually fresh and very cheap.

**City centre** *p174, maps p175 and p176*
¶¶¶ **Au Manoir de Khai**, 251 Dien Bien Phu St, District 3, T08-9303394, daily 1100-2200. Au Manoir is Khai's (of **Khaisilk** fame) French restaurant. As one would expect, it scores well in the design and style departments.

● *For an explanation of sleeping and eating price codes used in this guide, see inside the*
● *front cover. Other relevant information is found in Essentials, see pages 29-32.*

The villa is nicely restored and the garden is beautiful. Food is lavishly presented.

**An Vien**, 178A Hai Ba Trung St, T08-8243877, daily 1000-2300. Excellent and intimate restaurant that serves the most fragrant rice in Vietnam. Attentive service and rich decor: carpets, tasseled lampshades and silk-embroidered cushions. The *banh xeo* and crispy fried squid are recommended.

**Bi Bi**, 8A/8D2 Thai Van Lung St, T08-8295783, Mon-Sat 1000-2300, Sun 1700-2300. Ideal for long lunches. A relaxed, brightly decorated and informal restaurant, popular with diplomats and bankers, serving excellent French food. Most highly recommended is the superb Chateaubriand (for 2) and the tiger shrimp with parsley and cognac. The set-menu lunch of 3 courses plus coffee is good value.

**Kabin**, Renaissance Riverside Hotel, T08-8220033. One of the city's best Chinese restaurants; it sometimes features visiting chefs from China.

**La Fourchette**, 9 Ngo Duc Ke St, T08-8298143, daily 1200-1430, 1830-2230. Truly excellent and authentic French bistro offering a warm welcome, well-prepared dishes and generous portions of tender local steak. Booking advised. Recommended.

**Mandarin**, 11A Ngo Van Nam St, T08-8229783, daily 1130-1400, 1730-2300. One of the finest restaurants in HCMC serving up a culinary mix of exquisite flavours from across the country amid elegant decor including stunning, richly coloured silk tablecloths. The food is delicious but it's not very Vietnamese and the service is a little over the top.

**Qucina**, 7 Lam Son Sq, T08-8246325, Mon-Sat 1800-2300. Smart and stylish Italian restaurant in the basement of the Opera House. The sophisticated menu includes grilled tuna in black butter and rolled chocolate cake with vanilla cream – enough to satisfy any gourmet.

**La Camargue**, 16 Cao Ba Quat St, corner of Thi Sach St, T08-8243148, daily 1800-2300. One of HCMC's longest-standing restaurants and bars, and remains one of the most successful and popular places in town. Large French villa with a lovely upstairs open-air terrace restaurant. Consistently excellent food from an international menu with a strong French

bias. Downstairs is a relaxing garden area and the ever popular **Vasco** nightclub (see Bars and clubs).

**Pacharan**, 97 Hai Ba Trung St, T08-8256024, daily 1100-late. A hit from the beginning, this Spanish restaurant is nearly full every night with happy and satisfied customers. The open-air rooftop bar that overlooks the Opera House is a winner when there's a cool breeze blowing through the terrace. Fans of Spanish fare will love the (expensive) Iberian cured ham from rare, semi-wild, acorn-fed black-footed pigs as well as staples such as anchovies, olives, mushrooms and prawns;all the tapas are beautifully presented.

**Restaurant Nineteen**, Caravelle Hotel, Lam Son Sq, T08-8234999, daily 1130-1430, 1745-2200. Japanese sushi, Chinese dim sum, seafood, cheeses and puddings galore. The food is stacked up so luxuriously and abundantly, it is like a gastro-cinematic experience. Weekends are especially extravagant with tender roast beef. The free wine makes it tremendous value for money.

**Temple Club**, 29 Ton That Thiep St, T08-8299244, daily 1100-1400, 1830-2230. Beautifully furnished club and restaurant open to non-members. French-colonial style and tasty Vietnamese dishes. Excellent value. The restaurant is popular so it's wise to book.

**Augustin**, 10 Nguyen Thiep St, T08-8292941, Mon-Sat 1100-1400, 1800-2230. Fairly priced and some of the best, unstuffy French cooking in HCMC; tables pretty closely packed, congenial atmosphere. Excellent onion soup, baked clams and rack of lamb.

**Blue Ginger** (Saigon Times Club), 37 Nam Ky Khoi Nghia St, T08-8298676, daily 0700-1430, 1700-2200. A gorgeous restaurant that offers a feast of Vietnamese food for diners with more than 100 dishes on the menu. Dine indoors in the cellar-like restaurant or outdoors in a small courtyard. Charming staff offer courteous and discrete service.

**Cay Xoai** (Mango), Thi Sach St, open all day. Offers a wide range of fish and crustacea. It is rightly famous for its delicious crab in tamarind sauce. All very tasty and it remains very good value for money.

**Hoa Vien**, 28 bis Mac Dinh Chi St, T08-8290585, daily 0900-2400. A vast Czech bierkeller boasting Ho Chi Minh City's first microbrewery. Freshly brewed dark and light beer available by the litre or in smaller measures. Grilled mackerel, pork and sausages are very useful for soaking up the alcohol.

**Le Jardin**, 31 Thai Van Lung St, T08-8258465, daily 1100-1400, 1700-2130. Excellent French café, part of the **French Cultural Institute**. Eat inside or in the shady garden, good food, fairly priced.

**Pomodoro**, 79 Hai Ba Trung St, T08-8238957, daily 1000-1400, 1830-2200. This is an excellent Italian restaurant. Authentic dishes, well prepared. Good service.

**Saigon India**, first floor, 73 Mac Thi Buoi St, T08-8245671, daily 1115-1430, 1730-2230. Proving to be a very popular Indian restaurant it has a wide range of dishes from the north and south with tandoori dishes and plenty of vegetarian options. Delicious garlic nan bread.

**Underground**, 69 Dong Khoi St, T08-8299079, daily 1000-24000. Instantly recognizable by its London Underground symbol, this bar in its stygian gloom is an unlikely place to find some of HCMC's best food. The menu spans the full Mediterranean-Mexico spectrum and is superb. Portions are gigantic and prices are reasonable. Lunchtime specials are excellent value. There's often a shortage of tables. This is a popular venue for watching televised sporting events, particularly rugby.

**Al Fresco's**, 27 Dong Du St, T08-8227317, daily 0830-1400, 1830-2300. A huge success from its first day. Australian run. Specializes in ribs, steak, pizzas, hamburgers and Mexican dishes which are all excellent and highly popular. Book or be prepared to wait. Delivery available.

**Ashoka**, 17A/10 Le Thanh Ton St, T08-8231372, daily 1100-1400, 1700-2230. Delicious food from an extensive menu. Its set lunch lists 11 options with a further, extraordinary 19 curry dishes. Highlights are the mutton shami kebab, prawn vindaloo and kadhai fish – barbecued chunks of fresh fish cooked in kadhai (a traditional Indian-style wok with Peshwari ground spices and sautéd with onion and tomatoes. Sweet tooths should try the bizarre Coke with ice cream for pudding.

**Chao Thai**, 16 Thai Van Lung St, T08-8241457, daily 1100-1400, 1730-2230. Considered the best Thai restaurant in town. Attractive setting and attentive service.

**Huong Lai**, 38 Ly Tu Trong St, T08-8226814, daily 1200-1400, 1800-2115. An interesting little place, behind the City Hall, operated rather successfully by former street children. Try sautéed shrimp with coconut sauce. The set lunch menu of 6 dishes is good value. The young staff are eager to please.

**13 Ngo Duc Ke**, 13 Ngo Duc Ke St, T08-8239314, daily 0600-2230. Fresh, well cooked, honest Vietnamese fare. Chicken in lemon grass (no skin, no bone) is a great favourite and *bo luc lac* melts in the mouth. Popular with locals, expats and travellers.

**Au Parc**, 23 Han Thuyen St, T08-8292772, daily 0700-2100. Facing on to the park in front of the old Presidential Palace, this attractive café serves snacks and light meals including sandwiches, salads, juices and drinks. Also does a good Sun brunch 1100-1530. Delivery available.

**Com Nieu Saigon**, 6C Tu Xuong St, District 3, T08-9326388, daily 1000-2200. Best known for the theatrics which accompany the serving of the speciality baked rice: one waiter smashes the earthenware pot before tossing the contents across the room to his nimble-fingered colleague standing by your table. Deserves attention for its excellent food and selection of soups.

**Hoang Yen**, 5-7 Ngo Duc Ke St, T08-8231101, daily 1000-2200. Utterly plain setting and decor but absolutely fabulous Vietnamese dishes, as the throngs of local lunchtime customers testify. Soups and chicken dishes are ravishing.

**Kem Bach Dang**, 26-28 Le Loi Blvd. On opposite corners of Pasteur St. A very popular café serving fruit juice, shakes and ice cream. Try the coconut ice cream (*kem dua*) served in a coconut.

**Luong Son** (aka Bo Tuong Xeo), 31 Ly Tu Trong St, T08-8251330, daily 0900-2200. Noisy, smoky, chaotic and usually packed, this large canteen specializes in *bo tung xeo* (sliced beef barbecued at the table served with mustard sauce). The beef, barbecued squid and other delicacies are truly superb. Also the place to sample unusual dishes such as scorpion, porcupine, fried cricket and cockerel's testicles. Recommended.

**Pacific**, 15A Le Thanh Ton St. Central and excellent *bia hoi* which is packed with locals and visitors every night. The beer is served in a pint glass as soon as you arrive and is ridiculously cheap. Also a decent range of simple dishes: venison, beef, squid and chips, barbecued goat and hot pot with snakehead fish. Amiable and welcoming waiters.

**Pho**, 37 Dong Khoi St, T08-8296415, daily 0700-2400. This is a new Japanese-run *pho* shop. A bowl of *pho* is cheap but drinks are (by comparison) a bit expensive. Attractively and eccentrically furnished with heavy wooden tables and chairs and an interesting collection of pictures and ornaments.

**Pho Hoa Pasteur**, 260C Pasteur St, daily 0600-2400. Probably the best known *pho* restaurants and packed with customers and dizzying aromas. The *pho*, which is good, and costs more than average comes in 10 options. Chinese bread and wedding cake (*banh xu xe*) provide the only alternative in this specialist restaurant.

### Foodstalls

Just north of the centre on the south side of Tan Dinh market **Anh Thu**, 49 Dinh Cong Trang St (and numerous other stalls nearby) serve excellent *cha gio, banh xeo, bi cuon* and other Vietnamese street food.

Also head north of the market to the foodstalls on Hia Ba Trung St. Everyone has their favourite but nos **362-376** and no **381** (Hong Phat) are particularly good. All charge just over US$2 for steamed chicken and rice (*com gà hap*) with soup.

### Pham Ngu Lao *p179, map p179*

Pham Ngu Lao, the backpacker area, is chock-a-block with low-cost restaurants many of which are just as good as the more expensive places elsewhere. All restaurants here are geared to the habits and tastes of Westerners.

**Good Morning Vietnam**, 197 De Tham St, T08-8371894, daily 0900-2400. Italian owned and serving authentic Italian flavours. Good but not cheap. The pizzas are delicious and salads are good.

**Cappuccino**, 258 and 222 De Tham St, T08-8371467, daily 0800-2300. A good range of well-prepared Italian food at sensible prices. Very good lasagne and zabaglione. Also at 86 Bui Vien St, T08-8989706.

**Cay Bo De** (Original Bodhi Tree), 175/4 Pham Ngu Lao St, T08-8371910, daily 0800-2200. HCMC's most popular vegetarian eatery. Excellent food at amazing prices. Mexican pancake, vegetable curry, rice in coconut and braised mushrooms are classics.

**Kim Café**, 268 De Tham St, T08-8368122, open all day. Wide range of food, popular with travellers and expats. The breakfast must rate among the best value in the country.

**Lac Thien**, 28/25 Bui Vien St, T08-8371621, daily 0800-2300. Vietnamese food. Outpost of the well-known Lac Thien in Hué and run by the same family. *Banh xeo* (savoury pancake) is a major feature on the menu.

## Bars and clubs

Some of these bars sometimes succeed in staying open until 0200 or 0300 but at other times the police shut them down at 2400. Those in the Pham Ngu Lao area tend to be busy later at night and tend to stay open longer than those in the centre. Many also have pool tables.

### Ho Chi Minh City *p172, maps p172, p175, p176 and p179*

**La Fenêtre Soleil**, 2nd floor, 135 Le Thanh Ton St (entrance at 125 Nam Ky Khoi Nghia), T08-8225209, Mon-Sat café 0900-1900 bar 1900-2400. Don't be put off by the slightly grimy side entrance; climb up into the boho-Indochine world of this gorgeous café/bar, artfully cluttered with antiques, lamps, comfy sofas and home-made cakes, muffins, smoothies and other delights. The high-energy drinks of mint, passion fruit, and ginger juice are lovely. Highly recommended.

**Apocalypse Now**, 2C Thi Sach St, free admission for Westerners. This legendary venue remains one of the most popular and successful bars and clubs in HCMC. Draws a very wide cross section of punters of all ages and nationalities. Quite a large outside area at the back where conversation is possible.

**Blue Gecko** 31 Ly Tu Trong St, T08-8243483. This bar has been adopted by HCMC's Australian community so expect cold beer and Australian flags above the pool table.

**Bop**, 8a1/d1 Thai Van Lung, T08-8251901, daily 1630-2400. HCMC's first jazz club. All-white, sleek musical venue, with photographic images of skyscrapers lining the walls. Top cocktails and good live tunes daily.

**Heart of Darkness**, 17B Le Thanh Ton St, T08-8231080, daily 1700-2400 (often until later), ladies get free gin from 1900-2100. Off-shoot of the famous Phnom Penh bar. Khmer in style with Cambodian-style carvings and decor.

**Q Bar**, 7 Lam Son Square, T08-8233479, daily 1800-late. Haunt of a wide cross-section of HCMC society: the sophisticated, intelligent, witty, rich, handsome, cute, curvaceous, camp, glittering and famous are all to be found here. Striking decor and design, with Caravaggio-esque murals.

**Rex Hotel Bar**, 14 Nguyen Hue Blvd. The open-air rooftop bar that is the height of bad taste, with giant animal statues, strange fish tanks, song birds and topiary. Come for the good views, cooling breeze, snacks – and for a link with history (page 174).

**Saigon Saigon**, 10th floor, Caravelle Hotel, 19 Lam Son Sq, T08-8243999. Breezy and cool, with large comfortable chairs and superb views by day and night. Excellent cocktails but not cheap.

**Underground**, 69 Dong Khoi St, T08-8299079. Screens football, rugby, F1 racing and other sporting events. As the evening wears on, tables are packed away and the space fills with drinkers and dancers.

**Vasco**, La Camargue restaurant (see Eating), 16 Cao Ba Quat St, T08-8243148. A great spot any evening but only gets busy after 2200 Fri and Sat when a live band plays. The small dance floor generates a lot of energy. Also has a garden. Very popular with younger expats.

**163 Cyclo Bar**, 163 Pham Ngu Lao St, T08-9201567, daily 0700-2400. A clean, civilized and very welcome addition to this neighbourhood. There's an open bar downstairs; upstairs has a/c and live music from 2000 nightly. Inexpensive drinks and light meals.

**Evening cafés**

Vietnamese tend to prefer non-alcoholic drinks. Young romantic couples sit in virtual darkness listening to Vietnamese love songs, all too often played at a deafening volume, while sipping coffee. The furniture tends to be rather small for the Western frame but these cafés are an agreeable way of relaxing after dinner in a more typically Vietnamese setting.

**Thien Ha Café** at 25A Tu Xuong, District 3, which features piano and violin duets, is a prime and popular example.

## ⦿ Entertainment

**Ho Chi Minh City** *p172, maps p172, p175, p176 and p179*

**Cinemas**

**French Cultural Institute (Idecaf)**, 31 Thai Van Lung, T08-8295451. French films are screened here.

**Diamond Plaza**, 34 Le Duan St. The cinema on the 13th floor of this shopping centre screens English-language films.

## ⦿ Shopping

**Ho Chi Minh City** *p172, maps p172, p175, p176 and p179*

**Antiques**

Most antique shops are on Dong Khoi, Mac Thi Buoi and Ngo Duc Ke streets but for less touristy stuff visitors would be advised to spend an hour or so browsing the shops along Le Cong Trieu St. It runs between Nam Ky Khoi Nghia and Pho Duc Chinh streets just south of Ben Thanh market. Among the bric-à-brac are some interesting items of furniture, statuary and ceramics. Bargaining essential.

**Lac Long**, 143 Le Thanh Ton St, T08-8293373, daily 0800-1900. Mr Long sometimes has some unusual items for sale even if there is nothing of interest on display.

**Art, crafts and home accessories**

**Ancient/Apricot**, 50-52 Mac Thi Buoi St, T08-8227962, www.apricot-artvietnam.com. Specializes in famous artists and commands high prices.

**Dogma**, 29A Dong Khoi St, www.dogma.
vietnam.com. Sells propaganda posters,
funky T-shirts and postcards.
**Nguyen Freres**, 2 Dong Khoi St,
T08-8239459, www.nguyenfreres.com.
An absolute Aladdin's cave. Don't miss
this – even if it's just to potter amongst
the collectable items.
**Gaya**, 39 Ton That Thiep, T08-9143769,
www.gayavietnam.com, daily 0900-2100.
A 3-storey shop with heavenly items.
The 1st floor has embroidered tablecloths,
bamboo bowls, ceramics and screens.
The 2nd floor is stuffed with silk designer
clothes by Romyda Keth.
**Mosaique**, 98 Mac Thi Buoi, T08-8234634,
daily 0900-2100. Like its sister store in Hanoi,
this boutique is a home accessories parlour.
**Hanoi Gallery**, 43 Le Loi Blvd, T098-2038803
(mob). Like its counterpart in Hanoi it sells
original or reproduction propaganda posters.
**Lotus Gallery**, 55 Dong Khoi St, T08-829
2695. Another expensive gallery at the top
end of the market. Many are members of the
Vietnam Fine Arts Association and many
have exhibited around the world.
**Saigon Kitsch**, Ton That Thiep St, daily
0900-2000, www.saigonkitsch.com.
Communist kitsch ranging from big propaganda art posters to place mats and mugs.
Also retro bags and funky jewellery on sale.

### Clothing and silk
Many female visitors head straight for Dong
Khoi St for Vietnamese silk and traditional
dresses (*ao dai*). Also check out Ben Thanh
market in Binh Thanh District.
**Khai Silk**, 107 Dong Khoi, T08-8291146. Part
of Mr Khai's growing empire. Beautifully
made, quality silks in a range of products
from dresses to scarves to ties.
**Song**, 76D Le Thanh Ton, T08-8246986,
daily 0900-2000, www.valeriegregorim
ckenzie.com. A beautiful clothes emporium.
Lovely, flowing summer dresses from
designer Valerie Gregori McKenzie plus other
stylish and unique pieces and accessories.

### Department stores
**Tax Department Store** (Russian market),
corner of Le Loi and Nguyen Hue sts. The
widest range of shopping under one roof in
HCMC: CDs, DVDs (all pirate, of course) and
a good selection of footwear, coats and shirts.

## ▲ Activities and tours

**Ho Chi Minh City** *p172, maps p172,
p175, p176 and p179*
**Tour operators**
**Asian Trails**, 5th floor, 21 Nguyen
Trung Ngan St, District 1, T08-9102871,
www.asiantrails.com. Southeast
Asia specialist.
**Buffalo Tours**, Suite 502, Jardine House,
58 Dong Khoi St, District 1, T08-8279170
(1-800-1583), www.buffalotours.com.
Organizes general tours, a Cu Chi cycling
trip with good bikes, overland trips to Dalat
and trips to Can Tho.
**Cuu Long Tourist**, 97A Nguyen Cu Trinh St,
District 1, T08-9200339, cuulongtourist@
hcm.vnn.vn. Branch of Vinh Long
provincial tourist authority. For tours
to the Mekong Delta.
**Delta Adventure Tours**, 267 De Tham St,
T08-9202112, www.deltaadventure
tours.com. Slow and express bus and boat
tours through the Mekong Delta to Phnom
Penh, Cambodia at very good prices.
**Exotissimo**, Saigon Finance Center,
9 Dinh Tien Hoang St, T08-8251723,
www.exotissimo.com. An efficient agency
that can handle all the travel needs of
visitors to Vietnam.
**Handspan Aventure Travel**, F7, Titan
Building, 18A Nam Quoc Cang, T08-925
7605, www.handspan.com. Reputable
and well-organized business. Specializes
in adventure tours.
**Kim Café**, 270 De Tham St, District 1,
T08-9205552, www.kimtravel.com.
Organizes minibuses to Nha Trang, Dalat,
etc and tours of the Mekong from US$7.
A good source of information.
**Luxury Travel Co, Ltd**, Suite 404, Eden Mall,
4 Le Loi St, T08-8243408, www.LuxuryTravel
Vietnam.com. Offers luxury travel to Vietnam,
Cambodia and Laos.
**Sinh Café**, 246-248 De Tham St, District 1,
T08-8367338, www.sinhcafevn.com. Tours
are generally good value and the open
ticket is excellent value. For many people,
especially budget travellers, **Sinh Café** is the
first port of call. Tours to the Mekong Delta
and Cambodia are organized from US$26.
**TM Brother's Café**, 228 De Tham St,
T08-8377764 and 4 Do Quang Dau St,
T08-8378394, tmbrothers_saigon@

yahoo.com. The genuine version is a reliable Open Tour Bus operator. It also runs trips around the Mekong Delta and on to Cambodia.
**Vidotour**, 145 Nam Ky Khoi Nghia St, District 1, T08-9330457, www.vidotourtravel.com. One of the most efficient organizers of group travel in the country.

### Around Ho Chi Minh City p181
### Swimming
**Saigon Water Park**, Go Dua Bridge, Kha Van Can St, Thu Duc District, T08-8970456, Mon-Fri 0900-1700, Sat and Sun 0900-2000, 70,000d for adults, 30,000d for children. A Western-style water park, 10 km outside HCMC. It has a variety of water slides of varying degrees of excitement and a child's pool on a 5-ha site. To get there jump in a taxi, 70,000d, or catch a bus from Ben Thanh market.

Some hotels may also allow non-residents to use their pool for a fee.

## ◉ Transport

**Ho Chi Minh City** p172, maps p172, p175, p176 and p179
### Air
See page 172. **Airline offices** Air France, 130 Dong Khoi St, T08-829 0981, www.airfrance.com. **Bangkok Airways**, Unit 103, Saigon Trade Center, 37 Ton Duc Thang St, T08-9104490, www.bangkokair.com. **Cathay Pacific**, 115 Nguyen Hue Blvd, T08-8223203, www.cathaypacific.com. **Emirates Airlines**, 170-172 Nam Ky Khoi Nghia, District 3, T08-9302939, www.emirates.com. **Eva Air**, 19-25 Nguyen Hue Blvd, T08-8217151, www.evaair.com. **Lao Airlines**, 93 Pasteur St, T08-8234789. **Lufthansa**, 19-25 Nguyen Hue Blvd, T08-8298529, www.lufthansa.com. **Pacific Airlines**, 177 Vo Thi Sau St, District 3, T08-9325979. **Qantas**, Saigon Trade Center, unit 102, first floor, 37 Ton Duc Thang St, T08-9105373, www.qantas.com.au. **Siem Reap Airways International**, 132-134 Dong Khoi St, T08-8239288. **Thai Airways**, 65 Nguyen Du St, T08-8292810, www.thaiair.com. **United Airlines**, ground floor, 17 Le Duan, T08-8234755. **Vietnam Airlines**, 116 Nguyen Hue Blvd, T08-8320320, www.vietnamairlines.com.

Bikes and motorbikes can be hired from some of the cheaper hotels and cafés, especially in Pham Ngu Lao St. They should always be parked in the roped-off compounds (gui xe), found all over town; they will be looked after for a small fee (500d by day, 1000d after dark, 2000d for motorbikes; always get a ticket).

### Bus
**Local** All city buses start from or stop by the Ben Thanh bus station opposite Ben Thanh Market, District 1, T08-8217182. A free map of all bus routes can also be obtained here. The buses are green or yellow and run at intervals of 10-20 mins depending on the time of day; during rush hours they are jammed with passengers and can run late. There are bus stops every 500 m. Tickets for all routes are 2000d per person.
  **Open Tour Buses** The buses leave from company offices in the centre, including **Sinh Café** in Pham Ngu Lao.

### Cyclo
Cyclos are a peaceful way to get around the city. They can be hired for approximately US$2-3 per hr or to reach a specific destination. Some drivers speak English. Some visitors complain that cyclo drivers in HCMC have an annoying habit of 'forgetting' the agreed price, however, the drivers themselves will argue that cyclos are being banned from more and more streets in the centre of HCMC, which means that journeys are often longer and more expensive then expected.

### Motorcycle taxi
Honda om or xe ôm are the quickest way to get around town and are cheaper than cyclos; just agree a price and hop on the back. Xe ôm drivers can be recognized by their baseball caps and their tendency to chain smoke; they hang around on most street corners.

### Taxi
All taxis are metered. **Airport** (white or blue), T08-8446666. **Mai Linh Taxi** (green and white, but note that the Deluxe version is more expensive), T08-8277979.

Saigontourist, T08-8464646. Vinasun (white), T08-8272727. **Vinataxi** (yellow), T08-8111111.

### Train

**Thong Nhat Railway Station**, 1 Nguyen Thong St, Ward 9, District 3, T08-5621683, is 2 km from the centre of the city. There is now also a **Train Booking Agency**, 275c Pham Ngu Lao St, T08-8367640, daily 0730-1130, 1330-1630, which saves a journey out to the station. Much improved facilities include a/c waiting room, post office and bank (no TCs). Daily connections with **Hanoi** and all points north. Express trains take between 36 and 40 hrs to reach Hanoi; hard and soft berths are available. Sleepers should be booked in advance. The **5 Star Express**, 297 Pham Ngu Lao St, T08-9206868, www.5starexpress.com.vn, is a new, very comfortable and enjoyable train. 5 Star Express leaves HCMC at 0615 for Nha Trang stopping off at Muong Man (for Phan Thiet/Mui Ne) and arriving in **Nha Trang** at 1333. There are a variety of carriages and tickets are priced accordingly; tickets range from US$10 one way for the entire route up to US$150. Buoyed by success, the company has already introduced a night train to Nha Trang leaving 2020 arriving 0620, US$56. Highly recommended.

## ⊙ Directory

**Ho Chi Minh City** *p172, maps p172, p175, p176 and p179*
### Banks
There are now dozens of ATMs in shops, hotels and banks. Remember to take your passport if cashing TCs and withdrawing money from a bank. **ANZ Bank**, 11 Me Linh Sq, T08-8232218, 2% commission charged on cashing TCs into US$ or VND, ATM. **HSBC, Hong Kong and Shanghai Bank**, 235 Dong Khoi St, T08-8292288, provides all financial services, 2% commission on TCs, ATM. **Vietcombank**, 8 Nguyen Hue Blvd (opposite the Rex Hotel).

### Embassies and consulates
**Australia**, Landmark Building, 5B Ton Duc Thang St, T08-8296035. **Cambodia**, 41 Phung Khac Khoan St, T08-8292751. **Canada**, Metropole Building, 235 Dong Khoi St, T08-8279899. **Laos**, 9B Pasteur St, T08-8297667. **New Zealand**, Room 909, Metropole Building, 235 Dong Khoi St, T08-8226907. **Thailand**, 77 Tran Quoc Thao St, District 3, T08-9327637. **United Kingdom**, 25 Le Duan St, T08-8298433. **USA**, 4 Le Duan St, T08-8229433.

### Immigration
**Immigration Office**, 254 Nguyen Trai St, T08-8322300. For visa extensions and to change visas to specify overland travel to Cambodia via Moc Bai (see page 197) or for overland travel to Laos or China.

### Internet
There are numerous internet cafés in all parts of town.

### Laundry
There are several places that will do your laundry around Pham Ngu Lao St.

### Medical services
**Columbia Asia** (Saigon International Clinic), 8 Alexander de Rhodes St, T08-8238888, international doctors. **Family Medical Practice HCMC**, Diamond Plaza, 34 Le Duan St, T08-8227848, www.vietnammedicalpractice.com, well-equipped practice, 24-hr emergency service and an evacuation service; Australian and European doctors. Also provides a useful major and minor disease outbreak service on its website. **International SOS**, 55 Nguyen Du St, T08-8298424, Comprehensive 24-hr medical and dental service and medical evacuation.

### Post office and telephone
The **GPO** is at 2 Cong Xa Paris (facing the cathedral), daily 0630-2100. Telex, telegram and international telephone services available.

# Far south

*At its verdant best the Mekong Delta is a riot of greens: pale rice seedlings deepen in shade as they sprout ever taller; palm trees and orchards make up an unbroken horizon of foliage. But at its muddy worst the paddy fields ooze with slime and sticky clay; grey skies, hostile clouds and incessant rain make daily life a misery and the murky rising waters, the source of all the natural wealth of the delta, also cause hundreds of fatalities.*

*Boat trips along canals and down rivers are the highlights of this region, as is a visit to Phu Quoc – Vietnam's largest island. Lying off the southwest coast, Phu Quoc remains largely undeveloped with beautiful sandy beaches along much of its coastline and forested hills inland.* ▸▸ *For Sleeping, Eating and other listings, see pages 199-204.*

## Ins and outs

**Getting there and around** There are several highways throughout the Mekong Delta linking the major towns. Highway 1 from Ho Chi Minh City goes to My Tho, Vinh Long and Can Tho and Highway 91 links Can Tho, Long Xuyen and Chau Doc. Beyond these towns, however, roads are narrow and pot-holed and travel is generally slow. Ferry crossings make travel more laborious still. The easiest way to explore the region is to take a tour from Ho Chi Minh City to Can Tho, My Tho or Chau Doc. There are also flights to Can Tho and, if money is no object, the Victoria hotel group runs boats from Ho Chi Minh City to Can Tho and Chau Doc. ▸▸ *For further information, see Transport, page 202; for transport to Phu Quoc Island, see page 203.*

**Best time to visit** December to May is when the Mekong Delta is at its best. During the monsoon, from June to November, the weather is poor, with constant background drizzle, interrupted by bursts of torrential rain. In October flooding may interrupt movement particularly in the remoter areas and around Chau Doc and Dong Thap Province.

## Background

The Mekong River enters Vietnam in two branches known traditionally as the Mekong (to the north) and the Bassac but now called the Tien and the Hau respectively. Over the 200 km journey to the sea they divide to form nine mouths, the so-called 'Nine Dragons' or Cuu Long of the delta. In response to the rains of the southwest monsoon, river levels in the delta begin to rise in June, usually reaching a peak in October and falling to normal in December. This seasonal pattern is ideal for growing rice, around which the whole way of life of the delta has evolved. Even prior to the creation of French Cochin China in the 19th century, rice was being transported from here to Hué, the imperial capital.

The region has had a restless history. Conflict between Cambodians and Vietnamese for ownership of the wide plains resulted in ultimate Viet supremacy (although important Khmer relics remain). From 1705 onwards Vietnamese emperors began building canals to improve navigation in the delta. This task was taken up enthusiastically by the French in order to open up new areas to rice cultivation and export. By the 1930s the population of the delta had reached 4.5 million with 2,200,000 ha of land under rice cultivation. The Mekong Delta, along with the Irrawaddy (Burma) and Chao Phraya (Thailand) became one of the great rice-exporting areas of Southeast Asia, shipping over 1.2 million tonnes annually. During the French and American wars, the Mekong Delta produced many of the most fervent fighters for independence.

Today, the Mekong Delta remains Vietnam's rice bowl. The delta covers 67,000 sq km, of which about half is cultivated. Rice yields are in fact generally lower than in the north but the huge area under cultivation and the larger size of farms means that both individual households and the region produce a surplus for export. In the Mekong Delta there is nearly three times as much rice land per person as there is in the north. It is this that accounts for the relative wealth of the region.

# My Tho ⊜🕭▲⊜🄲 ➠ *pp199-204. Colour maps 5, B3.*

My Tho is an important riverside market town on the banks of the Tien River, a tributary of the Mekong. The town has had a turbulent history: it was Khmer until the 17th century, when the advancing Vietnamese took control of the surrounding area. In the 18th century Thai forces annexed the territory, before being driven out in 1784. Finally, the French gained control in 1862. This historical melting pot is reflected in **Vinh Trang Pagoda** ① *60 Nguyen Trung Truc St, daily 0900-1200, 1400-1700 (best to go by bicycle or cyclo)*, which was built in 1849 and displays a mixture of architectural styles – Chinese, Vietnamese and colonial. The façade is almost fairytale in inspiration and the entrance to the temple is through an ornate porcelain-encrusted gate.

## Ins and outs
From Ho Chi Minh City to My Tho the main route is Highway 1. The majority of travellers join an inclusive tour or catch an Open Tour Bus, which allows greater flexibility. ➠ *For further information, see Transport, page 202.*

## Tien River islands
① *The best way of getting to the islands is to take a tour. Hiring a private boat is not recommended due to the lack of insurance, the communication difficulties and lack of explanations. Prices vary according to the number of people.* ➠ *For further information, see Activities and tours, page 201.*
There are four islands in the Tien River between My Tho and Ben Tre: Dragon, Tortoise, Phoenix and Unicorn. Immediately opposite My Tho is **Tan Long** (Dragon Island), noted for its longan cultivation. Honey tea is made on the islands from the longan flower, with a splash of kumquat juice to balance the flavour. There are many other fruits to sample here, as well as rice whisky. It is also pleasant to wander along the island's narrow paths.

The Island of the Coconut Monk, also known as **Con Phung** (Phoenix Island), is about 3 km from My Tho. The 'Coconut Monk' established a retreat on this island shortly after the end of the Second World War where he developed a new 'religion', a fusion of Buddhism and Christianity. He is said to have meditated for three years on a stone slab, eating nothing but coconuts. Persecuted by both the South Vietnamese government and by the Communists, the monastery on the island has since fallen into disuse.

On **Con Qui** (Tortoise Island) there is an abundance of dragon fruit, longan, banana and papaya. Here visitors are treated to singing accompanied by a guitar and Vietnamese monochord.

# Vinh Long and around ⊕⊘▲ℂ ⇒ pp199-204. Colour maps 5, B3.

Vinh Long is a rather ramshackle riverside town on the banks of the Co Chien River. It was one of the focal points in the spread of Christianity in the Mekong Delta and there is a cathedral and Roman Catholic seminary in town as well as a Cao Dai church. The main reason for visiting Vinh Long is to spend a night at a homestay on the lovely and tranquil island of An Binh.

## Ins and outs

**Tourist information** Cuu Long Tourist ① *No 1, 1 Thang 5 St, T070-823616, www.cuu longtourist.net, daily 0700-1700*, is one of the friendlier and more helpful of the state-run companies and runs tours and homestays. Ask for Mr Phu; he is helpful and has a good understanding of English and French.

## Around Vinh Long

The river trips taking in the islands and orchards around Vinh Long are as charming as any in the delta but can be expensive. Officially, **Cuu Long Tourist** has a monopoly on excursions by foreigners. Local boatmen are prepared to risk a fine and take tourists for one-tenth of the amount. **Binh Hoa Phuoc Island** makes a pleasant side trip (see also Sleeping, page 199) or you could spend a morning visiting the floating market at **Cai Be**, about 10 km from Vinh Long. It's not quite as spectacular as the floating markets around Can Tho (see page 196) but nevertheless makes for a diverting trip.

   **An Binh Island** is just a 10-minute ferry ride from Phan Boi Chau Street and represents a great example of a delta landscape, stuffed with fruit-bearing trees and flowers. It is a large island that is further sliced into smaller islands by ribbons of small canals. Sights include the ancient **Tien Chau Pagoda** and a *nuoc mam* (fish sauce factory). Travel is by sampan or walking down the winding paths that link the communities. If you choose to stay on the island, you will be given tea and fruit at a traditional house, see ricecakes and popcorn being made, and visit a brick factory, where terracotta pots are made and then fired in pyramid-shaped kilns. A dawn paddle in the Mekong, surrounded by floating water hyacinth and watching the sun rise, is the reward for early risers.

# Can Tho and around ⊕⊘▲⊜ℂ ⇒ pp199-204. Colour map 5, B2.

Can Tho is a large and rapidly growing commercial town situated in the heart of the Mekong Delta. Lying chiefly on the west bank of the Can Tho River, it is the largest city in the delta and also the most welcoming and agreeable. It is the launch pad for trips to some of the region's floating markets. A small settlement was established at Can Tho at the end of the 18th century, although the town did not prosper until the French took control of the delta a century later and rice production for export began to take off. Despite the city's rapid recent growth there are still strong vestiges of French influence apparent in the broad boulevards flanked by flame trees, as well as many elegant buildings. Can Tho was also an important US base.

## Ins and outs

**Getting there and around** Virtually all visitors arrive by road. With the My Thuan Bridge (near Vinh Long) there is now only one ferry crossing between Ho Chi Minh City and Can Tho, so journey times have fallen. Most of Can Tho can be explored on foot but the floating markets are best visited by boat. ⇒ *For further information, see Transport, page 202.*

**Hai Ba Trung Street**, alongside the river, is the heart of the town, where, at dusk, families stroll in the park in their Sunday best. There is also a bustling **market** here, along the bank of the river. Opposite the park, at number 34, is **Chua Ong Pagoda**, dating from 1894 and built by Chinese from Guangzhou. Unusually for a Chinese temple it is not free standing but part of a terrace of buildings. The right-hand side of the pagoda is dedicated to the Goddess of Fortune, while the left-hand side belongs to General Ma Tien, who, to judge from his unsmiling statue, is fierce and warlike and not to be trifled with.

## Floating markets

ⓘ *The daily markets are busiest at around 0600-0900. Sampans are available to rent in Hai Ba Trung St. Expect to pay about 30,000d per hr for 2 people. Set off as early as possible to beat the flotilla of tour boats.*

The river markets near Can Tho are colourful and bustling confusions of boats, goods, vendors, customers, and tourists. From their boats the market traders attach samples of their wares to bamboo poles, which they hold out to attract customers. Up to seven vegetables can be seen dangling from the staffs – wintermelon, pumpkin, spring onions, giant parsnips, grapefruit, garlic, mango, onions and Vietnamese plums – and the boats are usually piled high with more produce. Housewives paddle their sampans from boat to boat and barter, haggle, and gossip; small sampans are the best means of transport here as they can negotiate the narrowest canals to take the shopper (or the visitor) into the heart of the area. It is recommended to take at least a five-hour round trip in order to see the landscape at a leisurely pace.

# Chau Doc and around ⊜⊘⊜€ ⇥ *pp199-204. Colour map 5, B1.*

Chau Doc was once an attractive, bustling riverside town on the west bank of the Hau or Bassac River, bordering Cambodia. It is still a bustling market town but no longer so appealing, since it has become an important trading and marketing centre for the surrounding agricultural communities. One of its biggest attractions, however, is the nearby **Nui Sam** (Sam Mountain), which is dotted with pagodas and tombs, and from whose summit superb views of the plains below can be enjoyed.

## Ins and outs

**Getting there** Chau Doc is an increasingly important border crossing into Cambodia. There are connections by boat with Phnom Penh as well as by road. There are tours to Chau Doc from Ho Chi Minh City. It is also possible (but expensive) to arrive by boat from Can Tho or Ho Chi Minh City (private charter only or with the Victoria Hotel group boat for guests only).

**Getting around** Chau Doc itself is easily small enough to explore on foot and Nui Sam, the nearby sacred mountain, can be reached by motorbike. ⇥ *For further information, see Transport, page 202.*

**Best time to visit** Nui Sam is one of the holiest sites in southern Vietnam and, as such, has vast numbers of pilgrims visiting it on auspicious days. From a climatic viewpoint, the best time to visit is between December and April.

## Background

Until the mid-18th century Chau Doc was part of Cambodia: it was given to the Nguyen lord, Nguyen Phuc Khoat, after he had helped to put down an insurrection in the area. The area still supports a large Khmer population, as well as the largest Cham

## To Cambodia via Chau Doc and Moc Bai

The river crossing is on the Mekong at **Chau Doc** and the land crossing is at **Moc Bai**, close to Tay Ninh in Vietnam.

**Transport** Daily morning boat departures from Chau Doc through the crossing at Vinh Xuong can be arranged through tour operators in Chau Doc, 9 hrs, US$6-15. A quicker option is the fast boat offered by Victoria Hotels & Resorts, www.victoriahotels-asia.com, but it is open to hotel guests only, leaving Chau Doc at 0700, 5 hrs, US$50, minimum 2 people. The return leaves at 1330. There is also an uncomfortable 10-hour public bus ride from Chau Doc to Phnom Penh via Moc Bai. Sinh Café, 248 De Tham St, Ho Chi Minh City, T08-8369420, www.sinhcafevn.com, runs a 2-day tour through the Mekong Delta from Ho Chi Minh City to Phnom Penh by land, US$21. To travel direct from Ho Chi Minh City to Moc Bai takes about 3 hrs, and from Moc Bai to Phnom Penh a further 6 hrs, with one ferry crossing.

**Note** If you intend to enter Cambodia from Vietnam you will need to obtain a visa in advance (available from the Immigration Office in Ho Chi Minh City, page 192).

settlement in the delta. Cambodia's influence can be seen in the tendency for women to wear the *kramar*, Cambodia's characteristic chequered scarf, instead of the *non lá* conical hat, and in the people's darker skin, indicating Khmer blood.

## Nui Sam (Sam Mountain) → *Colour map 5, B1.*

Nui Sam, 5 km southwest of Chau Doc, is one of the holiest sites in southern Vietnam. Rising from the flood plain, it is a favourite spot for Vietnamese tourists who throng here, especially at festival time. The mountain, really a barren, rock-strewn hill, can be seen at the end of the continuation of Nguyen Van Thoai Street. It is literally honeycombed with tombs, sanctuaries and temples. It is possible to walk or drive right up the hill for good views of the surrounding countryside and from the summit it is easy to appreciate that this is some of the most fertile land in Vietnam.

The **Tay An Pagoda**, at the foot of the hill, facing the road, represents an eclectic mixture of styles – Chinese, Islamic, perhaps even Italian – and contains a bewildering display of more than 200 statues. A short distance on from the pagoda, to the right, past shops and stalls, is the **Chua Xu**. It is rather a featureless building, though highly revered by the Vietnamese and honours the holy Lady Xu, whose statue is enshrined in the new multi-roofed pagoda. From the 23rd to the 25th of the fourth lunar month the holy lady is commemorated, during which time, hundreds of Vietnamese flock to see her being washed and reclothed. Lady Xu is a major pilgrimage for traders and business from Ho Chi Minh City and the south, all hoping that sales will soar and profits leap during this auspicious time.

On the other side of the road is the tomb of **Thoai Ngoc Hau** (1761-1829); an enormous head of the man graces the entranceway. Thoai is a local hero having played a role in the resistance against the French but is known more for his engineering feats in canal building and draining swamps.

**Hang Pagoda** is a 200-year-old temple situated halfway up Nui Sam. In the first level of the temple are some vivid cartoon drawings of the tortures of hell. The second level is built at the mouth of a cave, which, last century, was home to a woman named Thich Gieu Thien. Her likeness and tomb can be seen in the first pagoda. Fed up with her lazy and abusive husband she left her home in Cholon and came to live in this cave, as an ascetic supposedly waited on by two snakes.

# Phu Quoc Island 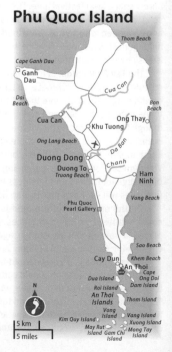  ▸ pp199-204. Colour map 6, C2.

Lying off the southwest coast of the country, Phu Quoc is Vietnam's largest island. It remains largely undeveloped, with beautiful sandy beaches along much of its coastline and forested hills inland. Most of the beaches benefit from crystal clear waters, making them perfect for swimming. The island's remoteness and lack of infrastructure means that tourism here is still in its infancy, and, although new resorts are planned, the pace of development is slow. After the rigours of sightseeing, Phu Quoc is well worth a visit for a few days' relaxation in southern Vietnam.

## Ins and outs

**Getting there and around**  You can get to Phu Quoc by plane from Ho Chi Minh City and most hotels will provide a free pick-up service from the airport if accommodation is booked in advance. There is also a high-speed boat service to the island from Rach Gia. There are only two asphalt roads on the island from Duong Dong to An Thoi and from Duong Dong to Ham Ninh. Hiring a motorbike is cheap and convenient but makes for dusty and very hot travelling; limited signposting can make some places pretty hard to find without local assistance. There are also plenty of motorbike taxis available, as well as cars with drivers at fairly reasonable prices; ask at hotels. ▸ For further information, see Transport, page 202.

## Around the island

Vietnamese fish sauce (*nuoc mam*) is produced on Phu Quoc. You'll see dozens of fish laid out to dry on land and on trestle tables, destined for the fish sauce factory at **Duong Dong**, the main town on the island. Here, 95 massive wooden barrels act as vats, each containing fish and salt weighing in at 14 tonnes and ringing in the till at US$5000 a barrel. If the sauce is made in concrete vats, the taste is lost and so the sauce is cheaper.

The island is also a centre for South Sea pearls, with 10,000 collected offshore each year. At the **Phu Quoc Pearl Gallery** ① *10 km south of Duong Dong, daily 0800-1800*; a video and gallery exhibits demonstrate the farming operation, the tasting of pearl meat and the pearl-making process. South of the pearl farm, on the coast road, are two **whale dedication temples**. Whales have long been worshipped in Vietnam. Ever since the days of the Champa, the whale has been credited with saving the lives of drowning fishermen. The Cham believed that Cha-Aih-Va, a powerful god, could assume the form of a whale in order to rescue those in need. Emperor Gia Long is said to have been rescued by a whale when his boat sank. After he ascended the throne, Gia Long awarded the whale the title 'Nam Hai Cu Toc Ngoc Lam Thuong Dang Than' – Superior God of the Southern Sea. Coastal inhabitants always try to help whales in difficulty and cut them free of their nets. If a whale should die, a full funeral is arranged.

## Phu Quoc Island

Thom Beach
Cape Ganh Dau
Ganh Dau
Cua Can
Dai Beach
Bon Beach
Cua Can
Ong Thay
Khu Tuong
Ong Lang Beach
Da Bon
Duong Dong
Duong To
Chanh
Truong Beach
Ham Ninh
Vong Beach
Phu Quoc Pearl Gallery
Sao Beach
Cay Dun
Khem Beach
An Thoi
Cape Ong Doi
Dua Island
Dam Island
Roi Island
An Thoi Islands
Thom Island
Vong Island
Kim Quy Island
Vang Island
May Rut Island
Xuong Island
Gam Chi Island
Mong Tay Island

N
5 km
5 miles

Inland, the **Da Ban** and **Chanh** streams and waterfalls are not very dramatic in the dry season but still provide a relaxing place to swim and walk in the forests.

The stunning, dazzling-white sands of **Sao Beach**, on the southeast coast, are worth visiting by motorbike but finding the beach can be difficult, as it is not well signposted, so you made need your resort or a tour operator to help you. One of the biggest draws are the boat trips around the **An Thoi islands**, which are scattered off the southern coast and offer opportunities for swimming, snorkelling and fishing.

## ⊜ Sleeping

**My Tho** *p194*

**B Chuong Duong**, No 10, 30 Thang 4 St, T073-870875, www.chuongduong hotel.com. This large, new hotel occupies a prime riverside location. It is by far the best hotel in town and is very good value. All the rooms overlook the river and have en suite facilities, satellite TV and minibar. The in-house restaurant provides good food and some tables enjoy river views.

**D-F Cong Doan**, No 61, 30 Thang 4 St, T073-874324, congdoantourist@hcm.vnn.vn. Clean hotel with 5 fan rooms that are cheaper than the 18 with a/c. Good views and location for the boat trips. Recommended.

**Vinh Long and around** *p195*

**A Mekong Homestays**, An Binh Island, Vinh Long. Organized by **Cuu Long Tourist**, page 195. Accommodation is basic, with camp beds, shared bathrooms and mosquito nets, and a home-cooked dinner of the fruits of the delta. Evening entertainment consists of sunset drinks and chatting with the owner. The price includes a boat trip around the island, transfers from Vinh Long, local guide, 1 dinner and 1 breakfast.

**B Cuu Long (B)**, No 1, 1 Thang 5 St, T070-823616, www.cuulongtourist.net. Set back from the river and conveniently opposite the quay where boats leave for An Binh Island. 34 a/c rooms; price includes breakfast (over the road at the **Phuy Thuong Restaurant**).

**C-D Nam Phuong**, 11 Le Loi St, T070-822226, phuong-mai9v9@ yahoo.com. These comfortable rooms have a/c and hot water; clean and cheap and very friendly.

**Can Tho** *p195*

**L Victoria Can Tho Resort**, Cai Khe Ward, T071-810111, www.victoriahotelsasia.com. This is one of the most beautiful hotels in Vietnam. With its riverside garden location, combined with an harmonious interior, breezy, open reception area and emphasis on comfort and plenty of genuine period features, it inspires relaxation. The centrepiece is the gorgeous, flood-lit pool, flanked by the lobby bar and restaurant. Rooms are elegantly decorated. Other facilities include a tennis court and therapies in divine massage cabins. The hotel offers a complimentary shuttle bus to the town centre. The boat shuttle may be up and running again by the time your read this.

**L-A Golf Hotel**, 2 Hai Ba Trung St, T071-812210, www.vinagolf.vn. Newest and tallest hotel in town. The staff are friendly, knowledgeable and multilingual. The rooms are well equipped with a/c, satellite TV, en suite facilities, decent-sized bathtub, well stocked minibar, electronic safe in the room. The restaurants provide fine dining and the views from the **Windy Restaurant** (8th floor) are superb. ATM on site.

**B Saigon Can Tho**, 55 Phan Dinh Phung St, T071-825831, sgcthotel@hmc.vnn.vn. A/c, comfortable, good value central business hotel in the competent hands of **Saigontourist**. The staff are friendly and helpful. Rooms are well-equipped with a/c, satellite TV, en suite facilities, minibar. There's a currency exchange, free internet for guests, sauna, and breakfast included.

**C-D Tay Ho**, 42 Hai Ba Trung St, T071-823392, kstayho-ct@hcm.vnn.vn. This lovely place has a variety of rooms and a great public balcony that can be enjoyed by those paying for back rooms. Some rooms have bathtubs and others share bathrooms and are cheaper. The staff are friendly.

**C-E Hau Giang B**, 27 Chau Van Liem St, T071-821950. A/c rooms all with hot water, TV and fridge. Used by backpacker tour groups from HCMC, good value. Virtually no English spoken.

### Chau Doc *p196*

**L Victoria Chau Doc**, 32 Le Loi St, T076-865010, www.victoriahotelsasia.com. This old, cream building with its riverfront pool is the perfect location in which to relax and look out on the busy, 3-way Mekong T-junction on which the hotel sits. All rooms are attractively decorated. The hotel group runs a speedboat to Phnom Penh.

**B Ben Da Sam Mountain Resort**, Highway 91, T076-861745. This resort consists of 4 hotels, a restaurant and bar. The staff speak good English. If you want a little bit of luxury then this would be the place to stay. Sam Mountain is 5 mins' walk away.

**C-D Thuan Loi**, 18 Tran Hung Dao St, T076-866134. A/c and good river views, clean and friendly, restaurant.

**D-F My Loc**, 51B Nguyen Van Thoai St, T076-866455. Some rooms with a/c, TV and fridge and others with fan and homestay showers. It's a friendly place in a quiet area.

**E-F Mekong Guesthouse**, Duong Len Tao Ngo, Nui Sam, T076-861870, mekongguesthouse@yahoo.com. This small place on the lower slopes of the mountain is a basic guesthouse and a good base for walking in the area. All rooms have fan, mosquito nets, blankets and homestay shower; some have a/c. The 2 dorms share a bathroom. Food is served all day and breakfast is less than US$1. Hammocks, DVDs, book exchange, internet access and bicycle hire make this an excellent value budget option.

### Phu Quoc Island *p198, map p198*

During peak periods, such as Christmas and Tet, it is advisable to book accommodation well in advance, otherwise accommodation is easily obtained on arrival at the airport. Representatives from different resorts meet most flights, providing free transfers and touting for business. Most of the resorts lie along the west coast to the south of Duong Dong and are within a few kilometres of the airport. Others are on On Lang Beach and in An Thoi.

**A Saigon Phu Quoc Resort**, 1 Trang Hung Dao St, Duong Dong, T077-846999, www.vietnamphuquoc.com. This resort, overlooking the sea, has a very attractive swimming pool surrounded by bungalows of varying prices and is set on a hillside garden. An enviable list of facilities includes a reasonably priced restaurant, internet, motorbikes for rent, fishing, tennis, massage, snorkelling, horse riding and bicycling.

**A-B Mango Bay Resort**, Ong Lang Beach, T090-3382207 (mob), www.mangobay phuquoc.com. A small and exclusive environmentally friendly private resort in tropical gardens located on the beach close to pepper farms. Bungalows are made from rammed earth and come with fans and coconut doorknobs and are kitted out with bamboo furniture and tiled floors. The 5 rooms share a wonderful, large communal veranda, some have outdoor bathrooms. The resort has information on birds and fish, a swimming pool and the restaurant provides a mixture of Vietnamese and Western food at very reasonable prices.

**A-B Tropicana Resort**, Duong Dong, T077-847127, www.tropicanaphuquoc.com. High-quality wooden bungalows and rooms set in a tropical garden next to the beach with a lovely pool. Prices vary according to the facilities required, although the beachfront balconied bungalows are overpriced. The resort has one of the best restaurants, a well-stocked bar and internet access.

**B-D Kim Hoa Resort**, Duong Dong, T077-3847039, http://vnrealty.com/pq/ kimhoa/index.html. This small resort offers typical wooden bungalows on a clean strip of sand in front of the resort. Bungalows have one double and one single bed and either have fan or a/c. The rooms which aren't on the beach have small bathrooms and are basic.

**C-D Thang Loi**, Ong Lang Beach, T077-3985002, www.phuquoc.de. A rustic hotel with wooden bungalows set in a remote coconut plantation on Ong Lang beach for those who want complete peace and quiet. Good bar and restaurant with friendly German owners. Bungalows are basically furnished with bamboo, fans and mosquito nets; some have hot water. There is a library, music and great food including *wiener schnitzel*. A newly built jetty juts out into the sea, a short walk from the bungalows.

## ● Eating

### My Tho *p194*
A speciality of the area is *hu tieu my tho* – a spicy soup of vermicelli, sliced pork, dried shrimps and fresh herbs. At night, noodle stalls spring up on the pavement on Le Loi St at the junction with Le Dai Han St.

**Ψ Banh Xeo 46**, 11 Trung Trac St. Serves *bánh xèo*, savoury pancakes filled with beansprouts, mushrooms and prawns; delicious.

**Ψ Hu Tien 44**, 44 Nam Ky Khoi Nghia St, 0500-1200. Specializes in *hu tien my tho*. At 8000d for a good-sized bowl filled to top.

### Vinh Long and around *p195*
There are a few restaurants along 1 Thang 5 St, just beyond Cuu Long Hotel (A).

**Ψ Nem Nuong**, 12 1 Thang 5 St, open all day. Sells grilled meat with noodles.

**Ψ Phuong Thuy Restaurant**, No 1, 1 Thang 5 St, T070-824786, 0600-2100. A 'stilt' restaurant on the river with Vietnamese and Western dishes and welcoming service. Cuttlefish and shrimp feature strongly.

### Can Tho *p195*
Hai Ba Trung St by the river offers a good range of excellent and very well-priced little restaurants; the riverside setting is an attractive one.

**ΨΨΨ-ΨΨ Victoria Can Tho Spices** (see Sleeping). Excellent location on the riverbank where it's possible to dine al fresco or inside the elegant restaurant. The food is delicious and the service is excellent.

**Ψ Mekong**, 38 Hai Ba Trung St. Perfectly good little place near the river in this popular restaurant strip. Serves decent Vietnamese fare at reasonable prices.

**Ψ Nam Bo**, 50 Hai Ba Trung St, T071-823908. This is a delightful French house with custard yellow and brown awnings on the corner of a street. Its balcony seating area overlooks the market clutter and riverside promenade. Tasty Vietnamese and French dishes. The set menu is US$6. Small café downstairs. Recommended.

**Ψ Phuong Nam**, 48 Hai Ba Trung St, T071-812077. Similar to the next door Nam Bo, good food, less stylish, a popular travellers' haunt and reasonable prices.

### Chau Doc *p196*
**ΨΨΨ-ΨΨ La Bassac**, in Victoria Chau Doc. The extravagant French and Vietnamese menus at this riverside restaurant include rack of lamb coated in Mekong herbs, sweet potato puree and pork wine reduction or spaghetti with flambéed shrimps in vodka paprika sauce.

**Ψ Bay Bong**, 22 Thung Dang Le St, T076-867271. Specializes in hot pots and soups and also offers a good choice of fresh fish. The staff are friendly.

**Ψ Lam Hung Ky**, 71 Chi Lang St. Excellent freshly prepared and cooked food.

### Phu Quoc Island *p198, map p198*
**ΨΨ-Ψ Tropicana Resort**. This is one of the best restaurants on the island where a sun-drenched terrace and well-stocked bar allows luxurious alfresco dining overlooking the sea. Enjoy succulent squid stir-fried with lemon grass, braised shrimps in coconut juice, Italian spaghettis or a range from the set menus.

**Ψ My Lan**, Sao Beach, T077-844447, dungmyt@yahoo.com, daily 0600-2100. A gorgeous setting on a gorgeous beach. Tables are under little thatched roofs. Sit back and enjoy a beer with the fresh seafood dishes. Recommended.

## ▲ Activities and tours

### My Tho *p194*
You can hire boats to take you to visit the islands. Once there, walk or cycle.

### Tour operators
**Chuong Duong Tourist**, next to the hotel, T073-870876, cdhoteltravel@vnn.vn.

**Tien Giang Tourist**, 63 Trung Trac St, Ward 1, T073-872105, www.tiengiangtourist.com. Dockside location is at No 8, 30 Thang 4 St, T073-873184. A boat trip to the islands costs US$16 for 1-3 people for 2½ hrs. It also offers dinner with traditional music on the Mekong US$28.

### Vinh Long and around p195
**Tour operators**
**Cuu Long Tourist**, No 1, 1 Thang 5 St, T070-823616, www.cuulongtourist.net. Trips to An Binh Island – a highlight of the area – include a visit to the small floating market of Cai Be. A tour of the area including homestay, dinner and breakfast costs US$67. A day trip to Cai Be passing the floating market, US$25; from HCMC, the tour costs US$120.

### Can Tho p195
**Boat trips**
**Trans Mekong**, 97/10 Ngo Quyen, P An Cu, T071-829540, www.transmekong.com. Operates the *Bassac*, a converted 24-m wooden rice barge which can sleep 12 passengers in 6, a/c cabins with private bathrooms. *Bassac II*, catering for 24 guests has been newly launched.

### Swimming
The **Victoria Can Tho**, has a pool open to the public for a fee.

### Therapies
The **Annam Pavilion, Victoria Can Tho**, see Sleeping, has several beautiful massage cabins right on the riverfront offering a host of treatments. Open to non-guests and recommended.

### Tour operators
**Can Tho Tourist**, 20 Hai Ba Trung St, T071-821852, www.canthotourist.com.vn. It's quite expensive and organizes tours in powerful boats – not the best way to see the delta. The staff are helpful and knowledge-able. Tours include trips to Cai Rang, Phong Dien and Phung Hiep floating markets, to Soc Trang, city tours, canal tours, bicycle tours, trekking tours and homestays that involve working with farmers in the fields.

**Phu Quoc Island** *p198, map p198*
**Diving**
**Rainbow Divers**, T091-3400964 (mob), www.divevietnam.com, operates out of the Rainbow Bar between the Saigon Phu Quoc resort and the Kim Hoa resort.

### Tour operators
**Discovery Tour**, Tran Hung Dao St, Duong Dong, T077-846587, daily 0700-1800. Run by the friendly Mr Loi.
**Tony's Tours**, T091-3197334 (mob), tonyphuquoc@yahoo.com. Tony knows Phu Quoc extremely well and speaks fluent English. He would be able to organize almost anything: island tours, snorkelling and deep-sea fishing excursions, car and motorbike rental and hotel and transport reservations.

## ● Transport

### My Tho p194
As in all Mekong Delta towns local travel to visit the orchards, islands and remoter places is often by boat. On land there are *xe ôms* and the *xe lôi*, the local equivalent of the cyclo, consisting of a trailer towed by a bicycle or a motorbike.

There are ferries to **Chau Doc** and **Vinh Long**. Enquire locally about departure times and prices as they vary.

### Can Tho p195
**Air**
**Vietnam Airlines**, 66 Chau Van Liem St. The airport is about 3 km from the centre of Can Tho and is currently being upgraded to international status. There are no flights at present.

### Boat
**Victoria Hotels & Resorts**, 2nd floor, 101 Tran Hung Dao St, District 1, HC MC, T08-8373031, www.victoria hotels-asia.com, runs boats from Can Tho to **Chau Doc** 1330, 3 hrs, US$35 per person, minimum 2 people. The same journey by chartered boat, US$300. Also by request to **HCMC**,1100, 5 hrs, US$55 per person, minimum 5 people; chartered boat, US$550.

The Can Tho ferry is 24 hrs and highly efficient, with not much waiting, 15,000d per car and 2000d per moto, 20 mins. A bridge is being built to Can Tho and is expected to be finished in 2010. **Vinashin**, T071-820527, www.cawaco.com.vn, operates a high-speed boat on Thu from 2 Hai Ba Trung St (the Ninh Kieu jetty) at 0700 to **Phnom Penh** (US$45) returning Sun at 0700 (US$35). The boat also stops at **Chau Doc** (US$10), 2 hrs from **Can Tho**, and **Long Xuyen** (US$5), 1½ hrs from Can Tho.

There is a boat to **Ca Mau** at 0700, 0800, 0900, US$7. Ask at **Can Tho Tourist** for details. To **Con Dao** on Fri, 0700, 3¾ hrs, US$44 return.

### Car

Cars with drivers can be hired from the larger hotels.

### Taxi
**Mai Linh Taxi**, T071-822266.

### Chau Doc *p196*
### Boat

There are daily ferries along the Vinh Te canal to **Ha Tien**, 10 hrs, US$5, a fascinating way to see village life (take plenty of food and water).

There are daily departures to Phnom Penh. A couple of tour operators in town organize boat tickets, see page 197 for further information.

### Phu Quoc Island *p198, map p198*
### Air

**Vietnam Airlines** fly from Ho Chi Minh City.

### Boat

There are 3 express boat services from **Rach Gia** on the mainland to Phu Quoc: **Hai Au**, 16 Trang Hung Dao, Duong Dong, T077-3981000, 160,000d adults on the top floor of the boat, 130,000d ground floor, children half price. Leaves for Rach Gia daily 1330, arriving at 1535. **Superdong**, Duong Dong, T077-846180. Leaves for Rach Gia at 1300, arriving 1535; adults 130,000d, children 70,000d.

**Trameco**, Khu Pho 1, Duong Dong, T077-980666, leaves for Rach Gia at 0830, 2 hrs 10 mins; adults 130,000d, children 70,000d.

### Car and bicycle

Cars and bicycles can be rented from resorts such as the **Tropicana** and **Saigon Phu Quoc**.

### Motorbike

Motorbikes can be rented from most resorts for about US$7-8 per day.

## ⓘ Directory

**My Tho** *p194*
**Bank** BIDV, 5 Le Van Duyet St. Offers a bureau de change service. **Internet** The post office and **Choung Dong** hotel are the best places. **Post office** No 59, 30 Thang 4 St. Also has facilities for international telephone calls, 0600-2100.

**Vinh Long and around** *p195*
**Banks** Nong Nghiep Bank (Agribank), 28 Hung Dao Vuong St. There's a Visa ATM next to the Cuu Long B hotel. **Internet** The post office and Cuu Long (B) hotel offer internet acces and there are a couple of email places on Ly Thuong Kiet St. **Post office** 12c Hoang Thai Hieu St, T070-825888, daily 0600-2100.

**Can Tho** *p195*
**Banks** Nong Nghiep Bank, 3 Phan Dinh Phung St. **Vietcombank**, 7 Hoa Binh Blvd, T071-820445. Bureau de change service. **Internet** No Gia, 71 Vo Van Tan St, and several others on the same street. Alternatively, the big hotels have email facilities. **Post office** 2 Hoa Binh Blvd, T071-827280. It offers internet access, 171 calling (cheap long-distance and international calls).

**Chau Doc** *p196*
**Banks** Nong Nghiep Bank, 51B Ton Duc Thang St. **Vietcombank**, 1 Hung Vuong St. **Internet** Available in the post office and also in Victoria Chau Doc Hotel. Medical services Located opposite the Victoria Chau Doc Hotel. **Post office** 73 Le Loi St, daily 0600-2100, internet access (0600-2100 only), 171 service and fax service.

**Phu Quoc Island** *p198, map p198*

**Banks** It is best to bring enough money with you to Phu Quoc. Some resorts will exchange traveller's cheques as will the banks in Duong Dong but rates are worse than on the mainland. **Phu Quoc Bank**, Duong Dong, cashes TCs. **Vietcom Bank**, daily 0700-1100, 1300-1700, has Visa and MasterCard ATM. **Medical services** The hospital is in Khu Pho, 1 Duong Dong, T077-848075. **Post office** Phu Quoc Post Office, Khu Pho 2, Duong Dong, daily 0645-2030, fax and internet access.

# Background

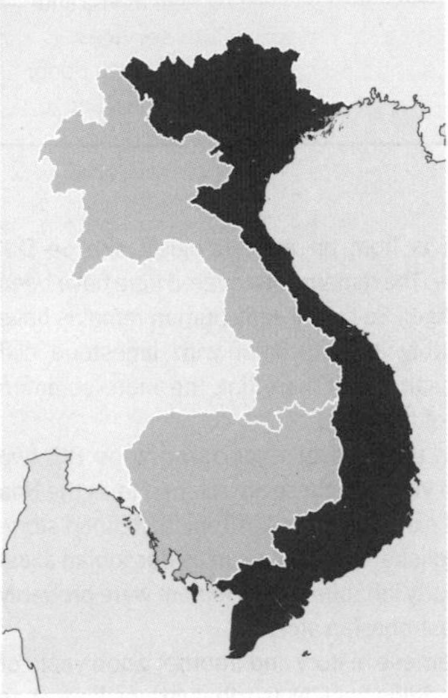



## Footprint features

# History

## Vietnam prehistory

The earliest record of humans in Vietnam is from an archaeological site on Do Mountain, in the northern Thanh Hoa Province. The remains discovered here have been dated to the Lower Palaeolithic (early Stone Age). So far, all early human remains have been unearthed in North Vietnam, invariably in association with limestone cliff dwellings. Unusually, tools are made of basalt rather than flint, the more common material found at similar sites in other parts of the world.

Archaeological excavations have shown that between 5000 and 3000 BC, two important Mesolithic cultures occupied North Vietnam: these are referred to as the **Hoa Binh** and **Bac Son** cultures after the principal excavation sites in Tonkin. Refined stone implements and distinctive hand axes with polished edges (known as Bacsonian axes) are characteristic of the two cultures. These early inhabitants of Vietnam were probably small, dark-skinned and of Melanesian or Austronesian stock.

There are 2000 years of recorded Vietnamese history and another 2000 years of legend. The Vietnamese people trace their origins back to 15 tribal groups known as the **Lac Viet** who settled in what is now North Vietnam at the beginning of the Bronze Age. Here they established an agrarian kingdom known as Van-lang that seems to have vanished during the third century BC.

A problem with early **French archaeological studies** in Vietnam was that most of the scholars were either Sinologists or Indologists. In consequence, they looked to Vietnam as a receptacle of Chinese or Indian cultural influences and spent little time uncovering those aspects of culture, art and life that were indigenous in origin and inspiration. The French archaeologist Bezacier for example, expressed the generally held view that 'Vietnamese' history only began in the seventh century AD. Such sites as Hoa Binh, Dong Son and Oc-Eo, which pre-date the seventh century, were regarded as essentially Chinese or Indonesian, their only 'Vietnamese-ness' being their location. This perspective was more often than not based on faulty and slapdash scholarship, and reflected the prevailing view that Southeast Asian art was basically derivative.

## Pre-colonial history

The beginning of Vietnamese recorded history coincides with the start of **Chinese cultural hegemony** over the north, in the second century BC. The Chinese dominated Vietnam for more than 1000 years until the 10th century AD and the cultural legacy is still very much in evidence, making Vietnam distinctive in Southeast Asia. Even after the 10th century, and despite breaking away from Chinese political domination, Vietnam was still overshadowed and greatly influenced by its illustrious neighbour to the north. Nonetheless, the fact that Vietnam could shrug off 1000 years of Chinese subjugation and emerge with a distinct cultural heritage and language says a lot for Vietnam's strength of national identity. Indeed, it might be argued, as William Duiker, an expert on Ho Chi Minh, does, that the Vietnamese nation "has been formed in the crucible of its historic resistance to Chinese conquest and assimilation".

### Ly Dynasty
The Ly Dynasty (1009-1225) was the first independent Vietnamese dynasty. Its capital, Thang Long, was at the site of present day Hanoi and the dynasty based its system of government and social relations closely upon the Chinese Confucianist model (see

The Vietnamese owe a considerable debt to the Chinese – mainly in the
spheres of government, philosophy and the arts – but they have always been
determined to maintain their independence. Vietnamese Confucianist scholars were
unsparing in their criticism of Chinese imperialism. Continuous Chinese invasions, all
ultimately futile, served to cement an enmity between the two countries, which is still in
evidence today – despite their having normalized diplomatic relations in October 1991.

The first Ly emperor, and one of Vietnam's great kings, was Ly Cong Uan who was
born in AD 974. He is usually known by his posthumous title, **Ly Thai To**, and reigned
for 19 years from 1009-28. Ly Cong Uan was raised and educated by monks and
acceded to the throne when, as the commander of the palace guard in Hoa Lu
(the capital of Vietnam before Thang Long or Hanoi) and with the support of his great
patron, the monk Van Hanh, he managed to gain the support of the Buddhist
establishment and many local lords. During his reign, he enjoyed a reputation not just
as a great soldier, but also as a devout man who paid attention to the interests and
well-being of his people. He also seemed, if the contemporary records are to be
believed, to have been remarkably sensitive to those he ruled. He tried to re-establish
the harmony between ruler and ruled which had suffered during the previous years
and he even sent his son to live outside the walls of the palace so that he could gain a
taste of ordinary life and an understanding of ordinary people. As he approached
death he is said to have increasingly retired from everyday life, preparing himself for
the everlasting.

Ly Cong Uan was succeeded by his son, Ly Phat Ma, who is better known as
**Ly Thai Tong** (reigned 1028-1054). Ly Phat Ma had been prepared for kingship since
birth and he proved to be an excellent ruler during his long reign. It is hard to
generalize about this period in Vietnamese history because Ly Phat Ma adapted his
pattern of rule no less than six times during his reign. Early on he challenged the
establishment, contending for example that good governance was not merely a
consequence of following best practice (which the logic of bureaucratic Confucianism
would maintain) but depended upon good kingship – in other words, depended upon
the qualities of the man at the helm. Later he was more of an establishment figure,
holding much greater store by the institutions of kingship. Perhaps his greatest
military success was the mounting of a campaign to defeat the Cham in 1044 from
which he returned with shiploads of plunder. His greatest artistic legacy was the
construction of the One Pillar Pagoda or Chua Mot Cot in Hanoi (see page 90).

Ly Phat Ma was succeeded by his son, Ly Nhat Ton, posthumously known as
**Ly Thanh Tong** (reigned 1054-1072). History is not as kind about Ly Thanh Tong as it is
about his two forebears. Nonetheless he did challenge the might of the Chinese along
Vietnam's northern borders – largely successfully – and like his father also mounted a
campaign against Champa (see page 212) in 1069. Indeed his expedition against the
Cham mirrored his father's in most respects and, like his father, he won. (But unlike his
father, he did not execute the Cham king.) Records indicate that he spent a great deal of
time trying to father a son and worked his way through numerous concubines and a
great deal of incense in the process. At last, after much labour (on his part, and
probably on the mother's too, although the texts do not say as much), a son was born
to a concubine of common blood in 1066 and named Ly Can Duc.

**Ly Can Duc** was proclaimed emperor in 1072 when he was only six years old and,
surprisingly, remained king until he died in 1127. During the early years of his reign the
kingdom faced a succession of crises, largely due to the fact that his young age meant
that there was no paramount leader. His death marks the end of the Ly Dynasty for he
left no heir and the crown passed to the maternal clan of his nephew. There followed a
period of instability and it was not until 1225 that a new dynasty – the Tran Dynasty –
managed to subdue the various competing cliques and bring a semblance of order to
the country.

**Vietnam** Background History

## ❧ Patriot games: Vietnamese street names

Like other countries that have experienced a revolution, the Vietnamese authorities have spent considerable time expunging street names honouring men and women who lack the necessary revolutionary credentials. Most obviously, Saigon had its name changed to Ho Chi Minh City following reunification in 1975. Most towns have the same street names and most are in memory of former patriots:

**Dien Bien Phu**  Site of the Communists' famous victory against the French in 1954.

**Duy Tan**  11th Nguyen emperor (1907-1916) until exiled to Réunion by the French for his opposition to colonial rule. Killed in an aircrash in Africa in 1945, his remains were interred in Hué in 1987.

**Hai Ba Trung**  The renowned Trung sisters who led a rebellion against Chinese overlords in AD 40.

**Ham Nghi**  The young emperor who joined the resistance against the French in 1885 at the age of 13 and thus gave it legitimacy.

**Hoang Van Thu**  Leader of the Vietnamese Communist Party, executed by the French in 1944.

**Le Duan**  Secretary-General of Lao Dong from 1959.

**Le Lai**  Brother-in-arms of Emperor Le Loi. Le Lai saved Viet forces by dressing in the Emperor's clothes and drawing away surrounding Chinese troops.

**Le Loi (Le Thai To)**  Leader of a revolt which, in 1426, resulted in the liberation of Vietnam from Ming Chinese overlords. Born into a wealthy family he had a life-long concern for the poor. Founder of the Le Dynasty, he ruled 1426-1433.

**Le Thanh Ton(g)**  A successor to Le Loi, ruled 1460-1498, poet king, and cartographer he established an efficient administration on strict Confucian lines and an enlightened legal code; literature and the arts flourished.

**Ly Thuong Kiet**  Military commander who led campaigns against the Chinese and Cham during the 11th century, and gained a reputation as a brilliant strategist. He died at the age of 70 in 1105.

## Tran Dynasty

Scholars do not know a great deal about the four generations of kings of the Tran Dynasty. It seems that they established the habit of marrying within the clan, and each king took queens who were either their cousins or, in one case, a half-sister. Such a long period of intermarriage, one imagines, would have had some far-reaching genetic consequences, although ironically the collapse of the dynasty seems to have been brought about after one foolish king decided to marry outside the Tran clan. The great achievement of the Tran Dynasty was to resist the expansionist tendencies of the Mongol forces who conquered China in the 1250s and then set their sights on Vietnam. In 1284 a huge Mongol-Yuan force, consisting of no fewer than four armies, massed on the border to crush the Vietnamese. Fortunately the Tran were blessed with a group of brave and resourceful princes, the most notable of whom was Tran Quoc Tuan, better known – and now immortalized in street names in just about every Vietnamese town – as **Tran Hung Dao**. Although the invading forces captured Thang Long (Hanoi) they never managed to defeat the Vietnamese in a decisive battle and in the end the forces of the Tran Dynasty were victorious.

**Nguyen Du (1765-1820)** Ambassador to Peking, courtier and Vietnam's most famous poet, wrote *The Tale of Kieu*.

**Nguyen Hue** Tay Son brother who routed the Chinese at the Battle of Dong Da. Later became Emperor Quang Trung.

**Nguyen Thai Hoc** Leader of the Vietnam Quoc Dan Dang Party (VNQDD) and the leader of the Yen Bai uprisings; captured by the French and guillotined on 17 June 1930 at the age of 28.

**Nguyen Trai** Emperor Le Loi's advisor and a skilled poet, he advised Le Loi to concentrate on political and moral struggle: "Better to conquer hearts than citadels."

**Nguyen Van Troi** Viet Cong hero who in 1963 tried, unsuccessfully, to assassinate Robert McNamara by blowing up a bridge in Saigon. He was executed.

**Phan Boi Chau** A committed anti-colonialist from the age of 19, he travelled to China and Japan to organize resistance to the French. Captured in Shanghai in 1925 he was extradited to Hanoi and sentenced to life imprisonment. Public pressure led to his amnesty in the same year and he spent the rest of his life in Hué where he died in 1940.

**Quang Trung** Leader of the Tay Son peasant rebellion of 1771; defeated both the Siamese (Thais) and the Chinese.

**Ton Duc Thang** Became President of the Socialist Republic of Vietnam; he took part in a mutiny aboard a French ship along with other Vietnamese shipmates in the Black Sea in support of the Russian Revolution.

**Tran Hung Dao** A 13th-century hero who fought and defeated the Yuan Chinese. Regarded as one of Vietnam's great military leaders and strategists, also a man of letters writing the classic *Binh Thu Yeu Luoc* in 1284.

**Tran Nguyen Han** A 15th-century general who fought heroically against the Ming Chinese occupiers.

**Tran Phu** The first Secretary General of the Communist Party of Indochina, killed by the French in 1931 at the age of 27.

**30 Thang 4 Street** Commemorates the capture of Saigon by the Communists on 30 April 1975.

# Le Dynasty and the emergence of Vietnam

## Le Loi

During its struggle with the Cham, nascent Dai Viet had to contend with the weight of Ming Chinese oppression from the north, often in concert with their Cham allies. Despite 1000 years of Chinese domination and centuries of internal dynastic squabbles the Viet retained a strong sense of national identity and were quick to respond to charismatic leadership. As so often in Vietnam's history one man was able to harness nationalistic sentiment and mould the country's discontent into a powerful fighting force: in 1426 it was Le Loi. Together with the brilliant tactician **Nguyen Trai** (see page 210), Le Loi led a campaign to remove the Chinese from Vietnamese soil. Combining surprise, guerrilla tactics and Nguyen Trai's innovative and famous propaganda, designed to convince defending Ming of the futility of their position, the Viet won a resounding victory which led to the enlightened and artistically distinguished Le period. Le Loi's legendary victory lives on in popular form and is celebrated in the tale of the restored sword in water puppet performances

## ⋮ Nguyen Trai

*Our country, Dai Viet, has long been
A land of ancient culture,
With its own rivers and mountains,
  ways and customs,
Different from those of the North.*
(Opening lines of *Proclamation of
Victory Over the Invaders*)

Nguyen Trai, mandarin, poet and nationalist, rose to prominence as an adviser to Le Loi during the 10-year campaign to eject the Ming from Dai Viet. His famous counsel "better to win hearts than citadels" (which mirrors similar advice during a war over 500 years later) was heeded by Le Loi who aroused patriotic fervour in his compatriots to achieve victory on the battlefield. It was on Nguyen Trai's suggestion that 100,000 defeated Ming troops were given food and boats to make their way home. After the war, Nguyen Trai accepted and later resigned a court post. He was a prolific composer of verse, which is considered some of the finest in the national annals.

On an overnight visit to Nguyen Trai, Emperor Le Thai Tong (Le Loi's son and heir) died unexpectedly. Scheming courtiers were able to fix the blame on Nguyen Trai who in 1442, along with three generations of his family, were executed, a punishment known as *tru di tam tôc*.

across the country. Following his victory against the Ming he claimed the throne in 1428 and reigned until his death five years later.

## Le Thanh Ton

With Le Loi's death the Le Dynasty worked its way through a succession of young kings who seemed to hold the throne barely long enough to warm the cushions before they were murdered. It was not until 1460 that a king of substance was to accede: Le Thanh Ton (reigned 1460-1497). His reign was a period of great scholarship and artistic accomplishment. He established the system of rule that was to guide successive Vietnamese emperors for 500 years. He also mounted a series of military campaigns, some as far as Laos to the west.

## Le expansion

The expansion of the Vietnamese state, under the Le, south from its heartland in the Tonkin Delta, followed the decline of the Cham Kingdom at the end of the 15th century. By the early 18th century the Cham were extinct as an identifiable political and military force and the Vietnamese advanced still further south into the Khmer-controlled territories of the Mekong Delta. This geographical over-extension and the sheer logistical impracticability of ruling from distant Hanoi, disseminating edicts and collecting taxes, led to the disintegration of the – ever tenuous – imperial rule. The old adage 'The edicts of the emperor stop at the village gate' was particularly apt more than 1000 km from the capital. Noble families, locally dominant, challenged the emperor's authority and the Le Dynasty gradually dissolved into internecine strife and regional fiefdoms, namely Trinh in the north and Nguyen in the south, a pattern that was to reassert itself some 300 years later. But although on paper the Vietnamese – now consisting of two dynastic houses, Trinh and Nguyen – appeared powerful, the people were mired in poverty.

There were numerous peasant rebellions in this period, of which the most serious was the **Tay Son rebellion** of 1771. One of the three Tay Son brothers, Nguyen Hue, proclaimed himself **Emperor Quang Trung** in 1788, only to die four years later.

## ⁑ Vietnamese dynasties

| Dynasty | Dates | Capital (province) |
|---|---|---|
| Hong Bang (legendary) | 2876-258 BC | Phong Chau (Son Tay) |
| Thuc | 257-207 BC | Loa Thanh (Vinh Phu) |
| Trieu | 207-111 BC | Phien Ngung (S China) |
| **under Chinese domination 111 BC-AD 23** | | |
| Trung Sisters | AD 40-43 | Me Linh (Son Tay) |
| **under Chinese domination AD 25-589** | | |
| Early Ly | 544-602 | various (Hanoi) |
| **under Chinese domination AD 603-938** | | |
| Ngo | 939-967 | Co Loa (Vinh Phuc) |
| Dinh | 968-980 | Hoa Lu (Ninh Binh) |
| Early Le | 980-1009 | Hoa Lu (Ninh Binh) |
| Ly | 1010-1225 | Thang Long (Hanoi) |
| Tran | 1225-1400 | Thang Long (Hanoi) |
| Ho | 1400-1407 | Dong Do (Hanoi) |
| Post Tran | 1407-1413 | |
| **under Chinese domination AD 1414-1427** | | |
| Le | 1427-1788 | Thang Long (Hanoi) |
| Mac | 1527-1592 | |
| Northern Trinh | 1539-1787 | Hanoi |
| Southern Nguyen | 1558-1778 | Hué |
| Quang Trung | 1787-1792 | |
| Nguyen of Tay Son | 1788-1802 | Saigon |
| Nguyen | 1802-1945 | Hué |

From the 16th to18th centuries there were up to four centres of power in Vietnam.

The death of Quang Trung paved the way for the establishment of the **Nguyen Dynasty** – the last Vietnamese dynasty – in 1802 when Emperor Gia Long ascended to the throne in Hué. Despite the fact that this period heralded the arrival of the French – leading to their eventual domination of Vietnam – it is regarded as a golden period in Vietnamese history. During the Nguyen Dynasty, Vietnam was unified as a single state and Hué emerged as the heart of the kingdom.

# History of the non-Viet civilizations

Any history of Vietnam must include the non-Vietnamese peoples and civilizations. The central and southern parts of Vietnam have only relatively recently been dominated by the Viets. Before that, these lands were in the hands of people of Indian or Khmer origins.

## Funan (AD 100-600)

According to Chinese sources, Funan was a Hindu kingdom founded in the first century AD with its capital, Vyadhapura, close to the Mekong River near the border with Cambodia. A local legend records that Kaundinya, a great Indian Brahmin, acting on a dream, sailed to the coast of Vietnam carrying with him a bow and arrow. When he arrived, Kaundinya shot the arrow and where it landed he established the capital of Funan. Following this act, Kaundinya married the princess Soma, daughter of the local King of the Nagas (giant water serpents). The legend symbolizes the union between Indian and local cultural traditions – the naga representing indigenous fertility rites and customs, and the arrow, the potency of the Hindu religion.

## Oc-Eo

Funan built its wealth and power on its strategic location on the sea route between China and the islands to the south. Maritime technology at the time forced seafarers travelling between China and island Southeast Asia and India to stop and wait for the winds to change before they could continue on their way. This sometimes meant a stay of up to five months. The large port city of Oc-Eo offered a safe harbour for merchant vessels and the revenues generated enabled the kings of the empire to expand rice cultivation, dominate a host of surrounding vassal states as far away as the Malay coast and South Burma, and build a series of impressive temples, cities and irrigation works. Although the Chinese chronicler K'ang T'ai records that the Funanese were barbarians – "ugly, black, and frizzy-haired" – it is clear from Chinese court annals that they were artistically and technologically accomplished. It is recorded for example that one Chinese emperor was so impressed by the skill of some visiting musicians in AD 263 that he ordered the establishment of an institute of Funanese music.

Funan reached the peak of its powers in the fourth century and went into decline during the fifth century AD when improving maritime technology made Oc-Eo redundant as a haven for sailing vessels. No longer did merchants hug the coastline; ships were now large enough, and navigation skills sophisticated enough, to make the journey from South China to the Malacca Strait without landfall. By the mid-sixth century, Funan, having suffered from a drawn-out leadership crisis, was severely weakened. Neighbouring competing powers took advantage of this crisis, absorbing previously Funan-controlled lands. Irrigation works fell into disrepair as state control weakened and peasants left the fields to seek more productive lands elsewhere. The Cham ultimately conquered Funan, having lost both the economic wealth and the religious legitimacy on which its power had been based.

What is interesting about Funan is the degree to which it provided a model for future states in Southeast Asia. Funan's wealth was built on its links with the sea, and with its ability to exploit maritime trade. The later rulers of Champa, Langkasuka (Malaya), Srivijaya (Sumatra) and Malacca (Malaya) repeated this formula.

## Champa (AD 200–1720)

In South Vietnam, where the dynastic lords achieved hegemony only in the 18th century, the kingdom of Champa – or Lin-yi as the Chinese called it – was the most significant power. The kingdom evolved in the second century AD and was focused on the narrow ribbon of lowland that runs north-south down the Annamite coast with its various capitals near the present-day city of Danang. Chinese sources record that in AD 192 a local official, Kiu-lien, rejected Chinese authority and established an independent kingdom. From then on, Champa's history was one of conflict with its neighbour; when Imperial China was powerful, Champa was subservient and sent ambassadors and tributes in homage to the Chinese court; when it was weak, the rulers of Champa extended their own influence and ignored the Chinese. ▸▸ See also box, page 214.

The difficulty for scholars is to decide whether Champa had a single identity or whether it consisted of numerous mini-powers with no dominant centre. The accepted wisdom at the moment is that Champa was more diffuse than previously thought and that only rarely during its history is it possible to talk of Champa in singular terms. The endless shifting of the capital of Champa is taken to reflect the shifting centres of power that characterized this 'kingdom'.

Like Funan, Champa built its power on its position on the maritime trading route through Southeast Asia. During the fourth century, as Champa expanded into formerly Funan-controlled lands, they came under the influence of the Indian cultural traditions of the Funanese. These were enthusiastically embraced by Champa's rulers who tacked the suffix '-varman' onto their names (for example Bhadravarman) and adopted the Hindu-Buddhist cosmology. Though a powerful trading kingdom, Champa was geographically poorly endowed. The coastal strip between the Annamite highlands to the west, and the sea to the east, is narrow and the potential for extensive rice cultivation limited. This may explain why the Champa Empire was never more than a moderate power: it was unable to produce the agricultural surplus necessary to support an extensive court and army, and therefore could not compete with either the Khmers to the south nor with the Viets to the north. But the Cham were able to carve out a niche for themselves between the two, and to many art historians, their art and architecture represent the finest that Vietnam has ever produced (see pages 142 and 145). Remains are to be found on the central Vietnamese coast from Quang Tri in the north, to Ham Tan 800 km to the south.

For over 1000 years the Cham resisted the Chinese and the Vietnamese. But by the time Marco Polo wrote of the Cham, their power and prestige were much reduced: "The people are idolaters and pay a yearly tribute to the Great Kaan which consists of elephants and nothing but elephants. In the year of Christ 1285 ... the King had, between sons and daughters, 326 children. There are a very great number of elephants in that country, and they have lignaloes (eagle wood) in great abundance. They have also extensive forests of the wood called Bonús, which is jet black, of which chessmen and pencases are made. But there is nought more to tell, so let us proceed." After 1285, when invading Mongol hordes were repelled by the valiant Viets, Champa and Dai Viet enjoyed an uneasy peace maintained by the liberal flow of royal princesses south across the Col des Nuages (Hai Van Pass) in exchange for territory. During the peaceful reign of Che A-nan a Franciscan priest, Odoric of Pordenone, reported of Champa "'tis a very fine country, having a great store of victuals and of all good things". Of particular interest, he refers to the practice of suti, writing "When a man dies in this country, they burn his wife with him, for they say that she should live with him in the other world also". Clearly, some of the ancient Indian traditions continued.

Champa saw a late flowering under King Binasuos who led numerous successful campaigns against the Viet, culminating in the sack of Hanoi in 1371. Subsequently, the treachery of a low-ranking officer led to Binasuos' death in 1390 and the military eclipse of the Cham by the Vietnamese. The demographic and economic superiority of the Viet coupled with their gradual drift south contributed most to the waning of the Cham Kingdom, but finally, in 1471 the Cham suffered a terrible defeat at the hands of the Vietnamese. Some 60,000 of their soldiers were killed and another 36,000 captured and carried into captivity, including the King and 50 members of the royal family. The kingdom shrank to a small territory in the vicinity of Nha Trang that survived until 1720 when surviving members of the royal family and many subjects fled to Cambodia to escape from the advancing Vietnamese.

## The colonial period

One of the key motivating factors that encouraged the **French** to undermine the authority of the Vietnamese emperors was their treatment of Roman Catholics. Jesuits had been in the country from as early as the 17th century – one of them, Alexandre-de-Rhodes, converted the Vietnamese writing system from Chinese characters to Romanized script – but persecution of Roman Catholics began only in the 1830s. Emperor Minh Mang issued an imperial edict outlawing the dissemination of Christianity as a heterodox creed in 1825. The first European priest to be executed was François Isidore Gagelin who was strangled by six soldiers as he knelt on a scaffold in Hué in 1833. Three days later, having

# ⋮ A Spanish account of Champa

This account of Champa is taken from an anonymous manuscript compiled in Manila about 1590-1595, possibly as part of the documentation assembled by Don Luis Perez das Marinas in justification of his scheme for the conquest of Indochina.

"It is a land fertile in foodstuffs and cows and oxen and very healthy in itself. It is not thickly populated and the people are swarthy and heathens. In this kingdom there is no money nor silver with which to sell anything; and in order to buy what they need, they exchange foodstuffs for cotton blankets and other things that they make for the purpose of buying and selling with each other. Nobody is allowed to go shod, save only the king, and nobody can be married with more than two wives.

### Food and drink

These people do not eat anything properly cooked, but only in raw or putrid condition; and in order to digest these foods, they are great drinkers of very strong spirits, which they drink little by little and very frequently, thinking it no disgrace to fall down from drinking too much.

### Seasons

They divide the year into six festivals, during the first of which the vast majority of his vassals pay tribute to the king. The king goes to a field, and there they assemble all these tributes, out of which they make alms to the souls of the dead and perform great obsequies and funeral rites in their memory.

The second festival also lasts two months and they spend the whole of this time singing to the exclusion of everything else, except when they are actually eating their meals. During these festivals the women, of whatsoever condition they be, have liberty to do what they like for the space of three days, during which they are not asked to account for their behaviour.

During the third festival they go to the seaside, where they stay fishing for another two months. They make merry, catching enough fish to last them for the year, pickling it in their jars, with just a little salt, and they eat it putrid in this manner. And they thrive very strong and lusty on this food.

When the king returns to the city, they display lights by night and day, putting on plays and races in public, in which the king participates. This is the fourth of their festivals.

The fifth is when the king goes hunting elephants, of which there are many in this land, taking with him the nobility and their female elephants; and the females go into the place where the wild elephants are, which follow the former into a little space which they have stockaded off for this purpose, and there they keep them for some days until they are tamed.

The last festival which they celebrate is a tiger-hunt. The tigers come to eat the buffaloes that are tied to a tree in

been told that Christians believe they will come to life again, Minh Mang had the body exhumed to confirm the man's death. In 1840 Minh Mang actually read the Old Testament in Chinese translation, declaring it to be 'absurd'.

Yet, Christianity continued to spread as Buddhism declined and there was a continual stream of priests willing to risk their lives proselytizing. In addition, the economy was in disarray and natural disasters common. Poor Vietnamese saw Christianity as a way to break the shackles of their feudal existence. Fearing a peasants' revolt, the Emperor ordered the execution of 25 European priests, 300 Vietnamese priests, and 30,000 Vietnamese Catholics between 1848 and 1860. Provoked by these killings, the French attacked and took Saigon in 1859. In 1862 **Emperor Tu Duc** signed a treaty ceding the three southern provinces to the French, certain places. They place sentinels over them, so that when the tigers approach, the king is informed. And as soon as this news arrives the king gets ready with a great number of Indians and nets, and they do with the tigers what they do with the elephants, surrounding them at once and killing them there and then. It is the custom with these Indians that at the time when they are occupied with this hunt, the king and his wife send out 100 or more Indians along the roads, with express order that they should not return without filling two gold basins which they give them, full of human gall, which must be from people of their own nation and not foreigners; and these emissaries do as they are told, not sparing anyone they meet, whether of high or low degree. As soon as they can catch a person on the road, they tie him at once to a tree, and there they cut out the gall … When all this is over the king and his wife bathe and wash with this human gall; and they say that in this way they cleanse themselves of their sins and their faults.

### Justice

The justice of this people is peculiar, for they have no fixed criminal code, but only their personal opinions, and when the case is a serious one, they investigate it with two witnesses. Their oaths are made with fire and boiling oil, and those condemned to death are executed with extreme barbarity.

Some are sentenced to be trampled to death by elephants; others are flogged to death; others are tortured for two or three days, during which time bits and pieces are cut out of their bodies with pincers until they die. And for very trifling and common offences, they cut off their feet, hands, arms and ears.

### Death

They have another custom invented by the Devil himself, which is that when any leading personage dies, they cremate the body, after it has been kept for eight or 10 days until they have made the necessary preparations in accordance with the quality of the deceased, when they burn it in the field. When such a person dies, they seize all the household servants and keep them until the same day on which they burn the body of their master, and then they throw them alive into the flames, so that they can serve them therewith in the other … Another custom which they have, which is a very harsh one for women, is that when the husband dies, they burn the wife with him. They say that this law was made to prevent wives from giving poisonous herbs to their husbands, for there are very great witchcrafts and knaveries in these lands. They say that if the wife realizes that her husband will not live any longer than her, she will take good care of his life and ease, and will not dare to kill him with poison.

thereby creating the colony of **Cochin China**. This treaty of 1862 effectively paved the way for the eventual seizure by the French of the whole kingdom. The French, through weight of arms, also forced the Emperor to end the persecution of Christians in his kingdom. In retrospect, although many Christians did die cruelly, the degree of persecution was not on the scale of similar episodes elsewhere: Minh Mang's successors Thieu Tri (1841-1847) and Tu Duc (1847-1883), though both fervently anti-Christian, appreciated French military strength and the fact that they were searching for pretexts to intervene.

The **French conquest of the north** was motivated by a desire to control trade and the route to what were presumed to be the vast riches of China. In 1883 and 1884, the French forced the Emperor to sign treaties making Vietnam a French protectorate. In

August 1883 for example, just after Tu Duc's death, a French fleet appeared off Hué to force concessions. François Harmand, a native affairs official on board one of the ships, threatened the Vietnamese by stating: "Imagine all that is terrible and it will still be less than reality ... the word 'Vietnam' will be erased from history." The emperor called on China for assistance and demanded that provinces resist French rule; but the imperial bidding proved ineffective, and in 1885 the **Treaty of Tientsin** recognized the French protectorates of Tonkin (North Vietnam) and Annam (Central Vietnam), to add to that of Cochin China (South Vietnam).

## Resistance to the French: the prelude to revolution

Like other European powers in Southeast Asia, the French managed to achieve military victory with ease, but they failed to stifle Vietnamese nationalism. After 1900, as Chinese translations of the works of Rousseau, Voltaire and social Darwinists such as Herbert Spence began to find their way into the hands of the Vietnamese intelligentsia, so resistance grew. Foremost among these early nationalists were Phan Boi Chau (1867-1940) and Phan Chau Trinh (1871-1926) who wrote tracts calling for the expulsion of the French. But these men and others such as Prince Cuong De (1882-1951) were traditional nationalists, their beliefs rooted in Confucianism rather than revolutionary Marxism. Their efforts and perspectives were essentially in the tradition of the nationalists who had resisted Chinese domination over previous centuries.

**Quoc Dan Dang (VNQDD)**, founded at the end of 1927, was the first nationalist party, while the first significant Communist group was the **Indochina Communist Party (ICP)** established by **Ho Chi Minh** in 1930 (see box, page 218). Both the VNQDD and the ICP organized resistance to the French and there were numerous strikes and uprisings, particularly during the harsh years of the Great Depression. The Japanese 'occupation' from August 1940 (Vichy France permitted the Japanese full access to military facilities in exchange for allowing continued French administrative control) saw the creation of the **Viet Minh** to fight for the liberation of Vietnam from Japanese and French control.

# The Vietnam wars

## The First Indochina War (1945-1954)

The Vietnam War started in September 1945 in the south of the country and in 1946 in the north. These years marked the onset of fighting **between the Viet Minh and the French** and the period is usually referred to as the First Indochina War. The Communists, who had organized against the Japanese, proclaimed the creation of the **Democratic Republic of Vietnam (DRV)** on 2 September 1945 when Ho Chi Minh read out the Vietnamese **Declaration of Independence** in Hanoi's Ba Dinh Square. Ironically, this document was modelled closely on the American Declaration of Independence. Indeed, the US was favourably disposed towards the Viet Minh and Ho. Operatives of the OSS (the wartime precursor to the CIA) met Ho and supported his efforts during the war and afterwards Roosevelt's inclination was to prevent France claiming their colony back. Only Winston Churchill's persuasion changed his mind.

The French, although they had always insisted that Vietnam be returned to French rule, were in no position to force the issue. Instead, in the south, it was British troops (mainly Gurkhas) who helped the small force of French against the Viet Minh. Incredibly, the British also ordered the Japanese, who had only just capitulated, to help fight the Vietnamese. When 35,000 French reinforcements arrived, the issue in the south – at least superficially – was all but settled, with Ca Mau at the southern extremity of the country falling on 21 October. From that point, the war in the south became an underground battle of attrition, with the north providing support to their southern comrades.

In the north, the Viet Minh had to deal with 180,000 rampaging Nationalist Chinese troops, while preparing for the imminent arrival of a French force. Unable to confront both at the same time, and deciding that the French were probably the lesser of two evils, Ho Chi Minh decided to negotiate. He is said to have observed in private, that it was preferable to 'sniff French shit for a while than eat China's all our lives'. To make the DRV government more acceptable to the French, Ho proceeded cautiously, only nationalizing a few strategic industries, bringing moderates into the government, and actually dissolving the Indochina Communist Party (at least on paper) in November 1945. But in the same month Ho also said: "The French colonialists should know that the Vietnamese people do not wish to spill blood, that it loves peace. But if it must sacrifice millions of combatants, lead a resistance for long years to defend the independence of the country, and preserve its children from slavery, it will do so. It is certain the resistance will win."

## Chinese withdrawal

In February 1946, the French and Chinese signed a treaty leading to the withdrawal of Chinese forces and shortly afterwards Ho concluded a treaty with French President de Gaulle's special emissary to Vietnam, Jean Sainteny, in which Vietnam was acknowledged as a 'free' (the Vietnamese word *doc lap* being translated as free, but not yet independent) state that was within the French Union and the Indochinese Federation.

It is interesting to note that in negotiating with the French, Ho was going against most of his supporters who argued for confrontation. But Ho, ever a pragmatist, believed at this stage that the Viet Minh were ill-trained and poorly armed and he appreciated the need for time to consolidate their position. The episode that is usually highlighted as the flashpoint that led to the resumption of hostilities was the French government's decision to open a customs house in Haiphong at the end of 1946. The Viet Minh forces resisted and the rest, as they say, is history. It seems that during the course of 1946 Ho changed his view of the best path to independence. Initially he asked: "Why should we sacrifice 50 or 100,000 men when we can achieve independence within five years through negotiation?" although he later came to the conclusion that it was necessary to fight for independence. The customs house episode might, therefore, be viewed as merely an excuse. The French claimed that 5000 Vietnamese were killed in the ensuing bombardment, versus five Frenchmen; the Vietnamese put the toll at 20,000.

In a pattern that was to become characteristic of the entire 25-year conflict, while the French controlled the cities, the Viet Minh were dominant in the countryside. By the end of 1949, with the success of the Chinese Revolution and the establishment of the Democratic People's Republic of Korea (North Korea) in 1948, the US began to offer support to the French in an attempt to stem the 'Red Tide' that seemed to be sweeping across Asia. At this early stage, the odds appeared stacked against the Viet Minh, but Ho was confident that time was on their side. As he remarked to Sainteny "If we have to fight, we will fight. You can kill 10 of my men for every one I kill of yours but even at those odds, I will win and you will lose". It also became increasingly clear that the French were not committed to negotiating a route to independence. A secret French report prepared in 1948 was obtained and published by the Viet Minh in which the High Commissioner, Monsieur Bollaert, wrote: "It is my impression that we must make a concession to Vietnam of the term, independence; but I am convinced that this word need never be interpreted in any light other than that of a religious verbalism."

## Dien Bien Phu (1954) and the Geneva Agreement

The decisive battle of the First Indochina War was at Dien Bien Phu in the hills of the northwest, close to the border with Laos. At the end of 1953 the French, with American

## ⦂ Ho Chi Minh: 'He who enlightens'

Ho Chi Minh, one of a number of pseudonyms Ho adopted during his life (see box, page 220), was born Nguyen Sinh Cung, or possibly Nguyen Van Thanh (Ho did not keep a diary during much of his life, so parts of his life are still a mystery), in Nghe An Province near Vinh on the 19 May 1890, and came from a poor scholar-gentry family. In the village, the family was aristocratic; beyond it they were little more than peasants. His father, though not a revolutionary, was a dissenter and rather than go to Hué to serve the French, he chose to work as a village school teacher. Ho must have been influenced by his father's implacable animosity towards the French, although Ho's early years are obscure. He went to Quoc Hoc College in Hué and then worked for a while as a teacher in Phan Thiet, a fishing village in South Annam.

In 1911, under the name Nguyen Tat Thanh, he travelled to Saigon and left the country as a messboy on the French ship *Amiral Latouche-Tréville*. He is said to have used the name 'Ba' so that he would not shame his family by accepting such lowly work. This marked the beginning of three years of travel during which he visited France, England, America (where the skyscrapers of Manhattan both amazed and appalled him) and North Africa. Seeing the colonialists on their own turf and

reading such revolutionary literature as the French Communist Party newspaper *L'Humanité*, he was converted to Communism. In Paris he mixed with leftists, wrote pamphlets and attended meetings of the French Socialist Party. He also took odd jobs: for a while he worked at the *Carlton Hotel* in London and became an assistant pastry chef under the legendary French chef Georges Escoffier.

An even more unlikely story emerges from Gavin Young's *A Wavering Grace*. In the book he recounts an interview he conducted with Mae West in 1968 shortly after he had returned from reporting the Tet offensive. On hearing of Vietnam, Mae West innocently said that she "used to know someone *very*, very important there ... His name was Ho ... Ho ... Ho something". At the time she was staying at the Carlton while starring in a London show, *Sex*. She confided to Young: "There was this waiter, cook, I don't know what he was. I know he had the slinkiest eyes though. We met in the corridor. We – well ..." Young writes that "Her voice trailed off in a husky sigh ..."

Gradually Ho became an even more committed Communist, contributing articles to radical newspapers and working his way into the web of Communist and leftist groups. At the same time he remained, curiously,

support, parachuted 16,000 men into the area in an attempt to protect Laos from Viet Minh incursions and to tempt them into open battle. The French in fact found themselves trapped, surrounded by Viet Minh and overlooked by artillery. There was some suggestion that the US might become involved, and even use tactical nuclear weapons, but this was not to be. In May 1954 the French surrendered – the most humiliating of French colonial defeats – effectively marking the end of the French presence in Indochina. In July 1954, in Geneva, the French and Vietnamese agreed to divide the country along the 17th parallel, so creating two states – the Communists occupying the north and the non-Communists occupying the south. The border was kept open for 300 days and over that period about 900,000 – mostly Roman Catholic – Vietnamese travelled south. At the same time nearly 90,000 Viet Minh troops along with 43,000 civilians went north, although many Viet Minh remained in the south to continue the fight there.

a French cultural chauvinist, complaining for example about the intrusion of English words like *le manager* and *le challenger* (referring to boxing contests) into the French language. He even urged the French prime minister to ban foreign words from the French press. In 1923 he left France for Moscow and was trained as a Communist activist – effectively a spy. From there, Ho travelled to Canton where he was instrumental in forming the Vietnamese Communist movement. This culminated in the creation of the Indochina Communist Party in 1930. His movements during these years are scantily documented: he became a Buddhist monk in Siam (Thailand), was arrested in Hong Kong for subversive activities and received a six month sentence, travelled to China several times, and in 1940 even returned to Vietnam for a short period – his first visit for nearly 30 years. Despite his absence from the country, the French had already recognized the threat that he posed and sentenced him to death in absentia in 1930. He did not adopt the pseudonym by which he is now best known – Ho Chi Minh – until the early 1940s.

Ho was a consummate politician and, despite his revolutionary fervour, a great realist. He was also a charming man, and during his stay in France between June and October 1946 he made a great number of friends. Robert Shaplen in his book *The Lost Revolution* (1965) talks of his "wit, his oriental courtesy, his savoir-faire ... above all his seeming sincerity and simplicity". He talked with farmers and fishermen and debated with priests; he impressed people wherever he travelled. He died in Hanoi at his house in the former governor's residence in 1969 (see page 90).

Since the demise of Communism in the former Soviet Union, the Vietnamese leadership have been concerned that secrets about Ho's life might be gleaned from old comintern files in Moscow by nosy journalists. To thwart such an eventuality, they have, reportedly, sent a senior historian to scour the archives. To date, Ho's image remains largely untarnished – making him an exception amongst the tawdry league of former Communist leaders. But a Moscow-based reporter has unearthed evidence implying Ho was married, challenging the official hagiography that paints Ho as a celibate who committed his entire life to the revolution. It takes a brave Vietnamese to challenge established 'fact'. In 1991, when the popular Vietnamese *Youth* or *Tuoi Tre* newspaper dared to suggest that Ho had married Tang Tuyet Minh in China in 1926, the editor was summarily dismissed from her post.

## The Second Indochina War (1954-1975)

The Vietnam War, but particularly the American part of that war, is probably the most minutely studied, reported, analysed and recorded in history. Yet, as with all wars, there are still large grey areas and continuing disagreement over important episodes. Most crucially, there is the question of whether the US might have won had their forces been given a free hand and were not forced, as some would have it, to fight with one hand tied behind their backs. This remains the view among many members of the US military.

## Ngo Dinh Diem

At the time of the partition of Vietnam along the 17th parallel, the government in the south was chaotic and the Communists could be fairly confident that in a short time their sympathizers would be victorious. This situation was to change with the rise of Ngo Dinh Diem. Born in Hué in 1901 to a Roman Catholic Confucian family, Diem wished to become a priest. He graduated at the top of his class from the French School of Administration and at the age of 32 was appointed to the post of minister of the interior at the court of Emperor Bao Dai. Here, according to the political scientist William Turley, "he worked with uncommon industry and integrity" only to resign in exasperation at court intrigues and French interference. He withdrew from political activity during the First Indochina War and in 1946 Ho Chi Minh offered him a post in the DRV government – an offer he declined.

Turley describes him as a man who was a creature of the past: "For Diem, the mandarin, political leadership meant rule by example, precept and paternalism. His Catholic upbringing reinforced rather

## ⦂ Ho Chi Minh pseudonyms

| | |
|---|---|
| Born 1890 | Nguyen Sinh Cung or Nguyen Van Thanh (Vinh) |
| 1910 | Van Ba (South Vietnam) |
| 1911 | Nguyen Tat Thanh (Saigon) |
| 1913 | Nguyen Tat Thanh (London) |
| 1914 | Nguyen Ai Quoc (Paris) |
| 1924 | Linh (Moscow) |
| 1924 | Ly Thuy (Moscow) |
| 1925 | Wang (Canton) |
| 1927 | Duong (Paris) |
| 1928 | Nguyen Lai, Nam Son, Thau Chin (Siam) |

than replaced the Confucian tendency to base authority on doctrine, morality and hierarchy. Utterly alien to him were the concepts of power-sharing and popular participation. He was the heir to a dying tradition, member of an elite that had been superbly prepared by birth, training, and experience to lead a Vietnam that no longer existed."

In July 1954 Diem returned from his self-imposed exile at the Maryknoll Seminary in New Jersey to become Premier of South Vietnam. It is usually alleged that the US administration was behind his rise to power, although this has yet to be proved. He held two rigged elections (in October 1955, 450,000 registered voters cast 605,025 votes) that gave some legitimacy to his administration in American eyes. He proceeded to suppress all opposition in the country. His brutal brother, Ngo Dinh Nhu, was appointed to head the security forces and terrorized much of Vietnamese society.

During the period of Diem's premiership, opposition to his rule, particularly in the countryside, increased. This was because the military's campaign against the Viet Minh targeted – both directly and indirectly – many innocent peasants. At the same time, the nepotism and corruption that was endemic within the administration also turned many people into Viet Minh sympathizers. That said, Diem's campaign was successful in undermining the strength of the Communist Party in the south. While there were perhaps 50,000-60,000 party members in 1954, this figure had declined through widespread arrests and intimidation to only 5000 by 1959.

The erosion of the Party in the south gradually led, from 1959, to the north changing its strategy towards one of more overt military confrontation. The same year also saw the establishment of Group 559 which was charged with the task of setting up what was to become the Ho Chi Minh Trail, along which supplies and troops were moved from the north to the south (see page 182). But, even at this stage, the Party's forces in the south were kept from open confrontation and many of its leaders were hoping for victory without having to resort to open warfare. There was no call for a 'People's War' and armed resistance was left largely to guerrillas belonging to the Cao Dai (see page 259) and Hoa Hao (Buddhist millenarian) sects. The establishment of the National Liberation Front of Vietnam in 1960 was an important political and organizational development towards creating a credible alternative to Diem – although it did not hold its first congress until 1962.

# The escalation of the armed conflict (1959-1963)

## Viet Cong

The armed conflict began to intensify from the beginning of 1961 when all the armed forces under the Communists' control were unified under the banner of the **People's Liberation Armed Forces** (**PLAF**). By this time the Americans were already using the term Viet Cong (or VC) to refer to Communist troops. They reasoned that the victory at Dien Bien Phu had conferred almost heroic status on the name Viet Minh. American psychological warfare specialists therefore invented the term Viet Cong, an abbreviation of *Viet-nam Cong-san* (or Vietnamese Communists) and persuaded the media in Saigon to begin substituting it for Viet Minh from 1956.

The election of **John F Kennedy** to the White House in January 1961 coincided with the Communists' decision to widen the war in the south. In the same year Kennedy dispatched 400 special forces troops and 100 special military advisers to Vietnam, in flagrant contravention of the Geneva Agreement. With the cold war getting colder, and Soviet Premier Nikita Khrushchev confirming his support for wars of 'national liberation', Kennedy could not back down and by the end of 1962 there were 11,000 US personnel in South Vietnam. At the same time the NLF had around 23,000 troops at its disposal. Kennedy was still saying that: "In the final analysis, it's their war and they're the ones who have to win or lose it". But just months after the Bay of Pigs debacle in Cuba, Washington set out on the path that was ultimately to lead to America's first large-scale military defeat.

The bungling and incompetence of the forces of the south, the interference that US advisers and troops had to face, the misreading of the situation by US military commanders, and the skill – both military and political – of the Communists, are most vividly recounted in Neil Sheehan's massive book, *A Bright Shining Lie*. The conflict quickly escalated from 1959. The north infiltrated about 44,000 men and women into the south between then and 1964, while the number recruited in the south was between 60,000 and 100,000. In August 1959, the first consignment of arms was carried down the **Ho Chi Minh Trail** into South Vietnam. Meanwhile, Kennedy began supporting, arming and training the Army of the Republic of Vietnam (ARVN). The US however, shied away from any large-scale, direct confrontation between its forces and the Viet Cong.

An important element in Diem's military strategy at this time was the establishment of **strategic hamlets**, better known simply as 'hamleting'. This strategy was modelled on British anti-guerrilla warfare during Malaya's Communist insurgency, and aimed to deny the Communists any bases of support in the countryside while at the same time making it more difficult for Communists to infiltrate the villages and 'propagandize' there. The villages which were ringed by barbed wire were labelled 'concentration camps' by the Communists, and the often brutal, forced relocation that peasants had to endure probably turned even more of them into Communist sympathizers. Of the 7000-8000 villages sealed in this way, only a fifth could ever have been considered watertight.

In January 1963 at **Ap Bac**, not far from the town of My Tho, the Communists scored their first significant victory in the south. Facing 2000 well-armed ARVN troops, a force of just 300-400 PLAF inflicted heavy casualties and downed five helicopters. After this defeat, many American advisers drew the conclusion that if the Communists were to be defeated, it could not be left to the ARVN alone – US troops would have to become directly involved. As Lieutenant Colonel John Vann, a US Army officer, remarked after the debacle to the American media (as cited in Neil Sheehan's *A Bright Shining Lie*): "A miserable damn performance. These people won't listen. They make the same goddam mistakes over and over again in the same way."

In mid-1963 a Buddhist monk from Hué committed suicide by dousing his body with petrol and setting it alight. This was the first of a number of **self-immolations**, suggesting that even in the early days the Diem regime was not only losing the military war but also the 'hearts and minds' war. He responded with characteristic heavy handedness by ransacking suspect pagodas. On 2 December 1963, Diem and his brother Nhu were both assassinated during an army coup.

## The American war in Vietnam

The US decision to enter the war has been the subject of considerable disagreement. Until recently, the received wisdom was that the US administration had already taken the decision, and manufactured events to justify their later actions. However, the recent publication of numerous State Department, Presidential, CIA, Defence Department and National Security Council files – all dating from 1964 – has shed new light on events leading up to American intervention (these files are contained in the United States Government Printing Office's 1108 page-long *Vietnam 1964*).

In Roger Warner's *Back Fire* (1995), which deals largely with the CIA's secret war in Laos, he recounts a story of a war game commissioned by the Pentagon and played by the Rand Corporation in 1962. They were asked to play a week-long game simulating a 10-year conflict in Vietnam. At the end of the week, having committed 500,000 men, the US forces were bogged down, there was student unrest and the American population had lost confidence in their leaders and in the conduct of the war. When the game was played a year later but, on the insistence of the US Airforce, with much heavier aerial bombing, the conclusions were much the same. If only, if only …

By all accounts, **Lyndon Johnson** was a reluctant warrior. In the 1964 presidential campaign he repeatedly said: "We don't want our American boys to do the fighting for Asian boys". This was not just for public consumption. The files show that LBJ always doubted the wisdom of intervention. But he also believed that John F Kennedy had made a solemn pledge to help the South Vietnamese people, a pledge that he was morally obliged to keep. In most respects, LBJ was completely in agreement with Congress, together with sections of the American public, who were disquietened by events in South Vietnam. The Buddhist monk's self-immolation, broadcast on prime-time news, did not help matters.

It has usually been argued that the executive manufactured the **Gulf of Tonkin Incident** to force Congress and the public to approve an escalation of America's role in the conflict. It was reported that two American destroyers, the *USS Maddox* and *USS C Turner Joy*, were attacked without provocation in international waters on the 2 August 1964 by North Vietnamese patrol craft. The US responded by bombing shore installations while presenting the Gulf of Tonkin Resolution to an outraged Congress for approval. Only two Congressmen voted against the resolution and President Johnson's poll rating jumped from 42% to 72%. In reality, the *USS Maddox* had been involved in electronic intelligence gathering while supporting clandestine raids by South Vietnamese mercenaries – well inside North Vietnamese territorial waters. This deception only became apparent in 1971 when the **Pentagon papers**, documenting the circumstances behind the incident, were leaked to the *New York Times* (the Pentagon papers were commissioned by Defense Secretary McNamara in June 1967 and written by 36 Indochina experts).

But these events are not sufficient to argue that the incident was manufactured to allow LBJ to start an undeclared war against North Vietnam. On 4 August, Secretary of State Dean Rusk told the American representative at the United Nations that: "In no sense is this destroyer a pretext to make a big thing out of a little thing". Even as late as the end of 1964, the President was unconvinced by arguments that the US should become more deeply involved. On 31 August, McGeorge Bundy wrote in a memorandum to Johnson: "A still more drastic possibility which no one is discussing is the use of substantial US armed forces in operation against the Viet Cong. I myself believe that before we let this country go we should have a hard look at this grim alternative, and I do not at all think that it is a repetition of Korea."

But events overtook President Johnson, and by 1965 the US was firmly embarked on the road to defeat. In March 1965, he ordered the beginning of the air war against

# Vietnam War

# ⁛ A war glossary

| | |
|---|---|
| **Agent Orange** | Herbicide used to defoliate forests. |
| **APC** | Armoured personnel carrier. |
| **ARVN** | Army of the Republic of Vietnam; the army of the South. |
| **Body Count** | The number of dead on a field of battle. |
| **BUFF** | Nickname for the B-52 bomber; stands for Big Ugly Fat Fellow or, more usually, Big Ugly Fat Fucker. |
| **COIN** | Counter-insurgency. |
| **DMZ** | Demilitarized zone; the border between North and South Vietnam at the 17th parallel. |
| **Dust-off** | Medical evacuation helicopter. |
| **DZ** | Parachute drop zone. |
| **FAC** | Forward air controller, an airborne spotter who directed bombers onto the target. |
| **Fire base** | Defence fortification for artillery, from which to support infantry. |
| **Fragging** | To kill or attempt to kill with a fragmentation grenade; better known as the killing of US officers and NCOs by their own men. In 1970 one study reported 209 fraggings. |
| **Gook** | Slang, derogatory term for all Vietnamese. |
| **Grunt** | Slang for a US infantryman; the word comes from the 'grunt' emitted when shouldering a heavy pack. |
| **Huey** | Most commonly used helicopter, UH1. |
| **LZ** | Helicopter landing zone. |
| **Napalm** | Jellified fuel, the name derives from two of its constituents, naphthenic and palmitic acids. To be burnt by napalm after an attack was terrible and one of the most famous photo images of the war (taken by Nick Ut) showed a naked local girl (Kim |

the north perhaps acting on Air Force General Curtis Le May's observation that "we are swatting flies when we should be going after the manure pile". **Operation Rolling Thunder,** the most intense bombing campaign any country had yet experienced, began in March 1965 and ran through to October 1968. In 3½ years, twice the tonnage of bombs was dropped on Vietnam (and Laos) as during the entire Second World War. During its peak in 1967, 12,000 sorties were being flown each month – a total of 108,000 were flown throughout 1967. North Vietnam claimed that 4000 out of its 5788 villages were hit. Most terrifying were the B-52s that dropped their bombs from such an altitude (17,000 m) that the attack could not even be heard until the bombs hit their targets. Each aircraft carried 20 tonnes of bombs. By the end of the American war in 1973, 14 million tonnes of all types of munitions had been used in Indochina, an explosive force representing 700 times that of the atomic bomb dropped on Hiroshima. As General Curtis Le May explained on 25 November 1965 – "We should bomb them back into the Stone Age". In the same month that Rolling Thunder commenced, marines landed at Danang to defend its airbase, and by June 1965 there were 74,000 US troops in Vietnam. Despite President Johnson's reluctance to commit the US to the conflict, events forced his hand. He realized that the undisciplined South Vietnamese could not prevent a Communist victory. Adhering to the domino theory, and with his own and the US's reputation at stake, he had no choice. As Johnson is said to have remarked to his press secretary Bill Moyers: "I feel like a hitchhiker caught in a hail storm on a Texas highway. I can't win. I can't hide. And I can't make it stop."

| | |
|---|---|
| | Phuc) running along a road at Trang Bang, northwest of Saigon after being burnt; the girl survived the attack by South Vietnamese aircraft and now lives in Canada. |
| **NLF** | National Liberation Front. |
| **NVA** | North Vietnamese Army. |
| **PAVN** | People's Army of Vietnam. |
| **Phoenix** | Counter-insurgency programme established by the US after the Tet Offensive of 1968 (see page 229). |
| **PLAF** | People's Liberation Armed Forces; the army of the Communist north. |
| **POW/MIA** | Prisoner of war/missing in action. |
| **Pungi stakes** | Sharpened bamboo stakes concealed in VC pits: accounted for 2% of US combat wounds. |
| **Purple Heart** | Medal awarded to US troops wounded in action. |
| **R&R** | Rest & Recreation; leave. |
| **ROE** | Rules of engagement. |
| **Rome Plow** | 20-tonne bulldozer designed to clear forest. Equipped with a curved blade and sharp protruding spike it could split the largest trees. |
| **Tunnel Rats** | US army volunteers who fought VC in the Cu Chi tunnels. |
| **VC, Charlie** | Viet Cong (see page 221); US term for Vietnamese Communist; often shortened to Charlie from the phonetic alphabet, Victor Charlie. |
| **Viet Minh** | Communist troops – later changed to Viet Cong (see above and page 221). |
| **WP, Willy Pete** | White phosphorous rocket used to mark a target. |

## Dispersal of the North's industry

In response to the bombing campaign, industry in the north was decentralized and dispersed to rural areas. Each province was envisaged as a self-sufficient production unit. In order to protect the population in the north, they too were relocated to the countryside. By the end of 1967 Hanoi's population was a mere 250,000 essential citizens – about a quarter of the pre-war figure. The same was true of other urban centres. What the primary US objective was in mounting the air war remains unclear. In part, it was designed to destroy the north's industrial base and its ability to wage war; to dampen the people's will to fight; to sow seeds of discontent; to force the leadership in the north to the negotiating table; and perhaps to punish those in the north for supporting their government. By October 1968 the US realized the bombing was having little effect and they called a halt. The legacy of Operation Rolling Thunder, though, would live on. Turley wrote: "… the bombing had destroyed virtually all industrial, transportation and communications facilities built since 1954, blotted out 10 to 15 years' potential economic growth, flattened three major cities and 12 of 29 province capitals, and triggered a decline in per capita agricultural output".

However, it was not just the bombing campaign that was undermining the north's industrial and agricultural base. Socialist policies in the countryside were labelling small land owners as 'landlords' – in effect, traitors to the revolutionary cause – thus alienating many farmers. In the cities, industrial policies were no less short-sighted. Though Ho's policies in the battlefield were driven by hard-headed pragmatism, in the field of economic development they were informed – tragically – by revolutionary fervour.

## 8 The Anzacs in Vietnam

In April 1964, President Johnson called for "more flags" to help defend South Vietnam. Among the countries that responded to his call were Australia and New Zealand. Australia had military advisers in Vietnam from 1962, but in April 1965 sent the First Battalion Royal Australian Regiment. Until 1972 there were about 7000 Australian combat troops in Vietnam, based in the coastal province of Phuoc Tuy, not far from Saigon. There, operating as a self-contained unit in a Viet Cong-controlled zone, and with the support of two batteries of 105 mm artillery (one from New Zealand), the Australians fought one of the most effective campaigns of the entire war.

As US Army Chief of Staff, General Westmoreland said: "Aggressiveness, quick reaction, the good use of firepower, and old-fashioned Australian courage have produced outstanding results."

Of the battles fought by the Australians in Phuoc Tuy, one of the most significant was **Long Tan**, on 18 August 1966. Although caught out by the advance of 4000 Viet Cong, the Australians successfully responded to inflict heavy casualties: 17 dead against about 250 VC. Following this they managed to expand control over large areas of the province, and then win the support of the local people. Unlike the Americans who adopted a policy of 'search and destroy', the Australians were more intent on a 'hearts and minds' strategy (COIN, or counter insurgency). Through various health, education and other civic action programmes, the Australians gained the confidence of many villagers, making it much harder for the VC to infiltrate rural areas of Phuoc Tuy.

This policy of gaining support of the local population was complemented by the highly effective use of small **Special Air Service** (SAS) teams who worked closely with the US Special Forces. Many of these men were transferred after fighting in the jungles of Borneo during the *Konfrontasi* between Malaysia and Indonesia. They came well trained in the art of jungle warfare and ended the war with the highest kill ratio of any similar unit: at least 500 VC dead, against none of their own to hostile fire. The Australians left Phuoc Tuy in late 1971, having lost 423 men. The ARVN were unable to fill the vacuum, and the Viet Cong quickly regained control of the area.

**William Westmoreland**, the general appointed to command the American effort, aimed to use the superior firepower and mobility of the US to 'search and destroy' PAVN forces. North Vietnamese bases in the south were to be identified using modern technology, jungle hideouts revealed by dumping chemical defoliants and then attacked with shells, bombs and by helicopter-borne troops. In 'free-fire zones' the army and air force were permitted to use whatever level of firepower they felt necessary to dislodge the enemy. 'Body counts' became the measure of success and collateral damage – or civilian casualties – was a cost that just had to be borne. As one field commander famously explained: 'We had to destroy the town to save it'. By 1968 the US had more than 500,000 troops in Vietnam, while **South Korean, Australian, New Zealand, Filipino** and **Thai** forces contributed another 90,000. The ARVN officially had 1.5 million men under arms (100,000 or more of these were 'flower' or phantom soldiers, the pay for whom was pocketed by officers in an increasingly corrupt ARVN). Ranged against this vastly superior force were perhaps 400,000 PAVN and National Liberation Front forces.

## ፤ The war in figures

**Vietnamese:**

| | |
|---|---:|
| Killed (soldiers of the North) | 1,100,000 |
| Killed (soldiers of the South) | 250,000 |
| Vietnamese civilians | 2,000,000 |

**Americans:**

| | |
|---|---:|
| Served | 3,300,000 |
| Killed | 57,605 |
| Captured | 766 (651 returned) |
| Wounded | 303,700 |
| MIA | 4993 |
| | (121 returned, 4872 declared dead) |

**Australians:**

| | |
|---|---:|
| Killed | 423 |
| Wounded | 2398 |

**At height of the war:**

| | |
|---|---:|
| Bombs dropped | 1.2 million tonnes per year |
| Cost of bombs | US$14 billion per year |
| Area defoliated | 2.2 million hectares (1962-1971) |
| US air attacks | 400,000 per year |
| Refugees | 585,000 per year |
| Civilian casualties | 130,000 per month |

### 1964-1968: who was winning?

The leadership in the north tried to allay serious anxieties about their ability to defeat the American-backed south by emphasizing human over physical and material resources. **Desertions** from the ARVN were very high – there were 113,000 from the army in 1965 alone (200,000 in 1975) – and the PAVN did record a number of significant victories. The Communists also had to deal with large numbers of desertions – 28,000 men in 1969. By 1967 world opinion, and even American public opinion, appeared to be swinging against the war. Within the US, **anti-war demonstrations** and 'teach-ins' were spreading, officials were losing confidence in the ability of the US to win the war, and the president's approval rating was sinking fast. As the US Secretary of Defense, Robert McNamara is quoted as saying in the *Pentagon Papers*: "... the picture of the world's greatest superpower killing or seriously injuring 1000 non-combatants a week, while trying to pound a tiny, backward nation into submission on an issue whose merits are hotly disputed, is not a pretty one".

But although the Communists may have been winning the psychological and public opinion wars, they were increasingly hard-pressed to maintain this advantage on the ground. Continual American strikes against their bases, and the social and economic dislocations in the countryside, were making it more difficult for the Communists to recruit supporters. At the same time, the fight against a vastly better equipped enemy was also taking its toll in sheer exhaustion. Despite what is now widely regarded as a generally misguided US military strategy in Vietnam, there were notable US successes (for example, the Phoenix Programme, see page 229). American GIs were always sceptical about the 'pacification' programmes that aimed to win the 'hearts and minds' war. GIs were fond of saying, 'If you've got them by the balls, their hearts and minds will follow'. At times, the US military and politicians appeared to view the average Vietnamese as inferior to the average American. This latent racism was reflected in General Westmoreland's remark that Vietnamese "don't think about death the way we do" and in the use by most US servicemen of the derogatory name "gook" to refer to Vietnamese.

At the same time as the Americans were trying to win 'hearts and minds', the Vietnamese were also busy indoctrinating their men and women, and the population in the 'occupied' south. In Bao Ninh's moving *The Sorrow of War* (1994), the main character, Kien, who fights with a scout unit describes the indoctrination that accompanied the soldiers from their barracks to the field: "Politics continuously. Politics in the morning, politics in the afternoon, politics again in the evening. 'We won, the enemy lost. The enemy will surely lose. The north had a good harvest, a bumper harvest. The people will rise up and welcome you. Those who don't just lack awareness. The world is divided into three camps.' More politics."

By 1967, the war had entered a period of military (though not political) stalemate. As Robert McNamara writes in his book *In Retrospect: the Tragedy and Lessons of Vietnam*, it was at this stage that he came to believe that Vietnam was "a problem with no solution". In retrospect, he argues that the US should have withdrawn in late 1963, and certainly by late 1967. Massive quantities of US arms and money were preventing the Communists from making much headway in urban areas, while American and ARVN forces were ineffective in the countryside – although incessant bombing and ground assaults wreaked massive destruction. A black market of epic proportions developed in Saigon, as millions of dollars of assistance went astray. American journalist Stanley Karnow once remarked to a US official that "we could probably buy off the Vietcong at US$500 a head". The official replied that they had already calculated the costs, but came to "US$2500 a head".

## The Tet Offensive, 1968: the beginning of the end

By mid-1967, the Communist leadership in the north felt it was time for a further escalation of the war in the south to regain the initiative. They began to lay the groundwork for what was to become known as the Tet (or New Year) Offensive – perhaps the single most important series of battles during the American War in Vietnam. During the early morning of 1 February 1968, shortly after noisy celebrations had welcomed in the New Year, 84,000 Communist troops – almost all Viet Cong – simultaneously attacked targets in 105 urban centres. Utterly surprising the US and South Vietnamese, the Tet Offensive had begun.

Preparations for the offensive had been laid over many months. Arms, ammunition and guerrillas were smuggled and infiltrated into urban areas and detailed planning was undertaken. Central to the strategy was a 'sideshow' at Khe Sanh. By mounting an attack on the marine outpost at **Khe Sanh**, the Communists successfully convinced the American and Vietnamese commanders that another Dien Bien Phu was underway. General Westmoreland moved 50,000 US troops away from the cities and suburbs to prevent any such humiliating repetition of the French defeat. But Khe Sanh was just a diversion, a feint designed to draw attention away from the cities. In this the Communists were successful; for days after the Tet offensive, Westmoreland and the South Vietnamese President Thieu thought Khe Sanh to be the real objective and the attacks in the cities the decoy.

The most interesting aspect of the Tet Offensive was that although it was a strategic victory for the Communists, it was also a considerable tactical defeat. They may have occupied the US embassy in Saigon for a few hours but, except in Hué, Communist forces were quickly repulsed by US and ARVN troops. The government in the south did not collapse nor did the ARVN. Cripplingly high casualties were inflicted on the Communists – cadres at all echelons were killed – morale was undermined and it became clear that the cities would not rise up spontaneously to support the

Communists. Tet, in effect, put paid to the VC as an effective fighting force. The fight was now increasingly taken up by the North Vietnamese Army (NVA). This was to have profound effects on the government of South Vietnam after reunification in 1975; southern Communists and what remained of the political wing of the VC – the government in waiting – were entirely overlooked as northern Communists were given all the positions of political power, a process that continues. This caused intense bitterness at the time and also explains the continued mistrust of many southerners for Hanoi. Walt Rostow wrote in 1995 that "Tet was an utter military and political defeat for the Communists in Vietnam", but adding "yet a political disaster in the United States". But this was not to matter; Westmoreland's request for more troops was turned down and US public support for the war slumped still further as they heard reported that the US embassy itself had been 'over-run'. Those who for years had been claiming it was only a matter of time before the Communists were defeated seemed to be contradicted by the scale and intensity of the offensive. Even President Johnson was stunned by the VC's successes for he too had believed the US propaganda. As it turned out the VC incursion was by a 20-man unit from Sapper Battalion C-10 who were all killed in the action. Their mission was not to take the embassy but to 'make a psychological gesture'. In that regard at least, the mission must have exceeded the leadership's wildest expectations.

The **Phoenix Programme**, established in the wake of the Tet Offensive, aimed to destroy the Communists' political infrastructure in the Mekong Delta. Named after the Vietnamese mythical bird the Phung Hoang, which could fly anywhere, the programme sent CIA-recruited and trained Counter Terror Teams – in effect assassination units – into the countryside. The teams were ordered to try and capture Communist cadres; invariably they fired first and asked questions later. By 1971, it was estimated that the programme had led to the capture of 28,000 members of the VCI (Viet Cong Infrastructure), the death of 20,000 and the defection of a further 17,000. By the early 1970s the countryside in the Mekong Delta was more peaceful than it had been for years; towns that were previously strongholds of the Viet Cong had reverted to the control of the local authorities. Critics have questioned what proportion of those killed, captured and sometimes tortured were Communist cadres, but even Communist documents admit that it seriously undermined their support network in the area. In these terms, the Phoenix Programme was a great success.

## The costs

The Tet Offensive concentrated American minds. The costs of the war by that time had been vast. The US budget deficit had risen to 3% of Gross National Product by 1968, inflation was accelerating, and thousands of young men had been killed for a cause that, to many, was becoming less clear by the month. Before the end of the year President Johnson had ended the bombing campaign. Negotiations began in Paris in 1969 to try and secure an honourable settlement for the US. Although the last American combat troops were not to leave until March 1973, the Tet Offensive marked the beginning of the end. It was from that date the Johnson administration began to search seriously for a way out of the conflict. The illegal bombing of Cambodia in 1969 and the resumption of the bombing of the north in 1972 (the most intensive of the entire conflict) were only flurries of action on the way to an inevitable US withdrawal.

## The Paris Agreement (1972)

US Secretary of State **Henry Kissinger** records the afternoon of 8 October 1972, a Sunday, as the moment when he realized that the Communists were willing to agree a peace treaty. There was a great deal to discuss, particularly whether the treaty would offer the prospect of peaceful reunification, or the continued existence of two states: a Communist north, and non-Communist south. Both sides tried to force the issue: the US mounted further attacks and at the same time strengthened and expanded the ARVN. They also tried to play the 'Madman Nixon' card, arguing that **President Richard Nixon** was such a vehement anti-Communist that he might well resort to the ultimate deterrent, the nuclear bomb. It is true that the PAVN was losing men through desertion and had failed to recover its losses in the Tet Offensive. Bao Ninh in his book *The Sorrow of War* about Kinh, a scout with the PAVN, wrote: "The life of the B3 Infantrymen after the Paris Agreement was a series of long suffering days, followed by months of retreating and months of counter-attacking, withdrawal, then counter-attack. Victory after victory, withdrawal after withdrawal. The path of war seemed endless, desperate, and leading nowhere."

But the Communist leadership knew well that the Americans were committed to withdrawal – the only question was when, so they felt that time was on their side. By 1972, US troops in the south had declined to 95,000, the bulk of whom were support troops. The north gambled on a massive attack to defeat the ARVN and moved 200,000 men towards the demilitarized zone that marked the border between north and south. On 30 March the PAVN crossed into the south and quickly overran large sections of Quang Tri province. Simultaneous attacks were mounted in the west highlands, at Tay Ninh and in the Mekong Delta. For a while it looked as if the south would fall altogether. The US responded by mounting a succession of intense bombing raids that eventually forced the PAVN to retreat. The spring offensive may have failed, but like Tet, it was strategically important, for it demonstrated that without US support the ARVN was unlikely to be able to withstand a Communist attack.

Both sides, by late 1972, were ready to compromise. Against the wishes of South Vietnam's President Nguyen Van Thieu, the US signed a treaty on 27 January 1973, the ceasefire going into effect on the same day. Before the signing, Nixon ordered the bombing of the north – the so-called Christmas Campaign. It lasted 11 days from 18 December (Christmas Day was a holiday) and was the most intensive of the war. With the ceasefire and President Thieu, however shaky, both in place, the US was finally able to back out of its nightmare and the last combat troops left in March 1973. As J William Fulbright, a highly influential member of the Senate and a strong critic of the US role in Vietnam, observed: "We [the US] have the power to do any damn fool thing we want, and we always seem to do it."

## The Final Phase (1973-1975)

The Paris Accord settled nothing; it simply provided a means by which the Americans could withdraw from Vietnam. It was never going to resolve the deep-seated differences between the two regimes and with only a brief lull, the war continued, this time without US troops. Thieu's government was probably in terminal decline even before the peace treaty was signed. Though ARVN forces were at their largest ever and, on paper, considerably stronger than the PAVN, many men were weakly committed to the cause of the south. Corruption was endemic, business was in recession, and political dissent was on the increase. The North's Central Committee formally decided to abandon the Paris Accord in October 1973; by the beginning of 1975 they were ready for the final offensive. It took only until April for the Communists to achieve total victory. ARVN troops deserted in their thousands, and the only serious resistance was offered at Xuan Loc, less than 100 km from Saigon. President Thieu resigned on 27 April. ARVN generals, along with their men, were attempting to flee as the PAVN advanced on Saigon. The end was quick: at 1045 on 30 April a T-54 tank (number 843) crashed its way through the gates of the Presidential Palace, symbolizing the end of the Second Indochina War. For the US, the aftermath of the war would lead to years of soul searching; for Vietnam, to stagnation and isolation. A senior State Department figure, George Ball, reflected afterwards that the war was "probably the greatest single error made by America in its history".

# Legacy of the Vietnam War

The Vietnam War (or 'American War' to the Vietnamese) is such an enduring feature of the West's experience of the country that many visitors look out for legacies of the conflict. There is no shortage of physically deformed and crippled Vietnamese. Many men were badly injured during the war, but large numbers also received their injuries while serving in Cambodia (1979-1989). It is tempting to associate deformed children with the enduring effects of the pesticide **Agent Orange** (1.7 million tonnes had been used by 1973), although this has yet to be proven scientifically; American studies claim that there is no significant difference in congenital malformation. One thing is certain: Agent Orange is detectable today only in tiny isolated spots, often near former military bases where chemicals were dumped. No scientific survey has found lingering widespread effects.

## Bomb damage

Bomb damage is most obvious from the air: well over five million tonnes of bombs were dropped on the country (north and south) and there are said to be 20 million bomb craters – the sort of statistic people like to recount, but no one can legitimately verify. Many craters have yet to be filled in and paddy fields are still pockmarked. Some farmers have used these holes in the ground to farm fish and to use as small reservoirs to irrigate vegetable plots. War scrap was one of the country's most valuable exports. The cities in the north are surprisingly devoid of obvious signs of the bombing campaigns; Hanoi remains remarkably intact. In Hué the Citadel and the Forbidden Palace were extensively damaged during the Tet offensive in 1968 although much has now been rebuilt.

## Psychological effect of the war

Even harder to measure is the effect of the war on the Vietnamese psyche. Bao Ninh in *The Sorrow of War* writes of a driver with the PAVN who, talking with Kien, the book's main character, observes: "I'm simply a soldier like you who'll now have to live with broken dreams and with pain. But, my friend, our era is finished. After this hard-won victory, fighters like you, Kien, will never be normal again. You won't even speak with your normal voice, in the normal way again." Later in the book, Kien muses about the opportunities lost due to the war. Although the book is a fictional story, the underlying tale is one of truth:

"Still, even in the midst of my reminiscences I can't avoid admitting there seems little left for me to hope for. From my life before soldiering there remains sadly little. ... Those who survived continue to live. But that will has gone, that burning will which was once Vietnam's salvation. Where is the reward of enlightenment due to us for attaining our sacred war goals? Our history-making efforts for the next generations have been to no avail."

The Vietnamese Communist Party leadership still seem to be preoccupied by the conflict and school children are routinely shown war museums and Ho Chi Minh memorials. But despite the continuing propaganda offensive, people harbour surprisingly little animosity towards America or the West. Indeed, of all westerners, it is often Americans who are most warmly welcomed, particularly in the south.

But it must be remembered that about 60% of Vietnam's population has been born since the US left in 1973, so have no memory of the American occupation. Probably the least visible but most lasting of all the effects of the war is in the number of elderly widowed women and the number of middle aged women who never married.

The deeper source of antagonism is the continuing divide between the north and south. It was to be expected that the forces of the north would exact their revenge on their foes in the south and many were relieved that the predicted bloodbath didn't materialize.

## ⁝ A nation at sea: the boat people

One of the most potent images of Vietnam during the 1970s and 1980s was of foundering, overloaded vessels carrying 'boat people' to Hong Kong, Thailand, Malaysia and the Philippines. Beginning in 1976, but becoming a torrent from the late 1970s, these boat people initially fled political persecution. Later, most were economic migrants in search of a better life. Now the tragedy of the boat people is almost at an end and fast becoming
a footnote in history as the last refugees are sent 'home' or onward to what they hope will be a better life.

Escaping the country was not easy. Many prospective boat people were caught by the authorities (often after having already paid the estimated US$500-US$3000 to secure a place on a boat), and sent to prison or to a re-education camp. Of those who embarked, it has been estimated that at least a third died at sea, from drowning or dehydration, and at the hands of pirates. The boats were usually small and poorly maintained, hardly seaworthy for a voyage across the South China Sea. Captains rarely had charts (some did not even have an experienced sailor on board) and most had never ventured further afield than the coastal waters with which they were familiar.

By 1977, the exodus was so great that some freighters began to stop heaving-to to pick up refugees – a habit which, until then, had been sacrosanct among sailors. Malaysia instructed their coastal patrol vessels to force boats back out to sea – and in the first six months of 1979 they did just that to 267 vessels carrying an estimated 40,000 refugees. One boat drifted for days off Malaysia, with the passengers drinking their own urine, until they were picked up – but not before two children had died of dehydration. The Singapore and Malaysian governments adopted a policy of allowing boats to replenish their supplies, but not to land – forcing some vessels to sail all the way to Australia before they were assured of a welcome (over 8000 km). Cannibalism is also reported to have taken place; one boy who had only just survived being killed himself told a journalist: "After the body [of a boy] had been discovered, the boat master pulled it up out of the hold. Then he cut up the body. Everyone was issued a piece of meat about two fingers wide."

As numbers rose, so did the incidence of piracy – an age-old problem in the South China Sea. Pirates, mostly Thai, realizing that the boats often carried families with all their possessions (usefully converted into portable gold) began to target the refugee boats. Some commentators have estimated that by the late 1970s, 30% of boats were being boarded, and the United Nations High Commissioner for Refugees (UNHCR) in 1981 reported that 81% of women had been raped. Sometimes the boats were boarded and plundered, the women raped, all the passengers murdered, and the boats sunk. Despite all these risks, Vietnamese continued to leave in huge numbers: by 1980 there were 350,000 awaiting resettlement in refugee camps in the countries of Southeast Asia and Hong Kong.

Most of these 'illegals' left from the south of Vietnam; identified with the

But few would have thought that this revenge would be so long lasting. The 250,000 southern dead are not mourned or honoured, or even acknowledged. Former soldiers are denied jobs and the government doesn't recognize the need for national reconciliation.

This is the multiple legacy of the War on Vietnam and the Vietnamese. The legacy on the US and Americans is more widely appreciated. The key question that still occupies the minds of many, though, is, was it worth it? Economic historian Walt former regime, they were systematically persecuted – particularly if they also happened to be ethnic Chinese or *Hoa* (the Chinese 'invasion' of 1979 did not help matters). But as conditions worsened in the north, large numbers also began to sail from Ha Long Bay and Haiphong. Soon the process became semi-official, as local and regional authorities realized that fortunes could be made providing boats and escorts. Large freighters began to carry refugees; the *Hai Hong* (1600 tonnes), which finally docked in Malaysia, was carrying 2500 passengers who claimed they had left with the cognizance of the authorities.

The peak period of the crisis spanned the years 1976-1979, with 270,882 leaving the country in 1979 alone. The flow of refugees slowed during 1980 and 1981 to about 50,000 and until 1988 averaged about 10,000 each year. But in the late 1980s the numbers picked up once again, with most sailing for Hong Kong and leaving from the north. It seems that whereas the majority of those sailing in the first phase (1976-1981) were political refugees, the second phase of the exodus was driven by economic pressures. Daily wage rates in Vietnam at that time were only 3000 dong (US$0.25), so it is easy to see the attraction of leaving for healthier economic climes. With more than 40,000 refugees in camps in Hong Kong, the Hong Kong authorities began to forcibly repatriate (euphemistically termed 'orderly return') those screened as economic migrants at the end of 1989 when 51 were flown to Hanoi. Such was the international outcry as critics highlighted fears of persecution that the programme was suspended. In May 1992, an agreement was reached between the British and Vietnamese governments to repatriate the 55,700 boat people living in camps in Hong Kong and the orderly return programme was quietly restarted. As part of their deal with China, the British government agreed to empty the camps before the handover date in 1997 (a target they failed to meet).

Ironically, the evidence is that those repatriated are doing very well – better than those who never left the shores of Vietnam – and there is no convincing evidence of systematic persecution, despite the fears of such groups as Amnesty International. With the European Community and the UN offering assistance to returnees, they have set up businesses, enrolled on training courses and become embroiled in Vietnam's thrust for economic growth.

In early 1996, around 37,000 boat people were still living in camps in Hong Kong (mostly), Indonesia, Thailand, the Philippines and Japan. The difficulty is that those who are left are the least attractive to receiving countries. As Jahanshah Assadi of the UNHCR put it at the end of 1994, "Our Nobel Prize winners left a long time ago for the West", adding "What we have now is the bottom of the barrel." Even Vietnam is not enamoured with the idea of receiving ex-citizens who clearly do not wish to return. For the refugees themselves, they have been wasted years. As the UNHCR's Jean-Noel Wetterwald said in 1996: "Leaving Vietnam was the project of their lives."

Rostow, ex-Singaporean prime minister Lee Kuan Yew and others would probably answer 'yes'. If the US had not intervened, Communism would have spread farther in Southeast Asia; more dominoes, in their view, would have fallen. In 1973, when the US withdrawal was agreed, Lee Kuan Yew observed that the countries of Southeast Asia were much more resilient and resistant to Communism than they had been, say, at the time of the Tet offensive in 1968. The US presence in Vietnam allowed them to reach this state of affairs. Yet Robert McNamara in his book *In Retrospect: the Tragedy and Lessons of Vietnam*, and one of the architects of US policy, wrote:

"Although we sought to do the right thing – and believed we were doing the right thing – in my judgment, hindsight proves us wrong. We both overestimated the effects of South Vietnam's loss on the security of the West and failed to adhere to the fundamental principle that, in the final analysis, if the South Vietnamese were to be saved, they had to win the war themselves."

# After the war

The Socialist Republic of Vietnam (SRV) was born from the ashes of the Vietnam War on 2 July 1976 when former North and South Vietnam were reunified. Hanoi was proclaimed as the capital of the new country. But few Vietnamese would have guessed that their emergent country would be cast by the US in the mould of a pariah state for almost 18 years. First President George Bush I, and then his successor Bill Clinton, eased the US trade embargo bit by bit in a dance of appeasement and procrastination, as they tried to comfort American business clamouring for a slice of the Vietnamese pie, while also trying to stay on the right side of the vociferous lobby in the US demanding more action on the MIA issue. Appropriately, the embargo, which was first imposed on the former North in May 1964, and then nationwide in 1975, was finally lifted a few days before the celebrations of Tet, Vietnamese New Year, on 4 February 1994.

On the morning of 30 April 1975, just before 1100, a T-54 tank crashed through the gates of the Presidential Palace in Saigon, symbolically marking the end of the Vietnam War. Twenty years later, the same tank – number 843 – became a symbol of the past as parades and celebrations, and a good deal of soul searching, marked the anniversary of the end of the War. To many Vietnamese, in retrospect, 1975 was more a beginning than an end: it was the beginning of a collective struggle to come to terms with the war, to build a nation, to reinvigorate the economy and to excise the ghosts of the past. Two decades after the armies of the South laid down their arms and the last US servicemen and officials frantically fled by helicopter to carriers waiting in the South China Sea, the Vietnamese government is still trying, as they put it, to get people to recognize that 'Vietnam is a country, not a war'. A further 20 years from now, it may seem that only in 1995 did the war truly end.

## Re-education camps
The newly formed Vietnam government ordered thousands of people to report for re-education camps in 1975. Those intended were ARVN members, ex-South Vietnam government members and those that had collaborated with the South regime including priests, artists, teachers and doctors. It was seen as a means of revenge and a way of indoctrinating the 'unbelievers' with Communist propaganda. It was reported in the Indochina Newsletter in 1982 that some 80 camps existed with an estimated 100,000 still languishing in them seven years after the war ended. Detainees were initially told that they would be detained for between three days and one month. Those that were sent to the camp were forced to undertake physical labour and survived on very little food and without basic medical facilities all the while undergoing Communist indoctrination.

## The boat people
Many Vietnamese also fled, first illegally and then legally through the Orderly Departure Programme. See box, page 232.

# Invasion of Cambodia

In April 1975, the Khmer Rouge took power in Cambodia. Border clashes with Vietnam erupted just a month after the Phnom Penh regime change but matters came to a head in 1977 when the Khmer Rouge accused Vietnam of seeking to incorporate Kampuchea into an Indochinese Federation. Hanoi's determination to oust Pol Pot only really became apparent on Christmas Day 1978, when 120,000 Vietnamese troops invaded. By 7 January they had installed a puppet government that proclaimed the foundation of the People's Republic of Kampuchea (PRK): Heng Samrin, a former member of the Khmer Rouge, was appointed president. The Vietnamese compared their invasion to the liberation of Uganda from Idi Amin – but for the rest of the world it was an unwelcome Christmas present. The new government was accorded scant recognition abroad, while the toppled government of Democratic Kampuchea retained the country's seat at the United Nations.

But the country's 'liberation' by Vietnam did not end the misery; in 1979 nearly half of Cambodia's population was in transit, either searching for their former homes or fleeing across the Thai border into refugee camps. The country reverted to a state of outright war again, for the Vietnamese were not greatly loved in Cambodia – especially by the Khmer Rouge. American political scientist Wayne Bert wrote: "The Vietnamese had long seen a special role for themselves in uniting and leading a greater Indochina Communist movement and the Cambodian Communists had seen with clarity that such a role for the Vietnamese could only be at the expense of their independence and prestige."

Under the Lon Nol and Khmer Rouge regimes, Vietnamese living in Cambodia were expelled or exterminated. Resentment had built up over the years Hanoi – exacerbated by the apparent ingratitude of the Khmer Rouge for Vietnamese assistance in fighting Lon Nol's US-supported Khmer Republic in the early 1970s. AS relations between the Khmer Rouge and the Vietnamese deteriorated, the Communist superpowers, China and the Soviet Union, polarized too – the former siding with Khmer Rouge and the latter with Hanoi.

The Vietnamese invasion had the full backing of Moscow, while the Chinese and Americans began their support for the anti-Vietnamese rebels.

Following the Vietnamese invasion, three main anti-Hanoi factions were formed. In June 1982 they banded together in an unholy alliance of convenience to fight the PRK and called themselves the Coalition Government of Democratic Kampuchea (CGDK), which was immediately recognised by the UN. The three factions of the CGDK were: The Communist Khmer Rouge whose field forces had recovered to at least 18,000 by the late 1980s. Supplied with weapons by China, they were concentrated in the Cardamom Mountains in the southwest and were also in control of some of the refugee camps along the Thai border. The National United Front for an Independent Neutral Peaceful and Co-operative Cambodia (Funcinpec) – known by most people as the Armée National Sihanoukiste (ANS). It was headed by Prince Sihanouk – although he spent most of his time exiled in Beijing; the group had fewer than 15,000 well-equipped troops – most of whom took orders from Khmer Rouge commanders. The anti-Communist Khmer People's National Liberation Front (KPNLF), headed by Son Sann, a former prime minister under Sihanouk. Its 5000 troops were reportedly ill-disciplined in comparison with the Khmer Rouge and the ANS.

The three CGDK factions were ranged against the 70,000 troops loyal to the government of President Heng Samrin and Prime Minister Hun Sen (previously a Khmer Rouge cadre.) they were backed by Vietnamese forces until September 1989.

In the late 1980s the Association of Southeast Asian Nations (ASEAN) – for which the Cambodian conflict had almost become its raison d'être – began steps to bring the warring factions together over the negotiating table. ASEAN countries were united in wanting the Vietnamese out of Cambodia. After Mikhail Gorbachev had come to power in the Soviet Union, Moscow's support for the Vietnamese presence in

# ⁝ Getting our children out of Vietnam: a personal story

(The following is a personal account by Ken Thompson and his wife Kim Chi. Ken flew in Vietnam and Laos as a Forward Air Controller (FAC). In Laos he was designated Raven 58.)

It was 1 April 1975. I was watching the news on television. The North Vietnamese had captured Qui Nhon. From my 26-month experience in the war zone of Vietnam, I knew immediately that South Vietnam was going to fall and we, myself and my Vietnamese wife, had to decide now to go to Vietnam to get our children out or possibly never see them again.

We had not heard from them in over a year and did not know if they were still with their grandmother in Luong Phuoc (a village 90 miles northeast of Saigon), whether their village had already been overrun, or if they were already dead. It had been a longer time since we had heard from our son and we believed that he had been killed.

Before, the North Vietnamese had moved south and captured Hué and Danang, only to be pushed back. But now they had captured Qui Nhon. They had outflanked the South Vietnamese Army and would now push south to Saigon. The country was lost.

We decided right then to go. In six days, we had our passports, shots and visas and were on our way to Saigon. We had been trying to get our girls out of Vietnam for over three years. But government red tape prevented us. Before going, everyone thought that we would not come back alive. So we taped our last wills to the kitchen cabinets in our home in Milford Center, Ohio.

We took as much money as possible and borrowed whatever we could. On 3 April, we left our 10-month-old daughter, Thao, with my parents and went to Washington DC to get my passport and our visas. Then we flew to the Philippines. But we had more delays. First, the flight to Saigon was delayed because the President's Palace in Saigon was being bombed. Then, during the delay, my passport was stolen. We went to the American Embassy in Manila and applied for an emergency passport. Realizing that Vietnam was about to fall to the North Vietnamese, the emergency passport was issued.

Finally, on 10 April 1975, we arrived in Saigon. We got a room in the Embassy Hotel and started to make enquiries about the status of the war. The police in Saigon told us that Luong Phuoc had been evacuated and the villagers were in Vung Tau, a former resort area turned into a refugee camp. Kim Chi went to Vung Tau to find our girls. They were not there and none of the villagers from Luong Phuoc were there. The police had told us the village had been evacuated so they would not have to go to Luong Phuoc to get the girls.

We had to find someone to go for us. We could not go. I, being an American, and Kim Chi now being too westernized, would both be killed by the Viet Cong or stopped by the South Vietnamese Army. Our cousin, Ty, in Saigon agreed to go and search for the girls in Luong Phuoc.

Our search for the girls was the main topic of interest at the Embassy Hotel, as none of the other Americans or Vietnamese staying there expected us to ever find them. We had received

Cambodia gradually evaporated. Gorbachev began leaning on Vietnam as early as 1987, to withdraw its troops. Despite saying their presence in Cambodia was 'irreversible', Vietnam completed its withdrawal in September 1989, ending nearly 11 years of Hanoi's direct military involvement. The withdrawal led to an immediate upsurge in political and military activity, as forces of the exiled CGDK put increased pressure on the now weakened Phnom Penh regime to begin a round of power-sharing negotiations.

word that Luong Phuoc was already cut off from Saigon. Ty had to go by boat in order to bypass the Viet Cong and arrived at Luong Phuoc to find Kim Chi's mother and the children. They left everything behind. Even then, they were stopped by the South Vietnamese Army and held for over an hour. The village came under attack by the North Vietnamese and Kim Chi's grandmother pushed the girls to the bottom of the boat and lay on top of them, yelling to the boatman to head for the sea. Under fire, they reached the safety of the ocean and headed south.

They reached Vung Tau and the following morning took a bus to Saigon. While waiting for the girls to arrive in Saigon, Kim Chi and I had been processing the papers required for their immigration to the US. However, on 20 April all that changed. The word had come down that all Vietnamese would be given refugee status if they accompanied an American out of Saigon. You could take anyone you wanted, just as long as you claimed they were a relative. (It really did not matter if they were or not. If an American thought that a Vietnamese should be given refugee status that was all that mattered.)

We arrived by bus at Tan San Nhut Airport while the outskirts of the city were being bombed by the North Vietnamese. After several hours, we boarded the Air Force C-141 Transport and flew to the Philippines where we slept on the gymnasium floor of the military base. We were there only four days before President Marcos kicked out all the refugees and we had to go to Guam where we were kept in a tent city constructed by the US Navy. Since we had most of our papers completed for the girls, Mai and Phuong (12 and seven years old), we were evacuated on 27 April 1975. We arrived in San Francisco on 28 April 1975, the day that Saigon fell to the North Vietnamese.

Nearly 15 years later, in 1989, Kim Chi returned to Vietnam to visit her mother. In 1995 she bought property near Luong Phuoc where we hope to eventually build a business.

(Footprint has managed to contact Ken and is pleased to report the following update. Ken's eldest daughter Mai has since married and has three children. She runs a property business with her husband in Columbus, Ohio, near to where Ken and Kim Chi live. The younger daughter, Phuong, has an engineering degree from Ohio State University and is working for a firm in Kentucky. She has one son who is in high school. Ken and Kim Chi had a further daugther in the US who trained with the Marine Corps and now works as a consultant for the military. She lives in Alexandria, Virginia, with her husband, also a Marine. Ken is a mathematical logician consultant for a professor at Indiana University.

Ken and Kim Chi returned to Vietnam in 1998 with their youngest daughter. Ken writes: "In 1998 while I was at our home, this older gentleman came riding in on his bicycle. He knew I was there and wanted to come and see me. We sat down and had some tea as my wife translated for him. He was the former VC general whose troops I had bombed and who had tried to capture my wife during the war. We sat and talked and had a good time together.")

## Border incursions with China

In February 1979 the Chinese marched into the far north of northern Vietnam justifying the invasion because of Vietnam's invasion of Cambodia, its treatment of Chinese in Vietnam, the ownership of the Paracel and Spratley Islands in the East Sea (South China Sea) also claimed by China and a stand against Soviet expansion into Asia (Hanoi was strongly allied with the then USSR). They withdrew a month later following heavy casualties although both sides have claimed to be victorious.

Vietnamese military hardware was far superior to the Chinese and their casualties were estimated to be between 20,000 and 60,000; Vietnamese casualties were around 15,000. In 1987 fighting again erupted on the Sino-Vietnamese border resulting in high casualties.

# Modern Vietnam

## Politics

The **Vietnamese Communist Party (VCP)** was established in Hong Kong in 1930 by Ho Chi Minh and arguably has been more successful than any other such party in Asia in mobilizing and maintaining support. While others have fallen, the VCP has managed to stay firmly in control. To enable them to get their message to a wider audience, the Communist Party of Vietnam have launched their own website, www.cpv.org.vn.

Vietnam is a one party state. In addition to the Communist Party the posts of president and prime minister were created when the constitution was revised in 1992. The president is head of state and the prime minister is head of the cabinet of ministries (including three deputies and 26 ministries), all nominated by the National Assembly. The current president is Nguyen Minh Triet and the current prime minister is Nguyen Tan Dung. Although the National Assembly is the highest instrument of state it can still be directed by the Communist Party. The vast majority of National Assembly members are also party members. Elections for the National Assembly are held every five years. The Communist Party is run by a politburo of 14 members. The head is the general secretary, currently Nong Duch Manh. The politburo, last elected in 2006 at the Tenth Party Congress, meets every five years and sets policy directions of the Party and the government. In addition, there is a Central Committee made up of 160 members, who are also elected at the Party Congress.

In 1986, at the Sixth Party Congress, the VCP launched its economic reform programme known as *doi moi*, which was a momentous step in ideological terms. However, although the programme has done much to free up the economy, the party has ensured that it retains ultimate political power. Marxism-Leninism and Ho Chi Minh thought are still taught to Vietnamese school children and even so-called 'reformers' in the leadership are not permitted to diverge from the party line. In this sense, while economic reforms have made considerable progress (but see below) – particularly in the south – there is a very definite sense that the limits of political reform have been reached, at least for the time being.

From the late 1990s to the first years of the new millennium there have been a number of arrests and trials of dissidents charged with what might appear to be fairly innocuous crimes (see The future of Communism in Vietnam, page 244) and, although the economic reforms enacted since the mid-1980s are still in place, the party resolutely rejects any moves towards greater political pluralism.

Looking at the process of political succession in Vietnam and the impression is not one of a country led by young men and women with innovative ideas. Each year commentators consider the possibility of an infusion of new blood and reformist ideas but the Party Congress normally delivers more of the same: dyed-in-the-wool party followers who are more likely to maintain the status quo than challenge it along with just one or two reformers. The Asian economic crisis did, if anything, further slow down the pace of change. To conservative party members, the Asian crisis – and the political instability that it caused – were taken as warnings of what can happen if you reform too far and too fast. The latest change of faces in the leadership occurred during the Ninth Party Congress in April 2001. The key change was the appointment of

# Provinces

100 km
100 miles

| Provinces | Ha Nam 7 | Ho Chi Minh City 14 |
|-----------|----------|---------------------|
| Hanoi 1 | Hung Yen 8 | Tien Giang 15 |
| Hà Tay 2 | Hai Duong 9 | Vinh Long 16 |
| Hai Phong 3 | Bac Ninh 10 | Dong Thap 17 |
| Thái Bình 4 | Vinh Phuc 11 | Hau Giang 18 |
| Nam Dinh 5 | Thai Nguyen 12 | Binh Duong 19 |
| Ninh Bình 6 | Ba Ria-Vung Tau 13 | |

67-year-old Nong Duc Manh as party general secretary, replacing the unpopular conservative Le Kha Phieu. Nong Duc Manh was re-elected as general secretary at the Tenth Party Congress in April 2006.

Nguyen Tan Dung was also re-elected and is now the country's prime minister. On his appointment as general secretary in 2001, Manh – who commentators are hoping will be a little more modern in his outlook than his predecessor – pledged to continue the modernization drive, reform the party and counter corruption. Nothing new there.

General Secretary Manh repeated his plan to tackle **corruption** at the Tenth Party Congress in the light of two high profile cases indicating that the authorities now mean business. In 2006 one case involving a minister for transport led his superior, the head of Transport Dao Dinh Binh to resign. Bui Tien Dun was sentenced to 13 years imprisonment along with others who were jailed for seven years in 2007. They had been accused of using US$760,000 of embezzled funds to place illegal bets on European football. Bui also was sentenced to a further seven years for bribery as he tried to cover up the bets.

Vietnam's former deputy trade minister was also convicted in 2007 of taking US$6000 bribes from textile companies who wanted to increase their US export quota above government-fixed figures (now no longer in place since Vietnam joined the WTO). He stood trial with 12 others, including his son and other high profile officials. He was sentenced to 14 years in prison; on appeal this was reduced to 12 years. Le Van Thang, former deputy director of the ministry's import-export department, was sentenced to 17 years for taking bribes.

For many westerners there is something strange about a leadership calling for economic reform and liberalization while, at the same time, refusing any degree of political pluralism. How long the VCP can maintain this charade, along with China, while other Communist governments have long since fallen (with the hardly edifying exceptions of Cuba and North Korea), is a key question. Despite the reforms, the leadership is still divided over the road ahead. But the fact that debate is continuing, sometimes openly, suggests that there is disagreement over the necessity for political reform and the degree of economic reform that should be encouraged. One small chink in the armour is the proposed bill to allow referenda. The draft report indicates that referenda would be held on the principles of universality, equality, directness and secret ballot but that the subject of referenda would be decided by the party.

In the country as a whole there is virtually no political debate at all, certainly not in the open. There are two reasons for this apparently curious state of affairs. First there is a genuine fear of discussing something that is absolutely taboo. The police have a wide network of informers who report back on a regular basis and no one wants to accumulate black marks that make it difficult to get the local police reference required for a university place, passport or even a job. Second, and more importantly, is the booming economy. Since the 1990s, **economic growth** in Vietnam has been unprecedented. In 2006 the growth rate was 8.2% and rising. As every politician knows, the one thing that keeps people happy is rising income. Hence with not much to complain about most Vietnamese people are content with their political status quo.

Nevertheless it would be foolish to think that everyone was happy. That political tensions are bubbling somewhere beneath the surface of Vietnamese society became clear in 1997 with **serious disturbances** in the poor coastal northern province of Thai Binh, 80 km southeast of Hanoi. In May, 3000 local farmers began to stage protests in the provincial capital, complaining of corruption and excessive taxation. There were reports of rioting and some deaths – strenuously denied, at least at first, by officials. However, a lengthy report appeared in the army newspaper *Quan Doi Nhan Dan* in September detailing moral decline and corruption in the Party in the province. For people in Thai Binh, and many others living in rural areas, the reforms of the 1980s and 1990s have brought little benefit. People living in Ho Chi Minh City may

## AIDS in Vietnam

Around 100 new infections are reported every day in Vietnam according to www.unaids.org.vn.

Like other countries in Southeast Asia, Vietnam is thought to have the potential for 'rapid increase' in the HIV/AIDS epidemic. The first case of AIDS was reported (ie admitted) in 1990 in Ho Chi Minh City. The number of HIV cases more than doubled between 2000-2006 from 122,000 to 280,000 and UNAIDS estimates that there were an estimated 14,000 AIDS-related deaths in 2005. The low levels of infection reported in the early 1990s reflected the absence of research and a reluctance to admit that the Vietnamese were susceptible to this 'foreign disease', rather than the absence of a problem. UNAIDS reports that HIV incidence among the adult population has risen from 0.28% to 0.53% in 2006 (one in 200 people). In the early years of this century of all reported cases around 60% were injecting drug users. Now the majority of new infections are via sexual transmission. The much-feared crossover into the normal population is proceeding rapidly. UNICEF attributes this to the fact that it is officially classified as a 'social evil' and the stigma surrounding the disease means the infected and those at risk deny their infection or even susceptibility. UNICEF now says that is young men's sexual and drug-taking behaviour that is driving the epidemic in Vietnam. Male and female injecting sex workers have high rates of HIV. In Ho Chi Minh City, a generalized epidemic has been realised with 1.2% of the population being HIV positive. Quang Ninh, Haiphong and Hanoi provinces are also on their way to epidemic status.

Another route of transmission that also alarmed authorities was tattooing in Dong Nai Province.

In 2000 all 60 cases of new infection had a tattoo. Body art is becoming fashionable with women tattooing their lips to look fresh and rosy and men getting dragons blazoned across their chests.

In the early 1990s the government launched a visible but somewhat ineffective campaign against AIDS. AIDS was always referred to in Vietnam by its French name, SIDA, which Vietnamese pronounce with a rather sinister hissing sound. But bowing to pressure from the similarly acronymic Swedish International Development Agency, which has been very generous to Vietnam, the government adopted the more international sounding AIDS, a word few Vietnamese can pronounce. Star of the SIDA campaign, appearing on countless posters, was the durian fruit. With its putrid smell and perilous spikes the analogy between durian and HIV was presumably seen as an obvious and sufficient warning to Vietnamese youth, while still within the strict limits of decency set by the Culture and Information Department. Inevitably, the hapless durian is now dubbed *trai SIDA* (the AIDS fruit).

The ineffectiveness of the campaign can be gauged from the still commonly held belief that AIDS is spread by white foreign males only. Fortunately the protection offered by condoms – *ao mua* (raincoats) – is generally understood although *ao mua* are usually used only in pre- and extra-marital relationships for their contraceptive effect. Further complicating the matter, many good quality second-hand garments are donated from abroad to the poor. Popular belief was these were the clothes of westerners who had died of SIDA, hence the common street sign 'Ao SIDA' advertising a second-hand clothing stall.

tout mobile phones and drive cars and motorbikes, but in much of the rest of the country average monthly incomes are around US$50. The Party's greatest fear is that ordinary people might lose confidence in the leadership and in the system. The fact that many of those who demonstrated in Thai Binh were, apparently, war veterans didn't help either. Nor can the leadership have failed to remember that Thai Binh was at the centre of peasant disturbances against the French. A few months later riots broke out in prosperous and staunchly Roman Catholic Dong Nai, just north of Ho Chi Minh City. The catalyst to these disturbances was the seizure of church land by a corrupt Chairman of the People's Committee. The mob razed the Chairman's house and stoned the fire brigade. Clearly, pent up frustrations were seething beneath the surface for Highway 1 had to be closed for several days while the unrest continued. While the Dong Nai troubles went wholly unreported in Vietnam, a *Voice of Vietnam* broadcast admitted to them and went on to catalogue a list of previous civil disturbances, none of which was known to the outside world; it appears the purpose was to advise Western journalists that this was just another little local difficulty and not the beginning of the end of Communist rule. But reports of disturbances continue to filter out of Vietnam. At the beginning of 2001 thousands of ethnic minorities rioted in the Central Highland provinces of Gia Lai and Dac Lac and the army had to be called in to re-impose order. All foreigners were banned from the Central Highlands.

Again in April 2004 **violence** between ethnic minorities and the government flared in the Central Highlands, resulting in 'unknown numbers of dead and injured and reports of people missing' according to Amnesty International. Once more the cause was religious freedom and land rights although the government persists in its implausible conspiracy theory about 'outside forces' and extremists in the US wanting to destabilize it; a pretext, some fear, for the use of the jackboot and the imprisonment of trouble makers. To its shame (not that they are aware of such a concept) the Cambodian government simply hands refugees – many of who are asylum seekers in the strictest meaning – straight back to the Vietnamese forces. Much of the border area is a no-go zone in both countries, neither country allowing representatives of UNHCR anywhere near.

In 2006 Brad Adams, Asia director at Human Rights Watch (HRW) said: "The Vietnamese government continues to persecute Montagnards once they are out of the sight of international observers. The international community should oppose their forced return to the Central Highlands as long as the authorities continue to persecute them." He continued: "Vietnamese officials continue to force Montagnard Christians to sign pledges renouncing their religion, despite the passage of new regulations banning such practices. Authorities in some areas restrict freedom of movement between villages – in particular for religious purposes not authorized by the government – and ban Christian gatherings in many areas unless they are presided over by officially recognized pastors."

HRW reports than more than 350 ethnic minority people from the Central Highlands have been jailed, charged under Vietnam's Penal Code.

In more recent years, others have been prepared to voice their views. In 2006 Bloc 8406, a pro-democracy group named after its founding date of 8 April 2006, was set up. Catholic priest Father Nguyen Van Ly, editor of the underground online magazine *Free Speech* and a founding member of Bloc 8406, was sentenced to eight years in jail for **anti-government activity**. Four others were also sentenced with him. His trial can be seen on You Tube, including images of him having his mouth covered up and being bundled out of the courtroom. In March 2007 Nguyen Van Dai and Le Thi Cong Nhan, two human rights lawyers, were arrested on the grounds of distributing material "dangerous to the State" and were sentenced to four and five years in prison respectively.

As well as Bloc 8406, other pro-democracy movements include the US-based Viet Tan Party, www.viettan.org, with offices also in Australia, France, Japan, and the People's Democratic Party, among others.

242

**Vietnam** Background Modern Vietnam

# International relations

In terms of international relations, Vietnam's relationship with the countries of the **Association of Southeast Asian Nations (ASEAN)** have warmed markedly since the dark days of the early and mid-1980s and in mid-1995 Vietnam became the association's seventh – and first Communist – member. The delicious irony of Vietnam joining ASEAN was that it was becoming part of an organization established to counteract the threat of Communist Vietnam itself – although everyone was too polite to point this out. No longer is there a deep schism between the capitalist and Communist countries of the region, either in terms of ideology or management. The main potential flashpoint concerns Vietnam's long-term historical enemy – China. The enmity and suspicion which underlies the relationship between the world's last two real Communist powers stretches back over 2000 years. Indeed, one of the great attractions to Vietnam of joining ASEAN was the bulwark that it created against a potentially aggressive and actually economically ascendant China.

China and Vietnam, along with Malaysia, Taiwan, Brunei and the Philippines, all claim part (or all) of the South China Sea's **Spratly Islands**. These tiny islands, many no more than coral atolls, would have caused scarcely an international relations ripple were it not for the fact that they are thought to sit above huge oil reserves. Whoever can prove rights to the islands lays claim to this undersea wealth. Over the last decade China has been using its developing blue water navy to project its power southwards. This has led to skirmishes between Vietnamese and Chinese forces, and to diplomatic confrontation between China and just about all the other claimants. Although the parties are committed to settling the dispute without resort to force, most experts see the Spratly Islands as the key potential flashpoint in Southeast Asia – and one in which Vietnam is seen to be a central player. The **Paracel Islands** further north are similarly disputed by Vietnam and China.

## Rapprochement with the US

One of the keys to a lasting economic recovery was a normalization of relations with the US. From 1975 until early 1994 the US made it largely illegal for any American or American company to have business relations with Vietnam. The US, with the support of Japan and other Western nations, also blackballed attempts by Vietnam to gain membership to the IMF, World Bank and Asian Development Bank, thus cutting off access to the largest source of cheap credit. In the past, it has been the former Soviet Union and the countries of the Eastern Bloc that have filled the gap, providing billions of dollars of aid (US$6 billion 1986-1990), training and technical expertise. But in 1990 the Soviet Union halved its assistance to Vietnam, making it imperative that the government improve relations with the West and particularly the US.

In April 1991 the US opened an official office in Hanoi to assist in the search for Missing in Action (MIAs), the first such move since the end of the war, and in December 1992 allowed US companies to sign contracts to be implemented after the US trade embargo had been lifted. In 1992, both Australia and Japan lifted their embargoes on aid to Vietnam and the US also eased restrictions on humanitarian assistance. Support for a **full normalization of relations** was provided by French President Mitterand during his visit in February 1993, the first by a Western leader since the end of the war. He said that the US veto on IMF and World Bank assistance had "no reason for being there", and applauded Vietnam's economic reforms. He also pointed out to his hosts that respect for human rights was now a universal obligation, which did not go down quite so well. Nonetheless he saw his visit as marking the end of one chapter and the beginning of another.

This inexorable process towards normalization continued with the full lifting of the trade embargo on 4 February 1994 when President Bill Clinton announced the normalization of trade relations. Finally, on 11 July 1995 Bill Clinton declared the full normalization of relations between the two countries and a month later Secretary of State Warren Christopher opened the new American embassy in Hanoi. On 9 May 1997 Douglas 'Pete' Peterson, the first 'post-war' American ambassador to Vietnam and a former POW who spent six years of the war in the infamous 'Hanoi Hilton', took up his post in the capital.

The progress towards normalization was so slow because many Americans still harbour painful memories of the war. With large numbers of ordinary people continuing to believe that servicemen shot down and captured during the war and listed as MIAs were still languishing in jungle jails, presidents Bush and Clinton had to tread exceedingly carefully. In a sense, it was recognized long ago that the embargo no longer served American interests, it was just that the public were not yet ready to forgive and forget.

Even though the embargo is now a thing of the past, there are still the families of over 2000 American servicemen listed as Missing in Action who continue to hope that the remains of their loved ones might, some day, make their way back to the US. (The fact there are still an estimated 300,000 Vietnamese MIAs is, of course, of scant interest to the American media.) It was this, among other legacies of the war, which made progress towards a full normalization of diplomatic and commercial relations such a drawn-out business.

The normalization of trade relations between the two countries was agreed in a meeting between Vietnamese and US officials in July 1999 and marked the culmination of three years' discussions. But conservatives in the politburo prevented the agreement being signed into law worried, apparently, about the social and economic side effects of such reform. This did not happen until 28 November 2001 when Vietnam's National Assembly finally ratified the treaty. It has led to a substantial increase in bilateral trade. In 2003 the USA imported US$4.5 billion worth of Vietnamese goods, roughly four times more than it exported to Vietnam. And not only goods: by 2004 the US Consulate General in Ho Chi Minh City handled more applications for American visas than any other US mission in the world.

### Recent progress

More good news came for Vietnam when it became the 150th member of the World Trade Organization in January 2007. The immediate effect was the lifting of import quotas from foreign countries thereby favouring Vietnamese exporters. Full benefits are expected to be realised when Vietnam gains full market economy status in 12 years' time. In June President Nguyen Minh Triet became the first president of Vietnam to visit the US. He met with George W Bush in Washington to discuss relations between the two countries; trade between the two former enemies now racks up US$9 billion a year. And, in October 2007 to round off a promising year, Vietnam was elected to the UN Security Council from 1 January 2008 as a non-permanent member for two years.

# The future of Communism in Vietnam

In his book *Vietnam at the Crossroads*, BBC World Service commentator Michael Williams asks the question: "Does Communism have a future in Vietnam?" He answers that "the short answer must be no, if one means by Communism the classical Leninist doctrines and central planning". Instead some bastard form of Communism has been in the process of evolving. As Williams adds: "Even party leaders no longer appear able to distinguish between Communism and Capitalism".

There is certainly **political opposition** and disenchantment in Vietnam. At present this is unfocused and dispersed. Poor people in the countryside,

## Cyber dissidents

Human Rights Watch (HRW) has condemned Vietnam for its witch-hunt of those trying to disseminate information about democracy via the internet and urges the release of cyber prisoners. Despite the amnesties mentioned below, Vietnam continues to imprison those writing about democracy on the web. According to Amnesty International, Vietnam has asked internet café owners and Internet Service Providers (ISPs) to monitor activity.

Vietnam has imprisoned several internet dissidents on charges of espionage and disseminating propaganda against the state in the last five years. Physician Dr Nguyen Dan Que was sentenced to 2½ years' imprisonment after he sent an email on state censorship of the media to the US. (He was later released in an amnesty in February 2005.) In 2003 Pham Hong Son was sentenced to 13 years' imprisonment plus three years' house arrest for, among other charges, translating an article from the US Embassy website in Vietnam entitled 'What is Democracy?'. (Pham Hong Son was released by amnesty in August 2006 but is still serving his three years' house arrest.) Journalist Nguyen Vu Binh was sentenced to seven years' imprisonment and three years' house arrest in 2002 after he provided the US Congress with written reports of human rights abuses. He was granted an amnesty in June 2007. "Harsh prison sentences and vaguely worded charges of spying appear designed to intimidate not only government critics, but everyone in Vietnam who uses the internet," reported HRW.

especially in the north, resent the economic gains in the cities, particularly those of the south (see the section on serious disturbances, page 240, in Thai Binh). But this rump of latent discontent has little in common with those intellectual and middle class Vietnamese itching for more political freedom or those motivated entrepreneurs pressing for accelerated economic reforms or those Buddhist monks and Christians demanding freedom of worship and respect for human rights. Unless and until this loose broth of opposition groups coalesces, it is hard to see a coherent opposition movement evolving.

Nonetheless, each year a small number of brave, foolhardy or committed individuals challenge the authorities. Most are then arrested, tried, and imprisoned for various loosely defined crimes including anti-government activity (see page 242). There is always the possibility that cataclysmic, and unpredictable, political change will occur. As one veteran, but anonymous, Central Committee member said in an interview at the end of 1991: "If the CPSU [Communist Party of the Soviet Union], which had been in power for 74 years, can fall to pieces in 72 hours, we have at least to raise that possibility in Vietnam." Major General Tran Cong Man highlighted these fears when he remarked that: "the collapse of the Soviet Union was a devastating blow for [Vietnam] ... [It] was our support, ideologically and psychologically, also militarily and economically. It was our unique model. Now we find it was a false model".

The tensions between reform and control are constantly evident. A **press law** which came into effect in mid-1993 prohibits the publication of works "hostile to the socialist homeland, divulging state or [Communist] party secrets, falsifying history or denying the gains of the revolution". Ly Quy Chung, a newspaper editor in Ho Chi Minh City, described the Vietnamese responding to the economic reforms "like animals being let out of their cage". But, he added, alluding to the tight control the VCP maintains over political debate, "Now we are free to graze around, but only inside the fences". The Party's attempts to control debate and the flow of information have extended to the internet. In 1997 a National Internet Control Board was established and all internet and email usage is strictly monitored. The authorities attempt to firewall topics relating to Vietnam in a hopeless attempt to censor incoming information. By 2004 a number of 'cyber-activists' were held on charges of disseminating information deemed injurious to national interests, see box above. The Vietnamese cyber police clearly credit the information highway with greater influence than any surfer.

# People

Vietnam is home to a total of 54 ethnic groups including the Vietnamese themselves. The ethnic minorities vary in size from the Tay, with a population of about 1.3 million, to the Odu, who number only 300 individuals. Life has been hard for many of the minorities who have had to fight not only the French and Vietnamese but often each other in order to retain their territory and cultural identity. Traditions and customs have been eroded by outside influences such as Roman Catholicism and Communism although some of the less alien ideas have been successfully accommodated. Centuries of Viet population growth and decades of warfare have taken a heavy toll on minorities and their territories; increasingly, population pressure from the minority groups themselves poses a threat to their way of life.

## Highland people: the Montagnards of Vietnam

The highland areas of Vietnam are among the most linguistically and culturally diverse in the world. In total, the highland peoples number around seven million. As elsewhere in Southeast Asia, a broad distinction can be drawn in Vietnam between the peoples of the lowlands and valleys and the peoples of the uplands. The former tend to be settled, cultivate wet rice and are fairly closely integrated into the wider Vietnamese state; in most instances they are Viet. The latter are often migratory, cultivate upland crops often using systems of shifting cultivation and are comparatively isolated from the state. The generic term for these diverse peoples of the highlands is Montagnard (from the French, Mountain People), in Vietnamese *nguoi thuong* (highland citizen) or, rather less politely, *moi* (savage or slave). As far as the highland peoples themselves are concerned, they identify with their village and tribal group and not as part of a wider grouping, as highland inhabitants.

The French attitude towards the Montagnards was often inconsistent. The authorities wanted to control them and sometimes succumbed to the pressure from French commercial interests to conscript them into the labour force, particularly on the plantations. But some officials were positively protective; one, Monsieur Sebatier, refused missionaries access to the territory under his control, destroyed bridges to prevent access and had three tribal wives. He recommended total withdrawal from their lands in order to protect their cultural integrity. In *A Dragon Apparent*, Norman Lewis provides a wonderful account of the Montagnards and their way of life and perceptively examines the relationship between them and the French.

Relations between the minorities and the Viet have not always been as good as they are officially portrayed. Recognizing and exploiting this mutual distrust and animosity, both the French and American armies recruited from among the minorities. In 1961 US Special Forces began organizing Montagnards into defence groups to prevent Communist infiltration into the Central Highlands from the north. Since 1975 relations between minorities and Viet have improved but there is still hostility and in recent years this has flared into vicious fighting. Official publications paint a touching

## ░ Visiting minorities: house rules

Etiquette and customs vary between the minorities. However, the following are general rules of good behaviour that should be adhered to whenever possible.

1. Dress modestly without displaying too much flesh.
2. Ask permission before photographing anyone (old people, pregnant women and mothers with babies often object).
3. Only enter a house if invited.
4. Do not touch or photograph village shrines.
5. Do not smoke opium.
6. Avoid sitting or stepping on door sills.
7. Avoid excessive displays of wealth and be sensitive when giving gifts (for children, pens are better than sweets).
8. Avoid introducing Western medicines.
9. Do not sit with the soles of your feet pointing at other people (eg sit cross-legged).
10. If offered a cup of rice wine it is polite to down the first cup in one (what the Vietnamese call *tram phan tram* – 100%).

picture portraying the relationship between Viet and minority peoples. Thus we read "successive generations of Vietnamese, belonging to 54 ethnic groups, members of the great national community of Vietnam, have always stood side by side with one another, sharing weal and woe, shedding sweat and blood to defend and build up their homeland". This illusion has been shattered by recent events so the government is keen to stress its role in improving health, eradicating poverty and introducing a settled rather than a nomadic existence among the minorities. But one serious consequence of a sedentary way of life has been the narrowing, blunting and elimination of cultural differences. In recent years the government has come to regard the minorities as useful 'tourist fodder' – with a splash of colour, primitive villages and ethnic dances, they provide a taste of the 'mystical East', which much of the country otherwise lacks.

Potentially tourism is a more serious and insidious threat to the minorities' way of life than any they have yet had to face. A great deal has been written about cultural erosion by tourism and any visitor to a minority village should be aware of the extent to which he or she contributes to this process. Traditional means of livelihood are quickly abandoned when a higher living standard for less effort can be obtained from the tourist dollar. Long-standing societal and kinship ties are weakened by the intrusion of outsiders. Young people may question their society's values and traditions that may seem archaic, anachronistic and risible by comparison with those of the modern tourist. And dress and music lose all cultural significance and symbolism if they are allowed to become mere tourist attractions.

Nevertheless, this is an unavoidable consequence of Vietnam's decision to admit tourists to the highland areas. Perhaps fortunately, however, for the time being at least, many of the minorities are pretty inaccessible to the average traveller. Visitors can minimize their impact by acting in a sensitive way; it is, for example, perfectly obvious when someone does not want their photograph taken. See also box above for general advice on visiting minority villages. In addition, you can report to provincial tourism authorities on arrival to check the latest on areas where travel is permitted. But the minority areas of Vietnam are fascinating places and the immense variety of colours and styles of dress add greatly to the visitor's enjoyment.

**Vietnam** Background People

**Bahnar (Ba-na)**

This is a Mon-Khmer-speaking minority group concentrated in the central highland provinces of Gia Lai-Kon Tum, numbering about 174,000. Locally powerful from the 15th to 18th centuries, they were virtually annihilated by neighbouring groups during the 19th century. Roman Catholic missionaries influenced the Bahnar greatly and they came to identify closely with the French. Some conversions to Roman Catholicism were made but Christianity, where it remains, is usually just an adjunct to Bahnar animism. Bahnar houses are built on stilts and in each village there is a communal house, or *rông*, which is the focus of social life. When a baby reaches his or her first full month he or she has their ears pierced in a village ceremony equivalent to the Vietnamese *day thang* (see box, opposite); only then is a child considered a full member of the community. Their society gives men and women relatively equal status. Male and female heirs inherit wealth and the families of either husband or wife can arrange marriage. Bahnar practise both settled and shifting cultivation.

## Coho (Co-ho, also Kohor, K'Ho, Xre, Chil and Nop)

These are primarily found on the Lam Dong Plateau in Lam Dong Province (Dalat) with a population of about 100,000. Extended family groups live in longhouses or *buon*, sometimes up to 30 m long. Unusually, society is matrilineal and newly married men live with their wives' families. The children take their mother's name; if the wife dies young her smaller sister will take her place. Women wear tight-fitting blouses and skirts. Traditional shifting cultivation is giving way to settled agriculture.

## Yao (Dao, also Mán)

The Yao live in northern Vietnam in the provinces bordering China, particularly in Lao Cai and Ha Giang. They number 6210,000 and include several sub-groupings, notably the Dao Quan Chet (Tight Trouser Dao), the Dao Tien (Money Dao) and the Dao Ao Dai (Long Dress Dao). As these names suggest, Yao people wear highly distinctive clothing although sometimes only on their wedding day. The **Dao Tien** or Money Dao of Hoa Binh and Son La provinces are unique among the Yao in that the women wear black skirts and leggings rather than trousers. A black jacket with red embroidered collar and cuffs, decorated at the back with coins (hence the name) together with a black red-tasselled turban and silver jewellery are also worn. By contrast men look rather plain in black jacket and trousers. Headgear tends to be elaborate and includes a range of shapes (from square to conical), fabrics (waxed hair to dried pumpkin fibres) and colours.

The women of many branches of Yao shave off their eyebrows and shave back their hair to the top of their head before putting on the turban; a hairless face and high forehead are traditionally regarded as attributes of feminine beauty.

Yao wedding customs are as complex as Yao clothing and vary with each group. Apart from parental consent, intending marriage partners must have compatible birthdays and the groom has to provide the bride's family with gifts worthy of their daughter. If he is unable to do this, a temporary marriage can take place but the outstanding presents must be produced and a permanent wedding celebrated before *their* daughter can marry.

The Yao live chiefly by farming: those in higher altitudes are swidden cultivators growing maize, cassava and rye. In the middle zone, shifting methods are again used to produce rice and maize, and on the valley floors sedentary farmers grow irrigated rice and rear livestock.

Spiritually the Yao have also opted for diversity; they worship *Ban Vuong*, their mythical progenitor, as well as their more immediate and real ancestors. The Yao also find room for elements of Taoism, and in some cases Buddhism and Confucianism, in their elaborate metaphysical lives. Never enter a Yao house unless invited; if tree branches are suspended above the gate to a village, guests are not welcome – reasons might include a post-natal but pre-naming period, sickness, death or special

## ⁞ Rite of passage: from baby to infant

In a poor country like Vietnam, staying alive for long enough to see one's own first birthday has not always been easy. Fortunately, infant mortality levels have fallen drastically (from 156 in 1000 in 1960 to 33 in 1000 in 1996 and 19 in 1000 in 2005) but remain high by Western standards. Perhaps not surprisingly therefore, Vietnamese families celebrate two important milestones in the early lives of their children.

*Day thang*, or full month, is celebrated exactly one month after birth. Traditionally, the mother remained in bed with her heavily swaddled baby for the first month keeping him or her away from sun, rain and demon spirits. At one month the child is beyond the hazardous neo-natal stage and the mother would leave her bed and go out of the house to introduce her baby to the village. Today, the parents hold a small party for their friends and neighbours.

*Thoi noi* is celebrated at the end of the first year; it marks the time the baby stops sleeping in the cot and, having reached a full year, it is also a thanksgiving that the child has reached the end of the most dangerous year of life. At the party the baby is presented with a tray on which are various items such as a pen, a mirror, scissors, some soil and food; whichever the baby takes first indicates its character and likely job: scissors for a tailor, pen for a teacher, soil for a farmer and so on. Babies are normally weaned at about this time: some Vietnamese mothers use remarkably unsubtle but effective means for turning the baby from the breast, smearing the nipple with charcoal dust or Tiger Balm!

ceremony. Since the Yao worship the kitchen god, guests should not sit or stand immediately in front of the stove.

## Ede (also Rhadê)

Primarily concentrated in the Central Highlands province of Dac Lac and numbering nearly 270,000, they came into early contact with the French and are regarded as one of the more 'progressive' groups, adapting to modern life with relative ease. Traditionally the Ede live in longhouses on stilts; accommodated under one roof is the matrilineal extended family or commune. The commune falls under the authority of an elderly, respected woman known as the *khoa sang* who is responsible for communal property, especially the gongs and jars, which feature in important festivals. Ede society is matrilocal in that after the girl's family selects a husband, he then comes to live with her. As part of the wedding festivities the two families solemnly agree that if one of the partners should break the wedding vow they will forfeit a minimum of one buffalo, a maximum of a set of gongs. Wealth and property are inherited solely by daughters. Shifting cultivation is the traditional subsistence system, although this has given way in most areas to settled wet rice agriculture. Spiritually the Ede are polytheist: they number animism (recognizing the spirits of rice, soil, fire and water especially) and Christianity among their beliefs.

## Giarai (Gia-rai, also Chó Ray)

Primarily found in Gia Lai and Kon Tum provinces (especially near Play Ku) and numbering 317,557, these are the largest group in the Central Highlands. They are settled cultivators and live in houses on stilts in villages called *ploi* or *bon*. The Giarai are animist and recognize the spiritual dimension of nature; ever since the seventh century they have had a flesh and blood King of Fire and King of Water whose spirit is invoked in rain ceremonies.

**Vietnam** Background People

**Hmong (Hmông, also Mèo and Mieu)**

These are widely spread across the highland areas of the country, but particularly near the Chinese border down to the 18th parallel. The Hmong number about 787,600 (over 1% of Vietnam's population) and live at higher altitudes, above 1500 m, than all other hill people. Comparatively recent migrants to Vietnam, the Hmong began to settle in the country during the 19th century after moving south from China. The Hmong language in its various dialects remained oral until the 1930s when a French priest attempted to Romanize it with a view to translating the Bible. A more successful attempt to create a written Hmong language was made in 1961 but has since fallen into disuse. Nevertheless – or perhaps because of this failure – the Hmong still preserve an extraordinarily rich oral tradition of legends, stories and histories. Hmong people are renowned for their beautiful folk songs. Each branch of the Hmong people preserves its own corpus of songs about love, work and festivals that are sung unaccompanied or with the accompaniment of the *khène*, a small bamboo pipe organ, a two-stringed violin, flutes, drums, gongs and jew's harps. Numerous Hmong dances also exist to celebrate various dates in the social calendar and to propitiate animist spirits.

They have played an important role in resisting both the French and the Vietnamese. Living at such high altitudes they tend to be one of the most isolated of all the hill people. Their way of life does not normally bring them into contact with the outside world that suits them well – the Hmong traders at Sapa are an exception (see page 111). High in the hills, flooding is not a problem so their houses are built on the ground, not raised up on stilts. Hmong villages are now increasingly found along the river valleys and roads as the government resettlement schemes aim to introduce them to a more sedentary form of agriculture. The Hmong practice slash-and-burn cultivation growing maize and dry rice. Traditionally opium has been a valuable cash crop. Although fields are often cleared on very steep and rocky slopes, the land is not terraced. There are a number of different groups among the Hmong including the White, Black, Red and Flower Hmong that are distinguishable by the colour of the women's clothes. Black Hmong wear almost entirely black clothing with remarkable pointed black turbans. White Hmong women wear white skirts and the Red Hmong tie their heads in a red scarf while the Flower Hmong wrap their hair (with hair extensions) around their head like a broad-brimmed hat. However, such numerous regional variations occur that even experts on ethnic minority cultures sometimes have problems trying to identify which branch of Hmong they have encountered. Serious social problems have occurred among the Hmong owing to opium addiction; with over 30% of the male population of some Hmong villages addicted, the drug has rendered many incapable of work, causing misery and malnutrition for their families and with the drug finding its way on to the streets of Vietnam's cities, the authorities have resolved to clamp down hard on opium production. This has had tragic consequences when the Hmong have tried to protect their livelihoods.

## Muong (Mường)

Numbering more than one million the Muong are the fourth largest ethnic minority in Vietnam. They live in the area between northern Thanh Hoa Province and Yen Bai but mainly in Hoa Binh Province. It is thought that the Muong are descended from the same stock as the Viets: their languages are similar and there are also close similarities in culture and religion. But whereas the Vietnamese came under strong Chinese cultural influence from the early centuries of the Christian era, the Muong did not. The Muong belong to the Viet-Muong language group; their language is closest to Vietnamese of all the ethnic minority languages. Muong practise wet and dry rice cultivation where possible, supplementing their income with cash crops such as manioc, tobacco and cotton. Weaving is still practised; items produced include pillowcases and blankets. Culturally the Muong are akin to the Thai Vietnamese ethnic minority and they live in stilt houses in small villages called *quel*; groupings of from

three to 30 quel form a unit called a *muong*. Muong society is feudal in nature with
each *muong* coming under the protection of a noble family (*lang*). The common
people are not deemed worthy of family names so are all called Bui. Each year the
members of a *muong* are required to labour for one day in fields belonging to the lang.

Marriages are arranged: girls, in particular, have no choice of spouse. Muong
cultural life is rich, literature has been translated into Vietnamese and their legends,
poems and songs are considered particularly fine.

## Mnong (Mnông)

The Mnong number some 92,000 people and predominantly live in Dak Lak, Binh
Phuoc and Binh Duong province with a smaller group living in Lam Dong province.
The Mnong are hunter-gatherers and grow rice. The Mnong village is characterised
by a longhouse on stilts although some groups live in normal sized stilt houses.
Families are matrilineal and tradition sees the women bare topped and with
distended earlobes. It is the Mnong who are the elephant catchers at Ban Don.

## Nung (Nùng)

Concentrated in Cao Bang and Lang Son provinces, adjacent to the Chinese border, the
Nung number approximately 860,000 people. They are strongly influenced by the
Chinese and most are Buddhist, but like both Vietnamese and Chinese the Nung practise
ancestor worship too. In Nung houses a Buddhist altar is placed above the ancestor altar
and, in deference to Buddhist teaching, they refrain from eating most types of meat. The
Nung are settled agriculturalists and, where conditions permit, produce wet rice; all
houses have their own garden in which fruit and vegetables are grown.

## Tay (Tày, also Tho)

The Tay are the most populous ethnic minority in Vietnam; they number about
1.5 million and are found in the provinces of northwest Vietnam stretching from
Quang Ninh east to Lao Cai. Tay society was traditionally feudal with powerful lords
able to extract from the free and semi-free serfs' obligations such as droit de seigneur.
Today Tay society is male dominated with important decisions being taken by men
and eldest sons inheriting the bulk of the family's wealth.

Economically the Tay survive by farming and are highly regarded as wet rice
cultivators, they are also noted for the production of fruits (pears, peaches, apricots and
tangerines), herbs and spices. Diet is supplemented by animal and fish rearing and
cash is raised by the production of handicrafts. The Tay live in houses on stilts, located
in the river valleys. Tay architecture is quite similar in design to that of the Black Thai,
but important differences may be identified, most notably the larger size of the Tay
house, the deeper overhang of the thatched or (among more affluent Tay communities)
tiled roof and the extent of the railed balcony which often encircles the entire house.

Like the Thai, Tay ancestors migrated south from southern China along with
those of the Thai and they follow the three main religions of Buddhism, Confucianism
and Taoism in addition to ancestor worship and animist beliefs. While Tay people
have lived in close proximity to the Viet majority over a period of many centuries, their
own language continues to be their primary means of communication. They hail from
the Austro-Asian language family and specifically the Thai-Kadai language group. Tay
literature has a long and distinguished history and much has been translated into
Vietnamese. During the French colonial period missionaries Romanized Tay script.

## Thai (Thái, also Tày DămTày)

Numbering more than one million this is the second largest ethnic minority in
Vietnam and ethnically distinct from the Thais of modern-day Thailand. There are two
main sub-groups, the Black (Thai Den), who are settled mainly in Son La, Lai Chan,
Lao Cai and Yen Bai provinces and the White Thái, who are found predominantly in

Hoa Binh, Son La, Thanh Hoa and Vinh Phu provinces, as well as many others, including the Red Thai (Thai Do). The use of these colour-based classifications has usually been linked to the colour of their clothes, particularly the colour of women's shirts. However, there has been some confusion over the origins of the terms and there is every reason to believe that it has nothing to do with the colour of their attire and is possibly linked to the distribution of the sub-groups near the Red and Black rivers. The confusion of names becomes even more perplexing when the Vietnamese names for the sub-groups of Thai people are translated into Thai. Some scholars have taken Thai Den (Black Thai) to be Thai Daeng – *daeng* being the Thai word for red, thereby muddling up the two groups. With the notable exception of the White Thai communities of Hoa Binh, traditional costume for the women of both the Black and White Thai generally features a coloured blouse with a row of silver buttons down the front, a long black skirt, a coloured waist sash and a black headscarf embroidered with intricate, predominantly red and yellow designs.

The traditional costume of the White Thai women of Hoa Binh comprises a long black skirt with fitted waistband embroidered with either a dragon or chicken motif together with a plain pastel coloured blouse and gold and maroon sash.

Being so numerous the Thai cover a large part of northwest Vietnam, in particular the valleys of the Red River and the Da and the Ma rivers, spilling over into Laos and Thailand. They arrived in Vietnam between the fourth and 11th centuries from southern China and linguistically they are part of the wider Thai-Kadai linguistic grouping. Residents of Lac village in Mai Chau claim to have communicated with visitors from Thailand by means of this shared heritage.

The Thai tend to occupy lowland areas and they compete directly with the Kinh (ethnic Vietnamese) for good quality farmland that can be irrigated. They are masters of wet rice cultivation producing high yields and often two harvests each year. Their irrigation works are ingenious and incorporate numerous labour-saving devices including river-powered water wheels that can raise water several metres. Thai villages (*ban*) consist of 40-50 houses on stilts; they are architecturally attractive, shaded by fruit trees and surrounded by verdant paddy fields. Commonly located by rivers, one of the highlights of a Thai village is its suspension footbridge. The Thai are excellent custodians of the land and their landscapes and villages are invariably very scenic.

Owing to their geographical proximity and agricultural similarities with the Kinh it is not surprising to see cultural assimilation – sometimes via marriage – and most Thai speak Vietnamese. It's also interesting to note the extent to which the Thai retain a distinctive cultural identity, most visibly in their dress.

When a Thai woman marries, her parents-in-law give her a hair extension (*can song*) and a silver hair pin (*khat pom*) that she is expected to wear (even in bed) for the duration of the marriage. There are two wedding ceremonies, the first at the bride's house where the couple live for one to three years, followed by a second when they move to the husband's house.

## Sedang (Xó-dang)

Concentrated in Gia Lai and Kon Tum provinces and numbering about 127,000, the Sedang live in extended family longhouses and society is patriarchal. The Sedang practise both shifting agriculture and the cultivation of wet rice. A highly war-like people, they almost wiped out the Bahnar in the 19th century. Sedang thought nothing of kidnapping neighbouring tribesmen to sacrifice to the spirits; indeed the practice of kidnapping was subsequently put to commercial use and formed the basis of a slave trade with Siam (Thailand). Sedang villages, or *ploi*, are usually well defended (presumably for fear of reprisal) and are surrounded by thorn hedges supplemented with spears and stakes. Complex rules designed to prevent in-breeding limit the number of available marriage partners that sometimes results in late marriages.

## Other groups

These are Hre (Hrê), in Quang Ngai and Binh Dinh provinces, numbering 113,000 and Stieng/Xtieng (Xtiêng) in Song Be province, with 66,788.

## Viet (Kinh)

The 1999 census revealed that 86.2% of the population were ethnic Vietnamese. But with a well-run family planning campaign beginning to take effect in urban areas and higher fertility rates among the ethnic minorities it is likely that this figure will fall. The history of the Kinh is marked by a steady southwards progression from the Red River basin to the southern plains and Mekong Delta. Today the Kinh are concentrated into the two great river deltas, the coastal plains and the main cities. Only in the central and northern highland regions are they outnumbered by ethnic minorities. Kinh social cohesion and mastery of intensive wet rice cultivation has led to their numerical, and subsequently political and economic, dominance of the country. Ethnic Vietnamese are also in Cambodia where some have been settled for generations; recent Khmer Rouge attacks on Vietnamese villages have, however, caused many to flee to Vietnam.

## Cham

With the over-running of Champa in 1471 (see page 212) Cham cultural and ethnic identity was diluted by the more numerous ethnic Vietnamese. The Cham were dispossessed of the more productive lands and found themselves in increasingly marginal territory. Economically eclipsed and strangers in their own land, Cham artistic creativity atrophied, their sculptural and architectural skills, once the glory of Vietnam, faded and decayed like so many Cham temples and towers. It is estimated that there are, today, 132,873 Cham people in Vietnam, chiefly in central and southern Vietnam in the coastal provinces extending south from Quy Nhon. Small communities are to be found in Ho Chi Minh City and in the Mekong Delta around Chau Doc. They are artistically the poor relations of their forebears but skills in weaving and music live on.

The Cham of the south are typically engaged in fishing, weaving and other small scale commercial activities; urban Cham are poor and live in slum neighbourhoods. Further north the Cham are wet or dry rice farmers according to local topography; they are noted for their skill in wet rice farming and small-scale hydraulic engineering.

In southern Vietnam the majority of Cham are Muslim, a comparatively newly acquired religion although familiar from earlier centuries when many became acquainted with Islamic tenets through traders from India and the Indonesian isles. In central Vietnam most Cham are Brahminist and the cult of the linga remains an important feature of spiritual life.

## Hoa: ethnic Chinese

There are nearly one million ethnic Chinese or Hoa in Vietnam, 80% living in the south of the country. Before reunification in 1975 there were even more; hundreds of thousands left due to persecution by the authorities and a lack of economic opportunities since the process of socialist transformation was initiated. There are now large Vietnamese communities abroad, particularly in Australia, on the west coast of the US and in France. It has been estimated that the total Viet-kieu population numbers some two million. With the reforms of the 1980s, the authorities' view of the Chinese has changed; they now appreciate the crucial role they played, and could continue to play, in the economy. Before 1975, the Hoa controlled 80% of industry in the south and 50% of banking and finance. Today, ethnic Chinese in Vietnam can own and operate businesses and are once again allowed to join the Communist party, the army and to enter university. The dark days of the mid to late 1970s seem to be over.

**Viet Kieu: overseas Vietnamese**

Since 1988, overseas Vietnamese or Viet Kieu (most of whom are of Chinese extraction) have been allowed back to visit their relatives, in some cases helping to spread stories of untold wealth in the US, Australia and elsewhere. The largest community of overseas Vietnamese, about 1.1 million, live in the US. The next largest populations are resident in France (250,000) and Australia (160,000), with much smaller numbers in a host of other countries. In 1990, 40,000 returned to visit; in 2003, 340,000 returned 'home'. Amusingly, many from America come back for dental treatment as it is much cheaper in Vietnam.

Many Viet Kieu are former boat people (see box, page 232), while others left the country as part of the UN-administered Orderly Departure Programme that began in earnest in the late 1980s. A smaller number (and one wonders whether they are strictly classed as Viet Kieu) left Vietnam for one of the former COMECON countries at some point between the 1950s and 1980s either to study or to work. The largest number appear to have gone to East Germany from where many have returned to take up important political positions. Those fortunate enough to find themselves in dour East Germany at the time of reunification suddenly found themselves privileged to be citizens of one of the world's richest countries. In the upheavals occasioned by ridding Eastern Europe of Communism they showed sound business acumen and carved out a pivotal position in the German tobacco smuggling industry.

In America the Viet Kieu have often shown enormous perseverance and grit. Take the small Texan shrimping town of Palacios. Today there are around 300 Americans of Vietnamese extraction, mostly Roman Catholics, living in and around Palacios. When the first settlers arrived in 1976 escaping from the defeated South, most had nothing. Many faced bigotry from racist elements in the local community who feared competition from foreigners. But they worked and saved and by the early 1980s some families had managed to buy shrimping boats for themselves. Another 10 years on and the most successful boats were owned and operated by Vietnamese. By that time, many of their children had been born and raised in the local community, they had gone through local schools (often winning the top scholastic prizes) and few questioned their credentials to be counted as Americans. There are Little Saigons in many countries but the most famous is in Los Angeles. From this social and economic hub the Vietnamese diaspora has set about cornering several industries. The nail manicure business is now virtually synonymous with the Vietnamese. In California and increasingly in other parts of the world, nail bars are Vietnamese owned; 'Hollywood Nails' appears to be the name of choice. In California, it seems, almost every block has a Vietnamese pharmacy and a *pho* restaurant selling noodles. And now shoppers in malls from Virginia to San José can sit down to a good bowl of *pho bo* (beef noodle soup), surely one of the more surprising outcomes of the Vietnam War.

As the Viet Kieu have discovered some measure of prosperity in the West, the Vietnamese government is anxious to welcome them back – or rather, welcome their money. So far, however, flows of investment for productive purposes have been rather disappointing and largely concentrated in the service sector, particularly in hotels and restaurants. Far more is thought to have been invested in land and property as overseas Vietnamese have, since 2000, been able to purchase property in their own name. (This, incidentally, has contributed to property speculation and a dizzy spiral of price increases that have made land prices in Ho Chi Minh City and Hanoi some of the most expensive in Asia.) Part of the problem is that many Viet Kieu were escaping from persecution in Vietnam and of all people continue to harbour doubts about a government that is, in essence, the same as the one they fled. On the government's side, they worry that the Viet Kieu may be a destabilizing influence, perhaps even a Fifth Column intent on undermining the supremacy of the Communist Party. Again the leadership have cause for concern as the most vocal opponents of the US policy of rapprochement have been Viet Kieu. Nor are the Overseas

Vietnamese quite as rich as their ostentatious displays of wealth on the streets of Ho Chi Minh City and Hanoi would indicate. They do not have the economic muscle of the Overseas Chinese, for example, and in most cases have only been out of the country for less than 20 years, many having lost everything in their attempt to escape. Many young Viet Kieu have, however, equipped themselves with qualifications and skills overseas – often much needed in Vietnam – and can find lucrative employment back in Vietnam.

# Religion

Vietnam supports followers of all the major world religions, as well as those religions that are peculiarly Vietnamese: Theravada and Mahayana Buddhism, Protestant and Roman Catholic Christianity, Taoism, Confucianism, Islam, Cao Daism, Hoa Hao and Hinduism. In addition, spirit and ancestor worship (*To Tien*) are also practised. Confucianism, although not a formal religion, is probably the most pervasive doctrine of all. Nominal Christians and Buddhists will still pay attention to the moral and philosophic principles of Confucianism and it continues to play a central role in Vietnamese life.

Following the Communist victory in 1975, the authorities moved quickly to curtail the influence of the various religions. Schools, hospitals and other institutions run by religious organizations were taken over by the state and many clergy either imprisoned and/or sent to re-education camps. The religious hierarchies were institutionalized, and proselytizing severely curtailed.

During the late 1980s and into the early 1990s some analysts identified an easing of the government's previously highly restrictive policies towards religious organizations. At the beginning of 1993, former General Secretary of the Vietnamese Communist Party, Do Muoi, even went so far as to make official visits to a Buddhist monastery and a Roman Catholic church. However it is clear the Communist hierarchy is highly suspicious of priests and monks. They are well aware of the prominent role they played in South Vietnamese political dissension and are quick to crack down on any religious leader or organization that becomes involved in politics. In recent years this religious intolerance has been particularly manifest in the repression of the Montagnards in the Central Highlands, the closure of churches and imprisonment of church leaders, particularly protestant sects.

There is no question that more people today are attending Buddhist pagodas, Christian churches and Cao Dai temples. However, whether this rise in attendance at temples and churches actually means some sort of religious rebirth is questionable. Dang Nghiem Van, head of Hanoi's Institute of Religious Studies, poured scorn on the notion that young people are finding religion. They "are not religious", he said, "just superstitious. This isn't religion. It's decadence".

## Mahayana Buddhism

Although there are both Theravada (also known as Hinayana) and Mahayana Buddhists in Vietnam, the latter are by far the more numerous. Buddhism was introduced into Vietnam in the second century AD: Indian pilgrims came by boat and brought the teachings of Theravada Buddhism, while Chinese monks came by land and introduced Mahayana Buddhism. In particular, the Chinese monk Mau Tu is credited with being the first person to introduce Mahayana Buddhism in AD 194-195.

Initially, Buddhism was very much the religion of the elite and did not impinge upon the common Vietnamese man or woman. It was not until the reign of Emperor Ly Anh Tong (1138-1175) that Buddhism was promoted as the state religion, nearly 1000 years after Mau Tu had arrived from China to spread the teachings of the Buddha.

By that time it had begun to filter down to the village level, but as it did so it became increasingly syncretic; Buddhism became enmeshed with Confucianism, Taoism, spirituality, mysticism and animism. In the 15th century it also began to lose its position to Confucianism as the dominant religion of the court.

There has been a resurgence of Buddhism since the 1920s. It was the self-immolation of Buddhist monks in the 1960s which provided a focus of discontent against the government in the south, and since the Communist victory in 1975, monks have remained an important focus of dissent, hence the persecution of Buddhists during the early years following reunification. Mahayana Buddhists are concentrated in the centre and north of the country and the dominant sect is the Thien (Zen) meditation sect. Of the relatively small numbers of Theravada Buddhists, the majority are of Cambodian stock and are concentrated in the Mekong Delta. In Vietnam, Buddhism is intertwined with Confucianism and Taoism.

## Confucianism

Although Confucianism is not strictly a religion, the teachings of the Chinese sage and philosopher Confucius (551-479 BC) form the basis on which Vietnamese life and government were based for much of the historic period. Even today, Confucianist perspectives are, possibly, more strongly in evidence than Communist ones. Confucianism was introduced from China during the Bac Thuoc Period (111 BC-AD 938) when the Chinese dominated the country. The 'religion' enshrined the concept of imperial rule by the mandate of heaven, constraining social and political change.

In essence, Confucianism stresses the importance of family and lineage and the worship of ancestors. Men and women in positions of authority were required to provide role models for the 'ignorant', while the state, epitomized in the emperor, was likewise required to set an example and to provide conditions of stability and fairness for his people. Crucially, children had to observe filial piety. This set of norms, which were drawn from the experience of the human encounter at the practical level, were enshrined in the Forty-seven Rules for Teaching and Changing first issued in 1663. A key element of Confucianist thought is the Three Bonds (*tam cuong*) – the loyalty of ministers to the emperor, obedience of children to their parents and submission of wives to their husbands. Added to these are mutual reciprocity among friends and benevolence towards strangers. Not surprisingly the Communists are antipathetic to such a hierarchical view of society although ironically Confucianism, which inculcates respect for the elderly and authority, unwittingly lends support to a politburo occupied by old men. In an essay entitled 'Confucianism and Marxism', Vietnamese scholar Nguyen Khac Vien explains why Marxism proved an acceptable doctrine to those accustomed to Confucian values: "Marxism was not baffling to Confucians in that it concentrated man's thoughts on political and social problems. By defining man as the total of his social relationships, Marxism hardly came as a shock to the Confucian scholar who had always considered the highest aim of man to be the fulfilment of his social obligations ... Bourgeois individualism, which puts personal interests ahead of those of society and petty bourgeois anarchism, which allows no social discipline whatsoever, are alien to both Confucianism and Marxism."

## Taoism

Taoism was introduced from China into Vietnam at about the same time as Confucianism. It is based on the works of the Chinese philosophers Lao Tzu (circa sixth-fifth centuries BC) and Chuang Tzu (fourth century BC). Although not strictly a formal religion, it has had a significant influence on Buddhism (as it is practised in Vietnam) and on Confucianism. In reality, Taoism and Confucianism are two sides of the same coin: the Taoist side is poetry and spirituality; the Confucianist side, social ethics and the order of the world. Together they form a unity. Like Confucianism, it is not possible to give a figure to the number of followers of Taoism in with Christianity, Cao Daism and Hoa Hao. Of all the world's religions, Taoism is perhaps the hardest to pin down. It has no formal code, no teachings and no creed. It is a cosmic religion. Even the word Tao is usually left untranslated or merely translated as 'The Way'. The inscrutability of it all is summed up in the writings of the Chinese poet Po Chu-i: "Those who speak know nothing, Those who know keep silence. These words, as I am told, were spoken by Lao Tzu. But if we are to believe that Lao Tzu was himself one who knew, how comes it that he wrote a book of five thousand words?"

Or to quote Chuang Tzu even more inscrutably: "Tao is beyond material existence ... it may be transmitted, but it cannot be received [possessed]. It may be attained, but cannot be seen. It exists prior to Heaven and Earth, and, indeed, for all eternity ... it is above the Zenith, but is not high; it is beneath the Nadir, but it is not low. It is prior to Heaven and Earth, but it is not ancient. It is older than the most ancient, but it is not old."

Central to Taoist belief is a world view based upon yin and yang, two primordial forces on which the creation and functioning of the world are based. The yin-yang is not specifically Taoist or Confucianist, but predates both and is associated with the first recorded Chinese ruler, Fu-hsi (2852-2738 BC). The well-known yin-yang symbol symbolizes the balance and equality between the great dualistic forces in the universe: dark and light, negative and positive, male and female. JC Cooper explains in *Taoism: the Way of the Mystic*, the symbolism of the black and white dots: "There is a point, or embryo, of black in the white and white in the black. This ... is essential to the symbolism since there is no being which does not contain within itself the germ of its opposite. There is no male wholly without feminine characteristics and no female without its masculine attributes." Thus the dualism of the yin-yang is not absolute, but permeable.

To maintain balance and harmony in life it is necessary that a proper balance be maintained between yin (female) and yang (male). This is believed to be true both at the scale of the world and the nation, and also for an individual, for the human body is the world in microcosm. The root cause of illness is imbalance between the forces of yin and yang. Even foods have characters: 'hot' foods are yang and 'cold', yin. Implicit in this is the belief that there is a natural law underpinning all of life, a law upon which harmony ultimately rests. Taoism attempts to maintain this balance and thereby harmony. In this way, Taoism is a force promoting inertia, maintaining the status quo. Traditional relationships between fathers and sons, between siblings, within villages, and between the rulers and the ruled, are all rationalized in terms of maintaining balance and harmony. Forces for change – like Communism and democracy – are resisted on the basis that they upset this balance.

## Christianity

Christianity was first introduced into Vietnam in the 16th century by Roman Catholic missionaries from Portugal, Spain and France. The first Bishop of Vietnam was appointed in 1659 and by 1685 there were estimated to be 800,000 Roman Catholics in the country. For several centuries Christianity was discouraged, and at times, outlawed. Many Christians were executed and one of the reasons the French gave for annexing the country in the late 19th century was religious persecution (see page 213). Today, 8-10% of the population are thought to be Roman Catholic; less than 1% are Protestant. This Christian population is served by around 2000 priests. Following reunification in 1975, many Roman Catholics in the former south were sent to re-education camps. They were perceived to be both staunchly pro-American and anti-Communist and it was not until 1988 that many were returned to normal life.

## ⁞ In Siddhartha's footsteps: a short history of Buddhism

Buddhism was founded by Siddhartha Gautama, a prince of the Sakya tribe of Nepal, who probably lived from 563 to 483 BC. He achieved enlightenment and the word buddha means 'fully enlightened one', or 'one who has woken up'. Siddhartha Gautama is known by a number of names. In the West, he is usually referred to as The Buddha, ie the historic Buddha (but not just Buddha); more common in South-east Asia is Sakyamuni, or Sage of the Sakyas (referring to his tribal origins).

Over the centuries, the life of the Buddha has become part legend and the Jataka tales that recount his various lives are colourful and convoluted. But central to Buddhist belief is that he was born under a sal tree, that he achieved enlightenment under a bodhi tree in the Bodh Gaya Gardens, that he preached the First Sermon at Sarnath, and that he died at Kusinagara (all in India or Nepal).

The Buddha was born at Lumbini (in present-day Nepal) as Queen Maya was on her way to her parents' home. She

had had a very auspicious dream before the child's birth of being impregnated by an elephant, whereupon a sage prophesied that Siddhartha would become either a great king or a great spiritual leader. His father, being keen that the first option of the prophesy be fulfilled, brought him up in all the princely skills – at which Siddhartha excelled – and ensured that he only saw beautiful things, not the harsher elements of life.

Despite his father's efforts Siddhartha saw four things while travelling between palaces: a helpless old man, a very sick man, a corpse being carried by lamenting relatives, and an ascetic, calm and serene as he begged for food. The young prince renounced his princely origins and left home to study under a series of spiritual teachers. He finally discovered the path to enlightenment at the Bodh Gaya Gardens in India. He then proclaimed his thoughts to a small group of disciples at Sarnath, near Benares,

Today, Roman Catholics are still viewed with suspicion by the state and priests felt to be drifting from purely religious concerns into any criticism of the state (seen as anti-government activity) are detained, such as Father Nguyen Van Ly. And this is the key point: the Vietnamese remain tolerant and open in matters of religion and spirituality. It is the political overtones that come with any established religion that the authorities find impossible to accept. While memories of the role of the Roman Catholic church in the downfall of Polish Communism linger relations between Hanoi and the Vatican are not warm and often strained and Rome finds it difficult to appoint bishops. However, in 2007 the prime minister became the first head of government to be received at the Vatican to discuss relations. More generally, the authorities have been slow to permit Vietnamese men to become ordained, and they have limited the production and flow of religious literature. Nevertheless centuries of existence in what for the Roman Catholic church has been the hostile environment of Vietnam has enabled it to reach a degree of acceptance. Doubtless the brighter of the Communist leaders realize the Roman Catholic church will be around long after their Party has disappeared.

Protestant sects have a much tougher time. This is partly due to the evangelical nature of much Protestantism that makes the authorities distinctly uneasy. Evangelical protestants have faced the brunt of the crackdowns in the last couple of years.

### Islam and Hinduism

The only centres of Islam and Hinduism are among the Cham of the central coastal plain and Chau Doc. The Cham were converted to Islam by Muslim traders. There are several mosques in Ho Chi Minh City and Cholon, some of them built by Indians from Kerala.

and continued to preach and attract followers until he died at the age of 81 at Kusinagara.

In the First Sermon at the deer park in Sarnath, the Buddha preached the Four Truths, still seen as the root of Buddhist belief and experience: suffering exists; there is a cause of suffering; suffering can be ended; and to end suffering it is necessary to follow the 'Noble Eightfold Path' – right speech, livelihood, action, effort, mindfulness, concentration, opinion and intention.

Soon after the Buddha began preaching, a monastic order – the Sangha – was established. As the monkhood evolved in India, it also began to fragment into different sects. An important change was the belief that the Buddha was transcendent: he had never been born, nor had he died; he had always existed and his life on earth had been mere illusion. The emergence of these new concepts helped to turn what up until then was an ethical code of conduct, into a religion. It eventually led to a new Buddhist movement, Mahayana Buddhism, which split from the more traditional Theravada 'sect'.

Despite the division of Buddhism into two sects, the central tenets are common to both. Specifically, the principles pertaining to the Four Noble Truths, the Noble Eightfold Path, the Dependent Origination, the Law of Karma, and nirvana. In addition, the principles of non-violence and tolerance are also embraced by both sects. The differences between the two are of emphasis and interpretation. Theravada Buddhism is strictly based on the original Pali Canon, while the Mahayana tradition stems from later Sanskrit texts. Mahayana Buddhism also allows a broader interpretation of the doctrine. Other major differences are that while the Theravada tradition is more 'intellectual' and self-obsessed, stressing the attainment of wisdom and insight for oneself, Mahayana Buddhism emphasizes devotion and compassion.

## Cao Daism

Cao Dai took root in southern Vietnam during the 1920s after Ngo Van Chieu, a civil servant, was visited by 'Cao Dai' or the 'Supreme Being' and was given the tenets of a new religion. Ngo received this spiritual visitation in 1919 on Phu Quoc Island. The Cao Dai later told Ngo in a seance that he was to be symbolized by a giant eye. The religion quickly gained the support of a large following of dispossessed peasants. It was both a religion and a nationalist movement. In terms of the former, it claimed to be a synthesis of Buddhism, Christianity, Taoism, Confucianism and Islam. Cao Dai 'saints' include Joan of Arc, the French writer Victor Hugo, Sir Winston Churchill, Sun Yat Sen, Moses and Brahma. Debates over doctrine are mediated through the spirits who are contacted on a regular basis through a strange wooden contraption called a *corbeille-à-bec* or planchette. The five Cao Dai commandments are: do not kill any living creature; do not covet; do not practise high living; do not be tempted; and do not slander by word. But, as well as being a religion, the movement also claimed that it would restore traditional Vietnamese attitudes and was anti-colonial and modestly subversive. Opportunist to a fault, Cao Dai followers sought the aid of the Japanese against the French, the Americans against the Viet Minh and the Viet Minh against the south. Following reunification in 1975, all Cao Dai lands were confiscated and their leadership emasculated. The centre of Cao Daism remains the Mekong Delta where – and despite the efforts of the Communists – there are thought to be perhaps two million adherents and perhaps 1000 Cao Dai temples. The Cao Dai Great Temple is in the town of Tay Ninh, 100 km from Ho Chi Minh City (see page 183).

**Hoa Hao**

Hoa Hao is another Vietnamese religion that emerged in the Mekong Delta. It was founded by Huynh Phu So in 1939, a resident of Hoa Hao village in the province of Chau Doc. Effectively a schism of Buddhism, the sect discourages temple building and worship, maintaining that simplicity of worship is the key to better contact with God. There are thought to be perhaps 1-1.5 million adherents of Hoa Hao, predominantly in the Chau Doc area.

# Land and environment

## The regions of Vietnam

The name Vietnam is derived from that adopted in 1802 by Emperor Gia Long: Nam Viet. This means, literally, the Viet (the largest ethnic group) of the south (Nam), and substituted for the country's previous name, Annam. The country is S-shaped, covers a land area of 329,600 sq km and has a coastline of 3000 km. The most important economic zones, containing the main concentrations of population, are focused on two large deltaic areas. In the north, there are the ancient rice fields and settlements of the Red River, and in the south, the fertile alluvial plain of the Mekong. In between, the country narrows to less than 50 km wide, with only a thin ribbon of fertile lowland suited to intensive agriculture. Much of the interior, away from the coastal belt and the deltas, is mountainous. Here ethnic minorities (Montagnards), along with some lowland Vietnamese resettled in so-called New Economic Zones since 1975, eke out a living on thin and unproductive soils. The rugged terrain means that only 25% of the land is actually cultivated. Of the rest, 20-25% is forested and some of this is heavily degraded.

The French subdivided Vietnam into three regions, administering each separately: Tonkin or Bac Ky (the north region), Annam or Trung Ky (the central region) and Cochin China or Nam Ky (the south region). Although these administrative divisions have been abolished, the Vietnamese still recognize their country as consisting of three regions, distinct in terms of geography, history and culture. Their new names are Bac Bo (north), Trung Bo (centre) and Nam Bo (south).

### Northern Highlands

Vietnam consists of five major geographical zones. In the far north are the northern highlands which ring the Red River Delta and form a natural barrier with China. The rugged mountains on the west border of this region – the Hoang Lien Son – exceed 3000 m in places. The tributaries of the Red River have cut deep, steep-sided gorges through the Hoang Lien Son, which are navigable by small boats. The eastern portion of this region, bordering the Gulf of Tonkin, is far less imposing; the mountain peaks of the west have diminished into foothills, allowing easy access to China. It was across these hills that the Chinese mounted their successive invasions of Vietnam, the last of which occurred as recently as 1979, see page 237.

### Red River Delta

The second region lies in the embrace of the hills of the north. This, the Red River Delta, can legitimately claim to be the cultural and historical heart of the Viet nation. Hanoi lies at its core and it was here the first truly independent Vietnamese polity was established in AD 939 by Ngo Quyen. The delta covers almost 15,000 sq km and extends 240 km inland from the coast. Rice has been grown on the alluvial soils of the Red River for thousands of years. Yet despite the intricate web of canals, dykes and

# ⁝ The Mekong: mother river of Southeast Asia

The Mekong River is one of the 12 great rivers of the world. It stretches 4500 km from its source on the Tibet Plateau in China to its mouth (or mouths) in the Mekong Delta of Vietnam. (On 11 April 1995 a Franco-British expedition announced that they had discovered the source of the Mekong – 5000 m high, at the head of the Rup-Sa Pass, and miles from anywhere.) Each year, the river empties 475 billion cu m of water into the South China Sea. Along its course it flows through Burma, Laos, Thailand, Cambodia and Vietnam – all countries constituting mainland Southeast Asia – as well as China. In both a symbolic and a physical sense it links the region. Bringing fertile silt to the land along its banks, but particularly to the Mekong Delta, the river contributes to Southeast Asia's agricultural wealth. In former times, a tributary of the Mekong that drains the Tonlé Sap (the Great Lake of Cambodia), provided the rice surplus on which the fabulous Angkor empire was founded. The Tonlé Sap acts like a great regulator, storing water in time of flood and then releasing it when levels recede.

The first European to explore the river was French naval officer Francis Garnier. His Mekong expedition (1866-68) followed the great river upstream from its delta in Cochin China (southern Vietnam). Of the 9960 km that the trip covered, 506 km were 'discovered' for the first time.

The motivation for the trip was to find a southern route into the Heavenly Kingdom – China. But they failed. The river is navigable only as far as the Lao-Cambodian border where the Khone rapids make it impassable. Nonetheless, the expedition report is one of the finest of its genre.

Today the Mekong itself is perceived as a source of potential economic wealth, not just as a path to riches. The Mekong Secretariat was established in 1957 to harness the waters of the river for irrigation and hydropower. The Secretariat devised a grandiose plan with a succession of seven huge dams that would store 142 billion cu m of water, irrigate 4.3 million ha of riceland and generate 24,200MW of power. But the Vietnam War disrupted construction. Only Laos' Nam Ngum Dam on a tributary of the Mekong was ever built and even though this generates just 150MW of power, electricity exports to Thailand are one of Laos' largest export earners. Now that the countries of mainland Southeast Asia are on friendly terms once more, the Secretariat and its scheme have been given a new lease of life. But in the intervening years, fears about the environmental consequences of big dams have raised new questions. The Mekong Secretariat has moderated its plans and is now looking at less ambitious, and less contentious, ways to harness the Mekong River.

Vietnam Background Land & environment

embankments, the Vietnamese have never been able to completely tame the river, and the delta is the victim of frequent and sometimes devastating floods. The area is very low-lying, rarely more than 3 m above sea level and often less than 1 m. The highwater mark is nearly 8 m above land level in some places. During the monsoon season, the tributaries of the Red River quickly become torrents rushing through the narrow gorges of the Hoang Lien Son, before emptying into the main channel that then bursts its banks. Although the region supports one of the highest agricultural population densities in the world, the inhabitants have frequently had to endure famines, most recently in 1989.

# Climate: temperatures, humidity and rainfall by place

## Hanoi

|  | Jan | Feb | Mar | Apr | May | Jun | Jul | Aug | Sep | Oct | Nov | Dec |
|---|---|---|---|---|---|---|---|---|---|---|---|---|
| Max (°C) | 33 | 35 | 37 | 39 | 43 | 40 | 40 | 39 | 37 | 36 | 36 | 32 |
| Min (°C) | 3 | 5 | 9 | 10 | 15 | 20 | 22 | 21 | 16 | 12 | 7 | 5 |
| Humidity (%) | 80 | 84 | 88 | 87 | 83 | 83 | 83 | 85 | 85 | 81 | 81 | 81 |
| Rainfall (mm) | 18 | 26 | 48 | 81 | 194 | 236 | 302 | 325 | 262 | 47 | 47 | 20 |

## Hué

|  | Jan | Feb | Mar | Apr | May | Jun | Jul | Aug | Sep | Oct | Nov | Dec |
|---|---|---|---|---|---|---|---|---|---|---|---|---|
| Max (°C) | 35 | 36 | 30 | 40 | 40 | 40 | 39 | 39 | 38 | 36 | 35 | 32 |
| Min (°C) | 9 | 11 | 12 | 14 | 18 | 21 | 19 | 21 | 19 | 16 | 13 | 11 |
| Humidity (%) | 90 | 90 | 88 | 84 | 80 | 76 | 73 | 77 | 84 | 88 | 88 | 90 |
| Rainfall (mm) | 188 | 89 | 57 | 64 | 78 | 104 | 76 | 124 | 498 | 744 | 693 | 346 |

## Danang

|  | Jan | Feb | Mar | Apr | May | Jun | Jul | Aug | Sep | Oct | Nov | Dec |
|---|---|---|---|---|---|---|---|---|---|---|---|---|
| Max (°C) | 31 | 34 | 34 | 36 | 39 | 40 | 39 | 40 | 38 | 35 | 34 | 32 |
| Min (°C) | 15 | 15 | 16 | 19 | 20 | 19 | 21 | 22 | 21 | 19 | 17 | 15 |
| Humidity (%) | 78 | 78 | 80 | 81 | 80 | 79 | 78 | 79 | 82 | 84 | 83 | 79 |
| Rainfall (mm) | 50 | 18 | 31 | 40 | 61 | 47 | 42 | 53 | 162 | 322 | 359 | 174 |

## Nha Trang

|  | Jan | Feb | Mar | Apr | May | Jun | Jul | Aug | Sep | Oct | Nov | Dec |
|---|---|---|---|---|---|---|---|---|---|---|---|---|
| Max (°C) | 31 | 34 | 34 | 36 | 39 | 40 | 39 | 40 | 38 | 35 | 34 | 32 |
| Min (°C) | 15 | 15 | 16 | 19 | 20 | 19 | 21 | 22 | 21 | 19 | 17 | 15 |
| Humidity (%) | 78 | 78 | 80 | 81 | 80 | 79 | 78 | 79 | 82 | 84 | 83 | 79 |
| Rainfall (mm) | 50 | 18 | 31 | 40 | 61 | 47 | 42 | 53 | 162 | 322 | 359 | 174 |

## Ho Chi Minh City

|  | Jan | Feb | Mar | Apr | May | Jun | Jul | Aug | Sep | Oct | Nov | Dec |
|---|---|---|---|---|---|---|---|---|---|---|---|---|
| Max (°C) | 36 | 39 | 39 | 40 | 39 | 36 | 35 | 35 | 35 | 35 | 35 | 36 |
| Min (°C) | 14 | 16 | 17 | 20 | 22 | 20 | 19 | 20 | 21 | 20 | 14 | 13 |
| Humidity (%) | 74 | 71 | 71 | 74 | 80 | 84 | 84 | 85 | 86 | 83 | 82 | 78 |
| Rainfall (mm) | 14 | 5 | 12 | 50 | 221 | 315 | 296 | 274 | 332 | 264 | 115 | 51 |

## South of the Red River Delta

South of the Red River Delta region lie the central lowlands and the mountains of the Annamite Chain. The **Annam Highlands**, now known as **Truong Son Mountain Range**, form an important cultural divide between the Indianized nations of the west and the

Sinicized cultures of the east. Its northern rugged extremity is in Thanh Hoa Province. From here the Truong Son stetches over 1200 km south, to peter out 80 km north of Ho Chi Minh City.

The highest peak is Ngoc Linh Mountain in Kon Tum Province at 2598 m. The Central Highlands form an upland plateau on which the hill resorts of **Buon Ma Thuot** and **Dalat** are situated. On the plateau, plantation agriculture and hill farms are interspersed with stands of bamboo and tropical forests. Once rich in wildlife, the plateau was a popular hunting ground during the colonial period.

## Central coastal strip

To the east, the Annamite Chain falls off steeply, leaving only a narrow and fragmented band of lowland suitable for settlement: the central coastal strip. In places the mountains advance all the way to the coast, plunging into the sea as dramatic rock faces and making north-south communication difficult. At no point does the region extend more than 64 km inland, and in total it covers only 6750 sq km. The soils are often rocky or saline, and irrigation is seldom possible. Nonetheless, the inhabitants have a history of sophisticated rice culture and it was here that the Champa Kingdom was established in the early centuries of the Christian era. These coastal lowlands have also formed a conduit along which people have historically moved. Even today, the main north-south road and rail routes cut through the coastal lowlands.

## Mekong Delta

Unlike the Red River Delta this region is not so prone to flooding and consequently rice production is more stable. The reason why flooding is less severe lies in the regulating effect of the Great Lake of Cambodia, the Tonlé Sap. During the rainy season, when the water flowing into the Mekong becomes too great for even this mighty river to absorb, rather than overflowing its banks, the water backs up into the Tonlé Sap, which quadruples in area. The Mekong Delta covers 67,000 sq km and is drained by five branches of the Mekong, which divides as it flows towards the sea. The vast delta is one of the great rice bowls of Asia producing nearly half of the country's rice and over the years has been cut into a patchwork by the canals that have been dug to expand irrigation and rice cultivation. Largely forested until the late 19th century, the French supported the settlement of the area by Vietnamese peasants, recognizing that it could become enormously productive. The deposition of silt by the rivers that cut through the delta, means that the shoreline is continually advancing, by up to 80 m each year in some places. To the north of the delta lies Ho Chi Minh City.

# Climate

Vietnam stretches more than 1800 km from north to south and the weather patterns in the two principal cities, Hanoi in the north and Ho Chi Minh City in the south, are very different. Average temperatures tend to rise the further south you go, while the seasonal variation in temperature decreases. The exceptions to this general rule of thumb are in the interior highland areas where the altitude means it is considerably colder.

## North Vietnam

The seasons in the north are similar to those of South China. The winter is November to April, with temperatures averaging 16°C and little rainfall. The summer begins in May and lasts until October. During these months it can be very hot, with an average temperature of 30°C, along with heavy rainfall and the occasional violent typhoon.

Central Vietnam experiences a transitional climate, halfway between that in the south and in the north. Hué has a reputation for poor weather: it's often overcast and an umbrella is needed whatever the month, even in the short 'dry' season from February to April. Hué's annual rainfall is 3250 mm. See page 122 for the best time to visit.

## South Vietnam

Temperatures in the south are fairly constant through the year (25°C-30°C) and the seasons are determined by the rains. The dry season runs from November to April (when there is virtually no rain whatsoever) and the wet season from May to October. The hottest period is during March and April, before the rains have broken. Typhoons are quite common in coastal areas between July and November.

## Highland Areas

In the hill resorts of Dalat (1500 m), Buon Ma Thuot and Sapa nights are cool throughout the year and in the 'winter' months between October to March it can be distinctly chilly with temperatures falling to 4°C. Even in the hottest months of March and April the temperature rarely exceeds 26°C.

---

# Flora and fauna

Together with overseas conservation agencies such as the Worldwide Fund for Nature (WWF), Vietnamese scientists have, in recent years, been enumerating and protecting their fauna and flora. The establishment of nature reserves began in 1962 with the gazetting of the Cuc Phuong National Park. Today there are a total of 87 reserves covering 3.3% of Vietnam's land area. However, some of them are too small to sustain sufficiently large breeding populations of endangered species and many parks are quite heavily populated. For instance 80,000 people live, farm and hunt within the 22,000 ha Bach Ma National Park. Vietnamese scientists with support from outside agencies, in particular the WWF, have begun the important task of cataloguing and protecting Vietnam's wildlife.

The **Javan rhinoceros** is one of the rarest large mammals in the world and until recently was thought only to survive in the Ujung Kulon National Park in West Java, Indonesia. However in November 1988 it was reported that a Stieng tribesman had shot a female Javan rhino near the Dong Nai River around 130 km northeast of Saigon. When he tried to sell the horn and hide he was arrested and this set in train a search to discover if there were any more of the animals in the area. Researchers discovered that Viet Cong soldiers operating in the area during the war saw – and killed – a number of animals. One former revolutionary, Tran Ngoc Khanh, reported that he once saw a herd of 20 animals and that between 1952 and 1976 some 17 animals were shot by the soldiers. With the Viet Cong shooting the animals whenever they chanced upon them, and the Americans spraying tonnes of defoliant on the area, it is a wonder than any survived through to the end of the war. However, a study by George Schaller and three Vietnamese colleagues in 1989 found tracks, also near the Dong Nai River, and estimated that a population of 10 to 15 animals probably still survived in a 750 sq km area of bamboo and dipterocarp forest close to and including Nam Cat Tien National Park.

This remarkable find was followed by, if anything, an even more astonishing discovery: of two completely new species of mammal. In 1992 British scientist Dr John MacKinnon discovered the skeleton of an animal now known as the **Vu Quang ox** (*Pseudoryx nghetinhensis*) but known to locals as *sao la*. The Vu Quang ox was the first new large mammal species to be found in 50 years; scientists were amazed that a large mammal could exist on this crowded planet without their knowledge. In June

1994 the first live specimen (a young calf) was captured and shortly afterwards a second one was caught and taken to the Forestry Institute in Hanoi. Sadly, both died in captivity but in early 1995 a third was brought in alive. The animals look anything but ox-like, and have the appearance, grace and manner of a small deer. The government responded to the discovery by extending the Vu Quang Nature Reserve and banning hunting of *sao la*. Local ethnic minorities, who have long regarded *sao la* as a tasty and not uncommon animal, have therefore lost a valued source of food and no longer have a vested interest in the animal's survival. *Sao la* must rue the day they were 'discovered'. In 1993 a new species of deer that has been named the **giant muntjac** was also found in the Vu Quang Nature Reserve. The scientists have yet to see it alive but villagers prize its meat and are reported to trap it in quite large numbers.

Large rare mammals are confined to isolated pockets where the government does its best to protect them from hunters. On Cat Ba Island, the national park is home to the world's last wild troops of white-headed langur. In North Vietnam tigers have been hunted close to extinction and further south territorial battles rage between elephants and farmers. Rampaging elephants sometimes cause loss of life and are in turn decimated by enraged villagers.

Among the **larger mammals**, there are small numbers of tiger (around 200), leopard, clouded leopard, Indian elephant, Malayan sun bear, Himalayan black bear, sambar deer, gibbon and gaur (wild buffalo). These are rarely seen, except in zoos. There are frequent news reports of farmers maiming or killing elephants after their crops have been trampled or their huts flattened. The larger reptiles include two species of crocodile, the estuarine (*Crocodilus porosus*) and Siamese (*Crocodilus siamensis*). The former grows to a length of 5 m and has been reported to have killed and eaten humans. Among the larger snakes are the reticulated python (*Python reticulatus*) and the smaller Indian python (*Python molurus*), both non-venomous constrictors. Venomous snakes include two species of cobra (the king cobra and common cobra), two species of krait and six species of pit viper.

Given the difficulty of getting to Vietnam's more remote areas, the country is hardly a haven for amateur naturalists. Professional photographers and naturalists have been escorted to the country's wild areas but this is not an option for the average visitor. Getting there requires time and contacts. A wander around the markets of Vietnam reveals the variety and number of animals that end up in the cooking pot, including deer, bear, snakes, monkeys and turtles. The Chinese penchant for exotic foods (such gastronomic wonders as tigers' testicles and bear's foot) has also become a predilection of the Vietnamese and most animals are fair game.

## Birds

Birds have, in general, suffered rather less than mammals from over-hunting and the effects of the war. There have been some casualties however: the eastern sarus crane of the Mekong Delta – a symbol of fidelity, longevity and good luck – disappeared entirely during the war. However, in 1985 a farmer reported seeing a single bird, and by 1990 there were over 500 pairs breeding on the now pacified former battlefields. A sarus crane reserve has been established in Dong Thap Province.

Among the more unusual birds are the snake bird (named after its habit of swimming with its body submerged and only its snake-like neck and head above the surface), the argus pheasant, which the Japanese believe to be the mythical phoenix, the little bastard quail of which the male hatches and rears the young, three species of vulture, the osprey (sea eagle), and two species of hornbill (the pied and great Indian). Vietnam also has colonies of the endangered white-winged wood duck, one of the symbols of the world conservation movement. The Vietnamese pheasant

(Vo Quy), thought to be extinct, was recently rediscovered in the wild and two males are now held in captivity in Hanoi zoo.

An incredible diversity of birds live in the forest and wetland habitats of **Nam Cat Tien National Park**, including an estimated 230 species of birds. Endangered birds that can be found here include Germain's peacock pheasant, green peafowl and the highly elusive orange-necked partridge. You can hire a jeep at the park headquarters to visit areas further afield such as Bird Lake to look for visiting waders or Crocodile Lake where grey-headed fish eagle, lesser adjutant and Asian golden weaver may be seen, as well as the reintroduced Siamese crocodiles. During the walk through the forest to Crocodile Lake look out for bar-bellied and blue-rumped pitta, red-and-black and banded broadbill and orange-breasted trogon. Other interesting species at Cat Tien include scaly-breasted partridge, Siamese fireback, woolly-necked stork and grey-faced tit-babbler and white-bellied, great slaty, pale-headed and heart-spotted woodpecker. On the trails or the headquarters road, green-eared, blue-eared, lineated and – if you're lucky – red-vented barbet can often be seen perched high up in the roadside trees.

Twenty minutes by road from Dalat at **Langbian Mountain**, the evergreen forests are home to many interesting birds including several endemic species. Key species to be found here include the silver pheasant, Indochinese cuckooshrike, Eurasian jay, mugimaki flycatcher, yellow-billed nuthatch and red crossbill. This is also the place to see three of Vietnam's most sought-after endemics: collared laughingthrush, Vietnamese cutia and Vietnamese greenfinch. Mount Langbian is best avoided at weekends and holidays when it is a popular destination for local tourists.

**Tuyen Lam Lake**, only 3 km from the centre of Dalat, is another hotspot for birders. Take a boat to far side of the lake where a track leads through the pines to areas of remnant tropical evergreen forest. With luck, the rare and endemic grey-crowned crocias, rediscovered in 1994 after not being seen for nearly 60 years, can be found. Other interesting species here include slender-billed oriole, maroon oriole, rufous-backed sibia, black-headed parrotbill and orange-breasted, black-hooded and white-cheeked laughingthrush.

**Ta Nung Valley**, around 10 km from Dalat, holds pockets of remnant evergreen forest where many of the Dalat specialities can still be found including orange-breasted, black-hooded and white-cheeked laughing thrush, blue-winged minla, grey-crowned crocias, black-headed parrotbill and black-throated sunbird.

At **Bach Ma National Park**, more than 330 species of bird have been recorded. Species include the annam partridge, crested argus, Blyth's kingfisher, coral-billed ground cuckoo, ratchet-tailed treepie, sultan tit and short-tailed scimitar babbler. Others include red-collared woodpecker, bar-bellied and blue-rumped pitta and white-winged magpie.

There are several good trails in the forested hills above the tourist resort of **Tam Dao**, which is 1½ hours by road from Hanoi. Specialities of Tam Dao include chestnut bulbul, grey laughingthrush, short-tailed parrotbill and fork-tailed sunbird. In the winter months look out for orange-flanked bush robin, black-breasted thrush, Japanese thrush and Fujian niltava.

In **Cuc Phuong National Park**, see page 93, an area of limestone hills covered with large tracts of primary forest, key bird species include silver pheasant, red-collared woodpecker, pied falconet, white-winged magpie and limestone wren-babbler and bar-bellied, blue-rumped and eared pitta.

# Cambodia

# Cambodia

# Phnom Penh

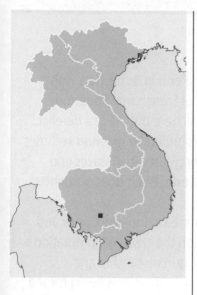

## ❂ Footprint features

# Introduction

It is not hard to imagine Phnom Penh in its heyday, with wide, shady boulevards, beautiful French buildings and exquisite pagodas. They're still all here but are in a derelict, dust-blown, decaying state surrounded by growing volumes of cars, pick-up trucks and motorcyclists. It all leaves you wondering how a city like this works. But it does, somehow.

Phnom Penh is a city of contrasts: East and West, poor and rich, serenity and chaos. Although the city has a reputation as a frontier town, due to drugs, gun ownership and prostitution, a more cosmopolitan character is being forged out of the muck. Monks' saffron robes are once again lending a splash of colour to the capital's streets, following the reinstatement of Buddhism as the national religion in 1989, and stylish restaurants and bars line the riverside. However, the amputees on street corners are a constant reminder of Cambodia's tragic story. Perhaps the one constant in all the turmoil of the past century has been the monarchy – shifting, whimsical, pliant and, indeed, temporarily absent as it may have been. The splendid royal palace, visible to all, was a daily reminder of this ultimate authority whom even the Khmer Rouge had to treat with caution. The royal palace area, with its glittering spires, wats, stupas, national museum and broad green spaces, is perfectly sited alongside the river and is as pivotal to the city as the city is to the country.

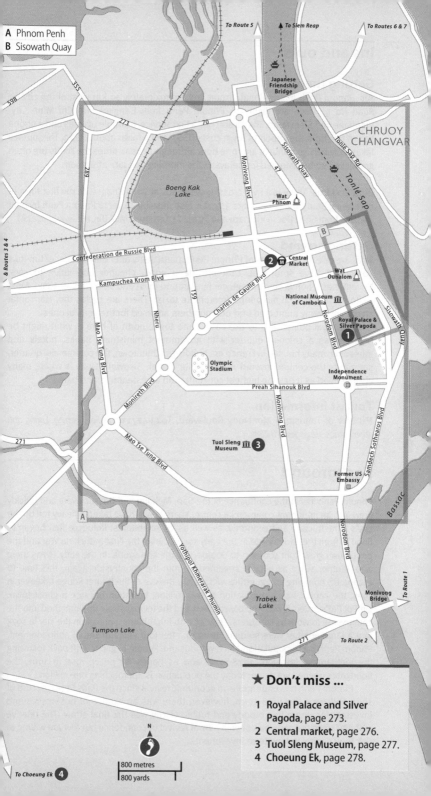

A Phnom Penh
B Sisowath Quay

# Ins and outs

## Getting there

**Air** Phnom Penh International airport lies approximately 10 km west of the city on Road No 4. There are flights to Phnom Penh from Bangkok, Ho Chi Minh City, Vientiane and Siem Reap. The airport has a taxi service, a couple of cafés and a phone box. A taxi from the airport to town costs US$7 and a moto about US$3. The journey takes between 40 minutes and one hour although at peak times the roads are often gridlocked so be prepared for delays in the morning and late afternoon.

**Boat and bus** There is a river crossing with Laos at Voen Kham with the first town of note being Stung Treng, see page 307. It is also possible to get to Phnom Penh by boat and bus from Chau Doc in Vietnam and by road crossing at Moc Bai. ▸▸ *See also page 197.*

## Getting around

Taxis are rare on the streets of Phnom Penh, particularly after dark. A fleet of tuk-tuks (*lomphata*) have sprung up that provide a good, cheaper alternative to cars. Nevertheless, hotels can arrange car hire around town and surrounding areas. Most visitors use the local motodops (motorbike taxis). There are cyclos too. Horizontal steets are evenly numbered and odd numbers are used for the vertical ones.

The royal quarter lies to the east of the town; north of here is what might be regarded as a colonial quarter with government ministries, banks, hotels and museums, many housed in French era buildings. Chinatown, the commercial quarter, surrounds the central covered market, Psar Thmei. Sisowath Quay is where many visitors head as it has the highest concentration of restaurants and bars.

## Tourist information

**Ministry of Tourism,** 3 Monivong Boulevard, T023-427130. ▸▸ *For Sleeping, Eating and other listings, see pages 278-288.*

# Background

Phnom Penh lies at the confluence of the Sap, Mekong and Bassac rivers and quickly grew into an important commercial centre. Years of war have taken a heavy toll on the city's infrastructure and economy, as well as its inhabitants. Refugees first began to flood in from the countryside in the early 1950s during the First Indochina War and the population grew from 100,000 to 600,000 by the late 1960s. In the early 1970s there was another surge as people streamed in from the countryside again, this time to escape US bombing and guerrilla warfare. On the eve of the Khmer Rouge takeover in 1975, the capital had a population of two million, but soon became a ghost town. On Pol Pot's orders it was forcibly emptied and the townspeople frog-marched into the countryside to work as labourers. Only 45,000 inhabitants were left in the city in 1975 and a large number were soldiers. In 1979, after four years of virtual abandonment, Phnom Penh had a population of a few thousand. People began to drift back following the Vietnamese invasion (1978-1979) and as hopes for peace rose in 1991, the floodgates opened yet again: today the population is approaching one million.

Phnom Penh has undergone an economic revival since the Paris Peace Accord of 1991. Following the 1998 coup, however, there was an exodus of businesses and investors for whom this bloody and futile atrocity was the final straw. The relative stability since the coup has seen a partial revival of confidence but few are willing to risk their capital in long-term investments.

# Sights

## Royal Palace and Silver Pagoda

ⓘ *Entrance on Samdech Sothearos Blvd. Daily 0730-1100, 1430-1700. US$3, plus US$2 for camera or US$5 for video camera.*

The Royal Palace and Silver Pagoda were built mainly by the French in 1866, on the site of the old town. The **Throne Hall**, the main building facing the Victory Gate, was built in 1917 in Khmer style; it has a tiered roof and a 59-m tower, influenced by Angkor's Bayon Temple. The steps leading up to it are protected by multi-headed nagas. It is used for coronations and other official occasions: scenes from the *Ramayana* adorn the ceiling. Inside stand the sacred gong and French-style thrones only used by the sovereign. Above the thrones hangs Preah Maha Svetrachatr, a nine-tiered parasol, which symbolizes heaven. There are two chambers for the king and queen at the back of the hall, which are used only in the week before a coronation when the royal couple are barred from sleeping together. The other adjoining room is used to house the ashes of dead monarchs before they are placed in a royal stupa.

The **Royal Treasury** and the **Napoleon III Pavilion** (summer house), built in 1866, are to the south of the Throne Room. The latter was presented by Napoleon III to his Empress Eugenie as accommodation for the princess during the Suez Canal opening celebrations. She later had it dismantled and dispatched it to Phnom Penh as a gift to the king.

The **Silver Pagoda** is often called the Pagoda of the Emerald Buddha or Wat Preah Keo Morokat after the statue housed here. The wooden temple was originally built by King Norodom in 1892 to enshrine royal ashes and then rebuilt by Sihanouk in 1962. The pagoda's steps are Italian marble, and inside, its floor comprises of more than 5000 silver blocks which together weigh nearly six tonnes. All around are cabinets filled with presents from foreign dignitaries. The pagoda is remarkably intact, having been granted special dispensation by the Khmer Rouge, although 60% of the Khmer treasures were stolen from here. In the centre of the pagoda is a magnificent 17th-century emerald Buddha statue made of Baccarat crystal. In front is a 90-kg golden Buddha studded with 9584 diamonds, dating from 1906. It was made from the jewellery of King Norodom and its vital statistics conform exactly to his – a tradition that can be traced back to the god-kings of Angkor.

## National Museum of Cambodia

ⓘ *Entrance is on the corner of streets 13 and 178. Daily 0700-1130, 1400-1730. US$2, plus US$3 for camera or video; photographs only permitted in the garden. French- and English-speaking guides are available, mostly excellent.*

The National Museum of Cambodia was built in 1920 and contains a collection of Khmer art – notably sculpture – throughout the ages (although some periods are not represented). Galleries are arranged chronologically in a clockwise direction. Most of the exhibits date from the Angkor period but there are several examples from the pre-Angkor era (that is from the kingdoms of Funan, Chenla and Cham). The collection of Buddhas from the sixth and seventh centuries includes a statue of Krishna Bovardhana found at Angkor Borei showing the freedom and grace of early Khmer sculpture. The chief attraction is probably the pre-Angkorian statue of Harihara, found at Prasat Andat near Kompong Thom. There is a fragment from a beautiful bronze statue of Vishnu found in the West Baray at Angkor, as well as frescoes and engraved doors.

To Boat Piers & Route 5

French Embassy

British Embassy

International Mosque

Calmette Hospital

*Boeng Kak Lake*

US Embassy

Monivong Blvd

Confederation de Russie Blvd

To Airport & Routes 3 & 4

Kampuchea Krom Blvd

Nehru Blvd

Charles de Gaulle Blvd

Psar Thmei (Central Market)

Wat Koh

Croix Rouge

Mao Tse Tung Blvd

Olympic Stadium

Wat Moha Montrei

Preah Sihanouk Blvd

Monireth Blvd

To Choeung Ek

Thai

Tuol Sleng Museum

Mao Tse Tung Blvd

Wat Tuol Tom Pong

Psar Tuol Tom Pong (Russian Market)

Rajana

**Related maps**
*Sisowath Quay, page 277*

**Sleeping**

Anise **20** *E4*
Aram **28** *D5*
Billabong **1** *C3*
Boddhi Tree **2** *E3*
Café Freedom **4** *B3*
Cambodiana **30** *D5*
Capitol **5** *D3*
Diamond **6** *C3*
Flamingo **8** *C4*
Golden Gate **10** *D4*
Grandview Guesthouse **12** *A3*
Happy Guesthouse **14** *D3*

Hello Guesthouse **15** *D3*
Himawari **30** *D5*
Holiday Villa **16** *C3*
Imperial Garden Villa **11** *D5*
Juliana **19** *C2*
KIDS Guesthouse **7** *C4*
Lazy Fish Guesthouse &
    Restaurant **21** *B3*
Le Royal **22** *B3*
L'Imprévu **13** *F4*
Narin Guesthouse **24** *D3*
New York **25** *C3*
Number 10 Lakeside
    Guesthouse **27** *B3*
Palm Resort **17** *F4*
Pavilion **38** *D5*
Phnom Penh **29** *A3*
Regent Park **31** *D5*
Royal Phnom Penh **23** *F5*
Scandinavia **32** *E4*
Simon 2 Guesthouse **34** *B3*
Spring Guesthouse **35** *D3*
Sunway **36** *B3*
Walkabout **37** *C4*

**Eating**

Asia Europe Bakery **1** *D3*
Baan Thai **2** *E4*
Boeung Bopha **5** *A4*
Comme à la Maison **3** *E4*
Elsewhere **6** *D4*
Family **7** *B3*
Garden Centre Café **4** *E4*
Gasolina **8** *F4*
Jars of Clay **11** *F3*
Java **10** *D5*
Khmer Surin **12** *E4*
La Marmite **13** *B4*
Lazy Gecko **14** *B3*
Living Room **29** *E4*
Monsoon **35** *B4*
Mount Everest **15** *D4*
Origami **16** *D5*
Pancho Villa **18** *B4*
Peking Canteen **17** *C3*
Pyong Yang **19** *E3*
Rendezvous **20** *B4*
Sam Doo **21** *C3*
Shiva Shakti **22** *D4*
Tamarind **23** *D4*
Tell **25** *B3*
The Deli **36** *C4*
The Shop **24** *D4*
Topaz **28** *E4*

**Bars & clubs**

Cathouse **26** *C4*
Heart of Darkness & Howie's **27** *C4*
Manhattan at Holiday International
    Hotel **30** *A3*
Peace Café **32** *E4*
Pontoon **40** *B4*
Q-Bar **41** *D4*
Sharkys **9** *C4*
Zepplin **34** *C3*

Cambodia Phnom Penh Sights

## ⦂ Phnom de guerre

Of the original population of Phnom Penh thousands died during the Pol Pot era so the population of the city now seems rural in character. The population tends to vary from season to season: in the dry season people pour into the capital when there is little work in the countryside but go back to their farms in the wet season when the rice has to be planted.

Phnom Penh has long faced a housing shortage – two-thirds of its houses were damaged by the Khmer Rouge between 1975 and 1979 and the rate of migration into the city exceeds the rate of building. Apart from the sheer cost of building new ones and renovating the crumbling colonial mansions, there has been a severe shortage of skilled workers in Cambodia: under Pol Pot 20,000 engineers were killed and nearly all the country's architects.

Exacerbating the problem is the issue of land ownership as so many people were removed from their homes. These days there are many more qualified workers but sky-rocketing property prices coupled with the confusing issue of land title has created a situation where a great land grab is occuring with people being tossed out of their homes or having them bulldozed to make way for profitable developments.

### The riverside and Wat Ounalom

Sisowath Quay is Phnom Penh's Left Bank. A broad pavement runs along the side of the river and on the opposite side of the road a rather splendid assemblage of colonial buildings looks out over the broad expanse of waters. The erstwhile administrative buildings and merchants' houses today form an unbroken chain – almost a mile long – of bars and restaurants, with the odd guesthouse thrown in. While foreign tourist commerce fills the street, the quayside itself is dominated by local Khmer families who stroll and sit in the cool of the evening, served by an army of hawkers.

Phnom Penh's most important wat, **Wat Ounalom**, is north of the national museum, at the junction of Street 154 and Samdech Sothearos Boulevard, facing the Tonlé Sap. The first building on this site was a monastery, built in 1443 to house a hair of the Buddha. Before 1975, more than 500 monks lived at the wat but the Khmer Rouge murdered the Patriarch and did their best to demolish the capital's principal temple. Nonetheless it remains Cambodian Buddhism's headquarters. The complex has been restored since 1979 although its famous library was completely destroyed. The stupa behind the main sanctuary is the oldest part of the wat.

### Central Market, Wat Phnom and Boeng Kak Lake

The stunning Central Market (Psar Thmei) is a perfect example of art-deco styling and one of Phnom Penh's most beautiful buildings. Inside a labyrinth of stalls and hawkers sell everything from jewellery through to curios. Those after a real bargain are better off heading to the Russian Market where items are much cheaper.

**Wat Phnom** stands on a small hill and is the temple from which the city takes its name. It was built by a wealthy Khmer lady called Penh in 1372. The sanctuary was rebuilt in 1434, 1890, 1894 and 1926. The main entrance is to the east; the steps are guarded by nagas and lions. The principal sanctuary is decorated inside with frescoes depicting scenes from Buddha's life and the *Ramayana*. At the front, on a pedestal, is a statue of the Buddha. There is a statue of Penh inside a small pavilion between the vihara and the stupa, with the latter containing the ashes of King Ponhea Yat (1405-1467). The surrounding park is tranquil and a nice escape from the madness of the city. Monkeys with attitude are in abundance but they tend to fight between themselves.

**Boeng Kak Lake** is the main area budget travellers stay in. The lakeside setting with the all important westerly aspect – eg sunsets – appeals strongly to the nocturnal instincts of guests. Some bars and restaurants open 24 hours a day. The lake is quite beautiful, but close to the guesthouses it becomes more like a floating rubbish tip.

## Around Independence Monument

South of the Royal Palace, between Street 268 and Preah Sihanouk Boulevard, is the **Independence Monument**. It was built in 1958 to commemorate independence but has now assumed the role of a cenotaph. **Wat Lang Ka**, on the corner of Sihanouk and Norodom boulevards, was another beautiful pagoda that fell victim to Pol Pot's architectural holocaust. Like Wat Ounalom, it was restored in Khmer style on the direction of the Hanoi-backed government in the 1980s. It is a really soothing getaway from city madness and the monks here are particularly friendly. They hold a free meditation session every Monday and Thursday night at 1800; anyone is welcome to join in.

## Tuol Sleng Museum ('Museum of Genocide')

ⓘ *Street 113, Tue-Sun 0800-1100, 1400-1700; public holidays 0800-1800. US$2; free film show at 1000 and 1500.*

After 17 April 1975 the classrooms of Tuol Svay Prey High School became the Khmer Rouge main torture and interrogation centre, known as Security Prison 21 or S-21. More than 20,000 people were taken from S-21 to their executions at Choeung Ek extermination camp, see below. Countless others died under torture and were thrown into mass graves in the school grounds. Only seven prisoners survived because they were sculptors and could turn out countless busts of Pol Pot. One block of classrooms is given over to photographs of the victims.

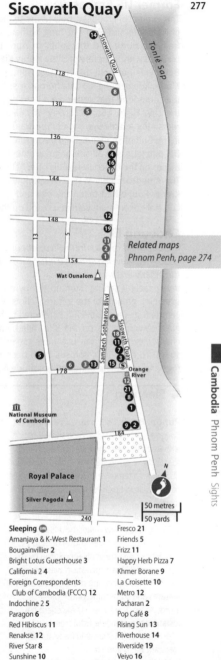

Related maps
Phnom Penh, page 274

**Sleeping** 🛏
Amanjaya & K-West Restaurant 1
Bougainvillier 2
Bright Lotus Guesthouse 3
California 2 4
Foreign Correspondents
  Club of Cambodia (FCCC) 12
Indochine 2 5
Paragon 6
Red Hibiscus 11
Renakse 12
River Star 8
Sunshine 10

Fresco 21
Friends 5
Frizz 11
Happy Herb Pizza 7
Khmer Borane 9
La Croisette 10
Metro 12
Pacharan 2
Pop Café 8
Rising Sun 13
Riverhouse 14
Riverside 19
Veiyo 16

**Eating** 🍴
Bali 1
Cantina 3
Chiang Mai Riverside 4
Fortune Pho 15

**Bars & clubs** 🍸
Ginger Monkey 6
Memphis Pub 17
Pink Elephant Pub 18
Salt Lounge 20

The former US Embassy, now home to the Ministry of Fisheries, is at the intersection of Norodom and Mao Tse Tung boulevards. As the Khmer Rouge closed on the city from the north and the south in April 1975, US Ambassador John Gunther Dean pleaded with Secretary of State Henry Kissinger for an urgent airlift of embassy staff. But it was not until the very last minute (just after 1000 on 12 April 1975, with the Khmer Rouge firing mortars from across the Bassac River onto the football pitch near the compound that served as a landing zone) that the last US Marine helicopter left the city. Flight 462, a convoy of military transport helicopters, evacuated the 82 remaining Americans, 159 Cambodians and 35 other foreigners to a US aircraft carrier in the Gulf of Thailand. Their departure was overseen by 360 heavily armed marines. Despite letters to all senior government figures from the ambassador, offering them places on the helicopters, only one, Acting President Saukham Khoy, fled the country. The American airlift was a deathblow to Cambodian morale. Within five days, the Khmer Rouge had taken the city and within hours all senior officials of the former Lon Nol government were executed on the tennis courts of the embassy.

## Choeung Ek

① *Southwest on Monireth Blvd, about 15 km from town. US$2. Return trip by moto US$2-5, however, a shared car (US$10) is far more comfortable because of the dust on the mainly unsurfaced road.*

In a peaceful setting, surrounded by orchards and rice fields, Choeung Ek was the execution ground for the torture victims of Tuol Sleng, the Khmer Rouge extermination centre, S-21 (see above). It is referred to by some as 'The killing fields'. Today a huge glass tower stands on the site, filled with the cracked skulls of men, women and children exhumed from 129 mass graves in the area (which were not discovered until 1980). To date 8985 corpses have been exhumed from the site. Rather disturbingly, rags and crumbling bones still protrude from the mud.

## Sleeping

**Phnom Penh** *p270, maps p274 and p277*
Boeung Kak Lake has become somewhat of a Khaosan Rd, with most backpackers opting to stay there. Street 182 also offers a selection of cheaper alternatives. The majority of hotels organize airport pick-up and most of them for free.
**LL Le Royal**, St 92, Phnom Penh, T023-981888, www.raffles-hotelleroyal.com. A wonderful colonial era hotel built in 1929 which has been superbly renovated by the Raffles Group. The renovation was done tastefully, incorporating many of the original features and something of the old atmosphere. The hotel has excellent bars, restaurants and a delightful tree-lined pool. 2 for 1 cocktails 1600-2000 daily at the Elephant Bar is a must.
**L-AL Himawari**, 313 Sisowath Quay, T023-214555, www.himawarihotel.com.

With luxurious designer apartments/suites, the Himawari offers an upmarket spot on the river. The usual a/c, cable TV and en suite facilities enhance great river views. Good restaurants, gym and nice pool.
**L-A Cambodiana**, 313 Sisowath Quay, T023-426288, www.hotelcambodiana.com. Originally built for Prince (as he was then) Sihanouk's guests. This eyesore of a building has more than a few Communist touches and it's not surprising that in a former life under the Lol Non regime, it was a military base. The place is redeemed by its vista, which overlooks the confluence of the Mekong, Tonlé Sap and Bassac rivers. 300 rooms, every one of which is equipped with an internet connection. Exceptional facilities.
**L-A Phnom Penh Hotel**, 54 Monivong Blvd, T023-724851, www.phnompenhhotel.com. This hotel comes most recommended from

● *For an explanation of sleeping and eating price codes used in this guide, see inside the*
● *front cover. Other relevant information is found in Essentials, see pages 29-32.*

almost everyone in Cambodia's tourism industry. 407 well-appointed rooms with TV, a/c, internet. Health club, spa and an outdoor swimming pool. Exceptional value.

**AL Amanjaya**, corner St 154 and Sisowath Quay, T023-219579, www.amanjaya.com. Gorgeous rooms full of amenities, beautiful furniture and creative finishing touches. The balconies have some of the best views on the river. Service can be a little ragged – you'll be asked to pay in full when you check-in – but they get enough right to make this probably the nicest place by the river. Free Wi-Fi and awesome breakfast are both included in the room rate. Good location. Recommended.

**AL-A Imperial Garden Villa and Hotel**, 315 Sisowath Quay, T023-219991, www.imperialgarden-hotel.com. Another unsightly archictectural development. The term 'garden', in this context, seems to refer to an area of concrete with the odd plant chucked in for good measure. The rooms (and suites) have a reasonably good view over the river, with wide screen TV, safe and all modern conveniences. Swimming pool, tennis, massage centre, restaurant.

**AL-A Sunway**, No 1 St 92, T023-430333, asunway@online.com.kh. Overlooking Wat Phnom, this is an adequate hotel in an excellent location. 140 ordinary though well-appointed rooms, including 12 spacious suites, provide comfort complemented by facilities and amenities to cater for the international business and leisure traveller.

**A Aram**, St 244, T012-565509, www.boddhitree.com. Nice little guesthouse tucked away in a small street near the palace. The stylish rooms are a bit small and overpriced.

**A Bougainvillier Hotel**, 277G Sisowath Quay, T023-220528, www.bougainvillier hotel.com. Lovely riverside boutique hotel, rooms decorated in a very edgy, modern Asian theme, with a/c, safe, cable TV and minibar. Good French restaurant.

**A Foreign Correspondents Club of Cambodia (FCCC)**, 363 Sisowath Quay, T023-210142, www.fccccambodia.com. Known locally as the FCC. 3 decent sized rooms are available in this well-known Phnom Penh landmark.

**A Juliana**, No 16, St 152, T023-366070, www.julianacambodia.com.kh. A very attractive resort-style hotel with 91 rooms, and decent sized pool in a secluded garden which provides plenty of shade; several excellent restaurants.

**A The Pavilion**, 227 St 19, T023-222280, www.pavilion-cambodia.com. A popular and beautiful small, 10-room hotel set in an old French colonial villa. Each room is unique with a/c, en suite and TV. The restaurant also serves decent food. However, the manage-ment has a reputation for being prickly and a penchant for banning organisations and individuals. Children are completely banned (unless friends of the owner) – we've had several reports of the management abruptly and unceremoniously asking women with children to leave the restaurant.

**A Royal Phnom Penh**, Samdech Sotheros Blvd, T023-982673, royalphnompenh@ bigpond.com.kh. On the Bassac River, a short drive south of the centre, this hotel is set in a large park. A tad run down but still sufficient. Swimming pool, spacious rooms.

**A-B Diamond**, 172-184 Monivong Blvd, T023-217221/2, diamondhotels@online. com.kh. Hotel in a good central location. A little overshadowed by some of the newer and better hotels but the staff are exceptionally helpful and friendly. Rooms are clean with TV and bath.

**A-B Holiday Villa**, 89 Monivong Blvd, T023-990888, www.holidayvilla.com.my. A bit 1970s but well appointed, with bath, internet, TV,safe, IDD phone. Breakfast included.

**A-B Regent Park**, 58 Samdech Sotheros Blvd, T023-427131, regentpark@online. com.kh. The well-designed lobby belies a collection of ordinary rooms and apartment-style suites. Still, it's reasonable value and in a good location. Thai and European restaurant. Price includes breakfast.

**B Flamingo Hotel**, No 30, St 172, T023-221640, reservation@flamingo.com.kh. Reasonably new hotel, bit garish from the outside but good facilities. Well-fitted rooms with all the amenities, including a bath. Free internet, a gym and a restaurant.

**B Red Hibiscus**, No 277c Sisowath Quay, T023-990691, www.redhibiscus.biz. Stylish rooms, some with river views, in an excellent location. A/c, en suite and with TV.

**B Renakse**, 40 Samdech Sothearos Blvd, T023-215701, renakse-htl@camnet.com.kh. Splendid yellow French colonial building in large grounds immediately opposite the Royal Palace. This hotel has the feel of a bygone era. Rooms are decorated in a tasteful, modern Asian style, with Thai-style cushion seats and adjoining mosaic-tiled bathroom.

**B River Star Hotel**, corner of Sisowath Quay and St 118, T023-990501, river_star_hotel@yahoo.com. Decent hotel on the riverfront. The only thing extraordinary about the rooms is the view. All rooms have a/c, bathroom and seating area.

**B Scandinavia Hotel** No 4, St 282, T023-214498, nisse@online.com.kh. Well-appointed, clean rooms with a/c and TV. Very clean. Rooftop restaurant/bar. Pool and Finnish sauna.

**B-C Anise**, 2c St 278, T023-222522, www.anisehotel.com. Excellent value in the heart of a busy area. All rooms are en suite with cable TV, a/c. Pay a little more and you'll get a room with a bathtub and private balcony. Included in the price is laundry, internet and breakfast. Recommended.

**B-C Golden Gate Hotel**, No 9 St 278 (just off St 51), T023-721161, goldengate htls@hotmail.com. Very popular and comparatively good value for the facilities offered. Clean rooms with TV, fridge, hot water and a/c. Within walking distance to restaurants and bars. Visa/MasterCard.

**B-C New York Hotel**, 256 Monivong Blvd, T023-214116, www.newyorkhotel.com.kh. The rooms aren't going to set the world on fire but the facilities are good for the price – massage centre, sauna, restaurant and in-room safe.

**B-C Palm Resort**, on Route 1, 5 km out of Phnom Penh, T023-3086881. Beautiful bungalows surrounded by lush gardens and a very large swimming pool. A/c rooms with very clean bathrooms. Excellent French restaurant. Recommended.

**B-D Paragon Hotel**, 219b Sisowath Quay, T023-222607, info_paragonhotel@yahoo.com. The Paragon gets the simple things right – it's a well-run and friendly hotel. The best and priciest rooms have private balconies overlooking the river – uncomplicated decoration with enough elegant touches to give it character. The cheaper rooms at the back are dark but still some of the best value in this part of town. Each room has colour TV, hot water and private shower or bath, a/c or fan. Recommended.

**C Billabong**, No 5, St 158, T023-223703, www.billabongcambodia.com. Reasonably new hotel with well-appointed and well-decorated rooms. Breakfast included. Swimming pool, poolside bar and deluxe rooms with balconies overlooking the pool. Internet.

**C-D Boddhi Tree**, No 50, St 113, T016-865445, www.boddhitree.com. A tranquil setting. Lovely old wooden building with guest rooms offering simple amenities, fan only, some rooms have private bathroom. Great gardens and fantastic food at very reasonable prices.

**C-D Bright Lotus Guesthouse**, No 22 St 178 (near the museum), T023-990446, sammy_lotus@hotmail.com. Fan and a/c rooms with private bathroom and balconies. Restaurant.

**C-D Hotel California 2**, No 317 Sisowath Quay, T023-982182. One block up from the FCC, overlooking the Tonlé Sap. TV, a/c, attached hot water bathroom with bathtub. Bored-looking staff. Front rooms are single only but with splendid views of the river.

**C-D Indochine 2 Hotel**, No 28-30 St 130, T023-211525. Great location and good, clean, comfortable rooms.

**C-D KIDS Guesthouse**, No 17A, St 178, T012-410406, ryan@ryanhem.com. Rather a good find. Guesthouse of the Khmer Internet Development Service (KIDS) set in a small tropical garden, spotted with a couple of cabana-style internet kiosks. A couple of rooms are a decent size, quite clean and equipped with a huge fridge. Discount on internet use for guests. Welcoming, safe and free coffee.

**C-D L'Imprévu**, on Highway Number 1, 6 km past the Monivong Bridge, T023-360405, imprecas@everyday.com.kh. French-run. Lovely bungalows with TV, fridge and hot water. Good pool and garden. Tennis court, petanque, snooker, table tennis and a gym.

**C-E Sunshine**, No 253 Sisowath Quay, T023-725684. F023-18256. 50 rooms, a few with a glimpse of the river. Facilities, from a/c to fan, in accordance with price.

**C-E Walkabout Hotel**, corner of St 51 and St 174, T023-211715, www.walkabouthotel.com. A popular Australian-run bar, café and guesthouse. 23 rooms ranging from small with no windows and shared facilities to large rooms with own bathroom and a/c. Rooms and bathrooms are okay but lower-end rooms are a little gloomy and cell-like. 24-hr bar.

**D Spring Guesthouse**, No 34, St 111 (next to the German Embassy), T023-222155, spring_guesthouse@yahoo.com. Newly established guesthouse in good location. Fan, cable, a/c, hot shower.

**D-F Capitol**, No 14, St 182, T023-364104, capitol@online.com.kh. As they say, 'a Phnom Penh institution'. What, in 1991, was a single guesthouse has expanded to 5 guesthouses all within a stone's throw. All aim at the budget traveller and offer travel services as well as a popular café and internet access. There are a number of other cheap guesthouses in close proximity, such as **Happy Guesthouse** (next door to Capitol Guesthouse) and **Hello Guesthouse** (No 24, 2 St 107) – all about the same ilk.

**D-F Narin Guesthouse**, No 20 St 111, off Sihanouk Blvd, T023-986131, touchnarin@ hotmail.com. In the western part of the city, not far from the Olympic stadium. Popular but has a bit of a seedy feel to it. Some with en suite bathroom, some with shared. Travel arrangements made.

**E-F Simon 2 Guesthouse**, the road in front of the lake. This place has the largest, cleanest rooms.

**F Café Freedom**, lakeside, T012-807345, www.cafefreedom.org.uk. There are only 7 rooms so more often than not this place is booked out. Nice, relaxing atmosphere, except for the fierce guard dogs.

**F Grandview Guesthouse**, just off the lake, T023-430766. This place is streets ahead of local competition. Clean, basic rooms. A few extra bucks gets you a/c. Nice rooftop restaurant affording good sunset views, with large breakfast menu, pizza, Indian and Khmer food. Travel services and internet.

**F Happy Guesthouse and Restaurant**, No 11, St 93, lakeside, T023-877232. If your idea of good accommodation is staying in a cupboard, then this is the place for you. 40 basic rooms, most with shared facilities but a few with private bathroom. Restaurant, free pool and lovely veranda area.

**F Lazy Fish Guesthouse and Restaurant**, No 16 St 93, lakeside, T012-703368. Very basic guesthouse with shared bathroom facilities.

**F No. 10 Lakeside Guesthouse**, No 10 St 93, Boeng Kak Lake, T012-454373. It is rather dingy and stuffy. Hammocks, pool tables and lockers.

## 🍴 Eating

**Phnom Penh** *p270, maps p274 and p277*
Most places are relatively inexpensive – US$3-6 per head. There are several cheaper cafés along Monivong Blvd, around the lake, Kampuchea Krom Blvd (St 128) in the city centre and along the river. Generally the food in Phnom Penh is good and the restaurants surprisingly refined. One of the most remarkable assemblages of restaurants is to be found on Highway 6, several kilometres beyond the Japanese Friendship (or Chruoy Changvar) Bridge. Also around here is an area that the expats refer to as the 'hammock bar stretch'. A strip of restaurants and beer parlours with a multitude of hammocks which boast great sunset views. Excellent, cheap Khmer food and loads of cold beer, a must. To get there just look for the anchor beer signs on the side of the road.

🍴🍴🍴 **Bougainvillier Hotel**, 277G Sisowath Quay, T023-220528. Upmarket French and Khmer food. Superb foie gras and you can even find truffles here. Fine dining by the river. Recommended.

🍴🍴🍴 **Comme à la Maison**, No 13, St 57, T023-360801. Great French delicatessen-type restaurant-cum-café. Good pizzas and breakfast is exceptional.

🍴🍴🍴🍴 **Elsewhere**, No 175, St 51, T023-211348. An oasis in the middle of the city offering delectable modern Western cuisine. Seats are speckled across wonderful tropical gardens, all topped off by a well-lit pool. This place has everything right – the food, the setting, the music.

🍴🍴🍴 **Foreign Correspondents Club of Cambodia (FCCC)**, No 363 Sisowath Quay, T023-210142. A Phnom Penh institution that can't be missed. Superb colonial building, 2nd floor bar and restaurant overlooks the Tonlé Sap. Extensive menu with an international flavour, fantastic pizzas and creative salads.

**K-West**, Amanjaya Hotel, corner of St 154 and Sisowath Quay, T023-219579. 0630-2200. Beautiful, spacious restaurant offering respite from the outside world. Khmer and European food plus extensive cocktail list. Surprisingly, the prices aren't that expensive considering how upmarket it is. Come early for the divine chocolate mousse – it sells out quickly. Great salads as well. Free Wi-Fi. Recommended.

**Origami**, No 88 SotheAros Blvd, T012-968095. Best Japanese in town, delectable, fresh sushi and sashimi. Pricey – one local describes it as where "good things come in very small, expensive packages".

**Pacharan**, 389 Sisowath Quay, T023-224394, 1100-2300. Excellent Spanish tapas and main courses in a old colonial villa with views across the river and an open kitchen. Stylish Mediterranean feel to it. While the tapas are good value the prices of the main courses are about the highest in town. Part of the FCC empire. Recommended.

**Red Hibiscus**, 277c Sisowath Quay, T023-990691. Eclectic range of crocodile and ostrich steaks on sale at this riverside establishment – the cow steaks are not bad either.

**Riverhouse**, corner of St 110 and Sisowath Quay, T023-220180. Mediterranean/Thai restaurant in a lovely restored building overlooking the river. Brilliant food, particularly the steak, which is cooked to perfection. Upstairs is a comfortable lounge bar which also serves light meals.

**Shiva Shakti**, 70 Sihanouk Blvd, T012-813817. Open until 2230, closed Mon. Facing the Independence Monument. Indian and Moghul specials, vegetarian and meat dishes. The option of pavement eating does not appeal by the side of this busy boulevard but the calm and aromatic atmosphere of the interior is enormously attractive. Quite expensive for Phnom Penh but a good range of excellent food. Selection of cigars.

**Tell**, No 13 St 90, T023-430650. Restaurant closes at 2300, bar at 2400. Swiss German specials including excellent raclette, fondue and wurst. Generous portions authentically prepared. Imported German beer. Owners maintain high standards in the kitchen and in the chalet-esque dining room. There's another branch in Siem Reap.

**Topaz**, 182 Norodom Blvd, T012-333276. 1100-1400, 1800-2300. Has set its sights on being the most upmarket place in town – a/c restaurant or outside dining, upstairs bar and cigar room. Recommended if you can afford it.

**Baan Thai**, No 2, St 306, T023-362991. 1130-1400, 1730-2200. Excellent Thai food and attentive service. Popular restaurant. Garden and old wooden Thai house setting with sit down cushions.

**Bali**, No 379 Sisowath Quay, T023-982211. 0700-2300. A wide range of very tempting Indonesian dishes on offer. Upstairs balcony facing the river.

**Boddhi Tree**, No 50, St 113, T016-865445, www.boddhitree.com. A delightful garden setting and perfect for lunch, a snack or a drink. Delicious salads, sandwiches, barbecue chicken and cheddar is exquisite. Very, very good Khmer food.

**Cantina**, No 347 Sisowath Quay. Great Mexican restaurant and bar opened by long-time local identity, Hurley Scroggins III. Fantastic food made with the freshest of ingredients. The restaurant attracts an eclectic crowd and can be a source of great company.

**Gasolina**, 56/58 St 57, T012-373009, 1100-late. Huge garden and decent French-inspired food await in this friendly, relaxed restaurant. The owner also arranges t'ai chi and capoeira classes. They normally have a BBQ at the weekends.

**Khmer Borane**, No 389 Sisowath Quay, T012-290092, open till 2300. Excellent Khmer restaurant just down from the FCC. Wide selection of very well prepared Khmer and Thai food. Try the Amok.

**La Croisette**, No 241 Sisowath Quay, T023-882221. Authentically French and good value hors d'oeuvres and steak. Sit on the broad pavement dining contentedly with Edith Piaf singing softly in the background. Good selection of wines.

**La Marmite**, No 80 St 108 (on the corner with Pasteur), T012-391746, closed Tue. Excellent value French food – some of the best in town. Extremely large portions.

**Living Room**, No 9 St 306, T023-726139. Tue-Thu 0700-1800, Fri-Sun 0700-2100. The Japanese owner has done a superlative job at this pleasant hangout spot, set in a villa amid a lot of soothing greenery. The food and coffee is spot-on and the set plates are great value but it's the laid back, calming vibe that is the clincher. Bring a book, curl up on the sofa and forget the chaos. There's a purpose-built kids play area downstairs. Free Wi-Fi if you spend over US$3. Highly recommended.

**Metro**, corner of Sisowath and St 148, 1000-0200. Huge, affordable tapas portions make this a great spot for lunch or dinner. The creme brulée smothered in passion fruit is life-affirming. Free Wi-Fi. Recommended.

**Monsoon**, 17 St 104, T016-355867, 1800-0200. They serve a damn fine curry at this funky South Asian restaurant-cum-wine bar. The drinks list is also pretty good and the soft furnishings should lull you into a state of somnolence. Recommended.

**Mount Everest**, 98 Sihanouk Blvd, T023-213821. 1000-2300. Has served acclaimed Nepalese and Indian dishes for 5 years, attracting a loyal following. There's also a branch in Siem Reap.

**Pancho Villa**, No 2 St 108 (just off Sisowath Quay). Good Mexican food, breakfast and coffee. The bar claims to be able to make any cocktail. The Hawaiian-shirt-clad owners are good for a chat.

**Pop Café**, 371 Sisowath Quay, T012-562892, 1100-1430, 1800-2200. Almost perfect, small, Italian restaurant sited next door to the FCC. Owned and managed by Italian ex-pat Giorgio, the food has all the panache you'd expect from an Italian. The home-made lasagne is probably one of the best value meals in town. Recommended.

**Pyong Yang Restaurant**, 400 Monivong Blvd, T023-993765. This North Korean restaurant is an all-round experience not to be missed. The food is exceptional but you need to get there before 1900 to get a seat before their nightly show starts. All very bizarre: uniformed, clone-like waitresses double as singers in the nightly show, which later turns into open-mic karaoke.

**Rendezvous**, No 239 Sisowath Quay, T023-736622. Large comfortable chairs, great place for breakfast or a leisurely lunch and very popular for its 2 for 1 happy hour everyday from 1600-1800. Khmer owned.

**Rising Sun**, No 20, St 178 (just round the corner from the FCC). English restaurant

with possibly the best breakfast in town. Ginormous roast and excellent iced coffee.

**Riverside**, corner 148 and Sisowath Quay, T023-766743. Enjoy omelettes and burgers while dining inside or out.

**Talking to a Stranger**, No 21 St 294, T012-798530, Wed-Sun. Fantastic bar and restaurant with beer garden. Run by a friendly Australian couple, Derek and Wendy. High on atmosphere, brilliant photographic display, wide selection of innovative meals.

**Tamarind**, No 31 St 240, T012-830139. Stylish place specializing in French and Mediterranean, great kebabs and couscous. Bar and tapas. Atmospheric.

**The Deli**, nr corner of St 178 and Norodom Blvd. Great cakes, bread, salads and lunch at this sleek little diner. Sandwich fillings, for the price, are a bit light, though.

**Veiyo** (River Breeze), No 237 Sisowath Quay, T012-847419. Pizza and pasta etc along with Thai and Khmer cuisine.

**Boeung Bopha**, Highway 6 (over the Japanese Friendship Bridge), T012-928353, open until 2300. Large Khmer restaurant with huge menu which includes a number of Khmer dishes and buffet.

**Chiang Mai Riverside**, No 227 Sisowath Quay, T011-811456, open until 2200. Riverfront location for this small but successful Thai restaurant. Simple picture menus (always a turn-off but common in Cambodia where little English is spoken). Endorsed by the Thai government.

**Family Restaurant**, St 93, lakeside. A small, unassuming family-run, Vietnamese restaurant serving brilliant (and quite adventurous) food at ridiculously low prices. Great service, lovely owners.

**Fortune Pho**, St 178, just behind the FCC, 0800-2100. Great Vietnamese noodles in this small shop. Unfortunately your eating experience can sometimes be ruined by dreadful service.

**Friends**, No 215, St 13, T023-426748. Non profit restaurant run by street kids being trained in the hospitality industry. The food is delicious and cheap.

**Frizz**, 335 Sisowath Quay, T023-220953. Awesome Khmer food. Friendly service and great location. One of the best spots to eat local food on the riverside. Incredibly cheap as well. Recommended.

‖ **Happy Herb Pizza**, No 345 Sisowath Quay, T023-332349. A Phnom Penh institution. Watch out for the 'happy' pizza full of hash – it has a nasty kick. Free pizza delivery.

‖ **Khmer Surin**, No 9, St 57, T023-363050, closes at 2230. Set in an attractive building with some traditional Thai-style seating on cushions, this restaurant is a little way south of Sihanouk Blvd. Quiet.

‖ **Lazy Gecko**, St 93, lakeside. Popular, chilled out restaurant/café/bar offering a good selection of sandwiches, burgers and salads in large portions. Good home-cooked Sunday roast. Affable owner, Juan, is a good source of information. Selection of new and used books for sale. Good trivia night on Thu.

‖ **Peking Canteen**, No 393, St 136, T011-909548, open till 2200. Hole in the wall Chinese restaurant famous for its cheap dumplings (which come either steamed or fried). Very busy at lunch time.

‖ **Sam Doo**, 56 Kampuchea Krom Blvd, T023-218773, open until 0200. Late night Chinese food and the best and cheapest dim sum in town.

‖ **The Shop**, No 39, St 240, T012-901964, 0900-1800. Deli and bakery serving sandwiches, juices, fruit teas, salads and lunches.

### Cafés and bakeries

**Asia Europe Bakery**, No 95 Sihanouk Blvd, T012-893177. One of the few Western-style bakery/cafés in the city. Delicious pastries, cakes and excellent breakfast and lunch menu. Recommended.

**Fresco**, 365 Sisowath Quay, T023-217041. Just underneath the FCC and owned by the same people. They have a wide-selection of sandwiches, cakes and pastries of mixed quality and high price.

**Garden Centre Café**, No 23, St 57, T023-363002. Popular place to go for lunch and breakfast, perhaps not surprisingly, the garden is nice too.

**Jars of Clay**, No 39 St 155 (beside the Russian Market). Fresh cakes and pastries.

**Java,** No 56 Sihanouk Blvd. Contenders for best coffee in town. Nice use of space – open-air balcony and pleasant surroundings. Delightful food. Features art and photography exhibitions on a regular basis.

**T&C Coffee World**, numerous branches – 369 Preah Sihanouk Blvd; Sorya Shopping Centre; 335 Monivong Blvd. Vietnamese-run equivalent of **Starbucks**, but better. Surprisingly good food and very good coffee. Faultless service.

## ⑪ Bars and clubs

**Phnom Penh** *p270, maps p274 and p277*
The vast majority of bars in Phnom Penh attract prostitutes.

**Elephant Bar**, Le Royal Hotel. Open until 2400. Stylish and elegant bar in Phnom Penh's top hotel, perfect for an evening gin. 2 for 1 happy hour every day with unending supply of nachos, which makes for a cheap night out in sophisticated surroundings. Probably the best drinks in town.

**Elsewhere,** No 175, St 51. Highly atmospheric, upmarket bar set in garden with illuminated pool and spot seating, lit by candle. Great cocktails and wine. Very popular with the expats, who have been known to strip off for a dip. Livens up on the last Sat of every month for parties.

**Foreign Correspondents Club of Cambodia (FCCC)**, 363 Sisowath Quay. Satellite TV, pool, *Bangkok Post* and *The Nation* both available for reading here, happy hour 1700-1900. Perfect location overlooking the river.

**Ginger Monkey**, No 29, St 178. Stylish, well decorated bar with faux Angkorian reliefs. Chilled out atmosphere. Quite popular with the younger expat crowd.

**Heart of Darkness**, No 26, St 51. Reasonable prices, friendly staff and open late. Has been Phnom Penh's most popular hangout for a number of years. Full of prostitutes, but your best bet for a night of dancing. There have been many violent 'incidents' here, so it is advisable to be on your best behaviour in the bar as they do not tolerate any provocation. An increasingly popular option is **Howie's Bar** next door.

**Hotel California 2**, 317 Sisowath Quay. Restaurant and bar, quite similar to the others on the riverfront. Staff not particularly helpful. US$0.75 pasties a major drawcard.

**La Croisette** has live music every Thu and Fri. See Eating.

**Manhattan**, in the rather dubious **Holiday International Hotel**, St 84, T023-427402. One of Phnom Penh's biggest discos. Security check and metal detectors at the door prevent you from bringing in small arms.

**Memphis Pub**, St 118 (off Sisowath Quay), open till 0200. Small bar off the river. Very loyal following from the NGO crowd. Live rock and blues music from Tue to Sat.

**Metro**, corner Sisowath and St 148, T023-217517, 1000-0200. As well as serving fine grub Metro is also home to a fabulous bar. A/c and smooth surroundings make it popular with rich Khmers and expansive ex-pats. Recommended.

**Peace Café (Sontipheap)**, No 234, St 258. Chilled-out bar with cheap drinks and friendly owner.

**Pink Elephant Pub**, 343 Sisowath Quay. Predominantly male bar with English football, pool, beer and bar food.

**Pontoon**, on the river at end of St 108, T012-572880, 1200-2330 weekdays, until late at weekends. Great little spot for a drink and dance. Hosts international Djs and serves good cocktails. Recommended.

**Q-Bar**, 96 Sothearos Bvld, T092-541821, 1600-0400. This bar has 'imported' (or stolen) most of its design from the famous Bed Supper Club in Bangkok. Expensive, Q-Bar attracts yuppie locals and wannabe foreigners.

**Riverside Bar**, 273a Sisowath Quay. Great riverfront bar. Tasty food. Recommended.

**Riverhouse Lounge**, No 6, St 110 (Sisowath Quay), 1600-0200. Upmarket, cocktail bar and club. Nice views of the river and airy open balcony space. Live music (Sun) and DJs (Sat).

**Salt Lounge**, No 217, St 136, T012-289905, www.thesaltlounge.com. Relatively new, funky minimalist bar. Very atmospheric and stylish. Gay friendly.

**Sharkys**, No 126 St 130. "Beware pickpockets and loose women" it warns. Large, plenty of pool tables and food served until late. Quite a 'blokey' hangout and advertized as the longest running rock and roll bar in Cambodia.

**Talking to a Stranger**, see Eating. Great cocktails and relaxed atmosphere. Recommended.

**The Cathouse**, corner of St 51 and St 118, open till 2400. Around since the UNTAC days of the early 1990s and one of the oldest running bars in the city. Not a bad place to have a beer and wonder what it would look like full of UN soldiers getting drunk, fighting and abusing women.

**The Rising Sun**, No 20, St 178, T023-970719, closes at 2400. Just around the corner from the FCCC. An English pub whose emphasis is just as much on food as beer.

**Zepplin Bar** aka Rock Bar, No 128, St 136 (just off Monivong beside the Central Market), open until late. Hole in the wall bar owned by a Taiwanese man named Joon who has over 1000 records for customers to choose from. Cheap beer and spirits. Truly unique concept and an excellent choice for rocking to your favourite songs.

## ☺ Entertainment

**Phnom Penh** p270, maps p274 and p277
Pick up a copy of the *Cambodia Daily* and check out the back page which details up-and-coming events.

### Dance

**National Museum of Cambodia**, St 70. Folk and national dances are performed by the National Dance group as well as shadow puppets and circus. Every Fri and Sat 1930, US$4.

### Live music

**Memphis Pub**, St 118 (off Sisowath Quay), open till 0200. Small bar off the river, very loyal following from the NGO crowd. Live rock and blues music from Tue-Sat.

**Riverhouse Lounge**, No 6, St 110 (Sisowath Quay). Usually has a guest DJ on the weekends and live jazz on Tue and Sun.

## ○ Shopping

**Phnom Penh** p270, maps p274 and p277
**Art galleries**
**Reyum Institute of Arts and Culture**, No 4, St 178, T023-217149, www.reyum.org. This is a great place to start for those interested in Cambodian modern art. Some absolutely world-class artists have been mentored and exhibit here.

### Handicrafts

Many non-profit organizations have opened stores to help train or rehabilitate some of the country's underprivileged.

**Disabled Handicrafts Promotion Association**, No 317, St 63. Handicrafts and jewellery made by people with disabilities.

**Le Rit's Nyemo**, 131 Sisowath Quay.
Non-profit shop with a wide range of
silk products.
**Orange River**, 361 Sisowath Quay (under
FCCC), T023-214594, has a selection of
beautifully designed decorative items and
a very good stock of fabrics and silks which
will leave many wishing for more luggage
allowance. Pricier than most other stores.
**Rajana**, No 170, St 450, next to the Russian
Market. Traditional crafts, silk paintings,
silver and jewellery.
**The National Centre for Disabled People**,
3 Norodom, T023-210140. Great store
with handicrafts such as pillow cases,
tapestries and bags made by people
with disabilities.

### Markets
**Central Covered Market** (Psar Thmei),
just off Monivong Blvd, distinguished by
its central art deco dome (built 1937),
is mostly full of stalls selling silver and
gold jewellery.
**Tuol Tom Pong**, between St 155 and St 163
to east and west, and St 440 and St 450 to
north and south. Known to many as the
Russian Market. Sells antiques (genuine
articles and fakes) and jewellery as well as
clothing, pirate CDs and computer software,
videos, sarongs, fabrics and an immense
variety of tobacco – an excellent place
for buying souvenirs, especially silk. Most
things at this market are about half the
price of the Central Market.

### Shopping centres
**Sorya Shopping Centre**, St 63, besides
the Central Market. The only 'mall' in the
whole country, a modern, 7-floor, a/c
shopping centre.

### Silverware and jewellery
Old silver boxes, belts, antique jewellery
along Monivong Blvd (the main
thoroughfare), Samdech Sothearos Blvd
just north of St 184, has a good cluster
of silver shops.

### Supermarkets
**Sharky Mart**, No 124, St 130 (below
Sharkys Bar), T023-990303. 24-hr
convenience store.

## ▲ Activities and tours

**Phnom Penh** *p270, maps p274 and p277*
**Cookery courses**
**Cambodia Cooking Class**, No 14, St 285,
T023-882314, www.cambodia-cooking-
class.com.

### Language classes
**The Khmer School of Language**, No 529,
St 454, Tuol Tumpung 2, Chamcar Morn,
T023-213047, www.camb comm.org.uk/ksl.

### Tour operators
**Asian Trails Ltd**, No 22, St 294, Sangkat
Boeng Keng Kong I, Khan Chamkarmorn, PO
Box 621, T023-216555, www.asiantrails.com.
Offers a broad selection of tours: Angkor, river
cruises, remote tours, biking trips.
**Capitol Tours**, No 14AE0, St 182 (see
**Capitol Guesthouse**), T023-217627,
www.bigpond.com.kh/users/capitol.
Cheap tours around Phnom Penh's main
sites. Also organizes tours around the
country. Targeted at budget travellers.
**Exotissimo Travel**, 46 Norodom Blvd,
T023-218948, www.exotissimo.com. Wide
range of day trips and classic tours covering
mainstream destinations: Angkor, Sihanouk-
ville, etc. Also offers tailor-made trips.
**PTM Tours**, No 333B Monivong Blvd,
T023-986363, www.ptm-travel.com.
Reasonably priced package tours to Angkor
and around Phnom Penh. Also offers cheap
hotel reservations.
**RTR Tours**, No 54E Charles de Gaulle Blvd,
T023-210468, www.rtrtours.com.kh.
Organizes tours plus other travel services,
including ticketing. Friendly and helpful.

## ⊙ Transport

**Phnom Penh** *p270, maps p274 and p277*
**Air**
Royal Phnom Penh Airways has
connections with **Siem Reap** and **Stung
Treng**. Bangkok/Siem Reap Airways has
connections with **Siem Reap**.

**Airline offices** Most airline offices are
open 0800-1700, Sat 0800-1200. **Air France**,
Samdeck Sothearos Blvd (Hong Kong
Centre), T023-2192200. **Bangkok/Siem Reap
Airways**, No 61A, St 214, T023-426624,

www.bangkokair.com. **Lao Airlines**, 58C Sihanouk Blvd, T023-216563. **President Airlines**, 13-14, 296 Mao Tse Toung Blvd, T023-993088/89. **Silk Air**, Himawari Hotel, 313 Sisowath Quay, T023-426808, www.silkair.com. **Thai**, 294 Mao Tse Tung Blvd, T023-890292. **Vietnam Airlines**, No 41, St 214, T023-363396/7, www.vietnamairlines.com.

### Bicycle
Hire from guesthouses for about US$1 per day. Cycling is probably the best way to explore the city. It's mostly flat, so not too exhausting.

### Boat
Ferries leave from wharves on the river north of the Japanese Friendship Bridge and from Sisowath Quay daily. There are supposed to be connections to **Siem Reap** (Angkor), **Kratie** and **Stung Treng**. In recent times the Mekong service (Kratie, Stung Treng) hasn't been running as they can't get enough customers now the roads have been improved. Fast boat connections (5 hrs) with **Siem Reap**, US$25 1-way, **Kratie**, US$7.85, and **Stung Treng** US$15.70. In the low season the trip to Siem Reap can take up to 6-7 hrs. Boats do sometimes break down and promised express boats often turn out to be old chuggers but it costs less than flying. All boats leave early, 0700 or earlier. Most hotels will supply ferry tickets (happy to collect the commission).

### Bus
Most buses leave southwest of Psar Thmei (Central Market) by the Shell petrol station. **Capitol Tours**, T023-217627, departs from its terminal, No 14, St 182. **GST**, T012-838910, departs from the southwest corner of the Central Market (corner of St 142). **Phnom Penh Public Transport Co** (formerly Ho Wah Genting Bus Company), T023-210359, departs from Charles de Gaulle Blvd, near the Central Market. To **Kratie**, 1 bus per day (US$4); Capitol Tours runs a bus to **Kampot**, 0800, US$2.50. There are also frequent departures from the Central Market (Psar Thmei) bus terminal. Around Khmer New Year and during the peak season you will need to book tickets the day before travel. **Phnom Penh Bus Co** to **Sihanoukville**, 0700, 0730, 0830, 1230 and

1330. **GST** buses leave at 0715, 0815, 1230 and 1330, 4 hrs. To Siem Reap, see page 339.

### Car
Chauffeur-driven cars are available at most hotels from US$25 per day upwards. Several travel agents will also hire cars. Prices increase if you're venturing out of town. **Car Rental**, T012-950950.

### Cyclo
Plentiful but slow. Fares can be bargained down but are not that cheap – a short journey should be no more than 1000 riel. A few cyclo drivers speak English or French. They are most likely to be found loitering around the big hotels and can also be hired for the day (around US$5).

### Moto
'Motodops' are 50-100cc motorbike taxis and the fastest way to get around Phnom Penh. Standard cost per journey is around US$0.50 for a short hop but expect to pay double after dark. If you find a good, English-speaking moto driver, hang on to him and he can be yours for US$8-10 per day.

### Shared taxi
These are either Toyota pick-ups or saloons. For the pick-ups the fare depends upon whether you wish to sit inside or in the open; vehicles depart when the driver has enough fares. **Psar Chbam Pao**, just over Monivong Bridge on Route 1, for **Vietnam**. For **Sihanoukville** and **Siem Riep**, take a shared taxi from the Central Market (Psar Thmei). Leave early 0500-0600. Shared taxi to **Kampot** takes 2-3 hrs, US$4, leaving from Doeum Kor Market on Mao Tse Tung Blvd.

### Taxi
There are only a few taxis in Phnom Penh as the risk of being held up at gunpoint is too high. It is possible to get a taxi into town from the airport and one or two taxi companies can be reached by telephone but expect to see no cabs cruising and no meter taxis. **Taxi Vantha**, T012-855000/ 023-982542, 24 hrs.

Phnom Penh hotels will organize private taxis to **Sihanoukville** for around US$25.

# ❶ Directory

**Phnom Penh** *p270, maps p274 and p277*
**Banks**   **ANZ Royal Bank**, Russian Bvd,
20 Kramuon Sar (corner of street 67), has
opened a number of ATMs throughout
Phnom Penh: also near the Independence
Monument and at 265 Sisowath Quay.
**Canadia Bank**, No 126 Charles de Gaulle
Blvd, T023-214668; 265-269 Ang Duong St,
T023-215286. Cash advances on credit cards.
**Cambodia Commercial Bank**(CCB), No 130
Monivong Blvd (close to the Central Market),
T023-426208. Cash advance on credit cards,
TCs and currency exchange. **Union
Commercial Bank** (UCB), No 61, St 130,
T023-724931. Most banking services, charges
no commission on credit card cash advances.

### Embassies and consulates
**Australia**, No 11, St 254, T023-213470,
australia.embassy.cambodia@dfat.gov.au.
**Canada**, No 11, St 254, T023-213470,
pnmpn@dfait-maeci.gc.ca. **France**,
1 Monivong Blvd, T023-430020,
sctipcambodge@online.com.kh. **Laos**,
15-17 Mao Tse Tung Blvd, T023-983632.
**Thailand**, 196 Norodom Blvd, T023-7263
0610, thaipnp@mfa.go.th. **United Kingdom**,
No 29, St 75, T023-427124,
britemb@online.com.kh. **USA**, No16, St 228,
T023-216436, usembassy@camnet.com.kh

(A new US Embassy was under construction
near Wat Phnom at the time of publication).
**Vietnam**, 436 Monivong Blvd, T023-362531,
embvnpp@camnet.com.kh.

### Immigration
Opposite the international airport.
Visa extensions, photograph required,
1-month US$30.

### Internet
Cheap and ubiquitous. Rates can be as low
as US$0.50 per hr although in many places
they are higher.

### Medical services
It is highly advisable to try and get to
Bangkok if you are seriously ill or have
injured yourself as Cambodia's medical
services are not up to scratch. **Calmette
Hospital**, 3 Monivong Blvd, T023-426948,
is generally considered the best. 24-hr
emergency. **Surya Medical Services**, No 39,
St 294, T016-8450000, Mon-Fri 0700-2000,
Sat-Sun 0700-1800. General medicine and
tropical medicine. After hours emergency
care available 24-hrs. **Pharmacy de la Gare**,
81 Monivong Blvd, T023-526855.

### Post office
Main post office, St 13, possible to make
international telephone calls from here.

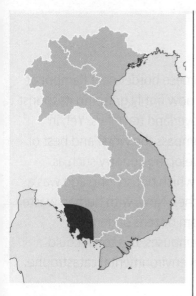

# Southern Cambodia

## Footprint features

# Introduction

With the opening of the Vietnamese border near Kampot at Ha Tien, southern Cambodia is now firmly grasping its tourist potential as a staging post for overland travellers. Yet, in many ways it manages to encompass the worst and best of what tourism can offer to a developing country such as Cambodia. Take Sihanoukville, which not so long ago was a sleepy port offering idyllic beaches. Now, with human waste pouring directly into the sea from dozens of generic backpacker shanty bars and flophouses, this town could almost offer a textbook study in environmental catastrophe.

Travel down the coast to Kep and Kampot, and things couldn't be more different. An old French trading port overlooking the Prek Kamping Bay River and framed by the Elephant Mountains, low-key Kampot, is filled with decrepit dusty charm. Just outside Kampot is Kep, the resort of choice for France's colonial elite, which is now slowly reasserting its position as a place for rest and recuperation. Don't go to Kep expecting wild nights or even a great beach, but perfect views, good seafood and serenity are on offer here.

Northwest from Sihanoukville is Koh Kong province, a vast, wild and untamed expanse of jungle that smothers the stunning Cardamom Mountain range in a thick green blanket. There's now a sealed road through here linking Sihanoukville with Thailand. With logging companies waiting in the wings, this area is now facing an uncertain future.

★ **Don't miss ...**

1 Kampot, page 296.
2 Bokor Hill Station, page 297.
3 Kep, page 298.

20 km
20 miles

*Gulf of Thailand*

CAMBODIA

VIETNAM

PHNOM PENH

KOMPONG CHAM

PREY VANG

KANDAL

TAKEO

AN GIANG

KAMPOT

KOMPONG SPEU

KOH KONG

PURSAT

# Sihanoukville 🏨🍴🚌▲🎷 » *pp298-302. Colour map 6, C2.*

If Sihanoukville was being tended with care it would occupy a lovely site on a small peninsula whose nobbly head juts out into the Gulf of Thailand. The first rate beaches, clean waters, trees and invigorating breezes are slowly being replaced with human effluvia, piles of stinking rubbish and nasty flophouses. Cambodia's beaches could be comparable to those in Thailand but are slowly being horribly degraded. Most people head for beaches close to the town which, starting from the north, are Victory, Independence, Sokha, Ochheauteal and, a little further out, Otres. Sihanoukville's layout is unusual, with the 'town' itself, acting as a satellite to the roughly equidistant three beaches. The urban area is pretty scattered and has the distinct feel of a place developing on an ad hoc basis. It has a few large Chinese hotels, a market, petrol stations and a couple of bars.

## Ins and outs

From Phnom Penh there are regular departures in comfortable, well-maintained, a/c coaches to Sihanoukville, costing US$3-4. Buses generally leave every half hour from 0700 until 1330. Taxis cost US$20-30. Without a proper bus linking Sihanoukville to Kampot and Kep, journey along the shoreline is not always the easiest though there are plentiful buses from Phnom Penh to these coastal jewels. Departing from Sihanoukville there are taxis to Kampot and Phnom Penh around 0700-0800, US$5-6. You can travel to Koh Kong via the brand new road (a whole series of bridges are due to open in late 2008) from Sihanoukville or Hat Lek, Thailand. » *For further information, see Transport, page 302.*

## Background

Sihanoukville, or Kompong Som as it is called during the periods the king is in exile or otherwise 'out of office', was founded in 1964 by Prince Sihanouk to be the nation's sole deep-water port. It is also the country's prime seaside resort. In its short history it has crammed in as much excitement as most seaside towns see in a century – but not of the sort that resorts tend to encourage. Sihanoukville was used as a strategic transit point for weapons used in fighting the USA, during the Vietnam War. In 1975, the US bombed the town when the Khmer Rouge seized the container ship *SS Mayaguez*.

   Sihanoukville has now turned a corner, however, and with rapid development has firmly secured its place in Cambodia's 'tourism triangle', alongside Phnom Penh and Angkor Wat. Not much of this development is sustainable and nearly every single island has now been bought up by Koreans and Russians, with incredibly bad taste, tacky and overpriced resorts already being built. While a liberal attitude towards the smoking of marijuana attracts a youthful crowd, no amount of intoxicants can cover up the fact that Sihanoukville is rapidly becoming an environmental stain on this already horribly scarred country. If it all becomes too much there are vast unspoiled areas close by in the coastal Preah Sihanouk 'Ream' National Park.

## Sights

**Victory Beach** is a thin, 2-km-long beach on the north of the peninsula, just down from the port, and at its extremes offers reasonably secluded beaches. Beach hawkers are ubiquitous and outnumber tourists at a ratio of about three to one. The area does afford a good sunset view, however. **Independence Beach** was at one time the sole preserve of the once bombed and charred – and now beautifully restored – **Independence Hotel**. The location of the hotel is magnificent and the grounds are a reminder of the place's former grandeur. With the restoration of this sleek hotel complete, its re-opening will do a lot to revive Independence Beach's fortunes. **Sokha**

**Beach** is arguably Sihanoukville's most beautiful beach. The shore laps around a 1-km arc and even though the large **Sokha Beach Resort** has taken up residence it is very rare to see more than a handful of people on the beach. It is stunning and relatively hassle-free. **Ochheauteal Beach** lies to the south and, bizarrely, is the most popular with hordes of backpackers and 'sex-pats'. What was once a sparkling stretch of white sand has been reduced to an unending dustbin of rickety, badly planned budget bars, restaurants and accommodation. Much of this has been built directly on the beach, with concrete foundations poured into what could be a stunning waterfront. Coupled with this is a complete lack of proper sewerage and stinking waste pours straight into the sea. Even more astonishing are the tourists and travellers who seem content to swim opposite the pipe openings, the once white foam of the waves turning a yucky brown. If all this isn't enough to put you off, then there is the unrelenting hassle you will get from hawkers and hordes of child vendors pursuing sales very aggressively. Watch your stuff as theft is also common here. The beach commonly referred to as **Serendipity Beach** is at the very north end of Ochheauteal and is basically Ochheauteal-like, complete with stinking sewer pipes. This little strand has gained flavour with travellers due in part to being the first beach

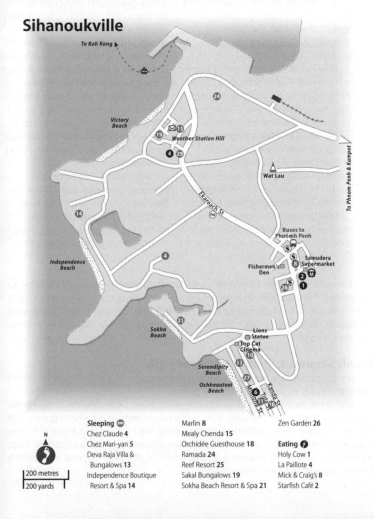

# Sihanoukville

*To Koh Kong*

*Victory Beach*

*Weather Station Hill*

*Ekareach St*

*Wat Lau*

*To Phnom Penh & Kampot*

Buses to Phnom Penh

Samudera Supermarket

Fishermen's Den

*Independence Beach*

*Sokha Beach*

Lions Statue
Top Cat Cinema

*Serendipity Beach*

*Ochheauteal Beach*

*Tola St*
*Mithona St*
*Kanda St*

N

200 metres
200 yards

**Sleeping**
Chez Claude **4**
Chez Mari-yan **5**
Deva Raja Villa &
  Bungalows **13**
Independence Boutique
  Resort & Spa **14**

Marlin **8**
Mealy Chenda **15**
Orchidée Guesthouse **18**
Ramada **24**
Reef Resort **25**
Sakal Bungalows **19**
Sokha Beach Resort & Spa **21**

Zen Garden **26**

**Eating**
Holy Cow **1**
La Paillote **4**
Mick & Craig's **8**
Starfish Café **2**

## Sihanoukville's islands

More than 20 beautiful islands and pristine coral reefs lie off Sihanoukville's coastline. Most of the islands are uninhabited except Koh Russei (Bamboo Island), Koh Rong Salaam and a few others that contain small fishing villages.

Diving and snorkelling around the islands is pretty good. The coast offers an abundance of marine life including star fish, sea anemones, lobsters and sponge and brain coral. Larger creatures like stingrays, angel fish, groupers, barracuda, moray eels and giant clams are ubiquitous. Baby whale sharks and reef sharks also roam the waters. More elusive are the black dolphins, pink dolphins, common dolphins and bottle-nosed dolphins but they are sighted from time to time. It is believed that further afield (closer to Koh Kong) are a family of dugongs (sea cows). No one has sighted these rare creatures except for one hotel owner who sadly saw a dugong head for sale in Sihanoukville's market.

The islands are divided into three separate groups: the Kampong Som Group, the Ream Group and the Royal Islands. The **Kampong Som Islands** are the closest to Sihanoukville and have quite good beaches. Here the visibility stretches up to 40 m. Koh Pos is the closest island to Sihanoukville, located just 800 m from Victory Beach. Most people prefer Koh Koang Kang also known as Koh Thas, which is 45 minutes from shore. This island has two beautiful beaches (with one named after Elvis) and the added attraction of shallow rocky reefs, teeming with wildlife, which are perfect for snorkelling. More rocky reefs and shallow water can be found at the **Rong Islands**. Koh Rong is about two hours west of Sihanoukville and has a stunning, 5-km-long sand beach (on the southwest side of the island). To the south of the Koh Rong is Koh Rong Salaam, a smaller island that is widely considered Cambodia's most beautiful. There are nine fantastic beaches spread across this island and on the east coast a lovely heart-shaped bay. It takes about 2½ hours to get to Koh Rong from Sihanoukville. Koh Kok, a small island off Koh Rong Salaam, is one of the firm favourite dive sites, warranting it the nickname 'the garden' and takes 1¾ hours to get there.

During winter (November to February) the **Ream Islands** are the best group to visit as they are more sheltered than some of the other islands but they are a lot further out.

The Ream Islands encompass those

in Sihanoukville to offer a wide range of budget accommodation. At the time of publication, the many guesthouses and restaurants lining the shore of Serendipity and the extended Ochheauteal Beach area were at the centre of a land dispute with developers hankering to clear the budget accommodation to make way for large Thai-style resorts.

### Preah Sihanouk 'Ream' National Park → *Colour map 6, C2.*

ⓘ *To12-875096, daily 0700-1715. Boat trip (half or 1 day), US$30 for 4 people. Nature trek with a guide (3- to 5-hrs), US$5 per person.*

This beautiful park is a short 30-minute drive from Sihanoukville, hugging the coastline of the Gulf of Thailand. It includes two islands and covers 21,000 ha of beach, mangrove swamp, offshore coral reef and the Prek Tuk Sap Estuary. Samba deer, endangered civet species, porcupines and pangolin are said to inhabit the park, as well as dolphins. To arrange a guided tour visit the park office or arrange one through a guesthouse in Sihanoukville.

islands just off the Ream coast: Prek Mo Peam and Prek Toek Sap, which don't offer the clearest waters. The islands of Koh Khteah, Koh Tres, Koh Chraloh and Koh Ta Kiev are best for snorkelling. Giant mussels can be seen on the north side of Koh Ta Kiev island. Some 50 km out are the outer Ream Islands which, without a doubt, offer the best diving in the area. The coral in these islands though has started to deteriorate and is now developing a fair bit of algae. Kondor Reef, 75 km west of Sihanoukville, is a favorite diving spot. A Chinese junk filled with gold and other precious treasures is believed to have sunk hundreds of years ago on the reef and famous underwater treasure hunter, Michael Archer, has thoroughly searched the site but no one can confirm whether he struck gold.

Koh Tang, Koh Prins and Paulo Wai are 7 hours away to the southwest. These islands are believed to have visibility that stretches for 40 m and are teeming with marine life, they are recommended as some of the best dive sites. It is believed that Koh Prins once had a modern shipwreck and sunken US helicopter but underwater scavengers looking for steel and US MIA guys have completely cleared the area. Large schools of yellow fin tuna are known to inhabit the island's surrounding waters. Koh Tang is worth a visit but is quite far from the mainland so an overnight stay on board might be required. Many local dive experts believe Koh Tang represents the future of Cambodia's diving. The island became infamous in May 1975 when the US ship *SS Mayaguez* was seized by the Khmer Rouge just off here. The area surrounding Paulo Wai is not frequently explored, so most of the coral reefs are still in pristine condition.

Closer to Thailand lies Koh Sdach (King's Island), a stop off on the boat ride between Sihanoukville and Koh Kong. This undeveloped island is home to about 4000 people, mostly fishing families. The beaches are a bit rocky but there is some fabulous snorkelling. At the time of publication a guesthouse was being built on the island so it should be possible to stay.

The Cambodian diving industry is still in its fledgling years. The positive in this is that most of the islands and reefs are still in relatively pristine condition and the opportunities to explore unchartered waters limitless.

Some of the islands mentioned above now have guesthouses and hotels, see page 299 for details.

# Koh Kong and around 🏨🍴🚌🛈 ➤ pp299-302. Colour map 6, C1.

Dusty Koh Kong is better known for its brothels, casinos and 'Wild West' atmosphere than for lying at the heart of a protected area with national park status (granted by Royal Decree in 1993). It is also often confused with its beautiful offshore namesake Koh Kong Island. The town is also reputed to have the highest incidence of HIV infection of anywhere in Cambodia and is a haven for members of the Thai mafia trying to keep their heads down and launder large sums of money through the casino. The place is only really used by travellers as a transit stop on the way to and from Thailand or two of the most scenic places in Cambodia – Koh Kong Island and the Cardamom Mountains.

## Central Cardamoms Protected Forest

ⓘ *The area remains relatively inaccessible but over the next few years it is anticipated that ecotourism operators will flock to the area. For now, it is best to make short trips into the park as the area is sparsely populated and heavily mined (so stay on clearly*

**To Thailand via Koh Kong**

The border crossing is 12 km from Koh Kong, across the river (15-20 mins). The border is open 0700-2000.

Transport The trip to the border at Cham Yem costs ฿60 by moto, ฿50 by shared taxi and US$6 with own taxi. There are public minibuses on the Thai side to Trat (84 km, 1¼ hrs, until 1800, ฿150). You can find private taxis after 1800 but bidding will start at A1000. From Trat buses run to Pattaya, Bangkok and Bangkok airport.

*marked paths). Take a motorbike (with an experienced rider) or a boat. The latter option is more convenient in Koh Kong. There are usually several men with boats willing to take the trip down the Mohaundait Rapids, cutting through the jungled hills and wilderness of the Cardomoms. The cost of the trip is between US$25-30.*

In 2002, the government announced the creation of the **Central Cardamoms Protected Forest**, a 402,000-ha area in Cambodia's Central Cardamom Mountains. With two other wildlife sanctuaries bordering the park, the total land under protection is 990,000 ha – the largest, most pristine wilderness in mainland Southeast Asia. The extended national park reaches widely across the country, running through the provinces of Koh Kong, Pursat, Kompong Speu and Battambang. Considering that Cambodia has been severely deforested and seen its wildlife hunted to near-extinction, this park represents a good opportunity for the country to regenerate both flora and fauna. The Cardamoms are home to most of Cambodia's large mammals and half of the country's birds, reptiles and amphibians. The mountains have retained large populations of the region's most rare and endangered animals, such as the Indochinese tigers, Asian elephants and sun bears. Globally threatened species like the pileated gibbon and the critically endangered Siamese crocodile, which has its only known wild breeding population here, exist in the Cardamoms. Environmental surveyors have identified 30 large mammal species, 30 small mammal species, more than 500 bird species, 64 reptiles and 30 amphibians, that reside in the park. Conservationists are predicting they will discover other animals that have disappeared elsewhere in the region such as the Sumatran rhinoceros. With virgin jungles, waterfalls, rivers and rapids this area represents a huge untapped ecotourism potential. However, tourist services to the area are still quite limited.

## Koh Kong Island → *Colour map 6, C1.*

ⓘ *The island is accessible by bridge from the mainland.* The island (often called Koh Kong Krau) is arguably one of Cambodia's best islands. There are six white powdery beaches each stretching kilometre after kilometre, while a canopy of coconut trees shade the glassy-smooth aqua waters. It's a truly stunning part of the country and has been earmarked by the government for further development, so go now, while it's still a little utopia. There are a few frisky dolphin pods that crop up from time to time – both from the black and the white species. Their intermittent appearances usually take place in the morning and in the late afternoon.

# Kampot and around 🔵🔵🔺🔵🔵 ›› *pp299-302. Colour map 6, C2 and C3.*

Kampot is a charming riverside town that was established in the early 1900s by the French. The town lies at the base of the Elephant Mountain Range, 5 km inland on the river Prek Thom and was for a long time the gateway to the beach resort at Kep (see page 298). On one side of the river are tree-lined streets, crumbling mustard yellow French shop fronts and a sleepy atmosphere, whilst on the other side you will find locals working in the surrounding salt pans. The town has the feel of another era – with a dabbling of Chinese architecture and overall French colonial influence – which, with a bit of restoration work, could easily be compared to UNESCO World Heritage Sites such as Hoi An in Vietnam and Luang Prabang in Laos. Life is very laid-back in Kampot and the town has become a regular expat retreat with Phnom Penh-ites ducking down here for a breath of fresh air and a cooler climate.

## Bokor Mountain National Park → *Colour map 6, C2.*

ⓘ *42 km (90 mins) from Kampot. US$5. Park rangers can speak some English and have a small display board on the flora and fauna in the park at their office. There are dorms (US$5) and double rooms (US$20) and a few basic dishes available. A moto and driver for the day will cost around US$15 or a car for around US$30.*

Bokor Mountain National Park's plateau, at 1040 m, peers out from the southernmost end of the Elephant Mountains with a commanding view over the Gulf of Thailand and east to Vietnam. Bokor Hill (Phnom Bokor) is densely forested and in the remote and largely untouched woods scientists have discovered 30 species of plants unique to the area. Not for nothing are these called the Elephant Mountains and besides the Asian elephant there are tigers, leopards, wild cows, civets, pigs, gibbons and numerous bird species. At the peak of the mountain is **Bokor Hill Station**, where eerie, abandoned, moss-covered buildings sit in dense fog. The buildings were built by the French, who attracted by Bokor's relative coolness, established a 'station climatique' on the mountain in the 1920s. In 1970 Lon Nol shut it down and Bokor was quickly taken over by Communist guerrillas; it later became a strategic military base for the Khmer Rouge. In more recent years there was a lot of guerrilla activity in the hills, but the area is now safe, with the exception of the danger, ever-present in Cambodia, of landmines. The ruins are surprisingly well preserved but bear evidence of their tormented past. There is a double waterfall called **Popokvil Falls**, a 2-km walk from the station, which involves wading through a stream, though in the wet season this is nigh on impossible.

# Kampot

*To 6*

*To Bokor Mountain National Park (42 km) & Sihanoukville*

*To Phnom Penh (Route 3) & Caves*

Prek Thom

Riverside Walk

Old Market

Canadia $

Obelisk Roundabout

Acleda $

Taxis
Naga Statue

Statue of 3 Soldiers

*To Kep (25 km) & Caves*

N

200 metres
200 yards

**Sleeping**
Blissful Guesthouse 3
Bodhi Villa 6
Bokor Mountain Lodge 9
Borey Bokor 1 1

Little Garden Bar 5
Long Villa 13
Molieden 7

**Eating**
Epic Arts Café 2
Jasmine 3
Rusty Key Hole 4

Cambodia Southern Cambodia Kampot & around

**Kbal Romeas caves and temple** → *Colour map 6, C3.*

Ten kilometres outside Kampot, on the roads to both Phnom Penh and to Kep, limestone peaks harbour interesting caves with stalactites and pools. It is here that you can find one of Cambodia's hidden treasures – an 11th-century temple slowly being enveloped by stalactites and hidden away in a cave in Phnom Chhnok, next to the village of Kbal Romeas. The temple, which is protected by three friendly monks, was discovered by Adhemer Leclere in 1866. Many motos and cars now do trips.

---

# Kep ●🏛🍴🚌 → *pp300-302. Colour map 6, C3.*

ⓘ *Jul-Oct Kep is subject to the southeast monsoon, occasionally rendering the beach unswimmable because of the debris brought in.*

Tucked in on the edge of the South China Sea, Kep was established in 1908 by the French as a health station for their government officials and families. The ruins of their holiday villas stand along the beachfront and in the surrounding hills. They were largely destroyed during the civil war under Lon Nol and by the Khmer Rouge and were then further ransacked during the famine of the early 1980s when starving Cambodians raided the villas for valuables to exchange for food.

At the time of publication, Kep still hadn't hit the radar of many international touritsts. It is very popular on weekends with holidaying Cambodians who have managed to keep this idyllic town one of the country's best kept secrets. Beautiful gardens and lush green landscape juxtaposed against the blue waters make it one of the most wonderfully relaxing places in the country. The town itself only has one major beach, a pebbly murky water pool which doesn't really compare with Sihanoukville beaches but they can be found at almost all of the 13 outlying islands where you can snorkel and dive although this is better around the islands off Sihanoukville; Kep is considerably more beautiful than Sihanoukville and much more relaxing. It is famous for the freshly caught crab which is best eaten on the beach (US$1.50 per kilo) and the *tik tanaout jiu,* palm wine. From Kep it is possible to hire a boat to **Rabbit Island** (Koh Toensay). Expect to pay about US$10 to hire a boat for the day. There are four half-moon beaches on this island which have finer, whiter sand than Kep beach.

---

## ● Sleeping

**Sihanoukville** *p292, map p293*
**L-AL The Independence Boutique Resort and Spa**, Independence Beach, T034-934300. Undoubtedly the most groovy and gorgeous hotel in town, The Independence has been beautifully restored to all its modernist glory. The rooms are minimalist, chic and complete with a/c, TV, bathtub and other luxuries. Great sea views from the hilltop perch, it's also set in some pleasing gardens with a pool. This is exactly the kind of thing Sihanoukville needs to pull itself out of its current malaise. You can also haggle the rates down when it is quiet. Highly recommended.
**AL-A Ramada Hotel and Resort**, Port Hill, T034-393916. The most expensive accommodation in its part of town. All mod cons in this upmarket though faintly dull property. Pool and tennis courts.

**L-A Sokha Beach Resort and Spa**, Street 2 Thnou, Sangkat 4, Sokha Beach, T034-935999, www.sokhahotels.com. A deluxe, 180-room beachfront resort and spa, set amid an expansive 15 ha of beachfront gardens and fronting a pristine white sandy beach. Guests have a choice between hotel suites or private bungalows dotted in the tropical gardens. The hotel has fantastic facilities including a landscaped pool, tennis court, archery range, children's club and in-house Philipino band at night. Rooms are impressive, with beautiful Italian linen and lovely bathtubs. The hotel also has a somewhat incongruous stretched SUV, fitted out with minibar, karaoke and a 15-seat lounge (US$50). The hotel has very low occupancy, so check if it can offer a discount as it's always running special deals.

**B Chez Claude**, between Sokha Beach and Independence Beach, T012-824870. A beautiful hillside spot with 9 bungalows representsing a cross-section of indigenous housing. The restaurant has fantastic views.

**B Reef Resort**, Serendipity Beach, T012-315338, www.reefresort.com.kh. well run, small hotel at the top of the hill near the garish golden lions roundabout. Rooms are a touch overpriced but there is a nice, little pool and mammoth breakfast included. Probably the best mid-range place in town and always full, so book ahead. Has a bar and restaurant which serves average food. Recommended.

**B Deva Raja Villa and Bungalows**, Serendipity Beach, T012-1600374, www.devarajavilla.com. Great little boutique type affair with stylish rooms, en suite facilities with nice bathtubs, a/c. Good restaurant. Recommended.

**C-D Chez Mari-yan**, Sankat 3, Khan Mittapheap, T034-916468. Currently the best bungalow-style place to stay in this end of town. Offers a block of hotel rooms and simple wooden and concrete bungalows perched on stilts at the top of a hill affording nice sea views. Restaurant sports a short menu which features fish, squid and crab.

**C-D Marlin Hotel**, Ekareach St, T012-890373. Recent refurb at this friendly downtown hostelry. Serves food and hosts a bar and there's Wi-Fi too. Good value a/c and fan rooms, but don't expect anything too fancy.

**C-D Orchidée Guesthouse**, Tola St, T034-933639, www.orchideeguest house.com. Does not belie its name and the courtyard full of beautiful orchids provides an auspicious welcome. Well run, properly maintained, clean and well-aired rooms, with a/c and hot water. Restaurant with Khmer and Western seafood. Nice pool area, a 5-min walk to the Ochheauteal Beach.

**D-F Mealy Chenda**, on the crest of Weather Station Hill, T034-670818. Very popular hotel offering accommodation to suit a wide range of budgets from dorm rooms through to a/c double rooms. Sparkly clean with fantastic views from the restaurant.

**E-F Sakal Bungalows**, near the end of Weather Station Hill, T012-806155, 012806155@mobitel.com.kh. 10 simple but cheap bungalows in a garden setting. Restaurant and bar, cheap internet. Closest bungalows to Victory Beach.

**F Zen Garden**, just south of downtown area, T011-262376. Nice setting in an old wooden building in a relaxed back street. Rooms are very basic but very cheap. Good budget option. Also have dorms and serve food.

**Sihanoukville Islands**
There are currently 3 accommodation options.
**L Mirax Hotel**, Koh Dek Koul Island, T012-966503, www.miraxresort.com. Grotesque island resort that epitomizes everything nasty about Cambodian tourism.

**C-F Jonty's Jungle Camp**, Koh Ta Kiev Island, T092-502374, www.jontysjungle camp.com. Basic, hammock-style camping accommodation in this gorgeous island retreat. Don't come expecting any mod cons but you will be given a mosquito net. Price drops if you stay for more than one night. Great snorkelling nearby, idyllic if you like this sort of thing. Serve their own basic food. Price includes long-tail to and from the island.

**D Koh Ru**, Koh Russie Island, T012-388860. Run by the owner of Bar Ru this is a quaint collection of simple fan bungalows in a lovely beachside location. Totally relaxed and quiet, this is a decent spot to really get away from it all. Food and drink available.

**Koh Kong and around** p295
Many of the small guesthouses scattered around the town double as brothels.
**D-E Bopha Koh Kong**, 2 blocks east of the boat pier, T035-963073. Good, clean rooms with all amenities – a/c, cable, fridge. More expensive rooms have bathtub and hot water. Pretty good value. Also has a restaurant.

**E-F Otto's**, a block south of the boat pier, T012-924249, 012924249@mobitel.com.kh. Basic fan rooms in a nice wooden house. Shared bath, fan, mosquito net, rather random and kitsch decor. Old wooden structure, feels like a bungalow, bit dirty, good size though. The German owner also runs the best restaurant in town serving Western, Khmer and Thai food. Otto is a good source of tourist information. Books for sale/swap. Internet. Recommended.

**Kampot and around** p296, map p297
There is now a good range of accommodation in Kampot. Some guesthouses seem to have been set up to indulge their owner's ganja smoking habits

and you may feel left out if you're not interested in engaging in this past-time.

**B Bokor Mountain Lodge**, 033-932314, www.bokorlodge.com. Old colonial property on the river front that has had several incarnations and was once even an HQ for the Khmer Rouge. It has bags of atmosphere and is probably the best spot in town for an icy sundowner. All rooms en suite with a/c, cable TV. Recommended.

**C Little Garden Bar**, T033-256901, www.littlegardenbar.com. Basic, clean rooms, fan and bathroom. Restaurant offering panoramic views of Mount Bokor.

**C-D Borey Bokor Hotel 1**, T012-820826. In an ostentatious style with all rooms offering a/c, fridge and comfy beds.

**D-E Molieden**, a block from the main bridge, T033-932798, chuy_seth@yahoo.com. A surprisingly good find, its hideous façade gives way to a very pleasant interior. Large, tastefully decorated modern art deco rooms with TV and fan. The rooftop restaurant also serves some of the best Western food in town. Very good value.

**E-F Blissful Guesthouse**, next to Acleda Bank. Converted colonial building with lovely surrounding gardens. Rooms are simple with mosquito net, fan and attached bath. High on atmosphere and very popular with locals and expats alike. Affable Khmer manager, Elvis, and owner, Angela, make this a very pleasant place to stay. Recommended.

**E-F Bodhi Villa**, 2 km northwest of town on Teuk Chhou Rd, T012-728884. Cheap and popular budget guesthouse in nice location just outside town, set on the riverbank. Owners seem well-intentioned, linking into local volunteer projects, though the hedonistic atmosphere and roaring speed boat which they've introduced to the peaceful river detracts from their efforts. Basic rooms, simple bungalows and US$1 a night dorm.

**E-F Long Villa**, T092-251418. Very friendly, well-runguesthouse. The unspectacular though functional rooms vary from en suite with a/c and TV through to fan with shared facilities. Recommended.

**Bokor Mountain National Park** *p297*

The park rangers run a simple guesthouse at the hill station – youth-hostel style. There are bunk beds (US$5) and doubles (US$20), with clean shared toilets and showers. Bring your own food: there is a large kitchen available for guests. Pack warm clothes and waterproofs.

**Kep** *p298*

Accommodation in Kep is better and cheaper than in the rest of the country.

**L Knai Bang Chatt**, T012-349742, www.knaibangchatt.com. Set in a splendidly restored 20th-century modernist villa, this property seeks to recreate an elitist and colonial atmosphere. High walls keep the locals and other undesireables out, while the infinity pool and hackneyed contemporary Asian designer trim of dark woods and white walls offer nothing particularly original. Some people will love the banality of exclusivity – others may judge that their would be better spent elsewhere. Rooms come with all the usual luxury amenities.

**A-B La Villa**, T012-1702648, www.lavilla kep.com. An interesting old French villa forms the centre-piece of this brand-new bungalow operation set by the sea. It's worth just taking a look at the villa if you're passing by. A giant tree grows through the back of the structure much like Ta Prohm in Angkor and the whole restored edifice seems to defy gravity. The bungalows are well-appointed with verandas, a/c, en suite bathrooms, Wi-Fi and cable TV. There are plans to open a restaurant and art space in the villa. Recommended.

**A-D Verandah Resort and Bungalows**, next door to N4, further up Kep Mountain, T012-888619. Superb accommodation. Large wooden bungalows set in a enchanting garden of ripe fruits, vines and tropical flowers which weave around the stairways criss-crossing the hillside. Each bungalow includes a good-sized balcony, fan, mosquito net and nicely decorated mosaic bathroom. The more expensive of these include very romantic open-air beds. A few extra upmarket bungalows are about to be built (a/c and hot water). The restaurant offers the perfect vista of the ocean and surrounding countryside. Epicureans will love the variety of international cuisines including poutine of Quebec, smoked ham linguini, fish fillet with olive sauce (all under US$3). Recommended.

**B The Beach House**, T012-240090, www.the beachhousekep.com. Arguably the nicest spot to stay in Kep. Great rooms, nearly all of which look out onto the mesmeric ocean – all have a/c, hot water, TV. They have a small pool and soothing chill-out area. Unpretentious and good value. The staff can sometimes appear to be half-asleep but are very friendly when provoked. Recommended.

# ❶ Eating

**Sihanoukville** *p292, map p293*

**Ψ Ψ Ψ Chez Mari-yan**, Victory Beach area. Has a good seafood restaurant with probably the nicest setting in Sihanoukville.

**Ψ Ψ Ψ-Ψ Ψ La Paillote**, top of Weather Station Hill. This is the finest dining establishment in town and one of the best in the country. It has everything right: the service can't be surpassed and it is high on atmosphere – cocooned from the noisy street and lit by soft glowing candles. The chef from Madagascar greets the customers (often to explain that he uses ganja as a flavour and not as a 'happy herb' style ingredient) and the food, is superb.

**Ψ Ψ Holy Cow**, Ekareach St, on the way out of town. Ambient restaurant offering a selection of healthy, Western meals – pasta, salads, baked potatoes. The English owner is a long-term resident and very good source of local information. To his credit he has created a lovely atmosphere and provides impeccable working conditions for his staff.

**Ψ Ψ Mick and Craig's**, Ochheauteal Beach. Thankfully, the menu here is a lot more creative than the venue's name. Sufficiently large meals with a bit of pizzazz – pizzas, burgers, hummus, etc. The restaurant also offers 'themed food nights', Sunday roast, BBQ and 'all you can eat' nights.

**Ψ Ψ Starfish Café**, behind **Samudera Super market**, T034-952011. Small café-cum-bakery in a very peaceful garden setting. Here you can eat great food, while knowing that you are supporting a good cause. The organization was originally established to help rehabilitate people with disabilities and has extended its services to cover a range of poverty-reducing schemes. A very positive place that oozes goodness in its food, environment and service – good Western breakfasts, cakes, sandwiches, salads and coffees. A non-profit massage business has also opened on premises.

**Koh Kong** *p295*

There are several places around town that sell Thai food – be warned, it tends to be a pale imitation of the real thing.

**Ψ Ψ-Ψ Moto Bar**, awesome Western breakfasts – one of the best in the country. Also serves other meals but it's at its best first thing.

**Ψ Otto's Restaurant**, big menu with Western breakfasts, baguette sandwiches, schnitzels, seafood, soups, Khmer standards and lots of vegetarian options. Recommended.

**Kampot and around** *p296, map p297*

**Ψ Ψ Ψ Molienden Restaurant**, see Sleeping. On the roof of the guesthouse. Extensive selection of pastas, spaghetti, soup and Italian seafood dishes. Fantastic food. Recommended.

**Ψ Ψ Bokor Mountain Lodge**, see Sleeping. Has recently relaunched its entire menu. Great sandwiches made with the best ingredients – the fish and chicken amok is also divine. Recommended.

**Ψ Ψ Jasmine**, is a new riverside eaterie set up by a switched on Khmer woman (Jasmine) and her American photographer partner. They offer a slightly more up-market experience than many of the other places along the riverfront and the food ain't bad as well. Khmer and Western dishes. Recommended.

**Ψ Ψ Rusty Key Hole Bar and Restaurant**, River Rd, past **Bamboo Light**. Run by the very down to earth Mancunian, Christian, Rusty's is now something of a local legend. Western food served. Friendly and the best place to watch football in town. The BBQ seafood and ribs come highly recommended.

**Ψ Ψ-Ψ Little Garden Bar**, T012-994161. This is an attractive and relaxed bar and restaurant on the riverfront offering delicious Khmer and Western food for reasonable prices. The rooftop bar is the place to be for spectacular sunsets over the Elephant Mountains.

**Ψ Epic Arts Cafe**, is a brilliant little NGO-run establishment in the centre of Kampot. Set up as a project to employ local disabled people, they produce some delicious cakes. The date cake is arguably the best slice in the country and when served with a mug of British tea, makes for a perfect afternoon distraction.

**Kep** *p298*

There are scores of seafood stalls on the beach, just before the tourist centre, that specialize in cooking freshly caught crab. At the tourist office itself there is also a row of restaurants serving crab, shrimp and fish. Nearly every hotel or guesthouse also serves food – see also Sleeping entries.

♚♚♚ **The Riel**, is now Kep's only proper restaurant-cum-café-cum bar. Great friendly atmosphere and decent food should make this establishment a winner. Good rock 'n' roll stories from the owner as well.

## ⊙ Bars and clubs

**Sihanoukville** *p292, map p293*
**Papagayo**, Weather Station Hill. Pool tables, cheap cocktails, email, comfy cane lounges. The US$2 tapas is exceptionally good value.

## ⊙ Tour operators

**Sihanoukville** *p292, map p293*
**Diving**
**Scuba Nation Diving Centre**, Weather Station Hill, T012-604680, www.divecambodia.com. This company has the best reputation in the town and is the longest-established PADI dive centre. Prices vary depending on what you want. An Open Water Course is US$350, dive trips are US$70.

**Fishing**
**The Fishermen's Den**, 1 block back from Ekareach St, next to the **Small Hotel**. Runs daily fishing trips for US$25 per person. If you have caught something worth eating, the proprietor, Brian, will organize the restaurant to prepare a lovely meal from the catch. The boat is fully equipped with showers, toilets, life jackets, etc.

## ⊙ Transport

**Sihanoukville** *p292, map p293*
Motos cost 2000 riel around town or 3000 from the centre to a beach. Taxis charge US$5 to a beach.

Bus to **Phnom Penh** leaves from the station on the corner of Ekareach and Sopheakmongkol St; Phnom Penh Public Transport Co, 0710, 0800, 1215, 1310, 1400 and GST 0715, 0815, 1230, 1315. There are no longer security risks on this route. To **Kampot** shared taxi, around 10,000 riel per person, 4 hrs.

**Koh Kong and around** *p295*
Small minibuses/vans go to **Phnom Penh** leaving Koh Kong Riverside Guesthouse, 0900, 5-6 hrs, ฿600. From Raksmei Bun Thaim Guesthouse at 0830, 5-6 hrs, ฿500.

A shared taxi to **Sihanoukville**, 5-6 hrs, leaves from market, US$10 person (6 per car), US$60 own car, from 0600 onwards.

**Kampot and around** *p296, map p297*
Motos charge about 1000 riel for short trips across town. They gather around the Sokimex petrol station on the way into town.

There are 2 buses in both directions run by the **Phnom Penh Sorya Transport Co.** between Kampot and **Phnom Penh**. These services also stop in **Kep**. There are presently no regular bus services between Kampot and **Sihanoukville**. However, a private service has emerged run by the **G'Day Mate guesthouse** in Sihanoukville. However, at the time of writing the timetable wasn't being adhered to and the promised twice-weekly service wasn't operating.

Vehicles leave from the truck station next to the Total gas station for **Phnom Penh** at 0700 until 1400 for US$3.50, private taxi US$20. Most guesthouses can arrange transport and tickets. To **Sihanoukville**, shared taxi, US$3, private US$18. To **Kep**, US$8, return US$14-15.

**Kep** *p298*
Kep is 25 km (30-45 mins) from **Kampot** on a good road. A large white horse statue marks the turn-off to Kep. Buses now run twice a day between Kep/Kampot and Phnom Penh.

## ⊙ Directory

**Sihanoukville** *p292*
**Banks** There are 4 banks in town (often shut): Acleda, UCB, Canadia and the Mekong Bank, all on Ekareach St. UCB and Canadia do Visa/MasterCard cash advances. Cash advances are also available at Samudera Supermarket, in town, 5% commission. Lucky Web, on Weather Station Hill, charges 4% commission. **Internet** All tourist areas in Sihanoukville have internet within 1-2 mins' walking distance. Prices vary from 3000-8000 riel per hr.

**Kampot and around** *p296, map p297*
**Banks** Canadia Bank, close to the Borey Bokor 1 Hotel. Cash advances on Visa and MasterCard (no commission). **Internet** There is a cluster of cafés on the road between the river and the central roundabout, US$1 per hr. International calls can be made and vary between 600-900 riel per min.

# Northeast Cambodia

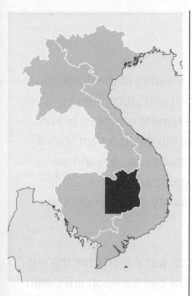

## ♣ Footprint features

# Introduction

A wild and rugged landscape, consisting of the three provinces of Ratanakiri, Mondulkiri and Stung Treng, greets any visitor to Cambodia's remote northeast region. Vast forested swathes of sparsely inhabited terrain spread north and eastwards toward Vietnam and Laos and are home to several distinct ethnic groups. The thick jungles also provide sanctuary to the majority of Cambodia's few remaining tigers.

During the civil war, the Northeast was cut off from the rest of the country. Then came years of bad transport links, with only the most committed making the arduous run up from up Phnom Penh. Yet the Northeast, much like the rest of the country, is now developing. A brand new Chinese-built road, including an arcing road bridge over the river in Stung Treng, forms a strong link between Cambodia and Laos, cutting hours off the journey time.

Framing its western edge, and cutting it off from the rest of the country, is the Mekong River. It bifurcates, meanders and braids its way through the country and represents in its width a yawning chasm and watery superhighway that connects the region with Phnom Penh. Stung Treng and Kratie are located on this mighty river and despite the lack of any kind of riverboat service are still becoming excellent places to view the elusive Irrawaddy River Dolphin.

The dust-blown and wild frontier town of Ban Lung, the capital of Ratanakiri, is slowly emerging as a centre of trekking and adventure travel.

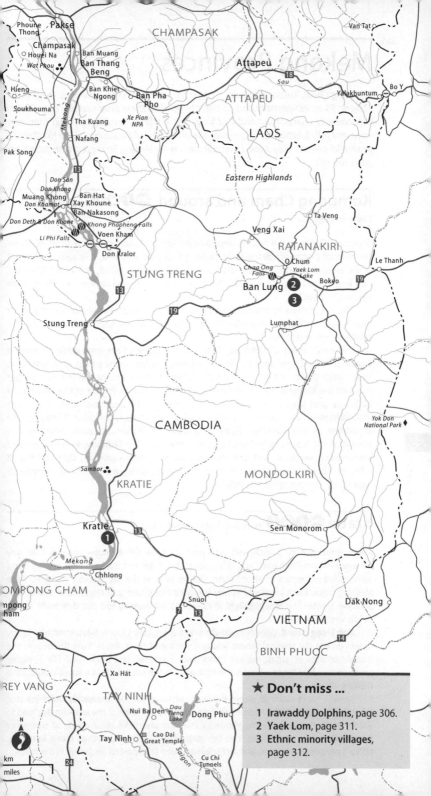

★ Don't miss ...

1 Irawaddy Dolphins, page 306.
2 Yaek Lom, page 311.
3 Ethnic minority villages, page 312.

# Mekong Provinces

*Kompong Cham, Kratie and Stung Treng make up the Mekong Provinces. Despite the Mekong River, its waterway and perpetual irrigation, these provinces are surprisingly economically unimportant and laid back. But with the new Chinese-built road now open and fully functioning – its easily one of the best in the country – the Northeast's provincial charms may soon be eradicated.* ➤➤ *For Sleeping, Eating and other listings, see pages 308-310.*

## Kompong Cham and around ⊟✈🚌ℂ ➤➤ pp308-310.

*Colour map 6, B4.*

Kompong Cham is the fourth largest town in Cambodia and is a town of some commercial prosperity owing to its thriving river port and also, it is said, as a result of preferential treatment received from local boy made good, the Prime Minister, Hun Sen. Town and province have a combined population of more than 1½ million people.

There is nothing in or around Kompong Cham to detain the visitor for long, most merely pass through, en route for Stung Treng and the northeast, but it is a pleasant enough town to rest awhile.

The small town of **Chhlong**, between Kompong Cham and Kratie, is one of Cambodia's best-kept secrets. The small town, nestled on the banks of the Mekong, 41 km from Kratie and 82 km from Kompong Cham, is one of the few places that survived the Khmer Rouge's ransacking and contains a multitude of French colonial buildings and traditional wooden Khmer houses. Of particular interest are the foundations of 120 antique houses and a 19th-century wooden Khmer house supported by 100 columns. Formerly a base for workers to surrounding rubber plantations, it is easy to feel nostalgic for a bygone era in Chhlong, with its wats and monasteries, an old school and charming market set in a colonial-style building. It takes four hours to get there get there by minibus, US$5; a whole boat, carrying 10 people, can be chartered for US$60.

## Kratie ⊟✈🚌ℂ ➤➤ pp308-310. Colour map 6, B4.

Kratie (pronounced 'Kratcheay') is a port town on the Mekong roughly half way between Phnom Penh and Laos. It is a delightful place with a relaxed atmosphere and some good examples of shophouse architecture. In the dry season the deep blue Mekong peels back to reveal sandy beaches like those you might find at the Thai seaside. Sunset is a real highlight in Kratie, as the burning red sun descends slowly below the shore line.

**Koh Trong Island**, directly opposite Kratie town, has a lovely 8-km stretch of sandy dunes (in the dry season) where you can swim and relax. Aside from the beach, the island consists of small market farms and a simple, laid-back rural life – highly recommended for those who want to chill out. On the south side is a small Vietnamese floating village.

Kratie's main claim to some modicum of fame are the **Irrawaddy dolphins** that inhabit this portion of the Mekong (Kampi pool), 15 km north of the town on the road to Stung Treng. The best time to glimpse these rare and timid creatures is at sunrise or sunset when they are feeding. You can go by moto, US$3 return, then hire a longboat, US$2-3 per person per hour, at the official viewpoint (signposted on the left of the road).

### To Laos via Koh Chheuteal or Don Kralor

**Lao immigration** The border is open daily from 0700-1700. You should aim to cross early in the day to avoid hassles and travelling at night. You will need to arrange visas beforehand in either Phnom Penh or Vientiane. Many tourists have encountered problems including inflated transportation costs and having to pay bribes, so try and be patient and keep smiling.

**Transport** A boat from Stung Treng to the Laos border (Koh Chheuteal) costs US$7 (per person or US$35 for the whole boat) and takes roughly one hour 10 minutes. Boats depart quite regularly (depending on passengers), approximately every two hours between 0700 and 1600. A departure tax of US$1-3 (depending on how hungry the customs officials are) will need to be paid at each side. Most hotels can organize tickets. Daily buses leave from Phnom Penh to Stung Treng but you wouldn't be able to make the trip from Phnom Penh across the border in a day. Phnom Penh Public Transport Co buses leave from Psar Thmei, Phnom Penh at 0700 and the journey takes nine-10 hours, 40,000 riel.

Few people choose to stay in Stung Treng, as the town is short on charm. However, there is plenty of accommodation should you get stranded. Most tourists head to Kratie three to four hours south of Stung Treng. To get to Kratie from Phnom Penh takes six-seven hours and both the Hour Lean Bus Company, T012-535387, and Phnom Penh Transport Company, T012-523400, both run buses to Kratie for US$4.50 at 0730, departing from Psar Thmei, Phnom Penh. Pick-ups and share taxis also regularly connect Phnom Penh with Kratie.

**Kampi Rapids** ① *1000 riel* (also known as Kampi resort), 3 km north of Kampi Dolphin Pool, provides a refreshing and picturesque area to take a dip in the clear Mekong waters (during the dry season). A bridge leads down to a series of scenic thatched huts which provide shelter for the swimmers.

Twenty one kilometres further north of the Kampi pool is **Sambor**, a pre-Angkorian settlement, but today unfortunately not a single trace of this ancient heritage exists. The highpoint of a trip to Sambor is more in the getting there, as you pass through beautiful countryside, than in the temples themselves. Replacing the ancient ruins are two temples. The first and most impressive is the 100-column pagoda, rumoured to be the largest new pagoda in the country. It is a replica of the 100-column, wooden original, which was built in 1529. During the war, Pol Pot based himself out of the complex, killing hundreds of people and destroying the old pagoda. The new one was built in 1985 (perhaps the builders were slightly overzealous – it features 116 columns). Three hundred metres behind the gigantic pagoda sits a much smaller and arguably more interesting temple. The wat still contains many of its original features including a number of wooden pylons which date back 537 years.

# Stung Treng ●●●▲●● ›› *pp308-310. Colour map 6, A4.*

Yet another eponymous provincial capital on the Mekong, Stung Treng is just 40 km from Laos and a stopping off place on the overland route to Ratanakiri. The town has a frontier feel to it though it is now set to lose its wild and remote feel due to the building of the mammoth Chinese road and a striking bridge that has created good links to Laos. Pigs, cows and the odd ox-cart still wander through the town's busy streets but there isn't a lot for tourists around Stung Treng. Some tour guides will organize a boat run to the Laos border to see riverine life and some waterfalls but you will need a Laos visa in order to do this. **Lbak Khone,** the 26 km rocky area that the Mekong rapids flow through en route to the Laos border, is one of the country's most stunning areas. Many tour operators will offer land transport to this area (as only the very, very brave would try by boat).

## Sleeping

### Kompong Cham and around *p306*
**D Mekong**, on the river, T042-941536. A large hotel with 60 rooms, fan and a/c, fridge, TV and with bathrooms attached. Easily the best hotel in town and popular with the NGO community. Excellent views from the rooms.

**D Rana**, T012-696340. Set in a small village just outside Kampong Cham, this is a well-run and engaging homestay programme run by Kheang and her American husband, Don. Set up more for educational purposes than as a business you can get a real insight into rural life here. Rates include full-board but accommodation is basic. They offer free moto pick up from Kampong Cham if you book for 2 or more nights. Recommended.

### Kratie *p306, see map*
**D Santepheap Hotel**, on the river road, T072-971537. Rooms are adequate in this reasonable hotel. It has a quiet atmosphere and the clean and airy rooms come with attached bathrooms, fridge, fan or a/c.

**D-E Oudom Sambath Hotel**, 439 River Rd, T072-971502. Well-run place with a friendly English speaking Chinese-Khmer owner. The rooms are huge, with a/c, TV, hot water etc. The more expensive rooms are fit for royalty with large ornate bath tub and very regal looking furniture. The huge rooftop balcony is a perfect spot for sunset gazing with the best views of the Mekong in town – they have rooms up here as well but these fill quickly. Also has a decent and very cheap restaurant attached, complete with comically surly teenage-girl staff. Recommended.

**E Star Guesthouse**, beside the market, T072-971663. This has gained the reputation of being the friendliest guesthouse in town. It is very popular with travellers and its rooms are nicely appointed.

**E-F You Hong Guesthouse**, between the taxi rank and the market, T012-957003. Clean rooms with attached bathroom and fan. US$1 extra gets you cable TV. Friendly, helpful owners. The restaurant is often filled with drunk backpackers.

### Stung Treng *p307*
**C-E Ly Ly Guesthouse**, opposite the market, T012-937859. Decent Chinese-style hotel with varying types of rooms – all come with private shower/toilet and cable TV. The ones at the back of the building have balconies and are the best value – you have the option of a/c or fan throughout. Friendly with some English spoken. Recommended.

**C-E Stung Treng Hotel and Guest House**, on main road near the river, T016-888335. Decent enough rooms in a good location – a reasonable second option.

**F Richies**, on the River Rd, T012-686954. Very friendly English speaking Khmer owner, Richie, offers 2 small and basic rooms in this riverside guesthouse. Great food as well.

**Kratie**

To Snuol & Stung Treng

Street 5
Street 6
Taxis
Pagoda Wat
Street 7
Ferry Port
Street 8
Street 9   Phnom Penh
Public Transport Co
Street 10
Food Stalls
Hour Lean
Street 11
Acleda

To Koh Trong Island & Vietnamese Floating Village

Mekong
Preah Soramarit St

To Phnom Penh

N
Not to scale

**Sleeping**
Oudom Sambath 4
Santepheap 3
Star Guesthouse 1
You Hong Guesthouse 8

**Eating**
Red Sun Falling 1

## ● Eating

**Kompong Cham** *p306*

**♥ Ho An Restaurant**, Monivong St, T042-941234. Large, Chinese restaurant with a good selection of dishes. Friendly service.

**♥♥-♥ Mekong Daze**, on the riverfront. British owner Simon provides alcohol, cakes, fish and chips and Khmer food from this new and friendly riverside establishment. He also has a free pool-table and you can grab the latest football on his TV. A good source of local info Simon can link you up with locals who rent boats and also local homestay programmes. Recommended.

**Kratie** *p306, map p308*

There are a number of food stalls set up along the river at night serving great fruit shakes. The market also sells simple dishes during the day.

**♥♥-♥ Red Sun Falling**, on the river road. Probably the best restaurant in town, it offers a variety of excellent Western dishes and a few Asian favourites. The full monty breakfast is fantastic. Good cocktails. The very friendly proprietor, Joe, also runs a very good bookshop on the premises. Closed Sun. Recommended.

**♥♥-♥ Star Guesthouse**, Street 10. A decent enough menu but sometimes the prices (almost US$1 for a squeeze of honey) and quality let the place down. Good array of Western food and the home-made bread is excellent.

**Stung Treng** *p307*

**♥ Richies**, on the river road near Sekong. One of the best places to eat in the region. Friendly Khmer owner, Richie offers great Khmer and Western food. Highly recommended.

## ● Shopping

**Kratie** *p306, map p308*

The central market sells most things. There are a couple of pharmacies opposite the market. A good camera shop, Konica, is on the River Rd.

## ▲ Activities and tours

**Stung Treng** *p307*

**Richies** (see Eating). Richie of guesthouse and restaurant fame, can offer all manner of tours and boatrides to Laos, Irrawaddy Dolphin spotting and to local waterfalls.

## ● Transport

**Kompong Cham** *p306*
**Boat**
Due to improved roads the boat service to and from Kompong Cham is non-existent. The boat service from Phnom Penh has also been curtailed.

**Moto/tuk-tuk/taxi**
Local transport is by moto, tuk-tuk or taxi. A moto for a day is between US$6-8 and between 500-1000 riel for short trips. Local tuk-tuk driver and guide **Mr Vannat** has an excellent reputation and is fluent in French and English, T012-995890. US$20 a day for a boat ride.

**Shared taxi**
The town is 120 km northeast of Phnom Penh via the well-surfaced Routes 5, 6 and 7. There are regular connections with **Phnom Penh** by shared taxi, US$1.85, 7000 riel. Several bus companies run services, US$2, 8000 riel, from Central Market, around 2 hrs, 8 buses a day. Pick-ups and shared taxis plough through to **Sen Monorom**, via **Snuol**, 2 hrs, US$3-4.

**Kratie** *p306, map p308*
**Boat**
The future of the express boat to and from Phnom Penh is uncertain but most believe the service won't resume.

**Bus**
Getting to Kratie is easy now the roads have improved. **Hour Lean Bus Company**, T012-535387, on Kratie's riverfront runs daily buses to **Phnom Penh** 0715, 7 hrs, US$4.50. **Phnom Penh Public Transport Co** also runs the trip to Phnom Penh for the same price – the bus leaves at 0715 from the Central Market. The same bus company

also charters buses to **Stung Treng** at around 1200. It is sometimes possible to hop on one of the buses coming from Phnom Penh to go to **Stung Treng** but seats can't be relied upon unless booked a few days in advance.

#### Motodop
Local transport by motodop US$1 per hr or US$6-7 per day.

#### Shared taxi
Shared taxis to **Stung Treng**, 3 hrs, US$4 per person. Shared taxis and pick-up to **Snuol** 0700, 2 hrs, US$2-3. Snuol is a good staging post for destinations such as **Sen Monorom** (a further 3 hrs away). Via Snuol, 5-6 hrs, US$4-5.

#### Stung Treng *p307*
#### Boat
There are no longer any vessels plying the **Phnom Penh/Kratie** route and with the new road bridge opening in early 2008 the future of the boat from Stung Treng to the **Lao border** is now in doubt and services are very likely to cease in the near future. Ask at **Richies** for an update when you arrive in town. He can also arrange private boat transfer should you need it. Most hotels (Sekong, Riverside, etc) can organize tickets. Alternatively, you can go directly to the taxi/bus rank.

#### Bus
Buses to **Phnom Penh** leave from the bus stand (near the park but this office was declared 'temporary' at the time of writing) at 0700, 10 hrs, US$10. The same bus will stop at **Kratie**, US$5.

#### Shared taxis and pick-ups
Pick-ups and shared taxis connect regularly with **Phnom Penh** via **Kratie** and with

recent road construction the roads should be okay to travel along (a little bumpy). Shared taxis to **Phnom Penh** leave at 0600 from the taxi rank near the river, 7 hrs, US$15. To **Ban Lung** at 0700 from the taxi rank, 4-5 hrs, US$10.

Please note that all shared taxi services will not run unless the driver has a full car, so departure times and fares will vary depending on the number of passengers.

## Directory

### Kompong Cham *p306*
**Banks** There are 2 banks in town – **Acleda** and **Canadia Bank**. Acleda, 0800-1600, will do Western Union transfers and Canadia will do advances on Visa and MasterCard.
**Internet** **ABC computers**, in the centre of town, was the only internet shop operating at the time of writing, US$1 per hr and overseas phone calls available. A new internet café was due to open on Pasteur St, opposite the Mekong Crossing.

### Kratie *p306, map p308*
**Banks** There is an **Acleda Bank** half way down Street 11. It does not do advances on Visa or MasterCard but is a subsidiary for Western Union. **Internet** You Hong guesthouse offer a good, cheap connection. **Three Star Internet** US$4 per hr. There is another internet café near Phnom Penh Transport bus office but at the time of writing it was US$4 per hr.

### Stung Treng *p307*
**Banks** There are no banks in town.
**Internet** Internet is available at the computer shop opposite the market and the **Sekong Hotel**, US$4 per hr.
**Telephone** There are telephone shops all over town.

# Ratanakiri Province

*Ratanakiri is like another planet compared to the rest of Cambodia – dusty, red roads curl through the landscape in summer, while in the rainy season the area becomes lush and green. Adventure enthusiasts won't be disappointed, with waterfalls to discover, ethnic minorities to meet, elephants to ride, river trips to take and the beautiful Yaek Lom volcanic lake to take a dip in.* ▸ *For Sleeping, Eating and other listings, see pages 312-314.*

## Ban Lung and around ●●●●●● ▸ *pages 312-314.*
*Colour map 6, A5.*

Ban Lung has been the dusty provincial capital of Ratanakiri Province ever since the previous capital Lumphat was flattened by US bombers trying to 'destroy' the footpaths and tracks that made up the Ho Chi Minh Trail. There are no paved roads in or around the town, merely dirt tracks which in the dry season suffocate the town with their dust and in the wet season turn into rivers of mud. The town is situated on a plateau dotted with lakes and hills, many of great beauty, and serves as a base from which visitors can explore the surrounding countryside. At present you'll find basic guesthouse accommodation, and food and drink can be obtained in town.

### Ins and outs
**Getting there** Ban Lung is 13 hours from Phnom Penh. It is better to break your journey in Kratie and Stung Treng and take a pickup/taxi from there.

**Getting around** The chief mode of transport is the motorbike which comes with a driver, or not, as required (usually US$5 without driver and US$15 with, but you'll have to haggle). Bus services are sporadic. Cars with driver can be hired for US$40-50 a day.

### Sights around Ban Lung
The name Ratanakiri means 'jewel mountains' in Pali, and presumably comes from the wealth of gems in the hills, but it could just as easily refer to the beauty of the landscape. **Yaek Lom** ① *US$1 and a parking charge of 500 riel*, it is a perfectly circular volcanic lake about 5 km east of town and easily reached by motorbike. The crystalline lake is rimmed by protected forest dominated by giant emergents (dipterocarps and shoreas) soaring high into the sky. It takes about one hour to walk around the lake: in doing so you will find plenty of secluded bathing spots and, given the lack of water in town, it is not surprising that most locals and visitors bathe in the wonderfully clear and cool waters of the lake. There is a small 'museum' of ethnographia and a couple of minority stilt houses to be seen.

There are three **waterfalls** ① *all 2000 riel*, in close proximity to Ban Lung town. **Kachaang Waterfall** is 6 km away. The 12-m high waterfall flows year round and is surrounded by magnificent, pristine jungle and fresh mist rising from the fall. **Katien Waterfall** is a little oasis 7 km northwest of Ban Lung. Believed to have formed from volcanic lava hundreds of years ago, the 10-m plunging falls are sheltered from the outside world by a little rocky grotto. It is one of the better local falls to swim in as it is very secluded (most people will usually have the area to themselves), the water is completely clean. The best waterfall is arguably **Chaa Ong Falls**, with the 30-m falls plunging into a large pool. Those game enough can have a shower behind the crescent-shaped ledge. To get to the waterfalls, follow Highway 19 out of town and branch off 2 km out on the main road in the first village out of Ban Lung: Chaa Ong

Falls are 9 km northwest at the intersection, turn right at the village and head for about 5 km to head to Katien Waterfall (follow the signs), the same road heads to Kachaang Waterfall.

The trip to **Ou'Sean Lair Waterfall**, 35 km from Ban Lung, is a wonderful day excursion offering a fantastic cross-section of what is essentially Ratanakiri's main attractions (without the riverside element). From Ban Lung, fields of wind-bent, spindly rubber trees provide a canopy over the road's rolling hills, a legacy left from the French in the 1960s. Punctuating the mottled natural vista is an equally diverse range of ethnic minority settlements. Tampeun and Kreung villages are dotted along the road and about half way (17 km from Ban Lung), in a lovely valley, is a tiny Cham village. The perfect end to the journey is the seven-tiered Ou'Sean Lair falls. The falls were reportedly 'discovered' by a Tampeun villager five years ago, who debated as to whether he should tell the Department of Tourism of their existence. In return for turning over the falls, they were named after him. The falls are most spectacular in the wet season but are still pretty alluring during the dry season.

## Sleeping

**Ban Lung** *p311*
The sheer volume of red dust that blows in through the doors and open windows makes washing and cleaning quite futile so guesthouse owners very sensibly gave up the fight against nature many years ago.
**A-B Terres Rouges Lodge**, T/F075-974051, www.ratanakiri-lodge.com. Run by Frenchman Pierre Yves and his friendly Khmer wife Chenda, this hotel is housed in a large traditional wooden Khmer lodge overlooking the lake and offers cool, spacious and beautiful rooms, with the added bonus of a great CD collection in the comfortable sitting area. Pierre, like most other guesthouse and hotel owners in the area, runs a number of tour services, including elephant trekking and the use of a 4WD. This place mostly attracts small package-tour groups and is priced accordingly. You can haggle for a discount in the low-season.
**C-D Lakeside Chenglock Hotel**, beside Lake Konsaign, T012-957422. An exponential improvement on its town counterpart. The rooms are very comfortable with the cheapest being roomy with fan and attached bathroom and, the more expensive bungalow-type rooms fitted with lovely wooden furniture, attached bathroom with hot water and bath, a/c and a beautiful view over the lake. Good value and recommended.

**D Yaklom Hill Lodge**, near Yaklom Lake, 6 km east of Ban Lung, T012-644240, www.yaklom.com. This rustic ecolodge is a bit out of town but offers guests the opportunity to experience first-hand the wonderful surrounding environs. Bungalows are interspersed in the natural surroundings, with good-sized balconies to take in the starry-lit nights, and are decorated nicely with local handicrafts and fabrics. Fan, mosquito net, attached bathroom, shower and thermos (for those that wish to have a warm traditional scoop shower out of the earthenware pots provided). Power is supplied via generator and solar panels. The friendly owner, Sampon, is planning on turning the lodge into a bird sanctuary – with 22 different species identified on the premises at the time of publication.
**D-E Lake View Lodge**, overlooking the lake, Old Governors House, T092-785259, www.lakeviewlodge-ratanakiri.com. Managed by the very switched-on Sophat – a Khmer former highschool teacher – this is fast establishing itself as the budget traveller place of choice in Ban Lung. The rooms are nothing to get too excited about – from fan and coldwater through to a/c, TV and hotwater – but the welcome is exceptional. Sophat will pick you up from the bus station in the middle of the night, provides internet access, decent food and trekking tours to outlying villages – there's even a small restaurant attached. Recommended.

# Eating

**Ban Lung** *p311*

**TTT-TT Terres Rouges Lodge Restaurant** is considered the 'in' place to eat and is as fine dining as it gets in Ban Lung. Cambodian and French food. Pasta US$3, coq au vin US$8.50, beef steak US$5. Good wine list/bar and very ambient setting.
The food is nothing exceptional, the service can be dodgy and they do charge very high corkage fees (US$10) should you decide to bring your own wine.

**TT Tribal Hotel Restaurant** on the outskirts of town, T075-974001. Has lost some of its previous rep for good food at good prices. Might be worth a visit if you've tried everywhere else in town.

**T American Restaurant**, on the crossroads opposite the petrol station – look for the badly painted sign. At first you think you've stumbled into someone's front room and then you find out you have! The humble surroundings, just two tables, belie the fact that the food is awesome and served by a very sweet Khmer family – a true frontier town experience. The history of the name is that US MIA's were based here at some point. Highly recommended.

**T Cyber Sophat**, near the market. Great little internet café run by the guys from **Lake View Lodge** offering all kinds of coffee, cakes and bus tickets. A beacon of modernity in the wilds of Ratanakiri.

**T Ratanak Hotel Restaurant**. A quite popular restaurant that serves a spectacular barbecue which you cook at your table. Cambodian food between US$1-2.

**T Yaklom Hill Lodge** offers a good selection of tasty and cheap Lao, Khmer and Thai-inspired meals with a few dishes to please the more Western-orientated palate. Curry US$2, burgers US$1.50.

# O Bars and clubs

**Ban Lung** *p311*

Since the local disco burnt down the town has been lacking any vivid nightlife. There is only one bona fide bar – the **VP Bar**, opposite the **Ratanak Hotel**. A small, intimate setting. Here, miles from any light 'pollution', you can see incredibly clear skies.

# O Shopping

**Ban Lung** *p311*

Ban Lung market is large and set in a wasteland. Plastic bags blow in the wind, pigs trot around snorting for morsels and hungry dogs linger looking for scraps to eat. During the day there is very little of interest for purchase although a few shops sell handicrafts but these have yet to develop and there are no local textiles, hence the eagerness with which kramas and T-shirts will be received. However from 0600-0700 the market is a hive of activity as nearby villagers come to sell their honey, nuts and other produce and catch up on the morning gossip whilst eating their breakfast. From 1700-1800 the food market opens at the back and, if you can face it, you can try their specialities.

# ▲ Activities and tours

**Ban Lung** *p311*

**Lake View Lodge**, T092-785259, offer a variety of tours and other adventures. They can also procure motos and dirtbikes of varying quality for rent.

# Transport

**Ban Lung** *p311*
**Air**

There is an airport in Ban Lung but the old plane that used to fly from Phnom Penh crashed near Bokor, taking several Korean tourists with it. There are no plans at the time of writing to begin flights again.

**Pick-up/taxi**

If you are a glutton for punishment or just want another after-dinner story when you get home, it is possible to travel directly to **Phnom Penh** but be prepared to sit in a cramped pickup/taxi for around 13 hrs. Taxi to **Kratie**, leaving the taxi stand at approximately 0800, 7 hrs, US$12-13. Taxi to **Stung Treng**, 0830, 2-3 hrs, US$5-7.

You can only get a moto to take you to **Lumphat** for around US$15 for the day trip. The road from Stung Treng is fairly well graded now and is constantly improving due to its use by logging companies. The trip to Ban Lung from Stung Treng takes about 3 hrs (if you get yourself in a nice new Camry), US$10. Unfortunately the same cannot be said of the road from Kratie to Stung Treng which barely deserves such an appellation. However, the road was being overhauled at the time of publication.

Tourists commonly ask about travelling between Ban Lung and **Sen Monorom**. At the time of publication this overland odyssey really wasn't an option, as the roads are almost impassable and difficult to navigate. Only experienced dirt-bike riders with very good local knowledge should attempt this trip.

### Motorbike and moto

Several guesthouses have motorbikes for hire, or can arrange hire, for around US$5 per day without driver and triple that with a driver. There are no garages/petrol stops outside the town of Ban Lung, though there are a few roadside places offering bottles of fuel of dubious quality, so it is advisable to set off with a full tank. **Lake View Lodge** can also arrange moto and dirtbike for US$5-10 per day.

## Directory

**Ban Lung** *p311*

**Banks** Amazingly **ANZ** bank have opened an ATM near the airport. At the time of writing only locals could use it but foreign cards should be accepted by the time of publication. Beware of queues as the locals try to figure out how to use this new bit of technology. The **Mountain Guesthouse** and the **Ratanak Hotel** both change TCs but allow at least 3 days for your cheques to clear. **Internet** Cyber Sophat near the market claims the only broadband connection in the whole province. Otherwise expect slow dial-up download speeds. CIC near **Sovannikiri Hotel**. **Medical services** The hospital is on the road north towards O Chum. **Dr Vannara**, T012-970359, speaks very good English. **Post office** In the centre of town.

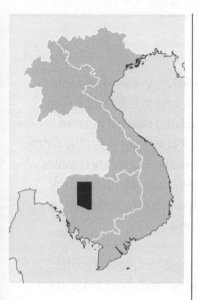

# Introduction

The huge temple complex of Angkor, the ancient capital of the powerful Khmer Empire, is one of the archaeological treasures of Asia and the spiritual and cultural heart of Cambodia. The empire reached its peak between the ninth and 15th centuries, when most of the legendary temples, sanctuaries, barays and roads were built. Henri Mouhot, the Frenchman who rediscovered it, wrote "it is grander than anything of Greece or Rome".

Angkor Wat is arguably the greatest temple within the complex, both in terms of grandeur and sheer magnitude. After all, it is the biggest religious monument in the world, its outer walls clad with one of the longest continuous bas-relief ever created. The diverse architectural prowess and dexterity of thousands of artisans is testified by around 100 brilliant monuments in the area. Of these the Bayon, with its beaming smiles; Banteay Srei, which features the finest most intricate carvings; and the jungle temple of Ta Prohm are unmissable. Others prefer the more understated but equally brilliant temples of Neak Pean, Preah Khan and Pre Rup.

The petite town of Siem Reap sits nearby the Angkor complex, and is home to a gamut of world-class hotels, restaurants and bars. A hop, skip and a jump from the town is Southeast Asia's largest lake, the Tonlé Sap, with floating villages, teeming with riverine life.

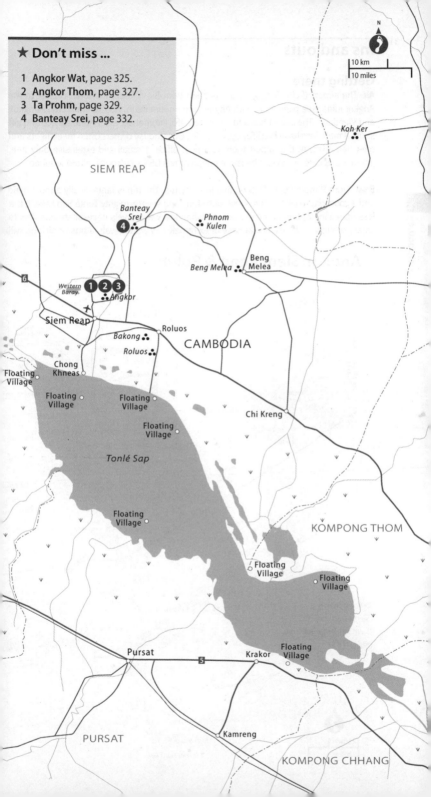

N

10 km
10 miles

Koh Ker

SIEM REAP

Banteay
Srei

Phnom
Kulen

Beng
Melea

Beng Melea

6

Western
Baray.

Angkor

Siem Reap

Roluos

CAMBODIA

Bakong

Roluos

Chong
Khneas

Floating
Village

Floating
Village

Floating
Village

Chi Kreng

Floating
Village

Tonlé Sap

Floating
Village

KOMPONG THOM

Floating
Village

Floating
Village

Pursat

Krakor

Floating
Village

5

Kamreng

PURSAT

KOMPONG CHHANG

# Ins and outs

## Getting there

**Air** The airport (REP), T063-963148, is 7 km from Siem Reap, the town closest to the Angkor ruins (see page 339), with flights from Phnom Penh, Ho Chi Minh City, Bangkok and Vientiane. The airport has a taxi service, café, internet access, phone service and gift shop. A moto into town is US$1, by taxi US$7. Guesthouse owners often meet flights and offer free rides. At the airport there is a post office, a small and expensive duty free, internet and café. Visas can be issued upon arrival US$20 (₡1000), photo required.

**Boat** From Phnom Penh, US$25, five to six hours. The trip is fantastically atmospheric and a good way to kill two birds with one stone and see the mighty Tonlé Sap Lake. It is a less appealing option in the dry season when low water levels necessitate transfers to small, shallow draft vessels. In case of extremely low water levels a bus or pick-up will

# Angkor, Siem Reap & Roluos

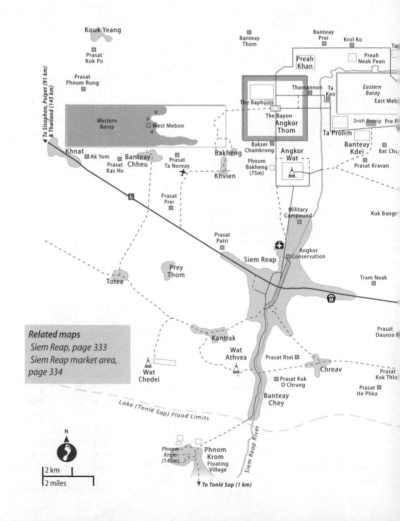

Related maps
Siem Reap, page 333
Siem Reap market area, page 334

2 km
2 miles

need to be taken for part of the trip. The mudbank causeway between the lake and the outskirts of Siem Reap is hard to negotiate and some walking may be necessary (it's 12 km from Bindonville harbour to Siem Reap). Boats depart from the Phnom Penh Port on Sisowath Quay (end of 106 Street) 0700, departing Siem Reap 0700 from Chong Khneas on the Tonlé Sap Lake. ▸▸ *For further information, see Transport, page 339.*

**Bus** The air-conditioned buses are one of the most convenient and comfortable ways to go between Phnom Penh and Siem Reap, US$3.50-4, six hours. Almost every guesthouse or hotel sells the tickets although it is easy enough to pick-up from the bus stations/terminal. In peak periods, particularly Khmer New Year, it is important to purchase tickets a day or two prior to travel. A shared taxi from Phnom Penh will cost you US$10.

## Getting around

Most of the temples within the Angkor complex (except the Roluos Group) are located in an area 8 km north of Siem Reap, with the area extending across a 25 km radius. The Roluos Group are 13 km east of Siem Reap and further away is Banteay Srei (32 km).

Cars with drivers and guides are available from larger hotels from around US$20 per day plus US$20 for a guide. The **Angkor Tour Guide Association** and most other travel agencies can also organize this. Expect to pay around US$7-8 per day for a **moto** unless the driver speaks good English in which case the price will be higher. This price will cover trips to the Roluos Group of temples but not to Banteay Srei. No need to add more than a dollar or two to the price for getting to Banteay Srei unless the driver is also a guide and can demonstrate to you that he is genuinely going to show you around. **Tuk-tuks** and their ilk have appeared on the scene in recent years and a trip to the temples on a motorbike drawn cart is quite a popular option for 2 people, U$10 a day (maximum of two people).

Bicycle hire, US$2-3 per day from most guesthouses, represents a nice option for those who feel reasonably familiar with the area. However, if you are on a limited schedule and only have a day or two at the temples you won't be able to cover an awful lot of the temples on a pedal bike as the searing temperatures and sprawling layout can take even the most advanced cyclists a considerable amount of time. Angkor Wat and Banteay Srei have official parking sites, 1000 riel (US$0.25) and at the other temples you can quite safely park and lock your bikes in front of a drink stall. For those wishing to see Angkor from a different perspective it is possible to charter a **helicopter. Elephants** are stationed near the Bayon or at the South Gate of Angkor Thom during the day. In the

## Beating the crowds

These days avoiding traffic within the Angkor complex is difficult but still moderately achievable. As it stands there is a pretty standard one-day tour itinerary that includes: Angkor Wat (sunrise), Angkor Thom, the Bayon, etc (morning), break for lunch, Ta Prohm (afternoon), Preah Khan (afternoon) and Phnom Bakheng (sunset). If you reverse the order, peak hour traffic at major temples is dramatically reduced. As many tour groups trip into Siem Reap for lunch this is an opportune time to catch a peaceful moment in the complex, just bring a packed lunch or eat at 1100 or 1400.

To avoid the masses at the draw-card attraction, Angkor Wat, try to walk around the temple, as opposed to through it. Sunset at Phnom Bakheng has turned into a circus fiasco, so aim for Angkor or the Bayon at this time as they are both relatively peaceful. Sunrise is still relatively peaceful at Angkor, grab yourself the prime position behind the left-hand pond (you need to depart Siem Reap no later than 0530), though there are other stunning early morning options, such as Srah Srang or Bakong. Bakheng gives a beautiful vista of Angkor in the early-mid morning.

evenings, they are located at the bottom of Phnom Bakheng, taking tourists up to the summit for sunset. ▸▸ *For further information, see Activities and tours, page 339.*

### Best time to visit

Angkor's peak season coincides with the dry season, November-February. Not only is this the driest time of year it is also the coolest (which can still be unbearably hot). The monsoon lasts from June to October/November. At this time it can get very muddy.

### Tourist information

**Guides** can be invaluable when navigating the temples, with the majority being able to answer most questions about Angkor as well as providing additional information about Cambodian culture and history. Most hotels and travel agents will be able to point you in the direction of a good guide. The **Khmer Angkor Tour Guide Association** ⓘ *on the road to Angkor, T063-964347,* has pretty well-trained guides. Most of the guides here are very well-briefed and some speak English better than others. The going rate is US$20-25 per day. If you do wish to buy an additional guidebook Dawn Rooney's *Angkor: An Introduction to the Temples* and *Ancient Angkor* by Michael Freeman and Claude Jacques are recommended.

**Temple fees and hours** One-day pass US$23, two- or three-day pass US$43, four- to seven-day pass US$63. Most people will be able to cover the majority of the temples within three days. If you buy your ticket after 1715 the day beforehand, you get a free sunset thrown in. For any ticket other than the one-day ticket you will need a passport photograph. The complex is open daily 0530-1830.

**Safety** Landmines were planted on some outlying paths to prevent Khmer Rouge guerrillas from infiltrating the temples; they have pretty much all been cleared by now, but it is safer to stick to well-used paths. Wandering anywhere in the main temple complexes is perfectly safe. Be especially wary of **snakes** in the dry season. The very poisonous Hanuman snake (lurid green) is fairly common in the area.

**Photography** A generalization, but somewhat true, is that black and white film tends to produce better-looking tourist pictures than those in colour. Plenty of hawkers have clicked onto this and sell Fuji SS fine-grain black and white film (US$2-3 a roll). The best colour shots usually include some kind of contrast against the temples, a saffron-clad monk or a child. Don't forget to ask if you want to include people in your shots. In general, the best time to photograph the great majority of temples is before 0900 and after 1630.

## Itineraries

The temples are scattered over an area in excess of 160 sq km. There are three so-called 'circuits'. The **Petit Circuit** takes in the main central temples including Angkor Wat, Bayon, Baphuon and the Terrace of the Elephants. The **Grand Circuit** takes a wider route, including smaller temples like Ta Prohm, East Mebon and Neak Pean. The **Roluos Group Circuit** ventures further afield still, taking in the temples near Roluos – Lolei, Preah Ko and Bakong. The order of visiting Angkor's temples is very much a matter of opinion and available time; here are some options:

**Half day** South Gate of Angkor Thom, Bayon, Angkor Wat.

**One day** Angkor Wat (sunrise or sunset), South Gate of Angkor Thom, Angkor Thom Complex (Bayon, Elephant Terrace, Royal Palace) and Ta Prohm. This is a hefty schedule for one day; you'll need to arrive after 1615 and finish just after 1700 the following day.

**Two days** The same as above but with the inclusion of the rest of the Angkor Thom, Preah Khan, Srah Srang (sunrise) and at a push, Banteay Srei.

**Three days** **Day 1** Sunrise at Angkor Wat; morning South Gate of Angkor Thom, Angkor Thom complex (aside from Bayon); Ta Prohm; late afternoon-sunset at the Bayon. **Day 2** Sunrise Srah Srang; morning Banteay Kdei and Banteay Srei; late afternoon Preah Khan; sunset at Angkor Wat. **Day 3** Sunrise and morning Roluos; afternoon Ta Keo and sunset either at Bakheng or Angkor Wat.

Those choosing to stay one or two days longer should try to work Banteay Samre, East Mebon, Neak Pean and Thomannon into their itinerary. A further two to three days warrants a trip to Prasat Kravan, Ta Som, Beng Melea and Kbal Spean.
▶▶ *For Sleeping, Eating and other listings, see pages 332-340.*

# Background

## Khmer Empire

Under **Jayavarman VII** (1181-1218) the Angkor complex stretched more than 25 km east to west and nearly 10 km north to south, approximately the same size as Manhattan. For five centuries (ninth-13th), the court of Angkor held sway over a vast territory. At its height Khmer influence spanned half of Southeast Asia, from Burma to the southernmost tip of Indochina and from the borders of Yunnan to the Malay Peninsula. The only threat to this great empire was a riverborne invasion in 1177, when the Cham used a Chinese navigator to pilot their war canoes up the Mekong. Scenes are depicted in bas-reliefs of the Bayon temple.

**Jayavarman II** (802-835) founded the Angkor Kingdom, then coined Hariharalaya to the north of the Tonlé Sap, in the Roluos region (Angkor), in 802. Later he moved the capital to Phnom Kulen, 40 km northeast of Angkor, where he built a Mountain Temple and Rong Shen shrine. After several years he moved the capital back to the Roluos region. **Jayavarman III** (835-877) continued his father's legacy and built a number of shrines at Hariharalaya. Many historians believe he was responsible for the initial construction of the impressive laterite pyramid, Bakong, considered the great precursor to Angkor Wat. Bakong, built to symbolize Mount Meru, was later embellished and developed by Indravarman. **Indravarman** (877-889) overthrew his predecessor violently and undertook a major renovation campaign in the capital Hariharalaya. The majority of what stands in the Roluos Group today is the work of Indravarman. A battle between Indravarman's sons destroyed the palace and the victor and new king **Yasovarman I** (889-900) moved the capital from Roluos and laid the foundations of Angkor itself. He dedicated the temple to his ancestors. His new capital at Angkor was called Yasodharapura, meaning 'glory-bearing city', and here he built 100 wooden ashramas, retreats (all of which have disintegrated today). Yasovarman selected Bakheng as the location for his temple-mountain and after flattening the mountain top, set about creating another Mount Meru. The temple he constructed was considered more complex than anything built beforehand, a five-storey pyramid with 108 shrines. A road was then built to link the former and present capitals of Roluos and Bakheng. Like the Kings before him, Yasovarman was obliged to construct a major waterworks and the construction of the reservoir – the East Baray (now completely dry) – was considered an incredible feat. After Yasovarman's death in 900 his son **Harshavarman** (900-923) assumed power for the next 23 years. During his brief reign, Harshavarman is believed to have built Baksei Chamkrong (northeast of Phnom Bakheng) and Prasat Kravan (the 'Cardamom Sanctuary'). His brother, **Ishanarvarman II** (923-928), resumed power upon his death but no great architectural feats were recorded in this time. In 928, **Jayavarman IV** moved the capital 65 km away to Koh Ker. Here he built the grand state temple Prasat Thom, an impressive seven-storey, sandstone pyramid. Following the death of Jayavarman things took a turn for the worst. Chaos ensued under **Harshavarman's II** weak leadership and over the next four years, no monuments were known to be erected. Jayavarman's IV nephew, **Rajendravarman** (944-968), took control of the situation and it's assumed he forcefully relocated the capital back to Angkor. Rather than moving back into the old capital Phnom Bakheng, he marked his own new territory, selecting an area south of the East Baray as his administrative centre. Here, in 961 he constructed the state temple, Pre Rup, and constructed the temple, East Mebon (953), in the middle of the baray. Srah Srang, Kutisvara and Bat Chum were also constructed, with the help of his chief architect, Kavindrarimathana. It was towards the end of his reign that he started construction on Banteay Srei, considered one of the finest examples of Angkorian craftsmanship in the country. Rajendravarman's son **Jayavarman V** (968-1001) became the new king in 968. The administrative centre was renamed Jayendranagari and yet again, relocated. More than compensating for the unfinished Ta Keo was Jayavarman's V continued work on Banteay Srei. Under his supervision the splendid temple was completed and dedicated to his father.

Aside from successfully extending the Khmer Empire's territory **King Suryavarman I** (1002-1049), made a significant contribution to Khmer architectural heritage. He presided over the creation of a new administrative centre – the Royal Palace (in Angkor Thom) – and the huge walls that surround it. The next in line was **Udayadityavarman II** (1050-1066), the son of Suryavarman I. The Baphuon temple-mountain was built during his relatively short appointment. After overthrowing his Great-Uncle Dharanindravarman, **Suryavarman II** (1112-1150), the greatest of Angkor's god-kings, came to power. His rule marked the highest point in Angkorian architecture and civilization. Not only was he victorious in conflict, having beaten the Cham whom couldn't be defeated by China, he was responsible for extending the borders of the Khmer Empire into Myanmar, Malaya and Siam. This aside, he was also considered one of the era's most brilliant creators. Suryavarman II was responsible for the construction of Angkor Wat, the current day symbol of Cambodia. Beng Melea, Banteay Samre and Thommanon are also thought to be the works of this genius. He has been immortalized in his own creation – in a bas-relief in the South Gallery of Angkor Wat the glorious King Suryavarman II sitting on top of an elephant. After a period of political turmoil,

## Motifs in Khmer sculpture

**Apsaras** These are regarded as one of the greatest invention of the Khmers. The gorgeous temptresses – born, according to legend, 'during the churning of the Sea of Milk' – were Angkor's equivalent of pin-up girls and represented the ultimate ideal of feminine beauty. They lived in heaven where their sole raison d'être was to have eternal sex with Khmer heroes and holy men. The apsaras are carved in seductive poses with splendidly ornate jewellery and clothed in the latest Angkor fashion. Different facial features suggest the existence of several races at Angkor. Together with the five towers of Angkor Wat they have become the symbol of Khmer culture. The god-king himself possessed an apsara-like retinue of court dancers – impressive enough for Chinese envoy Chou Ta-kuan to write home about it in 1296.

**Garuda** Mythical creature – half-man, half-bird – was the vehicle of the Hindu god, Vishnu, and the sworn enemy of the nagas. It appeared relatively late in Khmer architecture.

**Kala** Jawless monster commanded by the gods to devour his own body – made its first appearance in lintels at Roluos. The monster represented devouring time and was an early import from Java.

**Makara** Mythical water-monster with a scaly body, eagles' talons and an elephantine trunk.

**Naga** Sacred snake. These play an important part in Hindu mythology and the Khmers drew on them for architectural inspiration. Possibly more than any other single symbol or motif, the naga is characteristic of Southeast Asia and decorates objects throughout the region. The naga is an aquatic serpent and is intimately associated with water (a key component of Khmer prosperity). In Hindu mythology, the naga coils beneath and supports Vishnu on the cosmic ocean. The snake also swallows the waters of life, these only being set free to reinvigorate the world after Indra ruptures the serpent with a bolt of lightning. Another version has Vishnu's servants pulling at the serpent to squeeze the waters of life from it (the so-called churning of the sea, see page 300).

**Singha** Lion in stylized form; often the guardians to temples.

which included the sacking of Angkor, **Jayavarman VII** seized the throne in 1181 and set about rebuilding his fiefdom. He created a new administrative centre – the great city of Angkor Thom. The mid-point of Angkor Thom is marked by his brilliant Mahayana Buddhist state temple, the Bayon. It is said that the Bayon was completed in 21 years. Jayavarman took thousands of peasants from the rice fields to build it, which proved a fatal error, for rice yields decreased and the empire began its decline as resources were drained. The temple, which consists of sculptured faces of Avolokiteshvara (the Buddha of compassion and mercy) are often said to also encompass the face of their great creator, Jayavarman VIII. He was also responsible for restoring the Royal Palace, renovating Srah Srang and constructing the Elephant Terrace, the Terrace of the Leper King and the nearby baray (northeast of Angkor Thom), Jayatataka reservoir. At the centre of his reservoir he built Neak Pean. Jayavarman VII adopted Mahayana Buddhism; Buddhist principles replaced the Hindu pantheon, and were invoked as the basis of royal authority. This spread of Buddhism is thought to have caused some of the earlier Hindu temples to be neglected. The king paid tribute to his Buddhist roots through his monastic temples – Ta Prohm and Preah Khan.

## : The Churning of the Sea

The Hindu legend, the *Churning of the Sea*, relates how the gods and demons resolved matters in the turbulent days when the world was being created. The elixir of immortality was one of 13 precious things lost in the churning of the cosmic sea. It took 1000 years before the gods and demons, in a joint dredging operation – aided by Sesha, the sea snake, and Vishnu – recovered them all.

The design of the temples of Angkor was based on this ancient legend. The moat represents the ocean and the gods use the top of Mount Meru – represented by the tower – as their churning stick. The cosmic serpent offered himself as a rope to enable the gods and demons to twirl the stick.

Paul Mus, a French archaeologist, suggests that the bridge with the naga balustrades which went over the moat from the world of men to the royal city was an image of the rainbow. Throughout Southeast Asia and India, the rainbow is alluded to as a multi-coloured serpent rearing its head in the sky.

## The French at Angkor

Thai ascendency and eventual occupation of Angkor in 1431, led to the city's abandonment and the subsequent invasion of the jungle. Four centuries later, in 1860, Henri Mouhot – a French naturalist – stumbled across the forgotten city, its temple towers enmeshed in the forest canopy. Locals told him they were the work of a race of giant gods. Only the stone temples remained; all the wooden secular buildings had decomposed in the intervening centuries. In 1873 French archaeologist Louis Delaporte removed many of Angkor's finest statues for 'the cultural enrichment of France'. In 1898, the École Française d'Extrême Orient started clearing the jungle, restoring the temples, mapping the complex and making an inventory of the site. Delaporte was later to write the two-volume *Les Monuments du Cambodge*, the most comprehensive Angkorian inventory of its time, and his earlier sketches, plans and reconstructions, published in *Voyage au Cambodge* in 1880 are without parallel.

### Angkor temples → *Colour map 6, A2.*

The temples at Angkor were modelled on those of the kingdom of Chenla (a mountain kingdom centred on northern Cambodia and southern Laos), which in turn were modelled on Indian temples. They represent Mount Meru – the home of the gods of Indian cosmology. The central towers symbolize the peaks of Mount Meru, surrounded by a wall representing the earth and moats and basins representing the oceans. The devaraja, or god-king, was enshrined in the centre of the religious complex, which acted as the spiritual axis of the kingdom. The people believed their apotheosized king communicated directly with the gods.

The central tower sanctuaries housed the images of the Hindu gods to whom the temples were dedicated. Dead members of the royal and priestly families were accorded a status on a par with these gods. Libraries to store the sacred scriptures were also built within the ceremonial centre. The temples were mainly built to shelter the images of the gods – unlike Christian churches, Moslem mosques and some Buddhist pagodas, they were not intended to accommodate worshippers. Only priests, the servants of the god, were allowed into the interiors. The 'congregation' would mill around in open courtyards or wooden pavilions.

The first temples were of a very simple design, but with time they became more grandiose and doors and galleries were added. Most of Angkor's buildings are made from a soft sandstone which is easy to work. It was transported to the site from Phnom

Kulen, about 30 km to the northeast. Laterite was used for foundations, core material, and enclosure walls, as it was widely available and could be easily cut into blocks. A common feature of Khmer temples was false doors and windows on the sides and backs of sanctuaries and other buildings. In most cases there was no need for well-lit rooms and corridors as hardly anyone ever went into them. That said, the galleries round the central towers in later temples, such as Angkor Wat, indicate that worshippers did use the temples for ceremonial circumambulation when they would contemplate the inspiring bas-reliefs from the important Hindu epic, *Ramayana* (see page 57) and *Mahabharata* (written between 400 BC and AD 200).

Despite the court's conversion to Mahayana Buddhism in the 12th century, the architectural ground-plans of temples did not alter much – even though they were based on Hindu cosmology. The idea of the god-king was simply grafted onto the new state religion and statues of the Buddha rather than the gods of the Hindu pantheon were used to represent the god-king (see Bayon, page 327). One particular image of the Buddha predominated at Angkor in which he wears an Angkor-style crown, with a conical top which is encrusted with jewellery.

## Angkor Wat → *Colour map 6, A2.*

The awe-inspiring sight of Angkor Wat, first thing in the morning, is something you're not likely to forget. Angkor literally means 'city' or 'capital' and it is is the biggest religious monument ever built and certainly one of the most spectacular. The temple complex covers 81 ha. Its five towers are emblazoned on the Cambodian flag and the 12th-century masterpiece is considered by art historians to be the prime example of classical Khmer art and architecture. It took more than 30 years to build and is dedicated to the Hindu god Vishnu, personified in earthly form by its builder, the god-king Suryavarman II, and is aligned east to west.

## Angkor Wat

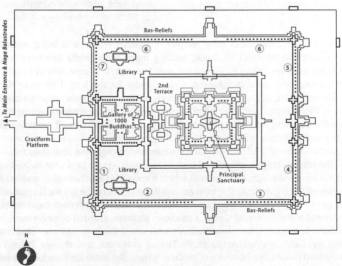

To Main Entrance & Naga Balustrades

Bas-Reliefs

Library

2nd Terrace

Gallery of 1000 Buddhas

Cruciform Platform

Library

Principal Sanctuary

Bas-Reliefs

N

500 metres
500 yards

See box overleaf for details

## ⠿ Anti-clockwise round Angkor Wat's bas-reliefs

**1 Western gallery** The southern half represents a scene from the Mahabharata of a battle between the Pandavas (with pointed head dresses, attacking from the right) and the Kauravas. The two armies come from the two ends of the panel and meet in the middle. The south-west corner has been badly damaged – some say by the Khmer Rouge – but shows scenes from Vishnu's life.

**2 Southern gallery** The western half depicts Suryavarman II (builder of Angkor Wat) leading a procession. He is riding a royal elephant, giving orders to his army before leading them into battle against the Cham. The rank of the army officers is indicated by the number of umbrellas. The undisciplined, outlandishly dressed figures are the Thais.

**3 Southern gallery** The eastern half was restored in 1946 and depicts the punishments and rewards one can expect in the after life. The damned are depicted in the bottom row, while the blessed, depicted in the upper two rows, are borne along in palanquins surrounded by large numbers of bare breasted apsaras.

**4 Eastern gallery** The southern half is the best-known part of the bas-relief – the churning of the sea of milk by gods and demons to make ambrosia (the nectar of the gods which gives immortality). In the centre, Vishnu commands the operation. Below are sea animals and above, apsaras.

**5 Eastern gallery** The northern half is an unfinished representation of a war between the gods for the possession of the ambrosia. The gate in the centre was used by Khmer royalty and dignitaries for mounting and dismounting elephants.

**6 Northern gallery** Represents a war between gods and demons. Siva is shown in meditation with Ganesh, Brahma and Krishna. Most of the other scenes are from the *Ramayana*, notably the visit of Hanuman (the monkey god) to Sita.

**7 Western gallery** The northern half has another scene from the *Ramayana* depicting a battle between Rama and Ravana who rides a chariot pulled by monsters and commands an army of giants.

Angkor Wat differs from other temples, primarily because it is facing westward, symbolically the direction of death, leading many to originally believe it was a tomb. However, as Vishnu is associated with the west, it is now generally accepted that it served both as a temple and a mausoleum for the king. Like other Khmer temple-mountains, Angkor Wat is an architectural allegory, depicting in stone the epic tales of Hindu mythology. The central sanctuary of the temple complex represents the sacred Mount Meru, the centre of the Hindu universe, on whose summit the gods reside. Angkor Wat's five towers symbolize Meru's five peaks; the enclosing wall represents the mountains at the edge of the world and the surrounding moat, the ocean beyond.

The temple complex is enclosed by a square moat – more than 5 km in length and 190 m wide – and a high, galleried wall, which is covered in epic bas-reliefs and has four ceremonial tower gateways. The main gateway faces west and the temple is approached by a 475-m-long road, built along a causeway, which is lined with naga balustrades. At the far end of the causeway stands a **cruciform platform**, guarded by stone lions, from which the devaraja may have held audiences; his backdrop being the three-tiered central sanctuary. Commonly referred to as the Terrace of Honour, it is entered through the colonnaded processional gateway of the outer gallery. The transitional enclosure beyond it is again cruciform in shape. Its four quadrants formed galleries, once stocked full of statues of the Buddha. Only a handful of the original 1000-odd images remain.

The cluster of **central towers**, 12 m above the second terrace, is reached by 12 steep stairways, which represent the precipitous slopes of Mount Meru. Many historians believe that the upwards hike to this terrace was reserved for the high priests and king himself. Today, anyone is welcome but the difficult climb is best handled slowly by stepping sideways up the steep incline. The five lotus flower-shaped sandstone towers – the first appearance of these features in Khmer architecture – are believed to have once been covered in gold. The eight-storey towers are square, although they appear octagonal, and give the impression of a sprouting bud. The central tower is dominant, as is the Siva shrine and principal sanctuary, whose pinnacle rises more than 30 m above the third level and, 55m above ground level. This sanctuary would have contained an image of Siva in the likeness of King Suryavarman II, as it was his temple-mountain. But it is now a Buddhist shrine and contains statues of the Buddha.

More than 1000 sq m of bas-relief decorate the temple. Its greatest sculptural treasure is the 2-m-high **bas-reliefs**, around the walls of the outer gallery. It is the longest continuous bas-relief in the world. In some areas traces of the paint and gilt that once covered the carvings can still be seen. Most famous are the hundreds of figures of deities and apsaras in niches along the walls.

# The royal city of Angkor Thom → Colour map 6, A2.

Construction of Jayavarman VII's spacious walled capital, Angkor Thom (which means 'great city'), began at the end of the 12th century: he rebuilt the capital after it had been captured and destroyed by the Cham. Angkor Thom was colossal: the 100-m-wide moat surrounding the city, which was probably stocked with crocodiles as a protection against the enemy, extended more than 12 km. Inside the moat was an 8-m-high stone wall, buttressed on the inner side by a high mound of earth along the top of which ran a terrace for troops to man the ramparts.

Four great gateways in the city wall face north, south, east and west and lead to the city's geometric centre, the Bayon. The fifth, Victory Gate, leads from the royal palace (within the Royal Enclosure) to the East Baray. The height of the gates was determined by the headroom needed to accommodate an elephant and howdah, complete with parasols. The flanks of each gateway are decorated by three-headed stone elephants, and each gateway tower has four giant faces, which keep an eye on all four cardinal points. Five causeways traverse the moat, each bordered by sculptured balustrades of nagas gripped, on one side, by 54 stern-looking giant gods and on the other by 54 fierce-faced demons. The balustrade depicts the Hindu legend of the churning of the sea (see page 324).

The **South Gate** provides the most common access route to Angkor Thom, predominantly because it sits on the path between the two great Angkor complexes. The gate is a wonderful introduction to Angkor Thom, with well-restored statues of asuras (demons) and gods lining the bridge. The figures on the left, exhibiting serene expression, are the gods, while those on the right, with grimaced, fierce-looking heads, are the asuras.

The **Bayon** was Jayavarman VII's own temple-mountain, built right in the middle of Angkor Thom; its large faces have now become synonymous with the Angkor complex. It is believed to have been built between the late 12th century to early 13th century, around 100 years after Angkor Wat. The Bayon is a three-tiered, pyramid-temple with a 45-m-high tower, topped by four gigantic carved heads. These faces are believed to be the images of Jayavarman VII as a Bodhisattra, and face the four compass points. They are crowned with lotus flowers, symbol of enlightenment, and are surrounded by 51 smaller towers each with heads facing north, south, east and west. There are more than 2000 large faces carved throughout the structure. The first two of the three levels feature galleries of bas-relief (which should be viewed clockwise); a circular central sanctuary dominates the third level. The **bas-reliefs** which decorate the walls of the Bayon are much less imposing than those at Angkor Wat. The sculpture is carved deeper but is more naive and less sophisticated than the bas-reliefs at Angkor Wat. The relief on the outside depicts historical events; those on the inside are drawn from the epic world of gods and legends, representing the creatures who were supposed to haunt the subterranean depths of Mount Meru. In fact the reliefs on the outer wall illustrating historical scenes and derring-do with marauding Cham were carved in the early 13th century during the reign of Jayavarman; those on the inside which illuminate the Hindu cosmology were carved after the king's death when his successors turned from Mahayana Buddhism back to Hinduism. Two recurring themes in the bas-reliefs are the powerful king and the Hindu epics. Jayavarman is depicted in the throes of battle with the Cham – who are recognizable thanks to their unusual and distinctive headdress, which looks like an inverted lotus flower. The other bas-reliefs give a good insight into Khmer life at the time – the warrior elephants, ox carts, fishing with nets, cockfights and skewered fish drying on racks. Other vignettes show musicians, jugglers, hunters, chess players, people nit-picking hair, palm-readers and reassuringly down-to-earth scenes of Angkor citizens enjoying drinking sessions. In the naval battle scenes, the water around the war-canoes is depicted by the presence of fish, crocodiles and floating corpses.

The **Royal Palace**, to the north of the Bayon, had already been laid out by Suryavarman I: the official palace was in the front with the domestic quarters behind, its gardens surrounded by a laterite wall and moat. Suryavarman I also beautified the royal city with ornamental pools. Jayavarman VII simply improved his designs. In front of the Royal Palace, at the centre of Angkor Thom, Suryavarman I laid out the

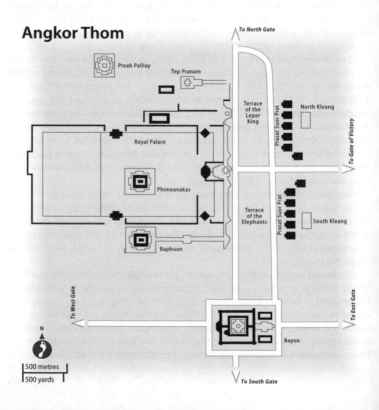

first Grand Plaza with the **Terrace of the Elephants** (also called the Royal Terrace). The 300-m-long wall derives its name from the large, life-like carvings of elephants in a hunting scene, adorning its walls. The 2.5-m wall also features elephants flanking the southern stairway. It is believed it was the foundations of the royal reception hall. Royalty once sat in gold-topped pavilions at the centre of the pavilion, and here there are rows of garudas (bird-men), their wings lifted as if in flight. They were intended to give the impression that the god-king's palace was floating in the heavens, like the imagined flying celestial palaces of the gods. At the northeast corner of the 'central square' is the 12th-century **Terrace of the Leper King**, which may have been a cremation platform for the aristocracy of Angkor. The 7-m-high double terrace has bands of bas-reliefs, one on top of the other, with intricately sculptured scenes of royal pageantry and seated apsaras as well as nagas and garudas which frequented the slopes of Mount Meru. Above is a strange statue of an earlier date, which probably depicts the god of death, Yama, and once held a staff in its right hand. The statue's naked, lichen-covered body gives the terrace its name – the lichen gives the uncanny impression of leprosy. The **Phimeanakas** (meaning Celestial or Flying Palace in Sanskrit) inside the Royal Palace was started by Rajendravarman and used by all the later kings. Lions guard all four stairways to the central tower. It is now ruined but was originally covered in gold.

South of the Royal Palace is the **Baphuon**, built by Udayadityavarman II. The temple was approached by a 200-m-long sandstone causeway, raised on pillars, which was probably constructed after the temple was built. **Preah Palilay**, just outside the north wall of the Royal Palace, was also built by Jayavarman VII.

# Around Angkor Thom

## Phnom Bakheng

ⓘ *Either climb the steep hill (slippery when wet), ride an elephant to the top of the hill (US$15) or walk up the gentle zig-zag path the elephants take.*

Yasovarman's temple-mountain stands at the top of a natural hill, Phnom Bakheng, 60 m high, affording good views of the plains of Angkor. A pyramid-temple dedicated to Siva, Bakheng was the home of the royal linga and Yasovarman's mausoleum after his death. It is composed of five towers built on a sandstone platform. There are 108 smaller towers scattered around the terraces. The main tower has been partially demolished and the others have completely disappeared. It was entered via a steep flight of steps which were guarded by squatting lions. The steps have deteriorated with the towers. Foliate scroll relief carving covers much of the main shrine – the first time this style was used. This strategically placed hill served as a camp for various combatants, including the Vietnamese, and suffered accordingly.

## Ta Prohm

For all would-be Mouhots and closet Indiana Joneses, the temple of Ta Prohm, is the perfect lost-in-the-jungle experience. Unlike most of the other monuments at Angkor, it has been only minimally cleared of its undergrowth, fig trees and creepers. It is widely regarded as one of Angkor's most enchanting temples.

Ta Prohm was consecrated in 1186 – five years after Jayavarman VII seized power. It was built to house the divine image of the Queen Mother. The outer enclosures of Ta Prohm are somewhat obscured by dense foliage but reach well-beyond the temple's heart (1 km by 650 m). The temple proper consists of a number of concentric galleries, featuring corner towers and the standard gopuras. Other buildings and enclosures were built on a more ad hoc basis.

Within the complex walls lived 12,640 citizens. It contained 39 sanctuaries or prasats, 566 stone dwellings and 288 brick dwellings. Ta Prohm literally translates to the 'Royal Monastery' and that is what it functioned as, home to 18 abbots and 2740 monks. By the 12th century, temples were no longer exclusively places of worship – they also had to accommodate monks, so roofed halls were increasingly built within the complexes.

The trees burgeoning their way through the complex are predominantly the silk-cotton tree and the aptly named strangler fig. Naturally, the roots of the trees have descended towards the soil, prying their way through the temples foundations in the process. As the vegetation has matured, growing stronger, it has forced its way further into the temples structure, damaging the man-built base and causing untold destruction.

## Banteay Kdei, Srah Srang, Prasat Kravan and Pre Rup

The massive complex of **Banteay Kdei**, otherwise known as 'the citadel of cells', is 3 km east of Angkor Thom. Some archaeologists think it may be dedicated to Jayavarman VII's religious teacher. The temple has remained in much the same state it was discovered in – a crowded collection of ruined laterite towers and connecting galleries lying on a flat plan, surrounded by a galleried enclosure. It is presumed that the temple was a Buddhist monastery and in recent years hundreds of buried Buddha statues were excavated from the site. Like Ta Prohm it contains a Hall of Dancers (east side), an open roof building with four separate quarters. The second enclosure runs around the perimeters of the inner enclosure. The third inner enclosure contains a north and south library and central sanctuary. The central tower was never finished. And the square pillars in the middle of the courtyard still can not be explained by scholars. There are few inscriptions here to indicate either its name or purpose, but it is almost certainly a Buddhist temple built in the 12th century, about the same time as Ta Prohm. The Lake (baray) next to Banteay Kdei is called **Srah Srang** – 'Royal Bath' – which was used for ritual bathing. The steps down to the water face the rising sun and are flanked with lions and nagas. This sandstone landing stage dates from the reign of Jayavarman VII but the Lake itself is thought to date back two centuries earlier. A 10th-century inscription reads 'this water is stored for the use of all creatures except dyke breakers', eg elephants. The baray (700 m by 300 m), has been filled with turquoise-blue waters for more than 1300 years. With a good view of Pre Rup across the lake, some archaeologists believe that this spot affords the best vista in the whole Angkor complex.

**Prasat Kravan**, built in 921, means 'Cardamom Sanctuary' and is unusual in that it is built of brick. By that time brick had been replaced by laterite and sandstone. It consists of five brick towers arranged in a line. The Hindu temple, surrounded by a moat, consists of five elevated brick towers, positioned in a North-South direction. Two of the five decorated brick towers contain bas-reliefs (the north and central towers). The central tower is probably the most impressive and contains a linga on a pedestal. The sanctuary's three walls all contain pictures of Vishnu.

Northeast of Srah Srang is **Pre Rup**, the State Temple of King Rajendravarman's capital. Built in 961, the temple-mountain representing Mount Meru is larger, higher and artistically superior than its predecessor, the East Mebon, which it closely resembles. Keeping with tradition of state capitals, Pre Rup marked the centre of the city, much of which doesn't exist today. The pyramid-structure, which is constructed of laterite with brick prasats, sits at the apex of an artificial, purpose-built mountain. The central pyramid-level consists of a three-tiered, sandstone platform, with five central towers sitting above. Its modern name, 'turning the body', derives from local legend and is named after a cremation ritual in which the outline of a body was traced in the cinders one way and then the other. The upper levels of the pyramid offer a brilliant, panoramic view of the countryside.

# Preah Khan

The 12th-century complex of Preah Khan, one of the largest complexes within the Angkor area, was Jayavarman VII's first capital before Angkor Thom was completed. Preah Khan means 'sacred sword' and is believed to have derived from a decisive battle against the Cham, which created a 'lake of blood', but was invariably won by Jayavarman VII. It is similar in ground-plan to Ta Prohm (see page 329) but attention was paid to the approaches: its east and west entrance avenues leading to ornamental causeways are lined with carved-stone boundary posts. Evidence of 1000 teachers suggests that it was more than a mere Buddhist monastery but most likely a Buddhist university. Nonetheless an abundance of Brahmanic iconography is still present on site. Around the rectangular complex, is a large laterite wall, surrounded by large garudas wielding the naga (each more than 5 m in height), the theme continues across the length of the whole 3-km external enclosure, with the motif dotted every 50 m. Within these walls lies the surrounding moat.

# Preah Neak Pean

To the east of Preah Khan is the Buddhist temple Preah Neak Pean built by Jayavarman VII. The exquisite temple of Neak Pean is also a fountain, built in the middle of a pool and representing the paradisiacal Himalayan mountain-lake, Anaavatapta, from Hindu mythology. It is a small sanctuary on an island in the baray of Preah Khan. Two nagas form the edge of the island, and their tails join at the back. The temple pools were an important part of the aesthetic experience of Preah Khan and Neak Pean – the ornate stone carving of both doubly visible by reflection.

---

# Outlying temples → *Colour map 6, A2 and B2.*

## The Roluos Group → *Colour map 6, B2.*

The Roluos Group receives few visitors but is worth visiting if time permits. Jayavarman II built several capitals including one at Roluos, at that time called Hariharalaya. This was the site of his last city and remained the capital during the reigns of his three successors. The three remaining Hindu sanctuaries at Roluos are **Preah Ko**, **Bakong** and **Lolei**. They were finished in 879, 881 and 893 respectively by Indravarman I and his son Yashovarman I and are the best-preserved of the early temples. All three temples are built of brick, with sandstone doorways and niches. Sculptured figures which appear in the Roluos group are the crouching lion, the reclining bull (Nandi – Siva's mount) and the naga (snake).

**Preah Ko**, meaning 'sacred ox', was named after the three statues of Nandi (the mount of the Hindu god, Siva) which stand in front of the temple. Orientated east-west, there is a cluster of six brick towers arranged in two rows on a low brick platform, the steps up to which are guarded by crouching lions while Nandi, looking back, blocks the way. The front row of towers was devoted to Indravarman's male ancestors and the second row to the female. Indravarman's temple-mountain, **Bakong**, is a royal five-stepped pyramid-temple with a sandstone central tower built on a series of successively receding terraces with surrounding brick towers. Indravarman himself was buried in the temple. Bakong is the largest and most impressive temple in the Roluos Group by a long way. A bridge flanked by a naga balustrade leads over a dry moat to the temple. The central tower was built to replace the original one when the monument was restored in the 12th century and is probably larger than the original. The Bakong denotes the true beginning of classical Khmer architecture and contained the god-king's Siva linga. **Lolei** was built by Yashovarman I in the middle of Indravarman's baray. The brick towers were dedicated to the king's ancestors, but over the centuries they have largely disintegrated; of the four towers two have partly collapsed.

Banteay Srei, 25 km from Ta Prohm along a decent road, was built by the Brahmin tutor to King Rajendravarman, Yajnavaraha, grandson of Harshavarman, and founded in 967. Banteay Srei translates to 'Citadel of Women', a title bestowed upon it in relatively recent years due to the intricate apsara carvings that adorn the interior. The temple is considered by many historians to be the highest achievement of art from the Angkor period. The explicit preservation of this temple reveals covered terraces, of which only the columns remain, which once lined both sides of the primary entrance. In keeping with tradition, a long causeway leads into the temple, across a moat, on the eastern side. The main walls, entry pavilions and libraries have been constructed from laterite and the carvings from pink sandstone. The layout was inspired by Prasat Thom at Koh Ker. Three beautifully carved tower-shrines stand side by side on a low terrace in the middle of a quadrangle, with a pair of libraries on either side enclosed by a wall. Two of the shrines, the southern one and the central one, were dedicated to Siva and the northern one to Vishnu; both had libraries close by, with carvings depicting appropriate legends. The whole temple is dedicated to Brahma. Having been built by a Brahmin priest, the temple was never intended for use by a king, which goes some way towards explaining its small size – you have to duck to get through the doorways to the sanctuary towers. Perhaps because of its modest scale Banteay Srei contains some of the finest examples of Khmer sculpture. Finely carved and rare pink sandstone replaces the plaster-coated carved-brick decoration, typical of earlier temples. All the buildings are covered in carvings: the jambs, the lintels, the balustered windows. Banteay Srei's ornamentation is exceptional – its roofs, pediments and lintels are magnificently carved with tongues of flame, serpents' tails, gods, demons and floral garlands.

# Siem Reap ⬤🍴🎭🛏️🏕️🔺🚌☕ » *pp332-340. Colour map 6, A2.*

The nearest town to Angkor, Siem Reap is seldom considered as anything other than a service centre and it is true that without the temples, few people would ever find themselves here. The town has smartened itself up quite substantially in the past couple of years and, with the blossoming of hotels, restaurants and bars, it is now a pleasant place in its own right.

The Old Market area is the most touristed part of the town. Staying around here is recommended for independent travellers and those staying more than two or three days. A sprinkling of guesthouses are here but a much greater selection is offered just across the river, in the Wat Bo area.

## 🛏️ Sleeping

**Siem Reap** *p332, maps p333 and p334*
**L Hotel de la Paix**, corner of Achemean and Sivatha, T063-966000, www.hoteldela paixangkor.com. Owned by the same company that also runs Bangkok's famous Bed Supper Club, this is probably Siem Reap's best value luxury hotel. The rooms offer simple contemporary design with giant bath tubs and plump bedding – all a/c and with cable TV. The pool is a maze of plinths and greenery and makes for a perfect spot to laze. Can feel a bit urban for Siem Reap but still a great hotel. Recommended.

**L Le Meridien Angkor**, main road towards temples, T063-963900, www.lemeridien. com/angkor. From the outside this 5-star hotel resembles a futuristic prison camp – severe, angled architecture with small, dark slits for windows. Walk into the lobby and it is immediately transformed into space and light, becoming, in a flash, a pretty decent place to lay your hat. Rooms are nicely designed and sized and all come with a/c, en suite and cable TV. Other facilities include spa, restaurants and pool. The garden is a lovely spot to take breakfast. Recommended.

# Siem Reap

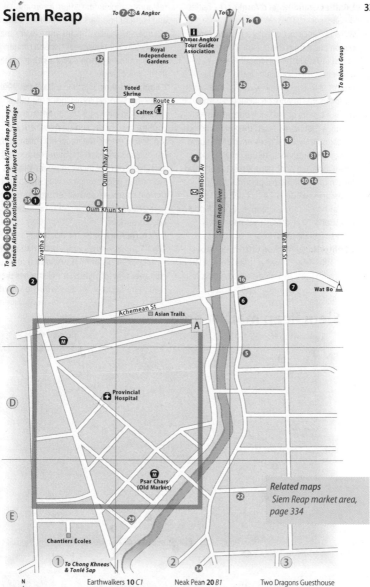

*Related maps*
*Siem Reap market area,*
*page 334*

N

100 metres
100 yards

**Sleeping** 🛏
Angkoriana **2** *A2*
Angkor Village Resort **1** *A3*
Apsara Angkor **3** *C1*
Bopha **5** *D3*
Borann **6** *A3*
Casa Angkor **8** *B1*

Earthwalkers **10** *C1*
Empress Angkor **11** *B1*
European Guesthouse **12** *B3*
FCC Angkor **4** *B2*
Golden Banana B&B **34** *E2*
Green Garden Home
  Guesthouse **35** *B1*
Home Sweet Home **14** *B3*
Jasmine Lodge **15** *B1*
La Residence D'Angkor **16** *C3*
La Villa Loti **17** *A2*
Le Meridien Angkor **7** *A2*
Mahogany Guesthouse **18** *B3*
Monoreach **19** *B1*

Neak Pean **20** *B1*
Paul Dubrule **9** *C1*
Passaggio **22** *E3*
Raffles Grand d'Angkor
  **13** *A2*
Rosy Guesthouse **25** *A3*
Secrets of Elephants
  Guesthouse **26** *B1*
Shinta Mani **27** *B2*
Sokha Angkor **21** *A1*
Sofitel Royal Angkor **28** *A2*
Sweet Dreams
  Guesthouse **31** *B3*
Ta Prohm **29** *E2*

Two Dragons Guesthouse
  **30** *B3*
Victoria Angkor **32** *A1*
Yaklom Angkor
  Lodge **33** *A3*

**Eating** 🍴
Abacus **1** *B1*
Barrio **2** *C1*
Madame Butterfly **5** *B1*
Moloppor **6** *C3*
Viroth's **7** *C3*
Pyongyang **3** *B1*

**L Raffles Grand Hotel d'Angkor**, 1 Charles de Gaulle Blvd, T063-963888, www.raffles.com. Certainly a magnificent period piece from the outside, Siem Reap's oldest (1930) hotel fails to generate ambience, the rooms are sterile and the design of the huge new wings is uninspired (unforgivable in Angkor). Coupled with this is a history of staff lock-outs and mass sackings that have caused the Raffles brand damage. However, it does have all the mod cons, including sauna, tennis, health and beauty spa, lap pool, gym, 8 restaurants and bars, nightly traditional performances, landscaped gardens, 24-hr valet service and in-house movie channels. Considering its astronomical rates guests have every right to feel disappointed.

**L Sofitel Royal Angkor**, Charles de Gaulle Blvd, T063-964600, www.sofitel.com. A large 238-room hotel in a garden-like setting, a large attractive swimming pool and 5 restaurants (including Asian, International and French) and bars. Other perks include an open-air jacuzzi, health and beauty spa. Rates include buffet breakfast and dinner. Not as intimate as some of the other hotels in this price range.

**L Sokha Angkor**, Sivatha St, T063-969999, www.sokhahotels.com. One of the few Cambodian-owned 5-star hotels in the country, the rooms and services here are top notch, even if the decor is a little gaudy (if you can't afford to stay here, do come and check out the incredibly over-the-top swimming pool, complete with faux temple structures and waterfalls). Also home to an excellent Japanese restaurant. Recommended.

**L Victoria Angkor Hotel**, Route 6, T063-760428, www.victoriahotels-asia.com. Perfection. A beautiful hotel, with that 1930s east-meets-west style that exemplifies the French tradition of 'art de vivre'. The superb

## Siem Reap market area

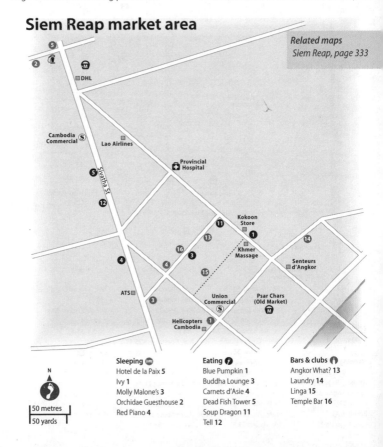

*Related maps*
*Siem Reap, page 333*

**Sleeping** 🛏
Hotel de la Paix **5**
Ivy **1**
Molly Malone's **3**
Orchidae Guesthouse **2**
Red Piano **4**

**Eating** 🍴
Blue Pumpkin **1**
Buddha Lounge **3**
Carnets d'Asie **4**
Dead Fish Tower **5**
Soup Dragon **11**
Tell **12**

**Bars & clubs** 🍸
Angkor What? **13**
Laundry **14**
Linga **15**
Temple Bar **16**

50 metres
50 yards

decor make you feel like you are staying in another era. Each room is beautifully decorated with local fabrics and fantastic furniture. Swimming pool, open-air salas, jacuzzi and spa. It's the small touches and attention to detail that stands this hotel apart from the rest. Highly recommended.

**L-AL Angkor Village Resort**, T063-963561, www.angkor village.com. Opened in 2004, the resort contains 40 rooms set in Balinese-style surroundings. The accommodation pays homage to traditional Asian architecture with lovely fittings, especially in the bathrooms. Traditional massage services, 2 restaurants, theatre shows and lovely pool. Elephant, boat and helicopter rides can be arranged. Recommended.

**L-AL Apsara Angkor Hotel**, Route 6 (between the airport and town), T063-964999, www.apsaraangkor.com. Pretty standard hotel for the money they are asking. Well-appointed rooms with all amenities but they are rather kitsch. Facilities include gym, internet, swimming pool. Visa/MasterCard/AMEX.

**L-AL Empress Angkor**, Airport Rd, opposite cultural village, T063-963999, www.empressangkor.com. One of the newest luxury hotels in town. The wooden interior is much nicer than you'd expect from the outside. 207 cosy guestrooms with all the usual inclusions, plus cable TV and balcony. Hotel facilities include restaurant (international and local cuisine), bar, massage, gym, swimming pool, jacuzzi spa and sauna. Visa/AMEX/MasterCard/JCB.

**L-AL La Residence D'Angkor Hotel**, River Rd, T063-963390, www.residence angkor.com. This is a hotel to aspire to. With its beautifully laid out rooms all lavishly furnished with marble and hardwoods, it is reassuringly expensive. Each room has a huge, free-form bathtub – which is the perfect end to a day touring the temples. The pool is lined with handmade tiles in a variety of green hues and, like the rest of the hotel, is in true Angkor style.

**L-AL Shinta Mani**, junction of Oum Khun and 14th St, T063-761998, www.shintamani.com. This 18-room boutique, luxury hotel is wonderful in every way: the design, the amenities, the food and the service. The hotel also offers a beautiful pool, library and has mountain bikes available. Provides vocational training to underprivileged youth.

**L-A FCC Angkor**, near the post office on Pokambor Av, T063-760280, www.fcc cambodia.com. The sister property of the famous FCC Phnom Penh this is a cute hotel set in the grounds of a restored, modernist villa. Rooms offer contemporary luxury and plenty of space but be warned – there is a massive generator at one end of the complex running 24/7 so make sure you are housed well away from here. Also tends to trade more on its reputation so service, food etc can be decidedly ropey.

**AL Monoreach Hotel**, Airport Rd, T063-760182, www.monoreach.com. Newly established international hotel, with 110 rooms and suites. Has a real Chinese-hotel feel to it. The room amenities include a/c, cable TV, IDD, minibar, hot water, bath tub. Onsite is a swimming pool, gym and restaurant. Rooms on average are about US$70 a night but there are a few more expensive ones that have pushed this hotel up into this category.

**A Ta Prohm**, T063-380117, www.angkor hotels.org/Ta_Prohm_Hotel. 95 large rooms in a well-kept and long-established property overlooking the river. Bathroom with bath tub. It is a touch overpriced but fair by Siem Reap standards. From the outside it can be difficult to tell whether the hotel is actually open but it is. Restaurant and tourist services.

**A-B Angkoriana Hotel**, 297 Phum Boeng Daun Pa, Khum (the main road to the temples), T063-760274, www.angkoriana hotel.com. Simply-furnished rooms with a/c, mini-bar, cable TV etc. Renovated restaurant serving Khmer and French cuisine. Pool.

**A-B Casa Angkor**, corner of Chhay St and Oum Khun St, T063-966234, www.casa angkorhotel.com. This is a good-looking, pleasant and well-managed 21-room hotel. 3 classes of room, all a decent size, well appointed and with cool wooden floors. Friendly reception and efficient staff. Restaurant, beer garden and reading room.

**A-B Molly Malone's**, Old Market area, T063-963533. Fantastic rooms with 4-poster beds and good clean bathrooms. Irish pub downstairs. Lovely owners. Recommended.

**A-B Neak Pean**, 53 Sivatha St, T063-924429, neakpean@camintel.com. 100 rooms, many in large wooden bungalows behind the main building. Swimming pool and garden. Large restaurant.

**A-B Passaggio**, near the Old Market, T063-760324, www.passaggio-hotel.com. 15 double and 2 family rooms, spacious, a/c, minibar and cable TV, internet, laundry service, bar and restaurant, outdoor terrace.

**B Borann**, T063-964740, borann@pig pond.com.kh. This is an attractive hotel in a delightful garden with a swimming pool. It is secluded and private. 5 small buildings each contain 4 comfortable rooms with terracotta floors and a lot of wood. Some rooms have a/c, some fan only: price varies accordingly.

**B La Villa Loti** (also known as Coconut House), 105 River Rd, T012-888403, resinf@lavillaloti.com. Fantastic French-run guesthouse, with 8 rooms in a big, wooden house. Good for laying back in a deckchair, amongst the tropical gardens, after a tiring day at the temples. Internet, massage, bicycles.

**B Secrets of Elephants Guesthouse**, Highway 6, Airport Rd, T063-964328, info@angkortravel.com. Traditional wooden Khmer house, with just 8 rooms. French-run but English spoken. The garden is a mini jungle. The house is beautifully furnished with antiques, silks, ornaments and hangings. All rooms have their own private bathroom but not necessarily en suite. Breakfast included and other meals prepared to order. Some rooms a/c, some fan only.

**B Yaklom Angkor Lodge**, Wat Bo St, T012-983510, www.yaklom.com. An attractive site and friendly, competent staff who speak good English. The 10 small, simple bungalows are built slightly too close together. Try to negotiate a discount. Breakfast and airport transfer included. Sawasdee Thai restaurant.

**B-C Bopha**, on the east side of the river, T063-964928, bopharesa@everyday.com.kh. Stunning hotel. Good rooms with all the amenities, decorated with local furniture and fabrics. Brilliant Thai-Khmer restaurant. Highly recommended.

**B-C Paul Dubrule Hotel and Tourism School**, airport road about 3km from town centre, T063-963672, www.ecolepaul dubrule.org. Set up by its namesake and founder of the Accor hotel group, the Paul Dubrule school has to be one of the best bargains in town. Sure, you'll be looked after by wide-eyed trainees and there's only a skeleton staff after 1800, but the rooms, themed on the local hotels that help sponsor the project, are excellent value. There are only 4 to choose from, the most expensive representing the best deal. All are a/c, with TV, hot water and include breakfast. Recommended.

**C Home Sweet Home**, T063-963245, sweethome@ camintel.com. Popular guesthouse and a favourite of the moto drivers (who get a kickback). Regardless, it is still quite good accommodation. Good clean rooms, some with TV and a/c.

**C-D Golden Banana Bed and Breakfast**, Wat Damnak Area (past Martini Bar), T012-885366, info@golden-banana.com. Good, clean rooms and decent restaurant.

**C-D Red Piano**, off Sivatha St (about 250 m from the restaurant), T063-963240, www.redpianocambodia.com. 15, clean a/c rooms with en suite bathroom.

**C-D Two Dragons Guesthouse**, Wat Bo Village, T012-868551. Really nice, clean rooms with beautiful photographs decorating them. Good little Thai restaurant. Gordon, the owner of this place, is one of the well-briefed guys in Siem Reap and runs www.talesofasia.com website. He can organize a whole range of unique and exciting tours in the area.

**D Green Garden Home Guesthouse**, down a small lane off Sivatha St, T012-890363. Price varies according to facilities required. A/c or fan, hot water or cold water etc, cable TV. Garden not as great as their PR would suggest.

**D Rosy Guesthouse**, east side of river before **Noria**, T063-965059, www.rosyguesthouse.com. Good, clean rooms with bathroom. Very popular.

**D-E Earthwalkers**, just off the Airport Rd, T012-967901, mail@earthwalkers.no. Popular European-run budget guesthouse. Good gardens and pool table. Bit far out of town.

**D-E European Guesthouse**, T012-846803, john_oc@hotmail.com. 12 fan rooms in a lane off Wat Bo St occupied by 3 guesthouses.

**D-E Ivy**, across from the Old Market, T012-800860. Reasonable rooms above the restaurant and bar.

**D-E Sweet Dreams Guesthouse**, off Wat Bo St, T012-783013, homesweethome@everyday.com.kh. Clean and well kept rooms in this small guesthouse in a quiet cul-de-sac. A favourite of the motos who obviously get a commission for bringing you here. Restaurant.

**D-F Jasmine Lodge**, Highway 6, Aiport Rd, T012-784980, jasmine lodge@camnet.com.kh. Good budget accommodation, clean rooms (the outside ones are better). Lots of travel services. Often gets booked out in advance so contact them first.

**D-F Orchidae Guesthouse**, T012-849716. A few houses down from the Naga Guesthouse and much better. Hammocks, restaurant and decent sized, clean rooms with shower or shared facilities. Recommended.

**E Mahogany Guesthouse**, Wat Bo St, T063-963417/012-768944, proeun@bigpond.com.kh. Fan and now some a/c. An attractive and popular guesthouse, lovely wooden floor upstairs (try to avoid staying downstairs), coffee-making facilities and a friendly crowd of guests.

## ⊘ Eating

### Angkor *p325*

Near the moat there are a number of cheap food and drink stalls, bookshops and posse of hawkers selling film, souvenirs, etc. Outside the entrance to Angkor Wat is a larger selection of cafés and restaurants including the sister restaurant to **Blue Pumpkin**, serving good sandwiches and breakfasts, ideal for takeaway.

### Siem Reap *p332, maps p333 and p334*

**₮₮₮ Abacus**, Oum Khun St, off Sivatha St, T012-644286. A little further out from the main Old Market area, this place is considered one of the best restaurants in town. Offering French and Cambodian, everything is fantastic here. The fish is superb, the steak is to die for. Recommended.

**₮₮₮ Barrio**, Sivatha St, away from the central area. Fantastic French and Khmer food. A favourite of the expats. Recommended.

**₮₮₮ Carnets d'Asie**, 333 Sivatha St, T016-746701. Primarily a French restaurant also offering some Khmer and Thai dishes. Outdoor and indoor seating in a garden, dotted with traditional Khmer parasols and a lovely water feature. Set menu and à la carte. Good Australian beef. Can't beat this one for atmosphere.

**₮₮₮ FCC**, Pokamber Av, T063-760280. Sister to the Phnom Penh restaurant, this one is a bit more schmick. Good range of world-class food and drinks, nice surroundings, great armchairs, sophisticated.

**₮₮₮ Madame Butterfly**, Airport Rd. Fantastic French and Khmer food. A favourite of the expats.

**₮₮ The Blue Pumpkin**, Old Market area, T063-963574. Western and Asian food and drinks. Sandwiches, ice cream, pitta, salads and pasta. Candidate for 'least likely eatery to find in Siem Reap' with its white minimalist decor reminiscent of the finest establishments in New York or London. Good breakfasts and cheap cocktails. Eat on the second level. Branches at both the International and domestic terminals at the airport and across from Angkor. Recommended if you need a retreat for half an hour.

**₮₮ Bopha**, on the east side of the river, slightly up from Passagio, T063-964928. Fantastic Thai-Khmer restaurant in lovely, tranquil garden setting. One of the absolute best in town. Highly recommended.

**₮₮ Buddha Lounge**, 184 Mondol St. Bar and restaurant offering mostly Western food.

**₮₮ Dead Fish Tower**, Sivatha Blvd, T063-963060. Thai and Khmer restaurant in a fantastically eclectic modern Thai setting. Multiple platforms, quirky decorations, sculptures, apsara dance shows, small putting green and a crocodile farm all add to the atmosphere of this popular restaurant.

**₮₮ Ivy**, across from the Old Market, T012-800860. Cosy, airy restaurant and bar servingBritish-style meals, plus a few Khmerdishes. Good breakfasts and roasts. Very popular.

**₮₮ Molly Malone's**, T063-963533. Lovely Irish bar and restaurant offering classic dishes like Irish lamb stew, shepherd's pie, roasts and fish and chips.

**₮₮ Pyongyang**, on the airport road about 1.5 km from the town centre. Excellent North Korean food is served in this twin restaurant of the eaterie with the same name in Phnom Penh. This place is a true oddity and has to be seen to be believed. Hosted by a bevy of North Korean beauties who perform a truly staggering dance routine every night at 2000, you'll find great *bulgolgi* (beef ribs), *kimchi* and other Korean specialties proffered here (including bear bile, by the way). Highly recommended.

**Soup Dragon**, T063-964933. Serves a variety of Khmer and Vietnamese dishes but its speciality is soups in earthenware pots cooked at the table. Breezy and clean, a light and colourful location sitting on a corner terrace surrounded by plants. Upstairs bar, happy hour 1600-1930.

**Tell**, 374 Sivatha St, T063-963289. Swiss, German, Austrian restaurant and bar. Branch of the long established Phnom Penh restaurant. Serves excellent fondue and raclette, imported beer and sausages. Reasonable prices and generous portions.

**The Red Piano**, northwest of the Old Market, T063-964750. An institution in Siem Reap, based in a 100-year-old colonial building. Coffee, sandwiches, salad and pastas. Cocktail bar, offering a range of tipples, including one dedicated to Angelina Jolie (who frequented the establishment while working on Tomb Raider).

**Viroth's Restaraunt**, No 246 Wat Bo St, T016-951800. Upmarket place offering very good modern Khmer cuisine plus a few Western staples. Looks more expensive than it actually is and is good value.

**Moloppor**, east of the river, near Bopha Hotel. Good cheap Japanese and pizzas.

**Orchidae Guesthouse**, fantastic Asian meals.

**Paul Dubrule Hotel and Tourism School**, airport road about 3km from town centre, T063-963672, www.ecolepauldubrule.org. As well as being a great place to stay, the school also offers a pretty good set lunch. It can be hit and miss but the quality is often very high and they are always eager to keep their guests happy. Your money will also go to support an excellent vehicle for development – some of the school's graduates have gone on to be well-paid chefs at some of Asia's top hotels and restaurants.

## ⊙ Bars and clubs

**Siem Reap** *p332, maps p333 and p334*
**Angkor What?**, Bar St, T012-631136. Open early evening to early morning. Bar run by friendly staff, popular with travellers and young expats.

**Dead Fish**, bar and informal diner serving Thai food.

**Easy Speaking**, T012-865332. Good little bar with inside and outside seating.

**Ivy**, popular bar and restaurant opposite Old Market. 0700 until late. Pool table, all-day breakfast for US$4.

**Laundry**, near the Old Market, turn right off Bar St, T016-962026. Funky little bar open till late.

**Linga**, Laneway behind Bar St, T012-246912. Gay-friendly bar offering a wide selection of cocktails. Great whisky sour.

**Red Piano**, Bar St, Old Market Area, T012-854150. A comfortable bar/diner furnished with large wicker armchairs.

**Temple Bar**, Bar St. Popular drinking hole, dimly lit, good music.

## ⊙ Entertainment

**Siem Reap** *p332, maps p333 and p334*
**Shadow puppetry** is one of the finest performing arts of the region. The **Bayon Restaurant**, Wat Bo road, has regular shadow puppet shows in the evening. Local NGO, Krousar Thmey, often tour its shadow puppet show to Siem Reap. The show is performed by underprivileged children (who have also made the puppets) at **La Noria Restaurant** (Wed, 1930 but check as they can be a tad irregular). Donations accepted.

A popular Sat evening attraction is the one-man concert put on by **Dr Beat Richner** (Beatocello), founder of the Jayavarman VII hospital for children. Run entirely on voluntary donations the 3 hospitals in the foundation need US$9 million per year in order to treat Cambodian children free of charge. He performs at the hospital, on the road to Angkor, at 1915, 1 hr, free admission but donations gratefully accepted. An interesting and worthwhile experience.

# O Shopping

**Siem Reap** *p332, maps p333 and p334*
Outside Phnom Penh Siem Reap is about
the only place whose markets are worth
browsing in for genuinely interesting
souvenirs. **Old Market (Psar Chars)** is not a
large market but stallholders and keepers
of the surrounding shops have developed
quite a good understanding of what tickles
the appetite of foreigners: Buddhist statues
and icons, reproductions of Angkor figures,
silks, cottons, kramas, sarongs, silverware,
leather puppets and rice paper rubbings of
Angkor bas-reliefs are unusual mementos.
**Chantiers Écoles**, down a short lane off
Sivatha St, T/F063-964097. School for
orphaned children which trains them in
carving, sewing and weaving. Products
are on sale under the name Les Artisans
d'Angkor and raise 30% of the school's
running costs.
**Senteurs d'Angkor**, opposite Old Market,
T063-964801. Sells a good selection of
handicrafts, carvings, silverware, silks,
handmade paper, cards, scented oils,
incense, pepper and spices.

# ▲ Activities and tours

**Siem Reap** *p332, maps p333 and p334*
**Therapies**
Khmer, Thai, reflexology and Japanese
massage are readily available. Many
masseuses will come to your hotel.
**Franginpani**, near old market, down the
side street opposite Kokoon, T063-757120.
Professional masseuse, offering
aromatherapy, reflexology and other
treatments.
**Seeing Hands** massage, T063-836487, by
seeing impaired individuals, US$3 an hr.
Highly recommended.

**Tour operators**
**Asian Trails**, No. 587, Hup Quan St,
Mondol 1, Khum Svaydangkum,
T063-964595, www.asiantrails.com. Offers
a broad selection of tours to Angkor and
beyond. Also cruises and biking trips.
**ATS**, Sivatha St, T063-760041. All manner
of local arrangements, boat tickets, minibus
tickets, car hire. Visa service. Internet service.

**Data Sight Travel**, 430 Sivatha St,
T063-963081, info@datasighttravel.com.
Very, very helpful travel agent. Organizes
tours, ticketing and a whole range of tourist
services. Ask for Lim.
**Exotissimo Travel**, No 300, Highway 6,
T063-964323, www.exotissimo.com.
Tours of Angkor and sites beyond.
**Hidden Cambodia Adventure Tours**,
T012-934412, www.hiddencambodia.com.
Specializing in dirt bike tours to some of
Cambodia's remote areas and off-the-
track temple locations. Recommended
for the adventurers.
**Journeys Within**, on the outskirts of Siem
Reap towards the temples, T063-964748,
www.journeys-within.com. Specializes
in private, customized tours, visiting
temples and experiencing the everyday
lives of Cambodians.
**RTR Tours**, No 331, Group 7, Modul 1
(in the Old Market Area) T063-964646,
www.rtrtours.com.kh. Organizes tours
plus other travel services, including
ticketing. Friendly and helpful.
**Terre Cambodge**, on Frangipani
premises, Old Market area, T012-843401,
www.terrecambodge.com. Tours with a
twist, including cruises on an old sampan.
Particularly good option for tours of the
floating villages of the Tonlé Sap. Not
cheap but worth it for the experience.

# ⊝ Transport

**Siem Reap** *p332, maps p333 and p334*
**Air**
Airline availability and flight schedules are
particularly prone to sudden change, so
ensure you check/book well in advance.
**Airline offices** Bangkok Airways/Siem
Reap Airways, Highway 6, T063-380191.
6 flights a day from Bangkok. **Helicopters
Cambodia**, near Old Market, T012-814500.
A New Zealand company offers chartered
flights around the temples. **Lao Airlines**,
opposite provincial hospital, T/F063-963283,
3 flights a week to Vientiane via Pakse.
**President Airlines**, Sivatha St, T063-964338.
**Vietnam Airlines**, Highway 6, T063-964488,
www.vietnamairlines.com. Also general
sales agent in town opposite provincial
hospital, T063-964929.

Khemara, opposite the Old Market, T063-964512, rents bicycles for US$2 per day.

**Bus**

Neak Krorhorm Travel, GST, Mekong Express and Capitol go to and from Siem Reap. Most buses depart Phnom Penh bus station between 0630 and 0800 and the same from Siem Reap (departing near the Old Market). The best bus service is the Mekong Express, US$6. It has the quickest service (about 5 hrs).

**Helicopter and balloon**

Helicopters Cambodia, Old Market area, Siem Reap, T012-814500, helicopter.cam.s@online.com.kh, run 8-min charter flights to Angkor Wat for US$204 per person (1-2 people) or US$68 (3-5 people) – great for gaining a perspective on the sheer scale of the complex. It also provides a longer 14-min tour to some of the outlying temples, US$360 per person (1-2 people) or US$120 per person (3-5 people). For charter flights further afield, the company charges a whopping US$1400 per hr. Credit cards accepted (3% surcharge). A cheaper (but not nearly as fun) alternative for a good aerial view is to organize a balloon ride above the temples. The tethered balloons float 200 m above Angkor Wat for about 10 mins, US$10 per trip. The balloon company is based about 1 km from the main gates from Angkor Wat, on the road from the airport to the temples.

## ⓘ Directory

**Siem Reap** *p332, maps p333 and p334*
**Banks** Cambodia Commercial Bank, 130 Sivatha St. Currency and TC exchange. Advance on Visa, MasterCard, JCB, AMEX. **Mekong Bank**, 43 Sivatha, Mon-Fri, Sat am, US dollar TCs cashed, 2% commission, cash advance on Visa and JCB cards only. **Union Commercial Bank**, north of Old Market, Mon-Fri and Sat am. Cash advance on MasterCard and Visa (no commission). Cash TCs. **Internet** Rates vary but should be around 3000 riel per hr. Most internet cafés now offer internet calls. **Medical services** The medical facilities are okay here but by now means of an international standard. In most cases it is probably best to fly to Bangkok. **Naga International Clinic**, Highway 6 (airport road), T063-965988. International medical services. 24-hr emergency care. **Post office** Pokamber Av, on the west side of Siem Reap river but can take up to a month for mail to be delivered, 0700-1700.

# History

## Pre-history

Archaeological evidence suggests that the Mekong Delta and the lower reaches of the river – in modern-day Cambodia – have been inhabited since at least 4,000 BC. But the wet and humid climate has destroyed most of the physical remains of the early civilizations. Excavated remains of a settlement at Samrong Sen on the Tonlé Sap show that houses were built from bamboo and wood and raised on stilts – exactly as they are today. Where these people came from is uncertain but anthropologists have suggested that there were two waves of migration; one from the Malay peninsula and Indonesia and a second from Tibet and China.

## Rise of the Lunar and Solar dynasties

For thousands of years Indochina was isolated from the rest of the world and was virtually unaffected by the rise and fall of the early Chinese dynasties. India and China 'discovered' Southeast Asia early in the first millennium AD and trade networks were quickly established. The Indian influence was particularly strong in the Mekong basin area. The Khmers adopted and adapted Indian script as well as their ideas about astrology, religion (Buddhism and Hinduism) and royalty (the cult of the semi-divine ruler). Today, several other aspects of Cambodian culture are recognizably Indian in origin – including classical literature and dance. Religious architecture also followed Indian models. These Indian cultural influences which took root in Indochina gave rise to a legend to which Cambodia traces its historical origins. An Indian Brahmin called Kaundinya, travelling in the Mekong Delta area, married Soma, daughter of the Naga (the serpent deity), or Lord of the Soil. Their union, which founded the 'Lunar Dynasty' of Funan (a pre-Angkorian Kingdom), symbolized the fertility of the kingdom and occupies a central place in Khmer cosmology. The Naga, Soma's father, helpfully drank the floodwaters of the Mekong, enabling people to cultivate the land.

### Funan

The kingdom of Funan – the forerunner of Kambuja – was established on the Mekong by tribal people from South China in the middle of the third century AD and became the earliest Hindu state in Southeast Asia. Funan was known for its elaborate irrigation canals which controlled the Mekong floodwaters, irrigated the paddy fields and prevented the incursion of seawater. By the fifth century Funan had extended its influence over most of present day Cambodia, as well as Indochina and parts of the Malay peninsula. Leadership was measured by success in battle and the ability to provide protection, and in recognition of this fact, rulers from the Funan period onward incorporated the suffix 'varman' (meaning protection) into their names. Records of a third century Chinese embassy give an idea of what it was like: "There are walled villages, places and dwellings. The men ... go about naked and barefoot. ... Taxes are paid in gold, silver and perfume. There are books and libraries and they can use the alphabet." Twentieth-century excavations suggest a seafaring people engaged in extensive trade with both India and China, and elsewhere.

The 'Solar Dynasty' of Chenla was a vassal kingdom of Funan, probably first based on the Mekong at the junction with the Mun tributary, but it rapidly grew in power, and was centred in the area of present day southern Laos. It was the immediate predecessor of Kambuja and the great Khmer Empire. According to Khmer legend, the kingdom was the result of the marriage of Kambu, an ascetic, to a celestial nymph named Mera. The people of Chenla – the Kambuja, or the sons of Kambu – lent their name to the country. In AD 540 a Funan prince married a Chenla princess, uniting the Solar and Lunar dynasties. The prince sided with his wife and Funan was swallowed by Chenla. The first capital of this fusion was at **Sambor**. King Ishanavarman (616-635) established a new capital at Sambor Prei Kuk, 30 km from modern Kompong Thom, in the centre of the country (the monuments of which are some of the best preserved of this period). His successor, Jayavarman I, moved the capital to the region of Angkor Borei near Takeo.

Quarrels in the ruling family led to the break-up of the state later in the seventh century: it was divided into 'Land Chenla', a farming culture located north of the Tonlé Sap (maybe centred around Champassak in Laos), and 'Water Chenla', a trading culture based along the Mekong. Towards the end of the eighth century Water Chenla became a vassal of Java's powerful Sailendra Dynasty and members of Chenla's ruling family were taken back to the Sailendra court. This period, from the fall of Funan until the eighth century, is known as the pre-Angkorian period and is a somewhat hazy time in the history of Cambodia. The Khmers remained firmly under Javanese suzerainty until Jayavarman II (802-850), who was born in central Java, returned to the land of his ancestors around AD 800 to change the course of Cambodian history.

## Angkor and the god-kings

**Jayavarman II**, the Khmer prince who had spent most of his life at the Sailendra court, claimed independence from Java and founded the Angkor Kingdom to the north of the Tonlé Sap in 802, at about the same time as Charlemagne became Holy Roman Emperor in Europe. They were men cast in the same mould, for both were empire builders. His far-reaching conquests at Wat Phou (Laos) and Sambhupura (Sambor) won him immediate political popularity on his return and he became king in 790. In 802 he declared himself a World Emperor and to consolidate and legitimize his position he arranged his for coronation by a Brahmin priest, declaring himself the first Khmer devaraja, or god-king, a tradition continued today. From then on, the reigning monarch was identified with Siva, the king of the Hindu gods. In the centuries that followed, successive devaraja strove to outdo their predecessors by building bigger and finer temples to house the royal linga, a phallic symbol which is the symbol of Siva and the devaraja. The god-kings commanded the absolute allegiance of their subjects, giving them control of a vast pool of labour which was used to build an advanced and prosperous agricultural civilization. For many years historians and archaeologists maintained that the key to this agricultural wealth lay in a sophisticated hydraulic – that is irrigated – system of agriculture which allowed the Khmers to produce up to three harvests a year. However, this view of Angkorian agriculture has come under increasing scrutiny in recent years and now there are many who believe that flood-retreat – rather than irrigated – agriculture was the key. Jayavarman II installed himself in successive capitals north of the Tonlé Sap, secure from attack by the Sailendras, and he ruled until 850, when he died on the banks of the Great Lake at the original capital, Hariharalaya, in the Roluos area (Angkor).

**Jayavarman III (850-877)** continued his father's traditions and ruled for the next 27 years. He expanded his father's empire at Hariharalaya and was the original founder of the laterite temple at Bakong. **Indravarman (877-889)**, his successor, was the first of the great temple-builders of Angkor and somewhat overshadowed the work of Jayavarman III. His means to succession are somewhat ambiguous but it is generally agreed that he overthrew Jayavarman III violently. Unlike his predecessor,

## A Chinese emissary's account of his stay at Angkor (1296-1297)

One of the most interesting documents relating to the great empire of Angkor is the Chinese emissary Chou Ta-kuan's short account of his stay there entitled *Notes on the customs of Cambodia*. The book was written in the late 13th or early 14th century, shortly after he had returned to China from a sojourn at Angkor between 1296 and 1297. His book describes the last days of the kingdom and his role as companion to the Chinese ambassador.

The book is divided into 40 short 'chapters' dealing with aspects of everyday and royal life ranging from childbirth, to justice, to clothing. The account also details aspects of the natural environment (fish and reptiles, birds), the economy of the empire (agriculture, trade, products), and technology (utensils, boats and oars). What makes the account so useful and unusual is that it describes not just the concerns and actions of great men and women, but of everyday life too. The extracts below are just a sample of the insights into everyday Cambodian life during the waning days of the Angkorian Empire. For those intending to visit the site of Angkor, the book is highly recommended. It brings to life the ruins of a city, helping you to imagine the place – now so empty – full of people and life.

**Cambodian dwellings** Out of the [royal] palace rises a golden tower, to the top of which the ruler ascends nightly to sleep. It is common belief that in the tower dwells a genie, formed like a serpent with nine heads, which is Lord of the entire kingdom. Every night this genie appears in the shape of a woman, with whom the sovereign couples. Not even the wives of the king may enter here. At the second watch the king comes forth

and is then free to sleep with his wives and his concubines. Should the genie fail to appear for a single night, it is a sign that the king's death is at hand. Straw thatch covers the dwellings of the commoners, not one of whom would dare place the smallest bit of tile on his roof.

**Clothing** Every man or woman, from the sovereign down, knots the hair and leaves the shoulders bare. Round the waist they wear a small strip of cloth, over which a large piece is drawn when they leave their houses. Many rules, based on rank, govern the choice of materials. Only the ruler may wear fabrics woven in an all over pattern.

**Women** Generally speaking, the women, like the men, wear only a strip of cloth, bound round the waist, showing bare breasts of milky whiteness. As for the concubines and palace girls, I have heard it said that there are from three to five thousand of these, separated into various categories. When a beautiful girl is born into a family, no time is lost in sending her to the palace.

**Childbirth** Once a Cambodian woman's child is born, she immediately makes a poultice of hot rice and salt and applies it to her private parts. This is taken off in 24 hours, thus preventing any untoward after-effects and causing an astringency which seems to renew the young mother's virginity. When told of this for the first time, my credulity was sorely taxed. However, in the house where I lodged a girl gave birth to a child, and I was able to observe beyond peradventure that the next day she was up carrying the baby in her arms and going with him to bathe in the river. This seems truly amazing!

Everyone with whom I talked said that the Cambodian women are highly sexed. One or two days after giving birth they are ready for intercourse: if a husband is not responsive he will be discarded. When a man is called away on matters of business, they endure his absence for a while; but if he is gone as much as 10 days, the wife is apt to say, "I am no ghost; how can I be expected to sleep alone?"

**Slaves** Wild men from the hills can be bought to serve as slaves. Families of wealth may own more than 100; those of lesser means content themselves with 10 or 20; only the very poor have none. If a slave should run away and be captured, a blue mark would be tattooed on his face; moreover, an iron collar would be fitted to his neck, or shackles to his arms or legs.

**Cambodian justice** Points of dispute between citizens, however trifling, are taken to the ruler. In dealing with cases of great seriousness, recourse is not had to strangulation or beheading; outside the West Gate, however, a ditch is dug into which the criminal is placed, earth and stones are thrown back and heaped high, and all is over. Lesser crimes are dealt with by cutting off feet or hands, or by amputation of the nose.

When a thief is caught red-handed, he may be imprisoned and tortured. Recourse is also had to another curious procedure. If an object is missing, and accusation brought against someone who denies the charge, oil is brought to boil in a kettle and the suspected person forced to plunge his hand into it. If he is truly guilty, the hand is cooked to shreds; if not, skin and bones are unharmed. Such is the amazing way of these barbarians.

**Products of Cambodia** Many rare woods are to be found in the highlands. Unwooded regions are those where elephants and rhinoceros gather and breed. Exotic birds and strange animals abound. The most sought-after products are the feathers of the kingfisher, elephant tusks, rhinoceros horns, and beeswax.

**Trade** In Cambodia it is the women who take charge of trade. For this reason a Chinese arriving in the country, loses no time in getting himself a mate, for he will find her commercial instincts a great asset.

**Utensils** For sleeping only bamboo mats are used, laid on the wooden floors. Of late, certain families have adopted the use of low beds, which for the most part are made by the Chinese.

**A prodigy** Within the Walled City, near the East Gate, a Cambodian man committed fornication with his younger sister. Their skin and their flesh were fused beyond the power of separating them. After three days passed without food, both parties died. My compatriot Mr Hsieh, who spent 35 years in this country declares he has known this to happen twice. If such be the case, it shows how well the Cambodians are policed by the supernatural power of their holy Buddha.

Notes on the customs of Cambodia was translated from the Chinese original into French by Paul Pelliot. J Gilman d'Arcy Paul translated the French version into English, and the Siam Society in Bangkok have republished this version with colour photographs and reproductions of Delaporte's fine lithographs of the monuments. The *Customs of Cambodia*, Siam Society: Bangkok, 1993.

Indravarman was not the son of a king but more than likely the nephew of Jayavarman's II Queen. He expanded and renovated the capital, building Preah Ko Temple and developing Bakong. Indravarman is considered one of the key players in Khmer history. Referred to as the "lion among kings" and "prince endowed with all the merits", his architectural projects established precedents that were emulated by those that followed him. After Indravarman's death his sons fought for the King's title. The victor, at the end of the ninth century was **Yasovarman I** (**889-900**). The battle is believed to have destroyed the palace, thus spurring a move to Angkor. He called his new capital Yasodharapura and copied the water system his father had devised at Roluos on an even larger scale, using the waters of the Tonlé Sap. After Yasovarman's death in 900 his son **Harshavarman** (**900-923**) took the throne, until he died 23 years later. Harshavarman was well regarded, one particular inscription saying that he "caused the joy of the universe". Upon his death, his brother **Ishanarvarman II**, assumed the regal status. In 928, **Jayavarman IV** set up a rival capital about 65 km from Angkor at Koh Ker and ruled for the next 20 years. After Jayavarman IV's death there was a period of upheaval as **Harsharvarman II** tried unsuccessfully to lead the empire. **Rajendravarman** (**944-968**), Jayarvarman's nephew, managed to take control of the empire and moved the court back to Angkor, where the Khmer kings remained. He chose to build outside of the former capital Bakheng, opting instead for the region south of the East Baray. Many saw him as the saviour of Angkor with one inscription reading: "He restored the holy city of Yashodharapura, long deserted, and rendered it superb and charming." Rajendravarman orchestrated a campaign of solidarity – bringing together a number of provinces and claiming back territory, previously under Yasovarman I. From the restored capital he led a successful crusade against the Champa in what is now Vietnam. A devout Buddhist, he erected some of the first Buddhist temples in the precinct. Upon Rajendravarman's death, his son **Jayavarman V** (**968-1001**), still only a child, took the royal reigns. Once again the administrative centre was moved, this time to the west, where Ta Keo was built. The capital was renamed Jayendranagari. Like his father, Jayavarman V was Buddhist but was extremely tolerant of other religions. At the start of his tenure he had a few clashes with local dissidents but things settled down and he enjoyed relative peace during his rule. The next king, **Udayadityavarman I**, lasted a few months before being ousted. For the next few years Suryavarman I and Jayaviravarman battled for the King's title.

The formidable warrior **King Suryavarman I** (**1002-1049**) won. He may originally have come from the Malay peninsula. He was a determined leader and made all of his officials swear a blood oath of allegiance. He undertook a series of military campaigns geared towards claiming Mon territory in central and southern Thailand and victoriously extended the Khmer empire into Lower Menam, as well as into Laos and established a Khmer capital in Louvo (modern day Lopburi in Thailand). Suryavarman holds the record for the greatest territorial expansion ever achieved in the Khmer Empire. The Royal Palace (Angkor Thom), the West Baray and the Phimeanakas pyramid temples were Suryavarman's main contributions to Angkor's architectural heritage (see page 329). He continued the royal Hindu cult but also tolerated Mahayana Buddhism.

On Suryavarman's death, the Khmer Kingdom began to fragment. His three successors had short, troubled reigns and the Champa kingdom captured, sacked and razed the capital. When the king's son, **Udayadityavarman II** (**1050-1066**), assumed the throne, havoc ensued as citizens revolted against him and some of his royal appointments.

When Udayadityavarman II died, his younger brother, Harsharvarman III (1066-1080), last in the line of the dynasty, stepped in. During his reign, there were reports of discord and further defeat at the hands of the Cham.

In 1080 a new kingdom was founded by a northern provincial governor claiming aristocratic descent. He called himself **Jayavarman VI (1080-1107)** and is believed to have led a revolt against the former king. He never settled at Angkor, living instead in the northern part of the kingdom. He left monuments at Wat Phou in southern Laos and Phimai, in Thailand. There was an intermittent period where Jayavarman's IV brother, **Dharanindravarman (1107-1112)** took the throne but he was overthrown by his grand-nephew **Suryavarman II (1113-1150)**, who soon became the greatest leader the Angkor Empire had ever seen. He worked prolifically on a broad range of projects and achieved some of most impressive architectural feats and political manoeuvres seen within the Angkorian period. He resumed diplomatic relations with China, the Middle Kingdom, and was held in the greatest regard by the then Chinese Emperor. He expanded the Khmer Empire as far as Lopburi, Siam, Pagan in Myanmar, parts of Laos and into the Malay peninsula. He attacked the Champa state relentlessly, particularly Dai Vet in Northern Vietnam, eventually defeating them in 1144-1145, and capturing and sacking the royal capital, Vijaya. He left an incredible, monumental legacy behind, being responsible for the construction of Angkor Wat, an architectural masterpiece that represented the height of the Khmer's artistic genius, Phnom Rung temple (Khorat) and Banteay Samre. A network of roads was built to connect regional capitals.

However, his success was not without its costs – his widespread construction put serious pressure on the general running of the kingdom and major reservoirs silted up during this time; there was also an intensified discord in the provinces and his persistent battling fuelled an ongoing duel between the Cham and Khmers that was to continue (and eventually be avenged) long after his death.

Suryavarman II deposed the King of Champa in 1145 but the Cham regained their independence in 1149 and the following year, Suryavarman died after a disastrous attempt to conquer Annam (northern Vietnam). The throne was usurped by **Tribhuvanadityavarman** in 1165, who died in 1177, when the Cham seized their chance of revenge and sacked Angkor in a surprise naval attack. This was the Khmer's worst recorded defeat – the city was completely annihilated. The 50-year-old **Jayavarman VII** – a cousin of Suryavarman – turned out to be their saviour. He battled the Cham for the next four years, driving them out of the Kingdom. In 1181 he was declared king and seriously hit back, attacking the Chams and seizing their capital, Vijaya. He expanded the Khmer Kingdom further than ever before; its suzerainty stretched from the Malay peninsula in the south to the borders of Burma in the west and the Annamite chain to the northeast.

Jayavarman's VII's first task was to plan a strong, spacious new capital – Angkor Thom; but while that work was being undertaken he set up a smaller, temporary seat of government where he and his court could live in the meantime – Preah Khan meaning 'Fortunate City of Victory' (see page 331). He also built 102 hospitals throughout his kingdom, as well as a network of roads, along which he constructed resthouses. But because they were built of wood, none of these secular structures survive; only the foundations of four larger ones have been unearthed at Angkor.

## Angkor's decline

As was the case duuring Suryavarman II's reign, Jayavarman VII's extensive building campaign put a large amount of pressure on the kingdom's resources and rice was in short supply as labour was diverted into construction.

Jayavarman VII died in 1218 and the Kambujan Empire fell into progressive decline over the next two centuries. Territorially, it was eroded by the eastern migration of the Siamese. The Khmers were unable to prevent this gradual incursion but the diversion of labour to the military rice farming helped seal the fate of Angkor. Another reason for the decline was the introduction of Theravada Buddhism in the 13th century, which undermined the prestige of the king and the priests. There is even a view that climatic change disrupted the agricultural system and led to Kambuja's demise. After Jayavarman VII, no king seems to have been able to unify the kingdom by force of arms or personality – internal dissent increased while the king's extravagance continued to place a crippling burden on state funds. With its temples decaying and its once-magnificent agricultural system in ruins, Angkor became virtually uninhabitable. In 1431 the royal capital was finally abandoned to the Siamese, who drove the Khmers out and made Cambodia a vassal of the Thai Sukhothai Kingdom.

## Explaining Angkor's decline

Why the Angkorian Empire should have declined has always fascinated scholars in the West – in the same way that the decline and fall of the Roman Empire has done. Numerous explanations have been offered, and still the debate remains unresolved. As Anthony Barnett argued in a paper in the *New Left Review* in 1990, perhaps the question should be "why did Angkor last so long? Inauspiciously sited, it was nonetheless a tropical imperium of 500 years' duration."

There are essentially five lines of argument in the 'Why did Angkor fall?' debate. First, it has been argued that the building programmes became simply so arduous and demanding of ordinary people that they voted with their feet and moved out, depriving Angkor of the population necessary to support a great empire. Second, some scholars present an environmental argument: the great irrigation works silted-up, undermining the empire's agricultural wealth. (This line of argument conflicts with recent work that maintains that Angkor's wealth was never based on hydraulic – or irrigated – agriculture.) Third, there are those who say that military defeat was the cause – but this only begs the question: why they were defeated in the first place? Fourth, historians with a rather wider view, have offered the opinion that the centres of economic activity in Southeast Asia moved from land-based to sea-based foci, and that Angkor was poorly located to adapt to this shift in patterns of trade, wealth and, hence, power. Lastly, some scholars argue that the religion which demanded such labour of Angkor's subjects became so corrupt that it ultimately corroded the empire from within.

# After Angkor – running scared

The next 500 years or so, until the arrival of the French in 1863, was an undistinguished period in Cambodian history. In 1434 the royal Khmer court under Ponheayat moved to Phnom Penh, where a replica of the cosmic Mount Meru was built. There was a short-lived period of revival in the mid-15th century until the Siamese invaded and sacked the capital again in 1473. One of the sons of the captured King Suryavarman drummed up enough Khmer support to oust the invaders and there were no subsequent invasions during the 16th century. The capital was established at Lovek (between Phnom Penh and Tonlé Sap) and then moved back to the ruins at Angkor. But a Siamese invasion in 1593 sent the royal court fleeing to Laos; finally, in 1603, the Thais released a captured prince to rule over the Cambodian vassal state. There were at least 22 kings between 1603 and 1848.

Politically, the Cambodian court tried to steer a course between its powerful neighbours of Siam and Vietnam, seeking one's protection against the other. King **Chey Chetta II** (1618-1628), for example, declared Cambodia's independence from Siam and in order to back up his actions he asked Vietnam for help. To cement the allegiance he was forced to marry a Vietnamese princess of the Nguyen Dynasty of Annam, and then obliged to pay tribute to Vietnam. His successors – hoping to rid themselves of Vietnamese domination – sought Siamese assistance and were then forced to pay for it by acknowledging Siam's suzerainty. Then in 1642, **King Chan** converted to Islam, and encouraged Malay and Javanese migrants to settle in Cambodia. Considering him guilty of apostasy, his cousins ousted him – with Vietnamese support. But 50 years later, the Cambodian **Ang Eng** was crowned in Bangkok. This see-saw pattern continued for years; only Siam's wars with Burma and Vietnam's internal disputes and long-running conflict with China prevented them from annexing the whole of Cambodia, although both took territorial advantage of the fragmented state.

By the early 1700s the kingdom was centred on Phnom Penh (there were periods when the king resided at Ondong). But when the Khmers lost their control over the Mekong Delta to the Vietnamese in the late 18th century, the capital's access to the sea was blocked. By 1750 the Khmer royal family had split into pro-Siamese and pro-Vietnamese factions. Between 1794-1811 and 1847-1863, Siamese influence was strongest; from 1835-1837 the Vietnamese dominated. In the 1840s, the Siamese and Vietnamese armies fought on Cambodian territory, devastating the country. This provoked French intervention – and cost Cambodia its independence, even if it had been nominal for several centuries anyway. On 17 April 1864 (the same day and month as the Khmer Rouge soldiers entered Phnom Penh in the twentieth century) King Norodom agreed to French protection as he believed they would provide military assistance against the Siamese. The king was to be disappointed: France honoured Siam's claim to the western provinces of Battambang, Siem Reap and Sisophon, which Bangkok had captured in the late 1600s. And in 1884, King Norodom was persuaded by the French governor of the colony of Cochin China to sign another treaty that turned Cambodia into a French colony, along with Laos and Vietnam in the Union Indochinoise. The establishment of Cambodia as a French protectorate probably saved the country from being split up between Siam and Vietnam.

# French colonial period

The French did little to develop Cambodia, preferring instead to let the territory pay for itself. They only invested income generated from tax revenue to build a communications network and from a Cambodian perspective, the only benefit of colonial rule was that the French forestalled the total disintegration of the country, which would otherwise have been divided up between its warring neighbours. French cartographers also mapped Cambodia's borders for the first time and in so doing forced the Thais to surrender the northwestern provinces of Battambang and Siem Reap.

For nearly a century the French alternately supported two branches of the royal family, the Norodoms and the Sisowaths, crowning the 18-year-old schoolboy **Prince Norodom Sihanouk** in 1941. The previous year, the Nazis had invaded and occupied France and French territories in Indochina were in turn occupied by the Japanese – although Cambodia was still formally governed and administered by the French. It was at this stage that a group of pro-independence Cambodians realized just how weak the French control of their country actually was. In 1942 two monks were arrested and accused of preaching anti-French sermons; within two days this sparked demonstrations by more than 1,000 monks in Phnom Penh. These demonstrations marked the beginning of Cambodian nationalism. In March 1945 Japanese forces ousted the colonial administration and persuaded King Norodom Sihanouk to proclaim independence. Following the Japanese surrender in August 1945, the French came back in force; Sihanouk tried to negotiate independence from France and they responded by abolishing the absolute monarchy in 1946 – although the king remained titular head of state. A new constitution was introduced allowing political activity and a National Assembly elected.

# Independence and neutrality

By the early 1950s the French army had suffered several defeats in the war in Indochina. Sihanouk dissolved the National Assembly in mid-1952, which he was entitled to do under the constitution, and personally took charge of steering Cambodia towards independence from France. To publicize the cause, he travelled to Thailand, Japan and the United States, and said he would not return from self-imposed exile until his country was free. His audacity embarrassed the French into granting Cambodia independence on 9 November 1953 – and Sihanouk returned, triumphant.

The people of Cambodia did not want to return to absolute monarchy, and following his abdication in 1955, Sihanouk became a popular political leader. But political analysts believe that despite the apparent popularity of the former king's administration, different factions began to develop at this time, a process which was the root of the conflict in the years to come. During the 1960s, for example, there was a growing rift between the Khmer majority and other ethnic groups. Even in the countryside, differences became marked between the rice-growing lands and the more remote mountain areas where people practised shifting cultivation, supplementing their diet with lizards, snakes, roots and insects. As these problems intensified in the late 1960s and the economic situation deteriorated, the popular support base for the Khmer Rouge was put into place. With unchecked population growth, land ownership patterns became skewed, landlessness grew more widespread and food prices escalated.

Sihanouk managed to keep Cambodia out of the war that enveloped Laos and Vietnam during the late 1950s and 1960s by following a neutral policy – which helped attract millions of dollars of aid to Cambodia from both the West and the Eastern Bloc. But when a civil war broke out in South Vietnam in the early 1960s, Cambodia's survival – and Sihanouk's own survival – depended on its outcome. Sihanouk believed the rebels, the National Liberation Front (NLF) would win; and he openly courted and backed the NLF. It was an alliance which cost him dear. In 1965-1966 the tide began to turn in South Vietnam, due to US military and economic intervention. This forced NLF troops to take refuge inside Cambodia (in 1966 half of Cambodia's rice supplies, normally sold abroad, were distributed to the NLF agents inside Cambodia). When a peasant uprising in northwestern provinces in 1967 showed Sihanouk that he was sailing close to the wind his forces responded by suppressing the rebellion and massacring 10,000 peasants.

Slowly – and inevitably – he became the focus of resentment within Cambodia's political élite. He also incurred American wrath by allowing North Vietnamese forces to use Cambodian territory as an extension of the **Ho Chi Minh Trail**, ferrying arms and men into South Vietnam. This resulted in his former army Commander-in-Chief, **Marshal Lon Nol** masterminding Sihanouk's removal as Head of State while he was in Moscow in 1970. Lon Nol abolished the monarchy and proclaimed a republic. One of the most auspicious creatures in Khmer mythology is the white crocodile. It is said to appear 'above the surface' at important moments in history and is said to have been sighted near Phnom Penh just before Lon Nol took over.

# The Third Indochina War and the rise of the Khmer Rouge

On 30 April 1970, following the overthrow of Prince Norodom Sihanouk, US President Richard Nixon officially announced **Washington's military intervention in Cambodia** – although in reality it had been going on for some time. The invasion aimed to deny the Vietnamese Communists the use of Sihanoukville port through which 85% of their heavy arms were reaching South Vietnam. The US Air Force had been secretly bombing Cambodia using B-52s since March 1969. In 1973, facing defeat in Vietnam, the US Air Force B-52s began carpet bombing Communist-controlled areas to enable Lon Nol's inept regime to retain control of the besieged provincial cities.

Historian David P Chandler wrote: "When the campaign was stopped by the US Congress at the end of the year, the B-52s had dropped over half a million tons of bombs on a country with which the United States was not at war – more than twice the tonnage dropped on Japan during the Second World War.

The war in Cambodia was known as 'the sideshow' by journalists covering the war in Vietnam and by American policy-makers in London. Yet the intensity of US bombing in Cambodia was greater than it ever was in Vietnam; about 500,000 soldiers and civilians were killed over the four-year period. It also caused about two million refugees to flee from the countryside to the capital."

As Henry Kamm suggested, by the beginning of 1971 the people of Cambodia had to face the terrifying realisation that nowhere in the country was safe and all hope and confidence in Cambodia's future during the war was lost. A year after the coup d'etat the country was shattered: guerrilla forces had invaded Angkor, the country's primary oil refinery, Lol Non had suffered a stroke and had relocated to Hawaii for months of treatment, Lol Non's irregularly paid soldiers were pillaging stores at gunpoint and extreme corruption was endemic.

By the end of the war, the country had become totally dependent on US aid and much of the population survived on American rice rations. Confidence in the Lon Nol government collapsed as taxes rose and children were drafted into combat units. At the same time, the **Khmer Rouge** increased its military strength dramatically and began to make inroads into areas formerly controlled by government troops. Although officially the Khmer Rouge rebels represented the Beijing-based Royal Government of National Union of Cambodia (Grunc), which was headed by the exiled Prince Sihanouk, Grunc's de facto leaders were Pol Pot, Khieu Samphan (who, after Pol Pot's demise, became the public face of the Khmer Rouge), Ieng Sary (later foreign minister) and Son Sen (Chief of General Staff) – all Khmer Rouge men. By the time the American bombing stopped in 1973, the guerrillas dominated about 60% of Cambodian territory, while the government clung tenuously to towns and cities. Over the next two years the Khmer Rouge whittled away Phnom Penh's defence perimeter to the point that Lon Nol's government was sustained only by American airlifts into the capital.

Some commentators have suggested that the persistent heavy bombing of Cambodia, which forced the Communist guerrillas to live in terrible conditions, was partly responsible for the notorious savagery of the Khmer Rouge in later years. Not only were they brutalized by the conflict itself, but they became resentful of the fact that the city-dwellers had no inkling of how unpleasant their experiences really were. This, writes US political scientist Wayne Bert, "created the perception among the Khmer Rouge that the bulk of the population did not take part in the revolution, was therefore not enthusiastic about it and could not be trusted to support it. The final step in this logic was to punish or eliminate all in these categories who showed either real or imagined tendencies toward disloyalty". And that, as anyone who has watched The Killing Fields will know, is what happened.

## The 'Pol Pot time': building year zero

On 1 April 1975 President Lon Nol fled Cambodia to escape the rapidly advancing Khmer Rouge. Just over two weeks later, on 17 April, the victorious Khmer Rouge entered Phnom Penh. The capital's population had been swollen by refugees from 600,000 to over two million. The ragged conquering troops wearing Ho Chi Minh

## Pol Pot – the idealistic psychopath

Prince Norodom Sihanouk once referred to Pol Pot as "a more fortunate Hitler". Unlike his erstwhile fascist counterpart, the man whose troops were responsible for the deaths of perhaps two million fellow Cambodians has managed to get away with it. He died on 15 April 1998, either of a heart attack or, possibly, at his own hands or somebody else's.

Pol Pot's real name was Saloth Sar – he adopted his nom de guerre when he became Secretary-General of the Cambodian Communist Party in 1963. He was born in 1928 into a peasant family in Kompong Thom, central Cambodia, and is believed to have lived as a novice monk for nine months when he was a child. His services to the Democrat Party won him a scholarship to study electronics in Paris. But he became a Communist in France in 1949 and spent more time at meetings of Marxist revolutionary societies than in classes. In his 1986 book *Sideshow*, William Shawcross notes that at that time the French Communist Party, which was known for its dogmatic adherence to orthodox Marxism, "taught hatred of the bourgeoisie and uncritical admiration of Stalinism, including the collectivization of agriculture". Pol Pot finally lost his scholarship in 1953.

Returning to newly independent Cambodia, Pol Pot started working as a school teacher in Phnom Penh and continued his revolutionary activities in the underground Cambodian Communist Party (which, remarkably kept its existence a secret until 1977). In 1963, he fled the capital for the countryside, fearing a crackdown of the left by Sihanouk. There he rose to become Secretary-General of the Central Committee of the Communist Party of Kampuchea. He was trained in guerrilla warfare and he became a

sandals made of used rubber tyres – which were de rigueur for guerrillas in Indochina – were welcomed as heroes. None in the crowds that lined the streets appreciated the horrors that the victory would also bring. Cambodia was renamed Democratic Kampuchea (DK) and Pol Pot set to work establishing a radical Maoist-style agrarian society. These ideas had been first sketched out by his longstanding colleague Khieu Samphan, whose 1959 doctoral thesis – at the Sorbonne University in Paris – analysed the effects of Cambodia's colonial and neo-colonial domination. In order to secure true economic and political independence he argued that it was necessary to isolate Cambodia completely and to go back to a self-sufficient agricultural economy.

Within days of the occupation, the rubber sandalled revolutionaries had forcibly evacuated many of the inhabitants of Phnom Penh to the countryside, telling citizens that the Americans were about to bomb the capital. A second major displacement was carried out at the end of the year, when hundreds of thousands of people from the area southeast of Phnom Penh were forced to move to the northwest.

Prior to the Khmer Rouge coming to power, the Cambodian word for revolution (*bambahbambor*) had a conventional meaning, 'uprising'. Under Pol Pot's regime, the word *pativattana* was used instead; it meant 'return to the past'. The Khmer Rouge did this by obliterating everything that did not subscribe to their vision of the past glories of ancient Khmer culture. Pol Pot wanted to return the country to **'Year Zero'** – he wanted to begin again. One of the many revolutionary slogans was "we will burn the old grass and new will grow"; money, modern technology, medicine, education and newspapers were outlawed. Khieu Samphan, who became the Khmer Rouge Head of State, following Prince Sihanouk's resignation in 1976, said at the time: "No, we have no machines. We do everything by mainly relying on the strength of our people. We work completely self-sufficiently. This shows the overwhelming heroism leader of the Khmer Rouge forces, advocating armed resistance to Sihanouk and his 'feudal entourage'. In 1975 when the Khmer Rouge marched into Phnom Penh, Pol Pot was forced out of the shadows to take the role of leader, 'Brother Number One'. Although he took the title of prime minister, he ruled as a dictator and set about reshaping Cambodia with his mentor, Khieu Samphan, the head of state. Yet, during the years he was in power, hardly any Cambodians – save those in the top echelons of the Khmer Rouge – had even heard of him.

The Vietnam-backed Hun Sen government, which took over the country after the overthrow of the Khmer Rouge in December 1978, calculated that by demonizing Pol Pot as the mastermind of the genocide, it would avert the possibility of the Khmer Rouge ever making a comeback. The Hun Sen regime showed no interest in analysing the complex factors which combined to bring Pol Pot to power. Within Cambodia, he has been portrayed simply as a tyrannical bogey-man. During the 1980s, 20 May was declared National Hate Day, when everyone reaffirmed their hatred of Pol Pot.

In a review of David Chandler's biography of Pol Pot (*Brother Number One: A Political Biography of Pol Pot*, Westview Press, 1992), Peter Carey – the co-director of the British-based Cambodia Trust – was struck by what he called "the sinister disjunction between the man's evident charisma ... and the monumental suffering wrought by his regime". Carey concludes: "one is left with the image of a man consumed by his own vision, a vision of empowerment and liberation that has little anchorage in Cambodian reality".

of our people. This also shows the great force of our people. Though bare-handed, they can do everything".

The Khmer Rouge, or *Angkar Loeu* ('The Higher Organization') as they touted themselves, maintained a strangle-hold on the country by dislocating families, disorientating people and sustaining a persistent fear through violence, torture and death. At the heart of their strategy was a plan to unfurl people's strongest bonds and loyalties: those that existed between family members. The term *kruosaa*, which traditionally means 'family' in Khmer, came to simply mean 'spouse' under the Khmer Rouge. In Angkar, family no longer existed. *Krusosaa niyum*, which loosely translated to 'familyism' (or pining for one's relatives) was a criminal offence punishable by death. Under heinous interrogation procedures people were intensively probed about their family members (sisters, brothers, grandparents and in-laws) and encouraged to inform on them. Those people who didn't turn over relatives considered adversaries (teachers, former soldiers, doctors etc.) faced odious consequences, with the fate of the whole family (immediate and extended) in danger.

Memoirs from survivors detailed in the book *Children of Cambodia's Killing Fields* repeatedly refer to the Khmer Rouge dictum "to keep you is no benefit to destroy you is no loss." People were treated as nothing more than machines. Food was scarce under Pol Pot's inefficient system of collective farming and administration was based on fear, torture and summary execution. A veil of secrecy shrouded Cambodia and, until a few desperate refugees began to trickle over the border into Thailand, the outside world was largely ignorant of what was going on. The refugees' stories of atrocities were, at first, disbelieved. Jewish refugees who escaped from Nazi occupied Poland in the 1940s had encountered a similarly disbelieving reception simply because (like the Cambodians) what they had to say was, to most

## King Norodom Sihanouk: latter-day god-king

An uncomplimentary profile of Prince Norodom Sihanouk in *The Economist* in 1990 said that over the preceding 20 years, he "twisted and turned, sulked, resigned many times, [was] humiliated and imprisoned. In one thing, however, he [was] consistent: his yearning to recover the face he lost in 1970, and return to Phnom Penh in triumph". The following year, on 14 November, Prince Sihanouk did exactly that, arriving in his former royal capital to a rapturous welcome, after 13 years of exile. In November 1991, as in 1953 when he returned from exile at Independence, he represented the one symbol Cambodia had of any semblance of national unity.

Norodom Sihanouk was crowned King of Cambodia at the age of 18 in 1941. He owed his accession to the throne to a method of selection devised by the French colonial regime who hoped that the young, inexperienced Sihanouk would be a compliant puppet-king. But in the event he turned out to be something very different. Using his position to great advantage, he became a nationalist leader and crusaded for independence in 1953. But following independence, his royal title worked against him: the 1947 constitution restricted the role the monarch could play in politics. So, he abdicated in favour of his father, Norodom Suramarit, in 1955 and, as Prince Sihanouk, was free to enter politics. He immediately founded the Sangkum Reastr Niyum – the Popular Socialist Community (PSC). The same year, the PSC won every seat in the National Assembly – as it did in subsequent elections in 1958, 1962 and 1966.

The old king died in 1960, but Sihanouk side-stepped the problem of succession by declaring himself Head of State, without ascending to the throne. Michael Leifer, a British political scientist, writes: "As Head of State, Prince Sihanouk became literally the voice of Cambodia. He articulated its hopes and fears within the country and to the outside world. He appeared as a popular figure revered especially in the rural areas as the father figure of his country." He was a populist of the first order.

Someth May, in his autobiography *Cambodian Witness*, describes Phnom Penh in the early 1960s: "Sihanouk's portrait was everywhere around town: in uniform with a sword, in a suit, in

people, unbelievable. Some left wing academics initially viewed the revolution as an inspired and brave attempt to break the shackles of dependency and neo-colonial domination. Others, such as Noam Chomsky, dismissed the allegations as right wing press propaganda.

It was not until the Vietnamese 'liberation' of Phnom Penh in 1979 that the scale of the Khmer Rouge carnage emerged and the atrocities witnessed by the survivors became known. The stories turned the Khmer Rouge into international pariahs – but only until 1982 when, remarkably, their American and Chinese sympathizers secured them a voice at the United Nations. Wives had been encouraged to denounce their husbands; children their mothers. Anyone who had smoked an American cigarette was a CIA operative; anyone with a taste for café crème was a French collaborator. During the Khmer Rouge's 44-month reign of terror, it had hitherto been generally accepted that around a million people died. This is a horrendous figure when one considers that the population of the country in 1975 was around seven million. What is truly shocking is that the work undertaken by a team from Yale University indicates that this figure is far too low.

monk's robes, dressed in white with a shaved head like an achar; on posters, on notebooks; framed in every classroom above the teacher's head; in the shops and offices. In the magazine that he edited himself we saw him helping a farmer dig an irrigation canal, reviewing the troops, shooting a film (for he was also a film-maker), addressing the National Assembly, giving presents to the monks, opening the annual regatta with his wife, Monique. On the radio we heard his speeches, and one year when he had a craze for singing you could hear his songs more than 10 times a day."

Sihanouk liked to run the show single-handedly and he is said to have treated his ministers like flunkies. In *Sideshow*, William Shawcross paints him as being vain – "a petulant showman who enjoyed boasting of his sexual successes. He would not tolerate criticism or dissent ... At the same time he had enormous political skill, charm, tenacity and intelligence."

With an American-backed right-wing regime in power after the coup in 1970, the former king went into exile in China, where his supporters formed an alliance with his former enemies, the Khmer Rouge: the Royal Government of National Union of Cambodia – otherwise known as the Grunc. When the Khmer Rouge marched into Phnom Penh in 1975, they restored Prince Sihanouk as Head of State.

He resigned in April 1976 as he became increasingly marginalized, and the Grunc was dissolved. Sihanouk was kept under house-arrest until a few days before the Vietnamese army occupied Phnom Penh in January 1979, whereupon he fled to Beijing. There Sihanouk and his supporters once again joined forces with the Khmer Rouge in a tripartite coalition aimed at overthrowing the Hanoi-backed government.

The peace settlement which followed the eventual Vietnamese withdrawal in 1989 paved the way for Sihanouk's return from exile. His past association with the Khmer Rouge had tarnished the prince's image, but to many Cambodians, he represented their hopes for a stable future. Following the elections of 1993, Sihanouk returned from Beijing to be crowned King on 24 September, thus reclaiming the throne he relinquished in 1955. In 2004 the King abdicated, making way for his son Sihamoni to fill his shoes.

Although the Khmer Rouge era in Cambodia may have been a period of unprecedented economic, political and human turmoil, they still managed to keep meticulous records of what they were doing. In this regard the Khmer Rouge were rather like the Chinese during the Cultural Revolution, or the Nazis in Germany. Using Australian satellite data, the team was expecting to uncover around 200 mass graves; instead they found several thousand. The Khmer Rouge themselves have claimed that around 20,000 people died because of their 'mistakes'. The Vietnamese have traditionally put the figure at two to three million, although their estimates have generally been rejected as too high and politically motivated (being a means to justify their invasion of the country in 1978/79 and subsequent occupation). The Documentation Center of Cambodia, involved in the heavy mapping project, said that 20,492 mass graves were uncovered containing the remains of 1,112,829 victims of execution. In addition, hundreds of thousands more died from famine and disease; frighteningly, the executions are believed to only account for about 30-40% of the total death toll.

How such a large slice of Cambodia's people died in so short a time (between 1975 and the end of 1978) beggars belief. Some were shot, strangled or suffocated;

## ⁑ Cambodia 1953-2008

**1953** Cambodian independence from France.

**1965** Prince Sihanouk's government cuts links with the United States following deployment of US troops in Vietnam.

**1966** Right-wing beats Sihanouk in the election; Lon Nol elected prime minister.

**1967** Lon Nol toppled following left-wing demonstrations.

**1969** Lon Nol becomes prime minister again.

**1970** Lon Nol topples Sihanouk in US-backed coup; US bombs Communist bases in Cambodia.

**1972** Lon Nol becomes first president of the Khmer Republic.

**1975** Lon Nol flees as Khmer Rouge seizes power; Sihanouk made head of government. December: Vietnam invades.

**1976** Cambodia renamed Democratic Kampuchea; Sihanouk resigns and Khieu Samphan becomes head of state, with Pol Pot as prime minister. Government moves people from towns to labour camps in the countryside.

**1981** Cambodia renamed the People's Republic of Kampuchea (PRK).

**1982** Coalition government-in-exile formed by anti-Hanoi resistance comprising Sihanoukists, Khmer Rouge and KPNLF. Sihanouk appointed President; Khieu Samphan, Vice-President and Son Sann, Prime Minister. Coalition backed by China and ASEAN.

**1984** Vietnam gains rebel-held territory along Thai border; Vietnamese civilians settle in Kampuchea.

**1989** People's Republic of Kampuchea renamed the State of Cambodia. September: last of the Vietnamese troops leave.

**1991** International Conference on Cambodia in Paris leads to peace treaty and deployment of UNTAC.

**1993** In May elections were held under the auspices of the United Nations Transitional Authority in Cambodia. A coalition government was formed and Norodom Sihanouk was re-crowned King in September.

**1996** Leng Sary (Brother Number Two) splits from Khmer Rouge and is granted a royal pardon.

many more starved; while others died from disease – malaria was rife – and overwork. The Khmer Rouge transformed Cambodia into what the British journalist, William Shawcross, described as: "a vast and sombre work camp where toil was unending, where respite and rewards were non-existent, where families were abolished and where murder was used as a tool of social discipline ... The manner of execution was often brutal. Babies were torn apart limb from limb, pregnant women were disembowelled. Men and women were buried up to their necks in sand and left to die slowly. A common form of execution was by axe handles to the back of the neck. That saved ammunition".

The crimes transcended all moral boundaries known to mankind – soldiers cooked and ate the organs of victims, removed while they were still alive. Sydney Schanberg's forward to *Children of Cambodia's Killing Fields* says of the memoirs: "painful though it may be to contemplate these accounts of young survivors, they desperately need to be passed, whole and without softening, from generation to generation. For it is only by such bearing of witness that the rest of us are rendered unable to pretend that true evil is exceedingly rare in the world, or worse, is but a figment".

The Khmer Rouge revolution was primarily a class-based one, fed by years of growing resentment against the privileged élites. The revolution pitted the

**1997** Hun Sen's coup ousts Ranariddh and Funcinp

**1998** Pol Pot dies. Elections and Hun Sen becomes so

**1999** Cambodia joins ASEAN.

**2001** Cambodian Senate approves a law to create a tribunal
charges against Khmer Rouge leaders.

**2002** First multi-party commune elections; the incumbent Cambodia
wins in all but 23 out of 1620 communes.

**2003** Major diplomatic upset with Thailand in January over comments attrib
Thai TV star that the Angkor Wat temple complex was stolen from Thailan
Angry crowds attack the Thai embassy and Thai-based businesses in
Phnom Penh.

**2003** Prime Minister Hun Sen's Cambodian People's Party wins the election in July
but fails to secure sufficient majority to govern alone. A political
deadlock arises.

**2004** After nearly a year of political stalemate, Prime Minister Hun Sen is re-elected
after his ruling Cambodian People's Party (CPP) forms a coalition with the
royalist Funcinpec party.

**2004** In August the parliament ratifies Cambodia's entry into World Trade
organization (WTO).

**2004** King Sihanouk abdicates in October and is succeeded by his son Norodom
Sihamoni.

**2005** Opposition leader Sam Rainsy flees the country after his parliamentary
immunity is stripped.

**2006** Hun Sen releases political detainees and allows Sam Rainsy to return to the
country.

**2007** Local elections pass off peacefully and give Hun Sen's CPP 61% of the vote.
The Khmer Rouge trial's finally get underway and all the main targets,
including Pol Pot's second in command, Brother No 2, Nuon Chea,
are arrested.

least-literate, poorest rural peasants (referred to as the 'old' people) against the educated, skilled and foreign-influenced urban population (the 'new' people). The 'new' people provided an endless flow of numbers for the regime's death lists. Through a series of terrible purges, the members of the former governing and mercantile classes were liquidated or sent to work as forced labourers. But Peter Carey, Oxford historian and Chairman of the Cambodia Trust, argues that not all Pol Pot's victims were townspeople and merchants. "Under the terms of the 1948 Genocide Convention, the Khmer Rouge stands accused of genocide," he wrote in a letter to a British newspaper in 1990. "Of 64,000 Buddhist monks, 62,000 perished; of 250,000 Islamic Chams, 100,000; of 200,000 Vietnamese still left in 1975, 100,000; of 20,000 Thai, 12,000; of 1800 Lao, 1000. Of 2000 Kola, not a trace remained." American political scientist Wayne Bert noted that: "The methods and behaviour compare to that of the Nazis and Stalinists, but in the percentage of the population killed by a revolutionary movement, the Khmer Rouge holds an unchallenged record."

It is still unclear the degree to which these 'genocidal' actions were controlled by those at the centre. Many of the killings took place at the discretion of local leaders, but there were some notably cruel leaders in the upper echelons of the Khmer Rouge and none can have been ignorant of what was going on. Ta Mok, who administered

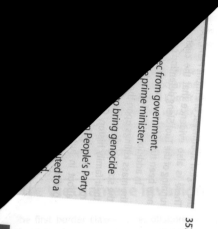

mass executions for example.
...t was directly involved in the
...least 20,000 people died. It has
...ust (see page 277).
...uol Sleng, there is the impact of
...of which is – to Western eyes –
..., if asked, matter-of-factly relate
...elling how the Khmer Rouge era
...family. Whereas death is talked
...ers have no such reservations,
...n all.

...etween Khmer Rouge forces and
...h after the Khmer Rouge came to
...uary 1977 when the Phnom Penh
government accused Vietn... incorporate Kampuchea into an
Indochinese federation. Hanoi's determination to oust Pol Pot only really became
apparent however, on Christmas Day 1978 when 120,000 Vietnamese troops
invaded. By 7 January (the day of Phnom Penh's liberation) they had installed
a puppet government which proclaimed the foundation of the People's Republic
of Kampuchea (PRK): Heng Samrin, a former member of the Khmer Rouge, was
appointed president. The Vietnamese compared their invasion to the liberation of
Uganda from Idi Amin – but for the Western world it was an unwelcome Christmas
present. The new government was accorded scant recognition abroad, while the
toppled government of Democratic Kampuchea retained the country's seat at the
United Nations.

The country's 'liberation' by Vietnam did not end the misery; in 1979 nearly half
Cambodia's population was in transit, either searching for their former homes or
fleeing across the Thai border into refugee camps. The country reverted to a state of
outright war again, for the Vietnamese were not greatly loved in Cambodia –
especially by the Khmer Rouge. American political scientist Wayne Bert wrote:
"The Vietnamese had long seen a special role for themselves in uniting and leading a
greater Indochina Communist movement and the Cambodian Communists had seen
with clarity that such a role for the Vietnamese could only be at the expense of their
independence and prestige."

Under the Lon Nol and Khmer Rouge regimes, Vietnamese living in Cambodia
were expelled or exterminated. Resentment had built up over the years in Hanoi –
exacerbated by the apparent ingratitude of the Khmer Rouge for Vietnamese
assistance in fighting Lon Nol's US-supported Khmer Republic in the early 1970s.
As relations between the Khmer Rouge and the Vietnamese deteriorated, the
Communist superpowers, China and the Soviet Union, polarized too – the former
siding with the Khmer Rouge and the latter with Hanoi. The Vietnamese invasion had
the full backing of Moscow, while the Chinese and Americans began their support for
the anti-Vietnamese rebels.

Following the Vietnamese invasion, three main anti-Hanoi factions were formed.
In June 1982 they banded together in an unholy and unlikely alliance of convenience
to fight the PRK and called themselves the Coalition Government of Democratic
Kampuchea (CGDK), which was immediately recognized by the United Nations.
The Communist **Khmer Rouge**, whose field forces recovered to at least 18,000 by
the late 1980s. Supplied with weapons by China, they were concentrated in the
Cardamom Mountains in the southwest and were also in control of some of the

refugee camps along the Thai border. The National United Front for an Independent
Neutral Peaceful and Co-operative Cambodia (Funcinpec) – known by most people as
the **Armée Nationale Sihanoukiste** (ANS) was headed by Prince Sihanouk although
he spent most of his time exiled in Beijing. The group had fewer than 15,000
well-equipped troops – most of whom took orders from Khmer Rouge commanders.
The anti-Communist **Khmer People's National Liberation Front** (KPNLF), headed by
Son Sann, a former prime minister under Sihanouk. Its 5000 troops were reportedly
ill-disciplined in comparison with the Khmer Rouge and the ANS.

The three CGDK factions were ranged against the 70,000 troops loyal to the
government of President Heng Samrin and Prime Minister Hun Sen (previously a
Khmer Rouge cadre). They were backed by Vietnamese forces until September 1989.
Within the forces of the Phnom Penh government there were reported to be problems
of discipline and desertion. But the rebel guerrilla coalition was itself seriously
weakened by rivalries and hatred between the different factions: in reality, the idea of
a 'coalition' was fiction. Throughout most of the 1980s the war followed the progress
of the seasons: during the dry season from November to April the PRK forces with their
tanks and heavy arms took the offensive but during the wet season this heavy
equipment was ineffective and the guerrilla resistance made advances.

## The road towards peace

In the late 1980s the Association of Southeast Asian Nations (ASEAN) – for which the
Cambodian conflict had almost become a raison d'être – began steps to bring the
warring factions together over the negotiating table. ASEAN countries were united
primarily in wanting the Vietnamese out of Cambodia. While publicly deploring the
Khmer Rouge record, ASEAN tacitly supported the guerrillas. Thailand, an ASEAN
member-state, which has had a centuries-long suspicion of the Vietnamese,
co-operated closely with China to ensure that the Khmer Rouge guerrillas over the
border were well-supplied with weapons.

After Mikhail Gorbachev had come to power in the Soviet Union, Moscow's
support for the Vietnamese presence in Cambodia gradually evaporated. Gorbachev
began leaning on Vietnam as early as 1987, to withdraw its troops. Despite saying
their presence in Cambodia was 'irreversible', Vietnam completed its withdrawal in
September 1989, ending nearly 11 years of Hanoi's direct military involvement.
The withdrawal led to an immediate upsurge in political and military activity, as
forces of the exiled CGDK put increased pressure on the now weakened Phnom Penh
regime to begin power-sharing negotiations (see page 361).

# Modern Cambodia

Until the mid-19th century, the outside world knew almost nothing of the interior of
Cambodia. From the 16th and 17th centuries, rumours began to surface in Europe –
based on tales from Portuguese and French missionaries – about a magnificent city,
hidden somewhere in the middle of the jungle. It is usually claimed that the ruins of
Angkor were 'discovered' by the French naturalist and explorer Henri Mouhot in 1861.
This is a travesty of history: Southeast Asians never forgot that Angkor existed. Truth,
as they say, is determined by the powerful, and in this case the West determined that
a Westerner should 'discover' what was already known. In a sense, Angkor is a great
weight on the collective shoulders of the Cambodian people. The usual refrain from
visitors is: 'How could a people who created such magnificence have also nurtured
Pol Pot and the Khmer Rouge?' A simple answer might be that only despotic rule could

create anything on the scale of Angkor. The totalitarianism of the Khmer Rouge echoed that of the Khmer kings, but as the kings built, so the Khmer Rouge destroyed. Nonetheless, it is easy enough to see a stark disjuncture between the glory of Angkor and the horrors of recent history. As Elizabeth Becker wrote at the beginning of 1995: "Cambodia's recent history is one of breathtaking tragedy; by comparison its immediate future looks small and venal. Today Cambodia resembles many of the striving, corrupt, developing nations trying to make up for time lost behind the iron curtain. The nation that bore the horrors of the Khmer Rouge seemed ready for a kinder if not a more prosperous transformation."

In his book *Sideshow*, the British journalist William Shawcross says the diplomats, journalists and tourists who visited Cambodia in the 1950s and 1960s described it as "an idyllic, antique land unsullied by the brutalities of the modern world". Paddy farmers laboured in their ricefields, mystical ruins lay hidden in the jungle, the capital had the charm of a French provincial town and pagodas dotted the landscape. "Such was the illusion," writes Shawcross, of "bucolic plenty, Buddhist serenity, neutralist peace". This was an illusion because for centuries Cambodia had been in a state of continuous social and political upheaval. Since the demise of the Angkorian Empire in the 15th century, the country has been at the mercy of its much larger neighbours, Siam (Thailand) and Vietnam, and of various foreign powers – China, France, the US and the former Soviet Union. This history of foreign domination is starkly overshadowed by the so-called 'Pol Pot time'. Between 1975 and 1979, Cambodians suffered one of the worst human tragedies to afflict any country since the Second World War – as we have seen, over a million people died out of a total population of about seven million. If the preceding period, during America's involvement in Indochina, is also taken into account, it is possible that around a fifth of Cambodia's population was killed.

The relics and reminders of those days are now firmly on the tourist's sightseeing agenda. These include the chilling Tuol Sleng Genocide Museum (see page 277), in the former high school where the Khmer Rouge tortured and killed at least 20,000 people and Choeung Ek (see page 278), a series of mass graves, the 'Killing Fields', 15 km southwest of Phnom Penh.

# Politics

Since the mid-1960s Cambodian politics has been chaotic, with warring and bickering factions, backed by different foreign powers and domestic cliques, and shifting alliances. The groups which battled for power following the Vietnamese invasion in 1979 are still in the political arena and although the country may have 'enjoyed' democratic elections in 1993, 1998 and 2002 civil society remains poorly developed. Gangsterism, political terrorism and extra-judicial killings remain very much part of the political landscape even after the end of the Khmer Rouge and despite the pretence of democracy. It is only the sheer horror of the Pol Pot years which gives the years since that ghastly episode a more rosy tint. Henry Kamm, for one, gave a dismal reading of Cambodia's prospects in his short article in *The New York Review*: "No equitable rule of law or impartial justice shelters Cambodians against a mean-spirited establishment of political and economic power, a cabal, dominated by Prime Minister Hun Sen, that is blind and deaf to the crying needs of an abused people" (August 13th 1998). While elements of Kamm's depressing take on Cambodia's prospects remain just as true today, the general picture over the last decade years has been one of modest improvement.

In September 1989, under pressure at home and abroad, the Vietnamese withdrew from Cambodia. The immediate result of this withdrawal was an escalation of the civil war as the rebel factions (see page 359) tried to take advantage of the supposedly weakened Hun Sen regime in Phnom Penh. The government committed itself to liberalizing the economy and improving the infrastructure in order to undermine the political appeal of the rebels – particularly that of the Khmer Rouge. Peasant farmers were granted life tenancy to their land and collective farms were substituted with agricultural co-operatives. But because nepotism and bribery were rife in Phnom Penh, the popularity of the Hun Sen regime declined. The rebel position was further strengthened as the disparities between living standards in Phnom Penh and those in the rest of the country widened. In the capital, the government became alarmed; in a radio broadcast in 1991 it announced a crackdown on corruption claiming it was causing a "loss of confidence in our superb regime ... which is tantamount to paving the way for the return of the genocidal Pol Pot regime".

With the withdrawal of Vietnamese troops, the continuing civil war followed the familiar pattern of dry season government offensives, and consolidation of guerrilla positions during the monsoon rains. Much of the fighting focused on the potholed highways – particularly Highway 6 which connects the capital with Battambang – with the Khmer Rouge blowing up most of the bridges along the road. Their strategy involved cutting the roads in order to drain the government's limited resources. Other Khmer Rouge offensives were designed to serve their own economic ends – such as their capture of the gem-rich town of Pailin.

The Khmer Rouge ran extortion rackets throughout the country, even along the strategic Highway 4 which ferried military supplies, oil and consumer goods from the port of Kompong Som (Sihanoukville) to Phnom Penh. The State of Cambodia – or the government forces, known as SOC – was pressed to deploy troops to remote areas and allot scarce resources, settling refugees in more secure parts of the country. To add to their problems, Soviet and Eastern Bloc aid began to dry up.

Throughout 1991 the four warring factions were repeatedly brought to the negotiating table in an effort to hammer out a peace deal. Much of the argument centred on the word 'genocide'. The Prime Minister, Hun Sen, insisted that the wording of any agreement should explicitly condemn the former Khmer Rouge regime's 'genocidal acts'. But the Khmer Rouge refused to be party to any power-sharing deal which labelled them in such a way. Fighting intensified as hopes for a settlement increased – all sides wanted to consolidate their territory in advance of any agreement.

Rumours emerged that China was continuing to supply arms – including tanks, reportedly delivered through Thailand – to the Khmer Rouge. There were also accusations that the Phnom Penh government was using Vietnamese combat troops to stem Khmer Rouge advances – the first such reports since their official withdrawal in 1989. But finally, in June 1991, after several attempts, Sihanouk brokered a permanent ceasefire during a meeting of the Supreme National Council (SNC) in Pattaya, South Thailand. The SNC had been proposed by the United Nations Security Council in 1990 and formed in 1991, with an equal number of representatives from the Phnom Penh government and each of the resistance factions, with Sihanouk as its chairman. The following month he was elected chairman of the SNC, and resigned his presidency of the rebel coalition government in exile. Later in the year, the four factions agreed to reduce their armed guerrillas and militias by 70%. The remainder were to be placed under the supervision of the United Nations Transitional Authority in Cambodia (UNTAC), which supervised Cambodia's transition to multi-party democracy. Heng Samrin decided to drop his insistence that reference should be made to the former Khmer Rouge's 'genocidal regime'. It was also agreed that elections should be held in 1993 on the basis of proportional representation.

Heng Samrin's Communist Party was promptly renamed the Cambodian People's Party, in an effort to persuade people that it sided with democracy and capitalism.

## The Paris Peace Accord

On 23 October 1991, the four warring Cambodian factions signed a peace agreement in Paris which officially ended 13 years of civil war and more than two decades of warfare. The accord was co-signed by 15 other members of the International Peace Conference on Cambodia. There was an air of unreality about the whole event, which brought bitter enemies face-to-face after months of protracted negotiations. There was, however, a notable lack of enthusiasm on the part of the four warring factions. Hun Sen said that the treaty was far from perfect because it failed to contain the word 'genocide' to remind Cambodians of the atrocities of the former Khmer Rouge regime and Western powers obviously agreed. But in the knowledge that it was a fragile agreement, everyone remained diplomatically quiet. US Secretary of State James Baker was quoted as saying "I don't think anyone can tell you there will for sure be lasting peace, but there is great hope."

Political analysts ascribed the successful conclusion to the months of negotiations to improved relations between China and Vietnam – there were reports that the two had held secret summits at which the Cambodia situation was discussed. China put pressure on Prince Norodom Sihanouk to take a leading role in the peace process, and Hanoi's new understanding with Beijing prompted Hun Sen's participation. The easing of tensions between China and Moscow – particularly following the Soviet Union's demise – also helped apply pressure on the different factions. Finally, the United States had shifted its position: in July 1990 it had announced that it would not support the presence of the Khmer Rouge at the UN and by September US officials were talking to Hun Sen.

On 14 November 1991, Prince Norodom Sihanouk returned to Phnom Penh to an ecstatic welcome, followed, a few days later, by Son Sen, a Khmer Rouge leader. On 27 November Khieu Samphan, who had represented the Khmer Rouge at all the peace negotiations, arrived on a flight from Bangkok. Within hours mayhem had broken out, and a lynch mob attacked him in his villa. Rumours circulated that Hun Sen had orchestrated the demonstration, and beating an undignified retreat down a ladder into a waiting armoured personnel carrier, the bloodied Khmer Rouge leader headed back to Pochentong Airport. The crowd had sent a clear signal that they, at least, were not happy to see him back. There were fears that this incident might derail the entire peace process – but in the event, the Khmer Rouge won a small public relations coup by playing the whole thing down. When the Supreme National Council (SNC) finally met in Phnom Penh at the end of December 1991, it was unanimously decided to rubberstamp the immediate deployment of UN troops to oversee the peace process in the run-up to a general election.

## The UN peace-keeping mission

The UN mission "... conducted a brief, profound and very welcome social revolution [in Cambodia]" (William Shawcross, *Cambodia's new deal: a report*, 1994).

The UN mission favoured "Phnom Penh's profiteers, the Khmer Rouge utopists, the Chinese businessmen of Southeast Asia, the annexationist neighbours ..." (Marie Alexandrine Martin, *Cambodia: a shattered society*, 1994).

Yasushi Akashi, a senior Japanese official in the United Nations, was assigned the daunting task of overseeing the biggest military and logistical operation in UN history. UNTAC comprised an international team of 22,000 peacekeepers – including 16,000 soldiers from 22 countries; 6000 officials; 3500 police and 1700 civilian employees and electoral volunteers. The first 'blue-beret' UN troops began arriving in November 1991, even before the SNC had agreed to the full complement of peacekeepers.

The UN Advance Mission to Cambodia (UNAMIC) was followed four months later by the first of the main peacekeeping battalions. The odds were stacked against them. Shortly after his arrival, Akashi commented: "If one was a masochist one could not wish for more."

## UNTAC's task

UNTAC's central mission was to supervise free elections in a country where most of the population had never voted and had little idea of how democracy was meant to work. The UN was also given the task of resettling 360,000 refugees from camps in Thailand and of demobilizing more than a quarter of a million soldiers and militiamen from the four main factions. In addition, it was to ensure that no further arms shipments reached these factions, whose remaining forces were to be confined to cantonments. In the run-up to the elections, UNTAC also took over the administration of the country, taking over the defence, foreign affairs, finance, public security and information portfolios as well as the task of trying to ensure respect for human rights.

By early 1993, UN electoral workers had successfully registered 4.7 million of roughly nine million Cambodians – about 96% of the population above voting age. With a US$2 billion price-tag, this huge operation was the most expensive mission ever undertaken by the UN. At the time, the UN was running 12 peacekeeping operations throughout the world, but two-thirds of its peacekeeping budget was earmarked for Cambodia. Over the months a steady stream of VIPs arrived to witness the operation – they included the UN Secretary-General, Boutros-Boutros Ghali, the Chinese Foreign Minister, Qian Qichen and President François Mitterrand of France.

UNTAC's job would have been easier if the different guerrilla factions and militias had stopped fighting once the Peace Accord was signed. In the months after their arrival UN troops had to broker successive ceasefires between government forces and the Khmer Rouge. During 1992, the Khmer Rouge refused to demobilize their fighters as required by the Accord and attempted to gain a foothold in the strategic central province of Kompong Thom in advance of the full deployment of UN peacekeeping forces. This prompted further scepticism among observers as to their commitment to the peace process. The Khmer Rouge – which was by then referred to (in politically neutral parlance) as the Party of Democratic Kampuchea, or the DK – made it as difficult as possible for the UN. It refused UN soldiers, officials and volunteers access to areas under its control. On a number of occasions in the months running up to the elections, UN military patrols were held hostage after entering Khmer Rouge-held territory.

## The Khmer Rouge pulls out

At the beginning of 1993 it became apparent that the Khmer Rouge had no intention of playing ball, despite its claim of a solid rural support base. The DK failed to register for the election before the expiry of the UN deadline and its forces stepped up attacks on UN personnel. In April 1993 Khieu Samphan and his entire entourage at the Khmer Rouge compound in Phnom Penh left the city. It was at this stage that UN officials finally began expressing their exasperation and anxiety over the Khmer Rouge's avowed intention to disrupt the polls. It was well known that the faction had procured fresh supplies of Chinese weapons through Thailand – although there is no evidence that these came from Beijing – as well as large arms caches all over the country.

By the time of the elections, the group was thought to be in control of between 10% and 15% of Cambodian territory. Khmer Rouge guerrillas launched attacks in April and May 1993. Having stoked racial antagonism, they started killing ethnic Vietnamese villagers and settlers, sending up to 20,000 of them fleeing into Vietnam. In one particularly vicious attack, 33 Vietnamese fishermen and their families were killed in a village on the Tonlé Sap. The Khmer Rouge also began ambushing and killing UN soldiers and electoral volunteers.

The UN remained determined that the elections should go ahead despite the Khmer Rouge threats and mounting political intimidation and violence between other factions, notably the Cambodian People's Party and Funcinpec. But it did not take any chances: in the week before the elections, 6000 flak jackets and helmets were flown into the country and security was tightened. In the event, however, there were remarkably few violent incidents and the feared co-ordinated effort to disrupt the voting failed to materialize. Voters took no notice of Khmer Rouge calls to boycott the election and in fact, reports came in from several provinces of large numbers of Khmer Rouge guerrillas and villagers from areas under their control, turning up at polling stations and casting their ballots.

## The UN-supervised elections

The voting was by proportional representation, province by province. The election was conducted under the aegis of 1400 International Polling Station Officers from more than 40 countries. The Cambodian people were voting for a 120-member Constituent Assembly to write a new constitution.

The days following the election saw a political farce – Cambodian style – which, as Nate Thayer wrote in the *Far Eastern Economic Review* "might have been comic if the implications were not so depressing for the country's future". In just a handful of days, the Phnom Penh-based correspondent went on, Cambodia "witnessed an abortive secession, a failed attempt to establish a provisional government, a royal family feud and the manoeuvres of a prince [Sihanouk] obsessed with avenging his removal from power in a military coup more than 20 years [previously]". The elections gave Funcinpec 45% of the vote, the CPP 38% and the BLDP, 3%. The CPP immediately claimed the results fraudulent, while Prince Norodom Chakrapong – one of Sihanouk's sons – announced the secession of the country's six eastern provinces. Fortunately, both attempts to undermine the election dissolved. The CPP agreed to join Funcinpec in a power sharing agreement while, remarkably, the Khmer Rouge were able to present themselves as defenders of democracy in the face of the CPP's claims of vote-rigging. The new Cambodian constitution was ratified in September 1993, marking the end of UNTAC's involvement in the country. Under the new constitution, Cambodia was to be a pluralistic liberal-democratic country. Seventy-year-old Sihanouk was crowned King of Cambodia, reclaiming the throne he relinquished in 1955. His son Norodom Ranariddh was appointed First Prime Minister and Hun Sen, Second Prime Minister, a situation intended to promote national unity but which instead lead to internal bickering and dissent.

## An uncivil society?

Almost from day one of Cambodia's rebirth as an independent state espousing the principles of democracy and the market, cracks began to appear in the rickety structure that underlay these grand ideals. Rampant corruption, infighting among the coalition partners, political intrigue, murder and intimidation all became features of the political landscape – and have remained so to this day. There are three bright spots in an otherwise pretty dismal political landscape. First of all, the Khmer Rouge – along with Pol Pot – is dead and buried. Second, while there have been coups, attempted coups, murder, torture and intimidation, the country does still have an operating political system with an opposition of sorts. And third, the trajectory of change since the last edition of this guide was published has been upwards. But, as the following account shows, politics in Cambodia makes Italy seem a model of stability and common sense.

From the elections of 1993 through to 1998, relations between the two key members of the ruling coalition, the CPP and Funcinpec, went from bad to quite appalling. At the end of 1995 Prince Norodom Sirivudh was arrested for plotting to kill Hun Sen and the prime minister ordered troops and tanks on to the streets of

Phnom Penh. For a while the capital had the air of a city under siege. Sirivudh, secretary-general of Funcinpec and King Norodom Sihanouk's half brother, has been a vocal critic of corruption in the government, and a supporter of Sam Rainsy, the country's most outspoken opposition politician and the bane of Hun Sen's life. The National Assembly voted unanimously to suspend Sirivudh's immunity from prosecution. Few commentators really believed that Sirivudh had plotted to kill Hun Sen. Though he had been outspoken, and occasionally rather injudicious in his public remarks, Sirivudh was not seen to be someone who would involve himself in such a serious conspiracy. The assumption, then, was that Hun Sen – a 'notorious bully' in the words of *The Economist* – was merely playing politics Cambodia-style. In the end Hun Sen did not go through with a trial and Sirivudh went into self-imposed exile.

In 1996, relations between the CPP and Funcinpec reached another low. First Prime Minister Prince Norodom Ranariddh joined his two exiled brothers – princes Chakkrapong and Sirivudh – along with Sam Rainsy, in France. Hun Sen smelled a rat and when Ranariddh threatened in May to pull out of the coalition his worries seemed to be confirmed. Only pressure from the outside prevented a meltdown. Foreign donors said that continuing aid was contingent on political harmony, and ASEAN sent the Malaysian foreign minister to knock a few heads together. Some months later relations became chillier still following the drive-by killing of Hun Sen's brother-in-law as he left a restaurant in Phnom Penh.

Things, it seemed, couldn't get any worse – but they did. In February 1997 fighting between forces loyal to Ranariddh and Hun Sen broke out in Battambang. March saw a grenade attack on a demonstration led by opposition leader Sam Rainsy outside the National Assembly leaving 16 dead and 150 injured – including Rainsy himself who suffered minor injuries. In April, Hun Sen mounted what became known as the 'soft coup'. This followed a complicated series of defections from Ranariddh's Funcinpec party to the CPP which, after much to-ing and fro-ing overturned Funcinpec's small majority in the National Assembly. In May, Hun Sen's motorcade was attacked and a month later, on 16 June, fighting broke out between Hun Sen and Ranariddh's bodyguards leaving three dead. It was this gradual decline in relations between the two leaders and their parties which laid the foundations for the coup of 1997.

In July 1997 the stage was set for Cambodia to join ASEAN, along with Laos and Myanmar (Burma). This would have marked Cambodia's international rehabilitation. Then, just a month before the historic day, on 5-6 June, Hun Sen mounted a coup and ousted Norodom Ranariddh and his party, Funcinpec, from government. It took two days for Hun Sen and his forces to gain full control of the capital. Ranariddh escaped to Thailand while the United Nations Centre for Human Rights reported that 41 senior military officers and Ranariddh loyalists were hunted down in the days following the coup, tortured and executed. In August the National Assembly voted to withdraw Ranariddh's immunity from prosecution. Five months later, in January 1998, United Nations High Commissioner for Human Rights Mary Robinson visited Cambodia and pressed for an investigation into the deaths – a request that Hun Sen rejected as unwarranted interference. ASEAN, long used to claiming that the Association has no role interfering in domestic affairs, found it had no choice but to defer Cambodia's accession. The coup was widely condemned and on 17 September the UN decided to keep Cambodia's seat vacant in the General Assembly.

Following the coup of 1997 there was some speculation that Hun Sen would simply ignore the need to hold elections scheduled for 26 July. In addition, opposition parties threatened to boycott the elections even if they did occur, claiming that Hun Sen and his henchmen were intent on intimidation. But despite sporadic violence in the weeks and months leading up to the elections, all parties ended up participating. It seems that intense international pressure got to Hun Sen who appreciated that without the goodwill of foreign aid donors the country would simply collapse. Of the

4.9 million votes cast – constituting an impressive 90% of the electorate – Hun Sen's Cambodian People's Party won the largest share at just over 41% while Ranariddh's Funcinpec secured 31.7% of the vote and the Sam Rainsy Party (SRP), 14.3%.

Hun Sen offered to bring Funcinpec and the SRP into a coalition government, but his advances were rejected. Instead Rainsy and Ranariddh encouraged a series of demonstrations and vigils outside the National Assembly – which quickly became known as 'Democracy Square', à la Tiananmen Square. At the beginning of September 1998, following a grenade attack on Hun Sen's residence and two weeks of uncharacteristic restraint on the part of the Second Prime Minister, government forces began a crack down on the demonstrators. A week later the three protagonists – Ranariddh, Sam Rainsy and Hun Sen – agreed to talks presided over by King Sihanouk in Siem Reap. These progressed astonishingly well considering the state of relations between the three men and two days later the 122-seat National Assembly opened at Angkor Wat on 24 September. Shortly before the talks, Cambodia's Queen Monineath put forward the suggestion that the three leaders should play more golf together – believing that this might lead to greater co-operation. (Southeast Asian leaders are great believers in the diplomatic powers of golf.) In mid-November further talks (it was not made clear whether these were before, during or after any golf match) between the CPP and Funcinpec led to the formation of a coalition government. Hun Sen became sole prime minister and Ranariddh chairman of the National Assembly. While the CPP and Funcinpec took control of 12 and 11 ministries respectively, with Defence and Interior shared, the CPP got the lion's share of the key portfolios. Sam Rainsy was left on the opposition benches. Even so King Sihanouk could say, before embarking on another round of medical tests in Beijing in November 1998 that "The big political crisis in our country has been solved, the political deadlock is over". It was only after the political détente that followed the elections that Cambodia was given permission to occupy its UN seat in December 1998. At a summit meeting in Hanoi around the same time, ASEAN also announced that they had agreed on the admission of Cambodia to the grouping – which finally came through on 30 April 1999.

## The press and the king

The years since the UN-supervised elections in 1993 have seen, in the eyes of some commentators, a gradual erosion of press freedoms as the government has become becoming increasingly authoritarian. In July 1995 a new press law gave additional powers to a state which has too often resorted to thuggery to convince its opponents. As one observer was quoted as saying in the *Far Eastern Economic Review* at the beginning of 1996, "many people's initial reactions in Cambodia are still violent". At times the sensitivity of politicians has descended into farce. In March 1995, Cambodian newspaper editor Chan Rottana was sentenced to a year in gaol for writing a "false and defamatory statement" that First Prime Minister Prince Norodom Ranariddh was "three times more stupid" than Second Prime Minister Hun Sen. In mid-1995 former foreign minister Sam Rainsy summed up the state of political affairs in the country when he said: "If you are satisfied with cosmetics, everything is OK, like some Americans tell me. But if you scratch a little bit below the surface, there is nothing democratic about the government. The parliament is a rubber stamp. The press is being killed … The judiciary is far from independent."

There is no doubt that by the mid-1990s the job of being a newspaper editor with opposition leanings was becoming increasingly dangerous. In May 1995, the *Khmer Ideal* newspaper was closed down and its publisher fined; in the same month, the editor of *New Liberty* was jailed for a year for penning an editorial entitled 'Nation of thieves', alluding to corruption in government ranks; a week after this, the government began proceedings against the editor of the *Morning News* – a man who was jailed in 1994 for a previous offending article. Human Rights Watch Asia reported that this series of actions "represent one of the most serious assaults yet on freedom of expression". In January 1996 the offices of the opposition Khmer Nation Party were raided by police, and in the following month Ek Mongkol, a radio commentator and Funcinpec member, was shot and seriously injured. In May 1996 anti-government newspaper editor Thun Bunly was gunned down in Phnom Penh and later died. Human Rights Watch reported that in 2003, Chou Chetharith, the deputy editor at royalist radio station, *Ta Prohm*, was shot and killed outside his office after Hun Sen publicly warned the station to stop broadcasting insults directed at the CPP. However, local journalists today claim they have more "press freedom" or as one Khmer journalist aptly put it "the party you are aligned with protects you". Many media outlets depend on financial support from political parties. Not surprisingly, Prime Minister Hun Sen and his allies control several broadcasters. A report by the United States Agency for International Development (USAID) into corruption in 2004 indicated that the media is far from free of bias – politicians will regularly pay journalists to run certain stories and pay them to not run others. It was reported that at the Poipet border, a quagmire of trafficking, corruption and lawlessness, journalists clued up on the pay-offs, regularly gather by the border and wait for officials to come and pay them off for not reporting the terrible border stories.

Most commentators also viewed former King Norodom Sihanouk as part of the problem, simply because he was so revered. He interfered in the political process, changed his mind constantly, and exasperated government ministers. Yet the respect held for him by Cambodians meant that he could not be ignored, or easily contradicted.

Nonetheless, in 1995 the government apparently had a stab at trying to reduce his influence and role. For a start the police confiscated all copies of a booklet entitled 'Only the King can save Cambodia' – reputed to call for the return of King Sihanouk to politics. But this council consists of a myriad of competing factions.

In 1996 William Shawcross returned to Cambodia and spent two hours with Sihanouk. The former King "was his usual charming and voluble self", Shawcross wrote of the meeting, "offering Tattinger champagne and chocolates". But he was also, apparently, a saddened man as he watched his country lurch from crisis to crisis. Sihanouk explained to Shawcross: "I am like a piece of ham in a sandwich, but not a delicious sandwich like those created by Lord Sandwich. I'm stuck instead between the government and the opposition. I am very miserable. Very, very miserable. I would like to conciliate. I cannot. I cannot reunite the two sides. My hope for Cambodia to become one of the world's most advanced liberal democracies is finished" (*The New York Review*, 14 November 1996).

After countless threats, on October 7, 2004, King Sihanouk abdicated; requesting by letter that all "compatriots please allow him [sic] to retire". Sihanouk's long-time battle with cancer was cited as his motivation. It is said that a fortune teller once predicted that he would not live past his 74th birthday, so he was already defying the odds. On his website the King explained: "My abdication allows me to give our country, our nation and our people a serious opportunity to avoid mortal turmoil the day after my death."

On October 14, the Cambodian Throne Council selected Prince Norodom Sihamoni to succeed Sihanouk as King. King Norodom Sihamoni officially ascended the throne in a coronation ceremony held on October 29.

Even though Cambodia's constitution, states that the king officially reigns as head of state but does not govern, Sihanouk king never stayed far from politics. Unlike his father, Sihamoni has no background in politics nor appears likely to head that way. Instead, the new King is renowned for his ballet prowess, having trained as a dancer in Prague in the 1970s. He later studied film in North Korea and served as Cambodia's envoy to the UNESCO in Paris.

Sihanouk, based in Beijing in 2005, continued to prove that out of sight wasn't out of mind, retaining an omnipresent voice. Having tried his hand as author, film maker, song writer, actor, and of course king, the serial multi-tasker, Sihanouk assumed a new hobby – blogging.

## A return to some kind of normality

The year 1997 was the low point in Cambodia's stuttering return to a semblance of normality. The Asian economic crisis combined with the coup (see above) to rock the country back on its heels. On 3 February 2002 free, fair and only modestly violent local commune elections were held. The CPP won the vote by a landslide and although there is little doubt that Hun Sen's party used a bit of muscle here and there, foreign election observers decided that the result reflected the will of the 90% of the electorate who voted. The CPP, despite its iron grip on power, does recognize that democracy means it has to get out there and make a case. Around one third of the CPP's more unpopular commune chiefs were replaced prior to the election. Funcinpec did badly, unable to shake off the perception that it sold out its principles to join the coalition in 1998. The opposition Sam Rainsy Party did rather better, largely for the same reason: the electorate viewed it as standing up to the might of the CPP, highlighting corruption and abuses of power.

In July 2002 Hun Sen took on the rotating chairmanship of ASEAN and used a round of high-profile meetings to demonstrate to the region, and the wider world, just how far the country has come. Hun Sen, who hardly has an enviable record as a touchy-feely politician, used the chairmanship of ASEAN to polish his own as well as his country's credentials in the arena of international public opinion. But despite the PR some Cambodians are concerned that Hun Sen is becoming a little like Burma's Ne Win. Like Ne Win, Hun Sen seems to be obsessed with numbers. His lucky number is nine; in 2002 he brought the local elections forward by three weeks so that the digits in the date would add up to nine. In 2001 he closed down all Cambodia's karaoke bars; fine if he was closing down drug dens, but karaoke bars? With over 20 years as prime minister there is no one to touch Hun Sen and he seems to revel in his strongman reputation. Judges bow to his superior knowledge of the judicial system; kings and princes acknowledged his unparalleled role in appointing the new king; many journalists are in thrall to his power. Hun Sen once said to foreign monitors that "international standards exist only in sports" (*The Economist*, 2.5.2002). If even the most fundamental of rights are negotiable then it would seem that only Cambodia's dependence on foreign largesse constrains his wilder impulses.

Compared to its recent past, the last 10 years has been a period of relative stability for Cambodia. Political violence and infighting between parties continues to be a major problem – by international standards the elections were borderline unacceptable, although most of the major parties were reasonably satisfied with the results which saw Hun Sen's landslide victory. The 2003 election wasn't smooth-sailing either. Prior to the June 2003 election the alleged instructions given by representatives of the CPP to government controlled election monitoring organizations were: "If we win by the law, then we win. If we lose by the law, we still must win." Nonetheless a political deadlock arose, with the CPP winning a majority of votes but not the two-thirds required under the constitution to govern alone. The incumbent CPP-led administration assumed power and took on a caretaker role, pending the creation of a coalition which would satisfy the required number of National Assembly seats to form government. Without a functioning legislature, the course of vital legislation was stalled. After almost a year-long stalemate, the National Assembly approved a controversial addendum to the constitution, which allowed a new government to be formed by vote. The vote took place on July 15 2004, and the National Assembly approved a new coalition government, an amalgam of the CPP and FUNCINPEC, with Hun Sen at the helm as Prime Minister and Prince Norodom Ranariddh as President of the National Assembly.

The government's democratic principles came under fire once again in February 2005, when opposition leader Sam Rainsy fled the country after losing his parliamentary immunity from prosecution. Rainsy is perceived as something of a threat due to his steadily gaining popularity with young urban dwellers, whose growing disenchantment with the current government he feeds off. On the one hand, his 'keep the bastards honest' style of politics has added a new dimension of accountability to Cambodian politics, but on the other, his nationalist, racist rantings, particularly his anti-Vietnamese sentiments, could be a very bad thing for the country. In May, 2005 Hun Sen said that Sam Rainsy would have to wait until the "next life" before he would guarantee his safety. However, having received a pardon in February 2006, he returned to the political fray soon thereafter.

## The lingering death of the Khmer Rouge

What many outsiders found hard to understand was how the Khmer Rouge enjoyed such popular support among Cambodians – even after the massacres and torture. UN officials working in Phnom Penh in 1992 and 1993 found this disquieting. In June 1994, the retiring Australian ambassador to Cambodia, John Holloway, in a leaked account of his 2½ years in Phnom Penh wrote: "I was alarmed in a recent dialogue with about 100 students from different groups at the University of Phnom Penh to hear them espousing a return to government by the Khmer Rouge ... They estimated that 60% of the student body favoured Khmer Rouge participation in government ... It is necessary for outsiders to understand, that for most Cambodians, the Vietnamese are a far more traumatic issue than the Khmer Rouge."

The Khmer Rouge was not, of course, just a political force. Its political influence was backed up and reinforced by military muscle. And it has been the defeat of the Khmer Rouge as an effective fighting force which seems to have delivered the fatal blow to its political ambitions.

In mid-1994 the National Assembly outlawed the Khmer Rouge, offering a six month amnesty to rank and file guerrillas. By the time the six months was up in January 1995, 7000 Khmer Rouge had reportedly defected to the government, leaving at that time somewhere between 5000 and 6000 hardcore rebels still fighting. A split in this core group can be dated to 8 August 1996 when Khmer Rouge radio announced that former 'brother number two', Ieng Sary, had betrayed the revolution by embezzling money earned from mining and timber contracts, and branded him a traitor.

This was the first evidence available to Western commentators that a significant split in the Khmer Rouge had occurred. In retrospect, it seems that the split had been brewing for some years – ever since the UN-sponsored elections had revealed a division between 'conservatives' and 'moderates'. The latter, apparently, wished to co-operate with the UN, while the former group desired to boycott the elections. In 1996 the moderate faction, headed by Ieng Sary, finally broke away from the conservatives led by Pol Pot and hardman General Ta Mok. Hun Sen announced soon after the radio broadcast in August 1996 that two Khmer Rouge commanders, Ei Chhien and Sok Pheap had defected to the government. At the end of September Ieng Sary held a press conference to declare his defection. He told an incredulous audience that he "had nothing to do with ordering the execution of anyone, or even the suggestion of it". On 14 September King Norodom Sihanouk granted Ieng Sary a royal pardon.

The Cambodian government's conciliatory line towards Ieng Sary seemed perplexing given the man's past. Although he cast himself in the mould of 'misguided and ignorant revolutionary', there are few who doubt that he was fully cognisant of what the Khmer Rouge under Pol Pot were doing even if, as Michael Vickery argues, he was not Brother Number Two, just Brother Number Four or Five. Indeed he has admitted as much in the past. Not only is he, as a man, thoroughly unpleasant – or so those who know him have said – but he was also a key figure in the leadership and was sentenced to death in absentia by the Phnom Penh government. Stephen Heder of London's School of Oriental & African Studies was quoted as saying after the September press conference: "It's totally implausible that Ieng Sary was unaware that people were being murdered [by the Khmer Rouge]". This was confirmed in October 1996 when Laurence Piq, formerly married to Suong Sikoeun an aide to Ieng Sary, wrote: "As in The Little Red Riding Hood, the hand he [Ieng Sary] extends for photographs is the better to grab you with. The jovial demeanour he affixes to his mouth is the better to bite you with. The red carpet is laid out. Abominable crimes are being erased. All shame is swallowed. The world's nations accept this under the pretext of peace. What kind of peace? A peace à la Khmer Rouge, dripping with the blood of genocide." The split in the Khmer Rouge and the defection of Ieng Sary deprived the Khmer Rouge of 3000-5000 men – halving its fighting force – and also denied the group important revenues from key gem mining areas around Pailin and many of the richest forest concessions.

The disintegration of the Khmer Rouge continued in 1997 after a complicated deal involving Pol Pot, Khieu Samphan, Son Sen and Ta Mok, as well as members of Funcinpec, collapsed. In early June Khieu Samphan, the nominal leader of the Khmer Rouge, was thought to be on the verge of brokering an agreement with Funcinpec that would give Pol Pot and two of his henchmen (Son Sen and Ta Mok) immunity from prosecution. This would then provide the means by which Khieu Samphan might enter mainstream Cambodian politics. It seems that Hun Sen, horrified at the idea of an alliance between Khieu Samphan and Funcinpec, mounted the coup of June 1997 to prevent the deal coming to fruition. Pol Pot was also, apparently, less than satisfied with the terms of the agreement and pulled out – killing Son Sen in the process. But before Pol Pot could flee, Ta Mok captured his erstwhile leader on June 19th at the Khmer Rouge stronghold of Anlong Veng.

A little more than a month later the 'Trial of the Century' began in this remote jungle hideout. It was a show trial – more like a Cultural Revolution lynching. A crowd of a few hundred people were on hand to shout slogans like 'Crush, crush, crush Pol Pot and his clique'. Pol Pot offered the usual Khmer Rouge defence: the revolution made mistakes, but its leaders were inexperienced. And, in any case, they saved Cambodia from annexation by Vietnam. (There is an argument purveyed by some academics that the Khmer Rouge was essentially involved in a programme of ethnic cleansing aimed at ridding Cambodia of all Vietnamese people and influences.) Show trial or not, few people had any sympathy for Pol Pot as he was sentenced by the Khmer Rouge 'people's' court to life imprisonment for the murder of Son Sen. A Khmer Rouge radio station broadcast that with Pol Pot's arrest and sentencing, a 'dark cloud' had been lifted from the Cambodian people.

Confirmation of this bizarre turn of events emerged in mid-October when journalist Nate Thayer of the *Far Eastern Economic Review* became the first journalist to interview Pol Pot since 1979. He reported that the former Khmer Rouge leader was "very ill and perhaps close to death". Even more incredibly than Ieng Sary's defence, Pol Pot denied that the Cambodian genocide had ever occurred and told Nate Thayer that his 'conscience was clear'. "I came to carry out the struggle, not to kill people", he said, adding "Even now, and you can look at me, am I a savage person?".

In March 1998 reports filtered out of the jungle near the Thai border that the Khmer Rouge was finally disintegrating in mutinous conflict. The end game was at hand. The government's amnesty encouraged the great bulk of the Khmer Rouge's remaining fighters to lay down their arms and in December 1998 the last remnants of the rebel army surrendered to government forces, leaving just a handful of men under hardman 'The Butcher' Ta Mok still at large. But even Ta Mok's days of freedom were numbered. In March 1999 he was captured near the Thai border and taken back to Phnom Penh.

# The death of Pol Pot

On 15 April 1998 unconfirmed reports stated that Pol Pot – a man who ranks with Hitler, Stalin and Mao in his ability to kill – had died in a remote jungle hideout in the north of Cambodia. Given that Pol Pot's death had been announced several times before, the natural inclination among journalists and commentators was to treat these reports with scepticism. But it was already known that Pol Pot was weak and frail and his death was confirmed when journalists were invited to view his body the following day. Pol Pot was reported to have died from a heart attack. He was 73.

## A new era?

The question of what to do with Ieng Sary was the start of a long debate over how Cambodia – and the international community – should deal with former members of the Khmer Rouge. The pragmatic, realist line is that if lasting peace is to come to Cambodia, then it may be necessary to allow some people to get away with – well – murder. As one Western diplomat pondered: "Do you owe fealty to the dead for the living?" This would seem to be Hun Sen's preferred position.

By late 1998, with the apparent end of the Khmer Rouge as a fighting force, the government seemed happy to welcome back the rank and file into mainstream Cambodian life – and even into the armed forces – while putting on trial key characters in the Khmer Rouge like Ta Mok, Khieu Samphan and Nuon Chea. While the government was considering what to do, former leaders of the Khmer Rouge were busy trying to rehabilitate their muddied reputations. After years of living pretty comfortable lives around the country, particularly in and around Pailin, by the end of 2007 the old guard of the Khmer Rouge were finally being brought to book. This turn of events was finally set in motion in March 2006 with the nomination of seven judges by the then Secretary General of the United Nations, Kofi Annan for the much anticipated Cambodia Tribunal. With Ta Mok dying in prison in early July 2006 the first charges were laid against the notorious head of the Tuol Sleng prison, Khang Khek Ieu – aka 'Comrade Duch'. Indicted on July 31st with crimes against humanity and after spending eight years behind bars Duch is likely to go on trial in early 2008. Yet it was with the arrests in late 2007 of Ieng Sary, Nuon Chea and Khieu Samphan that the tribunal finally began to flex its muscles. Each of these arrests made international news and it seems, almost 30 years after the Vietnam invasion ended the abhorrent Khmer Rouge regime, that Cambodia may finally be coming to terms with its horrific past (for more information on the Tribunal see box, page 372).

However, with only the few living key Khmer Rouge figures standing trial most of the minor – and probably equally murderous – cadre are still in circulation. It could be argued that the Tribunal is purely a diversion that allows this coterie of killers and Hun Sen's nefarious past to remain hidden from scrutiny.

What is obvious is that as the Tribunal progressed, many of the old divisions that have riven Cambodian society for generations where taking hold again. In late 2007 Cambodia was officially and internationally recognised as one of the most corrupt countries in history. Spend five minutes in Phnom Penh and this air of corruption is staring you in the face – Toyota Land Cruisers, giant, black Lexus SUVs and Humvees plough through the streets without regard for anyone or anything. When these vehicles do crush or kill other road users, the driver's well-armed body guards hop out, pistols waving, and soon dissuade any eager witnesses. This kind of event is commonplace and the poorer locals know this. Speak to a moto or tuk-tuk driver and you'll soon sense the resentment, "We hate the corrupt and we'd be happy to see them die", is a frequent comment reminiscent of Cambodia's darker times. The establishment of a new, rich elite is not leading to the trickle down of wealth but the entrenchment of certain groups who have no regard at all for building a new society. Even the aid community is complicit in this – one senior worker from a massive donor to Cambodia made this damning off-the-record

# Cambodia Tribunal

In 1997, with the country's interminable civil war set to end, the Cambodian government made an official approach to the United Nations to establish a court to prosecute the senior members of the Khmer Rouge. The thinking at the time was that Cambodia lacked the institutions and know-how to handle such a big trial and that outside expertise would be needed.

At first, things for the prosecution looked promising, with an agreed handing over of Pol Pot (was holed up in northern Cambodia in Anlong Veng), set to take place in April 1998. But he never made it to court, mysteriously dying the night before his supposed arrest. Some say from a heart attack, others that he took his own life.

In 1999, Kang Kek Iew aka 'Comrade Duch', the commandant of the infamous Tuol Sleng prison camp in Phnom Penh, surrendered to the Cambodian authorities. In the same year, Ta Mok, another blood-soaked Khmer Rouge leader, was also arrested (he died in custody seven years later in 2006). Initially, however, no power or legal authority existed to try them and it wasn't until 2001 that the Cambodian government agreed to pass a law setting up what came to be known as the 'Extraordinary Chambers in the Courts of Cambodia for the Prosecution of Crimes Committed during the Period of Democratic Kampuchea' or, for short, the Cambodia Tribunal.

Several more years passed, with the sometimes indifferent Cambodians stating that they had no money to finance the trials and the international community unwilling to fund a process in a country where corruption was so rampant. But despite this, in early 2006, buildings just outside Phnom Penh were requisitioned, the UN nominated its judges and by July of the same year a full panel of 30 Cambodian and UN judges were fully sworn in. A list of five main suspects was drawn up in July 2007 and the first person formally charged was the already incarcerated Comrade Duch on July 31st 2007.

Then, in late 2007, after years of snail-like progress, and with the main protagonists approaching their twilight years, a flurry of dramatic arrests occurred. Former Khmer Rouge ideologue and Foreign Minister Ieng Sary and his wife, the Minister of Social Affairs, Ieng Thirith, former Chief of State and Pol Pot's number two, Khieu Samphan, were all taken into custody and charged with war crimes and crimes against humanity.

As this book goes to press in early 2008, many commentators were in agreement that Cambodia has never really come to terms with its horrific past and that the trials, despite opening up extremely painful memories, are the only way forward. What is certain is that the trial of the old guard of the Khmer Rouge will be one of the most anticipated global news stories of the decade.

comment, "We view corruption as the only stabilising factor in Cambodian society. It is awful but what else is there?"

With elections planned for 2008 and no opposition to Hun Sen's rule to speak of, the international community and the Cambodian people can only expect more of the same.

# People

## Chinese

In the 18th and 19th centuries large numbers of ethnic Chinese migrated to Southeast Asia, where most became involved in commerce. Until the Khmer Rouge take-over in 1975, the Chinese played a central role in the economy, controlling trade, banking and transport. As in neighbouring Thailand, they assimilated to a greater degree than in other parts of Southeast Asia. In recent decades, most of Cambodia's urban and governing élite has had at least some Chinese blood – Lon Nol, for example had a Chinese grandparent. The Chinese started leaving the country when civil war broke out in 1970 – and many of those who did not get out before 1975 were killed during the Pol Pot years. The few who survived the Khmer Rouge era emigrated during the first months of the pro-Vietnam PRK rule. Officially, the Chinese population of Cambodia today constitutes around 1% of the total.

## Vietnamese

The southern part of Cambodia, particularly along the Mekong, has always had many inhabitants of Vietnamese descent, as well as the area around Phnom Penh. The Vietnamese live very separate lives to the Cambodians due to centuries of mistrust and animosity between the two groups. They are known by the Khmers as 'youn', a derogatory term meaning 'people from the north' and it is hard to find other Cambodians who have anything positive to say about Vietnamese settlers in the country. One human rights official was quoted as saying "Given a choice, a lot of people in this country would expel every single Vietnamese". And if the nationalistic fervour of Sam Rainsy ever comes to fruition, this could potentially happen. This dislike of the Vietnamese stems partly from historical fears – Vietnam absorbed large areas of the former Cambodian Empire in the 18th and 19th centuries; partly from Vietnam's role in Cambodia between 1979 and 1989; and partly from the sheer size of Vietnam – some 70 million inhabitants – when set against Cambodia's population of 10 million. As a result anti-Vietnamese sentiment is mainstream politics in the country. Inventing fanciful stories about Vietnamese commandos infiltrating the country, or Vietnamese control of the economy, is never likely to do harm to a budding populist politician. Many Vietnamese (and Cham) live in floating villages due to the foreign ownership laws relating to property.

## Cham-Malays

There are about 200,000 Cham-Malays, descended from the Cham of the royal kingdom of Champa based in present day central Vietnam. They now constitute the single largest ethnic minority in the country. In the 15th century the Vietnamese moving south drove many of the Cham living in the lower Mekong area into Cambodia. They now mainly live along the Mekong, north of Phnom Penh. The Chams were badly persecuted during the Pol Pot years and their population more than halved. They are Muslim and their spiritual centre is Chur-Changvra near Phnom Penh. They adopted their faith and script from Malays who settled in Kampot and interior regions on the invitation of the Muslim Khmer King Chan in 1642, after he had converted to Islam. The Cham are traditionally cattle traders, silk weavers and butchers – Theravada Buddhism forbids the Khmer to slaughter animals. Their batik sarongs are very similar to those found in Malaysia.

Although the Cham are now free to pursue their faith largely free from persecution, they still suffer from the stigma of being viewed, by many Cambodians, as second class citizens. Strangely perhaps, there is a close affinity between Christians and Muslims in Cambodia – in the face of an overwhelmingly dominant Buddhist faith.

**Other groups**

There are also a small number of Shans, Thai and Lao, most who live near Battambang, the descendants of miners and jewellers who came to work the ruby mines of Pailin during the French colonial era.

---

# Religion

## The god-kings of Angkor

Until the 14th century Buddhism and Hinduism existed side-by-side in Kambuja. In the pre-Angkor era, the Hindu gods Siva and Vishnu were worshipped as a single deity, Harihara. The statue of Harihara from Phnom Da (eighth century) is divided in half: the 'stern' right half is Siva (with wild curly hair) and the 'sublime' left half, Vishnu (who wears a mitre). The first city at Angkor, built by Jayavarman II in the early ninth century, was called Hariharalaya after this god. Early Angkor kings promoted various Hindu sects, mainly dedicated to Siva and Vishnu. During the Angkor period, Siva was the most favoured deity but by the 12th century Vishnu replaced him. Jayavarman VII introduced Mahayana Buddhism as the official court religion at the end of the 12th century. The constant chopping, changing and refining of state religion helped sustain the power of the absolute monarch – each change ushered in a new style of rule and historians believe refinements and changes of religion were deliberately imported to consolidate the power of the kings.

One reason the Khmer Empire was so powerful was its basis on the Hindu concept of the god-king or devaraja. Jayavarman II (802-850) crowned himself as a reincarnation of Siva and erected a Siva lingam (a phallic monument to the god) at Phnom Kulen, the source of power for the Khmer Dynasty. Siva-worship was not originally introduced by Jayavarman II, however – it had been previously practised in the old kingdom of Funan. The investiture of power was always performed by a Brahmin priest who also bestowed divinity on the king as a gift from Siva. This ceremony became an essential rite of kingship which was observed continuously – right into the 20th century. The king's spirit was said to reside in the lingam, which was enshrined in the centre of a monumental religious complex, representing the spiritual axis of the kingdom. Here, the people believed, their divinely ordained king communicated with the gods. Succeeding monarchs followed Jayavarman II's example and continued to install themselves as god-kings, evoking the loyalty of their subjects.

Very few of the statues of Vishnu and Siva and other gods left by the Khmer Empire were traditional representations of the deities. The great majority of the images were portraits of kings and princes and high dignitaries, each represented as the god into whom they would be absorbed at the end of their earthly existence. That the names given to the statues were usually a composite of the names of the man and the god, indicates that men were worshipped as gods.

The installation of the devaraja cult by Jayavarman II took place on the summit of Phnom Kulen. Under subsequent kings, it was transferred, in turn, to Bakong, Phnom Bakheng, Koh Ker and Phimeanakas. At the end of the 11th century, the Baphuon was constructed to house the golden lingam. The tradition of the god-king cult was so deeply rooted in the court that even Theravada Buddhism introduced in the 14th century bowed to its influence. Following the adoption of Mahayana Buddhism in the second half of the 12th century, the god-king left his lingam to enter the statue of the Buddha. Jayavarman VII built the Bayon to shelter the statue of the Buddha-king in the centre of the city of Angkor.

Temple-mountains were built as microcosms of the universe, with Mount Meru, the home of the gods, at the centre, surrounded by oceans (followed most perfectly at of an inherited tradition from India. At the summit of the cosmic mountain, at the centre of the city, the king, embodied by his own sacred image, entered into contact with the world of gods. Each temple was the personal temple of an individual king, erected by him during his life. When, after his death, his ashes or remains were deposited there (to animate the statue and give the cult a living image), the temple became his mausoleum. His successor always built another sanctuary to house the image of the god-king. During the Angkor period the Khmers did not seem to question this system. It ordered their lives, regulating everything from agriculture to birth and death rites. But the temples were not the products of a popular faith, like Christian cathedrals – they were strictly the domain of royalty and high priests and were reserved for the worship of kings and members of the entourage deified in the form of one of the Hindu or Buddhist gods.

## Theravada Buddhism

Despite the powerful devaraja cult, most Khmers also practised an amalgam of ancestor worship and animism. As Theravada Buddhism swept through Southeast Asia (well after the adoption of Mahayana Buddhism), propagated by missionary monks, its message of simplicity, austerity and humility began to undermine the cult of the god-king. As a popular religion, it had great attractions for a population which for so many centuries had been denied access to the élitist and extravagant devaraja cult. By the 15th century Theravada Buddhism was the dominant religion in Cambodia. ➤➤ *For further information on Theravada Buddhism, see page 524.*

## Buddhism in Cambodia

The Cambodian Buddhist clergy divide into two groups: the Mahanikay and Thommayuth (or Dhammayuttikanikay) orders. The latter was not introduced from Thailand until 1864, and was a reformist order with strong royal patronage. Theravada Buddhism remained the dominant and unchallenged faith until 1975.

It was a demonstration by Buddhist monks in Phnom Penh which first kindled Cambodian nationalism in the wake of World War II (see page 349). According to historians, one of the reasons for this was the intensifying of the relationship between the king and the people, due to the founding of the Buddhist Institute in Phnom Penh in 1930. The Institute was under the joint patronage of the kings of Laos and Cambodia as well as the French. It began printing and disseminating Buddhist texts – in Pali and Khmer. Historian David P Chandler wrote: "As the Institute's reputation grew, enhanced by frequent conferences, it became a rallying point for an emerging intelligentsia." The institute's librarian founded a Khmer-language newspaper (*Nagaravatta* – or 'Angkor Wat') in 1936, which played a critical role in articulating and spreading the nationalist message.

Before 1975 and the arrival of the Khmer Rouge, there were 3000 monasteries and 64,000 monks (*bonzes*) – many of these were young men who had become ordained to escape conscription – in Cambodia and rural life was centred around the wat (Buddhist monastery). Under Pol Pot, all monks were 'defrocked' and, according to some sources, as many as 62,000 were executed or died in the ricefields. Monasteries were torn down or converted to other uses, Pali – the language of Theravada Buddhism – was banned, and former monks were forced to marry. Ironically, Saloth Sar (Pol Pot) himself spent some time as a novice when he was a child. Buddhism was revived in 1979 with the ordination of monks by a visiting delegation of Buddhists from Vietnam; at the same time, many of the wats – which were defiled by the Khmer Rouge – were restored and reconsecrated. The two orders of Theravada Buddhism – the Thommayuth (aristocratic) and Mahanikay (common) – previously practised in Cambodia have now merged. The Hun Sen government softened the position on Buddhism to the degree that it was reintroduced as the

## Mudras and the Buddha image

An artist producing an image of the Buddha does not try to create an original piece of art; he is trying to be faithful to a tradition which can be traced back over centuries. It is important to appreciate that the Buddha image is not merely a work of art but an object of and for, worship. Sanskrit poetry even sets down the characteristics of the Buddha – albeit in rather unlikely terms: legs like a deer, arms like an elephant's trunk, a chin like a mango stone and hair like the stings of scorpions. The Pali texts of Theravada Buddhism add the 108 auspicious signs, long toes and fingers of equal length, body like a banyan tree and eyelashes like a cow's. The Buddha can be represented either sitting, lying (indicating paranirvana), or standing, and (in Thailand) occasionally walking. He is often represented standing on an open lotus flower: the Buddha was born into an impure world, and likewise the lotus germinates in mud but rises above the filth to flower. Each image will be represented in a particular mudra or 'attitude', of which there are 40. The most common are:

**Abhayamudra** – dispelling fear or giving protection; right hand (sometimes both hands) raised, palm outwards, usually with the Buddha in a standing position.

**Varamudra** – giving blessing or charity; the right hand pointing downwards, the palm facing outwards, with the Buddha either seated or standing.

**Vitarkamudra** – preaching mudra; the ends of the thumb and index finger of the right hand touch to form a circle, symbolizing the Wheel of Law. The Buddha can either be seated or standing.

**Dharmacakramudra** – 'spinning the Wheel of Law'; a preaching mudra symbolizing the teaching of the first sermon. The hands are held in front of the chest, thumbs and index fingers of both joined, one facing inwards and one outwards.

**Bhumisparcamudra** – 'calling the earth goddess to witness' or 'touching the earth'; the right hand rests on the right knee with the tips of the fingers 'touching ground', thus calling the earth goddess Dharani/Thoranee to witness his enlightenment and victory over Mara, the king of demons. The Buddha is always seated.

**Dhyanamudra** – meditation; both hands resting open, palms upwards, in the lap, right over left.

**Other points of note:**
**Vajrasana** – yogic posture of meditation; cross-legged, both soles of the feet visible.

**Virasana** – yogic posture of meditation; cross-legged, but with the right leg on top of the left, covering the left foot (also known as paryankasana).

**Buddha under Naga** – the Buddha is shown in an attitude of meditation with a cobra rearing up over his head. This refers to an episode in the Buddha's life when he was meditating; a rain storm broke and Nagaraja, the king of the nagas (snakes), curled up under the Buddha (seven coils) and then used his seven-headed hood to protect the Holy One from the falling rain.

**Buddha calling for rain** – the Buddha is depicted standing, both arms held stiffly at the side of the body, fingers pointing downwards.

**Bhumisparcamudra** – calling the earth goddess to witness. Sukhothai period, 13th-14th century.

**Dhyanamudra** – meditation. Sukhothai period, 13th-14th century.

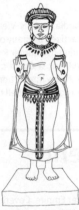

**Abhayamudra** – dispelling fear or giving protection. Lopburi Buddha, Khmer style 12th century.

**Vitarkamudra** – preaching, "spinning the Wheel of Law". Dvaravati Buddha, 7th-8th century, seated in the "European" manner.

**Abhayamudra** – dispelling fear or giving protection; subduing Mara position. Lopburi Buddha, Khmer style 13th century.

**The Buddha** 'Calling for rain'.

national religion in 1989 and young men were allowed to be ordained (previously restricted to men over 45 that were no longer able to serve in the army).

Today 90% of Cambodian citizens are Buddhist. In 2004, the country had almost 59,500 monks spread across the country's 3980 wats. Cambodian Buddhism is an easy-going faith and tolerates ancestor and territorial spirit worship, which is widely practised. The grounds usually consist of a *vihara* (Buddhist temple), Sala Thoama *saphea* (the hall where Dharma is taught) and *kods* (the quarters where the monks live). Traditionally, the vihara and the Buddha statues contained within them will face east in order to express gratitude to Lord Buddha for enlightenment and guide others toward the path of enlightenment. There are often small rustic altars to the guardian spirits (*neak ta*) in the corner of pagodas. Cambodians often wear *katha* – or charms – which are believed to control external magical forces. Most important ceremonies – weddings, funerals, coming of age – have both Buddhist and animist elements. Wats play an important role in education and it is fairly common to find schools built inside or beside wats.

## Other religions

There are around 60,000 Roman Catholics in Cambodia, mainly Vietnamese, and about 2000 Protestants. Islam, of the Sunni sect, is practised by many of the 200,000 (some commentators would say 500,000) Cham. During the Khmer Rouge period it was reported that Cham were forced to eat pork while most Cham mosques were destroyed, and only now are they being slowly rebuilt. A new International Mosque in Phnom Penh, built with Saudi money, was opened in 1994. Almost all the Chinese in Cambodia are Taoist/Confucianist.

# Land and environment

## Geography

Cambodia is all that remains of the once mighty Khmer Empire. Covering a land area of 181,035 sq km – about the size of England and Wales combined – the country is squeezed in between Thailand to the west, Vietnam to the east and Laos to the north. Cambodia holds many features of international conservation significance. The country has one of the highest proportions of land as natural habitat (forest and wetlands) in the world, and one of the least disturbed coastlines in continental Asia. The coastline stretches along the Gulf of Thailand for 435 km, supports 64 islands and extensive mangroves and coral reefs. The **Mekong** is as central to life in Cambodia as the Nile is to life in Egypt. The river runs through Cambodia for about 500 km, bisecting the east lowlands, north to south. It is navigable by cargo ships from the delta in Vietnam, right up to Phnom Penh and beyond. Near the centre of the country is the **Tonlé Sap** – the 'Great Lake' – the largest freshwater lake in Southeast Asia. It is connected to the Mekong via the short channel-like Tonlé Sap River. The Tonlé Sap basin includes all or part of eight of Cambodia's 24 provinces and covers 80,000 sq km (44% of Cambodia's total area) and is estimated to be home to 3.6 million people, one third of Cambodia's total population. When the Mekong floods between June and October – sometimes these floods can be devastating, as they were in 1991 – the Tonlé Sap River reverses its flow and the floodwaters fill the Great Lake, which doubles in size, covering the surrounding countryside.

North of Phnom Penh, the Mekong is known as the Upper Mekong – or just the Mekong; downriver from the capital it divides into the Lower Mekong and the Bassac rivers. These two tributaries then swing to the southeast across the fertile alluvial plain, towards the sprawling delta and the sea. The broad valley of the Mekong is a centuries-old trade route and its fertile central flood-plain is densely populated.

The alluvial soils are irrigated but have an even greater potential for agricultural production than is presently being realized. Throughout most of its course in Cambodia the river averages more than 1.6 km in width. There are viscous rapids at Kratie, northeast of Phnom Penh, and a succession of dramatic waterfalls – Li Phi and Khong Phapheng Falls – on the border with Laos.

The **central lowlands** are surrounded by savannah; in south Cambodia these plains run all the way to the Vietnamese border. But to the north, east and west, Cambodia is enclosed by mountain chains: the Cardamom Mountains and Elephant Range to the west and southwest, while the sandstone escarpment of the Dangrek Range forms a natural border with Thailand. The **Cardamom Mountains** (named after the spice) run in a gentle curve from just south of Battambang towards Phnom Penh. Phnom Aoral, in the Cardamoms, is Cambodia's highest peak at 1813 m and in 2004 Global Witness detected a large amount of illegal logging in the area. The **Elephant Mountains** run along the south coastline. All these mountains are densely forested and sparsely inhabited, making them perfect operational bases for Cambodia's rebel guerrilla factions, who fought the Phnom Penh government throughout the 1980s. On the south coast around Kompong Som is a lowland area cut off from the rest of the country by mountains. Because the Mekong was a major thoroughfare, the **coastal region** never developed into a centre of trade until a road was built with American aid from Kompong Som to Phnom Penh in the 1960s.

## Climate

The monsoons determine rainfall and temperature patterns in Cambodia. The southwest monsoon, from May to October, brings heavy rain throughout the country. This period accounts for between 75% and 80% of the total annual rainfall. The northeast monsoon blows from October to April and ushers in the dry season. In the mountain areas the temperature is markedly cooler and the dry season only lasts three months. Between the heat and rains there are transitional periods and the best time to visit the country is between November and January, before it gets too hot. Rainfall varies considerably from region to region. The Cardamom Mountains are the wettest. The mean temperature for Cambodia is 27.5°C. It is cooler – around 24°C – from November to January and hotter – around 32°C – between February and April. Humidity is generally high.

## Flora and fauna

The central plains are a predominantly agricultural area and are sparsely wooded but most of the rest of Cambodia – until recently – was still forested. In 1970, 73% of Cambodia's land area was thought to be forested but by 1995 the figure was less than 40%, and a paper published at the end of 1998 put the area at 30%. So the trend is rapidly down. The reasons for the alarming decline in Cambodia's forests are pretty clear – illegal logging (see below). In the southwest, around the Cardamom and Elephant Mountains, there are still large tracts of primary forest where teak predominates. There are also tracts of virgin rainforest in the west and the northeast. At higher elevations in these mountains there are areas of pine forest and in the north and east highlands, temperate forest.

Cambodia has a wide variety of fauna and, before war broke out in the 1970s, was on the international game-hunters' circuit; there were tigers (now an endangered species), buffalo, elephants, wild oxen, majestic birds, clouded leopards (also endangered) and bears, including Malaysian sun bears. Today, there are 630 types of protected wildlife, including 122 mammal species, 537 bird species, 114 are rodents from the rodent family, 40 are aquatic animals and 300 are insects and butterflies.

Even after all the fighting, game is still said to be abundant in forested areas, particularly in north-eastern provinces of Mondulkiri and Ratanakiri. Smaller animals include monkeys, squirrels, tree rats and shrews, flying foxes and numerous species of reptile, including several varieties of poisonous snake, the most common being Russell's viper, the banded krait, cobra and king cobra. Even around Phnom Penh one can see herons, cranes, grouse, pheasant, wild duck, pelicans, cormorants and egrets. The kouprey (meaning 'jungle cow') is Cambodia's most famous animal and a symbol of the Worldwide Fund for Nature. A wild ox, it was first identified in 1939 but is now virtually extinct worldwide. In 1963, King Sihanouk declared the animal Cambodia's national animal. Small numbers are thought to inhabit the more remote areas of the country, although some experts fear that the last specimens were either killed by guerrillas for meat or are being fatally maimed after treading on anti-personnel mines laid by the Khmer Rouge. An effort to capture and breed the kouprey is underway in Vietnam.

The Tonlé Sap area is particularly rich in fish-eating waterfowl and marine life. It supports possibly the largest inland fishing industry in the world. The lake is the lifeline for about 40% of the Cambodian population and provides almost 60% of the country's protein. In 1997 the government applied to UNESCO seeking the nomination of the great lake as a Biosphere Reserve, covering 300,000 ha including both the lake and its surrounding shores. Around 1.36 million Khmers are estimated to be wholly dependent on inland waterways for transport.

The lower reaches of the Mekong, marking the border between Cambodia and Laos, is also the last place in Indochina where the rare Irrawaddy dolphin (Orcaella brevirostris) is to be found. Unfortunately, fishermen in the area took to fishing using dynamite and this threatens the survival of the mammal. Countless numbers were also killed under the Khmer Rouge regime. It was also once found in Thailand's Chao Phraya River, but pollution put paid to that population years ago.

The poverty of most of Cambodia's population has made the trade in exotic fauna an attractive proposition. By 1997 the trade in wildlife had become 'rampant', according to the environmental NGO Global Witness. A case in point is the plight of the Malayan sun bear (Helarctos malayanus), which has been protected in Cambodia since 1992. But its paws and gall bladder are treasured by many Chinese and bear bile is said to command a price of US$100 per gramme in China due to its perceived medicinal properties. The animals are captured and caged and the bile siphoned off through a steel tube inserted into the gall bladder. There is also documentary footage of animals having their paws amputated while still alive. Once again, the failure to protect the sun bear, and many other wild animals, is not due to an absence of environmental legislation but due a lack of commitment to its implementation. Giant ibis and black-necked storks are sold for US$400-500 a pair, rewards are put out for black cranes, turtles and pythons are sold to Chinese and Korean restaurants, and the eggs and chicks of water birds are collected for sale in markets. Cambodia's fauna is being caught, sold and slaughtered on a truly grand scale.

## Timber tragedy

In 1995 the Cambodian government, to much fanfare, introduced a new environment law. This was heralded as the first step in the sustainable exploitation of Cambodia's forests and other natural resources. The introduction of the law was accompanied by other legislation, including a new Environmental Impact Assessment Law. At the end of 1996 the government seemed to go one step further when they outlawed the export of whole logs. But even in 1995 experts were sceptical about the ability of the Cambodian government to deliver on its environmental promises. The lack of transparency in many of the regulations, and the ease with which companies and individuals with political and economic power could – and still can – circumvent those regulations, makes environmental protection difficult to achieve in any systematic sense.

This scepticism was borne out later, in 1998, when the UK-based environmental group Global Witness claimed that, unless the rate of logging was reduced substantially, Cambodia was "heading toward deforestation of all saleable timber within three to five years". Patrick Alley, who has done much to highlight the plight of Cambodia's wild areas, claimed at a press conference that "the logging situation is out of control". Although Cambodia still has forests, it is believed 40-50% of the country's forests have been logged.

With foreign donors becoming increasingly frustrated at the Cambodian government's lack of commitment to protecting the environment, Prime Minister Hun Sen ordered a crack-down on illegal loggers in March 1999. The fact that some donors were moving towards making further aid dispersal contingent on forestry reform no doubt concentrated the mind of the Prime Minister. The difficulty for one of the poorest countries in the world is that forestry is one of Cambodia's major industries, accounting for 43% of foreign trade and contributing 15% of GDP in 1997. But even more crucial than the fact that forestry is important to the nation is that fact that timber is valuable to individuals.

The problem is that apparently just about everyone from senior government ministers through to senior army officers and foreign governments or their representatives are involved in illegal logging activities. As Ly Thuch, Under-Secretary for State for the Environment, told a meeting at the Foreign Correspondents Club in Phnom Penh, "the main destroyers of the environment are the Khmer Rouge and the rich and powerful". It is doubtful that even Cambodia's aid donors can make a difference. In mid-1996 international aid donors had become so worried about the failure of the Cambodian government to control logging that the IMF suspended a US$20 million budget-support payment. But Cambodia's two prime ministers continued to sign logging contracts – without cabinet discussion and in contravention of their own environmental laws.

In early 2000, Hun Sen vouched: "If I cannot put an end to the illegal cutting of trees, I will resign from my position of prime minister in the first quarter of 2001." True to his word? No. Needless to say the Cambodian government was still entering into illegal logging concessions in 2004-2005 breaking an international moratorium on logging that was due to expire in late 2005. Furthermore, those critical of the government's illegal activities have been threatened and hassled. In April 2002, a senior official with the independent forestry monitor Global Witness was beaten near her office. The next day she was sent an email instructing her to quit. The forestry monitor, Global Witness was later sacked by Hun Sen.

There are major ecological side effects of deforestation, particularly in a country where 80% of the population rely on subsistence agriculture. The ongoing rice crop failure and siltation of the waterways, effecting the valuable fisheries can largely be contributed to the rampant deforestation.

In an interview published in November 1996, William Shawcross suggested that illegal logging was "perhaps the most serious crisis of corruption in the regime". Nothing much has changed in the intervening years.

## National parks

Cambodia was the first country in Southeast Asia to establish protected areas, with the forests surrounding the Angkor temples declared a national park in 1925. By 1969, six wildlife sanctuaries had been established covering 2.2 million hectares or 12% of the country for the protection of wildlife, in particular large mammals. Towards the end of 1993, King Sihanouk signed a decree to create 23 protected areas, now covering over 21% of the country. Cambodia has one of the highest percentages of national territory within protected areas in the world and had the goal to increase that area to 25% by the end of 2005.

It may be rather ironic, but the dislocations caused by Cambodia's long-running civil war probably helped to protect the environment, rather than destroy it. Although larger animals like the kouprey may have suffered from the profusion of land mines that dot the countryside, other animals have benefited from the lack of development. Unlike Thailand and Vietnam, forest has not been cleared for agriculture and many regions became 'no-go' areas to all except for the foolhardy and the well-armed. This created conditions in which wildlife could survive largely undisturbed by the forces of 'development'. Now wildlife experts and environmentalists are arguing that Cambodia has a unique asset that should be preserved at all costs – and not just because it might be the morally 'right' thing to do. In addition, the growth in eco-tourism worldwide could create a considerable money-spinner for the country.

# Laos

# Laos

# Introduction

In 1563, King Setthathirat made the riverine city of Vientiane the capital of Laos. Or, to be more historically accurate, Wiang Chan, the 'City of the Moon', became the capital of Lane Xang. In those days it was a small fortified city on the banks of the Mekong with a palace and two wats, That Luang and Wat Phra Kaeo (built to house the Emerald Buddha). The city had grown prosperous from the surrounding fertile plains and taxes levied from trade going upriver.

Today Vientiane is, perhaps, the most charming of all Southeast Asia's capital cities. Cut off from the outside world and foreign investment for much of the modern period, its colonial heritage remains largely intact. While the last few years have brought greater bustle and activity, it is still a quiet city of tree-lined boulevards, where the image of the past is reflected in the present.

Snuggled in a curve of the Mekong, Vientiane is also the region's most modest capital. It is much more than a town, but it doesn't quite cut it as a conventional city. Here, colourless concrete Communist edifices sit alongside chicken farmers; outdoor aerobics fanatics are juxtaposed against locals making merit at the city's wats; and a couple of traffic lights command a dribble of chaotic cars, bikes, tuk-tuks and buses on the city's streets.

A short trip north of Vientiane is Vang Vieng, a favourite of adventure enthusiasts, with caving, kayaking, tubing, trekking and more on offer.

Hua Hin
Nam Nga

13

Ou

Houei Van

Sop Tiek

ak Ou Caves

Seng

Muang Muoi

13

1

LUANG
PRABANG

Vieng Thong

HUA PHAN

Hua Muong

*Sao Hintang*

Phou Lao
Nam Nouan

6

Sam Thong

Khan

Muang Kham

6

*Mat*

7

3

*Tran Ninh Highlands*

Muang Sui

Xang

Khien

Muang
Phou Khoun

Sen Kom

✈ Phonsavanh

LAOS

*Plain
of Jars*

Muang Khoune

Pha Sung

Phon

Sen Luang

XIENG
KHOUANG

13

a Tang

VIENTIANE

*Nam Ngum*

◆ *Phu Bia
(2819m)* ▲

Ta Viang

Khone Xa Na

■ *Tham Xang*

4 ● Vang Vieng

Tam Kalong

Muang Cha

Ban Houay
(North Port)

Muang
Muong Sam

XAYSOMBOON

Nam Cap

Hat Kham

Ban
Thalat

North Town

*Nam Ngum
Reservoir*

● South Port

Na Pho

Ban Hat
Khai

♨ *Tad Leuk*

Kouei

San

Nhiep

honhong
angxang

Ngum

Thulakhom

*Ang Nam
Leuk*

Muang Hom

Paksan

Ban Keun

Thabok

*Phou Khao
Khouay
NPA*

2

Ban Na

13

Na Kha

PREFECTURE DE
VIENTIANE

Tha Pabat
Phonsanh

Xieng Khuan
( Buddha
Park)

VIENTIANE

1 3

Tha
Deua

Nong Khai
Friendship Bridge

N

THAILAND

km

miles

# Vientiane region

*Vientiane's appeal lies in its largely preserved fusion of Southeast Asian and French colonial culture. Baguettes, plunged coffee and Bordeaux wines coexist with spring rolls, pho soup and papaya salad. Colourful tuk-tuks scuttle along tree-lined boulevards, past old Buddhist temples and cosmopolitan cafés. Hammer-and-sickle flags hang at ten-pin bowling discos, locals carry sacks of devalued currency and green and pink chickens wander the streets. But, as in the rest of Laos, the best thing about Vientiane, is its people. Take the opportunity to stroll around some of the outlying bans (villages) and meet the wonderful characters who make this city what it is.*

*Close to the city is Xieng Khuan, popularly known as the Buddha Park, a bizarre collection of statues and monuments, while, to the north, Vang Vieng, the adventure capital of Laos, attracts backpackers with a multitude of outdoor activities.*

▸▸ *For Sleeping, Eating and other listings, see pages 397-412.*

Laos Vientiane region

## Ins and outs → *Colour map 1, C3.*

### Getting there

**Air** Most visitors arrive in Vientiane by air, the great bulk on one of the daily connections from Bangkok, with **Thai Air** (www.thaiair.com) or **Lao Airlines** (www.lao airlines.com), which also run international flights to/ from Kunming, Phnom Penh and Siem Reap. **Vietnam Airlines** (www.vietnamairlines.com) runs flights between Hanoi and Ho Chin Minh City. **Wattay International Airport** lies 6 km west of the town centre (T021-212066). Vientiane is the hub of Laos' domestic airline system and to travel from the north to the south or vice versa it is necessary to change planes here. Both terminals have restaurants, telephones, a taxi service and an information booth. Only taxis are allowed to pick up passengers at the airport (US$5 to the centre of town, 20 minutes) although tuk-tuks can drop off here. Tuk-tuks can be taken from the main road and sometimes lurk at the far side of the airport, near the exit (40,000 kip to the centre).

A cheaper alternative from Thailand is to fly from Bangkok to **Udon Thani** on a budget airline (www.nokair.co.th, www.airasia.com) and then continue by road to Vientiane via the Friendship Bridge, which lies just 25 km downstream from the capital (allow three hours). Shuttle buses from Udon Thani airport, ฿150, usually run to the border after every flight. There are several flights a day between Udon Thani and Bangkok.

**Bus** There are three public bus terminals in Vientiane. The **Southern bus station** is 9 km south of the city centre on Route 13. Most international buses bound for Vietnam depart from here as well as buses to southern and eastern Laos. The station has a VIP room, restaurants, a few shops, mini-mart and there's a guesthouse nearby.

The **Northern bus station** is on Route T2, about 3 km northwest of the centre before the airport, T021-260255, and serves destinations in northern Laos. Most tuk-tuks will take you there from the city for 20,000 kip; ask for '*Bai Thay Song*'. There are English-speaking staff at the help desk.

The **Talaat Sao bus station** is across the road from the Morning Market, in front of Talaat Kudin, on the eastern edge of the city centre. This station serves destinations within Vientiane Province, buses to and from the Thai border and international buses to Nong Khai and Udon Thani in Thailand. It is also a good place to pick up a tuk-tuk.

▸▸ *For further information, see Transport, page 408.*

## Getting around

Vientiane is small and manageable and is one of the most laid-back capital cities in the world. The local catch phrase '*bopenyang*' (no worries) has permeated through every sector of the city, so much so that even the mangy street dogs look completely chilled out. The core of the city is negotiable on foot and even outlying hotels and places of interest are accessible by bicycle. Cycling remains the most flexible way to tour the city. It can be debilitatingly hot at certain times of year but there are no great hills to struggle up. If cycling doesn't appeal, a combination of foot and tuk-tuk or small 110-125cc scooters take the effort out of sightseeing.

Vientiane can be rather confusing for the first-time visitor as there are few street signs and most streets have two names, pre- and post-revolutionary but, because Vientiane is so small and compact, it doesn't take long to get to grips with the layout. The names of major streets or *thanon* usually correspond to the nearest wat, while traffic lights, wats, monuments and large hotels serve as directional landmarks. When giving directions to a tuk-tuk it is better to use these landmarks, as street names leave them a little bewildered.

## Tourist information

**Lao National Tourism Authority** ① *Lane Xang (towards Patuxai), T021-212251 for information, www.tourismlaos.gov.au*, can provide information regarding ecotourism operators and trekking opportunities. **The Tourist Police** ① *0830-1200, 1300-1600*, are upstairs. ▸▸ *For Sleeping, Eating and other listings, see pages 397-412.*

---

# Background

Vientiane is an ancient city. There was probably a settlement here, on a bend on the left bank of the Mekong, in the 10th century but knowledge of the city before the 16th century is sketchy. From the chronicles, scholars do know that King Setthathirat decided to relocate his capital here in the early 1560s. It seems that it took him four years to build the city, constructing a defensive wall (hence 'Wiang', meaning a walled or fortified city), along with Wat Phra Kaeo and a much enlarged That Luang. Vieng Chan remained intact until 1827 when it was ransacked by the Siamese; this is why many of its wats are of recent construction.

The city was abandoned for decades and erased from the maps of the region. It was only conjured back into existence by the French, who commenced reconstruction at the end of the 19th century. They built rambling colonial villas and wide tree-lined boulevards, befitting their new administrative capital, Vientiane. At the height of American influence in the 1960s, it was renowned for its opium dens and sex shows.

For the moment, the city retains its unique innocence: DJs are officially outlawed (although this is not enforced); there is a 2330 curfew; a certain percentage of music played at restaurants and bars every day is supposed to be Lao (overcome by banging out the Lao tune quota at 0800 in the morning) and women are urged to wear the national dress, the *sinh*. However, to describe the Lao government as autocratic is unfairly negative. Vientiane's citizens are proud of their cultural heritage and are usually very supportive of the government's attempts to promote it. The government has tried, by and large, to maintain the national identity and protect its citizens from harmful outside influences. This is already starting to change, as, with the government reshuffle in 2006 came a gradual loosening of the cultural stranglehold.

# Sights

Most of the interesting buildings in Vientiane are of religious significance. All tour companies and many hotels and guesthouses will arrange city tours and excursions to surrounding sights but it is just as easy to arrange a tour independently with a local tuk-tuk driver; the best English speakers (and thus the most expensive tuk-tuks) can be found in the parking lot beside Nam Phou. Those at the Morning Market (Talaat Sao) are cheaper. Most tuk-tuk drivers pretend not to carry small change, so make sure you have the exact fare with you before taking a ride.

## That Luang

ⓘ *That Luang Rd, 3.5 km northeast of the city centre; daily 0800-1200, 1300-1600 (except 'special' holidays); 2000 kip. A booklet about the wat is on sale at the entrance.*
That Luang is Vientiane's most important site and the holiest Buddhist monument in the country. The golden spire looks impressive at the top of the hill, overlooking the city.

According to legend, a stupa was first built here in the third century AD by emissaries of the Moghul Emperor Asoka. Excavations on the site, however, have only located the remains of an 11th- to 13th-century Khmer temple, making the earlier provenance doubtful in the extreme. The present monument, encompassing the previous buildings, was built in 1566 by King Setthathirat, whose statue stands outside. Plundered by the Thais and the Chinese Haw in the 18th century, it was restored by King (Chao) Anou at the beginning of the 19th century.

The reliquary is surrounded by a square cloister, with an entrance on each side, the most famous on the east. There is a small collection of statues in the cloisters, including one of the Khmer king Jayavarman VII. The cloisters are used as lodgings by monks who travel to Vientiane for religious reasons and especially for the annual **That Luang Festival** (see page 405). The base of the stupa is a mixture of styles, Khmer, Indian and Lao – and each side has a *hor vay* or small offering temple. This lowest level represents the material world, while the second tier is surrounded by a lotus wall and 30 smaller stupas, representing the 30 Buddhist perfections. Each of these originally contained smaller golden stupas but they were stolen by Chinese raiders in the

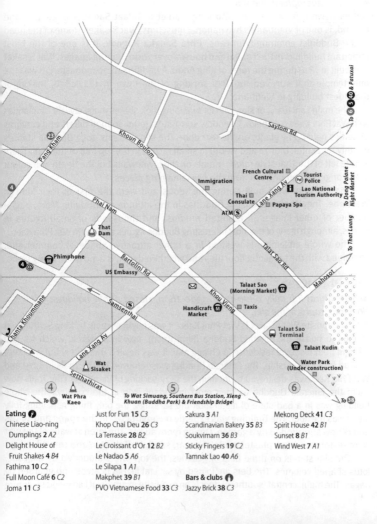

**Eating** 🍽
Chinese Liao-ning Dumplings **2** A2
Delight House of Fruit Shakes **4** B4
Fathima **10** C2
Full Moon Café **6** C2
Joma **11** C3
Just for Fun **15** C3
Khop Chai Deu **26** C3
La Terrasse **28** B2
Le Croissant d'Or **12** B2
Le Nadao **5** A6
Le Silapa **1** A1
Makphet **39** B1
PVO Vietnamese Food **33** C3
Sakura **3** A1
Scandinavian Bakery **35** B3
Soukvimarn **36** B3
Sticky Fingers **19** C2
Tamnak Lao **40** A6

**Bars & clubs** 🍸
Jazzy Brick **38** C3
Mekong Deck **41** C3
Spirit House **42** B1
Sunset **8** B1
Wind West **7** A1

19th century. The 30-m-high spire dominates the skyline and resembles an elongated lotus bud, crowned by a stylized banana flower and parasol. It was designed so that pilgrims could climb up to the stupa via the walkways around each level. It is believed that originally over 450 kg of gold leaf was used on the spire.

## Patuxai (Victory Monument)

ⓘ *Junction of That Luang Rd and Lane Xang Av; Mon-Fri 0800-1100, 1400-1630 (officially, but these hours seem to be posted only for fun); 3000 kip.*

At the end of That Luang is the Oriental answer to Paris's Arc de Triomphe and Vientiane's best-known landmark, the Victory Monument or Patuxai. It was built by the former regime in memory of those who died in the wars before the Communist takeover, but the cement ran out before its completion. Refusing to be beaten, the regime diverted hundreds of tonnes of cement, part of a US aid package to help with the construction of runways at Wattay Airport, to finish off the monument in 1969.

## Wat Sisaket

ⓘ *Junction of Lane Xang Av and Setthathirat Rd; daily 0800-1200, 1400-1600; 5000 kip. No photographs in the sim.*

Further down Lane Xang is the **Morning Market** or **Talaat Sao** (see page 405) and beyond, is one of Vientiane's two national museums, Wat Sisaket. Home of the head of the Buddhist community in Laos, **Phra Sangka Nagnok**, it is one of the most important buildings in the capital and houses over 7000 Buddha images. Wat Sisaket was built in 1818 during the reign of King Anou. A traditional Lao monastery, it was the only temple that survived the Thai sacking of the town in 1827-1828, making it the oldest building in Vientiane.

The main sanctuary, or **sim**, with its sweeping roof, shares many stylistic similarities with Wat Phra Kaeo (see below): window surrounds, lotus-shaped pillars and carvings of deities held up by giants on the rear door. The sim contains 2052 Buddha statues (mainly terracotta, bronze and wood) in small niches in the top half of the wall. There is little left of the Thai-style *jataka* murals on the lower walls but the depth and colour of the originals can be seen from the few remaining pieces.

The **cloisters** were built during the 1800s and were the first of their kind in Vientiane. They shelter 120 large Buddhas in the attitude of subduing Mara, plus a number of other images in assorted *mudras*, and thousands of small figures in niches, although many of the most interesting Buddha figures are now in Wat Phra Kaeo.

The whole ensemble is washed in a rather attractive shade of caramel and, combined with the terracotta floor tiles and weathered roof, is a most satisfying sight.

## Wat Phra Kaeo

ⓘ *Setthathirat Rd; daily 0800-1200, 1300-1600, closed public holidays; 5000 kip. No photographs in the sim.*

Almost opposite Wat Sisaket is Wat Phra Kaeo. It was originally built by King Setthathirat in 1565 to house the Emerald Buddha (Phra Kaeo), now in Bangkok, which he had brought from his royal residence in Chiang Mai. It was never a monastery but was kept instead for royal worship. The Emerald Buddha was removed by the Thais in 1779 and Wat Phra Kaeo was destroyed by them in the 1827 sacking of Vientiane. (The Thais now claim the Emerald Buddha as their most important icon in the country.) The whole building was in a bad state of repair after the sackings, the only thing remaining fully intact was the floor. The building was expertly reconstructed in the 1940s and 1950s and is now surrounded by a garden. During renovations, the interior walls of the wat were restored using a plaster made of sugar, sand, buffalo skin and tree oil.

The sim stands on three tiers of galleries, the top one surrounded by majestic, lotus-shaped columns. The tiers are joined by several flights of steps and guarded by nagas. The main, central (southern) door is an exquisite example of Lao wood sculpture

**To Thailand via the Friendship Bridge** → *Colour map 1, C3.*

The bridge is 20 km southeast of Vientiane. Shuttle minibuses take punters across the bridge every 20 minutes for 5000 kip, stopping at the Thai and Lao immigration posts where an overtime fee is charged after 1630 and at weekends. The border is open daily 0600-2200. Allow up to 1½ hours to get to the bridge and through formalities on the Lao side. The paperwork is pretty swift, unless you are leaving the country and have over-stayed your visa. 30-day visas are processed in about 15 minutes and cost between US$30 and US$42 depending on your nationality. You will require a passport-sized photograph and the name of the guesthouse or hotel you are staying at. You will need to bargain hard, but in a friendly way, for a good price on private transport from the border.

**Transport** Catch the Thai-Lao International bus from the Talaat Sao terminal (90 minutes, 15,000 kip), which runs every two hours from 0730 to 1530 and stops at Nong Khai bus station, or hire a tuk-tuk US$5-7 (see page 409) to the border and arrange transport across. The Thai side is über-efficient but not nearly as friendly. Tuk-tuks wait to take punters to Nong Khai (10 minutes), ฿50 per person; Udon Thani is another hour further on; taxis from the Thai side of the border charge about ฿700 to get you there; add another ฿300 if you organize the Thai taxi from the Lao side. From Udon Thani you can get to Bangkok easily by budget airline. Discount airlines (Air Asia, Nok Air) fly several times daily. Another option is to catch the overnight train from Nong Khai to Bangkok's Hualamphong Station (11 hrs, ฿800 for a sleeper). Buses also run from both Udon Thani and Nong Khai to Bangkok.

**Accommodation** If you get stuck in Nong Khai, Mut Mee Guesthouse is recommended.

*Laos Vientiane region*

with carved angels surrounded by flowers and birds; it is the only notable remnant of the original wat. (The central door at the northern end, with the larger carved angels supported by ogres, is new.) The sim now houses a superb assortment of Lao and Khmer art and some pieces of Burmese and Khmer influence, mostly collected from other wats in Vientiane. Although people regularly come and pray here the wat's main purpose is as a quasi-museum.

## Lao National Museum

ⓘ *Samsenthai Rd, opposite the Cultural Centre Hall; daily 0800-1200, 1300-1600; 5000 kip.*

Formerly called the Revolutionary Museum, in these post-revolutionary days it has been redesignated the National Museum. The museum's collection has grown over the last few years and now includes a selection of historical artefacts from dinosaur bones and pre-Angkorian sculptures to a comprehensive photographic collection on Laos' modern history. The rhetoric of these modern collections has been toned down from the old days, when photographic descriptions would refer to the 'running dog imperialists' (Americans). The museum features a dazzling array of personal effects from the revolutionary leader Kaysone, including his exercise machine and a spoon he once used. Downstairs there are ancient artefacts, including stone tools and poignant burial jars. Upstairs the museum features a range of artefacts and busts, as well as a small exhibition on various ethnic minorities. The final section of the museum comprises mostly photographs which trace, chronologically, the country's struggle against the 'brutal' French colonialists and American 'imperialists'.

## Phou Khao Khouay National Protected Area

Phou Khao Khouay National Protected Area (pronounced *poo cow kway*) is one of Laos' premier national protected areas. The area extends across 2000 sq km and incorporates an attractive sandstone mountain range. It is crossed by three large rivers, smaller tributaries and two stunning waterfalls at Tad Leuk and Tad Sae, which weave and weft their way in to the Ang Nam Leuk reservoir, a stunning man-made dam and lake that sits on the outskirts of the park. Within the protected area is a diverse array of wildlife, including wild elephants, gibbons, tigers, clouded leopards and Asiatic black bears.

Around the village of Ban Na (meaning rice field) the village's sugar cane plantations and river salt deposits attract a herd of wild elephants (around 30), which have, in the past, destroyed the villagers' homes and even killed a resident. This has limited the villagers' ability to undertake normal tasks, such as collecting bamboo, fearing that they may come across the wild elephants. To help compensate, the village, in conjunction with some NGOs, has constructed an elephant observation tower and has started running trekking tours to see these massive creatures in their natural habitat. The elephant tower is the primary attraction and it possible to stay over at the tower, 4 km from Ban Na, to try and catch a glimpse of the giant pachyderms who come to lap up salt from the nearby salt lick in the early evening hours. One-to three-day treks through the national park cross waterfalls, pass through pristine jungle and, with luck, offer the opportunity to hear or spot the odd wild elephant. It is too dangerous to get close.

This is an important ecotour that contributes to the livelihood of the Ban Na villagers and helps conserve the elephant population. Advance notice is required so it's advisable to book with a tour operator in Vientiane. If you are travelling independently you will need to organize permits, trekking and accommodation with the village directly. To do this, contact Mr Bounthanam, T020-2208286. Visit www.trekking centrallaos.com and contact the **National Tourism Authority** in Vientiane or **Green Discovery Tours** (see page 407). Visitors will need to bring drinking water and basic snacks. Do not try to feed the elephants, they are very dangerous.

**Ban Hat Khai** is home to 90 families from the Lao Loum and Lao Soung ethnic groups. It is also a starting point for organized treks through mountain landscapes, crossing the Nam Mang River and the Phay Xay cliffs. Most treks take in the Tad Sae Falls. Homestay accommodation is available in the village.

The park is northeast of Vientiane along Route 13 South. To get to Ban Na you need to stop at Tha Pabat Phonsanh, 80 km northeast of Vientiane; the village is a further 2 km from here. For Ban Hat Khai, 100 km northeast of Vientiane, continue on Route 13 to Thabok, where a songthaew or boat can take you the extra 7-8 km to the village. Buses to Paksan from the Talaat Sao bus station and That Luang market in Vientiane stop at Thabok.

*① Route 2 (25 km south of Vientiane); daily 0800-1700, 5000 kip, plus 5000 kip for
cameras. Food vendors sell drinks and snacks.*

Otherwise known as the **Garden of the Buddhas** or **Buddha Park**, Xieng Khuan is close
to the border with Thailand. It has been described as a Laotian Tiger Balm Gardens,
with reinforced concrete Buddhist and Hindu sculptures of Vishnu, Buddha, Siva and
various other assorted deities and near-deities. There's also a bulbous-style building
with three levels containing smaller sculptures of the same gods.

The garden was built in the late 1950s by a priest-monk-guru-sage-artist called
Luang Pu Bunleua Sulihat, who studied under a Hindu *rishi* in Vietnam and then
combined the Buddhist and Hindu philosophies in his own very peculiar view of the
world. He left Laos because his anti-communist views were incompatible with the
ideology of the Pathet Lao (or perhaps because he was just too weird) and settled
across the Mekong near the Thai town of Nong Khai, where he proceeded to build an
equally revolting and bizarre concrete theme park for religious schizophrenics, called
Wat Khaek. With Luang Pu's forced departure from Laos his religious garden came
under state control and it is now a public park.

To get there take the No 14 bus (1 hr) from the Talaat Sao bus station, a tuk-tuk
(100,000 kip), hire a private vehicle (US$15), or take a motorbike or bicycle because
the road follows the river and is reasonably level the whole way.

---

# Vang Vieng 🖼️🚻🧗⛰️🚌🎒 ›› *pp397-412. Colour map 1, C3.*

The drive from Vientiane to Vang Vieng, on the much-improved Route 13, follows the
valley of the Nam Ngum north and then climbs steeply onto the plateau where Vang
Vieng is located, 160 km north of Vientiane. The surrounding area is inhabited by the
Hmong and Yao hill peoples and is particularly picturesque: craggy karst limestone
scenery, riddled with caves, crystal-clear pools and waterfalls. In the early morning
the views are reminiscent of a Chinese Sung Dynasty painting.

The town itself is nestled in a valley on the bank of the Nam Song River, amid a
misty jungle. It enjoys cooler weather and offers breathtaking views of the imposing
mountains of Pha Tang and Phatto Nokham.

The town's laid-back feel has made it a popular haunt for the backpacker
crowd, while the surrounding landscape has helped to establish Vang Vieng as
Laos' premier outdoor activity destination, especially for rock climbing, caving and
kayaking. Its popularity in many ways has also become its downfall: neon lights,
pancake stands, 'happy' this and 'happy' that, and pirated *Friends* videos now
pollute this former oasis. Nevertheless, the town and surrounding area is still full of
wonderful things to do and see.

## Ins and outs

**Safety** Laos is a very safe country for tourists but a disproportionate number of
accidents and crimes seem to happen in Vang Vieng. **Theft** is routinely reported,
ranging from robberies by packs of kids targeting tubers on the river to the
opportunist theft of items from guests' rooms. Most guesthouses won't take
responsibility for valuables left in rooms, instead it is usually advisable to hand in
valuables to the management. Otherwise, you will need to padlock your bag.
Another major problem is the sale of illegal **drugs**. Police often go on sting
operations and charge fines of up to US$600 for possession. Legal issues aside,
numerous travellers have become seriously ill from indulging in the 'happy'
supplements supplied by the restaurants. ›› *For details of the significant safety risks
involved in adventure activities, see Activities and tours, page 407.*

Vang Vieng has become synonymous with tubing down the Nam Song. Tubes can be picked up from the Old Market area where the tubing company has formed a cartel. Without stops the 3 km tubing trip from the **Organic Mulberry Farm** to town can take one to two hours if done quickly, but most people do it in three to four hours, choosing to stop along the way and drink, play volleyball or use the flying fox swings at the many bars dotted along the river. ➤➤ *See also Tubing, page 408.*

Many tour operators organize kayaking trips as well. Popular routes include kayaking down the Nam Song to incorporate the caves (especially Tham Nam – water cave), or the trip back to Vientiane via the drop-off point at Nam Lik. If you want to break the journey, there are several nice guesthouses at Nam Lik. ➤➤ *See also Kayaking and rafting, page 408.*

## Caves
ⓘ *Each cave has an entrance fee of 3000 -10,000 kip and many have stalls where you can buy drinks and snacks. You can buy hand-drawn maps from the town but all the caves are clearly signposted in English from the main road so these are not really necessary.*

Laos Vientiane region

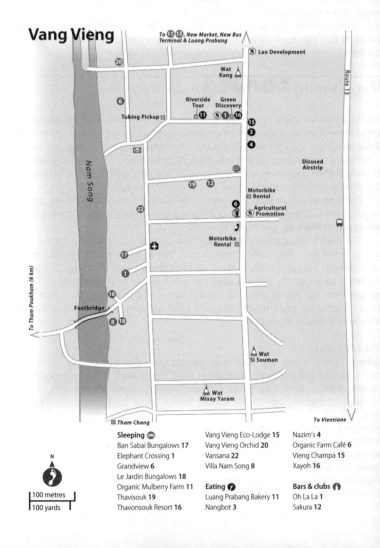

# Vang Vieng

To ⑪ ⑮, New Market, New Bus Terminal & Luang Prabang

Ⓢ Lao Development

⑳

Wat Kang

⑥

Riverside Tour  Green Discovery
Tubing Pickup ⬛ ⑪ Ⓢ ❶ ⑯

⑮
❸
❹

✉

Disused Airstrip

@

⑲ ⑫

Motorbike Rental ⬛

Ⓢ Agricultural Promotion ⑥❶

Nam Song

㉒

Motorbike Rental ⬛

⑰

✚

❶

⑯

Footbridge

❽ ⑱

To Tham Poukham (6 km)

Wat Si Souman

Wat Mixay Yaram

To Vientiane

Route 13

🚌

⬛ Tham Chang

**N**
| 100 metres |
| 100 yards |

**Sleeping** 🛏
Ban Sabai Bungalows **17**
Elephant Crossing **1**
Grandview **6**
Le Jardin Bungalows **18**
Organic Mulberry Farm **11**
Thavisouk **19**
Thavonsouk Resort **16**

Vang Vieng Eco-Lodge **15**
Vang Vieng Orchid **20**
Vansana **22**
Villa Nam Song **8**

**Eating** 🍴
Luang Prabang Bakery **11**
Nangbot **3**

Nazim's **4**
Organic Farm Café **6**
Vieng Champa **15**
Xayoh **16**

**Bars & clubs** 🍸
Oh La La **1**
Sakura **12**

Vang Vieng is best known for its limestone caves, sheltered in the mountains flanking the town. Pretty much every guesthouse and tour operator offers tours to the caves (the best of these is **Green Discovery**) and, although some caves can be accessed independently, it is advisable to take a guide to a few as they are dark and difficult to navigate. Often children from surrounding villages will take tourists through the caves for a small fee. Don't forget to bring a torch, or even better a head-lamp, which can be picked up cheaply at the market both in Vang Vieng and Vientiane.

Of Vang Vieng's myriad caves, **Tham Chang** is the most renowned of all. Tham Chang penetrates right under a mountain and is fed by a natural spring perfect for an early morning dip. From the spring it is possible to swim into the cave for quite a distance (bring a waterproof torch, if possible). The cave is said to have been used as a refuge during the 19th century from Chinese Haw bandits and this explains its name: *chang* meaning 'loyal' or 'steadfast'. Entrance is via Vang Vieng resort south of town. For your US$1 or 10,000 kip entry fee you get into the caves and the lighting system will be turned on. Although the cave is not the most magnificent, it serves as a superb lookout point.

Another popular cavern is **Tham Poukham** ① *7 km from Vang Vieng, 5000 kip*. The cave is often referred to as the cave of the Golden Crab and is highly auspicious. It's believed that if you catch a golden crab you will have a lifetime of fortune. To get there you need to cross the foot-bridge near the **Villa Nam Song**, and then follow the road for a further 6 km until you reach the village of Ban Nathong. From the village the cave is 1 km walk and a short climb up quite a steep hill. Mossy rocks lead the way into the main cavern area where a large bronze reclining Buddha is housed. Here there is an idyllic lagoon, with glassy green-blue waters, great for a swim.

**Tham None** ① *4 km north of Vang Vieng, 5000 kip*, is known locally as the 'Sleeping Cave' because 2000 villagers took refuge there during the war. The large cave is dotted with stalagmites and stalactites, including the 'magic stone of Vang Vieng', which reflects light. Lots of bats reside in the grotto.

**Tham Xang** ① *14 km north of Vang Vieng on the banks of the Nam Song, 2000 kip*, also known as the 'Elephant Cave', is named after the stalagmites and stalactites that have created an elephant formation (you may need to squint to see it). The cave also contains some Buddha images, including the Footprint of Buddha. Although the cave itself is relatively non-descript the bell used by monks is made of a former bomb. From this cave there is a signposted path that leads to **Tham Nam** (water cave) ① *15 km from town, 5000 kip*, a long spindly cave that is believed to stretch for at least 7 km. It takes about two hours to explore the cavern and at the entrance there is a crystal-clear pool. This is one of Vang Vieng's most interesting caves and in the wet season needs to be explored with an inner tube or by wading, while pulling yourself along a rope. It's not an easy task and should not be attempted alone. At times the cavern is an extremely tight fit and commando-type crawling is required; a hard helmet with lamp attached is necessary. However, this is an incredible caving experience. To get to these two caves follow Route 13 north and turn left at Km 14, follow this dirt road for 1 km until you reach the river. Boats charge 10,000 kip to cross the river to see Tham Xang; from there you can walk to Tham Nam.

*Laos Vientiane region Listings*

## ● Sleeping

**Vientiane** *p388, map p390*
There is very little quality accommodation in Vientiane under US$10 a night. There is a big difference in the quality of rooms between the US$10 and US$20-30 rooms, the extra US$10 is a worthwhile investment. Cheaper guesthouses will offer discounts in the wet season. Higher-end hotels offer

better rates on the internet than the rack rate given if you walk in off the street.
All of the guesthouses and boutique hotels, except for the most expensive, tend to get booked up so reserve in advance. As a rule of thumb, hotels priced over US$50 (eg our **A** category and above) accept major credit cards.

**LL Green Park Hotel,** Khou Vieng Rd, T021-264297, www.greenparkvientiane.com. Designed in a modern East-meets-West style, this hotel is set alongside Vientiane's primary park. Beautiful rooms with all the mod cons, Wi-Fi and super-duper bathtubs. Beautiful garden and excellent swimming pool. The only drawback is that it is set a little further out from the city centre and river, but is still within walking distance. A fantastic luxury option.

**LL-L Don Chan Palace Hotel**, Piawat Village (off Fa Gnum Quay) T021-244288, www.donchanpalace.com. This 14-storey hotel is the largest in Vientiane and probably the ugliest. It was built for the ASEAN summit and is so close to the river that locals joke it may fall in. Once you can get past the ugly exterior, the 230 rooms and facilities are outstanding and afford the best views of both the river and the city in town. There's a restaurant, private karaoke rooms, bar, poolside massage and gym.

**LL-L Settha Palace Hotel**, 6 Pang Kham Rd, T021-217581/2, www.sethapalace.com. The stunning **Settha Palace** was built in 1936 and opened as a hotel in 1999. Its French architecture, stunning colonial decor, period furniture and beautiful tropical gardens and pool sit more easily with the fundamental essence of Vientiane that the other top-level hotels. Often considered the best hotel in town. Recommended.

**A-B Beau Rivage Mekong**, Fa Ngum Rd, T021-243350, www.hbrm.com. One of the first Western-style boutique hotels in Vientiane, it is beautifully furnished, with artistic decoration and fantastic bathtubs. The pink exterior does not sit well with its surroundings but nonetheless this is a great hotel with superb Mekong river views. Its location, just out of the centre of town on the river, ensures peace and quiet but it's still only a 5-min walk to the hustle and bustle. Includes breakfast.

**A-B Lane Xang Hotel**, Fa Ngum Rd, T021-214100, www.lanexanghotel.com. This was the original 'luxury' hotel in Vientiane, built by the French in the 1960s. It has an indefinable charm, despite the fact that some of its retro-hip Soviet fittings and furniture have been ripped out to make way

for a more contemporary look. The a/c rooms are well equipped, with excellent bathrooms, making the hotel the best value in town. Opt for the deluxe room, with its own bar and velour bed fittings and indulge in a 1970s, porn-flick nostalgia trip. Other facilities include a dilapidated pool, nightclub and bar.

**A-B Orchid Hotel**, Chao Anou. T021-264138, www.laoorchid.com. Beautiful spacious rooms with stunning modern furnishings, polished floorboards and large showers. Outstanding value for the price and very popular with business travellers. 4½-star accommodation for a 3½-star price. Very busy so advanced bookings essential. Includes breakfast and Wi-Fi. Café and Zen fish pond. Visa and MasterCard accepted. Recommended.

**A-C Hotel Day Inn**, Pang Kham Rd, T021-222985, dayinn@laopdr.com. Run by a friendly Cambodian, this renovated villa is in a good position in a quiet part of town, just to the north of the main concentration of bars and restaurants. Attractive, airy, clean, large rooms, with a/c and excellent bathrooms. Bike hire.

**A-C Intercity Hotel**, 24-25 Fa Ngum Rd/Chou Anou (next to Wat Chan), T021-242842, www.laointerhotel.com. This Singaporean-owned hotel is one of the oldest in Vientiane, it has been operating for over 30 years. Renovations have made it sparkle: mosaics, relief sculptures and murals adorn the walls, and traditional shutters, silk hangings and furniture feature in every room. The a/c rooms are light and spacious, with slick bathrooms and fantastic balconies overlooking the Mekong. Lovely atrium and excellent gift shop with beautiful antique costumes.

**B Chanthapanya**, Nokeo Khoummane Rd, T021-244284, www.chanthapanyahotel.com. Fantastic modern Asian building. The rooms are new and very comfortable. Beautifully furnished with modern Lao wooden furniture, comfy beds, fridge, TV, hot water, phone and a/c. Includes breakfast.

**B-C Mali Namphu Guesthouse**, 114 Pang Kham Rd (next door to Phonepaseuth Guesthouse), T021-215093, malinamp@laotel.com. Difficult to spot as it looks like a small shopfront but the façade is deceiving, the foyer opens onto a beautifully manicured courtyard surrounded by quaint, terraced rooms. Clean, bright rooms are traditionally decorated with a modern twist and come with a/c, hot water, cable TV and a fantastic breakfast. The twin rooms are much nicer than the doubles. Friendly staff. Highly recommended.

**B-C Le Parasol Blanc**, behind National Assembly, close to Victory Gate (not very well marked), T021-216091. A very attractive leafy haven. Spacious a/c rooms, with wooden floors and sizeable bathrooms. Some look onto the garden, with sitting area in front, the most expensive are alongside the pool. Charming place, well run, mostly patronized by French visitors.

**B-C Vayakorn**, 91 Nokeo Khoummane Rd, T021-241911. The rooms are clean, beautifully decorated with modern furniture and very comfortable. Polished floors, hot water, a/c and TV. Sadly breakfast is no longer included with rooms but it is still excellent value. Great value and centrally located.

**C Douang Deuane**, Nokeo Khoummane Rd, T021-222301, www.bookings-asia.com/la/hotels/douangdeane. From the exterior, this dilapidated building looks like a classic Communist edifice, but the a/c rooms have charm and character: parquet wood floors, art deco furniture, excellent bathrooms and satellite TV. Try and get a balcony room for lovely patchwork views of the roofs of the city. Although the room rates are no longer competitive, it is a good centrally located option-B if the others within this price-range are fully booked. Good-value motorbike rentals, 40,000 kip per day.

**C-D Dragon Lodge**, Samsenthai Rd, T021-250112, dragonlodge2002@yahoo.com. Somewhere between a guesthouse and a hotel. Fun, colourful downstairs restaurant area – good for a party; if you're looking for quiet this probably isn't the best choice. Nice, simply decorated rooms, with hot water, TV and a/c. 5-star service. Visa accepted.

**D Thongbay Guesthouse**, off Luang Prabang Rd, turn right before the **Novotel**, Ban Non Douang, T021-242292, www.thongbay-guesthouses.com. Lovely traditional Lao house set in a lush tropical garden.

Rooms have traditional-style fittings, mosquito nets and fan or a/c. The guesthouse also runs cooking classes on request (US$10), which include buying ingredients at the local market. The only drawback of this place is the distance from the city centre. Perfect if you want to relax.

**D-E Saysouly**, 23 Manthathurath Rd, T021-218383. A variety of rooms, a bit on the musty side. Parquet floors, cheap US$5 single fan rooms with shared bathroom. The shared bathrooms are excellent with powerful showers. Extra for a/c. The more expensive US$10 rooms are quite good value.

**D-E Soukchaleun Guesthouse**, 121 Setthathirat Rd, T021-218723, soukchaleun_gh@yahoo.com. Quaint guesthouse with a variety of rooms ranging from US$5 with shared bathroom through to US$13 with a/c. Comfy, homely and very clean. The views are not scenic but the guesthouse is friendly and relatively good value.

**D-E Syri II Guesthouse**, Setthathirat Rd, T021-223178. This is probably one of the best options within the cheaper price range. 3-storey guesthouse with a variety of rooms including fan rooms with shared bathroom US$6 and private bathroom US$8. Clean and simply decorated with wooden furniture. Decorated with quirky curios from around Asia, with lounges and shared communal areas. Helpful staff. Recommended.

**E Joe Guesthouse**, 112 Fa Ngum Rd, T021-241936, joe_guesthouse@yahoo.com. Wonderful family-run guesthouse on the riverfront. Light, clean and airy. Good coffee shop downstairs. Fantastic service.

**E-F Mixok Guesthouse**, 188 Setthathirat Rd, T021-251606, bucnong@hotmail.com. This ain't the Ritz but you get what you pay for, rooms are amongst the cheapest in town. Very basic and pokey rooms, not for the claustrophobic, but they cost the same as hamburger and a Beer Lao. Shared bathroom with hot water. 11 rooms which are frequently booked out. Very friendly service and excellent location.

**Vang Vieng** *p395, map p396*
The town's popularity has ensured a uniformity among almost all places catering to budget tourists: most restaurants

feature the same menu and there isn't much individuality in the cheaper guesthouses either. The majority are geared to the needs of travellers and offer a laundry service, guides and bicycles. However, in the last 2 years a couple of higher-end hotels have cropped up, providing more attractive options. Although the accommodation in the centre of town is usually cheaper, try and get a room with a view of the river as it is simply stunning.

**A-B Vansana**, by the river, T023-511598, vansana@laotel.com. Despite its soulless exterior this hotel boasts the best rooms and facilities in town. Large bedrooms fitted with all the mod cons have stunning mountain and river views. Modern wooden furniture, minibar and local handicrafts decorate the room. Beautiful pool and bar by the river with deckchairs. Ask for a room with a view.

**A-C Thavonsouk Resort**, on the river, T021-511096, www.thavonsouk.com. Offers 5 different styles of accommodation across a sprawling riverfront premises. Bungalows range from US$18 to US$75. The US$35 bungalows are great value, with massive balconies fitted with sunbeds. There is a traditional Lao house, decorated with Lao furnishings, suitable for a family or big group, plus suites (TV, fridge, bath, a/c) and standard accommodation. Fantastic restaurant. Keep your eye out for local home-grown pop star, Aluna and her father Alom who run this family business.

**B Elephant Crossing**, on the Nam Song river, T023-511232, www.theelephant crossinghotel.com. A great mid-range option. Australian-owned riverfront hotel classically decorated with modern wooden furnishings. The big bathtub and sliding window between the bedroom and bathroom will be a big hit with romantics. All rooms have a view, fridge and a/c. Breakfast included.

**B Villa Nam Song**, reservation@villanamsong.com, milestone at the gate. Quaint terracotta villas set in manicured gardens overlooking the Nam Song. Parquet floors, hot water. Restaurant attached. Although this is a beautiful hotel there is better value for money in town.

**B-C Ban Sabai Bungalows**, on the banks of the river, T021-511088. A stunning complex of individual bungalows in a spectacular location, with all the modern fittings. Hot water, a/c and breakfast included.

**C-D Grandview**, on the river, T023-511474, grandviewguesthouse@gmail.com. This newcomer offers spotless rooms with attached hot water bathroom. The cheaper rooms don't have a view. Option of paying US$4 extra for a/c. Excellent value. Highly recommended.

**D-E Thavisouk**, in the centre of town, T023-511340. If you are looking for a budget option in town, this is perfect. No frills but very clean. Rooms with en suite bathrooms and hot water, US$3-4. While the accommodation is good value, their tours, tickets and other services aren't.

**D-E Vang Vieng Orchid**, on the river road, T023-5111172. Comfortable fan or a/c rooms. Hot water in the bathrooms, clean tiled floors and very comfortable rooms. Friendly owners. The rooms with the private balconies are well worth the few extra dollars for the phenomenal view.

**E-F Le Jardin Bungalows**, about 900 m from the centre of town along the river, T020-5474643. There are 3 sets of bungalows here: the best are superb; the worst, falling down and soulless, concrete blocks. It is far enough from town for the surrounding beauty to remain undisturbed but close enough for convenience. The views are remarkable and the restaurant is quite good too. The owners are lovely and don't suffer from the Vang Vieng jadedness quite often found in these cheaper bungalows.

## Out of town

The places on the outskirts of town are great for those who wish to escape into a more natural landscape. The lack of facilities and transport in the area ensures tranquillity but also makes it quite difficult to get to town.

**B-C Vang Vieng Eco-Lodge**, 7 km north of town, T020-2247323, tatluang@laotel.com. Although this isn't an eco-lodge it is still an exceptionally beautiful place to stay. Set on the banks of the river with stunning gardens and beautiful rock formations, it is a perfect place to get away from it all. The 10 chalet-style bungalows have been nicely decorated, with beautiful balconies, comfortable furnishings and big hot-water bathtubs. The Management ensures a tuk-tuk is just a phone call away. Good Lao restaurant. Also arranges activities and offers a low season discount.

**E-F Organic Mulberry Farm**, 3 km north of town, T021-511220, www.laofarm.org. This mulberry farm has basic rooms with mosquito nets, dorm accommodation and full board. Cheaper rates in the low season. Hugely popular restaurant, serving great starfruit wine and famous mulberry pancakes. It is a very popular drop-off spot for tubers.

## 🍴 Eating

**Vientiane** p388, map p390
The absolutely best place to get **Lao food** is from the open-air stalls that line the banks of the Mekong along **Fa Ngum**. The restaurants are ridiculously low in price and high in atmosphere, particularly at night with their flickering candles. From time to time the government kicks all the eateries off the patch but they usually return with a vengeance. The **Dong Palane Night Market**, on Dong Palane, and the night markets near the corner of **Chao Anou** and **Khoun Boulom Rd** are also good places to go for Lao stall food. There are various other congregations of stalls and vendors around town, most of which set up shop around 1730 and close down by 2100. Be sure to sample Lao ice cream with coconut sticky rice.

The **Chinese quarter** is around Chao Anou, Heng Boun and Khoun Boulom and is a lively spot in the evenings. There are a number of noodle shops here, all of which serve a palatable array of vermicelli, *muu daeng* (red pork), duck and chicken.

The **Korean-style barbeque**, *sindat*, is extremely popular, especially among the younger Lao, as it is a very social event and very cheap. It involves cooking finely sliced meat on a hot plate in the middle of the table, whilst forming a broth with vegetables around the sides of the tray. Reminiscent of a 1970s fondue evening. **Seendat** (see below) is a favourite amongst the older Lao.

**♦♦♦-♦♦ Le Nadao**, Ban Donmieng (on the right-hand side of the Patuxai roundabout). Daily 1100-1400, 1700-2230. This place is difficult to find but definitely worth every second spent searching the back streets of Vientiane in the dark. Sayavouth, who trained in Paris and New York, produces delectable French cuisine: soups, venison, lamb and puddings. The US$5 set lunch menu is one of the best lunches you will get in town. Fantastic.

**♦♦♦-♦♦ Le Silapa**, Sihom Rd, T021-219689. Mon-Sat 1130-1400, 1800-2200 (closed Sun and for a month in Jul). Anthony and Fred provide a fantastic French-inspired menu without blowing the budget. Innovative modern meals that would be just at home in the fine dining establishments of New York and London as they are here. Great set lunch menu. Part of the profits are donated to disadvantaged families, usually for expensive but life-saving surgical procedures.

**♦♦♦-♦ Sakura**, Luang Prabang Rd, Km 2/ Soi 3 (the soi runs along the side of the Novotel), T021-212274. Mon 1730-2200, Tue-Sun 1030-1400, 1730-2200. Regarded as the best Japanese food in town. Expensive for Vientiane but good value by international standards. The restaurant is in a converted private house.

**♦♦ Tamnak Lao Restaurant**, That Luang Rd, T021-413562. 1200-2200. It's well worth deviating from the main Nam Phou area for a bite to eat here. This restaurant and its sister branch in Luang Prabang have a reputation for delivering outstanding Lao and Thai food, usually prepared with a modern twist.

**♦♦-♦ La Terrasse**, 55/4 Nokeo Koummane Rd, T021-218550. Mon-Sat 1100-1400, 1800-2200. This is the best European restaurant in terms of variety and price. Large fail-safe menu offering French, European, Lao and Mexican food. Good desserts, especially the rich chocolate mousse, and a good selection of French wine. Fantastic service. Reasonable prices with an excellent 'plat du jour' each day. Great 1970s-style comfort food.

● *For an explanation of sleeping and eating price codes used in this guide, see inside the* ● *front cover. Other relevant information is found in Essentials, see pages 29-32.*

**Chinese Liao-ning Dumpling Restaurant**, Chao Anou Rd, T021-240811. Daily 1100-2230. This restaurant is a firm favourite with the expats and it isn't hard to see why: fabulous steamed or fried dumplings and a wide range of vegetarian dishes. The place is spotlessly clean but the birds in cages outside are a bit off-putting. No one is ever disappointed by the meals here. Highly recommended.

**Fathima**, Th Fa Gnum, T021-219097. Without a doubt the best-value Indian in town. Ultra-friendly service and a large menu with a range of excellent curries.

**Full Moon Café**, François Ngin Rd, T021-243373. Daily 1000-2200. Delectable Asian fusion cuisine and Western favourites. Huge pillows, good lighting and great music make this place very relaxing. Fantastic chicken wrap and some pretty good Asian tapas. The Ladybug shake is a winner. Also a book exchange and music shop for ipods.

**Just for Fun**, 57/2 Pang Kham Rd, opposite Lao Airlines. Good Lao food with vegetarian dishes, coffees, soft drinks and the largest selection of teas in Laos, if not Southeast Asia. The atmosphere is relaxed with a/c, newspapers and comfy chairs (also sells textiles and other handicrafts).

**Khop Chai Deu**, Setthathirat Rd, on the corner of Nam Phou Rd. Daily 0800-2330. This lively place housed in a former colonial building is one of the city's most popular venues. Garden seating, good atmosphere at night with soft lantern lighting, and an eclectic menu of Indian, Italian, Korean and international dishes (many of which come from nearby restaurants). While the food is okay most come for the bustling atmosphere. The best value are the local Lao dishes though, which are made on site and toned down for the falang palate. Also serves draft or bottled beer at a pleasant a/c bar. Excellent lunch buffet. Live performances.

**Makphet**, Setthathirat near Wat Inpeng, T021-260587, www.friends-international.org. Fantastic Lao non-profit restaurant that helps raise money for street kids. Run by the trainees, who are former street kids, and their teachers. Modern Lao cuisine with a twist. Selection of delectable drinks such as the iced hibiscus with lime juice. Beautifully decorated with modern furniture and painting by the kids. Also sells handicrafts and toys produced by the parents from vulnerable communities.

**PVO Vietnamese Food**, off Fa Gnum Quay. A firm favourite. Full menu of freshly prepared Vietnamese food but best known for baguettes, stuffed with your choice of pâté, salad, cheese, coleslaw, vegetables and ham. Bikes and motorbikes for rent too. Brilliant cheap food makes this a fantastic choice.

**Seendat**, Sihom Rd, T021-213855. Daily 1730-2200. This restaurant has been in existence for well over 20 years and is a favourite amongst the older Lao for its clean food (*sindat*) and good atmosphere. About US$1 per person more expensive than most other places but this is reflected in the quality.

**Soukvimarn**, T021-214441. 1100-1400, 1800-2100. Heavily influenced by traditional southern Lao flavours. Well worth the experience as it offers the opportunity to tempt the taste buds with a wider variety of Lao cuisine than most other eateries offer.

**Sticky Fingers**, François Ngin Rd, T021-215972, Tue-Sun 1000-2300. Very popular small restaurant and bar serving Lao and international dishes, including fantastic salads, pasta, burgers and such like. Everything from Middle Eastern through to modern Asian on offer. Fantastic comfort food and the best breakfast in town. Great cocktails, lively atmosphere, nice setting. Deliveries available. **Stickies** should be the first pit-stop for every visitor needing to get grounded quickly as, food aside, the expats who frequent the joint are full to the brim with local knowledge.

**Floating restaurants**
A couple of floating restaurants are docked on the Mekong. Off Fa Ngum Rd (just past the **Intercity Hotel**). At 1900 the restaurants cruise down the river for the sunset. The cruise is complimentary when you eat there. The food is as cheap as chips, so the cruises are exceptionally good value. Two of the better ones are:

**Champadeng**, a bit further along from Lane Xang Av, T020-5526911. Daily 1000-2200, cruise at 1930. This is probably the most popular of the two. Quite a good selection of Lao dishes and some hilarious English translations: fish fried flog, sansage and fried fish with three taste. The food

here is as good as you will find anywhere else and, when you get bored, you can pop down to the lower level and belt out a few tunes on the karaoke. When the river is too low the cruises won't run.
**Lane Xang**, T021-243397. Daily 1000-2230, cruise at 1900. It's a good idea to get in there early so you can watch the sunset, a lot of the cruise is actually in the dark.

### Cafés, cakeshops and juice bars
Pavement cafés are ten a penny in Vientiane. You need not walk more than half a block for some hot coffee or a cold fruit shake.
**Delight House of Fruit Shakes**, Samsenthai Rd, opposite the **Asian Pavilion Hotel**, T021-212200. Daily 0700-2200. A wonderful selection of fresh shakes and fruit salads for next to nothing.
**Joma**, Setthathirat Rd, T021-215265, bakers @laopdr.com. Mon-Sat 0700-2100. A very modern, chic bakery with efficient service. Wi-Fi and arctic-style a/c. However, it is starting to get a bit pricey.
**Le Croissant d'Or**, top of Nokeo Khoummane Rd, T021-223740. Daily 0700-1800. French bakery, great for pastries.
**Scandinavian Bakery**, 71/1 Pang Kham Rd, Nam Phou Circle, T021-215199, scandinavian@laonet.net. Daily 0700-2000. Delicious pastries, bread, sandwiches and cakes. Great place for a leisurely coffee and pastries. Pricey for Laos but a necessary European fix for many expats. The Nam Phou Circle outlet is much better value and has a wider selection of cakes and sandwiches.

**Vang Vieng** *p395, map p396*
There is a string of eating places on the main road through town. Generally, the cuisine available are hamburgers, pasta, sandwiches and basic Asian dishes. Most of the restaurants offer 'happy' upgrades – marijuana or mushrooms in your pizza, cake or lassi, or opium tea. Although many people choose the 'happy' offerings, some wind up very ill.
❦ **Luang Prabang Bakery Restaurant**, just off the main road, near BCEL. Excellent pastries, cakes and shakes and pretty delicious breakfasts. Make sure you ask for the freshest batch as they have a tendency to leave cakes on the shelf well past their use-by date. Recommended.

❦ **Nangbot**, on the main road, T021-511018. This proper sit-down restaurant is one of the oldest tourist diners in town and serves a few traditional dishes, such as bamboo shoot soup and *laap* with sticky rice, alongside the usual Western fare.
❦ **Nazim's**, on the main road, T021-511214. The largest and most popular Indian restaurant in town. Good range of South Indian and buriyani specialities, plus a selection of vegetarian meals.
❦ **Organic Farm Café**, further down the main road. Small café offering over 15 tropical fruit shakes and a fantastic variety of food. Mulberry shakes and pancakes are a must and the harvest curry stew is absolutely delicious. Try the fresh spring rolls with pineapple dipping sauce as a starter. The food is highly recommended, the service could do with a little work. The sister branch is at the **Organic Mulberry Farm** (see Sleeping).
❦ **Vieng Champa Restaurant**, on the main road, T021-511037. Refreshingly, this family-run restaurant seems to have a greater selection of Lao food than most other places on the street. Most meals are between 15,000 and 20,000 kip.
❦ **Xayoh**, Luang Prabang Rd, T023-511088. Restaurant with branches in Vientiane and Luang Prabang offering good Western food in a comfy environment. Pizza, soups and roast dinners.

## 🕪 Bars and clubs

**Vientiane** *p388, map p390*
**Bars**
There are a number of bar stalls, which set up in the evening along **Quai Fa Ngum** (the river road); a good place for a cold beer as the sun sets. Most bars will close at 2300 in accordance with the local curfew laws; some places seem to be able to stay open past this time although that varies on a day-to-day basis. Government officials go through phases of shutting down places and restricting curfews.
**Jazzy Brick**, Setthathirat Rd, near Phimphone Market. Very sophisticated, modern den, where delectable cocktails are served with jazz cooing in the background. Garish shirts banned. Decorated with an eclectic range of quirky and kitsch artefacts.

**Laos** Vientiane region Listings

Very upmarket. Head here towards the end of the night.

**Khop Chai Deu**, Setthathirat Rd (near the corner with Nam Phou). Probably the most popular bar for tourists in Vientiane. Casual setting with a nightly band.

**Mekong Deck**, Fa Gnum. Fantastic location on the river. Huge modern, open-air wooden deck. Limited drinks menu with beer, spirits and shakes but set to expand.

**Spirit House**, follow Fa Ngum Rd until it turns into a dirt track, past the Mekong River Commission, T021-243795. Beautiful wooden bar in a perfect river location. Range of snacks and decent sushi. Good for those wanting to catch the sunset in style. Wi-Fi.

**Sticky Fingers**, François Ngin Rd, opposite the **Tai Pan Hotel**. A fantastic bar and restaurant run by 2 Australian women. Brilliant cocktails, especially the renowned Tom Yum. Also serves food.

**Sunset Bar**, end of Fa Ngum Rd. Although this run-down wooden construction isn't much to look at, it is a firm favourite with locals and tourists hoping to have a quiet ale and take in the magnificent sunset.

**Wind West**, by traffic lights, Luang Prabang Rd. Usually stays open after 2300. Seedier than others; many wild nights happen here.

**Vang Vieng** *p395, map p396*
The latest hotspot in Vang Vieng changes week to week.

**Oh La La Bar**, off the main street. Very popular, open bar with pool table.

**Sakura Bar**, between the main road and the river, near **Erawan Restaurant**. Big open bar with loud, blaring and often live music.

## ● Entertainment

**Vientiane** *p388, map p390*
**Films and exhibitions**
**The French Cultural Centre**, Lang Xang Rd, T021-215764. Tue and Thu 1930, Sat 1530; US$1. Screens the occasional French film and also hosts the Southeast Asian film festival. Often holds art exhibitions and concerts. Check the *Vientiane Times* for up-to-date details.
**Lao International Trade Exhibition Centre (ITEC)**, Ban Phonethane Neua, T021-416374. Shows a range of international films.

Keep an eye in the *Vientiane Times* for international performances at the **Lao Cultural Centre** (the building that looks like a big cake opposite the museum).
**T-Shop Lai**, Th Inpeng (behing Wat Inpeng), T021-223178, has an exhibition upstairs devoted to Asian elephants.
**COPE Visitors' Centre**, National Rehabilitation Centre compound, Khou Vieng Road, www.copelaos.org, 0900-1600; 20,000 kip. At the time of publication COPE (Co-operative Orthotic & Prosthetic Enterprise) was setting up an exhibition on unexploded ordnance (UXO) and its effects on the people of Laos. The exhibition is very interesting and includes a small movie room, photography, UXO and a range of prosthetic limbs (some of which are crafted out of UXO). The exhibition helps raise money for the work of COPE, which includes the production of prosthetic limbs and rehabilitation of patients.

**Karaoke**
Could almost be the Lao national sport and there's nothing like bonding with the locals over a heavy-duty karaoke session. Karaoke places are everywhere. The more expensive, up-market **Don Chan Palace** lets you hire your own room. **Champadeng Cruise** has a good karaoke room below deck, and no one can hear your howling when you're out on the river.

**Traditional dance**
**Lao National Theatre**, Manthaturath Rd, T021-242978. Daily shows of Lao dancing, from 2030. Tickets, US$7. Performances represent traditional dance of lowland Lao as well as some minority groups. Performances are less regular in the low season.

## ● Festivals and events

**Vientiane** *p388, map p390*
**1st weekend in Apr** Pi Mai (Lao New Year) is celebrated with a 3-day festival and a huge water fight.
**12 Oct** Freedom of the French Day
**Oct** Boun Souang Heua (Water Festival) is a beautiful event on the night of the full moon at the end of Buddhist Lent. Candles are lit in all the homes and a candlelit

procession takes place around the city's wats and through the streets. Then, thousands of banana-leaf boats holding flowers, tapers and candles are floated out onto the river. The boats signify your bad luck floating away. On the second day, boat races take place, with 50 or so men in each boat; they power up the river in perfect unison. Usually, a bunch of foolhardy expats also tries to compete, much to the amusement of the locals.

**Nov** (movable) **Boun That Luang** is celebrated in all of Vientiane's *thats* but most notably at That Luang (the national shrine). Originally a ceremony in which nobles swore allegiance to the king and constitution, it amazingly survived the Communist era. On the festival's most important day, **Thak Baat**, thousands of Lao people pour into the temple at 0600 and again at 1700 to pay homage. Monks travel from across the country to collect alms from the pilgrims. It is a really beautiful ceremony, with monks chanting and thousands of people praying. Women who attend should invest in a traditional *sinh*. A week-long carnival surrounds the festival with fireworks, music and dancing.

## O Shopping

**Vientiane** *p388, map p390*
### Bookshops
**Kosila Books**, Nokeo Khoummane Rd, T021-241352. Small selection of second-hand books.
**Vientiane Book Centre**, 54/1 Pang Kham St (next door to **Just for Fun**), T021-212031. A limited but interesting selection of used books in a multitude of languages.
**Monument Books**, T021-243708. The largest selection of new books in Vientiane, Monument stock a range of Southeast Asian speciality books as well as coffee-table books. Good place to pick up Lao-language children's books to distribute to villages on your travels.

### Clothing and textiles
**Couleur d'Asie**, Nam Phou Circle. Modern-style Asian clothing. Pricey but high-quality fusion fashion.
**Lao Textiles by Carol Cassidy**, Nokeo Koummane Rd, T021-212123, Mon-Fri

0800-1200, 1400-1700, Sat 0800-1200. Exquisite silk fabrics, including *ikat* and traditional Lao designs, made by an American in a beautifully renovated colonial property. Dyeing, spinning, designing and weaving all done on site (and can be viewed). It's expensive, but many of the weavings are real works of art; custom-made pieces available on request.
**Mixay Boutique**, Nokeo Khoummane, T021-25717943, contact@mixay.com. Exquisite Lao silk in rich colours. Clothing and fantastic photographs and artefacts.
**Satri Laos**, Setthathirat, T021-244387. If Vientiane had a Harrods this would be it. Upmarket boutique retailing everything from jewellery, shoes, clothes, furnishings and homewares. Beautiful stuff, although most of it is from China, Vietnam and Thailand.

### Handicrafts and antiques
The main shops are along Setthathirat, Samsenthai and Pang Kham. The **Talaat Sao** (Morning Market) is also worth a browse, with artefacts, such as appliquéd panels, decorated hats and sashes, basketwork both old and new, small and large wooden tobacco boxes, sticky-rice lidded baskets, axe pillows, embroidered cushions and a wide range of silver work.
**CAMA crafts**, Mixay Rd, T021-241217. NGO which sells handicrafts produced by the Hmong ethnic groups. Beautiful embroidery, mulberry tea and Lao silk.
**T'Shop Lai Gallery**, Wat Inpeng Soi. Funky studio exhibiting local sculptures and art. Artists can be seen at work every day except Sun. Media include coconut shells, wood and metal. Proceeds from sales are donated to Lao Youth projects. Upstairs there is an exhibition on Asian elephants.

### Jewellery
**Tamarind**, Manthathurath, T020-5517031. Great innovative jewellery designs, nice pieces. Also stocks a range of beautiful clothes made in stunning silk and organza.

### Markets
Vientiane has several excellent markets. **Talaat Sao** (Morning Market), off Lane Xang Av. It's busiest in the mornings (from around 1000), but operates all day. There

are money exchanges here (quite a good rate), and a good selection of foodstalls selling Western food, soft drinks and ice cream sundaes. It sells imported Thai goods, electrical appliances, watches, DVDs and CDs, stationery, cosmetics, a selection of handicrafts, an enormous choice of Lao fabrics, and upstairs there is a large clothing section, silverware, some gems and gold and a few handicraft stalls.

There is also the newer addition to the Morning Market – a modern shopping centre-style market. This is not as popular as it is much pricier and stocked with mostly Thai products sold in baht. On the second floor there is an reasonable food court, *Talat Khua-Din*.

There is an interesting produce section at the ramshackle market on the other side of the bus stop. This market offers many of the same handicrafts and silks as the morning market but is a lot cheaper.

### Supermarkets
**Phimphone Market**, Setthathirath Rd, opposite **Khop Chai Deu Restaurant**. This supermarket has everything a foreigner could ask for in terms of imported food, drink, magazines, translated books, personal hygiene products, household items and much more (and the price to go with it). **Simuang Minimart**, Samsenthai Rd, opposite Wat Simuang. Supermarket with a great selection of Western products. Great place to pick up wine but double-check it is not past its use-by-date.

## ▲ Activities and tours

**Vientiane** *p388, map p390*
### Cooking
**Thongbay Guesthouse** (see Sleeping), T021-242292. Cooking classes, covering all of meal preparation, from purchasing the ingredients to eating the meal.

### Cycling
Bicycles are available for hire from several places in town, see Transport, page 409. A good outing is to cycle downstream along the banks of the Mekong. Cycle south on Tha Deua Rd until Km 5 (watch the traffic) and then turn right down one of the tracks (there are a number) towards the riverbank.

A path, suitable for bicycles, follows the river beginning at about Km 4.5. There are monasteries and drinks sellers en route to maintain interest and energy.

### Golf
**Santisuk Lane Xang Golf Club**, Km 14, Tha Deua, T021-812022. Daily 0700-1800. 9-hole course, open to the public, with modest green fees and caddies available. To get there, catch bus No 14 from the Morning Market or take a tuk-tuk (40,000 kip) **Vientiane Golf Club**, Km 6, Route 13 South, T021-515820. Daily 0630-sunset. Clubs for rent. To get there, turn right at Peugeot showroom (6 km south of town), left after bridge, right at the fork and right at top of hill.

### Gym
**Sengdara**, Dongpalane Rd, US$5. This is a very modern, well-equipped gym, with pool, sauna and massage.

Every afternoon at 1700 there is a free aerobics session in the outdoor gymnasium on the river. Completely bizarre but lots of fun.

### Kickboxing
**Soxai Boxing Stadium**, 200 m past the old circus in Baan Dong Paleb. Kickboxing is usually held on the last Fri of every month at 1700 (20,000 kip).

### Massage, saunas and spas
The best massage in town is given by the blind masseuses in a little street off Samsenthai Rd, 2 blocks down from Simuang Minimart (across from Wat Simuang). There are 2 blind masseuse businesses side-by-side and either one is fantastic: **Traditional Clinic**, T020-5659177, and **Porm Clinic**, T020-627633 (no English spoken). They are marked by blue signs off both Khou Vieng and Samsenthai roads. **Papaya Spa**, opposite Wat Xieng Veh, T021-216550. Daily 0900-2000. Surrounded by beautiful gardens. Massage, sauna, facials. They also have a new branch that is more accessible on Lane Xang Avenue just up from the Morning Market. **Mandarina**, Pang Kham just off Nam Phou, T021-218703. A range of upmarket treatments between US$5-30. Massage, facials, body scrubs, mini-saunas, oils, jacuzzi.

## Shooting
There is a shooting range in the Southern corner of the national stadium US$1-2 for a few rounds.

## Swimming and waterparks
Several hotels in town permit non-residents to use their fitness facilities for a small fee, including the Tai Pan Hotel (rather basic), the **Lao Hotel Plaza**, the **Lane Xang Hotel** and the luxurious **Settha Palace** (with a hefty entrance price to boot). **The Australian Embassy Recreation Club** Km 3, Tha Deua Rd, T021-314921, has a fantastic saltwater pool with superb Mekong views. At the time of publication a major **water park** was being constructed in the park on Khou Vieng Rd, just behind Talaat Kudin.

## Tenpin bowling
Bowling is a very popular local pastime. Although it might sound quite sedate, the bowling alleys are often the only bars that are open after curfew.
**The Lao Bowling Centre**, behind the Lao Plaza Hotel, T021-218661, is good value at US$1 per person, shoe hire is included but bring your own socks.

## Thak Baat
Every morning at day-break (around 0530-0600) monks flood out of the city's temples, creating a swirl of orange on the streets, as collect alms from city folk making merit. It is truly beautiful to see the misty, grey streets come alive with the robe-clad monks. Foreigners are more than welcome to participate, just buy some sticky rice or other food from the vendors and kneel beside others making merit.

## Tour operators
To organize any kind of ecotour, visit the **National Tourism Authority** for general travel information or specific recommendations. Most agents will use 'eco' somewhere in their title but this doesn't necessarily mean anything.
**Asian Trails**, PO Box 5422, Unit 10, Baan Khounta Thong, Sikotthabong District, T021-263936, www.asiantrails.com. Southeast Asia specialists.
**Diethelm Travel**, Nam Phou Circle, T021-213833, www.diethelm-travel.com.

**Exotissimo**, 6/44 Pang Kham Rd, T021-241861, www.exotissimo.com. Tours and travel services. Excellent but pricey. **Green Discovery Laos**, Setthathirat Rd, next to Kop Chai Deu T021-251564, www.greendiscoverylaos.com. Specializes in ecotours and adventure travel.

## Weaving and dyeing courses
**Houey Hong Vocational Training Centre**, Ban Houey Hong, 20 mins north of Vientiane, T021-560006, hhwt@laotel.com. This small NGO runs training courses for underprivileged ethnic minorities. Tourists are welcome to join in the course for US$15 per day. To get there ask a songthaew to drop you off at Talaat Houey Hong, and follow the track 200 m west. Call the centre in advance.

## Yoga
**Vientiane Yoga Studio**, Sokpaluang Rd, Soi 1 (first *soi* on the right after you turn onto Sokpaluang from Khou Vieng Rd). Tue-Thu 1700-1830, Fri-Sun 1000-1130 (50,000 kip), Hatha yoga classes, 1½ hrs duration, open level from beginner to experienced.

## Vang Vieng *p395, map p396*
Tour guides are available hiking, rafting, visiting the caves and minority villages from most travel agents and guesthouses. Safety issues need to be considered when taking part in any adventure activity. There have been fatalities in Vang Vieng from boating, trekking and caving accidents. The Nam Song River can flow very quickly during the wet season (Jul and Aug) and tourists have drowned here. Make sure you wear a life jacket during all water-borne activities and time your trip so you aren't travelling on the river after dark. A price war between tour operators has led to cost cutting, resulting in equipment that is not well maintained or does not exist at all. With all tour operators it is imperative you are given safety gear and that canoes, ropes, torches and other equipment are in a good state of repair. The more expensive, reputable companies are often the best option (see also Vientiane Tour operators, above). Reliable tour operators include:
**Green Discovery**, attached to Xayoh Café, T023-511440, www.greendiscoverylaoscom.

By far the best tour operator in town. Caving, kayaking, hiking and rock climbing. Very professional and helpful. Recommended. **Riverside Tour** T020-2254137, www.riversidetourlaos.com. Kayaking and adventure tours.

### Kayaking and rafting

See also tour operators, above. Kayaking is a very popular activity around Vang Vieng and competition between operators is fierce. There are a wide variety of trips available, ranging from day trips (with a visit to the caves and surrounding villages), to kayaking all the way to Vientiane via the stop-off point at Nam Lik, US$15-25, about 6 hrs, including a 40-min drive at the start and finish. All valuables are kept in a car which meets kayakers at the end of their paddle. A few companies also offer 2-day rafting trips down the Nam Ngum River. The trip includes several grade 4 and 5 rapids and usually an overnight camp. US$100 per person or less for groups of more than 3.

Be wary of intensive rafting or kayaking trips through risky areas during the wet season, as it can be very dangerous. Check equipment thoroughly before committing.

### Rock climbing

Vang Vieng is the only really established rock climbing area in the country, with over 50 sites in the locality, ranging from grade 5 to 8A+. Almost all of these climbs had been 'bolted'. There are climbing sites suitable for beginners through to more experienced climbers. **Green Discovery** (see Tour operators, page 407) runs climbing courses almost every day in high season (US$20-45 per day, including equipment rental). The best climbing sites include: **Sleeping Cave**, **Sleeping Wall** and **Tham Nam Them**.

### Trekking

Almost all guesthouses and agents in town offer hiking trips, usually incorporating a visit to caves and minority villages and, possibly, some kayaking or tubing. The best treks are offered through the major tour operators who will provide an English-speaking guide, all transport and lunch for US$10-15 per day.

### Tubing

No trip to Vang Vieng is complete without tubing down the Nam Song. Floating slowly along the river is an ideal way to take in the stunning surroundings of limestone karsts, jungle and rice paddies. The drop-off point is 3 km from town near the **Organic Mulberry Farm**, where several bars and restaurants have been set up along the river. Try and start early in the day as it's dangerous to tube after dark and the temperature of the water drops sharply. Women should take a sarong and avoid walking through town in a bikini, it is culturally unacceptable and highly offensive to the locals.

Tour operators and guesthouses offer tube rental, life jackets and drop-off for US$4. A US$7 fine is charged for lost tubes (people may offer to return the tubes for you; it is best to decline this offer). Dry bags can be rented for 10,000 kip. It is essential that you wear a life jacket as people have drowned on the river, particularly in the wet season (Jul and Aug) when the river swells and flows very quickly. Without stopping expect the journey to take 1-2 hrs. Most people stop along the way and make a day of it.

## ⊖ Transport

**Vientiane** *p388, map p390*
### Air
**Lao Airlines**, 2 Pang Kham Rd (near Fa Ngum), T021-212054, www.laoairlines.com, also at Wattay Airport; T021-212051 **Lao Air** office at Wattay Airport, T/F021-512027, laoair@laopdr.com. **Thai Airways**, Head Office, Luang Prabang Rd, not far past the Novotel, T021-222527/9, www.thaiairways.com, Mon-Fri 0830-1200, 1300-1500, Sat 0830-1200; also on Pang Kham Rd, next to the bookshop and at Wattay Airport, 1st floor, Room 106, T021-512024, daily 0700-1200, 1300-1600. **Vietnam Airlines**, Lao Plaza Hotel, T021-217562, www.vietnamairlines.com.vn, Mon-Fri 0800-1200, 1330-1630, Sat 0800-1200.

Prices and schedules are constantly changing, so always check in advance. **Lao Airlines** to **Bangkok** (80 mins) 3 flights daily; to **Luang Prabang** (40 mins) up to 3 flights daily; to **Pakse** (50 mins) daily. To **Oudomxay** and **Houei Xai** 4 flights a week; to **Siem Reap** 5 times a week, 3 times a week via Pakse; **Phnom Penh** (90 mins) twice a week via Pakse. **Kunming** 3 times a week (2½ hrs); **Chiang Mai** daily. **Hanoi** daily. Lao Airlines schedules prone to change. **Lao Air** operates flights to **Xam Neua** twice a week (50 mins) and **Phongsaly** twice a week (60 mins). **Thai Airways** to **Bangkok** (70 mins), daily. **Vietnam Airlines**, to **Hanoi** (60 mins), daily; to **HCMC** (3 hrs), daily and **Phnom Penh** daily.

## Bicycle and motorbike

For those energetic enough in the hot season, **bikes** are the best way to get around town. Many hotels and guesthouses have bikes available for their guests, expect to pay about 10,000 kip per day. There are also many bike hire shops around town. Markets, post offices and government offices usually have 'bike parks' where it is advisable to leave your bike. A small minding fee is charged.

**Motorbikes** are available for hire from many guesthouses and shops. Expect to pay US$5-10 per day and leave your passport as security. Insurance is seldom available anywhere in Laos on motorbikes but most places will also hire out helmets, a necessity. **KT bikes**, Manthathurath St, T020-5816816 offers the best range of well-serviced Suzukis (US$7 per day) and dirt bikes (US$20 per day); discounts available for longer hire.

**PVO**, off Fa Ngum, also has a reliable selection of bicycles and motorbikes. Often a driving licence can be used in lieu of a motorbike licence if the police pull you over.

## Bus

Vientiane has 3 main public bus terminals: Northern, Southern and Talaat Sao (Morning Market).

**Southern bus station** Route 13, 9 km south of the city centre. Public buses depart daily for destinations in southern Laos. At the time of writing bus prices were expected to increase by about 10,000 kip per trip. The southern bus station has a range of shops, a pharmacy and a massage place. To **Thakhek**, 4 daily, 6 hrs, 40,000 kip. To **Savannakhet**, 7 daily (early morning),

8 hrs, 55,000 kip. To **Pakse**, 9 daily, 15 hrs, 85,000 kip; **Muang Khong** 1030, 110,000 kip; **Veun Kham** 1000, 110,000 kip. There are also overnight VIP buses to Pakse, 11 hrs, 110,000 kip, and a VIP service daily at 2030 by **Thongli** T021-242657, which takes about the same time but has beds, water, snacks, etc, 130,000 kip. Make sure you book a double if you don't want to be stuck with a strange bedfellow. **KVT**, T021-213043, also run VIP buses to Pakse at 2030. Banag Saigon, T021-720175, run buses to **Hanoi**, 1900, US$20; **Vinh**, 1900, US$16; **Thanh Hoa**, 1900, US$16; **Hué**, 1930, US$20; **Danang**, 1930, US$20. These services run on odd days so check in advance.

**VIP buses** are very comfortable, usually allowing for a good night's sleep during the trip, but watch out that they don't swap the normal VIP bus for a karaoke one! Robberies have been reported on the night buses so keep your valuables somewhere secure.

**Northern bus station** Route 2, towards the airport, 3.5 km from the centre of town, T021-260255.

Northbound buses are regular and have a/c. For the more popular routes, there are also VIP buses which will usually offer snacks and service. To **Luang Prabang** (384 km), standard buses 5 daily, 11 hrs, 90,000 kip; a/c buses daily at 0630, 0900, 1930, 10-11 hrs, 1000,000 kip; VIP buses daily at 0800, 9 hrs, 120,000 kip. To **Udomxai** (578 km), standard buses twice daily, 14-15 hrs, 110,000 kip; a/c buses daily at 1600, 120,000 kip. To **Luang Namtha** (676 km), daily 0830, 19 hrs, 140,000 kip. To **Phongsali**, daily 0715, 26 hrs, 150,000 kip. To **Houei Xai**, Mon, Wed and Fri 1730, 30-35 hrs, 200,000 kip. To **Xam Neua**, 3 daily, 14-23 hrs (depending on whether it goes via Phonsavanh), 150,000 kip. To **Phonsavanh**, standard 4 daily, 10 hrs, 90,000 kip; a/c daily at 0730, 90,000 kip; VIP daily at 0800, 130,000 kip.

**Talaat Sao bus station** Across the road from Talaat Sao, in front of Talaat Kudin, on the eastern edge of the city centre. Destinations, distances and fares are listed on a board in English and Lao. Most departures are in the morning and can leave as early as 0400, so many travellers on a tight schedule have regretted not checking departure times the night before. There is a useful map at the station, and bus times and fares are listed clearly in Lao and English. However, it's more than likely you will need a bit of direction at this bus station: staff at the ticket office only speak a little English so a better option is to chat to the friendly chaps in the planning office, who love a visit, T021-216506. The times listed below vary depending on the weather and the number of stops en route.

To the **Southern bus station**, every 30 mins, 0600-1800, 2000 kip. To the **Northern bus station**, catch the Nongping bus (8 daily) and ask to get off at '*Thay song*' (1500 kip). To **Wattay Airport**, every 30 mins, 0640-1800, 3000 kip. Buses to Vang Vieng 5 daily, 3½ hrs, 15,000 kip.

There are numerous buses criss-crossing the province; most aren't very useful for tourists. To the **Friendship Bridge** (Lao side), every 30 mins, 0650-1710, 5000 kip. To **Nong Khai** (Thai side of the Friendship Bridge), 4 daily, 1 hr including immigration, 10,000 kip.

### Taxi

These are mostly found at the Talaat Sao (Morning Market) or around the main hotels. Newer vehicles have meters but there are still some ageing jalopies. Flag fall is 8000 kip. A taxi from the Morning Market to the **airport**, US$5; to **Tha Deua** (for the Friend- ship Bridge and Thailand), US$10, although you can usually get the trip much cheaper but the taxis are so decrepit that you may as well take a tuk-tuk, US$6 (see below). To hire a taxi for trips outside the city costs around US$20 per day.

Lavi Taxi, T021-350000. Is the only reliable call-up service in town but after 2000 you may not get an answer.

### Tuk-tuks

Tuk-tuks usually congregate around **Nam Phou**, **Talaat Sao** and **Talaat Kudin**. Tuk-tuks can be chartered for longer out-of-town trips (maximum 25 km, US$10-15) or for short journeys of 2-3 km within the city (10,000 kip per person). There are also shared tuk-tuks, which run on regular routes along the cities main streets. Tuk-tuks are available around Nam Phou until 2330 but are quite difficult to hire after dark in other areas of town. The tuk-tuks that

congregate on the city corners are generally part of a quasi cartel, it is thus much cheaper to travel on one that is passing through. To stop a vehicle, simply flag it down. A good, reliable driver is **Mr Souk**, T020-7712220, who speaks good English and goes beyond the call of duty.

### Vang Vieng p395, map p396
#### Bicycle and motorbike

There are many bicycles for rent along the road east up from the old market (10,000 kip per day). There are also a few motorbike rental places (US$5 per day), the best of these is opposite the **Organic Farm Café** in town .

#### Bus

Buses leave from the make-shift bus terminal on the east side of the airstrip, T021-511341. There are plans to relocate all buses to the terminal at the New Market, 2 km north of town. Check before going to either station. This station has been built for 2 years now and the buses still haven't relocated. Mini-buses leave from most guesthouses to both Vientiane and Luang Prabang – this service is notoriously unreliable with passengers packed in like sardines and minivans often breaking down. Best to opt for the local bus. You can catch northbound buses headed from **Vientiane** to **Luang Prabang** hourly between 1200 and 2000, 8-10 hrs, 70,000 kip. The bus en route from Vientiane to **Phonsovan** passes through town at 0900, 85,000 kip. Public buses leave for **Vientiane** 5 times daily, 3½-4 hrs 25,000 kip; songthaews depart every hr.

#### Private transport and VIP buses

Tickets are usually sold by guesthouses and will include a tuk-tuk pickup at your hotel to the bus. VIP buses leave for **Luang Prabang** at 1000, 6 hrs, US$10. The minivans leave at 0900. VIP Bus to **Vientiane** 1000 and 1300, 3 hrs, 55,000 kip (you are actually better off on the local bus for short stints like this). Minivan to Vientiane 0900, 3½ hrs, 70,000 kip (not recommended). Minibus to Luang Prabang 0900, 5 hrs, 105,000 kip. Every guesthouse and travel agent can book the VIP/minivans and they will pick up from your guesthouse. Seats get booked up really quickly and buses take at least 30 mins to make all their pick-ups, so expect long delays.

## Tuk-tuks

A day trip to the caves should cost US$10 but there have been reports of some drivers offering trips to the caves for 10,000 kip per person and then demanding an outrageous fee for the return leg. Make sure all prices are set in stone before setting off.

# ◐ Directory

## Vientiane *p388, map p390*

### Banks

See Money, page 41, for details on changing money in Laos. At the time of writing there were only a handful of multicard Visa and MasterCard ATMs in the city. The **Banque Pour le Commerce Exterieur (BCEL)**, corner of Fa Ngum and Pang Kham roads, takes all the usual credit cards (maximum withdrawal 700,000 kip; much less on Sun). Other multicard ATMs can be found in front of the Novotel, the Lao Plaza Hotel and beside the petrol station near Wat Simuang. Other **BCEL** ATMs such as those on Setthathirat and near the Morning Market only take MasterCard. More ATMs are planned in the next few years. **BCEL**, 1 Pang Kham Rd, traditionally offers the lowest commission (1.5%) on changing US$ TCs into US$ cash; there is no commission on changing US$ into kip; also has an international ATM. **Joint Development Bank**, Lane Xane Ave, T021-213535, offers good rates on cash advances. ATM.

### Embassies and consulates

**Australia**, Km3 Tha Deua Rd (from Apr 2008), T021-413602. **Britain**, contact the Australian Embassy. **Cambodia**, Tha Deua Rd, Km 3, T021-314952, visas daily 0730-1030; Cambodian visas US$20. **China**, Thanon Wat Nak Nyai T021-315105. Visas take 4-days. **France**, Setthathirat Rd, T021-215258. **Germany**, 26 Sok Paluang Rd, T021-312110/1. **Thailand**, Phon Kheng Rd, T021-900238 (consular section on That Luang arranges visas extensions), Mon-Fri 0830-1200. **USA**, That Dam Rd (off Samsenthai Rd), T021-267000. **Vietnam**, That Luang Rd, T021-413400, visas 0800-1045, 1415-1615. One-month visa costs US$50 and you must wait 3 days. An extra US$5 for the visa in 1 day.

## Immigration

Immigration office, Phai Nam Rd (near Morning Market), Mon-Fri 0730-1200, 1400-1700. Visa extensions can be organized for US$2 per day. For visa information, see Essentials page 49.

## Internet

Internet cafés have opened up all over the city, many on Setthathirat and Samsenthai roads. You shouldn't have to pay more than 100 kip per min. Internet phones are now very popular, with most cafés providing this service for under US$1 per min. Also, most major internet cafés are fitted with Skype and headphones. **Apollo Internet**, Setthathirat Rd, Mon-Fri 0830-2300, Sat and Sun 0900-2300.

## Medical services

There are 2 pretty good pharmacies close to the Talaat Sao Bus Station. **Australian Clinic**, Australian Embassy, T021-413603, Mon-Fri, Fri 0800-1200, 1400-1700, for Commonwealth patients only (except in emergencies). US$60 to see the doctor. **Mahasot Hospital**, Fa Gnum, T021-214021, suitable for minor ailments but for anything major it is advisable to cross the border to Nong Khai and visit **AEK Udon International Hospital**, T0066 42342555.

For other hospitals in Thailand, see page 39. In cases of extreme emergency where a medical evacuation is required, contact **Lao Westcoast Helicopters**, Hangar 703, Wattay Airport, T021-512023, which will charter helicopters to Udon Thani for US$1500-2000, subject to availability and government approval.

## Police

**Tourist Police Office**, Lang Xang Av (in the same office as the National Tourism Authority of Laos), T021-251128.

## Post

**Post Office**, Khou Vieng Rd/Lane Xang Av (opposite market), T021-216425, offers local and international telephone calls. Also a good packing service and a philately counter. To send packages, use **DHL**, Nong No Rd, near the airport, T021-214868, or **TNT Express**, Thai Airways Building, Luang Prabang Rd, T021-261918.

**Telephone**

The international telephone office is on Setthathirat Rd, near Nam Phou Rd, 24 hrs.

**Vang Vieng and around** *p395, map p396*

**Banks** Agricultural Promotion Bank and the Lao Development Bank, on the main road, both exchange cash, 0830-1530. BCEL, T021-511480, exchanges cash, TCs and will also do cash advances on Visa and MasterCard, 0830-1530. MasterCard ATM.

**Internet** There are a number of internet cafés along the main drag, all 300 kip per min (but is expected to go down once a new line to town is installed); most offer international internet calls from 3000 kip per min. **Magnet** is the best of the internet cafés and offers internet as well as music/movie transfer to ipod and cash advances from the EFTPOS facility for 3% commission.

**Medical services** Vang Vieng Hospital is located on the road that runs parallel to the river; it's terribly under-equipped. In most cases it is better to go to Vientiane.

**Post office** The post office is next to the former site of the old market, 0830-1600.

## ❊ Footprint features

# Introduction

Much of Laos' northern region is rugged and mountainous, a remote borderland. The key centre of the north is Luang Prabang, the enchanting former royal capital. A spell binding plethora of gilded temples, shrines, stupas and French colonial buildings decorate the magical town, which is surrounded by mountains and anchored at the crossways of the Nam Khan and Mekong rivers. Nearby are the Kwang Si Falls, where billowing cascades create natural, turquoise pools. The areas further north are home to a rich tapestry of wilderness, the vast tracts of jungle and jagged mountains inhabited by many ethnic minority groups. The areas around Muang Sing, Luang Namtha and Phongsali are perfect for trekking or just kicking back.

For something different, the northeast encompasses the mysterious Plain of Jars and Vieng Xai's Pathet Lao caves, both testament to the country's enigmatic, at times, horrific, history.

★ **Don't miss ...**

40 km
40 miles

# Luang Prabang and around

*Anchored at the junction of the Mekong and Nam Khan rivers, the former royal capital of Lane Xang is now a UNESCO World Heritage Site. It is home to a spellbinding array of gilded temples, weathered French colonial façades and art deco shophouses. In the 18th century there were more than 65 wats in the city. Yet for all its magnificent temples, this royal 'city' feels more like an easy-going provincial town: at daybreak, scores of monks in saffron robes amble silently out of the monasteries bearing gold-topped wooden boxes in which to collect offerings from the town's residents; in the early evening women cook, old men lounge in wicker chairs and young boys play takro in the streets.*

*The famous Pak Ou Caves and the Kwang Si Falls are located near the town.*

*➼ For Sleeping, Eating and other listings, see pages 423-431.*

### Ins and outs → *Colour map 1, B2.*

**Getting there** Flying is still the easiest option with daily connections from Vientiane, plus flights from Bangkok and Chiang Mai to **Luang Prabang International Airport** (LPQ) ① *4 km northeast of town, T071-212172/3.* The airport has a phone box, a couple of restaurants and handicraft shops. There is a standard US$2 charge for a tuk-tuk ride from the airport to the centre.

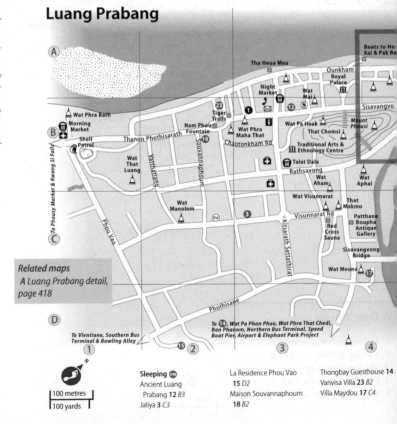

## Luang Prabang

*Related maps*
*A Luang Prabang detail,*
*page 418*

| 100 metres |
| 100 yards |

**Sleeping** 🛏
Ancient Luang
  Prabang **12** *B3*
Jaliya **3** *C3*

La Residence Phou Vao
  **15** *D2*
Maison Souvannaphoum
  **18** *B2*

Thongbay Guesthouse **14**
Vanvisa Villa **23** *B2*
Villa Maydou **17** *C4*

Route 13 is now safe, with no recent bandit attacks reported, and the road has been upgraded, shortening the journey from Vientiane to eight or nine hours. There are also overland connections with other destinations in northern Laos. Luang Prabang has two main bus stations: **Kiew Lot Sai Nuan** (northern bus station), located on the northeast side of Sisavangvong Bridge, for traffic to and from the north; and **Naluang** (southern bus station) for traffic to and from the south. Occasionally buses will pass through the opposite station to what you would expect, so be sure to double-check. The standard tuk-tuk fare to/from either bus station is 15,000 kip. If there are only a few passengers, it's late at night or you are travelling to/from an out-of-town hotel, expect to pay 20,000 kip. These prices tend to fluctuate with the international cost of petroleum. Another option is to travel by river: a firm favourite is the two-day trip between Luang Prabang and Houei Xai (close to the Thai border), via Pak Beng (see page 434). Less frequent are the boats to Muang Ngoi and Nong Khiaw, via Muang Khua. ▸▸ *For further details, see Transport, page 429.*

**Getting around** Luang Prabang is a small town and the best way to explore is either on foot or by bicycle. Bicycles can be hired from most guesthouses for US$1 per day. Strolling about this beautiful town is a real pleasure but there are also tuk-tuks and saamlors for hire.

**Best time to visit** Luang Prabang lies 300 m above sea level on the upper Mekong, at its confluence with the Nam Khan. The most popular time to visit the town is during the comparatively cool months of November and December but the best time to visit is from December to February. After this the weather is hotting up and the views are often shrouded in a haze, produced by shifting cultivators using fire to clear the forest for agriculture. This does not really clear until May or, sometimes, June. During the months of March and April, when visibility is at its worst, the smoke can cause soreness of the eyes, as well as preventing planes from landing.

**Tourist information** Luang Prabang Tourist Information Centre ① *Sisavangvong, T071-212487*, provides provincial information and offers a couple of good ecotourism treks (which support local communities), including one to Kwang Si and one in Chompet District. The Chompet trek receives quite good reviews and includes visits to hot springs, villages and the chance to watch a traditional performance from Hmong performers.

## Background

According to legend, the site of Luang Prabang was chosen by two resident hermits and was originally known as Xieng Thong – 'Copper Tree City'. Details are sketchy regarding the earliest inhabitants of Luang Prabang but historians imply the ethnic Khmu and Lao Theung groups were the initial settlers. They

Laos Northern Laos Luang Prabang & around

named Luang Prabang, Muang Sawa, which literally translates as Java, hinting at some kind of cross-border support. By the end of the 13th century, Muang Sawa had developed into a regional hub.

A major turning point in the city's history came about in 1353, when the mighty Fa Ngum barrelled down the Nam Ou River, backed by a feisty Khmer army, and captured Muang Sawa. Here, the warrior king founded Lane Xang Hom Khao (Kingdom of a Million Elephants, White Parasol) and established a new Lao royal lineage, which was to last another 600 years. The name of the city refers to the holy Pra Bang, Laos' most sacred image of the Buddha, which was given to Fa Ngum by his father-in-law, the King of Cambodia.

The city had been significantly built up by the time King Visounarat came to power in 1512 and remained the capital until King Setthathirat, fearing a Burmese invasion, moved the capital to Vieng Chan (Vientiane) in 1563.

Luang Prabang didn't suffer as greatly as other provincial capitals during the Indochina wars, narrowly escaping a Viet Minh capture in 1953. During the Second Indochina War, however, the Pathet Lao cut short the royal lineage, forcing King Sisavang Vatthana to abdicate and sending him to a re-education camp in northeastern Laos where he, his wife and his son died from starvation. Despite the demise of the monarchy and years of revolutionary rhetoric on the city's tannoy system, Luang Prabang's dreamy streets have somehow retained the aura of old Lane Xang.

# Sights

The sights are conveniently close together but, to begin with, it is worth climbing Phousi or taking a stroll along the river roads to get a better idea of the layout of the town. Most of Luang Prabang's important wats are dotted along the main road, Phothisarath.

## Mount Phousi

ⓘ *The western steps lead up from Sisavangvong Rd, daily 0800-1800. Admission at western steps 10,000 kip. If you want to watch the sun go down, get there early and jostle for position – don't expect to be the only person there.*

## Luang Prabang detail

**Sleeping** 🛏
Ammata Guesthouse **20** A3
Apsara **1** B4
Le Calao Inn **5** A4
Oui Guesthouse **21** B5
Pack Luck **7** A3
Sala Luang Prabang **9** A1

Sayo Guesthouse **11** A1
Silichit Guesthouse **12** A2
Three Nagas **14** B3
Villa Santi **16** B3
Villa Santi Annexe **22** B3

**Eating** 🍴
Blue Lagoon **21** A1
Café Ban Vat Sene **1** B3
Couleur Café **6** A2
Dao Fa **3** B2
L'Éléphant **7** A3
L'Étranger **8** B1

Directly opposite the Royal Palace is the start of the steep climb up Mount Phousi, the spiritual and geographical heart of the city and a popular place to come to watch the sunset over the Mekong, illuminating the hills to the east. Phousi is a gigantic rock with sheer forested sides, surmounted by a 25 m-tall *chedi*, **That Chomsi**. The *chedi* was constructed in 1804, restored in 1914 and is the designated starting point for the colourful Pi Mai (New Year) celebrations in April. Its shimmering gold-spired stupa rests on a rectangular base, ornamented by small metal Bodhi trees. Next to the stupa is a little sanctuary, from which the candlelit procession descends at New Year, accompanied by effigies of Nang Sang Kham, the guardian of the New Year, and Naga, protector of the city.

# Royal Palace

ⓘ *Sisavangvong Rd, daily 0800-1100, 1330-1600; 20,000 kip. No shorts, strappy dresses or short-sleeved shirts. No photography.*

Also called the **National Museum**, the Royal Palace is right in the centre of the city on the main road and close enough to the Mekong to allow royal guests ready access by river. Unlike its former occupants, the palace survived the 1975 revolution and was converted into a museum the following year.

It was built by the French for the Lao King Sisavang Vong in 1904 in an attempt to bind him and his family more tightly into the colonial system of government. Later work saw the planting of the avenue of palms and the filling in of one of two fish ponds. Local residents regarded the ponds as the 'eyes' of the capital, so the blinding of one eye was taken as inviting bad fortune by leaving the city unprotected. The subsequent civil war seemed to vindicate these fears. The palace is Khmer in style, cruciform in plan and mounted on a small platform of four tiers. The only indication of French involvement can be seen in the two French lilies represented in stucco on the entrance, beneath the symbols of Lao royalty. There are a few Lao motifs but, in many respects, the palace is more foreign than Lao: it was designed by a French architect, with steps made from Italian marble; built by masons from Vietnam; embellished by carpenters from Bangkok, and funded by the largesse of the colonial authorities.

The small ornate pavilion of **Wat Ho Prabang** is located in the northeast corner of the palace compound, to the right of the entrance to the Royal Palace. The chapel contains four Khmer Buddhas, ivories mounted in gold, bronze drums used in religious ceremonies and about 30 smaller Buddha images from temples all over the city. The Pra Bang, see below, is due to be moved here.

The main **entrance hall** of the palace was used for royal religious ceremonies, when the Supreme Patriarch of Lao Buddhism would oversee proceedings from his gold- painted lotus throne. It now contains a collection of 15th- to 17th-century Buddha statues. The room to the immediate right of the entrance was the King's reception room, also called the **Ambassadors' Room**. It contains French-made busts of the last three Lao monarchs, a model of the royal hearse (which is kept in Wat Xieng Thong) and a mural by French artist Alex de Fontereau, depicting a day in the life of Luang Prabang in the 1930s.

In comparison to the state rooms, the royal family's **private apartments** are modestly decorated. They have been left virtually untouched since the day the family

Related maps
Luang Prabang, page 416

Boats
Ou

Souvanna Khampong

ne

Wat
Pak Khan

(5)  (6)

ng Glory 23 *B3*
rind 22 *A3*
ak Lao 15 *B3*
Khaem Khong 4 *A1*

Khily Wine Bar 24 *B5*
Khob Jai 19 *B1*
Lao Lao Garden 26 *B1*
Pack Luck 25 *B2*

& clubs
8 *B1*

*Laos* Northern Laos *Luang Prabang & around*

left for exile in Xam Neua Province. To the rear of the entrance hall, the **Coronation Room** was decorated between 1960 and 1970 for Crown Prince Sisavong Vatthana's coronation, an event which was interrupted because of the war. The walls are a brilliant red with Japanese glass mosaics embedded in a red lacquer base with gilded woodwork and depict scenes from Lao festivals.

To the left of the entrance hall is the reception room of the **King's Secretary**, and beyond it, the **Queen's reception room**, which together house an eccentric miscellany of state gifts from just about every country except the UK.

To the far right of the entrance to the palace is a room (viewed from the outside) in which sits the Pra Bang, or **Golden Buddha**, from which the city derived its name. The Buddha is in the attitude of Abhayamudra or 'dispelling fear'. Some believe that the original image is kept in a bank vault, though most dispel this as rumour. It is 90% solid gold. Reputed to have originally come from Ceylon, and said to date from any time between the first and ninth centuries, the statue was moved to Cambodia in the 11th century, given to King Phaya Sirichanta, and was then taken to Lane Xang by King Fa Ngum, who had spent some time in the courts of Angkor and married into Khmer royalty. An alternative story has the Pra Bang following Fa Ngum to the city: it is said he asked his father-in-law, the King of Angkor, to send a delegation of holy men to assist him in spreading the Theravada Buddhist faith in Lane Xang. The delegation arrived bringing with them the Pra Bang as a gift from the Cambodian King. The Pra Bang's arrival heralded the capital's change of name, from Xieng Thong to Nakhon Luang Prabang, 'The great city of the big Buddha'. In 1563 King Setthathirat took the statue to Lane Xang's new capital at Vientiane. Two centuries later in 1779 the Thais captured it but it was returned to Laos in 1839 and rediscovered in the palace chapel in 1975. The Pra Bang is revered in Laos as its arrival marked the beginnings of Buddhism in Lane Xang.

## Wat Mai
ⓘ *Sisavangvong Rd, daily 0800-1700; 5000 kip.*
Next to the Royal Palace is Wat Mai. This royal temple, inaugurated in 1788, has a five-tiered roof and is one of the jewels of Luang Prabang. It took more than 70 years to complete. It was the home of the Buddhist leader in Laos, Phra Sangkharath, until he moved to That Luang in Vientiane. During Pi Mai (New Year), the Pra Bang is taken from the Royal Palace and installed at Wat Mai for its annual ritual cleansing, before being returned to the palace on the third day.

The façade is particularly interesting: a large golden bas-relief tells the story of Phravet (one of the last reincarnations of the Gautama or historic Buddha), with several village scenes, including depictions of wild animals, women pounding rice and people at play. Inside, the interior is an exquisite amalgam of red and gold, with supporting pillars similar to those in Wat Xieng Thong.

## Wat Sene (Wat Saen)
Further up the promontory, Wat Sene was built in 1718 and was the first sim in Luang Prabang to be constructed in Thai style, with a yellow and red roof. The exterior may lack subtlety, but the interior is delicate and rather refined, painted red, with gold patterning on every conceivable surface. Sen means 100,000 and the wat was built with a local donation of 100,000 kip from someone who discovered 'treasure' in the Khan River.

## Wat Xieng Thong
ⓘ *Xiengthong Rd, daily 0800-1700; 10,000 kip.*
**Wat Xieng Thong Ratsavoraviharn**, usually known as just Wat Xieng Thong, is set back from the road, at the top of a flight of steps leading down to the Mekong. It is arguably the finest example of a Lao monastery, with graceful, low-sweeping eaves,

beautiful stone mosaics and intricate carvings. The wat has several striking chapels, including one that houses a rare bronze reclining Buddha and another sheltering a gilded wooden funeral chariot. Inside, resplendent gold-stencilled pillars support a ceiling with *dharma* wheels. The striking buildings in the tranquil compound are decorated in gold and post-box red, with imposing tiled roofs and mosaics, making this the most important and finest royal wat in Luang Prabang. It was built by King Setthathirat in 1559, and is one of the few buildings to have survived the successive Chinese raids that marked the end of the 19th century.

The **sim** is a perfect example of the Luang Prabang style. Locals believe the roof has been styled to resemble a bird, with wings stretched out to protect her young. The eight central wooden pillars have stencilled motifs in gold and the façade is finely decorated. The beautiful gold-leaf inlay is predominantly floral in design but a few images illustrate *Ramayana*-type themes and the interior frescoes depict *dharma* wheels and the enigmatic King Chantaphanit. At the rear of the sim is a mosaic representation of the thong copper 'Tree of Life' in glass inlay.

Behind the sim are two red *hor song phra* (**side chapels**): the one on the left is referred to as **La Chapelle Rouge** (the Red Chapel) and houses a rare Lao reclining Buddha in bronze, dating from the 16th century. The exterior mosaics which relate local tales, were added in 1957 to honour the 2500th anniversary of the Buddha's birth, death and enlightenment. The other *hor song phra*, to the right of the sim, houses a standing image of the Buddha which is paraded through the streets of the city each New Year and doused in water.

The **Chapel of the Funeral Chariot** is diagonally across from the sim and was built in 1962. The centrepiece is the grand 12-m-high gilded wooden hearse, with its seven-headed serpent, which was built for King Sisavang Vong, father of the last sovereign, and used to carry his urn to the stadium next to Wat That Luang where he was cremated in 1959. It was built on the chassis of a six-wheel truck by the sculptor, Thid Tan. On top of the carriage sit several sandalwood urns, none of which contain royal ashes. Originally the urns would have held the bodies of the deceased in a foetal position until cremation. The mosaics inside the chapel were never finished but the exterior is decorated with some almost erotic scenes from the *Ramakien* (the local version of the *Ramayana*), sculpted in enormous panels of teak wood and covered with gold leaf.

## Wat Visunnarat (Wat Wisunarat) and That Makmo
ⓘ *Daily 0800-1700; 10,000 kip.*

This is better known as Wat Visoun and is on the south side of Mount Phousi. It is a replica of the original wooden building, constructed in 1513, which had been the oldest building in Luang Prabang, until it was destroyed by marauding Chinese tribes. The sim is virtually a museum of religious art, with numerous 'Calling to the Rain' Buddha statues: most are more than 400 years old and have been donated over the years by locals. Wat Visoun also contains the largest Buddha in the city and old stelae engraved with Pali scriptures (called *hiu chaluk*). The big stupa, commonly known as That Makmo ('melon stupa'), was built by Queen Visounalat in 1504. It is of Sinhalese influence with a smaller stupa at each corner, representing the four elements.

## Wat Phra Maha That
Close to the **Hotel Phousi** on Phothisarath, this is a typical Luang Prabang wat, built in the 1500s and restored at the beginning of this century. The ornamentation of the doors and windows of the sim merit attention, with their graceful, golden figures from the Phra lak phra lam (the *Ramayana*). The pillars, ornamented with massive nagas, are also in traditional Luang Prabang style and reminiscent of certain styles adopted in Thailand.

South of Wat That Luang, Wat Manolom was built by the nobles of Luang Prabang to entomb the ashes of King Samsenthai (1373-1416) and is notable for its large armless bronze Buddha statue, one of the oldest Lao images of the Buddha, which dates back to 1372 and weighs two tonnes. Locals maintain that the arm was removed during a skirmish between Siamese and French forces during the latter part of the 19th century. While it is not artistically significant, the temple – or at least the site – is thought to be the oldest in the city, dating back, so it is said, to 1375 and the reign of Fa Ngum.

## Wat Pa Phon Phao and Wat Phra That Chedi

ⓘ *3 km northeast of town, near Ban Phanom. Daily 0800-1000, 1300-1630; donation expected.*

Outside town, Wat Pa Phon Phao is a forest meditation centre renowned for the teachings of its famous abbot, Ajahm Saisamut, one of the most popular monks in Lao history. More famous to tourists, though, is Wat Phra That Chedi, known as the Peace Pagoda. It looks as though it is made of pure gold from a distance but is rather disappointing close up. The wat was started in 1959 but was only completed in 1988; the names of donors are inscribed on pillars inside. It is modelled on the octagonal Shwedagon Pagoda in Yangon (Rangoon) and its inner walls are festooned with gaily painted frescoes of macabre allegories. Less grotesque paintings, extending right up to the fifth floor, document the life of the Buddha. On the second level, it is possible to duck through a tiny opening to admire the Blue Indra statues and the view of Luang Prabang.

## Traditional Arts and Ethnology Centre

ⓘ *Ban Khamyong, T071-253364, www.taeclaos.org, Tue-Sun 0900-1800, 20,000 kip.*

A fantastic museum dedicated to the various ethnic groups in Laos. This non-profit centre has a permanent exhibition featuring fantastic photographs, religious artefacts, clothing, household objects and handicrafts. Within the exhibition there is a focus on the Hmong and their New Year celebrations; the Khmu and their baskets and art of backstrap looms; the Mien Yao embroidery and Lanten Taoist religious ceremonies, the Tai Dam bedding and Tai Lue culture. Truly this museum is a must-see in Luang Prabang – particularly for those that are venturing further north to go trekking. Attached to the centre is a handicraft shop that directly supports ethnic artisan communities. There's also a café and a small library.

# Around Luang Prabang

### Pak Ou caves → *Colour map 1, B3.*

ⓘ *US$1, free for children. Torches are available but candles make it possible to see reasonably well after your eyes have become accustomed to the dark. A boat trip from Luang Prabang is the best way to reach the caves. Rest houses, tables and a basic toilet are available.*

The Pak Ou Caves are perhaps the most popular excursion from Luang Prabang and are located 25 km upstream from the city, set in the side of a limestone cliff opposite the mouth of the Mekong's Nam Ou tributary (Pak Ou means 'Mouth of the Ou'). The two caves are studded with thousands of wood and gold Buddha images – 2500 in the lower cave and 1500 in the upper – and are one of the main venues for Pi Mai in April, when hundreds make the pilgrimage upriver from Luang Prabang.

The two sacred caves were supposedly discovered by King Setthathirat in the 16th century but it is likely that the caverns were associated with spirit (*phi*) worship before the arrival of Buddhism in Laos. For years the caves, which locals still believe to be the home of guardian spirits, were inhabited by monks.

# Kwang Si Falls → *Colour map 1, B3.*

ⓘ *30 km south Luang Prabang; 20,000 kip, parking 2500 kip. There are public toilets and changing rooms. Travel agents run tours or you can charter a tuk-tuk for about US$15 return. Slow boats take 1 hr down and 2 hrs back upriver, via Ban Muang Khai (a pretty little village), where it is necessary to take a tuk-tuk for the last 6 km or so to the falls.*

These waterfalls are on a tributary of the Mekong. The trip to the falls is almost as scenic as the cascades themselves, passing through small Hmong and Khmu villages and vivid, green, terraced rice paddies. The falls are stunningly beautiful, misty cascades flowing over limestone formations, which eventually collect in several tiered, turquoise pools. Best of all, and despite appearances, it's still possible to take the left-hand path halfway up the falls and strike out through the pouring torrents and dripping caves to the heart of the waterfall. Note that swimming is only permitted in designated pools and, as the Lao swim fully clothed, you should wear modest swimwear and bring a sarong.

# Hoykhua Waterfall (Tad Hoykhua)

ⓘ *14 km west of Luang Prabang in Ban Pakleung.*

Beautiful two-tiered cascades that plummet 50 m, with a deep pool at the bottom. There are several Hmong and Khmu villages in the vicinity. To get to the falls cross the Mekong by boat at Tha Heua (boat station) in Luang Prabang to Xiang Men Village and then travel the rest by road. There are three bungalows here at **Tad Hoykhua Guesthouse,** T020-557 0825.

**Laos** Northern Laos  Luang Prabang & around  Listings

# ⏺ Sleeping

**Luang Prabang** *p416, maps p416 and p418*
Accommodation in Luang Prabang continues to expand at the rate of knots. There were a few new places in development at the time of publication worth keeping an eye out for, in particular a new hotel from the **Amman** chain which will be in the old hospital and will probably be completed in 2008.

**LL La Residence Phou Vao**, on a hill slightly out of town, T071-2125303, www.residencephouvao.com. Best hotel in town by a mile. Every little detail in this plush hotel is perfect, from the fragrance of frangipani that wafts through the foyer, to the carefully lit pool with lines of lamps. Massive, beautiful rooms with lounge area, fresh fruit and a simply divine bathroom. A luxury hotel through and through. In the low season they drop their rates by about US$100.

**L Three Nagas Boutique Hotel (Auberge les 3 Nagas)**, Sakkaline Rd, T071-253888, www.3nagas.com. Housed in a beautifully restored building, with an annexe across the road, this boutique hotel is a running contender for best room in town. Attention to detail is what sets this hotel apart: from the 4-poster bed covered with local fabrics to the large deep-set bathtub with natural handmade beauty products. Private balconies or rooms leading onto a stunning courtyard. There's a lovely sitting area in each room, plus traditional *torchis* walls and teak floors. Breakfast (included) is served in the fantastic café downstairs. Internet facilities for those travelling with laptop.

**A Ancient Luang Prabang**, Sisavangvong Rd, T071-212264, www.ancientluangprabang.com. 12 fantastically designed open-plan rooms featuring a big modern bathtub (separate toilet). The perfect romantic retreat for couples but not the place to bunk down with your mother. At US$65 these rooms represent good value. Lovely wooden furnishings. Café downstairs with Wi-Fi and a good range of coffees including frappés.

**A Le Calao Inn**, river road, T071-212100, www.calaoinn.laopdr.com. Enclosed by yellow walls, this Portuguese/French colonial (1902) building boasts beautiful rooms in an incomparable position overlooking the Mekong. The balcony view is a real plus, so ensure you ask for a room with water views.

**A Maison Souvannaphoum**, Phothisarath, T071-212200, www.coloursofangsana. com/souvannaphoum/. Formally Prince Souvanna's residence, this place really is fit for royalty. There are 4 spacious suites and 18 rooms, with a/c, aromatherapy burners and special treats left in the rooms. The service is top-notch.

**A Pack Luck**, opposite L'Éléphant, T071-253373, packluck@hotmail.com. This boutique hotel has 5 rooms that you couldn't swing a cat in but are tastefully decorated with beautiful fabrics and have bathrooms with deep slate bathtubs.

**A Villa Maydou**, set very close to the grounds of Wat Meuna, T071-254601, www.villamaydou.com. Slightly on the expensive side but beautiful nonetheless. The hotel has a very evocative Buddhist feel due to its location right on the doorstep of Wat Meuna. The French-owned hotel is set in restored government buildings, originally built in 1925. Spacious airy a/c rooms simply decorated in a modern style with bathtub and minibar.

**A Villa Santi Hotel**, Sisavangvong Rd, T071-252157, www.villasantihotel.com. Almost an institution in Luang Prabang, this is a restored house from the early 20th century that served as the private residence of the first King Sisavong's wife and then Princess Manilai. It's a charming place, full of character and efficiently run but it is starting to get a it run down. There are 11 traditional rooms in the old building, each of a different size, and 14 newer rooms, with baths and showers, in a stylishly-built annexe. The daughter of the official royal cook rustles up mouth watering French cuisine in the **Princess Restaurant** and there are attractive seating areas inthe garden, lobby or on the balcony.

**A-B Sala Luang Prabang**, 102/6 Ounkham Rd, T071-252460, www.salaprabang. salalao.com. Very chic, renovated 100-year-old building overlooking the Mekong. Nice use of exposed beams and stone inlay in communal areas. Rooms have a minimalist, up-to-date edge with a/c, modern bathrooms, and doors either opening onto a small courtyard or river balcony (more expensive). Bus, car and bicycle hire available.

**A-C The Apsara**, Kingkitsarath, T071-212420, www.theapsara.com. Ivan Scholte, wine connoisseur and antique collector, has done a perfect job on this establishment. It oozes style. The stunningly beautiful rooms are themed by colour, with 4-poster beds, changing screen, big bathtub and lovely balcony. Very romantic with a modern twist. The rooms in second building are equally magnificent and have large terrazzo showers you could fit an elephant in. The foyer and lovely restaurant (see Eating) are decorated with Vietnamese lanterns, Burmese offering boxes and modern art. Room rate includes breakfast. Ivan has some very exciting plans in the pipeworks so watch this space. Get in early, this popular place gets booked up in advance.

**A-C Sayo Guesthouse**, Sotikoumman Rd, T071-252614, sayo@laotel.com. A lovely hotel set in colonial mansion. The front rooms are beautifully and tastefully decorated with local fabrics and woodwork, polished wooden floors and furniture, and they boast a fantastic view over Wat Xieng Muang – you can watch the monks carving, painting and woodworking. The back rooms aren't as good value but are still recommended.

**B Ammata Guesthouse**, T071-212175, phetmanyp@yahoo.com.au. Very popular guesthouse with largish rooms decorated simply and stylishly with wooden furniture and polished floorboards. Hot water and en suite bathroom.

**B Oui Guesthouse**, at the end of the peninsula in Ban Khille on Sukkaserm, T071-252374, ouisguesthouse@gmail.com. Charming little guesthouse with sparkling new rooms with polished floorboards, hot water, TV and fridge. Nicely decorated with local artefacts. Fantastic wine bar next door.

**B-D Silichit Guesthouse**, just off Ounkham Rd, T071-212758. Despite the dubious sounding name, this clean guesthouse is excellent value and well located. Comfortable rooms with fan, en suite bathroom and hot water. The very friendly owners speak English and French, and often invite guests to sit down for a family dinner or have a Beer Lao. As with most budget places, prices drop dramatically in the low season.

**E Vanvisa Villa**, T071-212925, vandara1@hotmail.com. Brightly coloured guesthouse down a quaint street. This is a little gem, with teak floors, large, characterful and immaculate rooms and friendly owners. The downstairs has beautiful handicrafts and antiques. It's a bit run down but has a homely feel.

**E-F Jaliya**, Phamahapasaman Rd, T071-252154. The ever-popular **Jaliya** has a range of bungalow-type rooms on offer, with varied facilities, from shared bathrooms and fan through to a/c and TV, so take a look around. Relaxing garden area with friendly pet deer. Bicycle and motorbike rental.

### Hotels out of Luang Prabang

**C Thongbay Guesthouse**, Ban Vieng May, 3 km southeast of the centre of Luang Prabang, T071-253234, www.thongbbay-guesthouses.com. Absolutely stunning set-up of modern bungalows overlooking the Nam Khan. 12 bungalows including 2 extra large family-sized ones. Beautiful tropical garden with a small pond as a centrepiece. The rooms overlooking the river are the best, affording fantastic views of the laid-back rural life. Bungalows have a fridge, 4-poster bed and hot water. Popular with tour groups so advanced booking is necessary. Recommended.

---

## ● Eating

**Luang Prabang** *p416, maps p416 and p418*
Note that, as Luang Prabang has a curfew; most places won't stay open past 2200.

The most famous local delicacy is *khai pehn*, dried river weed, mainly from the Nam Khan, which is mixed with sesame and eaten nationwide. *Chao bong*, a mildly hot pimento purée, is also popular throughout the country. Other delicacies include: *phak nam*, a watercress that grows around waterfalls and is commonly used in soups and salads; *mak kham kuan*, tamarind jam, and *mak nat kuan*, pineapple jam. One of the best local culinary experiences is to grab some Lao takeaway food from the

night market that runs off **Sisavangvong Rd**, 1600-2200. Here you can pick up fresh spring rolls (*nem nip*), papaya salad (*tom som*), sticky rice (*cow niao*), the local delicacy Luang Prabang sausage (*Sai Hua*), BBQ chicken on a stick (*gai*) or fish (*pa*), dried buffalo (*sin savanh*) and dried river weed. There are also a number of cheap buffets where you can get a selection of local curries and dishes. If you don't want your food too hot ask for '*bo pet*'.

**†††-†† L'Éléphant**, Ban Vat Nong, T071-252482, contact@elephantrestau.com. About as fine as dining gets in Luang Prabang. Very upmarket and utterly delectable cuisine. Pan-fried fillet of snapper, with capers and basil-flavoured mash is delicious, as are the simmered scallops. Also a number of Lao dishes. There are 3 set menus and an extensive wine list.

**††-† The Apsara**, see Sleeping. Beautifully decorated restaurant offering modern Lao/Thai cuisine. Try their delicious red curry cream soup with lentils and smoked duck or braised beef shin Chinese style. Great fish cakes. Good value.

**††-† Blue Lagoon**, beside the Royal Palace, www.blue-lagoon-cafe.com, T071-253698. This restaurant offers a great selection of delicious hearty European meals – especially Swiss-inspired meals such as the fondue chinoise. Great steaks, pasta and ice creams. Indoor and outdoor seating in comfortable candlelit garden setting.

**††-† Couleur Café/Restaurant**, Ban Vat Nong, T020-5621064. The French expats in town have nothing but praise for this place with its French and Lao meals and ambient setting. Good wine. This is the place for the carnivores as it has become renowned for its steaks.

**† Dao Fa**, Sisavangvong Rd, T071-215651, www.daofa-bistro.com. Great selection of teas and coffees, fab ice creams and tasty home-made pasta. The latter is the real draw and is recommended. Brightly decorated space with pavement seating.

**† Morning Glory**, Sakkaline Rd, 0800-1600. Small but cosy Thai restaurant decorated

---

● For an explanation of sleeping and eating price codes used in this guide, see inside the front cover. Other relevant information is found in Essentials, see pages 29-32.

with the proprietor's photographs and paintings. Intimate open-style kitchen serving up fantastic home-style meals – great juices, breakfasts and curries. Try the *Tom Kha Gai* and zesty juice.

¶ **Tamarind**, facing Wat Nong, T020-7770484, www.tamarindlaos.com, Mon-Sat 1100-1800. Brilliant restaurant offering modern Lao cuisine; an utterly exceptional dining experience. Try the five-bites (the Lao equivalent to tapas), the pumpkin soup is to die for and the tamarind juice is exceptional. Even better than their à la carte menu are the 'dining experiences' such as the traditional Lao Celebration meal 'Pun Pa', which includes succulent marinated fish and purple sticky rice dessert (60,000 kip per person, minimum 2 people), or the Adventurous Lao Gourmet degustation menu, which comes with clear explanations of what each dish is. They also do **market tours** with in-depth explanations of Lao delicacies (advance booking is essential) and can organize picnics. The owners Joy and Caroline have been receiving accolades from around the region.

¶ **Tamnak Lao**, Sisavangvong Rd, opposite **Villa Santi**, T071-252525. Brilliant restaurant, serving modern Lao cuisine, with a strong Thai influence. Very popular with tour groups. The freshest ingredients are used: try fish and coconut wrapped in banana leaf or pork-stuffed celery soup. Atmospheric surroundings, particularly upstairs, and exceptional service. Best for dinner. Unmissable.

¶ **View Khaem Khong**, Ounkham Rd, T071-212726. The most popular of the dining establishments along the river. Good for a beer at sunset. Tasty Luang Prabang sausage and *laap*.

### Cafés and bakeries

**Café Ban Vat Sene**, Sakkaline Rd. Great French food, more of a restaurant than a café, upmarket, great for breakfast.
**Joma**, Sisavangvong Rd, T071-252292. Serves an utterly delicious array of comfort foods. If you're planning a trek or boat trip get yout picnic food here.
**L'Étranger**, Kingkitsarath Rd, T020-54717036. This is a great little bookshop-cum-café. Outstanding breakfasts.

Books are rented here for 5000 kip per day. A movie is shown daily at 1900.

## 🍸 Bars and clubs

**Luang Prabang** *p416, maps p416 and p418*
**L'Éléphant**, **La Résidence Phou Vao** and **Apsara**, provide attractive settings for a drink. A sunset beer at the restaurants overlooking the river is divine. After everything closes between 2200 and 2300 most locals either head to the bowling alley for a beer (open until 0300) or have a bowl of soup and a cold beverage on Phou Vao Rd at one of the many *pho* noodle shops.

**Dao Fa nightclub** on the way to the South Bus Station. Extremely popular with locals, plays Asian dance music.
**Hive Bar**, Kingkitsarath Rd, next to **L'Étranger**. Luang Prabang's most happening bar-club is good for a dance, though it has become quieter now th at the competition around it has started to grow.
**Khily Wine Bar**, tucked away next door to Oui Guesthouse at the end of the peninsula. A secret hotspot for locals. This intimate bar has high chairs and a long bar stocked with an extensive selection of *lao-lao* and wine. Great for a quiet drink.
**Khob Jai**, Kingkitsarath Rd, opposite **Hive Bar** (sometimes known as **LPQ**). A dedicated gay bar but open to all and sundry.
**Lao Lao Garden**, Kingkitsarath Rd. A tiered landscaped terrace, with low lighting, that's become a favourite backpacker haunt with cheap, delicious cocktails.
**Pack Luck**, Sisavangvong Rd. For a more upmarket drink, this cosy wine bar has a great selection of tipples and well-selected wines. This modern establishment is high on atmosphere, with comfy beanbags, modern art adorning its walls and candlelit tables.

## 🎭 Entertainment

**Luang Prabang** *p416, maps p416 and p418*
**Theatre and dance**
Traditional dance performances are held Mon, Wed and Sat at 1800, at the **Royal Palace**; US$6-15.

## ❂ Festivals and events

**Luang Prabang** *p416, maps p416 and p418*
**Apr** Pi Mai (Lao New Year; movable) is
the time when the tutelary spirits of the
old year are replaced by those of the new.
It has special significance in Luang Prabang,
with certain traditions celebrated in the city
that are no longer observed in Vientiane.
It lasts 11 days.
**May** Vien Thiene (movable). Candlelit
festival.
**Sep** Boat races. Boats are raced by the
people living in the vicinity of each wat.

## ⦿ Shopping

**Luang Prabang** *p416, maps p416 and p418*
**Ban Khilly Paper Gallery**, Sakkaline St,
T071-212611. A *sa* crafts centre (*sa* is a
rough, leaf-effect paper). Sells scrolls,
paper lanterns and cards and beautifully
decorated and painted paper.
**Caruso Gallery**, Sisavangvong Rd
(towards the **Three Nagas Boutique Hotel**)
stunning but expensive wood furniture
and artefacts.
**Naga Creations**, Sisavangvong Rd,
T071-212775. A large collection of jewellery
and trinkets, combining Lao silver with
quality semi-precious stones. Both
contemporary and classic pieces. Some
truly innovative work by the jeweller
**Fabrice**, including beautiful use of beetle
wings (the same style that were once used
to adorn royal clothing).
**Ock Pop Tok**, near L'Éléphant restaurant,
T071-253219. **Ock Pop Tok**, which literally
translates as 'East meets West', truly
incorporates the best of both worlds in
beautiful designs and fabrics. It specializes
in naturally dyed silk, which is of a much
better quality than synthetically dyed silk
as it doesn't run. Clothes, household items,
hangings and custom-made orders are
also available (if ordered well in advance).
Check out the **Fibre2Fabric** gallery next
door to see the stories behind the
fabulous creations.
**Patthana Boupha Antique Gallery**, Ban
Visoun, T071-212262. This little gem can
be found in a partitioned-off area in a
fantastic colonial building. Antique
silverware and jewellery, Buddhas, old

photos and fine textiles. Less common are
furniture and household items. Reasonable
prices. Often closed, so ring beforehand.
**Satri Lao Silk**, Sisavangvong Rd, T071-
219295. Truly beautiful silks and handicrafts
for sale. Can sometimes be slightly overpriced, but definitely worth a look.

### Markets
The **night market** sprawls down several
blocks off Sisavangvong Rd (this market has
been moving around the last few years but
is expected to return to Sisavangvong Rd).
Daily 1700-2230. Hundreds of villagers flock
to the market to sell their handicrafts,
ranging from silk scarves through to
embroidered quilt covers and paper albums.
The market shouldn't be missed and most
visitors won't leave without a great souvenir
or two.
**Phousy market**, 1.5 km from the centre of
town. This market is a real gem: aside from
the usual fruit and vegetables, it is a fantastic
place to pick up quality silk garments.
Pre-made silk clothes are sold here for a
fraction of the price of the shops in town.
The clothes just need the odd button sewn
on here or the hem taken up there. Make
sure that you are very detailed with
instructions though and ensure the same
colour thread is used in any alterations.
**Talat Dala**, housed in a market building in
the middle of town on the corner of
Setthathirat and Chao Sisophon roads, at
the time of publication the market was
being gloriously revamped to become a
major market for artisans and jewellers to
sell their wares.

### Silver
There are several Lao silversmiths around
the Nam Phou area (fountain), where you
can watch the artisans ply their trade.
**Thit Peng**, signposted almost opposite
Wat That, is a workshop and small shop
with jewellery and pots.

## ▲ Activities and tours

**Luang Prabang** *p416, maps p416 and p418*
**Cookery classes**
There are a number of classes offered in
Luang Prabang. The cooking classes are
ordered in preference.

**Tamarind**, www.tamarindlaos.com, facing Wat Nong, T020-777 0484. This successful restaurant has been running specialized custom-made classes for 1 or 2 people at a time. However, due to their immense popularity they will expand these courses to larger groups. Recommended.

**Tamnak Lao**, T071-252525, www.laocookingcourse.com, US$25 per person for 1-day cooking class, including shopping at the markets.

**Tum Tum Cheng**, Sakkaline Rd, T071-253388, www.tumtumcheng.com. Mon-Sat. Popular cooking classes operating since 2001. 1 day, US$25; 2 day, US$45; 3 day, US$60. Advanced bookings are required.

### Elephants tours and activities

**Elephant Park Project**, 25 km from Luang Prabang (visits and activities can be organized through **Tiger Trails** office on Sisavangvong Rd, T071-252655, www.laos-adventures.com). This has been established in conjunction with Tiger Trails in Luang Prabang. They have bought old elephants that were chained up in Hongsa as they were no longer useful for hauling timber. In order to keep the old elephants active, the operators run a number of activities. Tourists can participate in up to 25 activities at the elephant park, including experiencing life as a *mahout* (elephant keeper), washing the elephants or trekking with them. There are a few other similar elephant park projects but these are pale imitations whichhave compromised on quality.

### Exhibitions and galleries

**Fibre2Fabric**, 71 Ban Vat Nong (next door to **Ock Pop Tok**), T071-254761, www.fibre2fabric.org. A fantastic gallery exhibiting textiles and a display on the culture surrounding the textiles of different ethnic groups. Exhibition with photography, weaving and explanations of local ethnic customs and cultures associated with textile production. Local weavers often on hand to explain the processes.

**Kop Noi**, Ban Aphay, www.kopnoi.com. This little shop has a rotating exhibition on the second storey of their shop. They also exhibit a selection of photographs from renowned Lao photographer Sam Sisombat.

**Kinnaly Gallery**, Sakkaline Rd, T020-555 7737. Gallery featuring photographic work and local art.

### Sauna and massage

**Aroma Spa**, Sisavangvong Rd, T020-7611255. Another mid-priced spa offering aromatherapy, facials, body scrubs, etc.

**Khmu Spa**, Sisavangvong Rd, T071-212092. A range of cheaply priced massages including the Khmu massage (gentler, lighter strokes), Lao massage (stretching, cracking and pressure points) and foot massage. Also has herbal sauna. Open until 2200.

**Maison Souvannaphoum** (see Sleeping). A spa with a range of luxurious and expensive treatments. For sheer indulgence.

**Red Cross Sauna**, opposite Wat Visunnarat, reservations T071-212303. Daily 0900-2100 (1700-2100 for sauna). Massage 30,000 kip per hr, traditional Lao herbal sauna 10,000 kip. Bring your own towel or sarong. Profits go to the Lao Red Cross.

**Spa Garden**, Ban Phonheauang, T071-212325, spagardenlpb@hotmail.com. More upmarket. Offers a wide selection of massage and beauty treatments including aromatherapy massage US$12 per hr, sports body massage, facial treatments, skin detox US$25 per hr. The best value for money in luxury massages, pedicure, manicure all set in a relaxing building with oil burners, wind chimes and dolphin-esque sounds playing in the background. Packages between US$5 and US$38.

**The Spa** at La Residence Phou Vao www.residencephouvao.com, T071-212530. Offers 3-hr massage courses, US$190 for 2 people. This includes a 1-hr massage for each person, the class, a handbook and oils.

### Tour operators

**All Laos Service**, Sisavangvong Rd. Large successful travel agency organizing ticketing and travel services.

**Green Discovery**, T071-212093, www.greendiscovery.com. A range of rafting and kayaking trips that pass through grade 1 and 2 rapids. Cycling trips around Luang Prabang and surrounding countryside. Homestays, rafting, kayaking, trips to Pak Ou caves, etc.

**Tiger Trail**, Sisavangvong Rd, T071-252655, www.tigertrail-laos.com. Adventure specialists: elephant treks, trekking, mountain biking tours, rafting, rock climbing, etc.

### Weaving

**Weaving Centre**, 2 km out of town on the river (bookings at **Ban Vat Nong Gallery**, T071-253219, info@ockpoptok.com). The team behind the fabulous creations at **Ock Pop Tok** have opened a weaving centre. Half-day dyeing classes introduce students to the world of silk dyes (US$35). A variety of 1- to 3-day weaving classes are offered at US$35 per day. Tailor-made courses are also available. Classes are run by professional weavers and their English-speaking assistants. At the time of publication a small café was going to be opened on the site.

## ⊙ Transport

### Luang Prabang *p416, maps p416 and p418*
**Air**
Luang Prabang International Airport (LPQ) about 4 km from town, T071-212172/3. **Lao Airlines**, Phamahapasaman Rd, T071-212172, has 3 daily connections with **Vientiane**, 40 mins, and a service to **Chiang Mai**, Pakse and Phonsavanh. They also run 3 flights a week between **Bangkok** and Luang Prabang. These flights are notoriously prone to change so check schedule well in advance. **Bangkok Airways** runs daily flights to **Bangkok**. In the high season (from November onwards) **Siem Reap Airways** flies to **Siem Reap** via Pakse.

Early morning departures are often delayed during the rainy season, as dense cloud can sometimes make Luang Prabang airport inoperable until about 1100. Airline tickets are more often than not substantially cheaper from travel agents (see Tour operators, above) than from the actual airline. Confirm bookings a day in advance and arrive at the airport early, as flights have been known to depart as soon as they're full.

### Bicycle
Bikes can be rented for about US$1 per day from most guesthouses.

**Boat**
**Tha Heua Mea Pier** is the most popular departure point and has a blackboard listing all the destinations and prices available (daily 0730-1130 and 1300-1600). Prices are largely dependent on the price of gasoline. There is also a dock at **Ban Don** (15 mins north of town by tuk-tuk, US$1-2).

**To Houei Xai/Pak Beng** The 2-day boat trip down the Mekong between Houei Xai and Pak Beng has become a rite of passage for travellers in Southeast Asia. There are a range of boat options to suit the flashpacker to the backpacker.

The **slow boat** to Houei Xai, leaves from the boat pier on Khem Khong Rd called the Tha Heua Mea pier, 2 days, with a break in Pak Beng after 6-7 hrs on the 1st day. It is US$11 for each leg of the trip and almost all travel agents sell tickets. It's often packed to the brim so wear something comfortable and bring some padding to sit on. Seats are usually basic wooden benches though you may luck out with one that has bus seats. The trip from Luang Prabang to Houei Xai (via Pak Beng overnight) is usually less busy than in the other direction. (If the boat to Pak Beng is full, you can charter your own for about US$200-300.) Tickets for the onward trip to Houei Xai, can be purchased in Pak Beng. Take a good book and a grab some goodies from one of the bakeries to take on board. Most boats will have a vendor selling basic drinks. The boat usually leaves between 0800 and 0900 (changeable so check) but it is necessary to get there early to secure yourself a good seat.

A mid-range option is the **Nagi**, a more comfortable, quicker boat than the regular slow boat. From Houei Xai the Nagi makes the trip to Luang Prabang in one day. The boat departs at 0830 and arrives at approximately 1730. Going upstream from Luang Prabang to Houei Xai the journey takes 2 days. Hot food and cold drinks are served on board. From Houei Xai to Luang Prabang – 1 day US$80; From Luang Prabang to Houei Xai (via Pak Beng) US$70 (not including accommodation in Pak Beng where you have to stay overnight).

The most luxurious way to make the trip is on the **Luangsay Cruise**, office on Sisavangvong Rd, T071-252553, www.asian-oasis.com, which makes the trip in 2 days and 1 night, stopping over at Pak Ou Caves en route and staying overnight at their luxurious lodge in Pak Beng. The boat is extra comfortable and has lounges, a stocked bar and lots of board games. Very popular in high season and will need to be booked 6 months in advance. In low season the boat runs from Houei Xai to Luang Prabang on Mon and Fri and in the opposite direction on Wed and Sat (US$243 twin/US$300 single). In the high season the boat runs from Houei Xai to Luang Prabang on Mon, Thu and Fri, and in the opposite direction Luang Prabang to Houei Xai on Tue, Wed and Sat (US$358 twin/ US$422 single). In the low season it may be possible to get a standby rate if there is availability.

Speedboats (which are not recommended) depart from Ban Don to **Houei Xai** (on the Thai border; see page 434), US$30, around 6 hrs, with a short break in **Pak Beng**. Tickets are available from most travel agents. The boats are horribly noisy and dangerous (numerous fatalities have been reported from boats jack-knifing when hitting waves). Ear plugs are recommended and ensure boatmen provide a helmet and life jacket.

A few boats travel up the Nam Ou to **Nong Khiaw**. However, these are infrequent, especially when the river is low. The journey usually takes 6 hrs to Nong Khiaw, 120,000 kip. The Nam Ou joins the Mekong near the Pak Ou Caves, so it is possible to combine a journey with a visit to the caves en route. The irregular travel dates to Nong Khiaw are posted on a board outside the boat pier or ask one of the travel agents on Sisavangvong Rd when the next departure is. It is possible to charter a boat for 1-6 people for US$150. Speedboats to Nong Khiaw sometimes leave from Ban Don, expect to pay 160,000 kip. These boats are hazardous, uncomfortable and not environmentally friendly.

### Bus/truck

The northern bus terminal is for north-bound traffic and the southern for traffic to/from the south. Always double-check which terminal your bus is using, as unscheduled changes are possible.

**From the northern terminal**  To **Luang Namtha**, daily 0900 and 1730, 10 hrs, usually via **Udomxai**, 70,000 kip. The 1730 bus has usually come from Vientiane and is often full. An alternative option is to break the journey by catching the bus to **Udomxai**, daily 0900 and 1130, 5 hrs, 45,000 kip, and then continuing on to Luang Namtha in the afternoon. There are also daily departures (usually in the morning) to **Houei Xai** on the Thai/Lao border, 11-12 hrs, 100,000 kip. A VIP bus to Houei Xai passes through on Mon, Wed, Fri and Sun, 1000, 10 hrs, 160,000 kip There is a very long bus journey to **Xam Neua**, 1630, they say it takes 14 hrs but it can take up to 20 hrs, 100,000 kip. **Phongsali** 1600, 13-15 hrs, 100,000 kip. To Nong Khiaw, by songthaew, regular departures usually in the morning, 32,000 kip.

**From the southern terminal**  There are up to 8 daily buses to **Vientiane**, though scheduled departures tend to decline in the low season, 10-11 hrs, 90,000 kip; most of these buses stop in **Vang Vieng**, 6 hrs, 75,000 kip. VIP buses to Vientiane depart 0800, 0900, 9 hrs, 115,000 kip; both these services stop in Vang Vieng, 100,000 kip.

To **Phonsavanh**, daily 0830, 8-9 hrs, 85,000 kip. It should cost 10,000-15,000 kip to get to the centre of town from the station.

### Saamlor and tuk-tuk

Lots around town which can be hired to see the sights or to go to nearby villages. A short stint across town should cost about 10,000 kip per person, but expect to pay 20,000 kip for anything more than 1 km. Most of the nearby excursions will cost US$5-10.

## ❶ Directory

**Luang Prabang** *p416, maps p416 and p418*
**Banks** Lao Development Bank, 65 Sisavangvong Rd, Mon-Sat 0830-1200, 1330-1530, will change US$/Thai ฿/TCs into dollars or kip, but doesn't accept credit cards. Banque pour le Commerce Exterieur Lao (BCEL), Sisavangvong Rd, Mon-Sat 0830-1200, 1330-1530; all transactions in kip, will exchange Thai ฿, US$, AU$, UK£, Euro and TCs, also offers cash advances on Visa cards. They also have an ATM but at the time of publication this was only for MasterCard.

Many of the jewellery stalls in the old market, plus restaurant and tourist shop owners, will change US$ and Thai ฿. Many of the travel agencies will do credit card advances if you get stuck after hours without money but charge a whopping 6-8% commission **Internet** There are a concentration of places on Sisavangvong Rd. **Medical services** The main hospital, on Setthathirat, T071-252049 is only useful for minor ailments. For anything major you're better off getting a flight to Bangkok.

There are a few reasonably well-equipped pharmacies towards Villa Santi on Sisavangvong Rd. **Post and telephone** The post and telephone office is on the corner of Chau Fa Ngum and Setthathirat, Mon-Fri 0830-1730, Sat 0830-1200, express mail service, international telephone facilities. Hotels and some guesthouses allow international calls from reception (about US$5 a min). It is dramatically cheaper to make international calls from one of the internet cafés, which usually have Skype.

# Far north

*The misty, mountain scenery of the far north conjures up classic Indochina imagery of striking rice terraces, golden, thatched huts and dense, tropical forests, all dissected by a cross-hatching of waterways. Here life is beautifully interwoven with the ebb and flow of the rivers. The mighty Mekong forges its way through picturesque towns, such as Pak Beng and Houei Xai, affording visitors a wonderful glimpse of riverine life, while, to the east, the Nam Ou attracts visitors to Nong Khiaw and, the latest traveller hot spot, Muang Ngoi Neua.*

*The wonderful upland areas are home to around 40 different ethnic groups, including the Akha, Hmong, Khmu and Yao, and it's not surprising that the country's best trekking is also found here.* ›› *For Sleeping, Eating and other listings, see pages 437-445.*

## Luang Namtha and around ⊞⊘▲⊟☺ ›› *pp437-445.*
*Colour map 1, A2 and B2.*

This area has firmly established itself as a major player in Laos' ecotourism industry, primarily due to the **Nam Ha Ecotourism Project**, which was established in 1993 by NTA Lao and UNESCO to help preserve Luang Namtha's cultural and environmental heritage in the Nam Ha National Protected Area. The Nam Ha NPA is one of the largest protected areas in Laos and consists of mountainous areas dissected by several rivers It is home to at least 38 species of large mammal, including the black-cheeked crested gibbon, tiger and clouded leopard, and over 300 bird species, including the stunning Blythe's kingfisher.

### Udomxai → *Colour map 1, B2.*
Heading northwest from Luang Prabang, travellers will reach Udomxai, the capital of Udomxai Province. It's a hot and dusty town, with a truck-stop atmosphere that doesn't enamour it to tourists and unfortunately, the other bad elements that come with major transport thoroughfares seem to be raising their heads here too, such as prostitution and increased HIV/AIDS. However, the town does make a decent stop-off point at a convenient junction; it's one of the biggest settlements in northern Laos and has excellent facilities. One only has to look around at the presence of Chinese flags on shop fronts to get an inkling of the large presence of Chinese workers and businesses in town.

Luang Namtha Province has witnessed the rise and decline of various Tai Kingdoms and now more than 35 ethnic groups reside in the province, making it the most ethnically diverse in the country. Principal minorities include Tai Lu, Tai Dam, Lanten, Hmong and Khmu. The provincial capital was obliterated during the war and the concrete structures erected since 1975 have little charm but there are a number of friendly villages in the area. As with all other minority areas it is advisable to visit villages with a local guide or endorsed tourism organization.

The **Luang Namtha Museum** ① *near the Kaystone Monument, daily 0800-1130, 1330-1630; 5000 kip.* (was undergoing renovations at the time of publication). The museum houses a collection of indigenous clothing and artefacts, agricultural tools, weapons, textiles and a collection of Buddha images, drums and gongs.

In the centre of town is a **night market** with a range of food stalls. It is only in its infancy but the local authorities have aspirations to expand the market to include ethnic handi- crafts, making it similar to the one in Luang Prabang.

## Surrounding villages

**Ban Nam Chang** is a Lanten village, 3 km along a footpath outside town; **Ban Lak Khamay** is quite a large Akha village 27 km from Luang Namtha on the road to Muang Sing. The settlement features a traditional Akha entrance; if you pass through this entrance you must visit a house in the village, or you are considered an enemy. Otherwise you can simply pass to one side of the gate but don't touch it. Other features of interest in Akha villages are the swing, located at the highest point in the village and used in the annual swing festival (you must not touch the swing), and the meeting house, where unmarried couples go to court and where newly married couples live until they have their own house. **Ban Nam Dee** is a small bamboo papermaking Lanten village about 6 km northeast of town. The name of the village means 'good water' and not surprisingly, if you continue on 1 km from Ban Nam Dee there's a waterfall. The trip to the village is stunning, passing through verdant rice paddies dotted with huts. A motorbike rather than a bicycle will be necessary to navigate these villages and sights, as the road can be very rocky. Villagers usually charge 3000 kip for access to the waterfall.

The small Tai Lue village of **Ban Khone Kam** is also worth a visit. The friendly villagers offer **homestays** here (30,000 kip per night, includes meals), for one or two nights. For trips between Luang Namtha and Houei Xai contact the **Luang Namtha Boat Station** ① *T086-211305,* or the environmentally friendly **Boat Landing Guesthouse** in Luang Namtha.

**Ban Vieng Nua** is a Tai Kolom village, 3 km from the centre of town, famous for its traditional house where groups can experience local dancing and a good luck baci ceremony (US$30 for the group). Contact the tourist information office to make a booking. Dinner can also be organized here at a cost of US$6 per head.

**Luang Namtha**

*To Muang Sing & Udomxai*

Luang Namtha Museum 🏛

Lao Telecom
BCEL
Bike Rental
Green Discovery

Luang Namtha Guide Service
Night Market

Morning Market

*To ⑩⑫, Boat Landing, Airport, Lao Airlines & Houei Xai*

N

100 metres
100 yards

**Sleeping** 
Boat Landing Guesthouse & Restaurant 12
Luang Namtha Guesthouse 7
Manychan Guesthouse 4
Vila Guesthouse 10
Zuela Guesthouse 5

**Eating** 
Banana 3
Coffee House 6
KNT Internet 5
Panda 2
Yamuna 4

Both Luang Namtha and Vieng Phouka are great bases from which to venture into the Nam Ha National Protected Area, one of a few remaining places on earth where the rare black-cheeked gibbon can be found. If you're lucky you can hear the wonderful singing of the gibbons in the morning. The 222,400 sq km conservation area encompasses more than 30 ethnic groups and 37 threatened mammal species. Organizations currently lead two- and three-day treks in the area for small groups of four to eight culturally sensitive travellers. Treks leave three to four times a week; check with the **Luang Namtha Guide Service Unit** or **Green Discovery** (see Tour operators, page 441) for departure days; an information session about the trek is given at the Guide's Office. The price will cover the cost of food, water, transportation, guides, lodging and the trekking permit. All the treks utilize local guides who have been trained to help generate income for their villages. Income for conservation purposes is also garnered from the fees for trekking permits into the area. ▸▸ *For further information, see Activities and tours, page 441.*

**Tubing** Several vendors on the main road offer inflated inner tubes for tubing on the Nam Ha River, though this is organized without the expertise in tubing and river awareness in other places in the country and is not always safe, particularly when the waters are high.

## Muang Sing and around → *Colour map 1, A2.*

Many visitors consider this peaceful valley to be one of the highlights of the north. The only way to get to Muang Sing is by truck or pickup from Luang Namtha. The road is asphalt but is sometimes broken and the terrain on this route is mountainous with dense forest. Muang Sing itself is situated on an upland plateau among misty, blue-green peaks. The town features some interesting old wooden and brick buildings and, unlike nearby Luang Namtha and several other towns in the north, it wasn't bombed close to oblivion during the struggle for Laos. Numerous hill peoples come to the market to trade, including Akha and Hmong tribespeople, along with Yunnanese, Tai Dam and Tai Lu.

**Muang Sing Ethnic Museum** ① *in the centre of town, Mon-Fri 0900-1200, 1300-1600; 5000 kip,* is a beautiful building housing a range of traditional tools, ethnic clothes, jewellery, instruments, religious artefacts and household items, like the loom. The building was once the royal residence of the Jao Fa (Prince), Phanya Sekong.

The population of the district is said to have trebled between 1992 and 1996, due to the resettlement of many minorities, either from refugee camps in Thailand or from highland areas of Laos and, as a result, it is one of the better places in northern Laos to visit ethnic villages. The town is predominantly Tai Lu but the district is 50% Akha, with a further 10% Tai Nua. The main activity for visitors is to hire bicycles and visit the villages that surround the town in all directions; several guesthouses have maps of the surrounding area and trekking is becoming increasingly popular. However, please do not undertake treks independently as it undermines the government's attempts to make tourism sustainable and minimize the impact on the culture of local villages. ▸▸ *For further information, see Activities and tours, page 441.*

From Muang Sing, trek uphill past **Phoutat Guesthouse** for 7 km up an 886-m hill to reach **That Xieng Tung**, the most sacred site in the area. The stupa was built in 1256 and is believed to contain Buddha's Adam's apple. It attracts lots of pilgrims in November for the annual full moon festival. There is a small pond near the stupa, which is also believed to be very auspicious: if it dries up it is considered very bad luck for Muang Sing. It is said that the pond once dried up and the whole village had no rice and starved. Most tourism operators will run to treks up to the stupa and will also stop at **Nam Keo** waterfall, a large cascade with a 10-m drop that trickles down into a little brook.

# Along the Mekong 🏠🚲⛰🏯 ›› *pp437-445. Colour map 1, B1 and B2.*

The slow boat along the Mekong between Houei Xai and Luang Prabang is a favourite option for visitors travelling to and from the Thai border. It's a charming trip through lovely scenery.

## Houei Xai → *Colour map 1, B1.*

Located southwest of Luang Namtha on the banks of the Mekong, Houei Xai is a popular crossing point to and from Thailand. Few people spend more than one night in the town. Boats run between here and Luang Prabang, two days' journey downstream, via Pak Beng. Most passengers arrive close to the centre at the passenger ferry pier. The vehicle ferry pier is 750 m further north (upstream). Although the petite, picturesque town is growing rapidly as links with Thailand intensify, it is still small and easy enough to get around on foot.

**Wat Chom Kha Out Manirath**, in the centre of town, is worth a visit for its views. The monastery was built at the end of the 19th century but, because it is comparatively well endowed, there has been a fair amount of re-building and renovation since then. There is also a large former French fort here called **Fort Carnot**, now used by the Lao army (and consequently out of bounds).

Most visitors who do stick around in Houei Xai do so to visit the **Gibbon Experience** ⓘ *To84-212021, experience@gibbonx.org, US$150 (price includes tree house accommodation, transport, food, access to Bokeo Nature Reserve and well-trained guides)*. This is a three-day trip into Bokeo Nature Reserve, where a number of tree houses have been built high up in the jungle canopy and linked by interconnected zip-lines. Staying in the trees and waking to the sound of singing gibbons is a truly awe-inspiring experience, as is zip-lining above the jungle canopy, through the mist. In the morning well-trained guides take visitors hiking to see if they can spot the elusive gibbons as well as other plant and animal species. Others to look out for are the giant squirrel, one of the largest rodents in the world, and the Asiatic black bear, whose numbers are in decline as they are hunted for their bile and gall bladders. First and foremost this is a very well-run conservation project. The **Gibbon Experience** was started to help reduce poaching, logging, slash-and-burn farming and the destruction of primary forest by working with villagers to transform the local economy by making a non-destructive living from their unique environment. Already the project has started to pay dividends: the forest conservation and canopy visits generate as much income year on year as the local logging company could do only once.

## Pak Beng → *Colour map 1, B2.*

This long thin strip of a village is perched halfway up a hill, with fine views over the Mekong. Its importance lies in its location at the confluence of the Mekong and the Nam Beng. There is not much to do here but it's a good place to stop en route between Houei Xai and Luang Prabang (or vice versa). The village is worth a visit for its traditional atmosphere and the friendliness of the locals, including various minorities. Just downstream from the port is a good spot for swimming in the dry season, but be careful as the current is strong. There are also a couple of monasteries in town. The locals are now organizing guided treks to nearby villages; check with the guesthouses.

In recent years the settlements of Nong Khiaw and Muang Ngoi Neua in the north of Luang Prabang Province have become firm favourites with the backpacker set. In fact, idyllic Muang Ngoi Neua is often heralded as the new Vang Vieng, surrounded by stunning scenery and the fantastic ebb of life on the river. It is far more pleasant to travel between Luang Prabang and Nong Khiaw/Ban Saphoun, just south of Muang Ngoi Neua, by long boat, than by bus. The Nam Ou passes mountains, teak plantations, dry rice fields and a movable waterwheel mounted on a boat, which moves from village to village and is used for milling. But with the improvements that have been made to Route 13, road travel has now become the preferred option for many – partly because it is cheaper, and partly because it is quicker. Route 13 north runs parallel with the river for most of the journey to Nam Bak. There is trekking around Muang Khua further north upriver.

## Nong Khiaw and Ban Saphoun → *Colour map 1, B3.*

Nong Khiaw lies 22 km northeast of Nam Bak and is a delightful, remote little village on the banks of the Nam Ou, surrounded by limestone peaks and flanked by mountains, the largest aptly named Princess Mountain. It is one of Laos' prettiest destinations. There are, in fact, two settlements here: Ban Saphoun on the east bank of the Nam Ou and Nong Khiaw on the west. Of the two, Ban Saphoun offers the best views and has the best riverside accommodation. Confusingly, the combined village is sometimes called one name, sometimes the other and sometimes Muang Ngoi, which is actually another town to the north (see below) and the name of the district.

One reason why the area has become a popular stopping place for travellers is because of its pivotal position on the Nam Ou, affording river travel from Luang Prabang to the north. It is also on the route between Udomxai and Xam Neau, which is one of the most spectacular in Laos, passing through remote villages. Despite its convenience as a staging post, this village is a destination in its own right. It is a beautiful spot, the sort of place where time stands still, journals are written, books read and stress is a deeply foreign concept. It is possible to swim in the river (women should wear sarongs) or walk around the town or up the cliffs. If you go to the boat landing it is also possible to organize a fishing trip with one of the local fishermen for very little money. You might need someone to translate for you. The bridge across the Nam Ou offers fine views and photo opportunities. There are caves in the area and the Than Mok waterfall.

**Tham Pha Thok cave** ① *2.5 km southeast of the bridge; 5000 kip* was a Pathet Lao regional base during the civil war. It was divided into sections – the hospital section, a police section and a military section. Old remnants exist like campfires and ruined beds but other than that there is little evidence of it being the PT headquarters until you see the bomb crater at the front. To get there you walk through beautiful rice paddies. There is a second cave about 300 m further down on the left, **Tham Pha Kwong**, which was the Pathet Lao's former banking cave. The cave is a tight squeeze and is easier to access with help from a local guide. It splits into two caves, one of which was the financial office and the other the accountant's office. A further 2 km along the road, at Ban Nokien is the **Than Mok** waterfall.

## Muang Ngoi Neua → *Colour map 1, B3.*

The town of Muang Ngoi Neua lies 40 km (one hour) north of Nong Khiaw, along the Nam Ou. This small town surrounded by ethnic villages has become very popular with backpackers over the last few years. The town is a small slice of utopia, set on a peninsula at the foot of Mount Phaboom, shaded by coconut trees, with the languid

# Phongsali

High up in the mountains at an altitude of about 1628 m, this northern provincial capital provides beautiful views and an invigorating climate. It is especially stunning from January to March, when wildflowers bloom in the surrounding hills. The town can be cold at any time of the year, so take some warm clothes. Mornings tend to be foggy and it can also be very wet. There is an end of an earth feel in the areas surrounding the main centre, with dense pristine jungle surrounded by misty mountains.

Phongsali was one of the first areas to be liberated by the Pathet Lao in the late 1940s. The old post office (just in front of the new one), is the sole physical reminder of French rule. The town's architecture is a strange mix of Chinese post-revolutionary concrete blocks, Lao wood-and-brick houses, with tin roofs, and bamboo or mud huts, with straw roofs. The town itself is home to about 20,000 people, mostly Lao, Phou Noi and Chinese, while the wider district is a pot pourri of ethnicities, with around 28 minorities inhabiting the area.

It is not possible to hire bikes, tuk-tuks or even ponies here so walking is the only way to explore the fantastic landscapes of this region. Many paths lead out of town over the hills; the walking is easy and the panoramas are spectacular. Climb the 413 steps to the top of Mount Phoufa for humbling views of the surrounding hills. The **Provincial Tourism Office** ① *on the way to Phou Fa Hotel (now simply a restaurant), T088-210098, Mon-Fri 0730-1130, 1330-1630*, can arrange guided ecotreks, including village homestays, for up to 5 nights. The rates depend on the number of people. Some people trek north from Phongsali to **Uthai**, staying in Akha villages en route. Uthai is probably as remote and unspoilt as it gets.

● D **Viphahone Hotel**, next to the post office, T088-210111. 3-storey building with restaurant and 24 very

river breeze wafting through the town's small paths. Most commonly known as Muang Ngoi, the settlement has had to embellish its name to distinguish it from Nong Khiaw, which is also often referred to as Muang Ngoi (see above). It's the perfect place to go for a trek to surrounding villages, or bask the day away swinging in your hammock. A market is held every 10- days and villagers come to sell produce and handicrafts. There are also caves and waterfalls in the area.

## Muang Khua → Colour map 1, A3.

Muang Khua is nestled into the banks of the Nam Ou, close to the mouth of the Nam Phak, in the south of Phongsali Province. Hardly a destination in itself, it's usually just a stopover between Nong Khiaw and Phongsali. It only has electricity from 1900 to 2200 nightly. The Akha, Khmu and Tai Dam are the main hilltribes in the area. The nearest villages are 20 km out of town and you will need a guide if you want to visit them. Trekking around Muang Khua is fantastic and still a very authentic experience as this region remains largely unexplored by backpackers. The friendly villages are very welcoming to foreigners, as they don't see as many here as in somewhere like Muang Sing. For these very reasons, it is very important to tread lightly and adopt the most culturally sensitive principles: don't hand out sweets and always ask before taking a photograph. Treks usually run for one to three days and involve a homestay at a villager's house (usually the Village Chief). ▸▸ *For further information, see Activities and tours, page 442.*

clean, large and airy twin and double rooms, with hot-water bathrooms, some with Western flush toilets.

● **Sengsaly Guesthouse**, up the hill and around the bend from the market, T088-210165. Worn but comfortable rooms, with squat toilets and scoop showers.

● **Yu Houa Guesthouse**, across the road from the market, has a short Lao and Chinese section on an English menu; cheap and good. **The Phongsali Hotel** is also a good bet and has a larger variety of dishes, including a few Thai, Chinese and Lao.

● You can travel from Muang Khua to Phongsali either by truck or by boat. Trucks also depart from Pak Nam Noi (near Muang Khua); buy lunch from the market before departure. The ride is long and difficult when the pick-up is full, but it's a great experience and the scenery near Phongsali is utterly breathtaking. Alternatively, catch a boat from Muang Khua to Hat Xa, 20 km or so to the northeast of Phongsali,

5-6 hrs, 100,000 kip. In the low season there may not be any scheduled boats so it might be necessary to gather a few extra tourists and charter a boat, US$80-100. Depending on the season, the river is quite shallow in places, with a fair amount of white water. It can be cold and wet so wear waterproofs and take a blanket. Note that you may find yourselves stuck in Hat Xa, as there are no onward buses to Phongsali after mid-afternoon. Alternative routes to Phongsali are by bus to/from Udomxai, 237 km, 9-10 hrs, 60,000 kip, or by plane to/from Vientiane, twice a week with Lao Airlines, T088-210794, although flights can be cancelled at short notice. More often than not they do not run and at the time of publication they had been discontinued. Another, newer option, is to fly with Lao Air, T021-512027, laoair@laopdr.com, which has 2 scheduled flights a week US$75, one way/US$150 return.

# ● Sleeping

### Udomxai p431

**D Surinphone**, T081-212789, srphone@lao tel.com. Very comfortable, clean and modern rooms with a/c rooms with TV, comfortable beds and hot-water bathrooms with bathtub. All in all a good choice. Very friendly.
**D-E Litthavixay Guesthouse**, about 100 m before the turning onto the airport road, T081-212175. This place has the best rooms in town, large single, double and triple rooms and all very clean. Rooms with lots of facilities including en suite hot-water shower. Best value internet in town. The restaurant has a small but good selection of foreign breakfast dishes.

### Luang Namtha p431, map p432

**B Boat Landing Guesthouse & Restaurant**, T086-312398. Further out of town than most other guesthouses, this place is located right on the river. Time stands still here. It's an

eco-resort that has got everything just right: pristine surroundings, environmentally friendly rooms, helpful service and a brilliant restaurant serving traditional northern Lao cuisine. The rooms are very homely, combining modern design with traditional materials and decoration. The gardens are beautiful and brimming with butterflies and birds. Great restaurant attached serving local indigenous dishes. Recommended.
**E Manychan Guesthouse**, on the main road in the centre of town, pposite the smaller bus station, T086-312209. One of the most popular places in town, probably due to the location and the restaurant. Decent, clean rooms with fan and hot-water bathrooms. Bikes can be hired next door for 15,000 kip per day. The staff are very friendly.
**E Vila Guesthouse**, on the south of the town, T086-312425. A 2-storey building with 11 of the cleanest rooms in town. Lounge and sparkling en suite bathrooms with hot water.

E **Zuela Guesthouse**, T086-312183.
Fantastic value guesthouse in a beautiful,
modern, wooden building with immaculate
fan rooms. Extremely comfortable beds, en
suite hot-water bathrooms and linen provided.
This family-run guesthouse is truly a league
apart from other budget options in town.
Restaurant attached. Highly recommended.
F **Luang Namtha Guesthouse**, 2 blocks
west of the main centre, T086-312087.
Run by 2 friendly Hmong brothers, one
of whom speaks English. The house is an
impressive building for Luang Namtha, with
a grand staircase. All rooms are beautifully
clean and furnished, with en suite hot-water
bathrooms and balconies. Satellite TV in the
more expensive rooms.

### Muang Sing *p433*
D **Phoulou 2**, at the southern end of town,
T086-212348. Has great double bungalows
and provides towels and bottled water.
The lack of scenery is its only downfall.
D **Phoutat Guesthouse/Black Stupa**,
6 km out of Muang Sing on the main road
towards Luang Namtha, T020-5686555.
This place changes its name about every
6 months but remains the best
accommodation in the vicinity. 10 wooden
bungalows perched on the side of a hill,
overlooking the small town, the mountains
and the rice paddies. Quaint gardens, home
to an abundance of butterflies, link the
bungalows via a small paved path. Hot
water, fan, Western toilet and fantastic
balcony. Stunningly beautiful. There is also
a decent restaurant on site, which affords
views extending all the way to China.
Very good value. Recommended.
D-E **Adima Guesthouse**, near Ban
Oudomsin, north of Muang Sing towards the
Chinese border, T020-2249008. A little hard
to get to but the location is scenic. Peaceful
bungalows constructed in traditional Yao
and Akha style, plus a lovely open-air
restaurant. A calm retreat surrounded by
rice fields. Minority villages are literally on
the doorstep. Footprint does not endorse
DIY treks using the guesthouse map, which
are having a negative effect on local villages.
If you wish to trek please visit the local
tourism office or **Exotissimo**, see page 441,
to organize a bonafide eco-trek. To get there,
take a tuk-tuk (20,000 kip) or hire a bike.

Alternatively, the owner runs in and out of
town about 3 times a day (depending on
bus arrival times) and will pick you up from
the bus station for a small fee.
F **Taileu Guesthouse**, above the restaurant
on the main road, T030-1212375. There are
8 very basic rattan rooms with bamboo
style 4-poster beds (the rickety backpacker
version not some romantic type), squat
toilets and temperamental hot water via
solar power. The owners are lovely people.

### Houei Xai *p434*
D-E **Arimid Guesthouse**, northwest end
of the town, T084-211040. The owners Mr
and Mme Chitaly speak excellent French
and a little English. Comfortable, rattan-style
bungalows with en suite bathrooms, hot
water, nice garden area and great balconies.
Some with a/c. Mme Chitaly will cook tasty
food and serve it to you at your bungalow.
Close to the slow boat terminal.
D-E **Taveensinh Guesthouse**, northwest
end of the town, T084-211502. The best
value rooms in town with fan, TV and
hot-water bathrooms. Great communal
balconies overlooking the river.
E **BAP Guesthouse**, on the main Sekhong
Rd, T084-211083. One of the oldest
guesthouses in town consisting of a
labyrinth of additions and add-ons as
their business has grown over the years.
A range of rooms, though the newer tiled
ones with hot-water bathroom are the
best. The female proprietor here is hard
as nails but has loads of charisma and a
wily sense of humour.
F **Thanormsub Guesthouse**, on the main
Sekhong Rd, T084-211095. Clean double
rooms with hot water, fan and satin
curtains to boot. Nice, helpful staff.

### Pak Beng *p434*
During peak season, when the slow boat
arrives from Luang Prabang, about 60 people
descend on Pak Beng at the same time.
As the town doesn't have an endless supply
of great budget guesthouses, it is advisable
to get someone you trust to mind your bags,
while you make a mad dash to get the best
room in town.
A-B **Pakbeng Lodge**. A wooden and
concrete construction, built in Lao style,
this stunning guesthouse sits perched on

a hillside above the Mekong and includes 20 rooms with fan, toilet and hot water. Good restaurant and wonderful views.

**B Luangsay Lodge**, about 1 km from the centre of town, T081-212296, www.mekongcruises.com. This is the most beautiful accommodation available in Pak Beng. An attractive wooden pathway curves through luscious tropical gardens to several wooden bungalows with fantastic balconies and large windows overlooking the river and the mountains. Hot-water bathrooms and romantic rooms make this a winner. Great restaurant. Book in advance.

**B Phetsoxkai Hotel**, T081-212299. Large, Lao-owned hotel that looks grand but doesn't live up to expectation. Nonetheless, the 28 rooms are beautifully decorated, though on the smallish side. hot-water bathroom, DVD player. Restaurant with Western, Lao and Thai cuisine. Very friendly owners.

**D-E Salika**, T081-212 306. This is an elegant structure on the steep cliff overlooking the river. Big, clean rooms with en suite toilet and shower (mostly cold), tiled floors. There is a great restaurant, serving reasonably priced meals (see Eating). Fantastic service.

**E-F Donevilisack Guesthouse**, T081-212 315. The popular **Donevilasack** offers a reasonable choice of rooms. In the older, wooden building are basic budget rooms with fan, mosquito net and shared hot-water showers. More expensive rooms are in the newer concrete building and have private homestay bathrooms.

**Nong Khiaw and Ban Saphoun** p435

**B-C Nong Khiau**, turn-off right beside the bridge in Ban Saphoun, T071-254770, www.nongkhiau.com. Stunning modern bungalows and restaurant. Beautifully decorated upscale rooms with 4-poster beds, mosquito nets and tiled hot-water bathrooms. For those looking for some-thing upmarket this exquisite place fits the bill perfectly. The restaurant has a great selection of wines and access to the internet. Book in advance as it is a favourite with tour groups. Recommended.

**F Phanoy Guesthouse, Bakery and Bookshop**, 50 m past the bridge, Ban Saphoun, T071-253919. Guesthouse has 7 basic but clean and comfortable thatched bungalows with mosquito nets and squat toilets. Inside bathroom. Fantastic verandas overlooking the river. Some bungalows (50,000 kip) have hot water. If you are very the owner will show you his collection of butterflies and beetles, and explain the history of each. Very nice family-owned business with a great atmosphere. The best of the cheaper options.

**F Sunset Guesthouse**, down a lane about 100 m past the bridge, Ban Saphoun, T071-253933. Slap bang on the bank of the river – you couldn't ask for a more picturesque setting from which to watch the sunset. The charming, sprawling bamboo structure looks out onto tables and sun umbrellas liberally arranged over the various levels of decking that serve as a popular restaurant in the evenings. Western toilet and hot-water shower outside. 8 rooms with hard mattresses. A bit dirty. Slow internet.

**Muang Ngoi Neua** p435

All the accommodation in town is dirt cheap and of the same standard: bungalows with extremely welcoming hammocks on their balconies. Most offer a laundry service for around 10,000 kip per kg and all have electricity 1800-2200 only. Rats are a problem here but, luckily, mosquito nets tend to keep them at bay.

**F Lattanavongsa**, concrete building housing relatively comfortable rooms with en suite bathroom.

**F Ning Ning Guesthouse**, beside the boat landing, with a great restaurant.

**F Phet Davanh Guesthouse**, on the main road, near the boat landing. Concrete rooms, restaurant, much cleaner than the other alternatives.

**Muang Khua** p436

**D Sernnali Hotel**, in the middle of town, near the top of the hill, T081-212445. By far the most luxurious lodging in town. 18 rooms with large double and twin beds, hot-water scoop showers and Western-

For an explanation of sleeping and eating price codes used in this guide, see inside the front cover. Other relevant information is found in Essentials, see pages 29-32.

style toilets, immaculately clean. Balconies overlook the Nam Ou. Chinese, Vietnamese and Lao food served in the restaurant.

**E-F Nam Ou Guesthouse & Restaurant**, follow the signs at the top of the hill, T081-210844. Looking out across the river where the boats land, this guesthouse is the pick of the ultra-budget bunch in Muang Khua. Singles, twins and doubles, some with hot-water en suites, and 3 newer rooms with river views. Great food (see Eating, below). A popular spot. Go for an upstairs room.

## ❼ Eating

### Udomxai *p431*
❡ **Sinphet Guesthouse & Restaurant**, opposite **Linda Guesthouse**. One of the best options in town. English menu, delicious iced coffee with ovaltine, great Chinese and Lao food. Try the curry chicken, *kua-mii* or yellow noodles with chicken.

**Litthavixay Guesthouse**, can whip up some good dishes, including Western-style pancakes and breakfasts.

### Luang Namtha *p431, map p432*
The night-market, though small, offers an interesting array of local cuisine with ubiquitous street food stands.

❡❡-❡ **Boat Landing Guesthouse & Restaurant** (see Sleeping), T086-312398. The best place to eat in town, with a beautiful dining area and exceptionally innovative cuisine. Serves a range of northern Lao dishes made from local produce, thereby supporting nearby villages. Highly recommended.

❡ **Banana Restaurant**, main road, towards the **KNT Internet**, T020-5718026. This restaurant is gaining favour with the locals and tourists for its good fruit shakes and Lao food. Also serves a few Western dishes.

❡ **Coffee House**, off the main road around the corner from **Green Discovery**, T030-5257842. This fantastic little hole-in-the-wall Thai restaurant serves a range of delicious meals all under 10,000 kip. The meals are served on brown rice imported from Thailand and include Massaman curry, Tom Yum soup and a variety of other Thai staples. Fantastic espresso coffee and cappuccinos. Mr Nithat, the owner's husband, is good for a chat. Recommended.

❡ **Panda Restaurant**, T086-211304. A goodie, housed in a beautiful stilted building overlooking rice paddies. Cheap and tasty food. The curries are outstanding. The friendly owner speaks English.

❡ **Yamuna Restaurant**, on the main road, T020-5405698. A delicious Indian restaurant with veg and non-veg dishes and halal cuisine. Extensive, predominantly south Indian menu.

### Cafés
For those with a sweet tooth, **KNT Internet** sells some fabulous home-made cakes.

### Muang Sing *p433*
❡ **Sengdeuane Guesthouse & Restaurant**. A quieter option with an English menu, which is mostly just for show. Nice garden setting and an ancient karaoke machine. Korean BBQ only (*sindat*). It opens from 1700. Popular with the locals.

❡ **Taileu Guesthouse & Restaurant** (see Sleeping), T081-212375. The most popular place to eat due to its indigenous Tai Leu menu. Unique and tasty meals, including baked aubergine with pork, soy mash and fish soup. One of the few places in the country where you can sample northern cuisine. Try their local piña colada with *lao-lao*, their *sa lo* (Muang Sing's answer to a hamburger) or one of the famous *jeow* (chilli jam) dishes. The banana flower soup is fantastic. Stand-out option in town and an eating experience you won't find elsewhere in Laos. Noi, the owner, is very friendly. Highly recommended.

❡ **Viengphone**, next door to the **Viengxai Restaurant**, T081-212368. This place has an English menu offering the usual fare. Excellent fried mushrooms, although the service is a bit *bopenyang*.

❡ **Viengxai Restaurant**. Very good food, with some of the best chips in Laos. English menu, friendly service, reasonable prices. Good selection of shakes. Clean.

### Houei Xai *p434*
❡❡-❡ **Riverside**, just off the main road, near the **Houay Xai Guesthouse**, T084-211064. Huge waterfront restaurant on large platform. Perfect position for taking in the sunset. Great shakes. Extensive menu that's a mixture of Lao and Thai food. The curries

are quite nice. Usually there is live music, some of it decidedly off-key, played here.

**⍾ Deen Restaurant**, on the main road, T020-5901871. Indian restaurant with an extensive menu of dishes, including a good selection of halal and vegetarian. Sparkly clean with very formal tablecloths and table settings. The owner is very accommodating.

**⍾ Khemkhong Restaurant**, across from the immigration stand. Good option for those who want a drink after the cross-border journey. Lao and Thai food.

**⍾ Nutpop**, on the main road, T084-211037. The fluorescent lights and garish beer signs don't give a good impression. However, this is quite a pleasant little garden restaurant, set in an atmospheric lamp-lit building, with good Lao food including fried mushrooms and curry. The fish here is excellent.

**Pak Beng** *p434*
**⍾ Kopchaideu Restaurant**, overlooking the Mekong. This restaurant has a large selection of Indian dishes with a few Lao favourites thrown in. Great shakes and fantastic service.
**⍾ Salika** (see Sleeping). An atmospheric restaurant with wonderful river views, fresh flowers on the table and an amazingly varied menu that includes cheese omelette. Interminably slow service.

**Nong Khiaw and Ban Saphoun** *p435*
Most of the guesthouses have cafés attached. For some fine dining the restaurant at the **Riverside** is absolutely fantastic, with an extensive wine menu to boot. For those on a budget the **Phanoy Guesthouse** and **Bakery Bookshop** does reasonably good food. Ask for dishes to be served with *jeow*, which is delicious. Good selection of cakes.

**Muang Ngoi Neua** *p435*
**⍾⍾-⍾ Sainamgoi Restaurant & Bar**, in the centre of town. Tasty Lao food in a pleasant atmosphere, with good background music. The bar, the only one in town, is in the next room.
**⍾ Nang Phone Keo Restaurant**, next to Banana Guesthouse. All the usual Lao food, plus some extras. Try the 'Falang Roll' for breakfast (a combination of peanut butter, sticky rice and vegetables).

**⍾ Sengdala Restaurant & Bakery**, on the main road, with a bomb casing out front. Very good, cheap Lao food, terrific pancakes and freshly baked baguettes.

**Muang Khua** *p436*
The **Nam Ou Guesthouse & Restaurant** (see Sleeping) is up the mud slope from the beach. An incomparable location for a morning coffee overlooking the river; it has an English menu and friendly staff.

---

## ▲ Activities and tours

**Luang Namtha** *p431, map p432*
**Tour operators**
**Green Discovery**, T086-211484, offers 1- to 7-day kayaking/rafting, cycling and trekking excursions into the Nam Ha NPA.
**Luang Namtha Guide Service Unit**, T086-211534. Information on treks into the Nam Ha NPA.

**Muang Sing** *p433*
**Trekking**
Trekking has become a delicate issue around Muang Sing as uncontrolled tourism was beginning to have a detrimental effect on some of the surrounding minority villages. Luckily some sensible procedures and protocols have been put in place to ensure low impact tourism which still benefits the villages concerned.
**Exotissimo**, www.exotissimo.com, in cahoots with **GTZ**, a German aid agency, have launched more expensive but thoroughly enjoyable treks such as the **Akha Experience**, which include tasty meals prepared by local Akha people. Closed on weekends.

The **tourism office and trekking centre**, in the centre of town, T020-2393534, can organize pretty good treks for 1, 2 or 3 days including accommodation and food. The guides are supposedly from local villages and can speak the native tongue, Akha or Tai Leu. Most treks cost around US$25 per day and have received glowing reports from tourists, particularly the **Laosee Trek**. Trek prices are reduced with larger numbers. The tourism office, next door to **Exotissimo**, is open from Mon-Fri 0800-1130, 1330-1700. Treks organized during the working week.

## Muang Ngoi Neua *p435*

Trekking, hiking, fishing, kayaking, trips to the waterfalls and boat trips can be organized through most of the guest-houses for US$10 per day. Tubing can be arranged for US$2 per day.

**Lao Youth Travel**, www.laoyouthtravel.com, 0730-1800. Half-day, day, overnight or 2-night treks. Also kayaking trips.

---

## ⊖ Transport

### Udomxai *p431*
**Air**

There are flights to **Vientiane**, Tue, Thu and Sat from Udomxai. **Lao Airlines** has an office at the airport, T081-312047.

### Bus, truck or songthaew

Udomxai is the epicentre of northern travel. If arriving into Udomxai to catch a connecting bus, it's better to leave earlier in the day as transport tends to peter out in the afternoon. These prices are subject to change.

The bus station is 1 km east of the town centre. Departures east to **Nong Khiaw**, 3 hrs, trucks are fairly frequent, most departing in the morning. If you get stuck on the way to Nong Khiaw it is possible to stay overnight in **Pak Mong** where there are numerous rustic guesthouses. The bus to **Nong Khiaw** leaves at 0900, 114 km. **Pak Mong**, 1400 and 1600, 2 hrs, 82 km, 22,000 kip. To **Luang Prabang**, 0800, 1100 and 1400, 5 hrs, 194 km, direct, 48,000 kip. Direct bus to **Vientiane**, 1530 and 1800, 15 hrs, 100,000 kip. Vientiane **VIP** bus, 1600 and 1800, 121,000 kip (also runs via **Luang Prabang**). **Xam Neua**, Tue-Sat 1230, 100,000 kip. **Luang Namtha**, 0800, 1130 and 1500, 4 hrs, 115 km, 32,000 kip. **Boten** (the Chinese border) 0800, 82 km, 28,000 kip. It is possible for some nationalities to obtain Chinese visas at the border. However, you will need to check if you are eligible in advance (at the time of publication UK citizens could, but US citizens could not get a Chinese visa at the border).

There are services north on Route 4 to **Phongsali**, 0800, 9 hrs, 232 km, 60,000 kip; this trip is long so bring something soft to sit on and try to get a seat with a view.

There are an abundance of songthaews on standby waiting to make smaller trips to destinations like **Pak Mong** and **Nong Khiaw**, if you miss one of the earlier buses it is worthwhile bargaining with the drivers, as if they can get enough money or passengers they will make the extra trip.

At the bus station there are a range of food stalls, a Chinese restaurant and a temperamental internet café, 10,000 kip per hr.

### Luang Namtha *p431, map p432*
**Air**

The airport is 7 km south of town – 15,000 kip by tuk-tuk. At the time of publication there were no domestic flights to or from Luang Namtha as the airport was being upgraded to an international airport. **Lao Airlines**, T086-312180, has an office south of town on the main road. When flights do reopen it is imperative to book in advance.

### Bicycles and motorbikes

Bicycles for hire from next door to the **Manychan Guesthouse**, opposite post office, for 15,000 kip a day. Motorbikes for hire for US$5 a day from **Zuela guesthouse**.

### Boat

Call T020-5686051 for information. Slow boats are the best and most scenic travel option but their reliability will depend on the tide and, in the dry season (Mar-May) they often won't run at all as the water level is too low. There isn't really a regular boat service from Luang Namtha, so you will have to either charter a whole boat and split the cost amongst the passengers or hitch a ride on a boat making the trip already. If you manage to organize a boat it should cost around US$150 to **Houei Xai**. It is cheaper to go from Luang Namtha to Houei Xai than vice versa. The **Boat Landing Guesthouse** is a good source of information about boats; if arrangements are made for you, a courtesy tip is appreciated.

### Bus, truck or songthaew

The main bus station and its ticket office, T086-312164, daily 0700-1600, are about 100 m north of the Morning Market. This bus station is set to be abolished to make way for a new Malaysian Hotel. A new bus station is planned on the corner near **Panda Restaurant** on the main road.

To **Muang Sing**, daily 0800, 1100 and 1400, 1½ hrs, 20,000 kip, additional pickups may depart throughout the day, depending on demand. To **Udomxai**, daily 0830, 1200 and 1430, 4-6 hrs, 100 km, 32,000 kip, additional services will leave in the early afternoon if there is demand, otherwise jump on a bus to Luang Prabang.

**Houei Xai**, 0900 and 1330, 55,000 kip. To **Luang Prabang**, daily 0930, 10 hrs, 70,000 kip. To **Vientiane**, 20 hrs, 140,000 kip. To get to **Nong Khiaw**, 60,000 kip you need to go via Udomxai (leave early)..

To **Boten** (Chinese border) daily 0800, 1100 and 1400, 1½ hrs, 25,000 kip. Many travellers have reported obtaining a visa at this; however, it is less risky to organize a visa in advance in Vientiane. Tourist visas between US$70-150 depending on nationality. US citizens are unable to obtain visas at this crossing. Check with the Chinese embassy beforehand.

## Muang Sing *p433*
### Bicycle
Available for rent from some guesthouses and bicycle hire shops on the main street for 10,000 kip per day. The Muang Sing tourism office also hires bikes for 20,000 kip per day.

### Boat
It is sometimes possible to charter boats from **Xieng Kok** downstream on the Mekong to **Houei Xai**, 3-4 hrs. This is expensive – around US$150-200.

### Bus or truck
The bus station is across from the main market. To **Luang Namtha**, by bus or pickup, daily 0800, 0900, 1100, 1300 and 1500, 2 hrs, 20,000 kip. To charter a songthaew or tuk-tuk to Luang Namtha costs at least 200,000 kip. Songthaews also leave sporadically for **Xieng Kok**, 4 hrs, 30,000 kip.

### Houei Xai *p434*
Lao National Tourism State Bokeo, on the main street up from immigration, T084-211555, can give advice on the sale of boat, bus, pickup and other tickets. Numerous travel agencies congregate around the immigration centre offering bus and boat ticket sales. See page 429 for information on boat travel between Houei Xai and Luang Prabang.

## Air
Houei Xai airport is located 5 km south of town and has flights to **Vientiane**, Tue, Thu. US$85 one way; US$162 return. Book in advance as it is a small plane and tends to fill up quickly.

## Boat
The **BAP Guesthouse** in Houei Xai is a good place to find out about boat services.

The 2-day trip down the Mekong to Luang Prabang has become part of the Southeast Asian rite of package. The slow boat to **Pak Beng** is raved about by many travellers. However, in peak season the boat can be packed to the rafters and the wooden chairs or ground extremely uncomfortable. It is advisable to bring something soft to sit on, a good book to read and a packed lunch. The boat leaves from a jetty 1½ km north of town, daily 0930-1000, 6-7 hrs, US$11 or US$22 for the 2-day trip (usually you buy the ongoing ticket at Pak Beng). If you can get enough people together it is possible to charter your own boat for US$600. It is worth noting that the trip, done in reverse, usually has fewer passengers.

For those looking for a luxury option there is the **Luangsay Cruise**, T071-252553, www.asian-oasis.com, which undertakes a 2-day/1-night cruise down the river in extreme comfort with cushioned deckchairs, a bar, wooden polished interior and games on board. Guests stay at the beautiful **Luangsay Lodge** in Pak Beng.

For a mid-range option, **Phoudoi Travel**, on the main road in Houei Xai, sells tickets for US$60 on a boat direct to Luang Prabang that is roomier than the standard cattle-class boat yet not as cosy as the Luangsay. The *Nagi*, for US$80, does the trip in 1 day in comfort. www.travel-thailand.com/article.php/cruise_the_mekong.

Speedboats are a noisy, nerve-wracking, dangerous alternative; they leave from the jetty south of town, to **Pak Beng**, 3 hrs, US$15 and to **Luang Prabang**, US$29. There have been reports of unscrupulous boatmen claiming there are no slow boats in the dry season to encourage travellers to take their fast boats. This is usually untrue.

## Bus, truck or songthaew
The bus station is located at the Morning Market, 7 km out of central Houei Xai, a

tuk-tuk to the centre costs 20,000 kip. Trucks, buses and minivans run to **Luang Namtha**, 0930 and1130, 7 hrs, 170 km, 65,000 kip; to **Udomxai**, 0930 and 1130, 7 hrs, 120,000 kip; to **Luang Prabang**, Fri 1130, 11 hrs, 140,000 kip; to **Vientiane**, 1130, 20 hrs, 200,000 kip.

### Pak Beng *p434*
### Boat

The times and prices for boats are always changing so it's best to check beforehand. The slow boat to **Houei Xai** leaves at around 0800-0900 from the port and takes all day, US$11. The slow boat to **Luang Prabang** leaves around the same time. Get in early to get a good seat. Speedboats to Luang Prabang (2-3 hrs) and Houei Xai leave in the morning, when full.

### Bus, truck, songthaew

Buses and songthaews leave about 2 km from town in the morning for the route north to **Udomxai**, 6-7 hrs, 40,000 kip. Direct songthaews to **Udomxai** are few, so an alternative is to take one to **Muang Houn** and catch a rather more frequent service from there. The road to Udomxai passes through spectacular scenery.

### Nong Khiaw and Ban Saphoun *p435*
### Boat

Boat services have become irregular following road improvements, although you may find a service to **Muang Noi Neua**, 1 hr, 20,000 kip, from the boat landing. However, these boats won't run unless there are enough passengers. Likewise, boats to Luang Prabang only run if there are enough people, so you might find yourself waiting a couple of days. Some vessels also head upriver to **Muang Khua**, 5 hrs, 100,000 kip. The river trips from Nong Khiaw are absolutely spectacular. It is possible to charter boats to both of these destinations.

### Bus/truck

Buses en route from surrounding destinations stop in Nong Khiaw briefly. As the buses usually arrive from Vientiane or Luang Prabang, the timetables are unreliable. Basic timetables are offered but buses can be hours early or late, so check details on the day. It is often a matter of waiting at the bus station for hours and hoping to catch the bus on its way through. Plonking yourself in a restaurant on the main road usually suffices but you will need to flag down the bus as it plies through town. Regular connections to **Luang Prabang**, 0830 and 1100, 3-4 hrs, 32,000 kip. Also several departures daily to **Nam Bak**, 30 mins, 10,000 kip and on to **Udomxai** 1130, 4 hrs, 31,000 kip. Alternatively, take one of the more regular songthaews to **Pak Mong**, 1 hr, 20,000 kip, where there is a small noodle shop-cum-bus station on the west side of the bridge, and then catch a vehicle on to Udomxai/Vientiane.

Travelling east on Route 1, there are buses to **Vieng Thong**, 2 hrs, 25,000 kip, and a village 10 km from **Nam Nouan**, where you can change and head south on Route 6 to **Phonsavanh** and the **Plain of Jars**. There are direct buses north to **Xam Neua** and the village near Nam Nouan, which can be caught from the toll gate on the Ban Saphoun side of the river when it comes through from Vientiane at around 2000-2200, 100,000 kip; it's usually quite crowded. If you miss a bus to/from Nong Khiaw you can always head to **Pak Mong** which is a junction town sitting at the crossroads to Luang Prabang, Nong Khiaw and Udomxai. Aim to get here earlier in the day to catch through traffic otherwise you may have to stay overnight. (If you do, try the **Pak Mong Guesthouse Restaurant**, T020-5795860, or any of the other 6 places in town.)

### Muang Ngoi Neua *p435*
### Boat

From the landing at the northern end of town, slow boats travel north along the beautiful river tract to **Muang Khua**, 5 hrs, US$10, or charter your own for US$50 per boat. Slow boats also go south (irregularly) to **Nong Khiaw**, 1 hr, 20,0000 kip, and **Luang Prabang**, 8 hrs, US$100 per boat. Departure times vary and whether they depart at all depends on whether there are enough passengers. For more information and tickets, consult the booth at the landing.

## Muang Khua p436
### Boat
Road travel is now more popular but irregular boats still travel south on the Nam Ou to **Muang Ngoi/Nong Khiaw**, 4-5 hrs, 100,000 kip, if there is enough demand. Also north to **Phongsali** via Hat Xa, 100,000 kip. Boats can be charted to Phongsali for around US$110. A jeep or truck transports travellers on from Hat Xa to Phongsali, 20 km, 2 hrs along a very bad road, 50,000 kip. Alternatively, charter a jeep, US$15.

### Songthaew or truck
To get to **Phongsali**, take a songthaew to **Pak Nam Noi**, 0800, 1 hr, 30,000 kip, then take the songthaew or bus that passes through from Udomxai at around 1000, 50,000 kip.

To **Udomxai**, pick-ups and buses leave 0700-0800 from the bus station alongside the market, 4 hrs, US$5 and Luang Prabang, 8 hrs, US$7.

## Directory

### Udomxai p431
**Banks** Lao Development Bank, Udomxai, just off the road on the way to Phongsali, changes US$, Thai ฿ and Chinese ¥. The BCEL Bank, on the main road, offers the same services. No credit card advances. **Internet** Available at Litthavixay Guesthouse, at the bus station, on the main road at Samlaan Cycling and around the corner from there at the English school 100-200 kip per min. Quite often the whole town's internet is down.

### Luang Namtha p431, map p432
**Banks** Banks open Mon-Fri only. Lao Development Bank, changes US$ and Thai ฿ to kip, also exchanges TCs but charges a sizeable commission. The BCEL changes US$ and Thai ฿ and does cash advances on Visa. The BCEL has an ATM but it only accepts MasterCard. **Internet** KNT Computers, 200 kip per min. **Telephone** You can make international calls from Lao Telecom. **Shopping** Panfa Art, on the main road, offers a range of beautiful handicrafts, silk and other local artefacts. There are

also plans to develop the small night market into a more extensive handicraft market, yet at the time of publication this looked unlikely.

### Muang Sing p433
**Banks** There is a small branch of the Lao Development Bank opposite the market which will exchange Thai ฿, US$ and Chinese ¥.

### Houei Xai p434
**Banks** Banks open Mon-Fri only. Lao Development Bank, next to the immigration office, changes TCs, US$ cash and ฿. **Immigration** At the boat terminal, daily 0800-1800, a small overtime fee is charged Sat and Sun and after 1600. Quite possibly the most friendly immigration post in the country. **Internet** There is a small internet shop on the main street which charges 15,000 kip per hr.

### Pak Beng p434
**Bank** There is no bank in Pak Beng, but most of the guesthouses and restaurants will exchange Thai ฿ and US$ cash at a hefty commission. **Internet** Available at the ferry office for a whopping 500 kip per min. High-speed internet is also available past the Pak Beng Market, 500 kip per min. **Massage** Next door to Bounmee Guesthouse, is an understated but fantastic massage place.

### Nong Khiaw and Ban Saphoun p435
**Internet** Sunset Guesthouse and Riverside Guesthouse, offer internet for 300 kip per min.

### Muang Khua p436
**Bank** Lao Development Bank, near the truck stop, Mon-Fri 0800-1130, 1300-1630, can change US$, Thai ฿ and Chinese ¥ for kip at quite bad rates. It won't change TCs or do cash advances on credit cards, so make sure you have plenty of cash before you come here. **Electricity** Daily 1830-2200. **Telephone** International calls can be made from the Telecom office, a small unmarked hut with a huge satellite, halfway up the winding road, behind the bank.

# Plain of Jars and the northeast

*Apart from the historic Plain of Jars, Xieng Khouang Province is best known for the pounding it took during the war. Many of the sights are battered monuments to the plateau's violent recent history. Given the cost of the return trip and the fact that the jars themselves aren't that spectacular, some consider the destination oversold. However, for those interested in modern history, it's the most fascinating area of Laos and helps one to gain an insight into the resilient nature of the Lao people. The countryside, particularly towards the Vietnam frontier, is beautiful – among the country's best – and the jars, too, are interesting by dint of their very oddness: as if a band of carousing giants had been suddenly interrupted, casting the jars across the plain in their hurry to leave.* ›› *For Sleeping, Eating and other listings, see pages 452-454.*

## Background

Xieng Khouang Province has had a murky, blood-tinted, war-ravaged history. The area was the most bombed province in the most bombed country, per capita, in the world as it became a very important strategic zone that both the US and Vietnamese wanted to retain control of. The town of Phonsavanh has long been an important transit point between China to the north, Vietnam to the east and Thailand to the south and this status made the town a target for neighbouring countries. What's more, the plateau of the Plain of Jars is one of the flatter areas in northern Laos, rendering it a natural battleground for the numerous conflicts that ensued from the 19th century to 1975. While the enigmatic Plain of Jars is here, this region will also hold immense appeal for those interested in the modern history of the country.

Once the French departed from Laos, massive conflicts were waged in 1945 and 1946 between the Free Lao Movement and the Viet Minh. The Pathet Lao and Viet Minh joined forces and, by 1964, had a number of bases dotted around the Plain of Jars. From then on, chaos ensued, as Xieng Khouang got caught in the middle of the war between the Royalist-American and Pathet Lao-Vietnamese. The extensive US bombing of this area was to ensure it did not fall under the Communist control of the Pathet Laos. The Vietnamese were trying to ensure that the US did not gain control of the area from which they could launch attacks on North Vietnam.

During the 'Secret War' (1964-1974) against the North Vietnamese Army and the Pathet Lao, tens of thousands of cluster bomb units (CBUs) were dumped by the US military on Xieng Khouang Province. Other bombs, such as the anti-personnel plastic 'pineapple' bomblets were also used but by and large cluster bombs compromised the majority dropped. The CBU was a carrier bomb, which held 670 sub-munitions the size of a lemon. As the CBU was dropped each of these smaller bombs was released. Even though they were the size of a tennis ball, they contained 300 metal ball-bearings which were propelled hundreds of metres. As 30% of the original bombs did not explode these cluster bombs continue to kill and maim today. The Plain of Jars was also hit by B-52s returning from abortive bombing runs to Hanoi, who jettisoned their bomb loads before heading back to the US air base at Udon Thani in northeast Thailand. Suffice it to say that, with over 580,944 sorties flown (one-and-a-half times the number flow in Vietnam), whole towns were obliterated and the area's geography was permanently altered. Today, as the **Lao Airlines** Y-12 turbo-prop begins its descent towards the plateau, the meaning of the term 'carpet bombing' becomes clear. On the final approach to the town of Phonsavanh, the plane banks low over the cratered paddy fields, affording a T-28 fighter-bomber pilot's view of his target, which in places has been pummelled into little more than a moonscape. Some of the craters are 15 m across and 7 m deep. Testament to the Lao people's resilience, symbolically, many of these craters have been turned into tranquil fish ponds; the bombs transformed into fences and the CBU carriers serving as planter pots. Because the war was 'secret', there are few records of what was dropped and where and, even when the unexploded ordnance (UXO) have been uncovered, their workings are often a mystery – the Americans used Laos as a testing ground for new ordnance so blueprints are unavailable. The UK-based **Mines Advisory Group** (MAG) ① *on the main road in the centre of town, daily 0800-1200, 1300-2000 (except the 12th and 18th of every month)*, is currently engaged in clearing the land of Unexploded Ordnance (UXO). They have an exhibition of bombs, photographs and information on the bombing campaign and ongoing plight of Laos with UXO. Usually there are staff on hand to explain exactly how the bombs were used. All T-shirts sold here help fund the UXO clearance of the area and are a very worthwhile souvenir.

Xieng Khouang remains one of the poorest provinces in an already wretchedly poor country. The whole province has a population of only around 250,000, a mix of different ethnic groups, predominantly Hmong, Lao and a handful of Khmu.

## Plain of Jars and Phonsavanh ⊞🖉✿▲🚌🌀

→ *pp452-454. Colour map 2, C2.*

The undulating plateau of the Plain of Jars (also known as Plaine de Jarres or **Thong Hai Hin**) stretches for about 50 km east to west, at an altitude of 1000 m. In total there are 136 archaeological sites in this area, containing thousands of jars, discs and deliberately placed stones, but only three are open to tourists. Note that the plateau can be cold from December to March. **Phonsavanh** is the main town of the province today – old Xieng Khouang having been flattened – and its small airstrip is a crucial transport link in this mountainous region. It's the only base from which to explore the Plain of Jars, so it has a fair number of hotels and guesthouses. Note that travel agents and airlines tend to refer to Phonsavanh as Xieng Khouang, while the nearby town of 'old' Xieng Khouang is usually referred to as Muang Khoune.

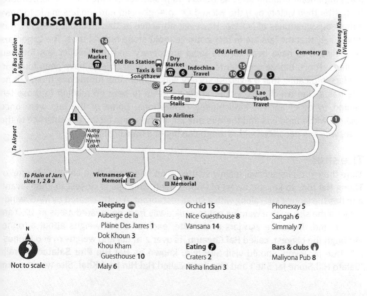

## Phonsavanh

**Sleeping** 🛌
Auberge de la
  Plaine Des Jarres **1**
Dok Khoun **3**
Khou Kham
  Guesthouse **10**
Maly **6**

Orchid **15**
Nice Guesthouse **8**
Vansana **14**

**Eating** 🍴
Craters **2**
Nisha Indian **3**

Phonexay **5**
Sangah **6**
Simmaly **7**

**Bars & clubs** 🍸
Maliyona Pub **8**

Not to scale
N

Laos Northern Laos Plain of Jars & the northeast

**Ins and outs**

**Getting there** Phonsavanh Airport (aka Xieng Khouang airport) is 4 km west of Phonsavanh. A tuk-tuk to town costs 20,000 kip per person. The most direct route by road from Luang Prabang to Xieng Khouang is to take Route 13 south to Muang Phou Khoun and then Route 7 east. An alternative, scenic, albeit convoluted, route is via Nong Khiaw (see page 435), from where there are pick-ups to Pak Xeng and Phonsavanh via Vieng Thong on Route 1 or Nam Nouan.

The bus station is 4 km west of Phonsavanh on Route 7, although many buses still pass by the old bus station near the dry market; a tuk-tuk to/from the centre costs 10,000 kip.

**Getting around** Public transport is limited and sporadic. Provincial laws have occasionally banned tuk-tuks and motorbikes from ferrying customers around the area. These regulations have been relaxed recently but don't be surprised if they are brought into force again. It should be possible to drive from Phonsavanh to the Plain of Jars, see Site one and return to town in two hours. Expect to pay in the region of US$30 for an English-speaking guide and vehicle for four people, or US$60 for seven people and a minivan. A tuk-tuk to Site one costs approximately US$7 per person. Alternatively, hotels, guesthouses and tour companies in Phonsavanh run set tours to the Plain of Jars, Muang Khoune (Xieng Khouang) and Hmong villages northeast of Phonsavanh. If you arrive by air, the chances are you'll be inundated with official and unofficial would-be guides as soon as you step off the plane. Note that it is not possible to walk from the airport to Site one as there is a military base in between. It is recommended that you hire a guide, for at least a day, to get an insight into the history of the area. The cost of admission to each site is 7000 kip. ▸▸ *For further information, see Activities and tours and Transport, pages 453.*

## Background

Most of the jars are generally between 1 m to 2.5 m high, around 1 m in diameter and weigh about the same as three small cars. The largest are about 3 m tall. The jars have long presented an archaeological conundrum, leaving generations of theorists nonplussed by how they got there and what they were used for. Local legend relates that King Khoon Chuong and his troops from Southern China threw a stupendous party after their victory over the wicked Chao Angka and had the jars made to brew outrageous quantities of *lao-lao*. However, attractive as this alcoholic thesis is, it is more likely that the jars are in fact 2000-year-old stone funeral urns. The larger jars are believed to have been for the local aristocracy and the smaller jars for their minions. Tools, bronze ornaments, ceramics and other objects have been found in the jars, indicating that a civilized society was responsible for making them but no one has a clue which one, as the artefacts seem to bear no relation to those left behind by other ancient Indochinese civilizations. Some of the jars were once covered with round lids and there is one jar, in the group facing the entrance to the cave, which is decorated with a rough carving of a dancing figure.

## The sites

More than 300 jars survive, mainly scattered on one slope at so-called 'Site one' or **Thong Hai Hin**, 10 km southwest of Phonsavanh. This site is closest to Phonsavanh and has the largest jar – along with a small restaurant. A path, cleared by MAG, winds through the site, with a warning not to walk away from delineated areas as UXO are still around. There are 250 jars at the site, each of which weighs about a tonne although the biggest, called **Hai Cheaum**, is over 2 m tall and weighs over 6 tonnes.

True jar lovers should visit Site two, known as **Hai Hin Phu Salatao** (literally 'Salato Hill Stone Jar Site') and Site three called **Hai Hin Laat Khai**. Site two is 25 km rather beautiful location, affording scenic views. A further 10 km south of Site two, Site three is the most atmospheric of all the sites, set in verdant green rolling hills, swiss-cheesed with bomb craters. To get there you have to walk through some rice paddies and cross the small bamboo bridge. There are more than 130 jars at this site, which are generally smaller and more damaged than at the other sites. There's also a very small, basic restaurant, serving *feu* (noodle soup).

## Tham Piu

① *The cave is to the west of the Muang Kham-Xam Neua Road, just after the 183 km post, entry 5000 kip. A rough track leads down to an irrigation dam, built in 1981. To get there from Phonsavanh you can either go the easy way and hire a vehicle US$30-40, or go the hard way, by public transport. For the latter, take the bus to Nong Haet, and request to stop at the Tham Phiu turn-off. From here walk towards the towering limestone cliff and follow the small trails for the last kilometre. It is best to do this with a guide as UXOs still litter the area.*

This cave is more of a memorial than a tourist site but will be of interest to those fascinated by the war.

More evidence of the dirty war can be seen here. The intensity of the US bombing campaign under the command of the late General Curtis Le May was such that entire villages were forced to take refuge in caves. (Curtis Le May is infamously associated with bragging that he wanted to bomb the Communists "back into the Stone Age".) If discovered, fighter bombers were called in to destroy them. In Tam Phiu, a cave overlooking the fertile valley near Muang Kham, 365 villagers from near-by Ban Na Meun built a two-storey bomb shelter and concealed its entrance with a high stone wall. They lived there for a year, working in their rice fields at night and taking cover during the day from the relentless bombing raids which killed thousands in the area. On the morning of 8 March 1968 two T-28 fighter-bombers took off from Udon Thani air base in neighbouring Thailand and located the cave mouth which had been exposed on previous sorties. It is likely that the US forces suspected that the cave contained a Pathet Lao hospital complex. Indeed, experts are at odds whether this was a legitimate target or an example of collateral damage. There are a few people still alive whose families died in the cave, and they certainly see it as innocent civilians being targeted. The first rocket destroyed the wall, the second, fired as the planes swept across the valley, carried the full length of the chamber before exploding. There were no survivors and 11 families were completely wiped out; in total 374 people died, many reportedly women and children. Local rescuers claim they were unable to enter the cave for three days, but eventually the dead were buried in a bomb crater on the hillside next to the cave mouth. You will need a torch to explore the cave but there isn't much inside, just eerily black walls. The interior of the cave was completely dug up by the rescue parties and relatives and today there is nothing but rubble inside. It makes for a poignant lesson in military history and locally it is considered a war memorial. Further up the cliff is another cave, **Tham Phiu Song**, which fortunately didn't suffer the same fate. Before the stairway to the caves there is a little memorial centre which displays photographs from the war and is usually attended by a relative of the victims. A poignant sculpture of a soldier carrying a dead child marks the site, free of the victory and glory of most other war monuments. Many bomb craters around the site have been turned into fish ponds now bearing beautiful lotus.

## Sao Hintang

① *About 130 km north of Phonsavanh and 56.5 km southwest of Xam Neua on Route 6. For further information contact the tourist office in Xam Neua. Tours can also be organized from Phonsavanh through Mr Sousath of Maly Hotel (see Sleeping, page 453).*

## Vieng Xai (Viengsay) and the Pathet Lao caves

Tourists are often put off visiting Hua Phan Province by the long bus haul to get here but, considering the road passes through gorgeous mountain scenery, the trip is well worth it. The main roads in are the paved Route 6, from Phonsavanh and the south, and Route 1, from Vieng Thong and the west. **Xam Neua** (Sam Neua) is the main provincial town and the tourist office here can organize a car with driver to Vieng Xai caves. Summer is pleasant but temperatures plummet at night so you should bring a jumper. Mosquitoes are monstrous here; precautions against malaria are advised. Xam Neua is one of the most intriguing provincial capitals in Laos and is buzzing with a colourful outdoor food market and the eclectic dry market.

The village of **Vieng Xai** lies 31 km east of Xam Neua and the trip is possibly one of the country's most picturesque journeys, passing terraces of rice, pagodas, copper- and charcoal-coloured karst formations, dense jungle with misty peaks and friendly villages dotted among the mountains' curves. The limestone landscape is riddled with natural caves that proved crucial in the success of the Communists (Pathet Lao) in the 1960s and 1970s. From 1964 onwards, Pathet Lao operations were directed from cave systems at Vieng Xai, which provided an effective refuge from furious bombing attacks. The village of Vieng Xai grew from 4 small villages consisting of less than 10 families to

a thriving hidden city concealing over 20,000 people in the 100 plus caves in the area. The Pathet Lao leadership renamed the area Vieng Xai, meaning 'City of Victory' and it became the administrative and military hub of the revolutionary struggle. The village itself was built in 1973, when the bombing finally stopped and the short-lived Provisional Government of National Union was negotiated. Today the former capital of the liberated zone is an unlikely sight: surrounded by rice fields at the dead end of a potholed road, it features street lighting, power lines, sealed and kerbed streets and substantial public buildings – all in varying stages of decay. Nonetheless is truly one of the most beautiful towns in Laos, dotted with fruit trees, hibiscus and man-made lakes, and flanked by amazing karst formations.

7 caves, formerly occupied by senior Pathet Lao leaders (Prince Souphanouvong, Kaysone Phomvihane, Nouhak Phounsavanh, Khamtai Siphandon and Phoumi Vongvichit), and open to visitors and all are within walking distance of the village; tickets are sold at the **Viengxay Caves Visitor Centre** ① *T064-314321, viengxaycavesvisitorcentre@yahoo.com daily 0800-1200, 13 00-1630; guided tours are conducted at 0900 and 1300, 30,000 kip with guide.* Tours are usually conducted on bikes which can be rented from the office. If you want to take the tour outside the designated times you must pay an additional fee. You will need to start early in

At the billboard-sized sign at the turn-off in Ban Liang Sat, turn up the dirt road heading east. This road is quite rough in places so you'll need a 4WD car or an all-terrain motorbike in order to get there. About 3 km up the road is a sign for the Kechintang Trail, a 90-minute walking trail that takes you to some of the sites. The first is visible from the road after a further 3 km, with Site two located another 3 km after that.

the morning to see all the caves. If you plan on coming across from Xam Neua it is advisable to stay overnight.

The caves have a secretive atmosphere, with fruit trees and frangipani decorating the exteriors. They have been fitted with electric bulbs but you may find a torch useful. Each cave burrows deep into the mountainside and features 60 cm-thick concrete walls, encompassing living quarters, meeting rooms, offices, dining and storage areas. Most visitors to Vieng Xai and the caves stay in Xam Neua and take a day trip. There is accommodation in Vieng Xai if required:

E **Naxay Guesthouse** (there are 2 by this name), opposite the Vieng Xai Cave Visitor Centre, T064-314330. 5 beautiful new bungalows with hot water, comfortable beds and a Western toilet. Recommended.

F **Naxay Guesthouse**, T064-314336. Very rustic accommodation with shared bathrooms. Beds as hard as rocks. There is a very pleasant restaurant beside the main lake in Vieng Xai – the fish here is a winner. In Xam Neua choose from

E-F **Kheamxam Guesthouse**, T064-312111. Offers a wide range of fairly well appointed rooms with attached hot-water bathrooms, some with a/c.

E **Shuliyo**, about 100 m from the songthaew station. Comfortable, modern rooms with hot-water bathrooms.

The colourful fresh food market in Xam Neua offers a wonderful selection of local dishes. **Kittavanh Restaurant**, opposite the Nam Xam river near the end of the market, offers great Lao food, particularly feu, with a good English menu on a whiteboard. **Dan Xam Muang**, a block back from the river, near the bridge, T064-314126. A good option. The fried fish is excellent as is the *feu*, *laap* and French fries. Good service.

There are regular songthaews from Xam Neua to Vieng Xai, 60-90 mins, 20,000 kip, although there are virtually no services after 1500 in either direction. If you get stuck you can charter a vehicle for a whole day for US$30-40, 50 mins.

Xam Neua bus station is about 2 km from the centre of town and costs 5000 kip in a songthaew. Buses depart from Xam Neua to Vieng Xai 5 times daily in the morning, 20,000 kip; to Nameo (the Vietnam border) at 0630, 25,000 kip; Nam Nouan 0700 (4 hrs), 27,000kip; Vieng Thong, 0720, 40,000 kip; Phonsavanh, 0800, 70,000 kip (10 hrs); Luang Prabang, 0800, 16 hrs, 100,000 kip; Vientiane 0800 and 1230, 24 hrs, 150,000 kip; Udomxai Sat 0900, 100,000 kip; Thanh Hoa (Vietnam) Sat 0800, 100,000 kip. The Luang Prabang bus goes via Nong Khiaw, 12 hrs, 70,000 kip.

Lao Air runs flights to Xam Neua, Sat and Mon, US$62 one way. Xam Neua airport is 2 km from the centre of town.

There are hundreds of ancient upright stone pillars, menhirs and discs, gathered in Stonehenge-type patterns over a 10-km area, surrounded by jungle. This enigmatic site is as mysterious as the Plain of Jars: no one is quite sure who, or even which ethnic group, is responsible for erecting the stones and they have become steeped in legend. It is believed that the two sites are somehow linked, as they are fashioned from the same stone and share some archaeological similarities. ▶ *For further information, see Activities and tours, page 453.*

**To Vietnam via Nam Xoi**

It is possible to cross over to Vietnam from here at the Nam Xoi (Laos)/Nameo (Vietnam) border crossing if you have a Lao/Vietnam visa. The border is open 0730-1130, 1330-1700. It may be necessary to pay a processing or overtime fee at weekend and after 1630.

**Transport** The trip is two hours from Vieng Xai and songthaews leave at 0640 from the main road between Xam Neua and Nameo, 1 km from the centre of Vieng Xai; 20,000 kip. It is also possible to travel from Xam Neua to the border by songthaew from the station at 0630 and 0715, 3-4 hrs, 30,000 kip or to charter a songthaew for about US$50. There have been several complaints about tourist operators on the Vietnamese side of this border charging a fortune for transport. A motorbike taxi to Quan Son should cost around US$10. If you get really stuck on the Vietnam side contact Mr Pham Xuan Hop in Nameo, T0084-9-9237425 who may be able to organize minivan rental, US$50 to Quan Son.

**Accommodation** There are 2 basic guesthouses in Nameo; Phucloc Nha Tru and Minhchien which both offer rudimentary facilities for US$3-5.

## ⬛ Sleeping

**Phonsavanh** *p447, map p447*
None of the streets in Phonsavanh are named – or at least the names aren't used.
**A-B Auberge de la Plaine des Jarres** (aka Phu Pha Daeng Hotel), 1 km from the centre, T/F021-312044. In a spectacular position on a hill overlooking the town are 16 attractive stone and wood chalets, with living room, fireplace and shower room (occasional hot water). Clean and comfortable with flowers planted around the chalets. Restaurant serves good food. More expensive Oct-May. They sell keyrings made of bullets.
**A-B Vansana**, on a hill 1 km out of town, T061-213170. Big, modern rooms with telephone, TV, minibar, polished floorboards and tea/coffee-making facilities. Phenomenal views of the countryside. Opt for the rooms upstairs, with free-form bathtub and picturesque balcony views. Restaurant offers Lao and foreign cuisine. Excellent value, especially the VIP room for US$50. Highly recommended.
**B-D Maly Hotel**, down the road from local government offices, T061-312031. All rooms have hot water and are furnished with a hotchpotch of local artefacts, including a small (defused!) cluster bomb on the table. More expensive rooms on the upper floors have satellite TV, internet for those who have laptops, out-of-place bathtubs, a sitting area and other luxuries.

Restaurant. The owner, Mr Sousath Phetrasy, runs tours.
**C-D Orchid**, just off the main road in the centre of town, T061-312403. You can't miss this big green-blue building. Guesthouse, not quite at hotel standard but close enough to it for this place to be good value. Rooms with TV, hot water, comfy beds and bath. Nicely decorated. Free breakfast and airport pickup (if you ring in advance).
**E Khou Kham Guesthouse**, on the main road through town. A Hmong-owned hotel. Large rooms with bathroom and hot water, but the beds are a bit like sleeping on a rock face. Mai and Khou, the friendly owners, speak English. A large selection of ethnic hats for sale in the foyer.
**E Nice Guesthouse**, on the main road, T0205616246, naibthoj@hotmail.com. Has a Chinese feel about it but owned by local Lao. Clean decent sized rooms with hot water and comfy beds. Reasonable value.
**E-F Sabaidee**, a block back from the main road, sabaidee2000@hotmail.com. Tiled, clean rooms with hot-water bathroom. Very low hobbit-like doors. Central location, family atmosphere.
**F Dok Khoun**, Route 7, T061-312189. Tiled rooms with desk. So clean that the smell of ammonia could knock you out. The bathroom is in what looks like a cupboard.

## Eating

**Phonsavanh** *p447, map p447*

**Maly Hotel**, see Sleeping. A great little restaurant serving fantastic food from a very extensive menu: everything from duck curry to beef steak.

**Craters**, main street, T020-7805775. Modern, Western restaurant offering burgers, pizza and sandwiches. Comfortable cane sofas, good music, attentive service. Delectable but pricey cocktails.

**Nisha Indian**, on the main road. The most unexpected find in Phonsavanh: north and south Indian food.

**Phonexay**, on the main road, towards the Tourism Office. Excellent fruit shakes and good Asian dishes – fried noodles, sweet and sour. Exceptionally friendly.

**Sangah**, main street. Thai, Lao and Vietnamese (good noodle soup) dishes available, as well as some Western fare including steak and chips. Enormous portions.

**Simmaly**, main street, T061-211013. What this place lacks in atmosphere it makes up 10-fold with food. Fantastic *feu* soup. Great service and immensely popular. Recommended.

### Drinking

**Maliyona Pub**, on the main road. This graffiti-decorated bar on the main drag sticks out like a sore thumb. Ear-blastingly loud hip-hop and Thai music. Beer Lao and BYO spirits. Rather devoid of customers.

## Festivals and events

**Phonsavanh** *p447, map p447*

**Dec** **National Day** on the 2 Dec is celebrated with horse-drawn drag-cart racing. Also in Dec is **Hmong New Year** (movable), which is celebrated in a big way in this area.

## Activities and tours

**Phonsavanh** *p447, map p447*
**Tour operators**
There are no shortage of tour operators in Phonsavanh and most guesthouses can now arrange tours and transport. A full-day tour for 4 people, travelling about 30 km into the countryside, should cost up to US$50-60, although you may have to bargain for it.

Most of the travel agencies are located within a block of each other on the main road.
**Indochina Travel**, on the main road, T061-312409. Expensive but well-regarded minivan tours (cheaper if you can organize a group).
**Lao Youth Travel**, on Route 7, T020-5761233, www.laoyouthtravel.com. Offers a wide range of tours to the jars and post conflict sites.

The most knowledgeable tour guide, however, is the owner of the **Maly Hotel** (see Sleeping). **Sousath Phetrasy** spent his teenage years in a cave at Xam Neua (see page 450) during the war.

## Transport

**Phonsavanh** *p447, map p447*
**Air**
Lao Airlines T061-212027, runs flights to **Vientiane**, 30 mins, everyday except Tue and Thu. In peak season it is often possible to fly via **Luang Prabang**.

**Bus**
To **Luang Prabang**, daily 0800 (both local and VIP bus), 265 km on a sealed road, 90,000 kip. To **Vientiane**, daily 0700, 0930 and 1600, 9-10 hrs, 90,000 kip, also a VIP bus daily at 0730, 100,000 kip. To **Vang Vieng**, daily 0720, 75,000 kip, and a VIP bus 0730, 100,000 kip. To **Muang Kham**, 3 hrs, 30,000 kip. Also north to **Nam Nouan** 0900, 4 hrs, 35,000 kip (change here for transport west to **Nong Khiaw**). **Xam Neua**, daily 0800 and 1600, 70,000 kip, a 10-hr haul through some of the country's most beautiful scenery and some very windy roads towards the end (you may want to take something for motion sickness). Buses also travel to **Vinh**, Vietnam on Tue, Thu and Sat, 0630, 12 hrs, US$12. If you want to cross the border here you will need to organize a visa in advance as there is no consulate in Phonsavanh and no agencies to send your passport to Vientiane.

**Nam Noaun** is a staging post that travellers bound for **Xam Neua** or **Nong Khiaw** will invariably find themselves stopping at. The through traffic for Xam Neua is relatively frequent and most buses/songthaews from

Phonsavanh stop on the way through. Getting a connecting bus to Nong Khiaw is a little more complicated as Nam Noun sits 7 km south of the junction between Routes 1 and 6, the junction village is called **Ban Sam Nyay**. You can get to the junction by songthaew or by asking one of the locals for a lift on a motorbike. Most buses to/from Nong Khiaw stop at the village and not Nam Nouan. It is a pleasant Khmu village but there is very little there in the way of amenities. If you are coming from Nong Khiaw you will probably arrive disorientated and dishevelled at some ungodly hour. Locals may try to charge you an extortionate rate to get a pickup to Nam Nouan, if that is the case just see if you can grab a lift with someone on a motorbike for US$5-6.

### Car

A full car with driver to the **Plain of Jars** will cost US$20 (US$5 each) to Site one, or US$30-40 to all 3 sites. To hire a songthaew to go to **Tham Phiu** is US$30-40 for the day, a minivan costs US$60.

## ❶ Directory

**Phonsavanh** *p447, map p447*
**Banks** Lao Development Bank, Mon-Fri 0800-1200, 1330-1600, near Lao Airlines Office, 2 blocks back from the dry market. Changes cash and TCs. No advances on Visa. **Indochine Travel** has an exchange booth with Visa advance, the only place in town, but they charge a whopping 6.9% commission. Moneygram service.
**Hairdressers** Unlikely that you would want a new hairstyle here but there are several hairdressers dotted around town that will give you a good head massage and hairwash for 10,000 kip. **Internet** At the photo shop, 200 kip per min, and across from the songthaew station in town. Slow internet access. **Medical services** Lao-Mongolian Hospital, T061-312166. Sufficient for minor ailments. Pharmacies are ubiquitous in town. **Post office and telephone** The post office is opposite the dry market and has IDD telephone boxes outside. **Shopping** West of the town centre is the Chinese Market, which stocks a good variety of ethnic clothes and jewellery as well as many cheap and tacky imported goods.

# Southern Laos

## ⁑ Footprint features

# Introduction

Laos' southern provinces offer a varied array of enticements and a different character from the north of the country. Base yourself in the region's unofficial capital, Pakse, to explore the many attractions of Champasak Province, including the romantic, pre-Angkorian ruins of Wat Phou and Ban Kiet Ngong, with its elephants. Inland from Pakse is the Boloven Plateau, an area that was earmarked by the French for settlement and coffee production. The rivers running off the plateau have created a series of spectacular falls, including towering Tad Fan and stunning Tad Lo.

A highlight of any trip down south is Siphandon, where the Mekong divides into a myriad channels and 'Four Thousand Islands'. The idyllic, palm-fringed Don Khone, Don Deth and Don Khong provide perfect places to relax and absorb riverine life, as fisherman cast nets amongst lush green islets and children frolic on the sand bars.

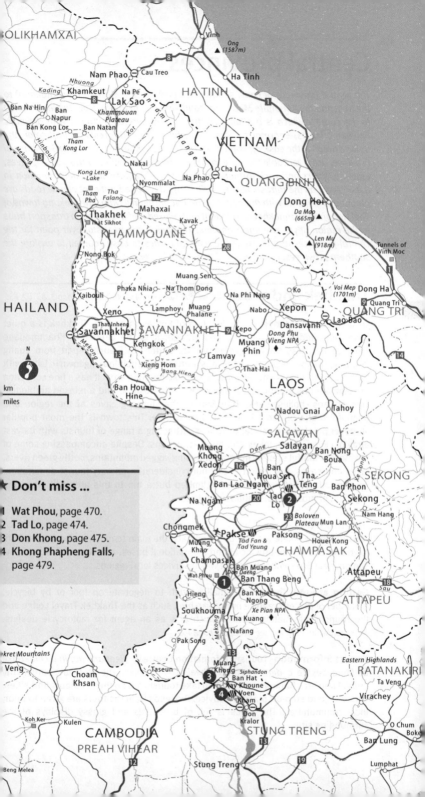

# Central provinces

*The central provinces of Laos, sandwiched between the Mekong (and Thailand) to the west and the Annamite Mountains (and Vietnam) to the east, are the least visited in the country which is a shame as the scenery here is stunning, with dramatic limestone karsts, enormous caves, beautiful rivers and forests. In particular, the upland areas to the east, off Route 8 and Route 12, in Khammouane and Bolikhamxai Province, are a veritable treasure trove of attractions, mottled with scores of caves, lagoons, rivers and rock formations. Visitors will require some determination in these parts, as the infrastructure is still being developed but a lot of new roads are planned to coincide with the near-finished Nam Theun II Dam. The Mekong towns of Thakhek and Savannakhet are elegant and relaxed and are the main transport hubs in the region. If you are short on time, Thakhek is the best stopover point for the central provinces and Pakse is the optimum place to base yourself to explore the southern provinces.* ▸▸ *For Sleeping, Eating and other listings, see pages 464-467.*

## Thakhek and around ⬤🚲🚌 ▸▸ *pp464-467. Colour map 3, A2, B2, B3.*

Located on the Mekong, at the junction of Routes 13 and 12, Thakhek is a quiet town, surrounded by beautiful countryside. It is the capital of Khammouane Province and was founded in 1911-1912, under the French. Apart from Luang Prabang, Thakhek is probably the most outwardly French-looking town in Laos, with fading pastel villas clustered around a simple fountain area. It has a fine collection of colonial-era shophouses, a breezy riverside position and a relaxed ambience. One of Laos' holiest sites, That Sikhot, the stunning caves of the region and beautiful Mahaxai can all be visited from here. This town is the most popular stopover point in the central provinces, attracting a range of tourists with its vast array of caves, rivers, lakes and other attractions. Despite encompassing some of the most beautiful scenery in Laos: imposing jagged mountains, bottle green rivers, lakes and caves, the region is still not considered a primary tourist destination. Tourism infrastructure is still quite limited but a trip to this area will prove the highlight of most visitors' holidays to Laos.

### Ins and outs

**Getting there** There are two bus terminals: the main terminal is about 5 km from town and offers inter-provincial and international buses, and the small songthaew station, near Soksombook market which services local regions.

**Getting around** Thakhek is small enough to negotiate on foot or by bicycle. A number of places organize motorbike hire, such as the **Thakhek Travel Lodge** and the Tourism Information Centre, which acts as an agent for motorcycle dealers. ▸▸ *For further information, see Transport, page 466.*

**Tourist information** Tourism Information Centre ① *Vientiane Rd, in a chalet-like building beside a derelict Ferris wheel, T052-212512.* The staff are particularly helpful and are champing at the bit to take tourists out on their ecotours and hikes. This is a good stop-off place for advice. Proceeds from the tours are given to poor, local communities. The office is full of brochures and glossy displays of the surrounding sites.

① *6 km south of Thakhek, daily 0800-1800; 2000 kip. Tuk-tuk 10,000 kip.*

That Sikhot or **Sikhotaboun** is one of Laos' holiest sites. It overlooks the Mekong and the journey downstream from Thakhek, along a quiet country road, reveals bucolic Laos at its best. The *that* is thought to have been built by Chao Anou at the beginning of the 15th century and houses the relics of Chao Sikhot, a local hero, who founded the old town of Thakhek.

According to local legend, Sikhot was bestowed with Herculean strength after eating some rice he had stirred with dirty – but as it turned out magic – sticks. At that time, the King of Vientiane was having a problem with elephants killing villagers and taking over the country (hard to believe now but Laos was once called Land of a Million Elephants). The King offered anyone who could save the region half his Kingdom and his daughter's hand in marriage. Due to his new-found strength, Sikhot was able to take on the pachyderms and secure most of the surrounding area as well as Vientiane, whereupon he married the King of Vientiane's daughter. The King was unhappy about handing over his kingdom and daughter to this man, and plotted with his daughter to regain control. Sikhot foolishly revealed to his new wife that he could only be killed through his anus, so the King of Vientiane placed an archer at the bottom of Sikhot's pit latrine (a messy business that does not bear thinking about) and when the unfortunate Oriental Hercules came to relieve himself, he was killed by an arrow.

That Sikhot consists of a large gold stupa raised 29 m on a plinth, with a viharn upstream built in 1970 by the last King of Laos. A major annual festival is held here in July and during February.

## Kong Leng Lake

① *33 km northeast of Thakhek.*

This site is usually incorporated into hikes as there isn't direct road access to the lake. This stunning lake is steeped in legend and locals believe an underground Kingdom lies beneath the surface of the 100-m-deep lake. As a result, you must request permission to swim in this lake from the local village authority and you can only swim in the designated swimming zone. Fishing is not permitted. The beautiful green waters of the lake morph into different shades season to season due to the dissolved calcium from the surrounding limestone crops. It is very difficult to get to on your own and the track sometimes is completely inaccessible except on foot. The Tourism Information Centre organizes excellent treks to the lake.

## Tham Pha (Buddha Cave) → *Colour map 3, A2 and B2.*

① *Ban Na Khangxang, off Route 12, 18 km from Thakhek; 2000 kip. A songthaew will cost US$15, use of boat 5000 kip. Women will need to hire a sinh (sarong) at the entance, 2000 kip.*

A farmer hunting for bats accidentally stumbled across the Buddha Cave (also known Tham Pa Fa, or Turtle Cave) in April 2004. On climbing up to the cave's mouth, he found 229 bronze Buddha statues, believed to be more than 450 years old, and ancient palm leaf scripts. These Buddhas were part of the royal collection believed to have been hidden here when the Thais ransacked Vientiane. Since its discovery, the cave has become widely celebrated, attracting pilgrims from as far away as Thailand, particularly around Pi Mai (Lao New Year). A wooden ladder and eyesore concrete steps have now been built to access the cave, but it is quite difficult to get to as the dirt road from Thakhek is in poor condition. It is recommended that you organize a guide through the **Thakhek Tourism Information Centre** to escort you. In the wet season, it is necessary to catch a boat. The journey itself is half the fun as the cave is surrounded by some truly stunning karst formations sprawling across the landscape like giant dinosaur teeth.

## Tham Kong Lor (Kong Lor cave)

① *Entrance fee at cave 5000 kip.* Tham Kong Lor cave can only be described as sensational. The Nam Hinboun River has tunnelled through the mountain, creating a giant rocky cavern, 6 km long, 90 m wide and 100 m high, which opens out into the blinding bright light at Ban Natan on the other side. The cave is apparently named after the drum makers who were believed to make their instruments here. Although very rare, it is also home to the largest living cave-dwelling spiders in the world, though it took conservationists decades to spot them so it is unlikely you will have a run in with the massive arachnid. It is almost impossible to do the nine-to 10-hour return trip from Ban Na Hin to Kong Lor in a day, as boat drivers won't travel in the dark. The first stage of the journey is by songthaew or tractor from Ban Na Hin to Ban Napur. From Ban Napur catch a boat along the Nam Hinboun to either Ban Phonyang where **Sala Hin Boun** is located (see Sleeping, page 465), or to Ban Kong Lor, the closest village to the caves, where you can find a homestay for 50,000 kip, including food. Beyond Ban Phonyang the river route to Tham Kong Lor is gorgeous, with small fish skipping

## Route 12 and the 'Loop' → *Colour map 3, A2, B2, B3.*

① *Contact Thakhek Travel Lodge (see Sleeping, page 464) for details of the 'Loop' route and for motorbike hire.*

The impressive karst landscape of the Mahaxai area is visible to the northeast of town and can be explored on a popular motorbike tour from Thakhek, known as the **Loop**, which runs from Thakhek along Route 12 to Mahaxai, then north to Lak Sao, west along Route 8 to Ban Na Hin and then south back to Thakhek on Route 13, taking in caves and other beautiful scenery along the way. The circuit – if done quickly – should take approximately three days but allow four to five, particularly if you want to sidetrack to Tham Kong Lor and the other caves along the way.

The 'Loop' is mostly for motorcyclists, who pick up a bike in Thakhek and travel by road. For those with more patience the trip can be undertaken on public transport. The whole loop covers an area over 400 km (without the side-trips). This includes 50 km from Thakhek to the Shell Station before the turn-off to Mahaxai; 45 km between the shell Station and Nakai; 70 km between Nakai and Lak Xao; 66 km between Lak Xao and Ban Na Hin; 60 km between Ban Na Hin and Ban Lao and then 100 km between Ban Lao and Thakhek. The trip between Ban Lao and Ban Na Hin offers some spectacular views.

If on a motorbike pack light: include a waterproof jacket, a torch, a few snacks, a long-sleeved shirt, sunglasses, sun block, closed-toe shoes, a *sinh* or sarong (to use as a towel, to stop dust and – for women – to bathe along the way), a phrase book and a good map. It is a bumpy, exhausting but enjoyable ride. Few of the sites are particularly well signposted in English so you will need to ask around. Most sites charge a parking fee for motorbikes.

Note that this whole region is very susceptible to change due to the Nam Theun II dam, a US$1.45 billion hydropower project, and other developments in the area. It is imperative that you check for up-to-date information before travelling. Check on the status of the roads at the Tourism Information Centre and check the logbook at the **Thakhek Lodge**. This trip is difficult in the wet season and will probably only be possible for skilled riders on larger dirt bikes. In the dry season it's very dusty.

The caves along Route 12 can also be visited on day trips from Thakhek, although some are difficult to find without a guide and access may be limited in the wet season. Many of the sights have no English signposts but locals will be more out of the water, languid buffalo bathing, kids taking a dip and ducks floating by – all surrounded by a Lord of the Rings fantasyland of breathtaking cliffs and rocky outcrops. At the start of the cave, you will have to scramble over some boulders while the boatmen carry the canoe over the rapids, so wear comfortable shoes with a good grip. A torch or, better a headlamp (2000 kip at Thakhek market), is also recommended. About two-thirds of the way through the cave is an impressive collection of stalagmites and stalactites. It is possible to continue from Ban Natan, on the other side of Kong Lor, into the awesome Hinboun gorge. This is roughly 14 km long and, for much of the distance, vertical cliffs over 300 m high rise directly from the water on both sides. Don't expect the three- to four-hour boat trip to be cheap – it is around US$25 each way (if you are lucky). These prices will come down once the roads have improved and the boat drivers don't have a monopoly on transport. A new road, scheduled to be completed in 2008, is in the works and will take visitors the 50 km from Ban Na Hin (also known as Ban Khoun Kham) to Ban Kong Lor.

than obliging to confirm you are going in the right direction if you ask. Turn south off Route 12 at Km 7 to reach **Tham Xang** (Tham Pha Ban Tham), an important Buddhist shrine that contains some statues and a box of religious scripts. It is considered auspicious due to the 'elephant head' that has formed from calcium deposits and in the Lao New Year the locals sprinkle water on it. At Km 13, turn north on a track for 2 km to **Tha Falang** (Vang Santiphap – Peace Pool), a lovely emerald billabong on the Nam Don River, surrounded by pristine wilderness and breathtaking cliffs. It's a nice place to spend the afternoon or break your journey. In the wet season it may be necessary to catch a boat from the Xieng Liab Bridge to get here. Turn south off Route 12 at Km 14 and follow the track south to reach **Tham Xiang Liab**, a reasonably large cave at the foot of a 300-m-high limestone cliff, with a small swimming hole (in the dry season) at the far end. It is not easy to access the interior of the cavern on your own and, in the wet season, it can only be navigated by boat, as it usually floods. This cave, called 'sneaking around cave' derived its name from a legend of an old hermit who used to meditate in the cave with his beautiful daughter. A novice monk fell in love with the hermit's daughter and the two lovebirds planned their trysts sneakily around this cave and Tham Nan Aen. When the hermit found out he flew into a rage and did away with the novice monk; the daughter was banished to the cave for the rest of her life.

At Km 17, beyond the narrow pass, turn to the north and follow the path for 400 m to reach **Tham Sa Pha In**, a cave containing a small Lake and a couple of interesting Buddhist shrines. Swimming in the lake is strictly prohibited as the auspicious waters are believed to have magical powers. South of Route 12, at Km 18, a path leads 700 m to the entrance of **Tham Nan Aen** ① *5000 kip*. This is the giant of the local caverns at 1.5 km long and over 100 m high. It has multiple chambers and the entrances are illuminated by fluorescent lighting; it also contains a small underground freshwater pool.

## Mahaxai → *Colour map 3, B2 and B3.*

Mahaxai is a beautiful small town 50 km east of Thakhek off Route 12. The sunset here is quite extraordinary but even more beautiful is the surrounding scenery of exquisite valleys and imposing limestone bluffs. A visit to Mahaxai should be combined with a visit to one or more of the spectacular caves along Route 12 and some river excursions to see the Xe Bang Fai gorges or run the rapids further downstream.

Close to Ban Na, 25 km northeast of Thakhek is **Nam Don Resurgence**. This beautiful lagoon is difficult to find without a local guide as it's located within a cave. It is shaded by a sheer 300 m cliff and filters off into an underground waterway network, believed to extend for 3 km.

# Savannakhet 🌐🚲⛰🏛☕ ↠ *pp464-467. Colour map 3, B2.*

Situated on the banks of the Mekong at the start of Route 9 to Danang in Vietnam, Savannakhet – or Savan as it is usually known – is an important river port and gateway to the south. The city has a sizeable Chinese population and attracts merchants from both Vietnam and Thailand, while the ubiquitous colonial houses and fading shopfronts are an ever-present reminder of earlier French influence. Savannakhet Province has several natural attractions, although the majority are a fair hike from the provincial capital. For those short on time in Laos, Pakse makes a better stopover than Savannakhet.

## Ins and outs

**Getting there and around** It is possible to cross into Vietnam by taking Route 9 east over the Annamite Mountains via Xepon. The border is at Dansavanh (Laos) and Lao Bao (Vietnam) (see page 131), 236 km east of Savannakhet, with bus connections direct from Savannakhet to Danang, Dong Ha and Hué. It is possible to cross the border into Mukdahan via the new Friendship Bridge or by one of the more infrequent ferries. The government bus terminal is near the Savan Xai market has connections with Vientiane, Thakhek, Pakse and Lao Bao; a tuk-tuk to the centre should cost about 10,000 kip. Just west of the bus station is the songthaew terminal, where vehicles depart to provincial destinations. Tuk-tuks, locally known as *Sakaylab*, criss-cross town. ↠ *For further information, see Transport, page 466.*

**Tourist information** The **Provincial Tourism Office** ① *T052-214203*, is one of the best in the country and runs a number of excellent ecotours and treks to Dong Natad and Dong Phu Vieng National Protected Areas, which should be organized in advance. The office can also arrange guides and drivers for other trips. ↠ *For further information, see Activities and tours, page 466.*

## Sights

Savan's **colonial heritage** can be seen throughout the town centre. Perhaps the most attractive area is the square east of the Immigration office between Khanthabouli and Phetsalath roads. **Wat Sounantha** has a three-dimensional raised relief on the front of the *sim*, showing the Buddha in the *mudra* of bestowing peace, separating two warring armies. **Wat Sayaphum** on the Mekong is rather more attractive and has several early 20th-century monastery buildings. It is both the largest and oldest monastery in town, although it was only built at the end of the 19th century. Evidence of Savan's diverse population is reflected in the **Chua Dieu Giac**, a Mahayana Buddhist pagoda that serves the town's Vietnamese population. The **Dinosaur Museum** ① *Khanthabouli Rd, Mon-Fri 0800-1200, 1400-1600; 5000 kip*, houses a collection of four different dinosaur and early mammalian remains, and even some fragments of a meteorite that fell to earth over 100 million years ago.

For those unable to get to the Ho Chi Minh Trail, there is some rusting war scrap in the grounds of the **Provincial Museum** ① *Khanthabouli Rd, Mon-Fri 0800-1130, 1300-1600, 5000 kip*, and a tank just to the north. The museum offers plenty of propaganda-style displays but little that is terribly enlightening unless you are interested in the former revolutionary leader Kaysone Phomvihane. If it looks closed just go across to the School of Medicine and knock on the curator's quarters, housed in the wooden building.

ⓘ *Any of the regular tuk-tuks which will make the trip for 80,000 kip return or take a shared songthaew to Xeno and ask to hop off at That Inheng. They will usually take you all the way there but if they drop you at the turning it is only a 3-km walk. Alternatively hire a bicycle in town and cycle.*

This holy 16th-century *that* or stupa is 12 km northeast of Savannakhet and is the second-holiest site in Southern Laos after Wat Phou. It was built during the reign of King Sikhottabong at the same time as That Luang in Vientiane, although local guides may try to convince you it was founded by the Indian emperor Asoka over 2000 years ago. Needless to say, there is no historical evidence to substantiate this claim. The wat is the site of an annual festival in February or March akin to the one celebrated at Wat Phou, Champasak (see page 470).

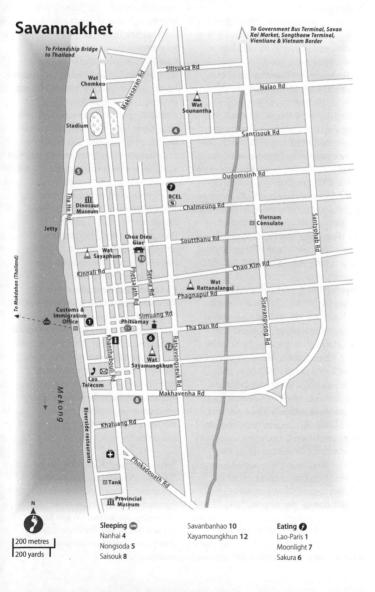

Savannakhet

200 metres
200 yards

**Sleeping** 🛏
Nanhai **4**
Nongsoda **5**
Saisouk **8**
Savanbanhao **10**
Xayamoungkhun **12**

**Eating** 🍴
Lao-Paris **1**
Moonlight **7**
Sakura **6**

**Dong Phu Vieng National Protected Area**

The Provincial Tourism Office (see Ins and outs, page 462) runs excellent treks through the Dong Phu Vieng National Protected Area, home to wildlife such as Siamese crocodiles, Asian elephants, the endangered Eld's deer, langurs and wild bison (most of which you would be incredibly lucky to see). Located within the NPA is a **Song Sa Kae** (Sacred Forest and Cemetery), revered by the local Katang ethnic group, who are known for their buffalo sacrifices. The well-trained local guides show how traditional natural produce is gathered for medicinal, fuel or other purposes. The tours are exceptionally good value. Most will only run during the dry season.

## ● Sleeping

**Thakhek** *p458*

Because of the irregular bus hours there is a small 'guesthouse' at the bus station, where you can rent a bed for 25,000 kip. Best avoided if possible.

**C-D Sooksomboon Guesthouse** (formerly the Sikhot Hotel), Setthathirat Rd, T051-250777. An immensely attractive building facing the Mekong that was once the provincial police station. The interior has been decorated with 1970s kitsch, deer antler decorations and padded walls, not to be cool but because it hasn't been renovated in the last 30 years. Once you get over the ghastly decor the place is actually very good value. The a/c rooms in the main house are best, with en suite bathrooms, bathtubs, fluffy chairs, fridge and TV. Also cheaper rooms in the motel-esque annexe. Excellent view across the river to Thailand. Run-down restaurant.

**D Mekong Hotel**, Setthathirat Rd (or Mekong Rd), T051-250777. Prime location overlooking the Mekong but housed in a hideous building painted in putrid baby blue. Exterior aside, the large 1950s hotel has 60 or so a/c rooms, with wide balconies perfect for the sunset vista. Large, plain but clean, with TV, telephone, fridge and bathtub. It's one of the best deals in town.

**D Southida Guesthouse**, Chao Anou Rd, T051-212568. Very popular guesthouse in the centre of town. Clean, comfortable rooms with a/c, TV and hot water. Very helpful staff and small restaurant downstairs, offering an eccentric mixture of dishes including sashimi. Often booked up.

**D-E Phoukanna**, Vientiane Rd, T030-212092. Nice gardens and good value, homely rooms with TV and hot water. Mini-mart and excellent restaurant on site. The hotel itself is fantastic, and popular with the NGO crowd,

if you can rouse the nonplussed staff from their sleep to organize a room.

**D-E Thakhek Travel Lodge**, 2 km from the centre of town, T030-5300145, travell@laotel.com. Popular guesthouse set in a beautifully restored and decorated house. Fantastic outdoor seating area and the furniture and embellishments are outstanding. The cheaper rooms are very basic. Good hotel restaurant particularly the Hawaiian curry, and BBQ (which needs to be ordered in advance), and the espresso machine. The owners provide travel advice, when they're around, and there's an excellent logbook for those intending to travel independently around the 'Loop'. Motorcycle hire, US$15 per day. Recommended for those planning adventure travel around the area. Ring them in advance if you're arriving on one of the midnight buses.

**F Khammuan International** (formerly the Chaleunxay Hotel), Kouvoravong Rd, T052-212171. Military owned hotel that has a soulless penitentiary feel. Smallish rooms without windows but some have a/c and the en suite bathrooms have hot-water showers. Cheaper single rooms with super-powerful ceiling fans are also available. Although the rooms are quite good value, you wouldn't put your mother up here as it may well double as a brothel.

**Towards Tham Kong Lor** *p460*

There are 2 guesthouses on Route 13 in **Ban Lao**, just past the Route 8 intersection, which are passable. Homestays are available in **Ban Kong Lor** and **Ban Natan**. The homestays charge about US$5 per person including breakfast.

**B-C Sala Hin Boun**, Ban Phonyang, 10 km from Kong Lor cave, T020-5614016, www.salalao.com. The best option. It enjoys a scenic location on the riverbank amongst karst rock formations and has 10 well-equipped and very pleasant rooms in 2 bungalows. Mr Kham, the manager, will arrange for a boat to pick you up in Napua for US$25, with advance notice. A tour to Kong Lor for 2-3 people is US$30 with picnic lunch. Discounts in low season.
**D-E Sala Kong Lor Lodge**, 6 km from Kong Lor cave, T051-214315. Lodge with 4 small huts with twin beds and a couple of rooms. There is also a campsite for US$2 per night.

**Mahaxai** p461
**F Mahaxai Guesthouse**. 10 large, clean and airy rooms with en suite showers. Upstairs rooms are brighter. There is an attractive balcony overlooking the river, ideal for watching the world go by.

**Savannakhet** p462, map p463
**B-C Nanhai**, Santisouk Rd, T041-212371. This 7-storey hotel is considered one of the better places in town. The 42 rooms, karaoke bars and dining hall are a prime example of a mainland Chinese hotel. Rooms have a/c, TV, fridge, IDD telephones and en suite bathroom but they smell musty and the single rooms are minuscule. The pool has no water. Decent restaurant.
**D Nongsoda**, Tha He Rd, T041-212522. Dodles of white lace draped all over the house. Clean rooms with a/c and en suite bathrooms with wonderfully hot water. During the low season the hotel drops its room rate. Motorbike hire.
**D-F Savanbanhao**, Senna Rd, T041-212202, sbtour@laotel.com. Made up of 4 colonial-styles houses set around a quiet concrete courtyard, with a range of rooms. Most expensive have en suite hot-water showers. Beware of the lethal Soviet water boiler. Some a/c. Large balcony. Savanbanhao Tourism Co is attached (see Activities and tours, page 466). Good for those who want to be in and out of Savannakhet quickly.
**E-F Xayamoungkhun** (English sign just reads 'Guest House'), 85 Ratsavongseuk Rd, T041-212426. An excellent little hotel with 6 rooms in an airy colonial-era villa.

Centrally positioned with a largish compound. Range of very clean rooms available, the more expensive have hot water, a/c and a fridge. Very friendly owners. Second-hand books and magazines available. Recommended.
**F Saisouk**, Makhavenha Rd, T041-212207. This breezy guesthouse has good-sized twin and double rooms, immaculately furnished and spotlessly clean, some a/c, communal bathrooms. Beautifully decorated with interesting objets d'art and what looks like dinosaur bones. Plenty of chairs and tables on the large verandas. Very friendly staff, reasonable English. Laundry service. Very friendly and homely.

## ⓓ Eating

**Thakhek** p458
There is the usual array of noodle stalls – try the one in the town 'square' with good fruit shakes. Warmed baguettes are also sold in the square in the morning. The best place to eat is definitely at one of the riverside restaurants on either side of fountain square, where you can watch the sunset, knock back a Beer Lao and tuck into tasty BBQ foods. Otherwise, most restaurants are attached to hotels.
**¶ Kaysone Restaurant**, in the centre of town, T051-212563. Although from the outside this looks like someone's backyard, once inside you'll discover a sprawling restaurant. Very popular with the locals. *Sindat*, Korean BBQ and an à la carte menu comprising of entrails and so forth. The ice cream here is fantastic. If you feel like belting out some tunes, there's karaoke on site. What more could one ask for?
**¶ Phoukanna**, see Sleeping. The best option, with good service and an array of Western and Lao dishes.
**¶ Southida Guesthouse**, see Sleeping. Good value and does a reasonable Western breakfast and has a very eclectic menu including sashimi.
**¶ Sukiyaki**, on Vientiane Rd, T020-5751533. A pokey but exceptionally friendly restaurant where a buffet of food is on offer which you can BBQ yourself at the table.
**¶ Thakhek Travel Lodge**, see Sleeping. Recommended for their BBQs and other meals.

Several restaurants on the riverside serve good food and beer. The market also has stalls offering good, fresh food, including excellent Mekong river fish.

¶ **Lao-Paris**, Simung St. A crumbling building with 4 tables on the grey veranda and a dingy inside. Tasty falang fare and Lao/Vietnamese dishes, opens at 0800 and serves a good breakfast. Cheap but definitely not haute cuisine.

¶ **Moonlight Restaurant**, Ratsavongseuk Rd, T030-5315718. Cosy café serving a range of reasonable Western dishes. Very popular with travellers and locals.

¶ **Sakura**, Sayamungkhun Rd, near the church, T041-212882. This is a bit of a shock find – in a good way. A very atmospheric lantern-lit garden, with a country and western meets Oriental sukiyaki feel. Good sukiyaki fondue and basic Asian fare, like fried rice, but it's the atmosphere that makes it special.

## ▲▲ Activities and tours

**Savannakhet** *p462, map p463*
**Savannakhet Provincial Tourism Authority**, T041-214203. The tourism authority runs excellent ecotours and treks to the national parks in the area. There are 14 keen, English-speaking guides who take tourists out to see the local culture and sights. 1- to 3-day treks have been established, with proceeds filtering down to local communities.
**Savanbanhao Tourism Co**, Savanbanhao Hotel, see Sleeping, T041-212944, Mon-Sat 0800-1200, 1330-1630. Tours and trips to most sights in the area and sells bus tickets to Vietnam.

## ⊖ Transport

### Thakhek *p458*
**Bus/truck**
Thakhek's **main bus station** is 4 km northeast of town. It is a large station with a mini-market and is open throughout the night. Frequent daily connections northbound to **Vientiane**, 346 km, 6-7 hrs, 40,000 kip; the VIP bus also dashes through town at 1300, 60,000-80,000 kip.

Southbound buses to **Savannakhet**, every hr, daily 1100-2200, 139 km, 2½ hrs, 20,000 kip; to **Pakse**, every hr until 2400, 6-7 hrs; also to **Sekong**, 1030, 1530 and 2300, 60,000 kip; to **Don Khong**, 1600, 15 hrs, 60,000 kip. To get to **Dong Ha** (Vietnam), Sat 0800, 80,000 kip. Buses to Hué daily 0800, 80,000 kip; Danang Mon-Fri 2000, 160,000 kip and Hanoi Sat 2000, 18 hrs, 160,000 kip. It costs 20,000-30,000 kip to get a tuk-tuk from the station to a guesthouse in town. It's best to call guesthouses in advance if you're arriving late, so they don't lock you out.

The **local bus station** is at Talaat Lak Sarm and services towns and villages within the province. From here songthaews depart hourly between 0700 and 1400 to Mahaxai, 50 km, 2-3 hrs, 20,000 kip; Nakai, 80 km, 2-4 hrs, 30,000 kip; Na Phao (Vietnam Border) 142 km, 6-7 hrs, 40,000 kip; Na Hin 45,000 kip. There is also a songthaew to Kong Lor village at 0730, 75,000 kip but this only runs when the road conditions are good (not in the wet season). Route 12 to the Vietnam border has been undergoing constant construction work but this should be complete in the next few years.

### Motorbikes
Bikes can be rented from **Thakhek Travel Lodge**, US$15 per day; and from the no-name rental shop, on the left-hand side, near the traffic lights, US$8 per day (ask for Mr Na). The Provincial Tourism Office can also organize motorbike rental.

### Mahaxai *p461*
Songthaews leave from the station in the morning. The last bus back to Thakhek leaves Mahaxai at 1500.

### Savannakhet *p462, map p463*
**Bus or truck**
From the bus station on the northern edge of town, frequent northbound buses depart daily to **Vientiane**, 8-9 hrs, 55,000 kip. Most of the Vientiane-bound buses also stop at **Thakhek**, 125 km, 2½-3 hrs, 25,000 kip. There are also scheduled buses to **Thakhek** daily 0730, 0915, 1015 and 1130.

Southbound buses to **Pakse** depart 6 times daily, 6-7 hrs, 30,000 kip; buses in transit from Vientiane to Pakse will also pick up passengers here. To **Don Khon**, 0700, 9-10 hrs, 50,000 kip.

Eastbound buses depart daily to **Xepon** and **Lao Bao** (Vietnam border, see page 131), 0630, 0930 and 1200, 5-6 hrs, 30,000 kip. A bus also departs daily 2200 for destinations within Vietnam, including **Hué**, 13 hrs, 110,000 kip; **Danang**, 508 km, 15 hrs, 140,000 kip, and **Hanoi**, 22 hrs, 200,000 kip; there are additional services Sat 0700 and 1800, and Sun 0700. Luxury Vietnam-bound buses can also be arranged through the Savanbanhao Hotel, see Sleeping, T041-212202, US$12.

Crossing the border with Thailand at Mukdahan: buses are expected to start running across the new Friendship Bridge. In the meantime though, ferries leave the boat pier at the centre of town at 0910, 1000, 1110, 1330, 1430 and 1600, 30 mins, 15,000 kip.

**Car, motorbike and bicycle**
Car and driver can be hired from the Savanbanhao Hotel, prices vary. They also rent motorbikes, US$10 per day. Lao-Paris Restaurant, rents bicycles for US$1 and motorbikes US$10 per day.

**Tuk-tuk**
Most tuk-tuks charge around 10,000 kip per person for a local journey.

## ❶ Directory

**Thakhek** *p458*
**Banks** Banque pour le Commerce Extérieur Lao (BCEL), Vientiane Rd, just across from the post office, T051-212686, will change cash and TCs and does cash advances on Visa. **Lao Development Bank**, Kouvoravong Rd (eastern end), exchanges cash but doesn't do cash advances. There is

also an exchange counter at the immigration pier. **Internet** Available at the Thakhek Travel Lodge and stationary shop in the main street in town, 300 kip per minute. **Post office** Kouvoravong Rd (at cross-roads with Nongbuakham Rd); inter-national calls can be made here.

**Savannakhet** *p462, map p463*
**Banks** Lao Development Bank, Oudomsinh Rd, will change most major currencies. **Banque pour le Commerce Exterieur Lao (BCEL)**, Chalmeung Rd, will exchange currency as well. There are exchange counters around the market, any currency accepted, and at the pier (bad rate). **Customs and immigration** Lao customs and immigration, Tha He Rd, at the passenger pier, for exit to Thailand and Lao visas, daily 0830-1200, 1300-1600, overtime fees payable Sat and Sun.
**Embassies and consulates** Vietnam Consulate, Sisavangvong Rd, T041-212737, Mon-Fri 0730-1100, 1400-1630. Provides Vietnamese visas in 3 days on presentation of 2 photos and US$50. **Thai Consulate**, Kouvoravong Rd, open 0830-1200 for applications, 1400-1500 for visa collection. Visas are issued on the same day if dropped off in the morning. **Internet** Phitsamay, Chaluanmeung Rd, is quite a decent internet café and shop in a convenient location. SPS Furniture Shop, Khanthabouli Rd, 100 kip per minute. Skype wasn't available at the time of publication.
**Medical services** Savannakhet Hospital, Khanthabuli Rd, T041-212051. **Police** A block back from the river, near the Tourist Office, T041-212069. **Post office** Khanthabouli Rd, daily 0800-2200.
**Telephone** Lao Telecom Office, next door to the post office, for domestic and international calls. There are also plenty of IDD call boxes scattered around town (including 1 next to the immigration office at the river).

# Far south

*The far south is studded with wonderful attractions: from pristine jungle scenery to the cooler Boloven Plateau and the rambling ruins of Wat Phou, once an important regional powerbase. The true gems of the south, however, are the Siphandon (4000 islands), lush green islets that offer the perfect setting for those wanting to kick back for a few days. This region, near the border with Cambodia, is an idyllic picture-perfect ending to any trip in Laos. The three main islands offer something for all tourists: the larger Don Khong is great for exploring the island, take in the stunning vista and traditional Lao rural life; Don Deth is a backpacker haven and is good for those who want to while away the days in a hammock with a good book; Don Khone is better for tourist sites such as the Li Phi falls or old colonial ruins. There are roaring waterfalls nearby and pakha, or freshwater dolphins, can sometimes be spotted here between December and May, when they come upstream to give birth to their young.*

▶ *For Sleeping, Eating and other listings, see pages 480-490.*

## Pakse (Pakxe) 🏠🕐⛰🚌🎵 ▶ *pp480-490. Colour map 3, C3.*

Pakse is the largest town in the south and is strategically located at the junction of the Mekong and Xe Don rivers. It is a busy commercial town, built by the French early in the 20th century as an administrative centre for the south. The town has seen better days but the tatty colonial buildings lend an air of old-world charm. Pakse is a major staging post

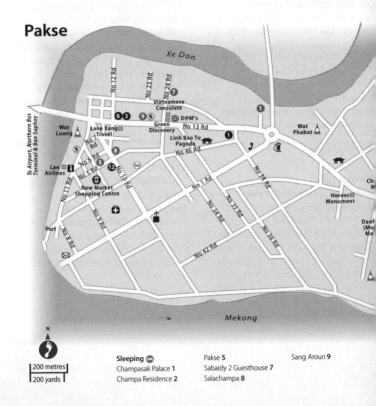

**Pakse**

Sleeping 
Champasak Palace **1**
Champa Residence **2**
Pakse **5**
Sabaidy 2 Guesthouse **7**
Salachampa **8**
Sang Aroun **9**

200 metres
200 yards

for destinations further afield such as the old royal capital of Champasak, famed for its pre-Angkor, seventh-century Khmer ruins of Wat Phou. Close to Pakse are ecotourism projects where elephant treks, bird watching and homestays are possible.

## Ins and outs

**Getting there** Pakse is Southern Laos' transport hub. The airport is 2 km northwest of town; tuk-tuks will make the journey for around 20,000 kip. There is a small café and BCEL exchange in the terminal building. International flights from Bangkok and Siem Reap, as well as domestic flights to/from Vientiane, run several times a week. There are three official bus terminals in Pakse: the Northern terminal (Km 7 on Route 13 north, T031-251508) is for buses to and from the north; the Southern terminal (Km 8 south on Route 13, T031-212981) is for buses to and from the south; and the VIP bus terminal is for northbound VIP buses. VIP buses to Ubon in Thailand are available from the evening market for ฿200. Tuk-tuks wait to transport passengers from terminals to the town centre; you shouldn't have to pay more than 7000 kip if there are multiple passengers but they will wait until the vehicle is jam-packed. ▶▶ *For further information, see Transport, page 488.*

**Getting around** Tuk-tuks and saamlors are the main means of local transport and can be chartered for half a day for about US$5. The main tuk-tuk 'terminal' is at the Daoheung market. Cars, motorbikes and bicycles are available for hire from some hotels and tour companies. The town's roads are numbered as if they were highways: No 1 Road through to No 46 Road.

**Tourist information** Champasak Provincial Department of Tourism ① *No 11 Rd, T031-212021, erratic hours but try Mon-Fri 0800-1200, 1400-1600.* They have some fantastic ecotours on offer to unique destinations (some are offered in conjunction with local travel agents, such as **Green Discovery** (see Activities and tours, page 486). Mr Phouvanh, head of the information office, is very nice and knowledgeable.

**Laos** Southern Laos Far south

# Champasak and around
🏠🚲🚌 ▶▶ *pp480-490. Colour map 3, C3.*

The agricultural town of Champasak, which stretches along the right bank of the Mekong for 4 km, is the nearest town to Wat Phou and with enough comfortable accommodation, is a good base from which to explore the site and the surrounding area. It is about 40 km south of Pakse. The sleepy town is quaint and charming and a fantastic place to spend the night, though the trip can be done in a day. The town itself is dotted with simply stunning colonial buildings. Of these, the former residence of Champasak hereditary Prince Boun Oun and former leader of the right wing opposition, who fled the country in 1975 after the Communist takeover, is quite possibly the most magnificent colonial building in Laos. His daughter-in-law now resides there and although it is not open to tourists it is certainly worth a look from the outside. Champasak is known for its wood handicrafts, and vases, and other carved ornaments are available for sale near the jetty.

**Tourist information** Champasak District Visitor Information Centre ⓘ *Mon-Fri 0800-1600, T020-2206215.* Can arrange boats to Don Daeng, guides to Wat Phou and tours to surrounding sites. Guides charge US$10 per day or US$5 for a half day.

## Ins and outs

**Getting there** Most songthaews run from Pakse's Southern bus terminal on Route 13 to Ban Lak Sarm Sip (which translates as 'village 30 km'), where they take a right turn to Ban Muang (2-3km). Here, people sell tickets for the ferry to Champasak (5000 kip; person and motorbike 8000kip). The ferry runs from 0600 until 2000. Public boats from Pakse make the journey to Champasak in two hours (60,000 kip). You can also charter a boat from Pakse, which makes sense for a larger group; expect to pay about US$50-60 for boat hire for 15 to 20 people. The boat will probably dock at Ban Wat Muang Kao, 4 km downstream from Champasak; take a bus or tuk-tuk from here. From Champasak there is a public bus to Pakse at 0630, 0730 and 0800, two hours (with a wait for the ferry), 15,000 kip.

## Wat Phou ✺ ›› *p470. Colour map 3, C3.*

ⓘ *The site is officially open 0800-1630 but the staff are happy to let you in if you get there for sunrise, even as early as 0530, and you won't get thrown out until 1800. The admission fee of US$3 or around 30,000 kip goes towards restoration (entry to the Exhibition Centre is included) . There are foodstalls at the gate. There is also the Wat Phu Exhibition Centre at the entrance; a surprisingly good museum with a fantastic array of artefacts such as the garuda and nandi bull. The centre closes at 1600. From the Champasak dock, you can catch a tuk-tuk to Wat Phou, 8-9 km, around 80,000 kip return. Most people prefer to hire a bicycle US$2 from one of the guesthouses in Champasak town and cycle to the ruins.*

The archaeological site of Wat Phou is at the foot of the Phou Pasak, 8 km southwest of Champasak. With its teetering, weathered masonry, it conforms exactly to the Western ideal of the lost city. The mountain behind Wat Phou is called **Linga Parvata**, as the Hindu Khmers thought it resembled a linga – albeit a strangely proportioned one. Although the original Hindu temple complex was built in the fifth and sixth centuries, most of remains today is believed to have been built in the 10th to 11th centuries.

Wat Phou was a work in progress and was constructed and renovated over a period spanning several hundred years. Most of the ruins date back to the fifth and sixth centuries, making them at least 200 years older than Angkor Wat. At that time, the Champasak area was the centre of power on the lower Mekong. The Hindu temple only became a Buddhist shrine in later centuries.

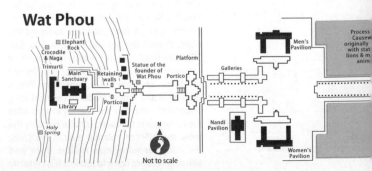

Wat Phou

Archaeologists and historians believe most of the building at Wat Phou was the work of the Khmer king, Suryavarman II (1131-1150), who was also responsible for starting work on Angkor Wat in Cambodia. The temple remained important for Khmer kings even after they had moved their capital to Angkor. They continued to appoint priests to serve at Wat Phou and sent money to maintain the temple until the last days of the Angkor Empire.

**Exploring the site** The king and dignitaries would originally have sat on the platform above the 'tanks' or *baray* and presided over official ceremonies or watched aquatic games. In 1959 a palace was built on the platform so the king had somewhere to stay during the annual Wat Phou Festival (see page 486). A long avenue leads from the platform to the pavilions. This **processional causeway** was probably built by Khmer King Jayavarman VI (1080-1107) and may have been the inspiration for a similar causeway at Angkor Wat.

The sandstone **pavilions**, on either side of the processional causeway, were added after the main temple and are thought to date from the 12th century (most likely from the reign of Suryavarman II). Although crumbling, with great slabs of laterite and collapsed lintels lying aesthetically around, both pavilions are remarkably intact. The pavilions were probably used for segregated worship by pilgrims, one for women (left) and the other for men (right). The porticoes of the two huge buildings face each other. The roofs were thought originally to have been poorly constructed with thin stone slabs on a wooden beam-frame and later replaced by Khmer tiles. Only the outer walls now remain but there is enough still standing to fire the imagination: the detailed carving around the window frames and porticoes is well-preserved. The laterite used to build the complex was brought from **Ou Mong**, also called Tomo Temple, another smaller Khmer temple complex a few kilometres downriver, but the carving is in sandstone. The interiors were without permanent partitions, although it is thought that rush matting was used instead, and furniture was limited – reliefs only depict low stools and couches. At the rear of the women's pavilion are the remains of a brick construction, believed to have been the queen's quarters.

Above the pavilions is a small temple, the **Nandi Pavilion**, with entrances on two sides. It is dedicated to Nandi, the bull (Siva's vehicle), and is a common feature in Hindu temple complexes. There are three chambers, each of which would originally have contained statues – these have been stolen. As the hill begins to rise above the Nandi temple, the remains of six brick temples follow the contours, with three on each side of the pathway. All six are completely ruined and their function is unclear. At the bottom of the steps is a portico and statue of the founder of Wat Phou, Pranga Khommatha.

The **main sanctuary**, 90 m up the hillside and orientated east-west, was originally dedicated to Siva. The rear section (behind the Buddha statue) is part of the original

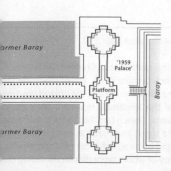

sixth-century brick building. Sacred spring water was channelled through the hole in the back wall of this section and used to wash the sacred linga. The water was then thrown out, down a chute in the right wall, where it was collected in a receptacle. Pilgrims would then wash in the holy water. The front of the temple was constructed later, probably in the eighth to ninth century, and has some fantastic carvings: apsaras, dancing Vishnu, Indra on a three-headed elephant and, above the portico of the left entrance, a carving of Siva, the destroyer, tearing a woman in two.

The Hindu temple was converted into a Buddhist shrine, either in the 13th century during the reign of the Khmer king Jayavarman VII or when the Lao conquered the area in the 14th century. A large Buddha statue now presides over its interior.

## Don Daeng Island

ⓘ *An ecotour is the way to get here, which can include treks and explorations of local villages. Contact the Provincial Tourism Office in Pakse or the Tourism Office in Champasak for further information. A trip by boat from Champasak will cost around US$1.*

This idyllic river island sits right across from Champasak. It stretches for 8 km and is the perfect place for those wishing to see quintessential village life, with basket weaving, fishing and rice farming, and without the cars and hustle and bustle. There is a path around the island that can be traversed on foot or by bicycle. A crumbling ancient brick stupa, built in the same century as Wat Phu, is in the centre of the island and there are a few ancient remnants in **Sisak Village** from the construction. The local inhabitants of **Pouylao Village** are known for their knife-making prowess. There is a lovely sandy beach on the Champasak side of the island, perfect for a dip. The island has only recently opened up to tourism, so it is important to tread lightly.

## Xe Pian National Protected Area

ⓘ *The provincial authorities are trying to promote ecotourism in this area. To organize an elephant trek go to the Visitor Centre in Ban Kiet Ngong, T030-5346547, or contact Kingfisher Ecolodge (see page 481).*

The Xe Pian National Protected Area (NPA) is home to large water birds, great hornbills, sun bears, Asiatic black bears and the yellow-cheeked crested gibbon. The area is rich in bird-life and is one of the most threatened land-types in Laos.

Ban Kiet Ngong Village, 1½ hrs from Pakse, has a community-based project which offers elephant trekking and homestay accommodation on the edge of the Xe Pian NPA. The village itself is at the Kiet Ngong Wetland, the largest wetland in Southern Laos. The villagers have traditionally been dependent on elephants for agricultural work and their treks can be organized to either the Xe Pian National Protected Area or the amazing fortress of **Phu Asa**. This ancient fortress is located 2 km from Kiet Ngong, at the summit of a small jungle-clad hill. It is an enigmatic site that has left archaeologists puzzled; it consists of 20 stone columns, 2 m-high, arranged in a semi-circle – they look a bit like a scaled-down version of Stonehenge. To reach the village from Pakse, follow Route 13 until you get to the Km 48 junction with Route 18 at Thang Beng Village (the Xe Pian National Protected Area office is here). Follow route 18 east for 7 km, turn right at the signpost for the last 1.5 km to Ban Kiet Ngong.

There are several other ecotourism two- to three-day trekking/homestay ecotours offered in the area, contact the Provincial Tourism Information Office in Pakse or the **Kingfisher Ecolodge**.

# Boloven Plateau ▲⊖ ►► *pp480-490. Colour map 3, C4.*

The French identified the Boloven Plateau, in the northeast of Champasak Province, as a prime location for settlement by hardy French farming stock. It is named after the Laven minority group that reside in the area. The soils are rich and the upland position affords some relief from the summer heat of the lowlands. However, their grand colonial plans came to nought and, although some French families came to live here, they were few in number and all left between the 1950s and 1970s as conditions in the area deteriorated. Today the plateau is inhabited by a colourful mix of ethnic groups, such as the Laven, Alak, Tahoy and Suay, many of whom were displaced during the

## Tahoy festival

There are several Tahoy settlements around the Boloven Plateau although the Tahoy population in Laos is only about 30,000. The village of Ban Paleng, not far from Tha Teng on Route 16, is a fascinating place to visit, especially in March (in accordance with the full-moon), when the animist Tahoy celebrate their annual three-day sacrificial festival. The village is built in a circle around the *kuan* (the house of sacrifice). A water buffalo is donated by each family in the village. The buffalo has its throat cut and the blood is collected and drunk.

The raw meat is divided among the families and surrounding villages are invited to come and feast on it. The head of each family throws a slab of meat into the *lak khai* – a basket hanging from a pole in front of the *kuan* – so that the spirits can partake too. The sacrifice is performed by the village shaman, then dancers throw spears at the buffalo until it dies. The villagers moved from the Vietnam border area to escape the war, but Ban Paleng was bombed repeatedly: the village is still littered with shells and unexploded bombs.

war. The premier attraction in the area is the number of roaring falls plunging off the plateau; Tad Lo and Tad Fan are particularly popular tourist destinations, while the grand Tad Yeung makes a perfect picnic destination. The plateau also affords excellent rafting and kayaking trips.

### Ins and outs

Tourist infrastructure is limited. Trips to **Tad Fan** and other attractions can be organized in Pakse through **Sabaidy 2** (see pages 480 and 487), and **Green Discovery Laos** (see page 487). Alternatively, the best base on the plateau is **Tad Lo** (see page 474), which can be reached by a bus or songthaew from Pakse, alighting at Ban Houa Set (2½ hrs from Pakse). There is a blue sign here indicating the way to Tad Lo – a 1.5-km walk along a dirt track and through the village of Ban Saen Wang. You can usually get a tuk-tuk from Ban Houa Set to Tad Lo for around 10,000 kip. Before you set off, pop in to **Tim's Guesthouse & Restaurant** (see Sleeping, page 482) for a quick chat to Soulideth (Tim's English-speaking husband). A great source of free and friendly information, he is the foremost authority on all there is to do in the area and is unbelievably helpful. He seems to be able to arrange tours and excursions with less hassle and more local involvement than anyone else. He'll also give you a map that you can copy, www.tadlo.laopdr.com. ▸▸ *For further information, see Activities and tours and Transport, pages 486 and 489.*

### Paksong (Pakxong) and around → *Colour map 3, C4.*

The main town on the Boloven Plateau is Paksong, a small town 50 km east of Pakse renowned for its large produce market. It was originally a French agricultural centre, popular during the colonial era for its cooler temperatures. The town occupies a very scenic spot, however, the harsh weather in the rainy season changes rapidly making it difficult to plan trips around the area.

On the way to Paksong, just past Km 38, is **Tad Fan**, a dramatic 120 -m-high waterfall, which is believed to be one of the tallest cascades in the country. The fall splits into two powerful streams roaring over the edge of the cliff and plummeting into the pool below, with mist and vapour shrouding views from above. One of the best viewing spots for the falls is the **Tad Fan Resort**'s restaurant (see Sleeping, page 481), which offers an unobscured view of the magnificent site.

Around 2 km from Tad Fan and 40 km from Pakse is Tad Yeung. The falls are about 1 km from the main road. Set amongst beautiful coffee plantations and sprinkled with wooden picnic huts, these falls are possibly the best on offer on the plateau as they offer both height and accessibility. Packing a picnic in Pakse and bringing it along for an afternoon trip is recommended. The cascades plummet 50 m to a pool at the bottom, where it's possible to swim in the dry season. During the wet season the waterways create numerous little channels and islands around the cascades. Behind the main falls sits a cave, however it's best to get someone to guide you here. There is a slippery walkway from the top of the falls to the bottom, where you can swim. The falls can be reached by taking a local bus from the Southern Bus station in Pakse to a village Km 40 (ask to go to **Lak See Sip**). The turn-off is on the right from Pakse (and on the left from Paksong). There is a sign on the main road which indicates **Sihom Sabaidy Guesthouse**, follow this road about 700 m to the falls. These falls are a great option if you are trying to avoid the backpacker hoardes.

Just 17 km from Paksong are the twin falls of **Tad Mone** and **Tad Meelook**. Once a popular picnic spot for locals, the area is now almost deserted and the swimming holes at the base of the falls are an idyllic place for a dip.

Some 35 km northwest of Pakse is **Pasuam Waterfall** and **Utayan Bajiang Champasak** ① *T031-251294, 5000 kip*, a strange ethnic theme park popular with Thai tourists. The large compound features small cascades, a restaurant, a model ethnic village, gardens and plenty of trails. There are bungalows, a tree house and rooms available for ₭1000. To get here from Pakse follow Route 13 towards Paksong and follow the left fork at 21 km and turn off at the 30-km mark.

---

# Tad Lo and around ⊟ 🕐 ✳ 🎒 ▲ 🖴 » *pp480-490. Colour maps 3, C4.*

Tad Lo is a popular 'resort' on the edge of the Boloven Plateau, nestled alongside three rolling cascades. There are several places to stay in this idyllic retreat, good hiking, an exhilarating river to frolic in (especially in the wet season) and elephant trekking. In the vicinity of Tad Lo there are also several villages, which can be visited in the company of a local villager. All the guesthouses in Tad Lo can arrange guided treks to Ban Khian and Tad Soung.

The **Xe Xet** (or Houai Set) flows past Tad Lo, crashing over two sets of cascades nearby: **Tad Hang**, the lower series, is overlooked by the **Tad Lo Lodge** and **Saise Guesthouse**, while **Tad Lo**, the upper, is a short hike away.

A new Community Guides office has been established with a number of trained guides offering treks around the Tad Lo area and to nearby Ngai villages. Elephant treks can also be arranged from here for US$5 per elephant for a 90-minute trek through the jungle and river.

There are two Alak villages, **Ban Khian** and **Tad Soung**, close to Tad Lo. Tad Soung is approximately 10 km away from the main resort area and are the most panoramic falls in the vicinity. The Alak are an Austro-Indonesian ethno-linguistic group. Most fascinating is the Alak's seeming obsession with death. The head of each household carves coffins out of hollowed logs for himself and his whole family (even babies), then stacks them, ready for use, under their rice storage huts. This tradition serves as a reminder that life expectancy in these remote rural areas is around 40 and infant mortality of around 100 per 1000 live births; the number one killer is malaria.

Katou villages such as **Ban Houei Houne** (on the Salavan-Pakse road) are famous for their weaving of a bright cloth used locally as a *pha sinh* (sarong). Tours to the village are run by **Saise Guesthouse**: at 150,000 kip per tour, it's best to set off in a group. **Tim's Guesthouse & Restaurant** can also make arrangements for you to get there.

# Don Khong ⬛🚰❀🚌🍸 ▸▸ *pp480-490. Colour map 3, C3.*

Don Khong is the largest of the Mekong islands at 16 km long and 8 km wide. It's a tremendous place to relax or explore by bicycle. Visitors might be surprised by the smooth asphalt roads, electricity and general standard of amenities that exist on the island but two words explain it all – Khamtay Siphandone – Laos' former president, who has a residence on the island.

## Ins and outs

**Getting there** The easiest way to get to all three major Siphandon islands from Pakse is by private minivan, 60,000 kip arranged by **Lane Xang Travel** and other operators in Pakse. The most luxurious way to get there is aboard the Vat Phou, www.asian-oasis.com, a beautiful boutique riverborne hotel that does a three day/two night cruise from Pakse to Champasak and Wat Phou to Don Khong and then back to Pakse. Departs Tuesdays, Thursdays and Saturdays from Pakse.

In the high season songthaews depart Pakse's Southern bus terminal hourly between 0800 and 1200. The occasional bus will also ply through but songthaews are the most common transport option. The journey to **Ban Hat Xai Khoune** (to catch a boat to Don Khong) should take between four and five hours and cost US$3; in most cases the bus/truck will board the car ferry (3000 kip) at **Ban Hat** (1 km south of Ban Hat Xai Khoune) and take you right across to **Ban Naa** on Don Khong (1 km south of Muang Khong).

There are also motorboats from Ban Hat Xai Khoune to Muang Khong (10,000 kip, depending on the number of passengers). If there is not a bus directly to Don Khong, catch a bus bound for **Ban Nakasang** (the stop-off for Don Deth and Don Khone) and jump off at Ban Hat Xai Khoune. If by chance you get dumped at Nakasang, you can arrange a boat to Don Khong from there; although this is a very pretty route it is time-consuming and not the most efficient way to get to the island. If you travel all the way from Pakse or Champasak by boat, alight at Ban Houa Khong on the northern tip of the island and arrange transport from there to Muang Khong (buses and tuk-tuks wait here). The boats often continue to **Ban Muang Saen Nua**, although they may arrive here considerably later, as they tend to visit neighbouring islands first.

**Getting around** All of the guesthouses can arrange bicycle hire for 10,000 kip per day. ▸▸ *For further information, see Transport, page 488.*

## Around the island

Don Khong's 'capital' is **Muang Khong**, a small former French settlement. Pigs and chickens scrabble for food under the houses and just 50 m inland the houses give way to paddy fields. There are two wats in the town. **Wat Kan Khong**, also known as Wat Phuang Kaew, is visible from the jetty: a large gold Buddha in the *mudra* of subduing Mara garishly overlooks the Mekong. Much more attractive is **Wat Chom Thong** at the upstream extremity of the village, which may date from the early 19th century but which was much extended during the colonial period. The unusual Khmer-influenced sim may be gently decaying but it is doing so with style. The wat compound, with its carefully tended plants and elegant buildings, is very peaceful. The naga heads on the roof of the main sim are craftily designed to channel water, which issues from their mouths.

Most people come to Muang Khong as a base for visiting the **Li Phi** and **Khong Phapheng Falls** (see page 479) in the far south. However, these trips, alongside the dolphin-watching trips are much easier to arrange from Don Deth or Don Khone. This island is a destination in itself and offers a great insight into Lao rural life without all the hustle and bustle found in more built-up areas. To a certain extent, save electricity, a sprinkling of cars and a couple of internet terminals, time stands still in Dong Khong.

The island itself is worth exploring by bicycle and deserves more time than most visitors give it. It is flat – except in the interior where there are approximately 99 hills – the roads are quiet, so there is less risk of being mown down by a timber truck and the villages and countryside offer a glimpse of traditional Laos. Most people take the southern 'loop' around the island, via **Ban Muang Saen Nua**, a distance of about 25 km (two to three hours on a bike). The villages along the section of road south of **Ban Muang Saen Nua** are wonderfully picturesque with buffalos grazing and farmers tending to their rice crops. Unlike other parts of Laos the residents here are fiercely protective of their forests and logging incurs very severe penalties.

About 6 km north of Ban Muang Saen Nua is a hilltop wat, which is arguably Don Khong's main claim to national fame. **Wat Phou Khao Kaew** (Glass Hill Monastery) is built on the spot where an entrance leads down to the underground lair of the nagas, known as **Muang Nak**. This underground town lies beneath the waters of the Mekong,

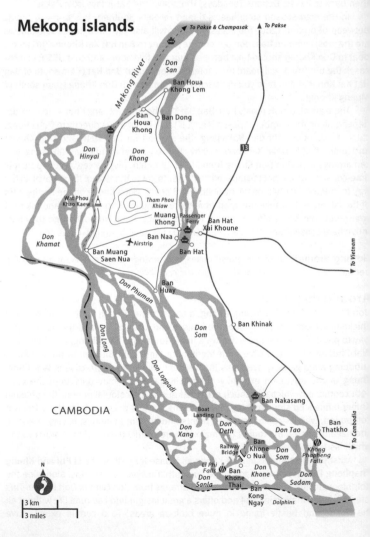

Mekong islands

Lao legend has it that the nagas will come to the surface to protect the Lao whenever the country is in danger.

**Tham Phou Khiaw** is tucked away among the forests of the **Green Mountain** in the centre of the island. It's a small cave, containing earthenware pots. Buddha images and other relics and offerings litter the site. Every Lao New Year (April) townsfolk climb up to the cave to bathe the images. Although it's only 15 minutes' walk from the road, finding the cave is not particularly straightforward except during Lao New Year when it is possible to follow the crowds. Head 1.5 m north from Muang Khong on the road until you come to a banana plantation, with a couple of wooden houses. Take the pathway just before the houses through the banana plantation and at the top, just to the left, is a small gateway through the fence and a fairly well-defined path. Head up and along this path and, after 300 m or so, there is a rocky clearing. The path continues from the top right corner of the clearing for a further 200 m to a rocky mound that rolls up and to the left. Walk across the mound for about 20 m, until it levels out, and then head back to the forest. Keeping the rock immediately to your right, continue round and after 40 m there are two upturned tree trunks marking the entrance to the cave.

On the northern tip of the island is a sandy beach. Note that swimming is generally not advised due to parasites in the water and potentially strong currents. There is a rumour that Laos' former president, Khamtay Siphandone, will be building a resort here in the next few years. In nearby **Wat Houa Khong**, approximately 13 km north of Muang Khong, is the former President's modest abode set in traditional Lao style.

# Don Deth, Don Khone and around ⊜⊘⊙▲⊜⊙

▶▶ *pp480-490. Colour map 6, A4.*

The islands of Don Khone and Don Deth are the pot of gold at the end of the rainbow for most travellers who head to the southern tip of Laos, and it's not hard to see why. The bamboo huts that stretch along the banks of these two staggeringly beautiful islands are filled with contented travellers in no rush to move on. Don Deth is more of a backpacker haven, not dissimilar to the Koh Phangans and Vang Viengs of the region, meanwhile Don Khone has been able to retain a more authentically Lao charm. Travelling by boat in this area is very picturesque: the islands are covered in coconut palms, flame trees, stands of bamboo, kapok trees and hardwoods; the river is riddled with eddies and rapids. In the distance, a few kilometres to the south, are the Khong Hai Mountains, which dominate the skyline and delineate the border between Laos and Cambodia.

In the area are the Li Phi (or Somphamit) Falls and Khong Phapheng Falls – the latter are the largest in Southeast Asia and reputedly the widest in the world.

The French envisaged Don Deth and Don Khone as strategic transit points in their grandiose masterplan to create a major Mekong highway from China. In the late 19th century, ports were built at the southern end of Don Khone and at the northern end of Don Deth and a narrow-gauge railway line was constructed across Don Khone in 1897 as an important bypass around the rapids for French cargo boats sailing upriver from Phnom Penh. In 1920, the French built a bridge across to Don Deth and extended the railway line to Don Deth port. This 5-km stretch of railway has the unique distinction of being the only line the French ever built in Laos. On the southern side of the island lie the rusted corpses of the old locomotive and boiler car. Before pulling into Ban Khone Nua, the main settlement on Don Khone, Don Deth's original 'port' is on the right, with what remains of its steel rail jetty.

A number of companies run tours to this area, especially from Pakse. To get to Don Deth or Don Khone independently from Pakse the bus/songthaew will need to drop you off at **Ban Nakasang**. This is not the most pleasant of Lao towns and several travellers have complained about being ripped off here. However, it has a thriving market, where most of the islanders stock up on goods, so it's worth having a look around before you head off, particularly if you need to pick up necessities like torches, batteries and film. It's a 500-m walk from the bus stop down to the dock. The 'ticket office' is located in a little restaurant to the right-hand side of the dock. However, you can ask anyone that's jumping across to the islands for a lift, at a dramatically reduced rate. The boats take about 15 to 20 minutes to make the easy trip to the islands and cost around US$3 per person. Prices will be higher (US$5-6) if you are travelling solo. A boat between Don Deth and Don Khone costs 30,000 kip; alternatively you can walk between the two islands, paying the 9000 kip charge to cross the bridge (also used as ticket to see Li Phi Falls). Both islands can easily be navigated on foot or bicycles can be rented from guesthouses for US$1 per day.
▶ *For further information, see Activities and tours, page 486, and Transport, page 490.*

## Don Deth → *Colour map 6, A4.*

The riverbank here is peppered with cheap-as-chips bamboo huts and restaurants geared to accommodate the growing wave of backpacker travellers that flood south to stop and recoup in this idyllic setting. A good book, hammock and icy beverage is the order of the day here, but those with a bit more energy should explore the truly stunning surroundings. It's a great location for watching the sunrises and sunsets, for walking through shady palms and frangipani trees and for swimming off the beaches, which attract the hordes in the dry season. Away from the picturesque waterfront, the centre of the island comprises rice paddies and farms; you should take care not to harm crops when exploring the island.

The national tourism authorities have been coordinating with locals to ensure that the beautiful island doesn't become 'Vang Vieng-ified', so you'll find no *Friends* DVDs here, although 'happy' shakes have started appearing. The island has no

Laos Southern Laos Far south

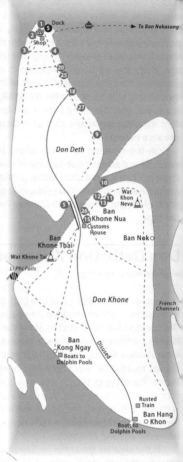

## Don Deth & Don Khone

600 metres
600 yards

**Sleeping** 😴
Auberge Sala Don
  Khone **11**
Boun Guesthouse **13**
Deng Guesthouse **18**
Lamphone Bungalows **25**
Mama Leuah **9**
Mama Mon & Papa **20**
Mama Tan On **4**
Miss Noy's **2**
Mr B's **3**
Mr Tho's **27**
Pan's Guesthouse **26**
Salaphae **10**
Santiphab Guesthouse **5**
Sompamit Guesthouse **12**
Souksan Guesthouse
  & Restaurant **1**
Xaymountry Residence **15**

**Eating** 🍴
Pool Room **5**

electricity (except for a generator supply 1800-2200), no cars (except for the odd truck) and few other modern conveniences. Internet has amazingly made its way to the island, however, and it's possible to get mobile phone coverage. There has been talk for years about electricity coming to the island but for now it seems unlikely. Most guesthouses run tours to the falls/dolphins. A few entrepreneurial types are starting to promote adventure tourism here. Kayaking and rafting trips can be organized through **Xplore-asia/Lang Xang Travel** (near the main port) for US$20 (minimum four people), T031-212893, www.xplore-asia.com. Several guesthouses also have tubes for rent for 5000 kip. It is definitely inadvisable to go tubing in the wet season and probably not a good idea all year round. Swimming, visiting the falls and other activities all need to be undertaken with the utmost caution here. The river's current is probably the strongest in all of Laos and several tourists have drowned here.

## Don Khone → *Colour map 6, A4.*

From the railway bridge, follow the southwest path through **Ban Khone Thai** and then wind through the paddy fields for 1.7 km (20 minutes' walk) to **Li Phi Falls** ① *9000 kip paid at the bridge.* Also known as Somphamitor or Khone Yai Falls, these are a succession of raging rapids, crashing through a narrow rocky gorge. In the wet season, when the rice is green, the area is beautiful; in the dry season, it is scorching. From the main vantage point on a jagged, rocky outcrop, the falls aren't that impressive, as a large stretch of them are obscured. 'Phi' means ghost, a reference, it is believed, to the bodies that floated down the river from the north during the war. It's best to visit Li Phi around June or July, when all the fishermen are putting out their bamboo fish traps. These are dangerous waterfalls, do not swim here.

The Mekong, south of Don Khone, is one of the few places in the world where it is possible to see freshwater dolphins. They can be spotted in the late afternoon from December to May, from the French pier at the end of the island, not far from the village of **Ban Hang Khon**. The walk across Don Khone from the railway bridge is some 4 km and bicycles can be hired. It is more likely, however, to catch a glimpse of the dolphins if you're in a boat (US$5), as they reside in deep water pools. In 1996 there were thought to be 30 dolphins, after which numbers seemed to decline and, according to local data, there were fears that only four or five were left, although a new calf has recently been spotted. The Laos-Cambodia border transects the dolphin pool and the Lao boatmen have to pay US$1 to the Cambodian authorities in order to access the waters in which the dolphins live. Cambodia gets a bit tetchy about these 'border incursions' and may, on the odd occasion, deny access. ▸▸ *For further information, see Activities and tours, page 486.*

## Khong Phapheng Falls → *Colour map 6, A4.*

① *Near Ban Thatkho, US$1. Guesthouses organize trips for around 60,000 kip per person (min 5 passengers), usually be booked in conjunction with a trip to see the dolphins.*

About 36 km south of Ban Hat Xai Khoune at Ban Thatkho, a road branches off Route 13 towards Khong Phapheng Falls, which roar around the eastern shore of the Mekong for 13 km. One fork of the road leads to a vantage point, where a large wooden structure, built up on stilts, overlooks the cascades for a fantastic head-on view of the falls. When you see the huge volume of white water boiling and surging over the jagged rocks below, it is hard to imagine that there is another 10 km width of river running through the other channels. A perilous path leads down from the viewpoint to the edge of the water. Be careful here. Unsurprisingly, the river is impassable at this juncture, as an 1860s French expedition led by adventurers Doudart de Lagrée and Francis Garnier discovered. Another road leads down to the bank of the Mekong, 200 m away, just above the lip of the falls; at this deceptively tranquil spot, the river is gathering momentum before it plunges over the edge. Boatmen will do a trip to both the falls and the dolphins for US$10, however, sometimes police will not allow them to make the trip. You can also visit the falls by catching a songthaew from Ban Nakasang, US$10 return.

# 🛌 Sleeping

**Pakse** *p468, map p469*

**A-B Champasak Palace**, No 13 Rd, T031-212263, champasak_palace_hotel@ yahoo.com. This is a massive chocolate box of a hotel with 55 rooms and lit up like a Christmas tree. It was conceived as a palace for a minor prince. There are some large rooms and 40 more modern, less elaborate rooms, which were added in 2000. It is quite bizarre seeing bellhops in traditional uniforms. Recent renovations have resulted in a loss of the original character in favour of modernity but some classic touches remain: wooden shutters, some art deco furniture and lovely tiles. The restaurant is one of the most atmospheric place to eat in town, set on a big veranda overlooking lovely frangipani trees. The friendly staff speak a smattering of English, there's a good terrace and the facilities are the best in town and include a massage centre. It's in a great position above the Xe Don and there are stunning views from the higher levels.

**B-C Champa Residence** (Residence du Champa), No 13 Rd, east of town near the stadium and museum, T031-212120, champare@laotel.com. Modern-style rooms, with a/c, minibar, hot water and satellite TV. Very clean and with some character. Attractive terrace and lush garden. Visa accepted and tours arranged. Includes breakfast.

**B-D Pakse Hotel**, No 5 Rd (facing the new market), T031-212131, www.hotel pakse.com. This is one of the nicest places to stay in town with 65 rooms. The French owner, Mr Jérôme, has integrated local handicraft decorations and tasteful furnishings into this slick hotel. Good rooftop restaurant with a perfect view over the city and river, the dimly lit eatery oozes ambience. Breakfast included. Wi-Fi.

**C Sang Aroun**, Route 13, T031-252111. The most modern hotel in town, 58 rooms with cable TV and a/c. The more expensive rooms have bathtubs. Modern but lacks character.

**C-D Salachampa**, No 10 Rd, T031-212273. The most characterful place in town. Choose a room in the main 1920s building: huge with wooden floors, large en suite bathrooms with warm-water showers; the upstairs rooms with balconies are best. There are also some additional, quaintly rustic rooms in a 'new' extension and a nice garden area between the two. Recommended for those looking for a touch of colonial elegance and friendly service. The rooms are exceptionally good value for money.

**E-F Sabaidy 2 Guesthouse**, No 24 Rd, T031-212992, www.sabaidy2laos.com. A wide range of rooms on offer, from dorms to rooms with private bathrooms and hot water. The rooms are quite basic but the service is exceptional. The proprietor, the effervescent Mr Vong offers tours, information and visa extensions. Mr Vong's grandfather, Liam Douang Vongsaa, was the first governor of Pakse and this building was the governor's residence, where Mr Vong was born in 1944. Very popular, you may need to book in advance. Basic food available. Motorbike rental.

**Champasak** *p469*

**D Souchitra**, along the river, T031-212366. A collection of cabins. Tiled rooms with fridge, a/c and hot water, many of which are decorated with tacky posters. The rooms in the newer annexe are better.

**D-F Anouxa Guesthouse**, 1 km north of the roundabout, T031-213272. A wide range of accommodation, from wooden bungalows to concrete rooms with hot water and either a/c (pay extra) or fan. The concrete villas are the best, with a serene river vista from the balconies. The restaurant is probably one of the best in town, overlooking the river and a shady cabana. The only drawback is that it is a little way out of town. Bikes for hire.

**D-F Vong Pasued Guesthouse**, 450 m south of the roundabout, T020-2712402. The grimy, dingy shop-front façade is deceiving, as out the back, beside the river, are a range of pleasant rooms to suit all budgets. The owners are very pleasant but there is a strange resident parrot that squawks 'cow' incessantly. A firm favourite with backpackers, this small family-run guesthouse offers pretty reasonable rooms. The US$5 rooms by the river are great value; clean with hot water. The more basic US$3 rooms (mosquito nets, thin walls and cold water) in an old longhouse are a bit run down. Good restaurant, perfect for a natter with fellow travellers.

**F Khamphouy Guesthouse**, west of Dokchampa. Delightful family-run place. Bright but basic rooms in the main house with shared facilities and 1 cottage (in the garden) with 2 rooms and an en suite shower. Clean, comfortable, friendly and relaxed. Bikes for hire.

**Don Daeng** *p472*

**A La Folie Lodge**, T030-5347603, www.lafolie-laos.com. 24 rooms housed in lovely wooden bungalows, each with its own balcony. The lodge has a swimming pool surrounded by landscaped tropical gardens. Restaurant with good wine and cocktail selection.

**F Homestays** are offered in a community-lodge in Ban Hua Don Daeng for US$2. The wooden lodge has 2 common rooms, sleeping 5 people and has shared bathrooms and a dining area.

**Xe Pian National Protected Area** *p472*

**B-C Kingfisher Ecolodge**, 700 m east of Kiet Ngong, T030-5345016, www.king fisherecolodge.com. Bonafide eco-lodge. In the main lodge, wooden and thatched rooms with shared bathroom. More expensive are the glass-fronted bungalows. The restaurant, set on the 2nd floor of the lodge affords simply stunning views over the Pha Pho wetlands.

**F Boun Home Guesthouse**, Ban Kiet Ngong, T030-5346293. Very basic guesthouse with wooden rooms and shared facilities.

**Paksong and around** *p473*

**B-C Tad Fan Resort**, T020-5531400, www.tadfane.com. Perched on the opposite side of the ravine from the falls is a series of wooden bungalows with nicely decorated rooms and en suite bathrooms, with hot showers. The 2nd floor of the excellent open-air restaurant offers the best view of the falls and serves a wide variety of Lao, Thai and Western food. Great service. Treks to the top of falls and the Dan-Sin-Xay Plain can be arranged.

**F Borlaven Guesthouse**, Route 23 about 2 km north of the market, beyond Paksong town, T030-5758086. The new brick and wood building has a cabin feel and is surrounded by coffee trees, cornfields and a flower garden. The simple rooms are bright (pink floral sheets) and clean with en suite bathrooms but no hot water. Very friendly owner speaks English.

**Tad Yeung** *p474*

**E Sihom Sabaidy Guesthouse,** at the time of writing Mr Vong from **Sabaidy 2** in Pakse was opening the new **Sihom Sabaidy Guesthouse** here. It is the only operational guesthouse in the vicinity of these falls. There are 8 basic rooms with shared hot-water bathrooms. There is an adjoining restaurant offering basic Lao meals, noodles, eggs, coffee. The guesthouse is set on a coffee plantation and tours are available to the waterfall as well as to nearby orchid areas and tours to see how coffee is made.

**Tad Lo and around** *p474*

**B-E Saise Guesthouse** (aka Sayse Guesthouse), T034-211886. The guesthouse, comprises 2 sections: the lower part sits near the restaurant at the foot of Tad Hang and consists of rooms and bungalows, all with hot water and fans. The more attractive and peaceful option is the so-called **Green House** (the roof's a giveaway) above the falls. This is a wooden chalet with 6 huge rooms, 4 with en suite shower and toilet, and 2 of those with balconies overlooking the river. The beautiful garden restaurant offers Lao and Thai food. Breakfast is included with most rooms.

**C Tad Lo Lodge**, T034-211889, souriya vincent@yahoo.com. Reception on the east side of the falls with chalet-style accommodation (13 rooms) built right on top of the waterfalls on the opposite side; it's a bit of a hike from one to the other. Rates include breakfast and hot water. It's an attractive location during the wet season and the accommodation is comfortable; cane rocking chairs on the balconies overlook the cascades on the left bank. Good restaurant serving plenty of Lao and Thai food.

● *For an explanation of sleeping and eating price codes used in this guide, see inside the front cover. Other relevant information is found in Essentials, see pages 29-32.*

E **Tim's Guesthouse & Restaurant**, down the bridge road, T020-5648820, soulideth@gmail.com. Twin and double wooden bungalows with hot water, fans, and lock boxes. Soulideth is full of local information and advice. Also offers internet access (expensive at 1000 kip per min), international calls, room service, a laundry service, book exchange and a substantial music collection. Runs a good range of services, including bike rentals and just about anything else you could ask for.

### Don Khong p475

Most of the guesthouses in Dong Khong have undergone name changes in recent years due to a change in legislation that requires any guesthouse with 14 or more rooms to be called a hotel and pay double the tax!

B **Senesothxeune Hotel**, Muang Khong, T031-5280577, www.ssxhotel.com. Tastefully designed, modern interpretation of colonial Lao architecture. Beautiful fittings, including carved wooden fish above each entrance way and brass chandeliers. Each room is fitted with mod cons like a/c, TV, hot water and minibar. Superior rooms have fantastic bathtubs. For those willing to splurge, upgrade to the suite that comes with spa and living area for US$70. The hotel has a modern internet café and restaurant. The menu is currently quite limited but this is due to change in the coming months. This relatively new hotel is the island's best accommodation by a long shot and is run by the gentle, softly spoken Mr Senesavath and his wife, both former mathematics professors from Don Dok University in Vientiane. Both speak English and French. Recommended.

B **Villa Muong Khong Hotel Guesthouse**, T031-2130111, www.khongislandtravel.com. This hotel is part chalet, part mock Tudor, part Lao and part Thai – all amalgamated together by someone with a fetish for wagon wheels and concrete. Despite the identity crisis architecture, this guesthouse is in a perfect location and offers affordable rooms. It is popular with tour groups. The rooms are large but a little spartan. Kitsch decorations but all the mod cons, including hot-water, bathtub and a/c. Internet available.

B-C **Auberge Sala Done Khong**, Muang Khong, T031-212077, www.salalao.com. This traditional wooden house, the former holiday home of the previous regime's foreign minister, was once the best place to stay on Don Khong but although the exterior is still stunning the rooms just aren't worth the price. There are 12 tastefully decorated, large rooms with a/c and en suite hot-water bathrooms; the best are in the main building on the 1st floor where there is an attractive balcony overlooking the Mekong with comfortable deckchairs. Starting to get a little bit run-down but clean and professionally run. Tours arranged, bicycles for hire, good food and very relaxing. Massages can be arranged. Slightly cheaper rate in the low season.

B-E **Mekong Hotel**, Muang Khong, T031-213668. Simple, spotless rooms with fans, some overlooking the Mekong and all with comfortable mattresses. Some rooms have a/c and hot-water showers (US$20). There are also cheaper rooms with shared facilities (equally clean) in a wooden building.

B-E **Souksan Hotel,** northern end of Muang Khong near Wat Chom Thong, T031-212071. The reception is in a homely building at the front, while the main accommodation area is set in a block further back. Well-designed a/c rooms with en suite bathrooms and hot water, set around a concrete garden. For US$5 the fan rooms represent exceptional value. If you want a/c the price is hiked to US$30. They also run one of the most up-market guesthouses on Don Deth.

C-E **KhangKong Villa Guesthouse**, back from the main road, central Muang Khong, T031-213539. Fantastic traditional Lao wooden building spruced up with some colourful paint. Spacious clean rooms, with or without a/c.

D-E **Pon Hotel and Restaurant**, Muang Khong, T031-214037. The large, spotless rooms are very good value, with hot-water showers, mosquito nets and comfortable beds (US$6). For US$10 you get a/c. Mr Pon, who speaks French and English, is perhaps the most helpful of all accommodation proprietors on the island and can offer an endless supply of tourist information and travel arrangements. Motorbike rental, US$10 or half-day,

US$5 and bicycles, US$1 per day. He can also arrange trips to the Cambodian border, to Don Deth and Don Khone and back to Pakse. Mr Pon is a regular Mr Fix-it and should be your first point of contact. Massage can be organized in your room for 50,000 kip. Recommended.

### Don Deth *p478, map 478*

Many people tend to make their choice of accommodation on the basis of word-of-mouth recommendations from other travellers; this is as good a way to choose as any, as the accommodation is all cheap and usually much of a muchness. It normally consists of spartan, threadbare bungalows with bed, mosquito net, hammock and shared squat toilets (unless otherwise stated). Always opt for a bungalow with a window, as the huts can get very hot. The wooden bungalows don't provide as much ventilation as the rattan equivalents but tend to attract fewer insects. Always check that the bungalow has a mosquito net. Other things to consider is the distance from the toilet to the bungalow (as a midnight bolt across a rice paddy isn't much fun), the state of the hammock, whether there is a restaurant attached and whether generator power is provided. Note that there may be a small price hike in the near future to ensure that tourism benefits all of the islands inhabitants, including the farmers. Costs are likely to double once the island gets electricity.

The accommodation runs across the both sides of the island, known as the Sunset Side and the Sunrise Side. There is a large conglomeration of accommodation towards the northern tip, which is a good option for those wishing to socialize and hop between the various establishments' restaurants/bars; this is also the most common drop-off point. As a general rule, if you want peace and quiet, head for the bungalows towards the mid-point along each coast; ask the boat drivers to drop you off directly at the bungalows as it can be a difficult hike with bags. There is really very little discernable difference between most lodgings on Don Deth, so if you're looking for truly inspirational accommodation pop across to Don Khone.

### Sunset Side

**D-E Souksan Guesthouse and Restaurant**, Houa Deth at the northern tip of the island, at the pinnacle of the Sunset and Sunrise sides, T031-212071. There are 20 or so twin and double rooms built from wood and bamboo with shared shower and toilets, not to mention a legendary Chinese restaurant. There are also a couple of concrete bungalows that are slightly more expensive. The beautiful garden is home to hundreds of butterflies, with little paths leading to the restaurant. This place unfairly get a bad rap by those looking for ultra-budget accommodation, however if you're looking for something a little more comfortable this is the island's only option. This is the hands-down winner on the island and more than worth the extra few bucks. That being said, Don Khone offers better accommodation at a more reasonable price.

**F Miss Noy's**, very close to the island tip and a small hike from the main drop-off point, this place offers an excellent view of the sunset. Restaurant is in a prime position with a good variety of dishes. The service here is exceptional. The owners are about to open several, clean concrete bungalows which should be very comfortable and one of the island's more promising offerings.

**F Mr B's**, near the northern tip. The bungalows and grounds themselves are a bit lacklustre and the chickens pecking around in the back yard don't make for the most pleasing surroundings. However, the river views and the helpful staff make this an outstanding option.

### Sunrise Side

**F Deng Guesthouse**, next to Mr Oudomsouk's. Wooden bungalows on stilts. Very popular with those who want to laze in a hammock overlooking the water. Scenic position.

**F Lamphone Bungalows**, mid-way down the island. 3 rattan bungalows, basic but lovely. The restaurant here is good and an added bonus is the resident Australian baker who cooks up a mean focaccia, and chocolate and banana doughnuts.

**F Mama Leuah**, on the south side of the former French concrete port towards the centre of the island. Several bungalows

Laos Southern Laos Far south Listings

that have seen better days. Shared squat toilet facilities.

**F Mama Mon and Papa**, on the northern peninsula. Typical thatched bamboo bungalows with mosquito nets and shared facilities. Nice shady position. The restaurant has battery-powered lights for the night-time blackout and serves a pretty exceptional lentil curry.

**F Mama Tan On**, T020-5835699. This place changes its name every year but the atmosphere remains unchanged. One of the first bungalows on the island. If you are having trouble finding it, try asking for some of its previous incarnations **Mama Rasta** or **Mama Tanon Rasta**. There is a beautiful view from the communal balcony and the effervescent Mama is good value, with her jovial demeanour and back-slapping, cheeky quips. Small library. The place is somewhat rundown, with rattan huts and communal facilities but it is a popular place to hang out in hammocks.

**F Mr Tho's**, T020-6567502. Wooden stilt bungalows, good hammocks and views of Don Khone. The staff are friendly. Rooms have been given unusual names, such as 'sticky rice bungalow' and 'bamboo bungalow'. Restaurant attached.

**F Santiphab Guesthouse**, far end of the island, facing Don Khone. 7 basic rattan bungalows right beside the bridge, most have the quintessential hammock. Idyllic setting, flanked by the Mekong on one side and rice paddies on the other. Good for those who want seclusion but also quick access to Don Khone. Very cheap restaurant serves tasty fare with buckets of atmosphere. Very little English spoken. A friendly, timeless place.

**Don Khone** *p479, map p478*

Although Don Deth attracts the vast majority of tourists, Don Khone holds its own by offering some very pleasant accommodation alternatives and close proximity to most of the attractions. In general, Don Khone evokes a much friendlier atmosphere.

**B-C Salaphae**, along from Auberge Sala Don Khone, T030-5256390, www.salalao.com. This is the most unique accommodation in the whole Siphandon area. 3 raft-houses (and 6 rooms) are managed by ex-lawyer Lesotho. Rooms have been decorated simply, with all the minor touches that can make accommodation outstanding. Hot-water bathrooms, a wonderful deck with seating overlooking the stunning river scenery and a fantastic restaurant. Starting to get a little rundown but still a fantastic option. The proprietor also plans to create a deluxe campsite and bungalows on another nearby island, Khon Pasoi which is 1.5 km from Don Khong. When these are completed they will be a great option for those tourists truly wanting to get away from it all. Check website for details.

**B-D Auberge Sala Don Khone**, Ban Khone Nua, T020-5633718, www.salalao.com. A former French hospital built in 1927, this is one of the nicest places to stay on the island. 2 traditional Luang Prabang-style houses have also been built in the grounds, with 6 rooms, all with en suite hot-water shower and toilet, some with a/c. The restaurant, across from the guesthouse, is one of the best places to dine on any of the 3 islands. It offers an unobscured waterfront view, comfy deckchairs and a good selection of food that offers a welcome change from the menus found in every other establishment. Generator 1800-2200. Reduced rate in low season. Organizes tours and boat trips. The manager is very informative and speaks excellent English.

**C Pan's Guesthouse,** opposite Xaymountry, T030-5346939. A relative newcomer to Don Khone, these wooden bungalows are exceptionally good value for money. 6 simple and very clean riverside bungalows with hot water, fan and comfy mattresses. The proprietor runs a small generator which means the fans in stay on into the early hours. The owner, Mr Pan, is truly one of the most helpful hosts in Siphandon and is at his guests' beck and call. Highly recommended for those on a limited budget.

**F Boun Guesthouse**, next door to Auberge Sala Don Khone. Mr Boun has built a couple of basic thatched bungalows with shared facilities, and a few newer wooden bungalows complete with en suite bathrooms.

**F Sompamit Guesthouse**, across from Boun Guesthouse, on the riverside, T020-5733145. Threadbare rattan thatched